GOVERNMENT AND POLITICS
IN THE UNITED STATES
NATIONAL EDITION

VAN NOSTRAND POLITICAL SCIENCE SERIES

Editor

Franklin L. Burdette
University of Maryland

Harwood L. Childs—*Public Opinion*

Russell W. Maddox, Jr.—*Issues in State and Local Government: Selected Readings*

Martin C. Needler—*Political Systems of Latin America*

Harold and Margaret Sprout—*Foundations of International Politics*

William G. Andrews—*European Political Institutions*

H. B. Sharabi—*Governments and Politics of the Middle East in the Twentieth Century*

Russell W. Maddox, Jr., and Robert F. Fuquay—*State and Local Government,* 2nd Ed.

Guy B. Hathorn, Howard R. Penniman, and Mark F. Ferber—*Government and Politics in the United States,* 2nd Ed.

Samuel Hendel—*The Soviet Crucible: The Soviet System in Theory and Practice,* 2nd Ed.

Harold Zink—*Modern Governments*

Harold Zink, Howard R. Penniman, and Guy B. Hathorn—*American Government and Politics: National, State, and Local*

Conley H. Dillon, Carl Leiden, and Paul D. Stewart—*Introduction to Political Science*

Benjamin Baker—*Urban Government*

Willis G. Swartz—*American Governmental Problems,* 2nd Ed.

William Goodman—*The Two-Party System in the United States,* 3rd Ed.

P. M. A. Linebarger, C. Djang, and A. W. Burks—*Far Eastern Governments and Politics—China and Japan,* 2nd Ed.

Elmer Plischke—*International Relations: Basic Documents,* 2nd Ed.

M. Jorrin—*Governments of Latin America*

Lane W. Lancaster—*Government in Rural America,* 2nd Ed.

R. G. Dixon, Jr., and Elmer Plischke—*American Government: Basic Documents and Materials*

Elmer Plischke—*Conduct of American Diplomacy,* 2nd Ed.

GOVERNMENT AND POLITICS

IN THE UNITED STATES

NATIONAL EDITION

GUY B. HATHORN

Associate Professor of Government and Politics
University of Maryland

HOWARD R. PENNIMAN

Professor of Government
Georgetown University

AND

MARK F. FERBER

University of California

SECOND EDITION

D. VAN NOSTRAND COMPANY, INC.

PRINCETON, NEW JERSEY

TORONTO   LONDON

NEW YORK

D. VAN NOSTRAND COMPANY, INC.
120 Alexander St., Princeton, New Jersey (*Principal office*)
24 West 40 Street, New York 18, New York

D. VAN NOSTRAND COMPANY, LTD.
358, Kensington High Street, London, W.14, England

D. VAN NOSTRAND COMPANY (Canada), LTD.
25 Hollinger Road, Toronto 16, Canada

Preface

This book has been tailored to meet the needs of those introductory courses that are concerned exclusively with the study of the national government. It contains all of the material, thoroughly revised, found in the larger book by the same authors, *Government and Politics in the United States,* except the eight chapters devoted to state and local governments.

The national government edition retains all of the features to be found in the longer book. It provides a realistic picture of the nation's institutions. It emphasizes the vitality and flexibility of those institutions to meet the ever increasing pressure for governmental action on both the domestic and foreign fronts.

As in the case of the longer edition, the opening of each chapter sets the stage for the rest of the chapter. A summary reminds the student of the general themes that have been discussed.

Since the publication of the first edition of *Government and Politics in the United States,* a number of significant events have taken place in the environment in which both government and politics are shaped. Hopefully, the most significant of these and their impact upon the American political system are covered in this substantially revised edition. Included among these events are the tragic assassination of John Fitzgerald Kennedy, the tradition-breaking presidential candidacy of Senator Goldwater with its implications for the party system, continued momentum in the area of civil rights, and the vastly expanded court rulings in the field of legislative re-apportionment which portend major alterations in the power base of many state legislatures and the national House of Representatives.

Internationally, the Test Ban Treaty stands as an enigma: a unique pause in the Cold War or the first in a series of steps leading to a more general disarmament.

While this new material has been incorporated into the text and older and less relevant sections have been discarded, we have preserved the general format. For students seeking to delve more deeply into a specific area, the bibliographic sections following each chapter have been updated.

As with the first edition, the authors wish to pay special thanks to Dr. Franklin L. Burdette for his encouragement and counsel.

HOWARD R. PENNIMAN
GUY B. HATHORN
MARK F. FERBER

Table of Contents

Government and Politics

Every profession or trade develops a specialized vocabulary. Often a word or phrase coined to describe a new object, concept, or procedure becomes a part of the general language of a people. Sometimes the connotation given a word by the general public is quite different from its original meaning. It is not unusual, particularly in the social sciences, for the specialists to argue among themselves as to the precise meaning of various terms, but often this apparent conflict is more a matter of degree than of absolute disagreement.

Much, if not most, of the terminology of political science is a part of the working vocabulary of the man in the street. Unfortunately, at least from the point of view of the political scientist, many people confidently and customarily use political terms in a sense somewhat removed from their established meanings.

The purpose of this chapter is to introduce the student to certain basic terms and concepts which are constantly used wherever politics is discussed (and that is everywhere). Some years ago a slogan advertising a well-known product proclaimed: "It's fun to be fooled, but it's more fun to know." So it is concerning the terminology of politics.

THE NATURE OF GOVERNMENT

Since the beginning of time mankind from birth to death has been restrained or impelled by societal standards of conduct. Whether in a primitive society or in a modern industrial community, individuals are enmeshed in a web of complex and sometimes contradictory customs, taboos, habits, and regulations. Of the many institutions exercising control and direction over people, government is unique in its relation to those within the orbit of its jurisdiction. Government stands above all other groups in the degree of coercion it may invoke together with the physical and psychological techniques it may employ to secure compliance with its policies. Failure to adhere to the rules of a social club may result in expulsion from the organization; conduct contrary to the mores of a community may lead to social ostracism; but violation of governmental laws may be punished by imprisonment or even death.

The State. Governments exercise authority within political associations designated as *states*. The concept of the state includes certain basic characteristics necessary to its being, including the elements of (1) population, (2) territory, (3) sovereignty, and (4) government.

The necessity of population and territory is obvious enough but it should be understood that the population dwells within demarcated territory. Sovereignty means that the actions of a government are not subject to control by any higher internal or external authority. One speaks of the sovereignty or authority of the state, but it is the *government*—the political agent of the state—which exercises the authority. *State* is an abstraction which serves to clarify the place of government in our society. The use of the term in this sense should not be confused with the word which designates one of the political units, i.e., California, within the United States. The term state as used here refers to sovereign political units such as France, Australia, Great Britain, or the Soviet Union. There are in the neighborhood of 130 states in the world today.

THE FORMS OF GOVERNMENT

From the time of the ancient Greek philosophers attempts have been made to classify governments into various types. One such classification, popularized by these philosophers, arranged governments according to the number of persons who determined policies.

Autocracy. Using this approach, a government in which *one* person is primarily responsible for making most of the significant political decisions may be designated as an *autocracy*. Note that this general term may be applicable to a wide range of commonly used expressions such as kingship, monarchy, emperorship, or dictatorship. Reiterating, the key to this classification is whether the king, monarch, emperor, or dictator really determines the policies of state in the final analysis. If he is merely the spokesman for a smaller group, or the symbol of state authority, then the system is not an autocracy. It may be argued that governmental power can never be concentrated absolutely in the hands of one individual so that this classification is meaningless. Yet it would appear justifiable to describe the regimes of such rulers as Napoleon and Hitler as autocracies.

Oligarchy. An *oligarchy* is a government in which a relatively small group of people dictates governmental policy. Again, oligarchy is a generic term which may cover a host of more specific popular terms. Thus a *plutocracy* is government by the wealthy; an *aristocracy* is a government by an elite group based usually on rank, wealth, or intellect; a *theocracy* would be a government dominated by a religious hierarchy. A good example of oligarchic government today would be the ruling of states by Communist Party leaders. It is probable that throughout the world more people are subject to oligarchic rule than any other type.[1]

Democracy. A *democracy* is government by the many. The most practical aspect of modern democracies is that the governmental officials who determine policy are subject to control and ultimately removal by a much larger body of citizenry. *Direct* democracy, in which the body of citizens vote directly on all governmental policies is an impossibility in large communities. *Representative* democracy, in which the people vote for officials who in turn make policy, is the form assumed by modern democratic governments. Democratic government is usually associated with the concept that a *majority* of the citizens are eligible to participate in the governmental process through voting. This is ordinarily the case at present with most democratic states permitting practically all adults to qualify as voters. Yet democratic government existed in the United States before 1920 even though most women could not vote in national elections. Even if the majority participation concept is disregarded, a government with relatively large numbers of persons participating, even though indirectly, is distinguishable from the autocratic or oligarchic type.

Monarchial or republican. Historically, two terms have been used to classify governments according to the method by which the titular head of the state is selected. In a *monarchy* the office of the titular ruler is hereditary. In a *republic* this office is filled by some system of election. James Madison distinguished between a "democracy" and a "republic," by defining the former as a system in which the people ruled directly and the latter as a system of representative government. This usage is obsolete, since "pure democracy" does not exist in modern states. This classification in itself does not determine whether a government is democratic or undemocratic. Thus even all communist states today are classified as republics since their titular leaders are subject to an elective process—at least in form. Great Britain, on the other hand, is a monarchy, but is at the same time a democracy.

Parliamentary or presidential. A *parliamentary* government concentrates the executive and legislative powers in a body of representatives chosen by the people. There is a titular executive usually known as President or King but his functions are for the most part symbolic or ceremonial. Certain parliamentary governments, as in Great Britain, are sometimes called cabinet governments and emphasize the leading role of the small group of cabinet officials, headed by a prime minister, who although responsible to parliament, initiates major governmental policies. Great Brit-

---

1 Certainly oligarchies of one kind or another have outnumbered democracies down through the ages. Democracy, at least in large countries, simply did not exist until the American experience and, as we shall see, the United States did not always operate as a democracy.

ain, Sweden, Italy, and the West German Republic are examples of parliamentary systems.

The *presidential* type of government on the other hand assigns real executive powers to an official, the President, who is elected for a set period of time, and whose tenure and prerogatives do not depend upon the parliament or national legislature. There is a separation of legislative and executive powers. There must be cooperation between the legislative and executive branches, but no single branch is so powerful as to negate the influence and authority of the other. The United States is the best example of a successful presidential system. Most Latin American Republics have adopted the presidential type of government. In 1958, France, under the leadership of General de Gaulle, initiated a constitution which seems to be something of a compromise between the traditional parliamentary and presidential governmental forms.

Federal or unitary. If a number of independent governments, without surrendering their independence, join together to handle certain problems, such as protection against external enemies, which they cannot take care of satisfactorily alone, it is said that a *confederation* has been formed. If the several governments go a step further, give up their independence, and form a new government, at the same time retaining certain powers, this is known as a *federal* type. Under this system part of the authority is conferred on the central government, while the remainder is reserved to the component subdivisions or to the people.[2]

The thirteen colonies after declaring their independence from Great Britain first entered into a confederation which was expected to handle defense and certain other difficult tasks. However, the confederation possessed such limited authority that it failed to provide a satisfactory solution to common problems. The convention of 1787, called to work out an arrangement for reducing the weaknesses of the confederation, decided to recommend an entirely new system of government which would be federal in character. Under this, the national government was given definite powers relating to foreign relations, national defense, interstate and foreign commerce, public finance, and other matters of common concern; the remaining authority was reserved to the states or the people.

The United States, Mexico, Canada, Brazil, the Soviet Union (according to its written constitution), and Switzerland are all examples of federal governments. Federalism in its modern form owes much to its successful operation in the United States. Its organizational structure is generally associated with states possessing rather large land areas, perhaps a tradition of strong local or regional government, and often a number of different

---

[2] The arrangement may be just the opposite. For example, in Canada specific authority is granted to the provincial governments, and the remaining authority is left to the national government. An excellent discussion of this form and its current applications is to be found in K. C. Wheare, *Federal Government* (rev. ed., New York: Oxford University Press, 1953).

language or cultural groupings. In the United States the phrase federal government is often used when referring to the national government. Actually, the federal government of the United States is the combination of state and national governments. There also appears to be a tendency on the part of many people to associate the phrase federal government with democratic government. The United States is both federal and democratic. On the other hand, the Soviet Union claims a federal system, but it is not a democratic government by the standards discussed earlier in this chapter.

If all of the power is conferred on a single government, a *unitary* form results. This does not mean that such a government cannot have subdivisions, since virtually all governments necessarily have to organize under some such arrangements for the purpose of administration and local government. But the final authority resides in the central government, and the subdivisions have only such power as the former sees fit to confer on them. As a matter of practice, the central government may delegate substantially the same measure of local home rule which is provided under the federal form; the test is not what power is given but the final seat of authority. Great Britain, in contrast to the United States, has long functioned as a unitary government, though she has been liberal in permitting the counties and the boroughs a considerable measure of leeway. A majority of the states of the world function under the unitary system. A common misconception is to link the unitary form with dictatorial or undemocratic types of government. Obviously, a unitary government may be democratic or undemocratic just as a federal government may be democratic or undemocratic.

Constitutional government or dictatorship. One of the most meaningful classifications of governments deals with their methods of exercising authority. A *constitutional* government is one in which there is a system of effective restraints upon governmental power. Herein there are established and respected rules of procedure for making political decisions and for questioning political decisions both before and after they are made. Means are available for holding governmental officials responsible if they ignore the predetermined "rules of the game."

In a *dictatorship* there are few if any regularized effective restraints upon political authority. Rules of procedure may vary at the whim of governmental officials. Important policy decisions are made and enforced without public debate or discussion. The "rules of the game" mean very little for they are subject to change without notice. The fact that a state has a document called a constitution does not of itself guarantee constitutional government.

Practically every state in the world today has a written constitution, but many of them are not practicing constitutional government. Great Britain is the prime example of a constitutional government without the benefit of a written document conveniently labelled the Constitution of Great Britain. Most governments do not fall at one extreme or the other on this particular scale of values. A government for the most part may act in a constitutional manner, but then in regard to a particular matter, or for a short period of time, may assume some of the characteristics of a dictatorship. In like manner a dictatorship may at times accept a degree of regularized restraint affecting its decisions.

ECONOMIC ORGANIZATION WITHIN THE STATE

All classifications of government mentioned have had to do with the political organization of the state. A primary purpose of governmental organization is to facilitate the making and enforcing of decisions. Decisions must be made as to the functions of government. Especially in the past fifty years bitter debate has raged, elections have been fought, and violent revolutions have been fomented because of decisions made or not made by governments as to their proper role in the economic organization of their territories.

Capitalism. In many respects the Constitution of 1787 reflects the concept of *laissez faire capitalism* which was especially popular with many of the influential members of the convention. According to this doctrine, government was to restrict its activities to a few though vital functions. It was to protect the people from outside enemies, maintain the public order at home, perhaps undertake a few essential public works, establish a stable monetary arrangement, and provide a fair system of courts so that, among other things, individuals would be given adequate protection of their property rights. In other words, the government was to play a negative role in respect to matters of economics. The production and distribution of economic goods was to remain outside the orbit of governmental control. The strongest selling point for the capitalistic system of the late eighteenth and early nineteenth century was that the general welfare of the individuals in the state would be best promoted by a minimal amount of governmental interposition in the economic process. This theory was a reaction to mercantilism in which the success of economic policies was largely measured in the benefits accruing to states. "Natural" economic forces such as the law of supply and demand and the free play of competition were to be the self-regulators of the system.

It has often been pointed out that no government, including our own, was ever able to quite live up to the negative role assigned to it by the more ardent *laissez faire* advocates. Governments were forced to adopt policies which sometimes favored one economic group over another or which were supposed to protect the individual from the natural laws of economics. By the beginning of the twentieth century, the United States government had moved far from any "hands off" policy toward economic matters—two outstanding legislative acts to the contrary being the Interstate Commerce Act (regulation of railroads) and the Sherman Antitrust Act. Following the great depression of the early 1930's no one could seriously argue that any system approaching *laissez faire* capitalism was operating in any major state of the world. In the United States the national government and the state governments have created a number of agencies which regulate various aspects of communication, transportation, labor-management relations, and business organization and finance. Agriculture, manufacturing, mining, the generation and distribution of electric power, and production of oil and natural gas represent an incomplete list of specific areas in which positive legislative action touches the economic front. Withal, the United States is still counted as the strongest capitalistic state in the world. Although its economy differs vastly from the *laissez faire* model, the primary means of production and distribution of economic goods remain in private not governmental hands. The fiction or reality, as the case may be, of competition in the market place continues to play an important part in American economic calculations. The profit motive remains of cardinal importance in the development of new products and the improvement of old ones.

With a few exceptions, the national government has been content to regulate various economic sectors in the interest of the general welfare, rather than assuming direct control of their operations, as would be the case in a socialistic economy.

Socialism. There are many varieties of socialistic theory but the one referred to here may be classified as evolutionary state socialism. According to this doctrine, the general welfare of the citizens can best be obtained through state (collective) ownership and operation of all the means of producing and distributing economic goods. The evolutionary socialist advocates the transition from capitalism to socialism through a gradual transfer of the major industries from private ownership to public ownership. He does not share the belief of many Marxian Socialists that the transfer from capitalism to socialism can only be achieved by violence. It may be accomplished, says the evolutionary socialist, through the normal democratic process in which the people's representatives, following full discussion, decide upon nationalization or socialization of various segments of the economy with fair compensation going to the owners. The British Labour Party program results from this type of socialist thinking. During its control of the British government from 1945 until 1951, the Labour Party was responsible for the nationalization of many key industries. Although only about 20 per cent of the British industry was ever nationalized, the government under both Labour and Conservative party leadership has assumed partial but powerful planning authority over many other sectors of the economy. Since World War II many states in all parts of the world have assumed operation of certain key industries and subjected others to strict regulation within a concept of governmental planning. In summary, socialism achieved through democratic processes is found in varying stages on all continents.

Communism. Marx spoke of governments as superstructures which were really the result of the control of the means of production. However today in practice, communism is commonly used to describe certain governmental methods, techniques, and organization of a dictatorial nature as well as the economic structure of the society within a state. The communist doctrine blames all the ills of society on capitalism. The theory predicts the inevitable destruction of capitalism, but nevertheless advocates violent revolution as a means of hastening its demise. The democratic political process is described by the communist as a sham which enables the capitalist to continue to dominate the political and economic ways of society. The ultimate goal of communism, according to its prophets, is a classless and stateless society in which the distribution of economic goods will be in accordance with the needs of the individual. Before this ultimate phase is reached, however, the party must direct the state through a period of socialism. This is the point the Soviet Union has now reached. The state has become the sole employer. Total planning for the entire economy is undertaken by the government, which is the creature of the Communist Party. In practice communist controlled states are both socialistic and totalitarian. Totalitarian refers to the state's policy of dominating every phase of the life of the individual.

THE WELFARE STATE

No matter what may be the political or economic organization of the state, there is a trend throughout the world for governments to use the collective resources of the community to enhance the economic and social well-being of its citizens. The reasons for this development are many and complex, and it is extremely difficult to separate cause from effect. The rise of nationalism, of modern industrialism, and the advance of technology in all areas, but particularly in the communication and transportation sectors, have all contributed to a redistribution of political power, because of the necessity of maintaining the sympathy and support of the masses for governmental policies.

In democratic states the influence of universal suffrage upon governmental policies is understandable. In such states there is power in numbers, and in the long run, if a majority of the people demand that the government undertake particular programs, the pleas will be heeded. The United States government has engaged in various welfare activities, not because of outside pressure, but because considerably more people in the United States favor these particular programs than oppose them. This is not to say that the concept of the welfare state has no weak points. As one author has written: "The important problems presented by the growth of the welfare state . . . do not involve evaluations of the possibility of turning back the clock but, rather, involve estimates of the extent to which welfare activity may or may not, at some stage, become dangerous to the economic health of the state and to the individual liberty and vitality of its citizens." [3]

In the United States the term welfare state has sometimes been used in a disdainful sense in noting the functions of government in socialistic or communistic societies. This usage is unfortunate because all major states of the world today are welfare states though in varying degrees. Manifestation of the welfare state trend in the United States would include governmental activities in such areas as old-age and survivors insurance (social security), public health, public education, public housing, unemployment insurance, and workmen's compensation.

THE WAYS OF DEMOCRACY

Day after day Americans are reminded on radio and television, in newspapers, periodicals, pamphlets, and books of the "challenge to democracy" with particular reference to the threat of world communism. Twenty years ago the menace appeared to be in the rise of the fascist states; undoubtedly, the future will witness a continuing competition involving democratic versus non-democratic governmental concepts. Neither concept is assured ultimate acceptance throughout the world, or in any particular state. Adherents of democratic government recognize inconveniences and potential dangers inherent in the system; non-democratic regimes are apt to preach the infallibility of their own particular brand of political control. The sustaining faith of the democratic creed is that in the long run its strength and advantages far outweigh its weaknesses and disadvantages.

A practical test of democracy in action is the responsiveness of the state to the public opinion of the community, provided that the community is given adequate opportunity to express opinions. The electoral system provides the most formal way for the people to register choices for officials and policies, but this is only the principal end product of a process which is in constant operation. Free discussion of all issues is a prerequisite to any intelligent choice between alternatives. A democratic society zealously guards the right of free discussion on all issues, even to the extent of permitting condemnation of policies which are already the law of the land.

Full debate may be largely sham unless there is some mechanism for translating convictions into policies. For this reason, the existence of more than one political party appears to be an essential for democracy's survival. One of the first steps taken by fascist and communist rulers has been to outlaw all opposition parties.

Democracy is predicated on the belief that the state and its governmental agent are means to ends rather than ends in themselves. This is in

---

[3] Daniel Wit, *Comparative Political Institutions* (New York: Henry Holt and Company, 1953), p. 466.

stark contrast to various philosophies which exalt the state as such, and in which an individual's worth is measured in terms of his contribution to the glory of the state. The rule of law is pre-eminent in a democratic society. State officials and private citizens are governed by the same regulations. Laws are publicized before taking effect; those accused of violating governmental rules are assured of a reasonable, regularized trial procedure.

Individualism, in its classic meaning, has suffered curtailment in all types of governments, including democracies. Authority versus liberty has been an age-old conflict since the establishment of government, with the scales tilting toward authority in modern times. Much has been written of the possible "tyranny of the majority" in a democratic state. Fortunately, democratic theory carries within it a counterbalancing doctrine of "minority rights." This concept is often formalized in bills of rights which establish certain fundamental guarantees to the individual such as freedom of speech, press, religion, and the right to a fair trial. The formal guarantees incorporated in a bill of rights are apt to be meaningless unless a consensus throughout the political community supports their application not sporadically but constantly. A democratic community furnishes support for the doctrine of minority rights.

Democracy is the most difficult type of government to establish and to operate. It appears to call for a political maturity in its citizens which can be developed only over a relatively long period. It has been said that the infant mortality rate of newborn democracies is extremely high, yet, once a democratic state has reached adulthood, its vitality is amazing.

POLITICS AND POLITICAL SCIENCE

Webster's Collegiate Dictionary defines politics as "the science and art of government." This definition is perhaps as good as any short one can be, but it needs elaboration. The science and art of government embraces individuals, institutions, and organizations having no formal connection with government *per se,* but who nevertheless affect government and are affected by governmental action. Professor Brewster has written: "Politics is the process of determining and applying public policy. It involves the establishment of constitutional foundations for the government, the fixing of governmental authority, the selection of officials, the determination of what laws and regulations are to be enacted, and the use of discretion in applying the laws." [4] In determining and applying public policy private individuals, pressure groups, and political parties compete and cooperate with each other in the political process, seeking to influence governmental action, i.e., public policy.

A popular but mischievous comparison is that which defines a politician

---

[4] R. Wallace Brewster, *Government in Modern Society* (Boston: Houghton Mifflin Company, 1958), p. 18.

as one who promotes selfish ends through artifices and intrigues, as distinguished from a statesman who is pictured as the fount of wisdom and virtue,
with the public welfare always his goal. "Politics," as used throughout this
book, covers the accomplishments and failures of both the saints and the
sinners. A realistic approach to an understanding of politics does not deny
that charlatans and demagogues may be significant influences in the process
of government, but the same realism must recognize that a non-political
statesman has never lived.

Many social scientists equate politics with a struggle for power. Again
misunderstanding may arise from such a description if the power struggle
is associated with base motives. The point to remember is that the techniques used to acquire power may be legal and/or moral as well as illegal
and/or immoral. The motivation and use of power may be socially acceptable and desirable as well as socially unacceptable and undesirable. If the
struggle for political power is viewed in its totality it becomes a realistic
descriptive phrase for politics.

Political science has been defined as "a branch of the social sciences
dealing with the theory, organization, and practice of the state." [5] But political science goes far beyond what the more literal minded reader might
infer from the foregoing definition. An understanding of its scope may be
gained by noting the various fields in which college courses in political
science are offered. One source identifies the following rather typical areas:

1. Political theory and/or philosophy.
2. Political parties, public opinion, and pressure groups (often
including propaganda and semantics). This cluster of courses is sometimes
titled "political dynamics."
3. Public law, frequently particularized into constitutional and
administrative law.
4. Public administration.
5. International relations, including diplomacy (or international
politics), international law, and international organization.
6. American government (national, state, and local).
7. Comparative (foreign) government. This is often bracketed with
American government as a single field.
8. Legislatures and legislation.
9. Government and business.[6]

SUMMARY

Governments acting for political units known as *states* exercise authority over people wherever they reside. *Politics* comprehends all concepts concerning the origin, establishment, nature, and necessity of states as well as

5 E. C. Smith and A. J. Zurcher (eds.), *A Dictionary of American Politics* (New York:
Barnes & Noble, Inc., 1944), p. 238.
6 C. C. Rodee, T. J. Anderson, and C. Q. Christol, *Introduction to Political Science*
(New York: McGraw-Hill Book Company, Inc., 1957), pp. 10-11.

theoretical and operational aspects of governments as to their creation, form, power, procedures, methods of choosing officials, and means of determining and executing public policy. *Political science* is the systematic study of politics.

Governments have been classified in many different ways but no single scheme is satisfactory for all purposes. The oldest classification is based on the number of individuals who determine state policies. An *autocracy* is characterized by one-man rule; an *oligarchy* involves the rule of the few; a *democracy* has many people shaping governmental policies.

Another classification is based upon how the titular head of the state is chosen. In a *monarchy* the office of the titular ruler is hereditary; in a *republic* the office is filled by a system of elections at least in outward form.

A *parliamentary* government concentrates the executive and legislative powers in a body of representatives chosen by the people. *Presidential* government grants considerable executive and administrative functions to an individual apart from the legislative body.

The method by which powers are distributed as between the central and lower units of a government determines whether a state is a unitary or federal form. In a *unitary* system the central government determines what functions are to be carried out by the lower levels of government. In a *federal* form both the central and local governments are allotted spheres of operations, usually defined in a written constitution which normally cannot be changed without participation by both levels of government.

Regularized restraint upon governmental powers results in *constitutional* government; in a *dictatorship* there exists no effective regularized restraint upon arbitrary governmental decisions.

States may also be described on the basis of their dominant form of economic organization. In a *capitalistic* state the primary means for the production and distribution of economic goods rests in private or corporate hands. *Socialism* is the state ownership and operation of economic factors. *Communism* originated as a type of socialistic economic theory, but preaching the necessity of a revolutionary, violent uprooting of the capitalistic system and proclaiming as an ultimate goal "the withering away" of states and governments. However, today communism is frequently used to describe certain governmental methods, techniques, and organization of a dictatorial nature as well as an economic theory.

BIBLIOGRAPHIC NOTE

Textbooks written as introductions to the study of political science include detailed discussions of most of the material covered in this chapter. Useful older studies in this category are J. W. Garner, *Political Science and Government* (New York: American Book Company, 1928); Francis G. Wilson, *The Elements of Modern Politics* (New York: McGraw-Hill Book Company, Inc., 1936); and Raymond Gettell, *Political Science* (2nd ed., Boston: Ginn and Company, 1949). More recent books of this type, which usually devote some attention to problems of methodology, include Conley H. Dillon, Carl Leiden, and Paul D. Stewart, *Introduction to Political Science* (Princeton, N. J.: D. Van Nostrand Company, Inc., 1958); R. Wallace Brewster, *Government in Modern Society* (Boston: Houghton Mifflin Company, 1958); Thomas R. Adam, *Elements of Government* (New York: Random House, 1960); Carlton C. Rodee, Totton J. Anderson, and Carl Q. Christol, *Introduction to Political Science* (New York: McGraw-Hill Book Company, Inc., 1957); and Austin Ranney, *The Governing of Men* (New York: Henry Holt and Company, 1958). For an extremely good book, stressing the sociological development of governmental institutions, see Robert M. MacIver, *The Web of Government* (New York: The Macmillan Company, 1947).

For two excellent books stressing democratic political institutions, see John P. Roche and Murray S. Stedman, Jr., *The Dynamics of Democratic Government* (New York: McGraw-Hill Book Company, Inc., 1954), and J. A. Corry and Henry J. Abraham, *Elements of Democratic Government* (3rd ed., New York: Oxford University Press, 1958). In Austin Ranney's and Willmoore Kendall's *Democracy and the American Party System* (New York: Harcourt, Brace and Company, 1956), the first four chapters focus attention on a "Model of Democracy." For a systematic treatment of the theories of democracy, see Henry B. Mayo, *Introduction to Democratic Theory* (New York: Oxford University Press, 1960. The uniqueness of American democracy is stressed in David J. Boorstin, *The Genius of American Politics* (Chicago: Chicago University Press, 1953). An analysis and description of the common traits of autocratic regimes is presented in C. J. Friedrich and Z. K. Brezinski, *Totalitarian Dictatorship and Autocracy* (Cambridge, Mass.: Harvard University Press, 1956).

Two of the best-known works on constitutionalism are C. H. McIlwain's *Constitutionalism, Ancient and Modern* (Ithaca, N. Y.: Cornell University Press, 1947); and C. J. Friedrich's *Constitutional Government and Democracy* (rev. ed., Boston: Ginn and Company, 1950).

A number of recent publications deal with the goals, methodology, and nature of political science. For example, see American Political Science Association, *Goals for Political Science,* Report of the Committee for the Advancement of Teaching (New York: William Sloane Associates, 1951); David Easton, *The Political System: An Inquiry into the State of Political Science* (New York: Alfred A. Knopf, 1953); Bernard Crick, *The American Science of Politics* (Los Angeles: University of California Press, 1959); Charles S. Hyneman, *The Study of Politics: The Present State of American Political Science* (Urbana: University of Illinois Press, 1959); and Roland Young, ed., *Approaches to the Study of Politics* (Evanston, Illinois: Northwestern University Press, 1958).

The number of publications concerned with the nature of the study of politics grows ever longer. Most recent contributions include George E. G. Catlin, *Systematic Politics: Elementa Politica et Sociologica* (Toronto: University of Toronto Press, 1962); Robert A. Dahl, *Modern Political Analysis* (Englewood Cliffs, N. J.: Prentice-Hall, 1963); Carl J. Friedrich, *Man and His Government: An Empirical Theory of Politics* (New York: McGraw-Hill, 1963); Bertrand de Jouvenel, *The Pure Theory of Politics* (New Haven: Yale University Press, 1963); Harold D. Lasswell, *The Future of Political Science* (New York: Atherton Press, 1963).

2

Political Experience Prior to 1789

I_T IS sometimes assumed that the United States came suddenly into being as a nation in 1789 without very much in the way of antecedents. Certainly the year 1789 occupies a bright place in the annals of Americans, but it should not be forgotten that the political experience of those living in the thirteen original states covered approximately as long a period prior to 1789 as has elapsed since. The first settlers arrived during the first half of the seventeenth century. And during the remainder of that century and through most of the eighteenth century a great deal of significant political experience was acquired. The founders of the new republic were aware of what had developed along political lines and they were influenced in no small measure by that knowledge in framing a constitution for the United States. We cannot here deal in detail with the political record of Massachusetts, Virginia, New York, and Pennsylvania during the seventeenth and eighteenth centuries, but a survey of political developments must be undertaken before proceeding to a discussion of the institutions and practices that have been established since 1789.

THE PRE-REVOLUTIONARY PERIOD

When the first settlements were made in what is now the United States may be a debatable question. The Vikings from the Scandinavian countries probably landed somewhere along the New England coast around the year 1000, but they established no permanent settlements and left no impact on political institutions. The Spaniards who came to the Southwest and Florida several centuries later were responsible for the first settlements and they have left an impact on certain areas, particularly New Mexico. The colonists from England, Holland, and other parts of western Europe founded various colonies along the Atlantic seaboard during the first half of the seventeenth century. Many of these proved permanent, and it was here that the political experience which was to make so great an impress on the constitution drawn up in 1787 was gained. The New England town or township goes back to the early seventeenth century. The first county was established in Virginia in 1634. New York City was probably the first formally chartered city or municipality, having received a Dutch charter in 1652 and an English charter in 1686.

These early colonists along the eastern seaboard did not start their political life in a vacuum. Most of them had emigrated from England where significant political experience had been accruing for more than a thousand years. Others came from France, Holland, and other places where political experience was also highly developed. These courageous and strong-minded men and women, frequently driven on by a desire for religious freedom which was lacking in their European homelands, brought with them at least rudimentary knowledge of governmental institutions and practices. Since the greatest number of the settlers came from England, the influence of English political and legal institutions was particularly notable. The pioneer governments set up in Massachusetts, Virginia, and certain other colonies were largely patterned after those left behind in England. In New York the Dutch experience left some mark. Elsewhere French and Spanish foundations are apparent.

It was in the thirteen colonies stretching along the Atlantic seaboard north of Florida that the most important developments took place, though the French impact on Louisiana and the Spanish contribution in California, Arizona, New Mexico, and Texas cannot be overlooked. The culmination of political developments in the thirteen colonies resulted in the Revolution which broke out in 1775. This led to the Declaration of Independence from England and subsequently to the establishing of the United States in 1789. But more than that, the political record in the thirteen colonies is worth attention because the settlers who crossed the Allegheny Mountains and eventually pushed to the Pacific largely came from these colonies. And they naturally took with them the knowledge arising out of their observation of and participation in the political organizations of these colonies and later states. The result was that the governments set up in these western areas were patterned more or less closely on those of the Atlantic colonies or states.

The thirteen colonies were settled by diverse groups who migrated to North America for varying reasons. Consequently there was a good deal of variation in the provisions made for government despite the more or less common English background. The Puritans of Massachusetts sought to mix religious ideas with their political organizations, whereas in Virginia religious motivation was far less. Royal colonies, like Massachusetts and Virginia, had a somewhat different political setup from those like Pennsylvania which started out as grants to proprietors. Climatic conditions also contributed to the diversity. Colonies that looked mainly to trade and small farming developed along somewhat different lines from those organized on the basis of large-scale agricultural undertakings. Thus Massachusetts and other New England colonies made the town (township) the basic unit of government, while the southern colonies, built around plantation life, organized their government around the county.

Nevertheless, if there was a considerable amount of diversity among the thirteen colonies, there was also a great deal of similarity. With the exception of Pennsylvania, Maryland, Connecticut, Delaware, and Rhode Island—quite an exception to be sure—all of the colonies became royal provinces, with governors appointed by the king of England. And it may be added that the non-royal provinces gradually became more and more like royal provinces under charters issued by the British crown. In every case the colonies had legislatures which increasingly sought to exercise authority over local affairs. The courts and legal systems of the thirteen colonies were rather similar, all following the rules of common law. To a greater or less degree, all of the colonies found themselves engaged in a common cause against the authorities in London. They saw their problems from the vantage point of the New World, whereas the officials in London looked upon the colonies as dependencies of the mother country.

In light of the revolution which eventually took place, it might be supposed that the colonies were ground down by the mother country, oppressed, and tyranically ordered about. Actually they enjoyed a large measure of autonomy; ironically it was this habit of freedom which perhaps led to their rebellion rather than any great degree of oppression. Though after 1707, one of the British secretaries of state was usually made responsible for the Scottish and colonial offices, the Colonial Office did not exist at this time and indeed there was no effective provision made by the English government for colonial control. The attitude of the officials in London may have been unsympathetic and lacking in understanding on occasion, but, with transportation and communication facilities still very simple and three thousand miles of ocean separating the mother country from the colonies, the colonies followed their own desires quite largely. If Parliament attempted to regulate colonial trade, the rules were usually evaded. Perhaps most incredible of all, the colonies paid no taxes into the English treasury. Instead of being garrisoned and forced to support British troops, the colonies ordinarily depended upon their own resources for protection. All of this established a pattern of self-reliance which placed them in a favorable position to make the transition from colonial to state status.

THE REVOLUTION AND DECLARATION OF INDEPENDENCE

After countenancing a large measure of colonial freedom, the British government, during the middle of the eighteenth century, decided that a more effective system of control over the American colonies should be inaugurated. They sent military contingents to serve as garrisons at various strategic points in order to protect their possessions against foreign aggression. It also seemed to them desirable to enforce the regulations relating to trade which had been on the statute books but were rarely observed across the Atlantic. They also maintained that it was reasonable to ask the colonies to pay a part of the cost arising out of colonial administration and therefore proposed to levy certain taxes, such as that on tea. But the colonies had enjoyed freedom too long to recognize the justice of these new measures. Though the taxes imposed were relatively light, the colonists objected violently to the principle involved, asserting that they should be expected to pay only those taxes which they or their representatives had

PAINTING OF THE COMMITTEE DRAFTING THE DECLARATION OF INDEPENDENCE   Thomas Jefferson, John Adams, Benjamin Franklin, Roger Sherman and Robert R. Livingston

voted. They disputed the right of Parliament to legislate for them, though they admitted their allegiance to the crown. The presence of British redcoats seemed to many colonists an irritation and even an insult rather than a measure for their protection. Consequently the tension between the colonies and mother country became more and more serious. Had there been a king who clearly understood matters or who displayed greater skill in dealing with a sensitive situation or had the ministers of the king been more far-sighted, the final break might have been avoided or at least postponed. As it was, revolution broke out in the colonies in 1775.

Rising dissatisfaction with the new controls imposed by England led to the calling of a First Continental Congress in Philadelphia in 1774. A

Second Continental Congress was convened in 1775; in 1776 this Congress finally decided to sever ties with the mother country. On June 7, 1776, Richard Henry Lee of Virginia moved three resolutions, one of which provided for a declaration of independence. John Adams of Massachusetts seconded the resolutions. On June 10, 1776, the Continental Congress adopted a motion which had the effect of setting up a committee composed of Thomas Jefferson, John Adams, Benjamin Franklin, Roger Sherman, and Robert Livingston to draft a resolution relating to independence. Thomas Jefferson was entrusted with the task of framing such a resolution, and he brought to the assignment one of the most gifted pens which has ever been set to the writing of a state paper. Jefferson consulted Adams and Franklin on various points, inserting in the draft various suggestions which they made. On June 28, 1776, the committee reported the resolution without change. On July 2, 1776, Congress adopted Lee's first resolution and so in the opinion of some authorities actually declared independence from England. However, the draft prepared by Jefferson was not adopted until July 4, 1776, after several changes had been made. July fourth is therefore regarded as the birthday of the United States.

It was one thing to declare independence and another to win independence. England was unwilling to see her American colonies sever their ties with the mother country and consequently took steps to put down the rebellion and nullify the Declaration of Independence. On a good many occasions the prospects of the colonies were far from bright. Many of the colonists were not very eager to serve in military forces, to pay taxes to support such forces, or to do much else to bring about independence. Colonial military forces were ill-trained, poorly equipped, and often far from dependable. After serving a few months, often in desultory fashion, members of the forces wanted to return to their homes and farms, and the discipline was so slight that many did leave their posts. It was a difficult task to raise any kind of military force and when commanding officers did receive recruits, they never knew how long they would be able to keep them.

The British also had their problems. Englishmen looked with little enthusiasm on serving in military forces intended to put down the American rebellion. Hence it was necessary to hire Hessians and other professional soldiers from the Continent to serve in the British military forces. Transport across three thousand miles of one of the world's most stormy and treacherous oceans constituted a serious problem. There was inefficiency and even some degree of corruption in supplying the British forces. Some of the British commanders were bumblers. The situation was complicated by war with France and the necessity of dividing British forces. Moreover, the French gave considerable material support to the revolting colonists. The result was that the revolution went on year after year, with neither the revolutionists nor the mother country able to bring about a decision. Some of those who had spoken loudly in favor of revolution seemed to lose their

FACSIMILE OF SIGNATURES ON THE DECLARATION OF INDEPENDENCE

ardor as time passed without a victory. Fortunately for the American cause, George Washington and a few others remained faithfully committed and refused to give up. Eventually the British admitted defeat, and the colonists gained their independence in 1783, but the struggle was long, drawnout, and exhausting on both sides. When victory was finally achieved, the prospects for the colonies did not immediately appear very bright, what with conflict among themselves, economic weakness, and difficulty in agreeing on steps to be taken to meet various pressing problems.

EARLY STATE CONSTITUTIONS AND GOVERNMENTS

When fighting broke out in 1774, colonial governors often left their posts to take refuge with British forces. Consequently some provision had to be made for carrying on government in the various places. Conventions were set up to deal with the emergency situation and the Continental Congress sent word to each revolting colony that it would be appropriate to reorganize its government in such a manner as to meet its individual requirements. As the revolution proceeded and independence became imminent, there was increasing dislike of the term "colony" which suggested dependence. Consequently it became customary to substitute the word "state" for "colony." What had been regarded in some quarters at least as temporary measures therefore came to be looked upon as permanent. With this attitude prevalent, it was to be expected that constitutions would be drafted for the several states.

Connecticut and Rhode Island, having royal charters which were deemed reasonably satisfactory, simply changed a few phrases here and there and by this process converted their charters into constitutions. The other states saw fit to prepare new constitutions for themselves. By 1780 the last of the states, Massachusetts, had taken this step. Some of these early state constitutions were very brief affairs which were hastily prepared. Others were more detailed and received more careful attention. Only in Massachusetts and New Hampshire were special conventions set up to draft the constitutions. The other states contented themselves with assigning this task to assemblies which had been established to deal with various public problems confronting the states. In about half of the states the documents were submitted to a popular vote for approval, but in the others they were put into effect by the process of legislative promulgation.

While the revolutionary constitutions varied a good deal in detail, they were characterized by a considerable degree of uniformity as far as basic matters went. In every instance they provided for a state government made up of three separate branches—executive, legislative, and judicial—each with certain checks over the other. A governor was everywhere authorized, but his scope was limited as a result of the experiences which the colonies had had with their royal governors. During the early days in all except four of the states, the governor was chosen by the legislature, and in ten of the states he received a term of only one year. Massachusetts was the only state originally to confer the veto power on the governor. In every case the governor was checked in making appointments by a council or by the legislature. Most of the states provided for bicameral legislative bodies, though Pennsylvania and Georgia contented themselves with a single house.[1] Everywhere the authority of the legislative branch was extensive, reflecting the popular distrust of the executive. Except in South Carolina, election to the lower house of the legislature was on an annual basis.

The court systems were taken over more or less intact from colonial days, with courts of three grades being authorized. Judges, who had been appointed by the crown in London during colonial days, were made elective by the legislature in about half of the states and in the others appointive by the governor, with the approval of a council or senate in some instances. Local government as it had existed under colonial administration was retained in large measure. The town (township) continued as the basic unit in the New England states, the county in the southern states, and a mixed system in the middle states. In general, the new constitutions laid strong emphasis on civil rights, though not all of them included formal bills of rights. Provisions for trial by jury, freedom of speech, religious tolerance, freedom of the press, and the writ of habeas corpus were commonplace. On the other hand, suffrage generally was limited to male property holders.

THE CONFEDERATION

It was not enough to transform colonial governments into state governments, for there were major problems which required attention from some agency at a higher level than that of the separate states. The Continental Congress recognized this need by drafting articles to serve as a basis for a confederation of the states in November, 1777. But the states displayed such local pride and were so jealous of their individual authority that Congress had to exercise a great deal of caution in taking action. It seemed feasible to do no more than set up a loose confederation of more or less independent states for the time being rather than a federal or unitary type of government. Under the Confederation the states retained a large measure of sovereignty and very reluctantly entered into an agreement to tolerate a central authority only to grapple with certain vexing matters, such as support for the revolutionary forces fighting against England, which they could not handle alone. Even with the concessions made to state pride, ratification of the Articles of Confederation was not completed until 1781, when Maryland was finally persuaded to accept the Articles.

The Articles of Confederation provided for a Congress to be made up of delegates or ambassadors from the various states, ranging from two to seven in number. The size of a state delegation was not very important, however, since each state had only one vote in Congress irrespective of the size of its del-

---

[1] Pennsylvania retained a unicameral legislature until 1790. Georgia contented itself with a unicameral legislature during the years 1777 to 1789. Vermont made use of a unicameral legislature for almost half a century from 1791 to 1836.

egation. Delegates were selected on an annual basis and paid by their own states. No delegate could serve more than three years out of any six. A majority of the delegates of a state determined the way the single state vote would be cast. Two-thirds of the states had to be in agreement to take any important action. There were no provisions for an effective executive or for courts of any character. The unanimous consent of the states had to be obtained to add amendments to the Articles of Confederation.

Under the Articles Congress was given full responsibility over many aspects of foreign relations. It could declare war and make peace, send and receive diplomatic representatives, enter into treaties and alliances, deal with Indian affairs, fix standards of coinage and of weights and measures, and organize a postal system. But the Confederation had no authority to tax and therefore it was forced to depend upon requisitions made upon the states. Unfortunately such requisitions were all too often not honored. Nor could Congress regulate interstate commerce or even commerce with foreign countries except indirectly through its treaty-making power. It is not difficult to see that these were extremely serious weaknesses, particularly under the circumstances confronting the revolting states. To make matters even more critical, a paralyzing depression made financial grants from the states most uncertain and at least partially explained a disposition on the part of the states to stifle what trade there was by resorting to tariffs and various commercial restrictions. Only about one-tenth of the amounts levied on the states by the Confederation was ever paid, and consequently the financial situation was desperate. All in all, the Confederation, weak to begin with because of the jealousy on the part of the states, could not even exercise in any very satisfactory manner the limited authority conferred on it. The result was that the situation became more and more critical as the months passed and the demand for some sort of change became insistent.

THE ALEXANDRIA AND ANNAPOLIS CONFERENCES

With financial bankruptcy threatened, widespread domestic disorder apparently in the offing and concern over the weak handling of relations with foreign countries, and numerous interstate commercial squabbles, there were various proposals as to possible courses of action. A conference was held at Alexandria, Virginia in 1785 to consider the disputes arising out of navigation on the Chesapeake Bay and the Potomac River between Maryland and Virginia. The conferees were able to work out an agreement on the immediate points involved, but it was apparent that the whole field of interstate commerce needed attention. Hence the Virginia legislature sponsored a meeting to be held at Annapolis in September, 1786. This meeting was attended by representatives of only five states, though others had been invited, and its limited representation restricted it to discussion of the underlying difficulties. As a result of the Annapolis conference, however, Alexander Hamilton drafted a report which pointed out in an incisive manner the general weaknesses of the Articles of Confederation. Though unable to accomplish practical results, itself, the Annapolis conference served a useful purpose by recommending the calling of another convention to be held in Philadelphia the following year, 1787. It was this convention, which proceeded to draft a new constitution for a United States of America to displace the Confederation.

SUMMARY

Political experience in what is now the United States began in the seventeenth century in the colonies along the Atlantic seaboard. The colonists who had emigrated from European countries, the largest number from England, brought with them a knowledge of political organization and practice on the other side of the Atlantic. But conditions in the new world were frequently different from those to be found in Europe and as time passed many modifications in existing political institutions were made to meet local needs. Such modification was made relatively easy if not encouraged by the degree of autonomy which the colonies were permitted by the English government. It is important to keep in mind that the colonists had had approximately a century and a half of experience in North America before the United States came into existence.

When the British government finally determined to tighten up on colonial administration, sent military forces to garrison certain colonies, and imposed some rather modest taxes on the colonists, revolution broke out. It led to a Declaration of Independence on July 4, 1776. A long drawn out war eventually led to independence. In the meantime the colonial governments were transformed into state governments and a Confederation was set up to give attention to various pressing problems. But the Confederation was given so little authority and displayed such serious weakness that a critical situation soon arose. This eventually led to the calling of a convention in Philadelphia in 1787 which drafted a constitution for a United States of America.

BIBLIOGRAPHIC NOTE

For detailed treatment of colonial developments C. M. Andrews, *The Colonial Period of American History* (4 vols., New Haven: Yale University Press, 1934-38), is very useful. L. W. Labaree's *Royal Government in America* (New York: Frederick Ungar Publishing Company, 1958) is particularly valuable for experience in the colonies under royal charters. Also see C. Bridenbaugh, *Cities in the Wilderness* (New York: Alfred A. Knopf, 1955) and *Cities in Revolt* (New York: Alfred A. Knopf, 1955).

On the revolution and the events leading up to it, see Carl L. Becker, *The Eve of the Revolution* (New Haven: Yale University Press, 1918); L. H. Gipson, *Coming of the Revolution* (New York: Harper & Brothers, 1954); Carl L. Becker,

Declaration of Independence (New York: Vintage Books, 1958); E. S. Morgan, *Birth of the Republic 1763-1789* (Chicago: University of Chicago Press, 1956); J. P. Boyd, *The Drafting of the Declaration of Independence* (Princeton: Princeton University Press, 1944); C. H. McIlwain, *The American Revolution; A Constitutional Interpretation* (New York: The Macmillan Co., 1923); C. L. Ward, *War of the Revolution* (2 vols., New York: The Macmillan Co., 1952); W. M. Wallace, *Appeal to Arms* (New York: Harper & Brothers, 1951); C. H. Van Tyne, *Causes of the War of Independence* (Gloucester: P. Smith, 1952); C. L. Rossiter, *Seedtime of the Republic* (New York: Harcourt, Brace & Company, 1953); J. R. Alden, *American Revolution 1775-1783* (New York: Harper & Brothers, 1954); and H. Clinton, *American Rebellion* (New Haven: Yale University Press, 1955).

A. Nevins, *The American States During and After the Revolution, 1775-1789* (New York: The Macmillan Company, 1924) deals with the transformation of the colonies into states. M. Jensen, *The Articles of Confederation* (Madison: University of Wisconsin Press, 1940) analyzes the provisions of the Articles of Confederation. A. C. McLaughlin, *The Confederation and the Constitution* (New York: Harper & Brothers, 1905) discusses the experience under the Confederation. J. B. Sanders, *Evolution of the Executive Departments of the Continental Congress, 1774-1789* (Chapel Hill: University of North Carolina Press, 1935) is worth consulting on the provisions made for an executive. W. W. Crosskey, *Politics and the Constitution in the History of the United States* (2 vols., Chicago: University of Chicago Press, 1953) seeks to uncover the actual record, both as to ideas and problems, of the period of the Confederation.

The aspects of our prenational life continue to fascinate historians and political scientists. Indeed, the broadening of their interests in current problems is matched by a similar broadening of interests as they look back on our early history. Some recent interesting and relevant books are Carl Berger, *Broadsides and Bayonets: The Propaganda War of the American Revolution* (Philadelphia: University of Pennsylvania Press, 1961); William N. Chambers, *Political Parties in a New Nation: The American Experiment, 1776-1809* (New York: Oxford University Press, 1963); Jackson T. Main, *The Anti-Federalists: Critics of the Constitution, 1781-1788* (Chapel Hill: University of North Carolina Press, 1961); John C. Miller (ed.), *The Colonial Image: Origins of American Culture* (New York: Harper and Row, 1960).

3

The Constitution and Its Development

T HERE are various meanings attached to the term "constitution" and a great deal has been written about this subject both in the United States and abroad. For our purpose two meanings must be kept carefully in mind. One regards a constitution as a single state paper drafted usually by a convention to serve as the foundation of a government. It is sometimes brief, running only to a few pages, or it may run to several hundred pages, as in the case of the new Indian constitution. Such a constitution is ordinarily divided into major sections dealing with the executive, legislative, and judicial branches; administrative agencies: public finance; and the like. The constitution which was drawn up in Philadelphia in 1787 is one of the best examples of this type of constitution. Most of the newer governments have a constitution of this type. The second meaning includes in a constitution the sum total of the elements which serve as the basic foundation of a government. Great Britain is the classic example of a country which has no constitution in the narrow sense noted above, but can point to one of the most famous constitutions in the broader sense. Here one finds major legislative acts, numerous usages and conventions, historic state papers such as the Great Charter, and the interpretations of courts. The United States has a constitution of the first type in the Constitution of 1787, but it also has a wider constitution consisting of the Constitution of 1787, major acts passed by Congress, executive decisions, decisions of the Supreme Court, and a body of customs and usages.

In order to avoid misunderstanding, it is essential that the meaning one is employing when using the term "constitution" is clear. It is quite correct to conceive of a constitution in either the limited or the broad sense, but what could be properly said about one might not accurately apply to the other. It is particularly dangerous to compare a constitution of the limited type with one of the broader sort. Yet many persons who should know better do fall into such an error. Hence they conclude that the broad British constitution has virtually no limitations, giving full freedom to the government to meet every problem which confronts it, whereas the formal Constitution of 1787 of the United States contains many restrictions which make it difficult for the United States to deal with pressing issues. If one is making comparisons, narrow constitutions should be set along side other narrow constitutions and broad constitutions should be measured against other broad constitutions. Because Great Britain has no constitution in the narrow sense, it is profitable to compare her constitution only with the broad constitution of the United States (or of other countries). If this is done, it is clear that there is not a great deal of difference in the actual authority exercised by the two governments of the United States and Great Britain. Both find it difficult on occasion to grapple with current problems because of powerful conventions or traditions, but both have substantial authority to take care of most of the major matters of state.

NARROW AND BROAD CONSTITUTIONS OF THE UNITED STATES

It is profitable to study various sections of the Constitution of 1787, the narrow constitution of the United States, but if one desires anything like a complete understanding of what goes on today, emphasis should be placed on the broader constitution. The Constitution of 1787 is a remarkable state paper which ranks high among public documents of the world. Considering the date of its drafting, its provisions strike a reader as exceptionally farsighted. But the Constitution of 1787 was prepared at a time when the United States consisted of a few million people residing along the Atlantic seaboard. The economy was largely of the manual variety and transportation had not even reached the horse and buggy days. A country with a population approaching the two hundred million mark and with problems so complex that they were hardly dreamed of a decade or so ago could not possibly handle its many affairs on the basis of the Constitution of 1787 alone. Hence, in this analysis of American government the broad constitution comes in for most attention.

The constitution in the broad sense is made up of six major elements. The first of these is the written Constitution of 1787. The formal amendments added since 1789 compose a second element. A third element of very great importance consists of the decisions of the Supreme Court and other courts which interpret the provisions of the narrow constitution and the amendments which have been added. A fourth element includes the statutes which Congress has passed in rather large numbers to elaborate, amplify, and implement the narrow constitution. A fifth element includes certain actions taken under the direction of the President. Finally, there are many customs, conventions, traditions, and usages which have grown up through the years and which often control political practices. Each one of these requires examination.

THE PHILADELPHIA CONVENTION OF 1787

A convention was called to meet in Philadelphia in 1787 to give attention to the weaknesses of the Confederation and certain problems which confronted the newly independent states. Congress added its approval to the call sent out by the Annapolis meeting, but Congress also stipulated that the convention should limit itself to proposing amendments to the Articles of Confederation thus implying that any changes would require the agreement of all of the thirteen states. No provision was made for the choosing of delegates, but they were selected in every instance by the state legislatures.

Seventy-three delegates were designated by twelve of the states—Rhode Island did not name delegates—but only fifty-five of these participated in the convention. A handful of the delegates exhibited such scant interest and displayed such little force that only their names remain to posterity. A somewhat larger number were men of moderate ability who had been active in the affairs of their respective states and were logical choices on that basis, irrespective of any special fitness for constitution-drafting. But a comparatively large proportion displayed ability and notable force. Perhaps never in the history of the United States has there been a public assemblage with as large a proportion of outstanding men as there was at the convention which met in Philadelphia in 1787.

First of all, there was George Washington with the immense prestige gained from leading the Continental Army through several years of adversity to eventual independence. Then there was Benjamin Franklin whose many years had been filled with a variety of public and private experiences of interest. He was so aged and infirm in 1787 that he could hardly speak above a whisper and had to be assisted to his feet when he addressed the convention. But his sage judgment proved most helpful at several critical stages. The brilliant young James Madison perhaps contributed more to the detailed provisions of the new constitution than any other delegate. James Wilson and Gouverneur Morris, though less striking as personalities than certain others, nevertheless performed very important services. Alexander Hamilton was less active than those named above, but he deserves to be named. Thomas Jefferson, who might have been an outstanding member, was not in attendance because he was in Europe as minister to France.

Certain aspects of the backgrounds of the delegates deserve attention. The group included an unusually large proportion of men under forty, several of whom exerted great influence. At a time when attendance at a university was quite unusual, many of the delegates present had had such education. In general, the delegates came from upper-middle-class groups and displayed somewhat conservative attitudes, especially in economic matters. Small farmers and laborers did not have sufficient strength at the time to gain any representation. Charles A. Beard who once studied the

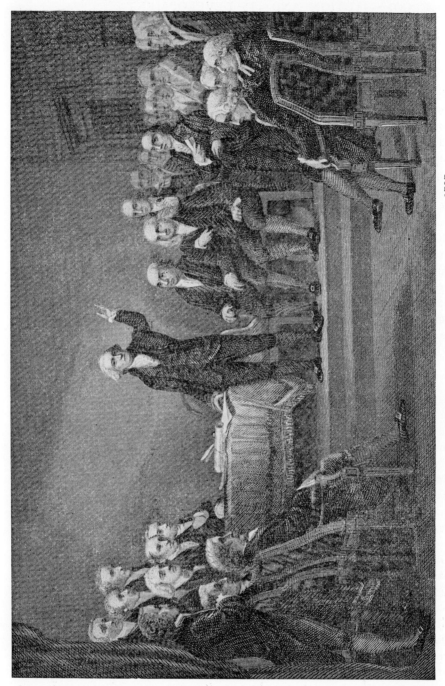

PAINTING OF WASHINGTON PRESIDING IN THE CONVENTION OF 1787

property interests of the delegates, found that many owned government securities, insurance stock, and western lands, and on this basis concluded that the work performed at Philadelphia can be interpreted largely if not entirely in economic terms.[1] But a more recent analysis throws a good deal of doubt on the validity of the Beard conclusions.[2] Many of the land and stock holdings seem to have been rather incidental, with their owners men of ideas and more than ordinarily broad in their interests. Certain delegates were probably more or less motivated by economic interests, but to explain the Constitution primarily on such a basis seems an unwarranted over-simplification. Experience under colonial administration, the writings of European authors, for example Montesquieu, and a deep-seated interest in the problems confronting the new nation had much to do with the attitudes of the delegates.

The call which went out specified that the convention would open on May 14, 1787, but when that day arrived only a small number of delegates had put in an appearance. For a time the prospects of holding a convention at all were far from bright. However, those on the scene waited more or less patiently; 29 delegates were present by May 25. On that day a meeting was held in Independence Hall and George Washington was chosen as presiding officer.

PROCEEDINGS OF THE PHILADELPHIA CONVENTION

For three and a half months, sessions of the convention were held during one of the hottest summers in memory. Rarely were there more than 30 or so in attendance. Despite the instructions to limit themselves to overhauling the Articles of Confederation, the delegates decided that a new constitution was called for and they set themselves to this bold task. Realizing the delicacy of their positions and fearing that their states might recall them if reports went out that they were engaged in drafting a new constitution, they ruled that their sessions should be closed to the public and discussions carried on within a closed circle.

For the most part, the delegates possessed such social graces that they enjoyed agreeable personal relations, but as representatives of the several states their views on public questions differed sharply. The most serious cleavage grew out of the conflict between the large states—notably Virginia, New York, Pennsylvania, and Massachusetts—and the states with smaller populations—such as Delaware and New Jersey. For a time there was such a gulf separating these two camps that there seemed little or no possibility of reconciling the two points of view. Had it not been for the

---

[1] See his *An Economic Interpretation of the Constitution of the United States* (New York: rev. ed., The Macmillan Company, 1935).

[2] R. E. Brown, *Charles Beard and the Constitution, A Critical Analysis of 'An Economic Interpretation of the Constitution of the United States'* (Princeton: Princeton University Press, 1956).

ability and persuasiveness of George Washington, it is possible that a hopeless deadlock might have brought an end to the convention.

The states with the larger populations supported a plan frequently referred to as the "Virginia Plan." This proposed a two-house legislative body. The lower chamber was to be representative of the states on the basis of population. This would have meant 16 or 17 seats for Virginia and only a single seat for Delaware and Rhode Island. The upper chamber was to be chosen by the lower house and consequently would also reflect large-state interests. Naturally the smaller states feared the result of such an arrangement and violently opposed the plan.

As a counter to the Virginia Plan, the smaller states drafted the so-called "New Jersey Plan." This provided for a legislative body in which every state would have an equal voice irrespective of population. Of course this proposal was not acceptable to the delegates of the more populous states. After protracted debate, which in the hot weather led to some frayed tempers, a compromise was finally worked out which made it possible for the convention to avoid a total breakdown and proceed to less controversial matters. To differentiate this compromise from others on lesser issues, it is sometimes called the "Great Compromise." [3] Considering the results such a title is amply warranted. Under this compromise a legislative body of two houses was agreed upon. The lower chamber would represent the states on the basis of their populations, while the upper would give each state, large or small, two seats and two votes. The members of the lower house were to be elected by direct popular vote. To give every possible safeguard to the individual states and perhaps to avoid excessive democracy the members of the upper chamber were to be chosen by the state legislatures.

With the thorny question of large-versus-small-state representation out of the way, the convention disposed of other issues more easily. In the matter of representation of a state, there were those who opposed any credit for slaves whatsoever in the lower house of Congress. The issue was complicated by the question of what status to give slaves in assessing direct taxes. A curious compromise was eventually reached which stipulated that a slave should be considered as three-fifths of a free person for both purposes: apportionment of legislative seats and direct taxation. This came to be known as the "Three-Fifths Compromise."

Under the Articles of Confederation very inadequate provision had been made for an executive, and the delegates were rather generally of the opinion that something should be done to strengthen the executive side of government. But should there be a single or a plural executive? Should the executive be given life tenure or a short term? What method of selection should be employed and what title should be used? Here there was a considerable divergence of opinion. It was finally decided that a single execu-

---

[3] Often called the Connecticut Compromise.

A PAINTING OF THE SIGNING OF THE CONSTITUTION AT PHILADELPHIA IN 1787

31

tive was desirable and that the holder of such an office should be called "President." An initial compromise between those who wanted life tenure and their opponents resulted in a provision for a single seven-year term, but this was changed at the last moment to a four-year term with no restriction on re-election. The electoral college was chosen as the method of selection. Some of the delegates seemed to have in mind a weak executive with a high social position, but the general sentiment supported the granting of extensive powers to the President. Nevertheless, remembering the difficulties with colonial governors, care was exercised lest the executive become too unlimited in authority. Provisions specifying checks by Congress found their way into the new Constitution.

On the question of what powers to give the central government in the field of regulating commerce, a split developed between the mercantile states of the North and the southern states which exported agricultural products and imported manufactured commodities. The former feared the possible use of such central authority over their local interests. It was eventually agreed that interstate trade and commerce with foreign nations might properly be regulated by Congress, leaving commerce within a single state under state control. No taxes on exports were to be permitted, though authorization for import taxes was given to the central government. Importation of slaves could not be prohibited until 1808; nor could a head tax exceeding $10 be levied on each person imported from abroad.

There was some difference of opinion among the delegates as to a system of courts. Certain delegates saw no need for any courts beyond the state level, but the general sentiment favored a federal Supreme Court with limited jurisdiction. There was considerable doubt as to whether lower federal courts were desirable. It was finally decided to dispose of the difficulty by giving Congress the power to establish such lower federal courts as it might deem necessary, but none were required below the Supreme Court. The jurisdiction of the federal judiciary was limited to federal matters, to disputes among the several states, and to cases involving a diversity of citizenship.

RATIFICATION

Wearied by its long debates and having settled the main points of disagreement, the convention approved the new Constitution in draft form and submitted it to the states for ratification. The Articles of Confederation provided that any amendment must be agreed to unanimously and, in view of their original intentions, the delegates might have seemed bound by such a stipulation in submitting the draft Constitution to the states. Being practical men, the delegates realized that it would be very difficult if not impossible to achieve unanimous ratification of their proposals; and hence they boldly specified that the Constitution should go into effect after nine states had ratified. Reactions to the draft were varied, as one might expect. Some felt quite strongly about the complete displacement of the Articles of Confederation. Others feared that the states would lose their sovereignty under such a system as was proposed. Still others objected to the lack of a formal bill of rights. In short, there were a good many criticisms of one sort and another, but no united hostility to any single provision. During the debate which followed submission to the states James Madison, Alexander Hamilton, and John Jay joined together to prepare a series of papers known

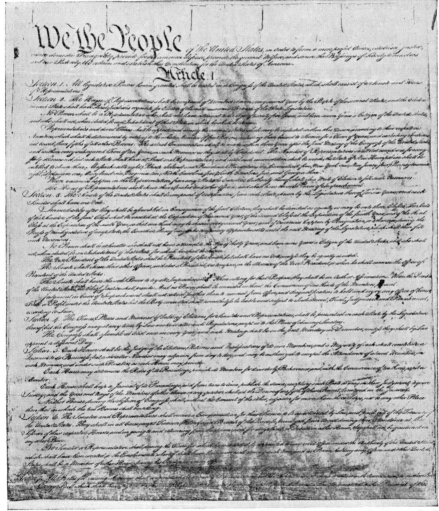

Courtesy The National Archives, Washington, D. C.

THE FIRST PAGE OF THE ORIGINAL CONSTITUTION

as *The Federalist* to assist in building up support for the new Constitution in New York where ratification appeared uncertain. These papers discussed various current problems and strongly urged ratification. They have long been regarded as notable both in their content and influence, but an iconoclastic study by W. W. Crosskey recently published sharply takes issue with such attitude, maintaining that they were more of the space-filler variety and employed in large measure to keep other points of view out of the papers.[4]

Some of the states ratified promptly; others hesitated. By the end of 1787, ratifications had started to come in, with Delaware the first to take action on December 7, 1787. Slightly over six months later New Hampshire became the ninth state to ratify. But the key states of New York and Virginia had not ratified, and it was hardly conceivable that the new government could be set up until both agreed to participate. On June 25, 1788, Virginia gave its consent by a vote of 89 to 79, and just over a month later New York gave its approval by a closely contested vote. North Carolina would not ratify until a bill of rights had been submitted to the states. Rhode Island did not see fit to call a convention to consider the ratification. On September 13, 1788, the Congress of the Confederation called on the states to choose presidential electors, senators, and representatives. The first Wednesday of March, 1789, was set as the date for getting the new United States of America under way; but majorities of both houses of Congress did not arrive in New York City, the temporary capital, to count the electoral votes until April 6. It was April 30 when Washington reached New York City to assume the office of President. Even then the new government existed only in skeletal form, because the Constitution left many steps to be taken by Congress. Administrative departments—the departments of State, War, and Treasury—had to be provided by congressional action. The establishment of a federal judiciary, the tax system, and other basic matters also depended upon legislative enactment. All of this required time and certain steps were delayed until 1790 or even later.

GENERAL CHARACTER OF THE CONSTITUTION OF 1787

The Constitution of 1787 is brief—only some ten printed pages. It is shorter than most national constitutions and indeed less than a tenth as voluminous as the longest of the state constitutions. At the time of the framing, there were those who expressed disappointment that certain omissions had been permitted; this was shortly remedied, to some extent at least, by the adding of the first ten amendments. In retrospect it has probably been the consensus of opinion that the brevity of the Constitution of 1787 has served as an asset rather than a liability. During early years more detailed

---

[4] See his *Politics and the Constitution in the History of the United States* (2 vols., Chicago: University of Chicago Press, 1953).

provisions might have saved some uncertainty, but times change rapidly and such details would perhaps have been outmoded long ago. The result might have been the necessity of complete overhauling or the handicap of an outworn guiding document. Because of its general character, details have been filled in by statute and other means, and these may be modified as occasion demands. Those who know constitutions both in the United States and abroad are usually impressed by the fine phraseology of the Constitution of 1787. Very few state papers of this or any other period equal it in clarity, well-chosen language, and orderliness. The framers included some sticklers for good form in writing, with the result that after the decisions had been made as to contents a careful restatement was executed by Gouverneur Morris.

The Constitution of 1787 consists of a preamble and seven rather brief articles. Article I, subdivided into ten sections, is approximately as lengthy as the remainder of the articles combined and has to do with the legislative branch of the government, dealing with its structure, powers, and limitations. Article II, divided into four sections, relates to the executive branch and is devoted largely to the presidency. Article III, with three sections, provides for the judicial branch. Article IV, having four sections, lays down a number of requirements in regard to interstate commerce and the relations between the central government and the states. Article V, a single paragraph, outlines the process of formally amending the Constitution, while Article VI, also consisting of a single section, makes the Constitution, laws passed in pursuance thereof, and treaties made under the authority of the United States the supreme law of the land. Article VII runs to only a single sentence of two printed lines and has to do with the ratification of the Constitution.

FORMAL AMENDMENTS

The second element of the broader Constitution of the United States, formal amendments, is not unimportant, but it occupies a considerably less distinctive place than judicial decisions, statutes, executive actions, and customs in elaborating and developing the Constitution of 1787. This may be accounted for in various ways, but the difficult character of the amending process has been a major factor.

The amending process. The Constitution of 1787 makes detailed provisions for the process of making formal amendments. Two stages, proposal and ratification, are specified and each of these may be handled in two ways. Amendments may be proposed by the two houses of Congress if two-thirds of the members voting thereon are favorable (a quorum must, of course, be present). It has been held by the Supreme Court that the amending process is distinct from that of ordinary law-making and hence that the signature of the President is not required. All amendments thus far submitted for ratification have been proposed by this method. However, the

Constitution declares that if the legislatures of two-thirds of the states so request, Congress shall call a special convention for proposing amendments though no mechanism is provided for assuring congressional compliance.

After amendments have been proposed, they are submitted for ratification to the states currently by the General Services Administrator. Ordinarily they go to the legislatures in the states, but an alternative is to submit them to state conventions—the decision resting with Congress. All amendments, with the single exception of the Twenty-first, have been ratified by state legislatures. In the case of the repeal of the Eighteenth Amendment, however, it was decided that a more accurate expression of public opinion might be secured through state conventions. When the legislatures or conventions of three-fourths of the states have ratified and when their governors have notified the General Services Administrator of such action, the amendment is proclaimed in effect.

There are four possible methods of amending the Constitution by formal action. The common procedure is through proposal by Congress and ratification by the legislatures of three-fourths of the states. On one occasion an amendment was accomplished as a result of proposal by Congress and ratification by conventions in three-fourths of the states. A third and fourth method, neither thus far employed, would involve proposal by a national convention called by Congress at the request of the legislatures of two-thirds of the states and ratification either by state legislatures or state conventions.

Some critics maintain that the process of formal amendment is too cumbersome. They point to the inconsistency of majority rule under a democratic system with provisions requiring two-thirds approval of Congress together with the ratification of three-fourths of the states. They are especially critical of the time which is ordinarily required to complete the process. Furthermore, they point to the extremely high mortality rate in the case of proposals to amend: out of some four thousand joint resolutions introduced in Congress proposing amendments less than thirty have been endorsed by the required majorities in both houses. Despite the fairly frequent attempts to bring about formal amendment of the Constitution, only twenty-three amendments have been added since 1789. It is clear that the chances of getting an amendment accepted by a two-thirds majority in both houses of Congress and ratified by a sufficient number of the states are not good. Foreign observers of the political process in the United States often comment on the complicated character of the amending process, concluding more often than not that the Constitution of the United States is one of the most rigid in the modern world. The actual situation is less critical than some suppose however, because the formal amendment process has been bypassed in many instances. Necessary changes have been brought about by judicial interpretation, by congressional statute, and by custom and usage when it has appeared that an amendment to the Constitution would be difficult to accomplish. The Constitution is less rigid than many commentators have maintained, but it must in all fairness be admitted that the amending process is such that it can claim little of the credit for keeping the United States abreast of changing conditions.

The twenty-four amendments. Ten of the twenty-four amendments were added almost immediately, in 1791, to meet the demands of such states as North Carolina which found the omission of a bill of rights in the document of 1787 a matter of serious concern. The first ten amendments have sometimes been regarded as a single amendment because they were put through during a single rather brief period and are often considered an appended bill of rights. Actually only eight of them deal with what would ordinarily be included in a bill of rights. The Ninth Amendment provided that "The enumeration in the Constitution of certain rights shall not be construed to deny or disparage others retained by the people." There was some feeling that the status of the states was not sufficiently safeguarded in the Constitution of 1787 and the Tenth Amendment categorically states that "The powers not delegated to the United States by the Constitution, nor prohibited by it to the States, are reserved to the States respectively, or to the people."

One of the early cases decided by the Supreme Court laid down the rule that a state could be sued in the federal courts by the citizens of another state.[5] Much consternation followed, with the states inclined to view the decision as an intolerable restriction on their sovereign powers. The Eleventh Amendment, proclaimed effective in 1798, was drafted to correct this situation and states that "The judicial power of the United States shall not be construed to extend to any suit in law or equity, commenced or prosecuted against one of the United States by citizens or another State, or by citizens or subjects of any foreign State." The election of 1800 made it apparent that the scheme for electing a President and a Vice-President was not suited to a system dominated by political parties. The Twelfth Amendment, which became a part of the Constitution in 1804, remedied this by specifying that the President and the Vice-President should be elected separately.

The Thirteenth, Fourteenth, and Fifteenth Amendments are sometimes referred to as the "Civil War Amendments," because they grew out of the conflict between the North and the South involving the status of Negroes. The first of these, proclaimed in effect in 1865, prohibits slavery and involuntary servitude. The Fourteenth Amendment, which is dated almost three years later, sought to guarantee the privileges and immunities of citizenship to the Negroes. It contains two of the most controversial and oft-quoted sections of the entire Constitution: "nor shall any State deprive any person of life, liberty, or property without due process of law" and "nor

---

[5] See *Chisholm* v. *Georgia*, 2 Dallas 419 (1796).

deny to any person within its jurisdiction equal protection of the laws." The first of these, although intended to protect Negroes, was long used primarily by corporations to avoid state regulation. The second has been thrown into the limelight during recent years by the series of Supreme Court cases dealing with such matters as equal educational opportunities for Negroes. Section 2 of the Fourteenth Amendment is an example of a part of the Constitution which has long been a dead letter. This declares that representation in the lower house of Congress shall be reduced in those states which deprive adult male citizens of their suffrage. The Fifteenth Amendment is another instance of a constitutional provision which has been frequently ignored. It states that neither the United States nor a state shall deny the voting privilege on "account of race, color, or previous condition of servitude."

Some students of the American Constitution believe that the Sixteenth Amendment should never have been considered necessary. This amendment authorizes Congress to levy income taxes irrespective of the source and without apportionment among the states. It was added in 1913 to remove doubt cast by *Pollock* v. *Farmers Loan and Trust Company* (1895)[6] as to the authority of Congress in this field. The rising tide of democracy beat upon the plan of indirect election of senators and substituted in the Seventeenth Amendment, put into effect in 1913, their direct election by the voters.

While there are several sections of the Constitution which are not at present generally heeded or which have been modified by subsequent amendment, there is but one example of outright repeal. The Eighteenth Amendment was added in 1919 as a result of intensive effort on the part of the anti-liquor forces over a period of years. It prohibited the "manufacture, sale, or transportation of intoxicating liquors." The Twenty-first Amendment, rushed through in record time in 1933, specifically repealed this prohibition.

The Nineteenth, Twentieth, and Twenty-second Amendments have been judged by many to be among the most important amendments. The first removed the suffrage discrimination in the case of women and thus doubled the number of qualified voters in the United States. The second, known as the "Lame Duck Amendment," reduced the period between the election of a Congress and its first session from thirteen months to two. It also advanced from March 4 to January 20 the beginning of a presidential term of office.[7] The third, on occasion the object of attempts to repeal, limits a President to two terms of office. A twenty-third amendment authorizes a presidential vote for residents of the District of Columbia. A twenty-fourth Amendment states that no one need pay a tax in order to vote.

The Supreme Court upheld as a reasonable limit a congressional stipu-

---

6 158 U. S. 601.
7 See p. 787.

lation that three-fourths of the states must ratify an amendment within a period of seven years.[8] In 1939 the Supreme Court was asked to rule on what happened when no time limit was set by Congress. It refused to specify the exact time, simply noting that a reasonable period should be permitted, leaving it up to Congress to decide whether an amendment is still before the states for ratification.[9] In a Kentucky case the Supreme Court has upheld Congress's decision that a state may ratify an amendment after having previously declined to take such an action.[10] On the other hand, the Supreme Court has laid down the rule that a state may not withdraw a favorable action on an amendment after the national government has been notified.[11] In *Hawke* v. *Smith* (1920) the Supreme Court disallowed an Ohio constitutional provision which permitted the state legislature to submit federal constitutional amendments to the voters of that state.[12]

JUDICIAL DECISIONS

During the early years of the republic the Supreme Court did not play an outstanding part in developing the Constitution; but, beginning with the nineteenth century, it assumed a much more vigorous role. In the last century or so, the decisions and interpretations of the Supreme Court have been a major factor in keeping the Constitution reasonably abreast of the times, far exceeding formal amendments in their influence. The landmark case of *Marbury* v. *Madison,* decided in 1803, may be regarded as a foundation on which later cases relating to the Constitution have been based.[13]

Shortly before leaving office President Adams sent to the Senate the name of John Marshall as Chief Justice of the United States, and the Senate confirmed this nomination as one of its last acts before Thomas Jefferson took over the Presidency. Since the Supreme Court was made up of judges who belonged to the opposite political camp, Jefferson was not disposed to be very cordial toward the Court, particularly resenting the last-minute action of his predecessor in filling vacancies on it. When one of the Adams' appointees to a minor justiceship of the peace applied to Jefferson's Secretary of State, James Madison, for his commission of office which had not been delivered, he received a cold reception. Failing to obtain his commission, Marbury, the appointee in question, turned to the Supreme Court for assistance. Citing the Judiciary Act of 1789, he asked for a writ of mandamus ordering the Secretary of State to give him the commission. It appeared that the Supreme Court would have little option in granting the petition of Mr. Marbury, but President Jefferson made it clear that any such mandamus would be ignored.

To the surprise of the President and the general public, the Supreme

8 *Dillon* v. *Gloss,* 256 U. S. 368 (1921).
9 *Coleman* v. *Miller,* 307 U. S. 433 (1939).
10 *Chandler* v. *Wise,* 307 U. S. 474 (1939).
11 *Coleman* v. *Miller,* 307 U. S. 433 (1939).
12 253 U. S. 221.
13 1 Cranch 137 (1803).

Court did not issue such a writ, though it noted that Mr. Marbury was entitled to the commission. In comparing the Judiciary Act of 1789, which provided for such jurisdiction on the part of the Supreme Court, with the provisions of the Constitution of 1787, the judges found a conflict. Article III of the latter gave the Supreme Court original jurisdiction in only two types of cases: those involving foreign diplomatic officials and those in which the states were parties. It was clear that the Marbury case did not belong to either of these categories. Hence the Supreme Court proceeded to declare null and void that section of the Judiciary Act of 1789 which required it to take jurisdiction. Whether the judges were fully aware of what a far-reaching precedent they were establishing in making this decision or whether they were primarily concerned with saving face in the embarrassing conflict with President Jefferson, cannot be definitely determined. At any rate the Marbury case has become the basis for the very important authority exercised by the Supreme Court in passing on the validity of acts of Congress and interpreting the provisions of the Constitution drafted in Philadelphia in 1787.

In lecturing at the Law School of Columbia University, the late Chief Justice Hughes, at that time governor of New York and not a justice of the Supreme Court, made an observation which has been widely quoted. He said: "We are under the Constitution, but the Constitution is what the judges say it is." [14] Taken out of its context this sentence sounds somewhat more categorical than was probably intended. Nevertheless, it does summarize in a few striking words a procedure which has been of far-reaching importance in developing the constitutional system of the United States. Many cases brought before the Supreme Court are relatively insignificant and indeed the majority of them are not given detailed consideration. However, during the course of the years, the Supreme Court has received cases involving almost every conceivable aspect of the Constitution of 1787 and the formal amendments. In deciding these cases it is frequently necessary for the Court to interpret the more or less general terms of the Constitution of 1787 and its amendments in a detailed and precise manner. It has been alleged that the Supreme Court has ignored the intent of the framers in making such interpretations and that it has followed a course of "sophistry" in arriving at conclusions.[15] Be that as it may, the fact remains that the interpretations of the Court must be accepted as law, at least until set aside by formal amendment. The many cases in which major interpretations have been made by the Supreme Court, few of which have ever been overturned though the Court at times has reversed itself, have contributed very heavily to the present Constitution of the United States.

If "the Constitution is what the judges say it is," it could be a very mere-

---

[14] See Charles E. Hughes, *Addresses* (New York: Harper & Bros., 1908), p. 139.

[15] W. W. Crosskey, in his *Politics and the Constitution in the History of the United States* (2 vols., Chicago: University of Chicago Press, 1953), charges the Supreme Court with ignoring the intent of the framers in the case of interstate commerce and with employing "sophistry" rather than logic in making interpretations.

tricious affair indeed. One group of judges would decide one way; anoth__ would prefer a different interpretation; and the result might be confusion. If the successive benches of judges who have constituted the Supreme Court decided cases on the basis of personal whim, there would, of course, be chaos. Actually, however, the judges are generally guided by the principle of precedent to a considerable degree. In other words, in interpreting clauses of the Constitution, they give careful consideration to previous cases involving similar points. At times the Supreme Court has been subjected to severe criticism because it has relied on precedent, and it is perhaps fair to say that such a course has at times made progress difficult. On the other hand, unless attention were paid to past decisions, there would be little or no relation between interpretations of yesterday, today, and tomorrow; and that would hardly be conducive to stability. Most of those who condemn the principle of precedent probably do not want its abandonment but rather its suspension in times of crisis, or possibly less attention to the letter of the law.

Some of the framers may have anticipated judicial review by the Supreme Court, but no vote was taken on the matter at Philadelphia and no specific provision was inserted into the Constitution of 1787 which conferred such power on the Court. In the last decade or so an activist Supreme Court has seemed to take not only a negative role in nullifying state legislation, but it has also taken positive action in promoting civil liberties and racial equality. This more aggressive role appeared particularly clearly in *Brown* v. *Board of Education of Topeka*[16] and in the other civil rights cases that followed. Professor Charles S. Hyneman has made the most thorough recent inquiry into the role of the Supreme Court in the American policy-making process.[17] He concludes that the Court has taken on a role not previously exercised by that body.

CONGRESSIONAL STATUTES

Few legislative bodies turn out anything like the enormous number of statutes, joint resolutions, and other types of acts produced every year by Congress. By no means all of these have any constitutional relevance—indeed only a comparatively small proportion contribute to the development of the constitutional system. The private bills, the appropriation measures, and the routine statutes may involve vast sums of money and affect the lives of millions of people, but they are not of such a character as to contribute to the Constitution. The relatively small number of congressional acts that do fall into this category are not distinguishable on their surface from the mass of ordinary legislation. They have the same general form and require only the ordinary majority of votes expected in the case of other acts. It is their con-

---

16 347 U. S. 483 (1954) and at the same time *Bolling* v. *Sharpe* 347 U. S. 497, which ended discrimination in the District of Columbia schools.

17 See Professor Hyneman's *The Supreme Court on Trial* (New York: Atherton Press, 1963).

tents that make them important from a constitutional standpoint. Just how many statutes of this type have been enacted by Congress during more than a century and a half is impossible to state, for no record is kept which separates these acts from ordinary ones. But the number is fairly large, running perhaps into the thousands.

Since the Constitution of 1787 is very general in character and brief in length, it is to be expected that Congress has had to fill in many details. The framers at Philadelphia specified a Supreme Court, but they left the creation of such a court and the establishment of other federal courts to Congress. Hence the composition, organization, and appellate jurisdiction of the Supreme Court have been provided for by congressional action. The other federal courts are left entirely to the discretion of Congress, with the result that the whole system of district, appellate, and special courts stems from congressional legislation. The judicial branch of the government is, then, largely the result of statutes passed by Congress from time to time. During recent years the administrative side of government has been receiving emphasis the world over. The Constitution of 1787 has no article devoted to administration and indeed hardly refers to such activities at all. All of the major administrative departments have been set up by congressional action. The civil service system, the budgetary setup, and the planning and reporting agencies are all at least generally provided for by statute, although in matters of detail they may depend upon executive orders. The Foreign Service of the United States, the Army, the Navy, the Marine Corps, and the Air Force are based on the statutes which Congress has passed under the broad terms of the Constitution of 1787 relating to diplomatic and military affairs. Many other examples of the role of statutes in developing the constitutional system could be cited, but it should be apparent from those given above that the total import is beyond that of formal amendments.

EXECUTIVE ACTION

The President is responsible for enforcing congressional legislation and constitutional provisions. In so doing, he frequently is forced to provide his own interpretation of the meaning of constitutional provisions. Later, the Supreme Court may rule on the constitutionality of the actions of the President, but it is he who holds the initiative in interpreting his own powers.

In the Constitution there is provision for the appointment of officers of the national government but no provision for their removal except in those cases covered by impeachment. Over the years various Presidents have removed many officials, and in a number of such instances the Court has been forced to rule so that it has been established that the President can remove a government official whose function is to carry out the will of the President. On the other hand, he is limited in his power to force out those who have quasi-legislative and quasi-judicial functions on independent commissions established by Congress.

In the international field, presidential interpretation of his authority has led to Supreme Court approval of his power to act in certain matters without prior authorizing legislation by Congress. Such power, the Court has said, is inherent in the nature of the executive function.

CUSTOMS, CONVENTIONS, AND USAGES

Every government is likely to develop certain ways of handling its problems which are not mentioned in any constitutional article or even in an ordinary law. The Anglo-Saxon countries, relying as they do on the common law perhaps give a larger place to conventions and the like than most other countries. The government of the United Kingdom is traditionally associated with a rich background of customs, frequently quite colorful in character. Although the United States is comparatively youthful in terms of English history, many customs and usages have grown up during the years. Some of these have little or no bearing on the constitutional system; others contribute quite significantly to it.

Even a casual observer recognizes the major role which political parties assume in the American political process. Indeed it is hardly possible to conceive of the national, state, or local governments in the absence of political groups of one kind or another. Yet the Constitution of 1787 makes no provision at all for political parties. There are various statutes which regulate political party practices, but for the most part political parties are the result of custom and usage.

Another example is in the cabinet for which there is no specific basis in the Constitution of 1787. Congressional statutes have established the departments from which cabinet members are drawn, but they do not provide for a cabinet. The early Presidents found it useful to have a small group of advisers to whom they could look for counsel. Other Presidents have continued the custom, until it would require great audacity to dispense with such a body. Some Presidents lean more heavily on the cabinet than others, but they all recognize it to some extent, although they have the power to abolish it at any time.

Custom and usage have had much to do with making the electoral college workable during these many years that political parties have assumed the responsibility for nominating candidates for the Presidency and Vice-Presidency. Under the provisions of the Constitution of 1787, electors are given a free hand in electing a President. Today electors are usually mere figureheads who cast their votes for the nominee of the party which has honored them. This change has been accomplished without formal amendment. It makes it clear that, in the absence of a formal constitutional stipulation, custom and usage may not only control, but may even operate to modify a formal provision of the Constitution of 1787.

Another illustration of the place of custom and usage involves the making of federal appointments. The framers of the Constitution of 1787 conferred such a responsibility primarily on the President, although they checked this power in some instances by requiring senatorial confirmation. The number of federal positions filled by presidential appointment has become so large and the duties of the President have multiplied to such an extent that it is not now feasible for the President to take the initiative very often. Through the years it has become the custom for the senators and even the representatives of the President's party to recommend persons to the Chief Executive for appointment to federal positions, with the result that the executive offices have become to some extent merely an avenue along which appointments pass from their inception in a congressional office to confirmation at the hands of the Senate. This usage has achieved such strength that it has led to what is known as "senatorial courtesy." Unless the President consults or indeed follows the recommendation of the senator—if of the President's party —from the state where the appointment is to be made, the Senate will normally refuse to confirm the appointment.

SUMMARY

The Constitution of the United States is made up of various elements, including the Constitution drafted at Philadelphia in 1787, twenty-three formal amendments, numerous decisions and dicta of the courts, a large number of statutes passed by Congress through the years, executive actions, and a considerable body of customs and usages. The Constitution of 1787 is a comparatively brief document which provides in general terms for a federal system of government and the national government. A bill of rights—in the first ten formal amendments—and the remaining amendments have resulted in fairly important changes. Because the process of formal amendment is cumbersome and time-consuming, other methods of developing the Constitution have been heavily relied upon. It is through these less formal devices that the Constitution has been kept reasonably abreast of the times. And it is through these latter devices that the Constitution of the United States has been flexible rather than rigid.

BIBLIOGRAPHIC NOTE

The literature relating to the Constitution is extensive—perhaps more so than in any other area of American government. This in itself may be considered significant, indicating the highly important role of the Constitution in the United States. However, the wealth of books, monographs, and other sources makes it difficult to prepare a bibliographic note within the space available. The omission of any particular study should not therefore be considered as a reflection on its worth.

General works on the Constitution which may be especially useful to university students include: C. B. Swisher, *American Constitutional Development* (rev. ed., Boston: Houghton Mifflin, 1954); C. H. Pritchett, *American Constitution* (New York: McGraw-Hill Book Company, 1959); R. G. McCloskey (ed.), *Essays on Constitutional Law* (New York: Alfred A. Knopf, 1957); E. S. Corwin, *The Constitution and What It Means Today* (rev. ed., Princeton: Princeton University Press, 1958); A. H. Kelley and W. A. Harbison, *The American Constitution; Its Origins and Development* (rev. ed., New York: W. W. Norton & Company, 1955); J. A. Rickard and J. H. McCrocklin, *Our National Constitution; Origins, Development, and Meaning* (Harrisburg, Penna.: Stackpole & Company, 1955); A. T. Mason and W. M. Beaney, *American Constitutional Law* (New York: Prentice-Hall Company, 1954); F. McDonald, *We the People* (Chicago: University of Chicago Press, 1958); J. Mussatti, *Constitution of the United States; Its Origins, Principles, and Problems* (Princeton, N. J.: D. Van Nostrand Company, Inc., 1956); and W. W. Crosskey, *Politics and the Constitution in the History of the United States* (2 vols., Chicago: University of Chicago Press, 1953).

Among the books dealing with the drafting of the Constitution of 1787 the following may be cited as specially useful to university students: Max Farrand, *The Records of the Federal Convention* (4 vols., New Haven: Yale University Press, 1937); G. Hunt and J. B. Scott (eds.), James Madison, *The Debates in the Federal Convention of 1787* (New York: Oxford University Press, 1920); A. T. Prescott, *Drafting the Federal Constitution* (Baton Rouge: Louisiana State University Press, 1941); Charles Warren, *Making of the Constitution* (Cambridge: Harvard University Press, 1947); C. L. Rossiter, *Seedtime of the Republic* (New York: Harcourt, Brace, and Company, 1953); and C. Van Doren, *The Great Rehearsal; The Story of the Making and Ratifying of the Constitution of the United States* (New York: The Viking Press, 1948). The records of the several states in ratifying may be found in J. Elliot, *Debates in the Several State Conventions on the Adoption of the Federal Constitution* (5 vols., Philadelphia: J. B. Lippincott Co., 1937).

The general works cited above deal with the development of the Constitution, but this aspect is especially treated in A. N. Holcombe, *Our More Perfect Union: From Eighteenth Century Principles to Twentieth Century Practice* (Cambridge: Harvard University Press, 1950); F. T. Fenn, *The Development of the Constitution* (New York: Appleton-Century-Crofts, Inc., 1948); and B. F. Wright, *Growth of American Constitutional Law* (New York: Reynal & Hitchcock, 1942). The formal amending process is discussed in detail in D. P. Myers, *The Process of Constitutional Amendment* (Washington, D. C.: Government Printing Office, 1940) and L. B. Orfield, *Amending of the Federal Constitution* (Ann Arbor: University of Michigan Press, 1942).

The development of the Constitution by judicial interpretation has received much attention during recent years. Among the books which may be useful to the student are the following: R. K. Carr, *The Supreme Court and Judicial Review* (New York: Farrar & Rinehart, 1942); O. J. Roberts, *Court and the Constitution* (Cambridge: Harvard University Press, 1951); E. S. Corwin, *Court over Constitution* (Gloucester: Peter Smith, 1957); J. S. Williams, *Supreme Court Speaks* (Austin: University of Texas Press, 1956); T. R. Powell, *Vagaries and Varieties in Constitutional Interpretation* (New York: Columbia University Press, 1956); and C. B. Swisher, *Historic Decisions of the Supreme Court* (Princeton, N. J.: D. Van Nostrand Company, Inc., 1958), and by the same author, *Supreme Court in Modern*

Role (New York: New York University Press, 1958). Collections of cases in which constitutional interpretation has figured are readily available and include those edited by Robert E. Cushman, Charles Fairman, C. Gordon Post, and Paul Bartholomew.

The following recent books of note are concerned with aspects of the Constitution and its development: Charles S. Hyneman, *The Supreme Court On Trial* (New York: Atherton Press, 1963); Walter F. Murphy, *Congress and the Court* (Chicago: University of Chicago Press, 1962): Robert S. Hirschfield, *The Constitution and the Court: The Development of the Basic Law Through Judicial Interpretation* (New York: Random House, 1962): William T. Hutchinson and William M. E. Rachal (eds.), *The James Madison Papers* (Chicago: University of Chicago Press, 1962).

4

The Federal System

Public debate is the hallmark of a thriving democratic government. Throughout our nation's history many of the most significant constitutional and political questions have arisen from the fact that the central government and the states are associated within the framework of a federal system.

The essence of a federal government is the distribution of powers between the national government and the constituent units. The Constitution provides for the basic division of powers, but the dynamic nature of the federal system is illustrated by the judicial and political interpretations which have made it possible for national problems to be solved by unilateral action on the part of the national government, through the cooperation of the central government and the states, or by cooperation among the states.

Centralization of power in the national government is a political fact of life almost everywhere in the world. The concept of "cooperative federalism" in the United States at least keeps many facets of this trend within the bound aries of the historic distribution of powers principle.

THE NATURE OF FEDERAL GOVERNMENT

The United States is to be credited with first developing the modern concept of a federal form of government. Interestingly enough, the words "federal" or "federation" do not appear anywhere within the Constitution, but nevertheless this document has always been referred to as the "federal constitution" and many of its principles have been adopted by subsequent federal unions.

It has been suggested that certain prerequisites are necessary for the federal form of government to come into being.[1] The associated units must desire to be under a single independent government for some purposes; conversely the component political units of a federal union must desire to retain independent governments for some matters.

---

[1] See K. C. Wheare, *Federal Government* (New York: Oxford University Press, 1947), pp. 35-36.

Even under the Articles of Confederation, the individual states placed most aspects of foreign affairs, and certain other matters, in the hands of the central government. Eventually, the desire to obtain greater economic strength persuaded the representatives of the states to call the constitutional convention which drafted the document that placed many additional powers in the hands of a national government. Since the states were already firmly established as political units, however, their representatives naturally reserved many areas of performance for the states alone.

Several points may be made concerning the American federal union with respect to the capacity of the people to make the system work. In the first place, the original states had already secured considerable experience in governing before the federal union was formed. Secondly, there was time to develop the system slowly, since there was small threat of foreign intervention. In the third place, our capacities to make the federal plan work have been severely tested, two examples being the Civil War and the disastrous economic depression of the 1930's. The altered nature of federal-state relations in the past three decades is in the final analysis a testimonial to the capacity of Americans to make the federal system work.

Advantages of federalism. Doubtlessly, the average American is not particularly concerned with defending the federal system. He is apt to believe that any criticism levied against American federalism is motivated by envy, jealousy, or ignorance. However, people in many areas of the world, particularly since World War II, have carefully assessed the advantages and disadvantages of the federal form of government before drawing up constitutions.

A federal union was the only plan acceptable to the states which would allow substantial powers to a central government. There was too great a gap between a confederation and a unitary type of government to be bridged by the delegates in 1787. Perhaps the strongest argument for federalism is that it permits regions with diverse cultural, religious, and ethnic groups voluntarily to form a central government to act upon general problems. The alternative, in many such cases, would be a national unity by force of arms, if it came at all.

It has often been suggested that a territorial distribution of power makes it more difficult for a national dictatorship to emerge. This argument has lost some of its force in these days when only the national government is capable of developing the weapons and manning the machinery for a modern military force.

Federalism encourages greater participation by citizens in the political process, since significant decisions must be made by the states and local governments. Local problems can be handled at the grass-roots level by the people who are most intimately associated with them. Certain governmental plans and devices have been tested at the state level, and proving worthwhile, have been adopted by the national government; the executive budget is a case in point. State and local governments have proved to be valuable training grounds for politicians and administrators who have eventually assumed responsible positions with the national government.

Disadvantages of federalism. A federal system is more complicated to operate than a unitary one. The division of powers between the central and state governments often leads to delay and indecision. In our own case, for many years there was a so-called "twilight zone" involving problems which neither the states nor the national government seemingly had the constitutional powers to solve. The diversity characteristic of federalism has disadvantages as well as advantages. It has led to a lack of uniformity in legislation and administration in many matters such as civil rights, divorce, insurance, banking, and traffic which fact at times has positively burdened many individuals. The disparity of wealth among the units within the federal union means that equality of opportunity, let us say in education, varies from state to state (as well as within states). Financially and administratively, there is costly duplication of effort. To those who view extensive economic and social planning on a national scale as necessary or desirable, the federal system may present a serious obstacle.

A satisfactory balance. To a great extent the arguments for and against federalism in the United States are scholastic. Our nation is wedded to the federal form of government. Actually, most of the pro and con arguments on the federalist issue are translated into political issues debated in Congress and in election campaigns. The implied power doctrine makes it possible for Congress to act on local matters if these affect national policies. It is a foolish fallacy for anyone to think that a unitary system would suddenly change the nature of the political problems in the United States. The same types of problems would remain, and success in the political process would still depend upon compromising group and regional interests.

THE PROCESS OF ADMITTING STATES

Under the Constitution, Congress is given wide latitude in admitting new states. The first step toward acquiring statehood is that of petitioning Congress for admission. The inhabitants of a territory may conduct a poll to indicate their sentiment or they may produce other good evidence of their desires. If Congress approves the request, an enabling act is passed which authorizes the election of delegates to a convention for drafting a tentative constitution. After this constitution has been accepted by a majority of the voters in the territory, it goes to Congress for review. Congress may reject it altogether, accept it without change, or indicate that modifications will be necessary before approval can be given. Finally, after all conditions laid down by Congress have been met, a joint resolution admits the territory to statehood.[2]

Alaska and Hawaii become states. The procedural process for admitting new states is simple enough, but the politics associated with the process is another matter as was shown most recently in the case of Alaska and Hawaii. In 1952, and again in 1956, the Republican and Democratic party platforms endorsed admission. The House of Representatives approved Hawaiian statehood bills three times and an Alaskan statehood bill one time, only to see them founder in the Senate. Many members argued against admitting non-contiguous territories. Alaskan statehood was opposed by some on the grounds of its small population and its relatively undeveloped economic status. The fact that Hawaii's population was only about 23 per cent Caucasian caused some members of Congress to vote against statehood. Southern members in the Senate saw in the admission of the two territories a further dilution of their power in fighting against federal civil rights measures. It is probably fortunate for the two newest states that one of them (Hawaii) has traditionally voted Republican and the other (Alaska) has usually been considered a Democratic party stronghold. This political division made it practical for both of them to be admitted within a short space of time, once the opposition on other grounds was overcome in Congress. President Eisenhower signed the Alaskan statehood bill on July 7, 1958. The Hawaiian statehood bill was signed by the President on August 21, 1959, and her two senators and one representative took their seats in Congress in that same month.

Status of special conditions imposed by Congress. Inasmuch as Congress has a free hand in prescribing conditions that must be satisfied before statehood will be conferred, a territory has no alternative but compliance with these demands, however unreasonable it may consider them to be. After Congress has acted favorably and statehood has been granted, there is no possibility of subsequent revocation. Consequently, the newly-admitted states sometimes disregard commitments which they were forced to make. When the conditions imposed by Congress would deprive a state of its political and legal equality as a part of the union, the Supreme Court has upheld the right of the states to ignore prerequisites for admission. Thus Oklahoma could move her capital in 1910 despite a provision in the enabling act which forbade such change prior to 1913.[3] However, if the change has to do with "contractual" rather than "political" matters, then the newly-admitted state cannot escape so easily. In the case of Minnesota, public lands were given to the new state with the specific stipulation that proceeds therefrom should be used for educational purposes. After admission the demand for improved roads became insistent, and it was decided that some of the revenue from land sales would be employed for road construction. The Supreme Court

---

[2] This joint resolution must be sent to the President even as an ordinary legislative measure, and, of course, is subject to a presidential veto.

[3] See *Coyle* v. *Smith*, 221 U. S. 559 (1911).

refused to permit this diversion on the ground that acceptance of the land by Minnesota carried with it a contractual obligation to use the proceeds for the purpose specified by Congress.[4]

Equality and inequality of the states. On a strictly legal basis the states are equal, for all of the states have the same relative power in enacting legislation and in handling local problems. The Supreme Court has emphasized that once a state is admitted it stands on an equal footing with all of the states in the Union. However, no one supposes that the states are equal in influence, wealth, population, area, or certain other respects. Currently New York is entitled to forty-one members in the House of Representatives, whereas Nevada, Alaska, and several other states must content themselves with only one. Texas has an area of more than a quarter of a million square miles, while Rhode Island, with 1,250 square miles, embraces less than one per cent as much territory. The aggregate wealth of Illinois is far greater than that of Mississippi, say, and the per capita wealth of the former is all out of proportion to that of the latter. In most national political relations, the large and wealthy states have proportionately more power and influence than the small and less well-to-do ones.

DISTRIBUTION OF POWERS IN THE FEDERAL SYSTEM

The essence of a federal form of government is the fact that governmental powers are divided between a general government, which in certain matters is independent of the associated parts, and regional governments, with certain powers independent of the general government. In either case, the government acting within its allotted sphere is not subordinate to the other. In a federal system both central and regional governments act directly on the people.

The Constitution of the United States fixes the broad outline of the distribution of powers between the national and state governments. The principle is easy to state, more difficult to apply, and impossible to understand if one views it as a static rather than as a developmental concept. Thus the interpretation of the developing Constitution has permitted the shifting of responsibility in innumerable areas from the states to the national government.

National government has delegated powers. The national government possesses only those powers which are delegated to it in the Constitution. As Chief Justice Marshall wrote: "The principle, that it can exercise only the powers granted to it, would seem too apparent to have required to be enforced by all those arguments which its enlightened friends, while it was depending before the people, found it necessary to urge. That principle is now universally admitted. *But the question respecting the extent of the*

---

4 See *Stearns* v *Minnesota*, 179 U. S. 223 (1900).

powers actually granted, is perpetually arising, and will probably continue to arise, as long as our system shall exist." [5]

The most obvious type of delegated powers are those *powers specifically enumerated in the Constitution.* Thus there have never been any arguments concerning the authority of the national government to coin money, establish a postal system, make treaties, raise armies, levy taxes, and to undertake many other functions mentioned by name. It is true, of course, that even in these areas the precise meaning and extent of the power has been questioned, but its existence has not been. However, a more fundamental question arose in the very first session of Congress. It was: Did the national government possess any powers which were not expressly enumerated?

Hamilton and others believed that the last paragraph in Article I, section 8, provided for *implied powers when it stated Congress shall have power,* "To make all laws which shall be necessary and proper for carrying into execution the foregoing powers, and all other powers vested by this Constitution in the government of the United States, or any department or officer thereof." In essence Hamilton argued, the Supreme Court has accepted, and Congress acts upon the assumption that the "necessary and proper" clause provides the basis for the passage of laws to make effective the broad purposes suggested by the enumerated powers.[6] The implied power principle gives the Constitution the flexibility which has permitted the national government to pass laws necessary for the solution of any truly national problem.

States have reserved powers. The states are not granted specific powers in the national Constitution. The Tenth Amendment makes explicit, what was already implicit, when it stated: "The powers not delegated to the United States by the Constitution, nor prohibited by it to the States, are reserved to the States respectively, or to the people." In contrast to the national government then, the states have inherent powers to legislate concerning their internal activities, so long as they do not run afoul of the national Constitution in doing so. It is now clear that the Tenth Amendment is not in itself a restriction upon the national government's powers.[7] If the central government has the authority to act, the amendment does not shield the people in the states from the effects of national law. It merely reiterates the distribution of power principle upon which the federal system is structured; it permits state actions in an undefined field rather than curtailing the national government in the exercise of its delegated powers.

National supremacy. Because our federal system is described as one in which both national and state governments have their allotted spheres of action, it is sometimes mistakenly understood that the two levels of government are of co-equal powers. This is far from being the case. The Constitu-

---

[5] Italics added. *McCulloch* v. *Maryland,* 4 Wheaton 316 (1819).
[6] For a more detailed discussion of the implied power doctrine, see p. 270.
[7] See *United States* v. *Darby Lumber Co.,* 312 U. S. 100 (1941).

tion specifically states: "This Constitution, and the laws of the United States which shall be made in pursuance thereof; and all treaties made, or which shall be made, under the authority of the United States, shall be the supreme law of the land; and the Judges in every State shall be bound thereby, anything in the Constitution or laws of any State to the contrary notwithstanding." [8] This clause does not mean that the national government may pass *any* law and make it the supreme law of the land; but it does mean that if the national government *has the power* to pass a law, or make a treaty,[9] state actions or instrumentalities may not be used to negate the national will. Significantly, also, is the fact that it is a national organ, the Supreme Court, which ultimately and authoritatively interprets the extent of the national government's powers.

RESPONSIBILITIES OF THE NATIONAL GOVERNMENT TO THE STATES

The Constitution charges the national government with certain specific responsibilities in its relations with the states as component parts of the national union. The central government is, however, the final judge of its own responsibilities with respect to the states.

Protection against invasion or domestic disturbance. The United States is charged with protecting each state against invasion, and "on application of the legislature, or of the executive (when the legislature cannot be convened) against domestic violence." [10] The requirement that the national government protect state territory against foreign invasion is, of course, a more or less obvious responsibility. The second part of this obligation is somewhat more meaningful, since it is a common responsibility of both the national and the state governments to suppress domestic disturbances throughout the land. In those cases where violence and internal upheavals reach such proportions that a state is itself unable to cope with the situation, the sending of federal forces is therefore guaranteed by the Constitution if state officials request such assistance. Except in very unusual circumstances state police facilities, or national guard units subject to state governors' direction, are capable of handling disturbances; consequently, it is uncommon for states to ask for federal aid. National authorities, alleging the primacy of federal property or rights, sometimes wish to take a hand when the state officials refuse to ask for assistance. President Eisenhower sent Federal troops into Arkansas and President Kennedy sent them into Mississippi to enforce court orders requiring integration, over the protests of the two governors. The power of the President to send troops to secure all rights entrusted by the Constitution to the national government without benefit of

---

8 Art. VI, sec. 2.
9 See p. 233 for discussion of this point with respect to treaties.
10 Art. IV, sec. 4.

an invitation from state officials has been upheld by the Supreme Court.[11]

A republican form of government. Under the terms of the Constitution the national government guarantees a republican form of government to the states.[12] This clause reads very well, but an examination of the facts reveals that it sometimes has comparatively little meaning in practice. In fact, the Constitution provides no definition of the meaning of the phrase "republican form of government." That is not to say that it does not have a good moral effect or that it might not be invoked if any widespread movement away from republican forms developed among the states. The trouble is that no adequate machinery is set up to enforce such a guarantee during ordinary times. The Supreme Court has repeatedly ruled that it is not for the courts to attempt to exercise such a function which, they say, falls under the political rather than the judicial category.[13]

It has, therefore, been left to Congress and the President to see that the states do have republican governments. The President, however, has numerous other duties to occupy his attention; moreover, it would frequently be unwise from a political standpoint for him to inquire too closely into the actual operation of the government of a certain state. Congress has the authority to refuse seats to senators and representatives of states that disregard republican principles and may also withhold federal appropriations from such states. But there is a wide chasm between the power to do something and the actual use of that power. If seats were refused or appropriations withheld, a great hue and cry would doubtless be raised. Moreover, the individual senators and representatives are very reluctant to establish a precedent that might sometimes be embarrassing to their own positions or states.

Territorial integrity. The framers of the Constitution were fearful that territory of their states might be alienated by the national government. They, therefore, inserted clauses which they believed would serve to prevent such action. Territory may not be taken from a state without its specific consent;[14] a state cannot be divided up into two or more states unless it agrees to such action;[15] and two or more states shall not be joined together to form a single state unless they so desire.

Equality of representation in the Senate. Article V details the procedure for adding formal amendments to the Constitution. A provision therein suggests that even the amending process may not be used to deprive a state of

---

11 *In re Debs,* 158 U. S. 564 (1895).

12 Art. IV, sec. 4.

13 Perhaps the best statement of the Supreme Court on this question is to be found in *Pacific States Telephone and Telegraph Co.* v. *Oregon,* 223 U. S. 118 (1912). See also *Luther* v. *Borden,* 7 Howard 1 (1849).

14 Art. IV, sec. 3. This does not prevent the national government from taking limited areas for post offices and forts by eminent domain.

15 The letter of the Constitution was adhered to in the case of West Virginia since a rump "loyalist" Virginia legislature consented to the breaking off of the western portion of the state.

its equality of representation in the Senate. Some authorities have argued that the amending process may not be thus restricted; but, in any case, the question is largely an academic one since the smaller states would surely block any proposed amendment on the subject.

PROHIBITIONS ON STATE AND NATIONAL GOVERNMENTS

Numerous prohibitions are imposed by the Constitution on both the state and national governments. These prohibitions are designed to secure to the individual certain areas of freedom beyond the reach of government, to protect the national interests as opposed to local interests, and conversely to protect the states' interests in certain areas from national control.

The accompanying chart shows most of the specific prohibitions found in the Constitution. Our discussion at this point is confined to those designed to protect the national interest against state action. The other types of prohibitions are discussed in subsequent chapters.

In general, the *states have all powers which are not delegated to the national government or reserved to the people.* Nevertheless, the framers felt it wise to lay down certain limitations on the exercise of those powers.

Restrictions upon the taxing power. The states under the Articles of Confederation had enjoyed the taxing power in its totality, while the central government had had to beg for the morsels that fell from the states' tables. The new Constitution remedied the weakness by giving the national government the direct authority to levy taxes, but it also left the power of the states in the tax field more or less unimpaired. It did, however, lay down several special specific prohibitions or restrictions, while the Supreme Court has read others into it.

The framers inserted a clause which forbade any state, without the consent of Congress, to lay "any imposts or duties on imports or exports, except what may be absolutely necessary for executing its inspection laws." [16] In this category may also be mentioned a prohibition relating to the levying of tonnage duties.[17] The due process clause of the Fourteenth Amendment, which commands a state not to deprive anyone of "life, liberty, or property without due process of law" has sometimes been applied by the courts in such a manner as to limit the taxing power of states. The contract and the equal-protection clauses of the Constitution have also been interpreted in like manner. While the Constitution contains no specific prohibition of state taxation of federal instrumentalities, the Supreme Court decided at an early date in the history of the republic that this was implied.[18] The Court declared that it would cause endless trouble if the states were permitted to hamper the federal government by levying such taxes. This general rule con-

---

16 Art. I, sec. 10.
17 *Ibid.* The consent of Congress may justify tonnage duties, but this is not given.
18 See *McCulloch* v. *Maryland,* 4 Wheaton 313 (1819).

THE DISTRIBUTION OF POWERS IN THE FEDERAL SYSTEM

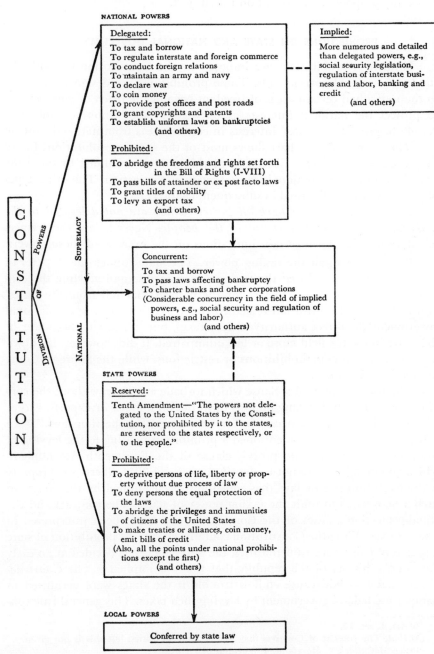

NATIONAL POWERS

Delegated:

To tax and borrow
To regulate interstate and foreign commerce
To conduct foreign relations
To maintain an army and navy
To declare war
To coin money
To provide post offices and post roads
To grant copyrights and patents
To establish uniform laws on bankruptcies
    (and others)

Prohibited:

To abridge the freedoms and rights set forth
    in the Bill of Rights (I-VIII)
To pass bills of attainder or ex post facto laws
To grant titles of nobility
To levy an export tax
    (and others)

Implied:

More numerous and detailed
than delegated powers, e.g.,
social security legislation,
regulation of interstate business and labor, banking and
credit
    (and others)

Concurrent:

To tax and borrow
To pass laws affecting bankruptcy
To charter banks and other corporations
(Considerable concurrency in the field of implied
    powers, e.g., social security and regulation of
    business and labor)
        (and others)

STATE POWERS

Reserved:

Tenth Amendment—"The powers not delegated to the United States by the Constitution, nor prohibited by it to the states,
are reserved to the states respectively, or
to the people."

Prohibited:

To deprive persons of life, liberty or prop-
    erty without due process of law
To deny persons the equal protection of
    the laws
To abridge the privileges and immunities
    of citizens of the United States
To make treaties or alliances, coin money,
    emit bills of credit
(Also, all the points under national prohibi-
    tions except the first)
        (and others)

LOCAL POWERS

Conferred by state law

CONSTITUTION

POWERS

OF

DIVISION

SUPREMACY

NATIONAL

tinues to apply. States are not permitted to tax the property of the national government unless specific consent is given.

Restrictions upon the power to regulate commerce. The authority to regulate interstate and foreign commerce is expressly given to the national government, leaving intrastate regulation to the states. As long as manufacturing, mining, agriculture, and labor-management relations, as well as local distribution, were included under intrastate commerce, the states had considerable regulatory authority. Since the national government, within the last quarter of a century, has been enabled to legislate in the first four fields mentioned above, the role of the states has been greatly reduced. Under their police powers the states may still regulate interstate commerce to a degree where Congress by silence or by law permits such regulation. For example, states may fix reasonable speed limits for interstate vehicles, or since Congress authorized it, determine the rates for various types of insurance policies, even though the insurance business has been declared to come within the regulatory powers of the national government. The primary point here is that Congress, not the states, determines under what conditions the states may affect interstate or foreign commerce.

Foreign relations. "No state shall enter into any treaty, alliance, or confederation . . . No state shall, without the consent of Congress, enter into any agreement or compact with another state or with a foreign power." [19] This constitutional provision has effectively eliminated treaties between the states and foreign countries and concentrated such authority in the central government. Compacts between a state and a foreign government are possible with the consent of Congress. Congress has not encouraged the latter procedure and would carefully evaluate the possible ramifications flowing from even a non-political agreement between a state and a foreign country before giving its consent. Congress did, however, give its consent to a compact between New York State and Canada concerning an international bridge.

Military affairs. States cannot, without the consent of Congress, "keep troops or ships of war in time of peace" or "engage in war, unless actually invaded or in such imminent danger as will not admit of delay." [20] Congress has, of course, made provision for the National Guard and in a few instances has permitted the operation of unimportant vessels of at least a semimilitary character. As for engaging in war, the states seem to be glad to have the national government assume that responsibility.

The monetary system. "No state shall coin money; emit bills of credit; make anything but gold and silver coin a tender in payment of debts." [21] The second part of the limitation was more or less avoided during the years prior to the Civil War by permitting state banks to issue notes and scrip

---

19 Art. I, sec. 10.
20 *Ibid.*
21 Art. I, sec. 10.

which served substantially the same purpose as state bills of credit. The abuses in connection with this particular practice, together with the desire of Congress to foster a strong system of national banks, led in 1866 to legislation taxing out of existence notes issued by state banks.[22]

Impairing the obligation of contracts. Finally, there is the important clause in the Constitution which reads: "No state shall pass any law impairing the obligation of contracts." [23] The constitutional fathers probably had in mind the ordinary executory contracts between individuals, which, before the Constitution, had frequently been interfered with by the enactment of "stay laws," legal tender laws, and other legislation for the benefit of insolvent debtors. In the first interpretation given the clause by the Supreme Court, however, it was applied to a grant of land by a state legislature, which it later sought to rescind.[24] In applying the clause to a state law in the famous Dartmouth College case,[25] the Supreme Court declared that New Hampshire could not legally take over the college. The donors of the original funds had entered into a contract which was recognized by the English crown at the time and accepted by the state of New Hampshire during the Articles of Confederation when the state could have revoked the charter. The Constitution protected the charter. Some years later the court modified the sweeping character of the Dartmouth College case to some extent by laying down the principle that states are not bound by implied terms of a contract.[26] Although the contract clause is still used by the courts to prevent state action, it is a less serious hindrance than might be imagined. The states ordinarily now protect themselves by inserting provisions in charters for revocation. The restrictions imposed on the states by the Fourteenth Amendment are much more important today as a protection for property rights than the obligation of contracts clause.

FEDERAL CENTRALIZATION

It has been said that the states have at present less exclusive power than ever before in their history, and yet they are more active than at any previous time. To a large extent, the current energy displayed by the state governments may be attributed to the greatly enlarged role of government in general in the United States. No doubt, states in some instances have felt compelled to undertake certain programs in an effort to ward off federal government participation in the same area. One can certainly argue that had the states been more aggressive in pursuing particular policies, as in the social security field, the federal government would have been less likely to have assumed responsibility for legislation affecting these matters.

---

[22] Upheld by the Supreme Court in *Veazie Bank* v. *Fenno,* 8 Wallace 533 (1869).
[23] Art. I, sec. 10.
[24] See *Fletcher* v. *Peck,* 6 Cranch 87 (1810).
[25] 4 Wheaton 518 (1819).
[26] See *Charles River Bridge* v. *Warren Bridge,* 11 Peters 420 (1837).

An extremely significant development, largely of twentieth century vintage, has been the trend toward federal centralization. Centralization refers to a higher level of government assuming authority or responsibility for functions which formerly rested with a lower level of government. At this point, our concern is with federal centralization with respect to the states, although states have also tended toward centralization in many areas which at one time were left to the local units of government.

Sometimes federal centralization is pictured as an indication of usurpation of power by the national government. It is true that the national government either undertakes programs on its own authority, or persuades the states to cooperate in various programs, to a degree which would have been unthinkable or even unconstitutional forty or fifty years ago. Until recently centralization was largely the result of either congressional or presidential action which was later upheld by the Supreme Court. In such instances, then, it was elected representatives who were taking the initiative in expanding national power. Since World War II, however, the Supreme Court has sometimes taken the initiative in expanding federal power. Each time this expansion has resulted from the Court's changing interpretations of its responsibilities under the Fourteenth Amendment. We have already noted its new role in civil rights. Since 1962 the Court has entered the field of state legislative apportionment and in 1964 took an active role in congressional redistricting within the several states. Both these developments will be discussed in later chapters.

Techniques of centralization. In the broadest sense centralization has progressed primarily because Congress has expanded the scope of its operations and the Supreme Court has upheld its enactments. The formal constitutional amendment process has played a relatively minor role in the centralization trend.

The *commerce power* is described in some detail in a subsequent chapter.[27] At this point, it is sufficient to say that Congress has used the commerce clause more frequently than any other section of the Constitution to regulate activities which at one time were considered subject only to state legislation. Agriculture, business, labor-management relations, wages and hours, and child labor practices are but a few of the areas or activities affected by national legislation under the commerce power.

In the famous case of *McCulloch* v *Maryland,* Chief Justice Marshall wrote that ". . . the power to tax involves the power to destroy." The federal *taxing power* has been used to destroy certain activities within the states,[28] but it has also been used to promote state legislation. The tax-offset device is an ingenious technique used by the national government in a few

---

27 See p. 442.
28 See p. 426.

instances to "persuade" the states to undertake certain programs. For example, when the national government wished the states to adopt unemployment insurance programs, it levied a payroll tax on employers. However, if a state adopted an unemployment insurance scheme, acceptable to the national government, up to 90 per cent of the federal tax within that state could be used for the support of the program. Under the pressure of the tax-credit device all of the states enacted appropriate unemployment insurance laws.[29]

Grants-in-aid. Although the national government may not pass any law because it believes the general welfare of the nation would benefit, it may spend money to promote that purpose. Through the *grant-in-aid system* the spending power has been developed as a potent weapon by the national government in securing state cooperation in many fields. In accepting the financial payment, states must agree to certain conditions attached to the grant. Thus states may be required:

(1) to match a certain proportion of the grant with their own funds;
(2) to establish an administrative agency through which the national government may work in dealing with the state;
(3) to create a merit system for the selection of state personnel to administer the program;
(4) to comply with certain engineering, professional, or technical requirements set by the national government;
(5) to use the grant only for the specific purpose authorized by national law;
(6) to permit national inspection of the program's administration; and
(7) not to discriminate against persons benefited by the program on account of race, color, or religion.

A multitude of national-state programs are now operating under the grant-in-aid approach. Among these are programs in highway construction and maintenance, education, agricultural research, public assistance and welfare, health administration, conservation, and housing. Within the past five years federal grant-in-aid expenditures have more than doubled. Over six billion dollars was allotted for such activities in the 1960 fiscal year. Many state governments derive 15 or 20 per cent of their total revenues from these federal funds.

The grant-in-aid technique has been criticized by some as "perverting in its influence," a "backstairs" approach to solving problems, and a violation of the spirit, if not the letter, of the Constitution. Some of the more prosperous states have argued that their taxes are paying for local programs in the poorer states. Also it is suggested that the technique has sent state taxes soaring because of the feeling or necessity that they must "keep up" with the other states.

Proponents of this type of grant, and they are in the majority, point

---

[29] For a fuller discussion of this scheme, see p. 527.

out that the programs are voluntary; that a state does not have to participate
They argue that the device actually slows down further federal centralization
and that the states at least can tailor the programs to meet local needs and
conditions. Many persons believe that a modern industrial nation must
furnish expanding social services, that the states were slow to move in this
direction, and that the grant-in-aid device permits desirable and necessary
programs to be developed within the framework of the federal system.

Many other powers of the national government such as the treaty, postal,
bankruptcy, and "war" powers have been used to further centralization.
Those mentioned above are the most frequently used.

OTHER ASPECTS OF FEDERAL-STATE RELATIONS

The federal and state governments cooperate in many areas where the
issue of centralization is seldom raised. Occasionally, the national government has used either the states or state officers as agents. Under the Selective
Service Act, state governors are permitted to name the local boards which pass
on the individual cases of those who are called for military training. The
F.B.I. has worked closely with state law enforcement officers for a number
of years. State and national officials collaborate in enforcing the Pure Food
and Drug Act. It has become a federal crime to flee from a state in order
to escape prosecution for a felony under state law. The national government
has divested itself of control over certain articles in interstate commerce (as
convict-made goods) so that the states may prohibit sales within their borders.
A great amount of informal cooperation between the two levels of government is achieved through consultation and conference, exchange of advisory
and educational facilities, and temporary loans of equipment or personnel.

INTERSTATE RELATIONS

In addition to the relation between the national government and the
states, the federal system also involves the relations among the states themselves. The founders were not unaware of this problem as evidenced by a
number of provisions in the Constitution bearing on the subject.

Full faith and credit. The Constitution, commands the states to give
"full faith and credit" to "public acts, records, and judicial proceedings of
every other state." [30] If every state clung churlishly to the minutiae of its own
forms and persistently refused to recognize records and acts of other states
which did not have exactly the same requirements, there would be great
confusion, inconvenience, and loss of time. To obviate such chaos the
framers agreed upon a provision which orders every state to accept at full
value the acts, public records, and court proceedings of all other states.

---

[30] Art. IV, sec. 1.

On its face, this stipulation would seem to apply to both civil and criminal cases, but the Supreme Court has decided that only civil matters are involved.[31]

Under the full-faith-and-credit clause states must give full recognition to the deeds, mortgages, notes, wills, contracts, and similar instruments of sister states as long as these have met all the requirements of the state where they originated. Nevertheless, the procedure for obtaining full faith and credit for various types of actions is not so simple as one might imagine. For example, suppose A obtained a judgment against B for payment of damages in a civil suit. Suppose B moves outside the jurisdiction of the state awarding the judgment. A will probably have to go to the second state and institute court proceedings to collect the judgment. The court of the second state cannot retry the issues leading to the original award. In other words, the second state is bound under the full-faith-and-credit clause to require B to pay A. The second court can, however, challenge the jurisdiction of the first state to render the judgment. In essence, this is the primary difficulty in the matter of giving full faith and credit to divorce decrees.

The full-faith-and-credit clause has presented many difficulties in connection with *divorce decrees*. The states vary as widely in their divorce laws as perhaps in any other field. If the persons securing a divorce are bona fide residents of the state granting the divorce, every other state must accept the judgment without question. However, the Supreme Court in *Williams* v. *North Carolina*[32] sustained the right of a North Carolina jury to determine that a six weeks sojourn in Nevada had not made bona fide Nevada residents out of two North Carolinians and that they were therefore not legally divorced from their former spouses. This reasoning was based on the proposition that under the circumstances the Nevada court did not have jurisdiction to grant the divorce, so it was not entitled to full faith and credit in North Carolina. The potential far-reaching effect of the Williams case was modified somewhat by a later decision when the Supreme Court held that a divorce granted in a contested proceeding in which the state court's jurisdiction was not questioned, must be accorded full faith and credit.[33]

Amending the Constitution to provide for uniform divorce proceedings has often been suggested, but no such proposal has ever been passed by Congress. Perhaps another solution to the numerous problems arising under the full-faith-and-credit clause, including divorce, lies in the language of the latter part of the clause itself. The Constitution states: "And the Congress may by general laws prescribe the manner in which such acts, records, and proceedings shall be proved, and the effect thereof." [34] Congress has passed two laws based on this authority, but they do little to clarify the un-

---

31 See *Wisconsin* v. *Pelican Insurance Co.,* 127 U. S. 265 (1888).
32 325 U. S. 226 (1945).
33 *Sherrer* v. *Sherrer,* 334 U. S. 343 (1948).
34 Art. IV, sec. 1.

certainties involved in many areas. It would seem reasonable to assume that, under the implied power doctrine, Congress could at least specify certain standards in some of the problem areas for guidance to the courts at all levels of government.

Rendition. To assist in the apprehension of criminals, the delegates to the constitutional convention inserted a declaration that states should surrender to sister states fugitives from justice. This process, known as "rendition" but frequently referred to as "extradition," serves a very useful purpose in preventing criminals from escaping punishment. The exact constitutional language is: "A person charged in any state with treason, felony, or other crime, who shall flee from justice, and be found in another state, shall on demand of the executive authority of the state from which he fled, be delivered up, to be removed to the state having jurisdiction of the crime." [35]

The Supreme Court has said that "the words of the clause . . . were made sufficiently comprehensive to include every offense against the laws of the demanding state, without exception as to the nature of the crime." [36] However, the words "it shall be the duty" have been interpreted as not being a mandatory requirement but as a declaration of the moral duty of the governor of the asylum state, to render the fugitive up to the requesting state's authorities.[37] Usually states cooperate in the matter of interstate rendition. Yet it is not infrequent for a governor to refuse to turn over a fugitive for one reason or another. Perhaps the governor feels that the individual will not get a fair trial if he is returned; or perhaps the fugitive is leading an exemplary life in the second state, and the governor does not believe that the ends of justice will be served by sending him back to the demanding state. Sometimes the refusal to cooperate may be based on the fact that the governor is not in sympathy with the purpose or application of the law under which the person has been charged, as when, in the period before the Civil War, some Northern governors opposed the fugitive slave laws.

Privileges and immunities of state citizenship. The Constitution requires that "the citizens of each state shall be entitled to all privileges and immunities of citizens in the several states." [38] Foreign corporations (incorporated in another state) are not considered citizens under this clause. A state may go so far as to exclude foreign corporations except where the corporation is engaged in interstate commerce or is performing a federal function. This fact is not nearly so important as it once was since the concept of what constitutes interstate commerce has expanded increasingly in the past thirty years.

There is no authoritative listing of the privileges and immunities of interstate citizenship, but several examples may be cited. Citizens may move

---

35 *Ibid.*
36 *Ex parte Reggel,* 114 U. S. 642 (1885).
37 *Kentucky* v. *Dennison,* 24 Howard 66 (1860).
38 Art. IV, sec. 2

freely from one state to another. They may establish businesses and own property in any state. They are entitled to the use of the state courts and judicial processes. Non-residents are entitled to protection by state and local authorities even as permanent residents.

Of course, a person moving into a state does not automatically bring with him all of the privileges associated with his former resident status. If he has been a voter in his old home, he must nevertheless meet the requirements of the second state before exercising the suffrage privilege. If he were practicing law in one state, he must pass the second state's bar examination or otherwise meet the requirement. If he has a high school teaching certificate in one state, this does not mean that he may teach in the schools of all of the states.

The privileges and immunities clause does not prevent state and local governments from reserving certain facilities for the use of permanent residents or giving them priority in their use. Many states give their own residents first choice in the use of camping and other facilities in state parks. All state universities require a higher tuition fee for out-of-state undergraduate students than for their own residents. Hunting licenses for residents of outside states cost more than for persons living within the state. In the latter two examples, a state may not discriminate among the states. Thus a person from California could not be required to pay more tuition to attend Pennsylvania State University than a student from Maryland.

Interstate trade barriers. One of the primary pressures for the calling of the constitutional convention stemmed from the stifling of trade and commerce throughout the United States because of discriminatory navigation, tax, and other laws passed by the individual states. The Constitution did not fully remove the possibility of the states erecting various types of trade barriers, and the states, particularly since the 1930's, have passed numerous laws and regulations designed to favor certain industries, businesses, and professions within their own borders, and to secure revenue from out-of-state persons and corporations. Once a state passes legislation which appears to be discriminatory against citizens of other states, there is a natural tendency for sister states to act in a similar fashion. It would be unfair to assume that all laws which are labeled as "discriminatory" are unreasonable or motivated by selfishness. No one would deny, for example, that a state should have a right to protect itself from the importation of diseased cattle. On the other hand, if this power is used as an excuse to favor local stockmen over out-of-state stockmen, it becomes an unreasonable barrier.

Police power trade barriers. Sometimes the police power of the state is used for discriminatory purposes. Minnesota enacted a law, subsequently invalidated by the Supreme Court, prohibiting the sale of meat not taken from animals inspected in the state within twenty-four hours before slaughter. Sometimes areas have been marked out from which milk may be shipped to local markets so as to discriminate in favor of local milk producers. In some instances, "fresh eggs" are only those produced in the state. Restrictive quarantine measures with respect to plants, produce, and animals often favor local producers. Limitations as to the weight and size of motor trucks and trailers that use the state's highways may be extremely discriminatory.

Tax and license barriers. Special taxes and license fees have been levied on foreign corporations for the privilege of doing local business. Chain store taxes, graded according to the number of units within the state, favor the independent merchant. Taxes on oleomargarine favor local dairy interests. Persons who obtain items outside of a state to avoid sales tax are frequently required to pay a "use" tax for the privilege of enjoying their purchases. Some states limit the amount of a particular commodity, such as liquor or cigarettes, that a person may bring into the state, even for his own use, unless he pays a tax equal in amount to that charged by the state in which they are to be consumed.

Proprietary power barriers. State and local governments spend millions of dollars for goods and services. It is not unusual for state laws or local ordinances to give preferential treatment to local businesses in regard to such matters. Thus a state law may prevent state officials from awarding a particular type of contract—perhaps a printing contract—to an out-of-state firm.

Relief from discriminatory trade barriers. The Supreme Court has negated certain types of discrimination primarily on the basis that they interfere with interstate commerce. Congress, no doubt, could do much more than it has done, particularly toward eliminating unreasonable restrictions with respect to interstate motor carriers. A third avenue of approach is through voluntary cooperation by the states themselves. The Council of State Governments[39] has made studies, called conferences, and generally encouraged the states to cooperate in the removal of various trade restrictions, with a fair measure of success in some areas.

Interstate cooperation. The complexity of interstate relations has given rise to various organizations which seek to secure voluntary cooperation among the states. As early as 1925 the American Legislators' Association was formed. In 1935 this organization fostered the establishment of the Council of State Governments.

The Council of State Governments does much of its work through commissions of interstate cooperation set up in every state. It serves as a secretariat, research agency, and clearing house for many national organizations of state officials such as the American Legislators' Association, the Governors' Conference, the National Association of Secretaries of State, the National Association of Attorneys General, the Conference of Chief Justices, the National Association of State Budget Officers, and the National Association of State Purchasing Officials. The Council spotlights interstate problems through its research activities, disseminates information, and sponsors many

---

[39] See below.

types of regional and national conferences dealing with areas of interest to most of the states. It publishes a regular monthly magazine, *State Government,* and a biennial *Book of the States,* which includes information about the work and personnel of all branches of state governments.

As early as 1889 the American Bar Association summoned a conference on uniform state laws—called *The National Conference of Commissioners on Uniform State Laws.* Since 1912 all of the states have appointed commissioners to serve at this conference. The conference has encouraged interstate cooperation by drafting model laws in many important fields. Only a few of the model statutes have been adopted by a majority of the states, but the conference has nevertheless had considerable influence on certain types of legislation even where its recommendations were not completely followed. A few of the subjects upon which recommendations have been made include negotiable instruments, stock transfer, proof of statutes, traffic regulations, desertion and non-support, criminal extradition, and declaratory judgments.

States may, with the consent of Congress, enter into *compacts with other states.* Prior to 1925 most interstate compacts dealt with boundary disputes. In the past thirty-five years compacts have been entered into by many states in an effort to solve regional or even national problems. Many of the regional compacts deal with such matters as flood control, construction of power dams, oil conservation, fisheries, education, sanitation, and stream pollution. On the other hand, the Interstate Crime Compact, setting up uniform methods of out-of-state supervision of parolees and probationers, has been entered into by all of the states. Once a state enters a compact agreed to by Congress the compact becomes enforceable through the federal court system.

Legislatures may authorize a state's administrative officials to enter into agreements with officials of other states with respect to many aspects of the privileges of state citizenship. These are *reciprocity agreements.* A state may say that it will recognize a license to practice a profession granted in another state if that other state similarly recognizes permits to practice the profession granted by the first state.

SUMMARY

The basic principles of our federal system as outlined in the Constitution are fairly easy to state. The national government possesses delegated powers, consisting of enumerated and implied powers. To the states are reserved all powers not delegated to the national government nor prohibited to the states. In certain areas, i.e., taxation, both national and state governments exercise concurrent powers. Various prohibitions are mentioned in the Constitution affecting the national government alone, only the states, or restrictive on both national and state governments. The national government is obligated to fulfill certain guarantees toward the states. However, the national government is the judge of its own powers and responsibilities;

also the "supreme law of the land clause" clearly establishes national supremacy over state constitutions and laws.

The application of these basic principles is not so simple as their enumeration. The outstanding feature of American federalism has been its adaptation of the constitutional principles to meet the developing needs of the nation. The doctrine of implied powers is the chief source of this adaptability; its acceptance by the judicial and political branches of the central government and its endorsement by the electorate has provided the national government with the constitutional means to legislate on practically any problem national in scope. The various techniques of centralization and cooperative federalism are the results of its application.

Article IV of the Constitution includes the full faith and credit, the rendition, and the privileges and immunities clauses, all concerned with interstate relations. These are all mandatory requirements upon the states as interpreted by the Supreme Court. These constitutional requirements are in turn supplemented by a number of optional devices used by the states to solve their mutual problems, the interstate compact being a prime example.

BIBLIOGRAPHIC NOTE

In recent years a number of studies have dealt with the general subject of federalism. Perhaps the most readable of these publications is by K. C. Wheare, *Federal Government* (4th ed., New York: Oxford University Press, 1963). Various aspects of the subject are covered by a number of authors in A. W. Macmahon (ed.), *Federalism: Mature and Emergent* (Garden City, N. Y.: Doubleday & Company, Inc., 1955). Probably the most comprehensive survey of the theory and practice of federalism is found in Robert R. Bowie and C. J. Friedrich (eds.), *Studies in Federalism* (Boston: Little, Brown and Company, 1954). William Livingston's *Federalism and Constitutional Change* (London: Oxford University Press, 1956) presents the thesis that federalism is largely a product of social, economic, political, and cultural forces which make the outward form necessary.

Among the publications concerned with American federalism, see L. D. White, *The States and the Nation* (Baton Rouge: Louisiana University Press, 1953), and William Anderson, *The Nation and States, Rivals or Partners?* (Minneapolis: University of Minnesota Press, 1955). The former study consists of three essays entitled, "The March of Power to Washington," "Strength and Limitations of the States," and "The Next Quarter Century"; the Anderson book is a plea for cooperative federalism. Another important study on American federalism is that of the President's Commission on Intergovernmental Relations, *A Report to the President for Transmittal to Congress* (Washington, D. C.: Government Printing Office, 1955).

The Committee on Government Operations, U. S. House of Representatives prepared a detailed bibliography on *Intergovernmental Relations in the United States* (84th Cong., 2nd Sess., 1956). For studies on the grant-in-aid system, see V. O. Key, *The Administration of Federal Grants to States* (Chicago: Public Administration Service, 1937); Rebecca L. Notz, *Federal Grants-in-Aid to States* (Chicago: Council of State Governments, 1956); and James A. Maxwell, *The Fiscal Impact of Federalism in the United States* (Cambridge, Mass.: Harvard University Press, 1946).

Important facets of national-state relations are discussed in Joseph E. Kallenbach's *Federal Cooperation With the States Under the Commerce Clause* (Ann Arbor: University of Michigan Press, 1942); Ruth L. Roettinger, *The Supreme Court and State Police Power: A Study in Federalism* (Washington, D. C.: Public Affairs Press, 1957); and J. R. Schmidhauser, *The Supreme Court as Final Arbiter in Federal-State Relations, 1798-1957* (Chapel Hill: University of North Carolina Press, 1958).

Among the studies dealing with interstate relations are: F. E. Melder, *State and Local Barriers to Interstate Commerce in the United States* (Orono, Me.: University of Maine Press, 1937); Robert H. Jackson, *Full Faith and Credit* (New York: Columbia University Press, 1942); Vincent V. Thursby, *Interstate Cooperation: A Study of the Interstate Compact* (Washington, D. C.: Public Affairs Press, 1953); F. L. Zimmerman and M. Wendall, *The Interstate Compact Since 1925* (Chicago: The Council of State Governments, 1951); and R. H. Leach and R. S. Sugg, Jr., *The Administration of Interstate Compacts* (Baton Rouge, La.: Louisiana State University Press, 1959).

Three recent studies dealing with the history of American federalism are Jackson T. Main, *The Antifederalists: Critics of the Constitution, 1781-1788* (Chapel Hill: University of North Carolina Press, 1961); Daniel J. Elazar, *The American Partnership: Intergovernmental Cooperation in Nineteenth Century United States* (Chicago: University of Chicago Press, 1962); Alpheus T. Mason, *The States Rights Debate: Antifederalism and the Constitution* (Englewood Cliffs: Prentice-Hall, 1964).

Two new books which are primarily concerned with modern problems of federalism in the United States are George C. S. Benson et al., *Essays in Federalism* (Claremont, Calif.: Institute for Studies in Federalism, 1961) and Robert A. Goldwin (ed.), *A Nation of States: Essays on the American Federal System* (Chicago: Rand McNally, 1963).

5

Citizens and Aliens

A<small>T LEAST</small> since the time of Moses the world has witnessed the flight of refugees from tyranny. Yet the twentieth century has added something new to the refugee problem. Today there is no place for many of the refugees to go. Stateless, homeless, hopeless, they live in the camps of Western Europe and of the Far East with the gates of both their totalitarian homelands and the freer lands to the west closed to them. Until the second decade of the twentieth century refugees could be counted in the thousands. Since the middle of the second decade the refugees have been counted first in the tens of thousands, then the hundreds of thousands, and for the past thirty years in the millions. Until the twentieth century a few men sought refuge outside their homelands because of religious or political persecution. With the coming of totalitarianism in Russia, Germany, Italy, and now in Communist China and the satellite countries of Eastern Europe hundreds of thousands of refugees have streamed out of their homelands. Later the totalitarians decided for propaganda reasons to stop their escape and destroy them or place them in concentration camps. Prior to the present century there was always some place for the refugees to go, some place where they could once more set up their own communities and build stable new societies. Today, the countries which welcomed the refugees of an earlier era are more densely populated. They choose the refugees whom they will accept. The pitiful, difficult cases are never solved. The latter will spend their natural lives in the refugee camps of the west or in the crowded make-shift hovels of the Far East.

America, the haven for the political and religious refugees of the eighteenth and nineteenth centuries and the hope for countless others whose futures seemed grim and unpalatable elsewhere, today still receives more immigrants than any other country in the world, although Canada and Australia have higher per capita rates. America still provides a home for a few hundred thousand of "the tired, the poor, and the huddled masses" of the rest of the world, but it no longer accepts half a million a year to its shores at the very time that the pressure of refugees has increased. The other large countries of the Americas—Canada, Brazil, and Argentina have also cut back on immigration. Australia, which still seeks more immigrants, has thrown up some barriers to their entrance.

Those who get to America and become citizens enjoy the same privileges and rights as all other citizens of this country. The nature of these privileges and rights has been defined, re-defined, and modified over the years. The nation at first had no definition of citizenship. There was no constitutional provision dealing with the matter until after the Civil War. After the Fourteenth Amendment defined the term it became necessary for the Courts to interpret the definition.

WHO IS A CITIZEN

Definitions. The Fourteenth Amendment provides that "All persons born or naturalized in the United States, and subject to the jurisdiction thereof, are citizens of the United States and of the State wherein they reside." This statement was made exactly ninety-two years after the Declaration of Independence and seventy-nine years after the Constitutional Convention. In the intervening period there had been no mention of the nature of citizenship in the Constitution and only the extraordinary decision in the Dred Scott case in 1857 [1] gave guidance concerning the character of citizenship. The provision of the Fourteenth Amendment just quoted was a direct reversal of Chief Justice Taney's opinion in the Dred Scott case. The Fourteenth Amendment also made clear that the United States was following essentially the English view of citizenship and not the one that prevailed in most other countries. Place of birth is at least as important as parentage in determining eligibility for United States citizenship.

Jus Soli. This Latin phrase refers to citizenship gained as a result of place of birth. Relating of place of birth to citizenship was the traditional English view. The Supreme Court in its earliest interpretation of the meaning of the citizenship clause suggested that it did not automatically grant citizenship merely because a person was born in this country. Later the Court clearly stated that the provision applied to anyone born in this country and subject to its jurisdiction even if his parents were ineligible to become citizens.[2] The Court in this instance ruled that a man whose parents could not become citizens because of the Chinese Exclusion Act was nonetheless a citizen himself if he were born in this country. This doctrine was challenged once more but was upheld in the case of a Japanese-American whose citizenship was contested by an ultranationalist group during World War II.[3]

Exempt from the rule of the citizenship because of the place of birth are all those who are not "subject to the jurisdiction" of the United States.

---

[1] 19 Howard 393.

[2] *United States* v. *Wong Kim Ark,* 169 U. S. 649 (1898).

[3] *Regan* v. *King,* 319 U. S. 753 (1943).

That qualifying phrase is intended primarily to cover persons born to parents who are foreign government officials assigned to the embassies and other official missions of the governments in the United States. These persons are subject to the jurisdiction of their own governments and therefore are not automatically citizens because of birth within our geographic limits. Most Americans are citizens by virtue of birth in this country.

Jus Sanguinis. A second means of defining citizenship is on the basis of the citizenship of one's parents, that is, on the basis of the law of blood. Most countries of Europe and Asia follow this rule. A few, like the United States, follow some combination of the two rules.[4] The United States as early as 1890 enacted legislation providing that a child born abroad of American parents was himself an American. Today that rule is still in effect with certain additions and modifications. If his parents are both Americans and either of them has resided in the United States prior to his birth, the child is considered a native born American. A child of one American and one non-American parent is considered a citizen, but his American parent must have lived in this country for five years after the age of fourteen and a total of ten years prior to the birth of the child. In addition the child must himself come to the United States before he is twenty-three and live in this country for five consecutive years during the period between his fourteenth and twenty-eighth birthdays.

Dual citizenship. Given the differences in the way in which countries define the basis of citizenship, it is not surprising that some persons are citizens of two countries or of none. The child of Italian parents born in the United States automatically acquires citizenship in Italy and in the United States. He is a citizen of the former because his parents were Italian and that country follows the rule of *jus sanguinis*. He is a citizen of this country under the rule of *jus soli*. Since the child normally remains in the United States, the fact of dual citizenship does not affect his life. If, however, he should go to Italy he faces certain problems arising out of this fact.

Some persons have no citizenship. They are stateless. Some countries provide that a woman shall lose her citizenship upon her marriage to a citizen of a foreign country. If her husband's native country, like the United States, does not automatically give citizenship to the foreign wife, the woman is stateless at least until naturalized. Other persons have given up their citizenship in one country and not acquired it in any other country. Still others may have lost citizenship in all countries for various other reasons.

Privileges of citizenship. Citizens normally have certain rights which are not available to non-citizens. The United States makes fewer distinc-

---

4 For a good brief discussion of the rules of *jus soli* and *jus sanguinis* see Austin Ranney, *Governing of Men* (New York: Henry Holt and Company, 1958).

tions than do most countries between the rights and privileges granted citizens and aliens. Most of the constitutional safeguards refer to "persons" making no distinctions between citizens and aliens. Within the boundaries of the United States both are assured government protection. Once outside of the United States, however, the alien resident does not receive the protection of the American government against actions of a foreign power, nor does he receive assistance of the American embassies should he desire their help. He is most vulnerable in the country of his birth.

Today the alien does not possess the right to vote in any of the 50 states, although there was a time when little distinction was made even with respect to this matter. Now the voter must be an American citizen as well as meet the other tests which are laid down locally concerning age, residence, literacy, and so forth.[5]

IMMIGRATION

Aside possibly from the native Indians, all Americans are either immigrants or the children of immigrants. During the colonial period most of the settlers were English although New York and New Jersey were settled first by persons of Dutch and Scandinavian parentage. By the time of the Declaration of Independence, roughly ninety per cent of the three million persons then in the colonies were English or of English decent. During the first sixty years of the new republic the English and Scotch-Irish continued to provide the vast majority of the immigrants. After 1840 new sources of immigration developed.

Immigration during the nineteenth century. Waves of Irish and German immigrants began to arrive before the middle of the nineteenth century and continued to come in large numbers until the turn of the century. The Germans were fleeing the tyrannies that periodically arose within that country. The Irish were fleeing poverty, famine, and the British. The Irish who came in such great numbers mid-way in the nineteenth century settled in the cities along the eastern seaboard or moved westward to participate as laborers in the building of the railroads and the canals then being developed to connect the east coast with the newer states of the old Northwest Territory. At the same time there was developing in most of the major cities a new interest in politics as the suffrage was extended to include all citizens who had attained their majority. The Irish who arrived were poor almost beyond present day conception. They had saved enough money, or had been sent funds by their kinfolk in America to pay passage from Ireland. They had to bring their own food and even the water to take care of their needs during the long passage. They arrived in New York and Boston without money, sick or weak from the trip and with no im-

---

[5] As late as 1838 at least one state, Arkansas, made no distinction between citizens and aliens in the matter of voting.

mediately available means of support. These new immigrants were greeted by those who would cheat them of their last pennies and by representatives of the political machines who would assure them of at least some assistance until they could begin to make their way in the new world. The immigrants gave their votes to the political machines in return for food, shelter, and jobs. From the middle of the nineteenth century until the third decade of the twentieth century, the immigrants provided the major support needed by the political organizations to maintain themselves in power; the machines in turn were the immigrants' link with the society of the new country. Without other roots in the society, despised by the "older" citizens, and without the money to compete, the Irish took up a business at which they excelled—politics. They took over the politics of almost every major city east of the Mississippi. They sent men to the legislatures of the states and to Congress. At the same time other Irish immigrants provided the physical labor needed to build the roads, streets, canals, and railroads of the country.

The German immigrants also came in large numbers beginning in the middle of the 19th century. Most of the Germans came not to escape famine or hardship, but to escape political persecution. Some had fought in unsuccessful uprisings and came to America to escape the vengeance of the victors. Some were liberals fighting for political reform. Later German immigrants included Marxist social democrats who worked in the trade unions and sought to create parties whose aim would be a socialistic America. These German immigrants dominated the left wing movements of the new world from 1880 to 1915. By the latter date many of the earlier immigrants had died. Their children felt no tie to a dogma which could be made to fit many American situations only by distortions of the most egregious sort. As the Germans of the second and third generations came to play a larger role in American politics, as they were more and more absorbed into American society, and as they became more and more dispersed throughout the country, their politics changed and they moved into the two major parties.

New sources of immigrants. The largest wave of immigrants to the United States came between 1880 and 1920, in large measure, from new areas of Europe—from the east, and Slavic areas, and from Italy on the south. Although the Irish, English, and Germans continued to come, they were far outnumbered by the newer immigrants. A total of 23,465,374 immigrants came to these shores between 1880 and 1920. Those from Eastern Europe replaced the Irish in the mines, the steel mills, and other hard but undesirable jobs across the country. Some of them also replaced the Germans as the leaders and members of the left wing movement. When the Socialist Party split in 1917, the vast majority of those leaving to establish the Communist Party (at that time under different names) were of Eastern European birth. The foreign language sections that dominated the new Communist Party outnumbered the English speaking sections of the party as much as ten to one in most areas. Furthermore, the languages were Eastern not Western European languages. Although only a fragment of the total number of immigrants participated in the communist movement, they constituted almost the entire membership.[6]

After the passage of the immigration acts of 1921 and 1924 the major waves of immigration came to an end. Except for the unusual problems arising out of World War II and the Hungarian Revolution, American immigration was reduced to a relative trickle of about 150,000 persons per year. Even with the limitations on immigration to this country, 20 per cent of all Europeans leaving their homes in the years after World War II came to the United States.

Regulation of immigration. The first regulation of immigrants came in 1798 with the Alien and Sedition Act which provided for the deportation of aliens under certain circumstances. The act was in effect for only two years during which time it was not used. In effect then there was no regulation of immigration for the first hundred years of American independence. For much of that period immigration was encouraged to help man the factories and till the land of the rapidly expanding country. In 1875 Congress passed the first act to exclude criminals and prostitutes.

A few years later the labor movement pressed the government to limit the immigration of orientals because of the competition for jobs and wages. Congress in 1882 passed the Chinese Exclusion Act which prevented further immigration of orientals to the United States. During the next few years Congress also placed severe limitations upon various forms of contract labor under which immigrants had been brought over by business groups to depress wages of workers already in America. Following the assassination of President William McKinley by an anarchist immigrant, Congress passed legislation preventing anarchists from immigrating to the United States. Later Congress excluded those who were mentally deficient, who could not earn their way in this country, and those afflicted with tuberculosis.

Development of rules of immigration. Following the Chinese Exclusion Act, Theodore Roosevelt worked out the "Gentlemen's Agreement" with Japan which limited the immigration of Japanese nationals. In 1921 the United States for the first time seriously limited the number of immigrants who could come to this country. That act excluded orientals, anarchists, criminals, and set a quota of the number of persons who could enter the country each year. The 1921 act was a temporary measure limited to two years of effectiveness. In 1924 a permanent act was passed limiting immigration to 150,000 persons per year and providing that a quota be set for each nationality based upon the number of persons from a particular

---

[6] See the excellent discussion of the East European immigrant strength in the Communist Party in Theodor Draper, *The Roots of American Communism* (New York: The Viking Press, 1957).

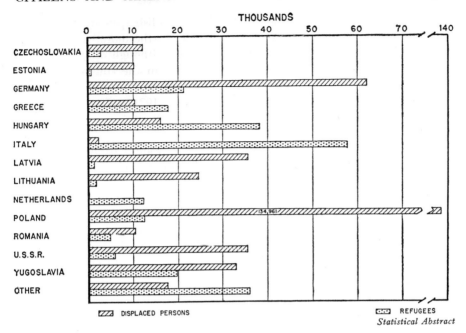

DISPLACED PERSONS ADMITTED BETWEEN 1948 AND 1955 AND REFUGEES ADMITTED BETWEEN 1951 AND 1959, BY COUNTRY OF BIRTH

country who were resident in the United States in 1920. The new arrangement meant that persons from the British Isles and northern Europe were favored over those who came from eastern and southern Europe.

The rise of Communism and Nazism in Europe led to further restrictions on immigration in 1940 when the Alien Registration Act was passed. That act provided that certain criminal and subversive persons not previously excluded should be excluded or deported. Aliens already in this country were forced to register and be fingerprinted to make possible closer surveillance of their activities. The Internal Security Act of 1950 added still more limitations on the admission of potential subversives and also made their expulsion simpler.

The Immigration and Nationality Act of 1952. Senator McCarran, Democrat from Nevada, began hearings by the Senate Judiciary Committee on the whole problem of immigration and naturalization in 1948. For two years the committee talked with immigrants, law enforcement officials, and others concerning the problem. A report was published by the committee in 1950.[7] Two years later the House of Representatives and the Senate under the leadership of Representative Francis E. Walter and Senator McCarran produced a bill which was passed by Congress, vetoed by

---

[7] "The Immigration and Naturalization Systems of the United States," by the Senate Judiciary Committee, Senate Report 1515, 81st Congress, Second Session 1950.

President Truman, and then passed over his veto. In his message President Truman criticized the measure because it had retained the 1924 provisions concerning national origins and did not take into account certain hardship problems. He also criticized some of the grounds set for exclusion and expulsion.

The 1952 act included a couple of matters which the President praised in his veto message. The law codified immigration rules which had developed in the preceding half century. Further, it removed the stigma attached to oriental birth by allowing some immigration from any country without regard to race. At the same time the act restricted the number of persons who could come into this country from the "Pacific triangle" to 100 immigrants per year each from China, Japan, and India. Using the 1920 base for setting quotas, it continued the bias in favor of persons from the British Isles and northern Europe.[8]

The McCarran-Walter Act, as the 1952 law was called, excluded persons on various economic, health, criminal, moral, and subversive grounds. The Attorney-General and the Secretary of State were authorized to waive some of the requirements for temporary immigrants. The act also laid down rules for the deportation of aliens who were subversives, criminals, narcotics law violators, and certain other undesirables.

Action since 1952. Various commissions, public and private, have looked into the immigration and naturalization policies of the United States since the passage of the McCarran-Walter Act. President Truman set up a commission which reported on January 1, 1953 that there should be an end to national quotas, that unified annual quotas should be based not on the 1920 census but on the most recent population figures, that a new agency be established to administer the immigration program, and that certain other liberalizing features be adopted. After 1956 President Eisenhower also submitted several proposals for revising the immigration and naturalization programs and procedures. In his last year in office, President Eisenhower asked Congress to pass legislation that would increase the quota by approximately one hundred per cent and that special consideration be given to refugees and to those coming from the Pacific Triangle. Congress failed to act on any of the major proposals made by President Truman and each of his three successors. Nor did it take action on somewhat similar recommendations of the American Bar Association. Some minor changes have been made in the basic law, and some special treatment has been given to refugees from Communist tyranny, but no major action has been taken in this field since 1952.

Refugee legislation. Shortly after the Republicans came into power in 1953 an act was passed which allowed the immigration of 214,000 refugees

---

[8] Britain and Northern Ireland received 65,361 of the total of 150,000 immigrants allowed annually.

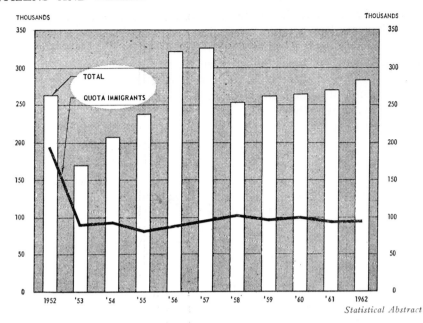

THOUSANDS   THOUSANDS

TOTAL

QUOTA IMMIGRANTS

Statistical Abstract

IMMIGRANTS ADMITTED BETWEEN 1950 AND 1962   The total number of immigrants admitted during the years 1950 to 1962 includes not only the non-quota immigrants normally exempt from the quota regulations, but also the refugees. Most of the latter came from countries now dominated by the Soviet Union.

from Iron Curtain countries without their being charged against the national quotas. The law expired in 1956 just as a drastic new need for refugee asylum developed. After the Hungarian Revolution had been crushed by the Russians in late 1956, President Eisenhower allowed Hungarians to come into the United States on a "parole" basis and asked Congress for modifications in the law. Congress, in 1957, eased the immigration laws to take the Hungarian tragedy into account. Further modifications were made in 1958 and 1959.

    Administration of immigration laws. Immigration is a national problem and not subject to state regulation.[9] It was first claimed for the national government as an aspect of foreign commerce control which was vested exclusively in Congress. By the end of the nineteenth century, however, the Supreme Court had abandoned the narrow grounds of the commerce clause and was stating that, as a sovereign nation, the United States must have the power to regulate immigration including the authority to forbid the entrance of particular foreigners into the country.[10] By the same reasoning the Supreme Court stated that the United States could also expel or deport aliens. According to a recent study of immigration law

    9 *The Passenger Cases,* 48 U. S. 283 (1849).
    10 *Ekiu* v. *United States,* 142 U. S. 651 (1892).

". . . there are no limits to the power of Congress to prescribe grounds for exclusion or deportation. . . . This apparently limitless power extends only to determining the classes of aliens subject to exclusion or expulsion. . . . While it has been doubted that due process of law is fully available to an alien seeking to enter the United States for the first time, such an alien is entitled to demand the rights and procedures accorded to him by Congress. . . . On the other hand an alien in the United States is completely protected and he cannot be deported unless he is given full procedural due process of law, including a fair hearing. . . ." [11]

The executive and immigration. The actual administration of immigration and deportation statutes is in the hands of the executive branch of government. Congress has delegated the executive some discretion in the matter, but has carefully limited the areas of discretion. When the regulation of immigration began, the Treasury Department was charged with administrative responsibility for its enforcement. At various times since 1882 responsibility has rested with the Department of Commerce and Labor, the Department of Labor, and finally with the Department of Justice. Other departments and agencies have limited responsibility in the field. Overseas personnel of the Department of State issue visas to persons seeking admission to the country; the Visa Division supervises this operation from Washington. The Health, Education and Welfare Department, through the Public Health Service, undertakes the necessary physical examinations of prospective immigrants to ascertain whether or not the applicants meet the very high standards of health set by the statutes. To a lesser extent other departments are concerned with the entrance of aliens into the United States.

The actual administration of the laws is in the hands of the Immigration and Naturalization Service in the Department of Justice. The Service is headed by a commissioner. Thirty-three district offices are to be found in various states and possessions of the United States. All applications are directed to the district offices.

A Board of Immigration Appeals, which is strictly an appellate board, exists within the Immigration and Naturalization Service. The Board of four members and a chairman is authorized to review certain carefully specified types of cases. It acts for the Attorney General in these matters and decides cases exclusively on the basis of the record without hearing any direct evidence.

Quite apart from the decisions of the executive agencies there is the possibility of admission to the country through an act of Congress. Many of the persons admitted by special act are those whose political activities would normally cause their exclusion, but who are thought by Congress to be worthy now of admission because of changes in their views and of their

---

[11] Charles Gordon and Harry N. Rosenfeld, *Immigration Law and Procedure* (Albany, N. Y.: Banks and Company, 1959).

current active opposition to totalitarian regimes. Congress has also established a Joint Congressional Committee on Immigration and Nationality Policy which oversees the work of the various administrative agencies charged with carrying out the laws.

Finally, along with the executive and legislative action in the field, there is extensive activity by certain private agencies. These groups work with possible immigrants overseas and continue to follow their progress through the entire immigration and naturalization process. The government has come to rely heavily on private agencies. During the periods of stress following World War II and the Hungarian Rebellion, the government actually depended on the private agencies not only for assistance in administering the law but also for aid in the development of the policies themselves. The government, as a consequence of its recognition of the value of the private organizations, has made funds available to these groups either by loans or through grants and contracts.

Role of the courts. The federal courts have relatively little role to play in the immigration program except to interpret the meaning of the Constitution and the laws. Occasionally, the courts may hear cases of individuals who claim citizenship but who have been denied citizenship by the administrative agencies. When the claims are serious and real doubt can be raised concerning the decision of the administrative group the district courts hear the entire cases and render the final decisions. Through interpretation of particular statutes, the courts have played perhaps their most significant role in deciding who is eligible to become a citizen.

NATURALIZATION

We have already noted that citizenship may be acquired either by birth in this country or by children born of American parents abroad. It may also be acquired through naturalization under the terms and by the methods prescribed by Congress. Further, Congress also determines the circumstances under which persons may be deprived of citizenship or may be expelled from the country.

Collective naturalization. Persons may secure citizenship in the United States by action of Congress conferring this privilege upon all persons in a specified group. Over our history Congress has taken this kind of action in only a very few instances. Indians were granted citizenship in 1924, although individual Indians had previously been able to acquire citizenship through the normal processes of naturalization. Congress conferred citizenship upon Texans when the Lone Star State was admitted to the Union. Citizenship may also be granted by treaty to persons in territories newly acquired by the United States. The treaties under which this country gained Louisiana, Alaska, Florida, and Hawaii provided that the inhabitants of the territories would become citizens of the United States.

After the Spanish-American War the United States took over control of the Philippine Islands, Puerto Rico, and Guam. In none of these instances did the island residents immediately acquire citizenship either as a result of the treaty of peace or of congressional action. Congress provided that certain rights were acquired by the residents of these islands, but it did not formally grant citizenship. As a matter of fact, although referred to by the courts as "nationals" and not as citizens or aliens, the residents received almost all of the privileges and rights possessed by American citizens. They could not vote in presidential elections and they did not have voting representation in Congress, but neither did the citizens of territories on the mainland. In almost every other respect they enjoyed the same protection as did natural born citizens. Ten years after the acquisition of the Virgin Islands from Denmark, Congress granted citizenship to all those who chose to relinquish their Danish citizenship.

Individual naturalization. The great bulk of the naturalized citizens of the United States have secured their citizenship by following certain procedures provided for in various acts of Congress. The present rules are laid down in the McCarran-Walter Act of 1952, but these procedures vary only slightly from the ones that had prevailed for at least a decade prior to that legislation.

The acquisition of citizenship by individuals begins with the arrangement to immigrate to this country with a permanent visa. Once in this country, the immigrant who has attained the age of 18 years must (a) live here a minimum of five years, (b) learn to speak and read the English language, and (c) come to understand enough of the history and institutions of the United States to pass a relatively simple examination concerning the basic characteristics of our government and history. In addition, a person seeking citizenship must be of good character and must not be associated with any organization that is dedicated to the overthrow of the government by force or violence. The applicant once needed to show that he was not a pacifist and therefore was willing to bear arms on behalf of the United States should war occur.[12] The Supreme Court in mid-1940's and later Congress in 1952 specifically provided that pacifists, at least religious pacifists, should not be barred from becoming citizens purely because of their unwillingness to bear arms for the United States.[13] While a person who has once arrived in this country as an immigrant seeking citizenship cannot be prevented from securing citizenship because of his pacifism, there is nothing in the law which requires that one who is a pacifist must be admitted to this country.

Thirty days after an alien has passed a preliminary examination following at least five years of residence, he becomes eligible to take out his

---

[12] See *MacIntosh* v. *United States,* 283 U. S. 605 (1931) and *United States* v. *Schwimmer,* 279 U. S. 644 (1929).

[13] See *Girouard* v. *United States,* 328 U. S. 61 (1946) and the McCarran Act of 1952.

final papers. At this stage he appears before a judge of either a federal or state court and there answers questions put by the judge in open court. If the answers of the prospective citizen are satisfactory to the judge, final papers are authorized and the applicant gains his citizenship.

U. S. Immigration and Naturalization Service

NEW CITIZENS TAKING THE OATH OF ALLEGIANCE AT A NATURALIZATION HEARING

Special situations in acquiring citizenship. In most countries of the world the wife takes the citizenship of her husband. For many years this rule applied in the United States. An American woman marrying a citizen of some other country became a citizen of that country. In like manner, a woman who was a citizen of another country automatically acquired American citizenship if her husband was an American citizen and if she was otherwise eligible. Today, American women and wives of American men are treated just as are their husbands. The women control their own citizenship so far as American law is concerned. An American woman need not give up her citizenship in this country simply because her husband happens to be a citizen of some other country. By the same token a woman born in another country no longer automatically acquires American citizenship merely because her husband is an American. By giving them priority in obtaining visas, our laws make it easier for spouses or persons affianced to American citizens to come to this country and thus avoid some of the difficulties. The question of becoming a citizen or remaining an alien, however, is left to the personal choice of the immigrant. Likewise, an American woman loses her citizenship only if she deliberately gives up her American citizenship and accepts that of her husband, or, for that matter, that of any other country with which she may choose to associate herself.

Expatriation. Any citizen, whether naturalized or native born, may give up his citizenship. Certain actions such as taking an oath of allegiance to another country, serving in the armed forces of another nation, and voting in its elections cause the loss of citizenship. Those who give up or lose their citizenship may either become stateless or the citizens of another country. Certain of the expatriates may regain their citizenship without concern for the quotas. For example, those who lost their citizenship by serving in the armed forces of an allied nation during World War II must be naturalized, but they may enter the country as non-quota immigrants.

Deportation. Congress has, as we have noted, full power over the expulsion of aliens who have entered this country. Aliens are here on suffrance with no rights to continue to stay here except as the government shall grant. There are in the neighborhood of 700 different grounds for deportation. The courts have been largely unwilling to upset any action of Congress in this field on grounds that its actions are either *ex post facto* laws or bills of attainder. The Court has held that deportation is not criminal punishment and therefore does not come under the heading of *ex post facto* laws. Since legislation with respect to the deportation of aliens always applies to a class, such as Communist Party members or those convicted of felonies, the legislation has not been considered as a bill of attainder. From time to time minorities of the Supreme Court and critics of our present policies dealing with deportation have suggested that deportation is in fact punishment and that greater protection should be provided the alien in our land. The alien is fully protected in procedural matters, although he does not have court protection against actions of Congress. In spite of the criticisms of some present policies and the degree of hardship which is suffered by an alien who has been uprooted and deported after living in this country for many years, there is little likelihood that the plenary powers of Congress over immigration and deportation will soon be curbed.

Congress has provided for the deportation of certain aliens since 1888 when contract laborers were allowed to remain in this country no longer than one year. Since then many other grounds for deportation have been laid down by Congress. These newer reasons include the commission of certain crimes, moral turpitude, and membership in subversive organizations. Under the 1952 act, aliens may be deported at any time for their failure, however long ago, to meet the tests of the law. The only time limits are not on action of the government against the offending alien but on the period in which certain actions or developments contrary to the law have taken place. Thus, a person who has become a public charge after residing in this country for five years is not deportable. An alien who does not join the Communist Party until after residing here for at least five years cannot be deported. If an alien voluntarily joins the Communist Party less than five years after coming to this country, he may be deported at any time during his life.

Denaturalization. A naturalized citizen may lose his citizenship for any of the reasons which cause the loss of citizenship for a natural born citizen. He may give it up voluntarily or by certain actions such as serving in a foreign army without the consent of this government or for treason. In addition, he may forfeit his citizenship if he has obtained it through fraud or for failing to provide essential information during the naturalization process. The Supreme Court ruled in 1964 that the Fifth Amendment's "due process" clause prevents any differentiation in the law between natural born citizens and those who acquired citizenship by naturalization.[14] Prior to this ruling the law had specified a number of grounds upon which a naturalized citizen could lose his citizenship which did not apply to the natural born citizen. No citizen may be deported.

SUMMARY

Prior to the ratification of the Fourteenth Amendment the Constitution contained no definition of citizenship. That amendment became necessary because of the extraordinary decision in the *Dred Scott* case which gave state citizenship priority over national citizenship in order to protect slave owners. In the United States citizenship may be the result of place of birth (*jus soli*), or parentage (*jus sanguinis*), or naturalization.

Persons may become naturalized citizens by act of Congress, by treaty, or by individual action. Individual naturalization is the method by which most aliens have become citizens. This process takes a minimum of five years and requires that the immigrant meet certain minimum standards of language, knowledge of American institutions, and morality.

The persons who first immigrated to the United States came primarily from England and Scotland. Later waves of immigrants came from Ireland, Germany, and other countries of northern Europe. After 1880 the great masses of immigrants came from eastern and southern Europe. This new influx of immigrants brought a reaction from the older citizens and from Congress. In 1924 a permanent quota system was established which limited the number of immigrants coming to this country to about 150,000 per year. The number allowed from each country was based on the number of persons from that country living in the United States in 1920. Persons from Asia were excluded from citizenship.

The 1924 law remained substantially unchanged until 1952 when the McCarran-Walter Act codified existing law, removed the provisions excluding Asians, and placed more stringent restrictions on the admission of persons who had been members of totalitarian groups in the countries of their

---

14 *Schneider* v. *Rusk*, 377 U. S. 163 (1964).

birth. The number of immigrants allowed from European countries remained roughly the same as before.

Exceptions to the immigration laws have been made during the years since World War II to help take care of some of the refugees from war and tyranny. The first exceptions were made immediately after the war. Later the Hungarian Revolution brought thousands more to America under presidential and later congressional waivers of the quota system. The United States has greatly restricted the number of persons who may come to this country each year but she still opens her doors to the victims of tyrants.

BIBLIOGRAPHIC NOTE

Problems of immigration and naturalization have forced themselves more and more on public attention as the refugees from communist dominated countries join the thousands already living in the camps of Europe and Asia. Articles abound in the journals of opinion dealing with the strengths and failures of American immigration policies. Law journals carry articles on various aspects of the administration of our immigration and naturalization programs.

While there are many articles on the subject, there is a dearth of important books that deal in a comprehensive manner with immigration. The best available book for reference purpose is Charles Gordon and Harry N. Rosenfield, *Immigration Law and Procedure* (Albany, New York: Banks and Company, 1959). Since the book seeks to reach several audiences, including the lawyer and administrator, much of it is highly technical. The early chapters, however, give a good brief history of immigration and naturalization and the laws affecting them in the United States. See also Frank L. Auerbach, *Immigration Laws of the United States* (Indianapolis: Bobbs-Merrill Company, 1961) and Hubert H. Humphrey, Jr., *The Stranger at Our Gates* (Public Affairs Pamphlet No. 202, 1954).

Two government publications are of value to the student. *Immigration and Nationality Act* (Government Printing Office, Washington, D. C., 1958) is a committee document prepared for the use of the Committee on the Judiciary of the House of Representatives. The 157 page booklet gives the present major legislation, the immigration quotas for each country at the time of publication, and amendments to the basic law of 1952. A second, older document is *Whom Shall We Welcome* (Government Printing Office, Washington, D. C., 1953). This document was prepared by the President's Commission on Immigration and Naturalization and was intended in part to start a movement for revising the recently enacted McCarran-Walter Act.

Oscar Handlin, *The Uprooted* (Boston: Little, Brown, and Company, 1951) is a scholarly book describing the story of American immigration. Other books can be found that describe the fate of the Hungarian escapees after the advent of the Russian armies in 1956.

Milton R. Konvitz has written two books on aspects of the immigration problem in the United States. The two books are *The Alien and the Asiatic in American Law* (Ithaca: Cornell University Press, 1946) and *Civil Rights in Immigration* (Ithaca: Cornell University Press, 1953). C. Herman Pritchett, *Civil Liberties and the Vinson Court* (Chicago: University of Chicago Press, 1954) devotes some pages to the handling of immigration cases. An old, but still useful book in the field is William C. Van Vleck, *The Administrative Control of Aliens* (New York: Commonwealth Fund, 1932).

For a consideration of the development of the United States policy toward

Asian nationals—a policy which was in effect from the nineteenth century until mid-way through the twentieth century—see Fred W. Riggs, *Pressure On Congress* (New York: King's Crown Press, 1950). In this book Professor Riggs discusses the passage of the Chinese Exclusion Act.

Most of the standard case books in constitutional law provide the student with at least a few cases in which the Supreme Court has ruled on problems related to eligibility of aliens for citizenship, deportation of aliens, and various other aspects of immigration and naturalization.

Henry Steele Commager has edited an interesting group of essays, *Immigration and American History* (Minneapolis: University of Minnesota Press, 1961) dealing with the interrelationships between the movement of persons and the passage of cultural values from the Old to the New World, and then back to the Old World again.

6

Civil Liberties in the United States

I$_N$ THE Declaration of Independence the founders of the United States announced to the world that they held these

> truths to be self-evident, that all men are created equal, that they are endowed by their Creator with certain unalienable Rights, that among these are Life, Liberty and the pursuit of Happiness. —That to secure these rights, Governments are instituted among Men, deriving their just powers from the consent of the governed,— That whenever any Form of Government becomes destructive of these ends, it is the Right of the People to alter or to abolish it, and to institute new Government, laying its foundation on such principles and organizing its powers in such form, as to them shall seem most likely to effect their Safety and Happiness.

The men who thus declared the freedom of the thirteen colonies from England were expressing or reaffirming doctrines that were already deeply rooted in Anglo-Saxon culture. When the framers of the Constitution worked out the basic document for our government, they made provision for protecting certain rights of persons living in the United States. More rights were added within four years after the Constitutional Convention in the Bill of Rights or the first ten amendments. Of these the first eight specify substantive or procedural rights.

The rights which are referred to in a general way in the Declaration of Independence and specifically mentioned in the Constitution and some of its amendments are not unique to our society. Most countries of the world claim to guarantee many of these same rights to their citizens. There seems to be a kind of universal recognition that a government must state that its people are free and that they have been guaranteed certain rights. In the more democratic countries these rights are not only mentioned in the basic documents but are recognized and protected by the government of the day.[1]

---

[1] Austin Ranney, *The Governing of Men* (New York: Henry Holt and Company, 1958), pp. 104-108.

CIVIL LIBERTIES UNDER DICTATORSHIPS

In totalitarian countries, and to some extent in all countries ruled by dictators, civil rights are mentioned in the public documents but they are neither respected nor enforced. In the Soviet Union and in Communist China these public documents set forth an impressive array of rights to which the citizen is supposedly entitled. Yet in practice no "right" has any standing against the government of either country. Substantive and procedural rights cannot be safe in a totalitarian society when the government carries out periodic purges. Even when a purge is not in full swing, no citizen dares to criticize the party leadership publicly or to organize for peacefully replacing it. If arrested, even on obviously false charges, a citizen has no protection against a government which is determined to convict him. Gustav Regler, in his autobiography, tells of asking Molotov what would happen if an innocent man were executed.[2] Molotov replied, "When that happens we shoot the judge."

The remark helps to make clear an aspect of totalitarian attitudes toward justice. When a purge is in progress the judge is a mere creature of the regime. If the government prosecutor asks the death sentence for the victims brought before him, the judge hands down the sentence as requested. Judge, prosecutor, secret police, and dictator are all parts of an apparatus of destruction. If, later, the dictator decides to take a new and more moderate tack, the prosecutors and the judges who carried out his wishes during the purge may be executed. But, justice still does not prevail. Vishinsky did not replace Yagoda because Yagoda had failed to do the work of the regime. Vishinsky took over and Yagoda was executed in order that the regime could rid itself of one who had been needed to present trumped up charges to justify the shooting of party leaders. When the fever of killing was nearing its end, the government could announce a shift to a temporarily more moderate position by destroying the symbol of the purge.

People whose lives are dependent upon the whims of totalitarian dictators can never live without fear. They can never be free to speak or to act as they please, because they are not allowed more than the most primitive means to protect themselves against governmental injustices.[3]

In countries governed by dictators with less than total authority, the citizens are faced with fewer reasons for fear. They have some areas for free

---

[2] *Owl of Minerva* (New York: Farrar, Straus and Cudahy, 1960), p. 257. Nikita Khrushchev's famous speech to the Twentieth Party Congress in 1956 gives massive evidence of the "justice" that prevailed in the USSR from 1917 to 1956. The evidence of thorough change since 1956 is scanty.

[3] In Communist China in 1957, Mao Tse-Tung requested all who wished to criticize the government to speak up. To Mao's surprise hundreds of intellectuals and others criticized his regime. Mao promptly arrested and punished them.

action, because the dictator either is not interested or cannot control their private activities. Normally, under a non-totalitarian dictatorship, citizens have greater freedom of movement and organization and have more subjects upon which they are free to speak. The dictator does not have an all-embracing ideology which all citizens are expected to accept and follow. These regimes are not interested in forcing other countries to accept their views of the nature of the universe. Citizens are relatively free to move in and out of these countries. Lovers of freedom may not be happy under ordinary dictators, but their freedom is greater and their survival chances much better than are those of people who live under totalitarian regimes.

CIVIL LIBERTIES IN A DEMOCRATIC SOCIETY

Most personal freedoms are closely related to each other. Freedom of speech has little value if there is no freedom to organize political parties to implement the views of the speaker. If the government can execute a critic without giving him an opportunity to defend his right to speak freely before a court of justice, then critics will be silent. The forms of defense allowed the citizen and the organization of the courts may differ from one democratic country to another, but they all provide the citizen protection against arbitrary and capricious action by the government. The formal guarantee of a fair trial is likely to be important to the citizens of those societies which allow the freedom to criticize its instruments of justice.

Fundamental to any belief in the freedom of the individual is the belief that the state exists to help men to live better and more freely than they could live outside the state. Equally fundamental is the belief that men, *as men,* are equal and that they should be given equal opportunities and receive equal treatment in similar situations.[4]

In order that men may be free and possess rights which the government will respect, there must be some centers of power in the community other than the state itself. If men are to be free, they need to be able to join political, social, and economic groups which are independent of the state. Totalitarian societies recognize this fact and, therefore, systematically destroy all agencies and potential centers of power not controlled by the regime. Even the family is coerced by the state. Children are used against their parents, while the latter are allowed only a minimum of control over the children. Other organizations in the society are allowed to continue only if they can be used as instruments of the state. The unions, the trade associations, and to some extent the churches are controlled by the regime and used to help the state dominate men's lives.

The farther one moves away from the totalitarian regime, the more men are allowed to choose their associates and organizations. The greater

---

4 See Austin Ranney, *op. cit.,* pp. 96-103 for a very good and brief description of the sources of the modern belief in the equality of man in society.

the freedom of choice in these matters, the more men's lives can be centered somewhere other than in the state and its instrumentalities. We call a society with many independent centers of power that are concerned with the various problems of the community a pluralistic society. Citizens in such a community may not always be in step with the demands of the state, but the community is likely to be one in which there is a considerable degree of freedom for most of its members.

Rights and duties. A democratic system works best if the vast majority of the citizens recognize that they not only receive rights from the community but that they also owe it some obligations. Each man who enjoys freedom of speech and press is obliged to recognize that same freedom for all others. Each citizen must be willing to assist in the preservation of the larger community. He must be willing to face death if necessary to defend it against outside force.[5]

Many duties and obligations of citizens could be listed, but no list can be fully inclusive nor would today's list correspond precisely with yesterday's or tomorrow's. Certain things are clear however. A democratic society requires that those who accept the responsibilities and obligations of the democratic belief be in a position to protect themselves against those who would destroy the democratic society. In wartime those who attempt to prevent the successful prosecution of the war are subject to punishment in order to preserve the nation. It is much less clear what limits should be placed upon those who deliberately refuse to respect their obligations to society in peacetime. Neither Congress nor the Supreme Court is sure what is the wisest policy for dealing with those who refuse to accept such obligations. Congress tends to be strict in regulating the activities of those in subversive organizations who shun their duties. The Supreme Court on the other hand tends to protect them in their refusal to cooperate. Some of the justices feel that restriction on the personal freedom of any citizen, even those in subversive groups, is dangerous; it may lead to the destruction of the rights of other citizens by an incompetent or oversuspicious administration.

THE LIMITS OF CIVIL LIBERTIES

Civil liberties include rights to fair procedures and various forms of freedom of expression. Those rights necessary for the citizens are freedom of speech, press, and religion, the right of one accused of a crime to have his day in court where he can expect fair treatment, the right to participate in elections, and many others. Where do these rights end and where may the government place limits on individual action for the good of the whole society? This question cannot be answered in a manner satisfactory to every-

---

5 Most countries of western Europe and the United States allow pacifists to refuse to bear arms, but these societies would face great difficulties if more than a handful of pacifists existed in each country.

one. For present purposes, let us agree that all of us recognize the need for some limitations on even our most basic rights. Freedom of movement, as Austin Ranney has suggested, does not include the right of an individual to drive on the left hand side of American highways. Nor, to use the example given by Justice Holmes, does the right of free speech cover the freedom of an individual to shout "fire" in a crowded theatre. Plural marriage is not allowed in the United States although the prohibition against polygamy prevents certain religious groups from putting into practice some of their beliefs. Even the freedoms which Americans possess carry with them some responsibilities which are difficult to avoid. False or slanderous comments about other persons can be costly if the victim of the remark brings the spokesman to court and requires that he prove the charges or pay damages, but a public official must prove "actual malice" to win his case.

The examples given above are ones on which we are all agreed. Other problems of civil liberties are more difficult. Should a man who exercises his right not to testify against himself before a grand jury or a congressional committee lose his job with the government because he has become suspect as the result of this refusal to testify? The Supreme Court seems to have answered this question both in the affirmative and negative, and Americans are sharply divided on the answer. Has a man the freedom to speak in favor of the violent overthrow of the government in order to establish a dictatorial regime? The Supreme Court has not been entirely clear on this matter either, and again the public is not of one mind on the issue. The Constitution tells us that a man is entitled to a fair trial, but what constitutes a fair trial? Is it a fair trial if an accused person has a jury of six men, or must the jury include twelve persons, or can a judge decide the issue himself? What constitutes cruel and unusual punishment? The constitution tells us what rights are possessed by citizens and residents of this country. Legislatures pass laws defining the limits of the guaranteed rights and executive officials carry out the laws. Each branch is in some manner responsible for the respect and maintenance of our civil liberties, but it is the Supreme Court which finally interprets the meaning of the provisions in the Constitution.

Constitutional provisions for civil liberties. The Constitution, as it emerged from the Philadelphia convention in 1787, included some prohibitions against the states, some against the national government, and some against both. The rights guaranteed in Article I and Article IV are primarily procedural rights. They protect the individual against either the national or the state governments in matters of *ex post facto* laws and bills of attainders. They guard against the national government's power to deny the right to the writ of *habeas corpus* and describe the procedures which shall govern trials for treason. The single substantive protection in the Constitution itself says that state governments shall make no laws "impairing the obligation of contract."

The Bill of Rights was added at the insistence of various state ratifying conventions as further protection against the national government. Very early in our history, the Supreme Court made clear that these amendments did not apply to the states but only to the national government.[6] In more recent years the Supreme Court has ruled that the provisions of the Fourteenth Amendment were intended to protect the individual against state action in some of the same ways the Bill of Rights protects him against the national government.[7] The first eight amendments to the Constitution include both substantive and procedural guarantees. On the substantive side, Congress is prohibited from making any laws restricting freedom of religion, speech, the press, the right to assemble peaceably, and to petition the government. The right of the people to keep and bear arms and to be free from the quartering of soldiers in time of peace is also protected. The remaining rights are of a procedural character, describing how the government is limited in bringing those accused of crimes to court and trying them. The Ninth Amendment states that the fact that some rights are listed in earlier amendments is not to suggest that there are no other rights. The Tenth Amendment says that, "The powers not delegated to the United States by the Constitution, nor prohibited by it to the States, are reserved to the States respectively, and to the people."

The Supreme Court and the Bill of Rights. Until the end of World War I few civil liberties cases arose under the Bill of Rights or the Fourteenth Amendment. By contrast, since 1938, the Supreme Court has turned its attention more and more to cases involving civil rights and liberties. No area of constitutional law has changed more rapidly since that date. Both in the substantive and procedural fields, the Court has modified or over-ruled many earlier decisions. The Court still seems to be feeling its way in interpreting some of the amendments. During the past two decades controversies have raged in Congress, in the press, and in public discussion concerning the reasonableness of certain of the Court rulings. No doubt the rulings of the Court on civil liberties problems will one day be stabilized; in the meantime, interpretations that seemed firm yesterday may be reversed today and reinstated tomorrow.[8]

PROCEDURAL GUARANTEES

Habeas corpus. The writ of *habeas corpus* requires that an incarcerated person be brought before the court in order that the court may determine whether or not there are sufficient grounds for his being held prisoner. It is

---

[6] *Barron* v. *Baltimore,* 7 Peters 243 (1833). Most state constitutions also included a statement of rights possessed by the citizen against the state.

[7] *Gitlow* v. *New York,* 265 U. S. 652 (1925).

[8] In later sections of this chapter we will have occasion to note some of the vacillations of the Supreme Court.

regarded by some as the most basic of all our civil rights. The late Zechariah Chafee suggested that all other rights can be retained in some manner in spite of the efforts of the government to prevent their use. A prison, however, can only be pierced by the writ of *habeas corpus.* "When imprisonment is possible without explanation or redress . . . every form of liberty is impaired. A man in jail cannot go to church or discuss or publish or assemble or enjoy property or go to the polls." [9]

The Constitution provides that the privilege of the writ cannot be suspended except when public safety demands it in time of war or rebellion. The Supreme Court has ruled that Congress alone has the authority to suspend the writ, but Congress may authorize the President to exercise some discretion in the matter.[10] The Court has sometimes been reluctant to order the Chief Executive to refrain from suspending the writ until after the danger has passed. Lesser officials have been forced by the courts to justify holding prisoners even in time of war.

Bills of attainder and ex post facto laws. The Constitution prohibits Congress and the states from passing any law that declares a person to be a criminal and provides for his punishment. Such a law is called a *bill of attainder.* The Court has held that this prohibition also prevents Congress from withholding funds for salaries of specific persons who are working for the government. To withhold the funds is to punish by legislative action and therefore is a bill of attainder.[11]

An *ex post facto* law, which is also prohibited by the Constitution, has been defined by the Court as a law which (a) applies only to criminal cases, (b) makes an act a crime which had not been a crime at the time the act took place, (c) increases the punishment for a crime after the act has taken place, or (d) makes it easier to convict a person after the crime has been committed.[12]

Grand jury. The Fifth Amendment provides that no person may be brought to trial for a "capital, or otherwise infamous crime, unless on presentment or indictment of a grand jury." A federal prosecuting attorney, in other words, cannot bring a man to trial on frivolous grounds simply to discredit him or to prevent him from taking some action not desired by the prosecutor. A federal grand jury consists of 12 to 23 jurors whose function is to review the evidence against any person charged with crime. The jury can either dismiss the case or agree that the person should stand before a regular court.

Some states provide for the use of the grand jury device while others do not. There must be some kind of protection of the individual against

---

[9] Quoted in Walter Gellhorn, *American Rights* (New York: The Macmillan Co., 1960), p. 12.

[10] *Ex parte Milligan,* 4 Wall. 2 (1866).

[11] *United States* v. *Lovett,* 328 U. S. 303 (1946).

[12] *Calder* v. *Bull,* 3 Dallas 386 (1798).

arbitrary charges, but the protection need not be that of a grand jury.[13] If, however, a state does provide for indictment by grand jury, then there must be no discrimination against the members of any group in the selection of the jury members.

Jury trial and right to counsel. Several provisions of the Constitution relate to guaranteeing the fair administration of justice in criminal cases. In addition to the grand jury requirement, there are also the rights of the accused to a "speedy and public trial, by an impartial jury . . . , and to be informed of the nature and cause of the accusation; to be confronted with witnesses against him; to have compulsory process for obtaining witnesses in his favor, and to have the assistance of counsel for his defense." Fair trial is required in the prosecution of alleged criminals in the states, but the Supreme Court has ruled that fair trial does not necessarily include the right to be heard by a jury of twelve persons which is the traditional number of jurors required under common law. The defendant may waive his right to a jury trial, but he must understand the situation clearly before doing so.[14] Where there is a jury trial there must be no discrimination in the selection of the members of the jury.[15]

The Court has stated that the Sixth Amendment guarantees an accused the right to counsel. He may waive his right, but he must first understand the right he is waiving.[16] The Court later ruled that the Fourteenth Amendment includes this protection in state courts and also that this right covers the pretrial period when police accuse a person of a crime.[16a]

Unreasonable searches and seizures. One of the most technical problems that has faced the Supreme Court has been the interpretation of the Fourth Amendment provision against unreasonable searches and seizures. Police officers now have improved methods of crime detection and new kinds of evidence may be secured and presented in the courts.[16b] Some of these newer methods may involve the invasion of a person's home or the unintended testifying by an accused against himself.

In general, no police officer of the United States government may search a man's property without a warrant signed by an authorized magistrate. The warrant must state clearly what property is to be searched and for what purpose. Certain exceptions have been made by the courts; they have, for example, allowed police to make searches in situations in which the suspect might easily destroy the evidence or where he could make his escape while warrants were being sought. In most of the exceptions allowed, the Supreme Court has recognized the time factor as of major importance.[17]

---

13 *Hurtado* v. *California,* 110 U. S. 516 (1884).

14 *Patton* v. *United States,* 281 U. S. 276 (1930).

15 *Norris* v. *Alabama,* 294 U. S. 587 (1935) and *Thiel* v. *Southern Pacific Company,* 328 U. S. 217 (1946).

16 *Johnson* v. *Zerbst,* 304 U. S. 458 (1938).

16a *Gideon* v. *Wainwright,* 372 U. S. 335 (1962), *Escobedo* v. *Illinois,* 378 U. S. (1961).

16b *Silverman* v. *United States,* 365 U. S. 505 (1961) barred planted microphones.

17 *United States* v. *Rabinowitz,* 339 U. S. 56 (1949).

In 1961 the Supreme Court for the first time said that the due process clause of the Fourteenth Amendment protected persons from unreasonable searches and seizures by state governments and ruled against use of evidence gained in such a manner by the states.[18]

The most celebrated problem growing out of modern methods of gathering information against suspected criminals involves the use of wire taps by federal officers. A sharply divided Supreme Court upheld the right of police officers to use evidence secured by wire tapping. The majority of the Court held that, since there was no actual entry, there was no invasion of a man's property or privacy. The minority argued that such a narrow interpretation made a mockery of the real intent of the Fourth Amendment.[19] Six years after the Court's action, Congress passed the Federal Communications Act of 1934, providing that no one could make public any information secured by wire tapping without the consent of the sender. In practice the Department of Justice still makes wire taps, but it does not introduce the evidence in court. Information gained by wire tapping, however, may very well suggest other information sources which can be used for prosecution of a suspect.[20]

Self incrimination. Closely related to the prohibition against unreasonable searches and seizures is the Fifth Amendment provision that no man "shall be compelled in any criminal case to be a witness against himself." Forcing a man to give up certain incriminating papers may not only be a violation of the "searches and seizures" prohibition but also may constitute a violation of the self-incrimination provision of the Fifth Amendment.[21]

At various times the Supreme Court has sought to define the meaning and limits of the self-incrimination rule. Among other things the Supreme Court has said that (1) a witness who voluntarily testifies on a subject cannot later refuse to answer questions on the same subject; (2) that the mere fact that answering questions may disgrace him is not enough to justify his use of the right; (3) after a pardon a man may no longer argue that testifying would involve self-incrimination; and (4) that Congress may provide immunity for a witness who may then be forced to testify, since he may no longer be prosecuted for what he says.[22]

In 1964 the Court reversed a long-standing ruling to say that the Fourteenth Amendment protects the individual against efforts to force him to testify against himself.[23] This new view seems compatible with rulings against confessions secured by either physical or psychological third

---

18 *Mapp* v. *Ohio,* 367 U. S. 643 (1961); also, *Aguilar* v. *Texas* 378 U. S. (1964).

19 *Olmstead* v. *United States,* 277 U. S. 438 (1928).

20 Robert E. and Robert F. Cushman, *Cases in Constitutional Law* (New York: Appleton-Century-Crofts, Inc., 1958), pp. 449-450.

21 *Boyd* v. *United States,* 116 U. S. 616 (1886).

22 *Brown* v. *Walker,* 161 U. S. 591 (1896). See also *Ullman* v. *United States,* 350 U. S. 322 (1956); *Murphy* v. *Waterfront Commission,* 378 U. S. 678 (1964).

23 *Malloy* v. *Hogan* 378 U. S. 653 (1964).

degree methods may not be introduced as evidence before a court.[24] Two unusual rulings of the Court in connection with the forcible collection of evidence from a suspect may be noted. The Supreme Court ruled that a stomach pumb could not be used to discover whether a suspect had actually swallowed some narcotics to hide evidence.[25] Later, however, the Court upheld the right of the police to extract blood in order to find out if a driver was drunk at the time of an accident. The Court allowed this action even though the test was made while the defendant was unconscious and obviously could not give his consent to the test.[26]

Self-incrimination and congressional committees. In recent years serious legal problems have resulted from the refusal of persons to testify before congressional committees, grand juries, and other public bodies concerning their possible activities connected with the communist movement. In this area some rules are clear, but some have still to be established. It is clear that a witness may not plead self-incrimination to protect a third party.[27] What a public agency can do about discontinuing the employment of one who has refused to testify before a congressional committee or some other legitimate official inquiry is not clear. In 1956 the Supreme Court, by a five to four decision, refused to allow the Board of Education of New York to fire a teacher under a provision of the charter which called for the dismissal of those who refused to testify on grounds of self-incrimination.[28] In 1960 the Court allowed Los Angeles county to discharge a temporary employee who had refused to testify about possible communist connections after he had been warned that his failure to do so would result in his firing.[29]

Since 1950 there has been widespread discussion of the meaning to be attached to the plea of self-incrimination in refusing to testify before congressional committees concerning possible communist activities. Can it be assumed that a man who refuses to testify has in fact engaged in communist activities which he will not discuss? At least three views of what constitutes the correct answer to this question are to be found. One group believes that the refusal to testify means the witness is guilty of some mis-doing. A second group, represented by Professor Sidney Hook, says that one cannot be certain of the guilt of those who refuse to testify, but he argues that it is difficult to avoid the "common sense" view that the refusal to testify raises

---

24 *Brown* v. *Mississippi*, 297 U. S. 278 (1936) and *Chambers* v. *Florida*, 309 U. S. 227 (1940).

25 *Rochin* v. *California*, 342 U. S. 165 (1952).

26 *Breithaupt* v. *Abram*, 352 U. S. 432 (1957).

27 *Rogers* v. *United States*, 340 U. S. 367 (1951).

28 *Slochower* v. *Board of Education*, 350 U. S. 551 (1956).

29 *Nelson* v. *County of Los Angeles*, 362 U. S. 1 (1960). The majority of the Court sought to distinguish this decision from the earlier Slochower decision. The minority of the Court and most commentators, however, looked upon the Globe decision as a retreat from a position that had earlier been very widely criticized. Furthermore, there had been significant changes in the membership of the Court during the intervening four years.

some doubts as to the witness's innocence and that these doubts should be taken into account in any future judgments about that person.[30] A third group, for which Dean Erwin N. Griswold of the Harvard Law School has been a spokesman, argues that one can make no assumptions at all about the guilt or innocence of a person simply because he refuses to testify on grounds of self-incrimination. This group argues that there may be many reasons for the refusal that relate to possible court action and yet leave room for the man to be completely innocent.[31] All these views are vigorously held and there seems little likelihood of agreement among the groups in the immediate future.[32]

Double jeopardy. The Fifth Amendment protects persons from being tried twice for the same offense. This provision applies against the national government, but it does not protect a man from being prosecuted under similar state and national laws. The Court has repeatedly held that, as long as both the state and national governments have authority to act in a particular field, each may punish the same act if that act violates the laws of both jurisdictions.[33] The Court has also allowed states, under certain circumstances, to bring a man to trial a second time for the same offense without violating the meaning of the "due process" clause of the Fourteenth Amendment.[34] In so doing the Court has pointed out that the "due process" clause of the Fourteenth Amendment includes some, but not all, of the same restrictions on the states that the Bill of Rights covers for the national government.

PERSONAL LIBERTY

Substantive as opposed to procedural rights may be divided into two categories—personal and property rights. Property rights received greater attention from the Supreme Court during the first century and a quarter of our history. The Supreme Court not only protected procedural rights for the defense of property, it also gave a "substantive" interpretation of the due process clause of the Fifth and Fourteenth amendments under which the Court prevented or modified government regulation of the economic order. This defense of property by the Supreme Court ended during the New Deal. Property rights are still protected procedurally, but no special attention is given to the substance of state and federal laws regulating property.

---

30 Sidney Hook, *Common Sense and the Fifth Amendment* (New York: Criterion Books, 1957).

31 Erwin N. Griswold, *The Fifth Amendment Today* (Cambridge: Harvard University Press, 1955).

32 For other problems related to congressional committee hearings see the later chapters on Congress.

33 *United States* v. *Lanza,* 260 U. S. 377 (1922).

34 *Palko* v. *Connecticut,* 302 U. S. 319 (1937).

Since World War I and particularly since 1938, a greater emphasis has been placed upon personal substantive rights—freedom of speech, the press, assembly, religion, and equality in certain political and social areas. It is difficult to say precisely why this change of emphasis came about, but there are certain possible explanations for the shift. Prior to 1910 relatively few cases involving substantive personal rights had come before the Supreme Court. The Court could not interpret the Constitution unless the questions were raised by litigants asking for a ruling. Perhaps one of the reasons that the Court was asked to decide so few cases was its own somewhat unsympathetic attitude in the cases which it did handle. A second reason for the failure of more cases to arise may have been related to the nature of the developing American society during the nineteenth and early twentieth centuries. Those who were discriminated against may either have been unable or unwilling to take their problems to the courts. Discrimination was practiced during the last century primarily against the negroes and against certain immigrant groups. Poverty, the struggle to remain alive and to establish roots in a new country, the lack of knowledge of the available channels for legal action, the reliance of the immigrants in the big cities on the political machines for their needs all helped prevent the injured parties from taking legal action. In the rest of the community there was an almost universal lack of knowledge about or interest in discrimination.

New interest in substantive rights. About the time of World War I several significant developments occurred here and abroad to change the apparent indifference to problems of civil liberties and civil rights. In 1920 various groups combined to found the American Civil Liberties Union (ACLU). This organization defended those who were still in prison because of their opposition to this nation's entry into the war. Later the ACLU supported others whose views were at variance with state and national legislation aimed at subversive activities. In 1917 the communists had come to power in Russia—a fact which alarmed most Americans but encouraged a few. Those who were alarmed by the rise of the communists reacted by passing legislation intended to prevent the party from getting a foothold in this country. Those who looked on the Russian Revolution with favor struck back through the facilities of the newly established American Communist Party. They introduced court cases in the hope of nullifying the restrictive legislation.

A second organization interested in interpretations of another area of constitutional law was the National Association for the Advancement of Colored People (NAACP). This organization was founded in 1909 to work for the improvement of the Negro's position in America. With its creation there was for the first time a source of advice and money to help bring the Negro's problems into court.

These organizations helped to increase the number of court cases and therefore increased the number of opportunities for interpretation of the rights guaranteed by the Constitution. Nevertheless, until 1937 the dominant interest of the Supreme Court was probably not in the field of civil liberties. In that year and the years immediately following, the Supreme Court handed down a number of decisions which allowed both the state and the national governments to legislate freely concerning the economic activities of the community. At about the same time the expanding bureaucracy was granted more regulatory authority, thus removing some of the reasons for appeal to the Supreme Court on economic issues. Earl Latham has suggested that it was at this point that the Court shifted its emphasis to civil liberties in order to carve out a new field of operations to replace the economic realm which it was abandoning.[35]

The Court's interest in civil liberties and civil rights has continued to grow since 1938, so that today more of the most interesting Court opinions are written in this field. A check of any recent constitutional law case book will show that the vast majority of the important cases concerning economic regulation or interpreting the relations among the three branches of government occurred before 1940. By contrast, most cases in civil liberties or civil rights have been decided since that date. The Court still seems somewhat uncertain about the relation that ought constitutionally to exist between the state and the individual, so that the important constitutional law developments of the next decades are likely to be largely in the civil liberties area.

FREEDOM OF RELIGION

The First Amendment to the Constitution forbids Congress to establish a state religion or to legislate against the free exercise of religion. The provision against an official state religion was written by men who had experienced or observed problems created by an established church in Europe and in some of the American colonies. These men had no desire to see that experience repeated here on a national scale. They or their forefathers, after all, had left their homelands in order to worship as they pleased. Actually, by the time the Constitution was adopted, there was very little possibility of any attempt to set up a national church. So many different denominations existed in the various states that a move to establish a national church would have met great resistance.

In recent years the courts have considered the question of the meaning of the phrase "established" church in modern America. It has given new content to the words in some of its major decisions since World War II.

Religion and the schools. In 1925 the Supreme Court invalidated an Oregon law which provided that all students must attend public schools. The Court stated that such a law denied parents the freedom to direct the development of their children, because it did not allow them to decide

---

[35] Earl Latham, "The Supreme Court and Civil Liberty," *American Government Annual, 1958-1959* (New York: Henry Holt and Company, 1958), pp. 1-27.

whether their children should attend a religious or a secular school. It further stated that parents are thus denied the protections of the Fourteenth Amendment which, said the Court, includes freedom of religion as guaranteed in the First Amendment against the national government.[36]

Parochial schools and other private schools may be required to comply with the standards prescribed by the state for all schools. Parents of children in private schools must also pay taxes to support public schools. In recent years the state governments have provided some financial assistance to private schools, especially parochial schools. Some states have contributed equally to both public and parochial schools for certain comparable activities carried out by both types of educational institutions. Louisiana, under the late Huey P. Long, provided for the purchase of school books for children without regard to the type of school which they attended. This action was upheld since the children and the state were the sole beneficiaries of the grant.[37]

The question of the extent to which the states may aid parochial schools was again raised in 1947 when New Jersey provided bus transportation for children going to parochial school as well as for those attending public school. Again the action was upheld on the ground that only the state and the children profited from the assistance. In the majority opinion, however, Justice Black stated that the Constitution intended to take away from the governments of the nation and the states the power to "tax, to support, or otherwise assist any or all religions." The First Amendment, he said, "has erected a wall between church and state. That wall must be kept impregnable." The dissenting judges went much farther than Justice Black. They agreed that there should be an absolute separation of church and state and asserted that therefore the states should not be permitted to furnish school buses for parochial school children.[38]

Religious training. A different kind of question has arisen with respect to the teaching of religion in the schools. Public school sponsorship of either Bible reading or prayers has been ruled by the Court to violate the constitutional restrictions against establishment of religion.[39] Religious education has been abolished in some schools because local authorities doubted the constitutionality of such actions or felt that uniform religious courses would create a furor among parents. In the absence of regular religious training, some schools have resorted to a system for releasing children from school to allow religious instruction by the representatives of the churches. In 1948 the Supreme Court ruled that public school property could not be

---

36 *Pierce* v. *Society of Sisters*, 268 U. S. 510 (1925).

37 *Cochran* v. *Louisiana State Board of Education*, 281 U. S. 370 (1930).

38 *Everson* v. *Board of Education*, 330 U. S. 1 (1947).

39 State approved prayers were ruled out in 1962 even though dissenting students were not required to participate, *Engel* v. *Vitale* 370 U. S. 421 (1962). Opening religious services were barred in 1963 in *Murray* v. *Curlett*, 374 U. S. 203.

used for religious instruction during the released time.[40] To allow such training, the Court said, would tear down the wall separating church and state of which both the minority and majority had spoken in the school bus case. This decision, along with the historical evidence which supported it, was vigorously attacked by church groups and leading constitutional scholars.[41] Four years later the Supreme Court upheld the right of the states or the local governments to allow "released time" for religious training so long as that training did not occur on public school property.[42]

In other decisions the Court has upheld so-called blue laws requiring most businesses to close on Sundays. These laws do not violate the First and Fourteenth Amendments, the Court said, because there are secular reasons for closing one day per week. The fact that the laws may have once had a religious foundation is not controlling.[43]

The second provision concerning religion states that Congress shall not interfere with its free exercise. As we have seen the Fourteenth Amendment has been interpreted as covering the protection of freedom of religion in the states and it is in connection with state law that most litigation has arisen. The guarantee of freedom is not absolute. No religious belief can, for example, be made to justify polygamous practice in this country.[44] The Jehovah's Witnesses, a small but extremely active group, has frequently been before the courts to challenge state and local legislation which has sought to control their activities. For a period local communities were upheld in their right to require all children to join other public school children in saying the oath of allegiance and saluting the flag even though the Jehovah's Witnesses thought such action constituted idolatrous worship.[45] Three years later the Court reversed itself and found that the requirement of flag saluting constituted a violation of religious freedom.[46] In other cases involving the Witnesses, the Court has vacillated on the question of taxing church solicitors in the same manner in which door-to-door salesmen are licensed.[47] As in other areas of civil liberties, the constitutional interpretation of freedom of religion remains only partially worked out.

FREEDOM OF SPEECH AND PRESS

History of national regulation. Shortly after the adoption of the First Amendment with its flat insistence that "Congress shall make no law. . . .

40 *Illinois ex rel McCollum* v. *Board of Education,* 333 U. S. 203 (1948).

41 Professor E. S. Corwin of Princeton was one of those most critical of the historical accuracy of the evidence cited in the opinion.

42 *Zorach* v. *Clauson,* 343 U. S. 306 (1952).

43 *McGowan* v. *Maryland,* 366 U. S. 420 (1961) makes the basic point.

44 *Reynolds* v. *United States,* 98 U. S. 145 (1879).

45 *Minersville School District* v. *Gobitis,* 310 U. S. 586 (1940).

46 *West Virginia State Board of Education* v. *Barnette,* 319 U. S. 624 (1943).

47 See the conflicting opinions in *Jones* v. *Opelika,* 316 U. S. 584 (1942) and *Murdock* v. *Pennsylvania,* 319 U. S. 105 (1943).

abridging the freedom of speech, or of the press. . . ." Congress and the Federalist administration made clear that they did not look upon that provision as an absolute protection for all things said either orally or in writing. In 1798, Congress passed and John Adams signed the Sedition Act which prohibited false and scandalous criticism of Congress or the President or criticism uttered with the intent of defaming them or exciting the hatred of the people against them or urging sedition. Conditions at the time were extremely tense.

Mobs had surrounded a house in which President Adams was staying and had shouted abuse and threats against him. Anti-British feeling ran high in one part of the society while anti-French feeling was strong in another part. The two groups coalesced around President Adams and the Federalists on the one hand and around Jefferson and the Republicans on the other. Each side denounced the other as traitorous to the United States. Since the Federalists were in office at the time they enforced the act in such a way as to punish the supporters of Jefferson. The Sedition Act carried a time limit of two years, so that it was no longer in effect at the time Jefferson took office in 1801. As soon as he became President, Jefferson pardoned those who had been jailed under the act and refused to allow prosecution of others who were under indictment. No cases were brought to the Supreme Court and no rulings were handed down concerning the constitutionality of the law.

Whatever the merits of the Sedition Act, this action by Congress so soon after the ratification of the First Amendment made it clear that many of the government officials of the period did not think of the amendment as a prohibition against all regulation of speech or press. No justice asserted the absolute character of the amendment until very recently when Justices Douglas and Black have occasionally made such statements in dissenting opinions. Strangely, few cases concerning free speech and press reached the Supreme Court until near the end of World War I. Speech and press had been restricted during earlier wars in which the United States engaged, but these restrictions usually occurred during periods of martial law, and the cases did not get up to the highest court as a result of the action of military officers.

"Clear and present danger." In the cases growing out of the Espionage Act of 1917, the Supreme Court for the first time began to work out the standards by which it would test the validity of legislation defining the relation of freedom of speech and press to national security. Mr. Justice Holmes in the first major case before the Court stated that obviously the First Amendment did not imply complete freedom to say or write anything. Congress has the right and duty to prevent speeches and writings which present a "clear and present danger." "The question," he said, "in every case is whether the words used are used in such circumstances and are of such a nature as to create a clear and present danger that they will bring about the substantive evils that Congress has the right to prevent. It is a question of proximity and degree." [48] Most of the persons tried under the Espionage Act were convicted by way of the Holmes' formula, but it raised a barrier against too loose an interpretation of the act or too great a willingness to punish men for speeches that had little connection with any danger to the country.

In 1925, the Fourteenth Amendment was interpreted by the Court to include the guarantee of freedom of speech against the actions of the state governments. In the case which made this new interpretation of the Fourteenth Amendment's protection of free speech, however, a majority of the Court also changed the "clear and present danger" doctrine to allow greater latitude to the governments for the regulation of speech and press. In this case, which involved some pamphlets written by the executive secretary of the Workers' (Communist) Party, the Court ruled that the danger to the government need not be imminent. States could also legislate against speeches and writings which showed a "bad tendency" toward a danger to the overthrow of the government by force and violence.[49] There the matter rested for more than a decade at least so far as subversive groups were concerned.

During the intervening period, the Court ruled that various activities that had previously been subject to control were in the area of free speech protected by the First and Fourteenth Amendments. Peaceful picketing was held to be an expression of free speech and could not be stopped merely because it might injure the income of the company being picketed.[50] The full force of the decision on picketing was cut back by later decisions which allowed restriction on union activities where violence occurred even if the violence was not directly the result of the picketing. Nor could there be picketing directed against a man's business for reasons unconnected with his business. Where right to work laws exist, state courts are allowed to enjoin picketing.

Early in the forties, four justices of the Supreme Court argued that, while in general it was desirable to uphold actions of state legislatures and Congress, the rights guaranteed in the First Amendment held a "preferred position." Before this doctrine reached the status of a firm Court ruling, however, two of the four judges had been replaced by more conservative appointees. Today only Justices Black and Douglas continue to argue for this interpretation. During the forties, however, the Court ignored the "bad tendency" test in favor of the "clear and present danger" test.

Following World War II, Americans became increasingly aware of the menace of international communism. The celebrated cases of espionage

---

48 *Schenck* v. *United States,* 249 U. S. 47 (1919).
49 *Gitlow* v. *New York,* 268 U. S. 652 (1925).
50 *Thornhill* v. *Alabama,* 310 U. S. 88 (1940).

that arose in the five years after the war, the spreading power of the Soviet Union, the communist takeover in China, and the aggression in Korea served to emphasize the danger. Congress as early as 1941 in the Smith Act had sought to prohibit activities aimed at the forceful overthrow of the government. This law was supplemented twice in the decade after the war with further legislation aimed at the communists. In 1951 the Supreme Court, in interpreting the Smith Act which was used to prosecute a dozen of the top American Communist Party members, set forth a doctrine of "clear and probable danger" which seemed in many respects to be very similar to the older and discarded "bad tendency" test.[51] When the public fears of communism seemed once more to abate, during the following five or six years, the Court again reverted to the "clear and present danger" doctrine. The Supreme Court also restricted the meaning of certain terms in the Smith Act so that further prosecution of the communist leaders was not pushed by the Attorney-General.[52]

In other cases a badly divided Court threw out municipal action to stop a meeting of extremist groups in which the speakers were denouncing Jews, communists, and democrats while an opposition group outside the building milled around shouting threats and throwing stones.[53] West Coast unionist Harry Bridges was upheld in his right to criticise the integrity of a court before a decision had been rendered by that court.[54]

The interpretation of the limits of free speech and press has varied considerably since the end of World War II. From 1949 to 1953 the Court's decisions stressed the right of the government to protect itself against subversive organizations. These decisions coincided with the period of greatest anxiety about communism, the Korean War, and also an era of relatively conservative judges. Some later opinions, delivered in a period of somewhat more liberal judges and less national fear of local communists, stressed freedom of speech rather than national security. This second period was followed by vigorous criticism of the Court in Congress. Several measures to limit the appellate jurisdiction of the Court very nearly passed Congress in the session following the Court's shift to a greater emphasis on freedom of speech and press rather than on security. In 1959 and 1960 the Supreme Court seemed to vacillate in its position on these matters. Without explicitly overruling its liberal decisions, the Court seemed less inclined in those years to reverse state and national action against those who accepted the communist faith. Except possibly in the first prosecution of the Communist Party leaders under the Smith Act, the majority of the Supreme Court has seldom seemed to look upon the Communist Party as an organized group with characteristics different from those of other political

51 *Dennis* v. *United States*, 341 U. S. 494 (1951).
52 *Yates* v. *United States*, 354 U. S. 298 (1957).
53 *Terminello* v. *Chicago*, 337 U. S. 1 (1949).
54 *Bridges* v. *California*, 314 U. S. 252 (1941).

organization. Yet in upholding the ruling of the Subversive Activities Control Board the Court clearly noted the conspiratorial nature of the Communist Party.[54a] More recently, however, the Court insisted that passports cannot be withheld from Communist Party members because the law does not distinguish between knowing and unknowing party members.[54b]

Postal censorship. Congress has given the Post Office Department powers that are closely related to the power of censorship. The Department is forbidden to carry materials that are obscene or seditious. It may cut off all service to those who would use the mails to ship obscene materials or to defraud. The Postmaster General may also deny magazines and newspapers the special rate normally accorded them under the second class mailing privileges and thus make it impossible for the paper or magazine affected to compete with others in the field. If second class mailing privileges are revoked, the paper or magazine cannot regain the special rate until the Postmaster General is convinced that future issues of the publication will not repeat the offenses which caused loss of the privilege. The Court has tended to uphold the Postmaster General's action when mails were denied to those who would defraud the public, but it has been less sympathetic to denials of access to the mails or second class mailing privileges because of alleged obscenity.[55] During World War I the Postmaster General denied second class privileges to a socialist publication on grounds it contained seditious material. This action was upheld by the Court.[56] No similar questions have reached the Supreme Court since that time.

The authority of the states to regulate or censor magazines, newspapers, and movies has also been limited. In 1931 the Supreme Court ruled that no prior censorship of a newspaper was legitimate even if the materials contained in the paper were untruthful, malicious, and calculated to bring the state or local government into disrepute. Still more recently the Court has ruled that public officials may not sue for damages merely because of false statements. They must prove "actual malice." [57]

State regulation of movies. When the states first regulated the showing of moving pictures, the courts ruled that the theaters and producers had no justifiable complaint because movies were like circuses and other spectacles that could be censored to prevent the presentation of obscene and salacious acts. More recently, movies have been defined as a means for the transmission of information and ideas and therefore protected by the freedom of the press provision of the First Amendment and, by

---

54a *Communist Party* v. *Subversive Activities Control Bd.,* 367 U. S. 1 (1961).
54b *Aptheker* v. *Secretary of State,* 378 U. S. 992 (1964).
55 *Summerfield* v. *Sunshine Book Co.,* 349 U. S. 921 (1955) and *Hannegan* v. *Esquire,* 327 U. S. 146 (1946).
56 *Milwaukee Social Democratic Publishing Co.* v. *Burleson,* 255 U. S. 407 (1921).
57 *Near* v. *Minnesota,* 283 U. S. 697 (1931) and in 1964 *New York Times* v. *Sullivan,* 376 U. S. 254.

absorption, the Fourteenth Amendment. States may not censor movies as sacrilegious. The Court, however, has stated that censorship of movies because of obscenity is possible if the definitions of obscenity are clearly written in the law.[58]

The Court has upheld some statutes and ordinances that have sought to prevent the distribution of books and other printed materials considered lewd and obscene by the officials. No firm rule can as yet be drawn from the decisions of the Court except that the more vague the definition of the things to be banned, the less likely it is that the convictions will stand up in court. Clearly, "dirt for dirt's sake" is not legitimate material for public sale and distribution,[59] but the problem is to define the line between literature that happens to have some objectionable language and the obscene materials written and distributed to appeal only to the prurient mind and with the possible consequences of unlawful or immoral action.[60]

PROTECTION OF PROPERTY

The Constitution provides that "No state shall . . . pass any . . . law impairing the obligation of contracts." Justice John Marshall, whose opinions played a major role in shaping the direction of government policies during the early years of the nineteenth century, interpreted that clause to mean that the states have no right to change contracts once entered into by private individuals or between the state and individuals.[61] Even if a state legislature had fraudulently given land to speculators, another legislature could not nullify the contract.[62] In the name of obligation of contract and later as an interpretation of "substantive" due process of law, the Supreme Court limited economic regulation by the states. The Court reviewed rates made by state commissions to determine their reasonableness, restricted state police power, and invalidated legislation aimed at improving the status of workers—men, women, and children. Between 1890 and 1937, the Court struck down much of the social legislation that came before it by invoking the due process clause of the Fourteenth Amendment.

In 1934, the Court agreed that the contract clause did not exclude a state from placing certain limitations on the provisions of private contracts in the interest of preserving the economy of the entire community.[63] In the same year the Court refused to intervene against state economic regulations so long as it could not be shown that the regulations were arbitrary or capricious.[64] By 1938 the Court had abandoned most of the

---

58 *Burstyn* v. *Wilson,* 343 U. S. 495 (1953), and *Times Film Corp.* v. *Chicago,* 365 U. S. 43 (1961).

59 *Kingsley Books* v. *Brown,* 354 U. S. 436 (1957).

60 *Winters* v. *New York,* 333 U. S. 507 (1948).

61 *Dartmouth College* v. *Woodward,* 4 Wheaton 518 (1819).

62 *Fletcher* v. *Peck,* 6 Cranch 58 (1810).

63 *Home Building and Loan Association* v. *Blaisdell,* 290 U. S. 398 (1934).

64 *Nebbia* v. *New York,* 291 U. S. 502 (1934).

limitations which it had once insisted must be applied against state economic regulation.

RACIAL EQUALITY

Development of racial inequalities. Following the end of the occupation of the South after the close of the Civil War, Negroes, who had gained a large measure of equality during the Reconstruction days, saw much of their status undermined by the return of the white southerners to power. Prior to the withdrawal of the northern armies, Congress had enacted legislation to preserve the improved position of the Negro, but these laws served little purpose. Southern legislation and pressure from private groups prevented the Negro from exercising his rights. The Supreme Court, with a few notable exceptions, provided the Negro little protection. The Court allowed national action to prevent the blocking of Negro voting by fraud or intimidation.[65] In other decisions the Negro fared less well. The Fourteenth Amendment was declared to apply only to states and not to individuals thus freeing private groups to discriminate against persons because of race,[66] When the white legislatures later wrote laws calculated to reduce Negro voting, the Court refused to nullify them unless the discrimination was clear within the acts themselves. The Court said it would not look behind the laws for any special unstated intent.[67] Further, it was held that the Fourteenth Amendment, with its equal protection of the laws clause, did not require that exactly the same facilities be made available to both Negroes and whites.

In order to provide equality in the sense intended by the amendment it was, said the Court, enough to provide "separate but equal facilities." [68] Later usage reduced the meaning of the phrase to "substantially equal." Under this new interpretation, Negroes were granted no assistance, if for example, a county, after providing schools for white children from which the Negro children were barred, flatly stated it had no money left to build a school for the Negro children. For a period Negroes had really no protection against discrimination by individuals or even by the states except the self-restraint of the potential offenders.

There were occasional breaks in the solid wall of discrimination, but these breaks were few and affected only a small number of Negroes. The "grandfather clause" was thrown out in Oklahoma, but this action gave no votes to the Negroes.[69] The Court refused to allow a state to grant a railroad the privilege of providing special facilities for whites without making available similar accommodations for Negroes. In spite of these infrequent

---

65 *Ex Parte Yarbrough,* 110 U. S. 651 (1884).
66 *Civil Rights Cases,* 109 U. S. 651 (1883).
67 *Williams* v. *Mississippi,* 170 U. S. 213 (1898).
68 *Plessy* v. *Ferguson,* 163 U. S. 537 (1896).
69 See chapter 7 for history of Negro suffrage.

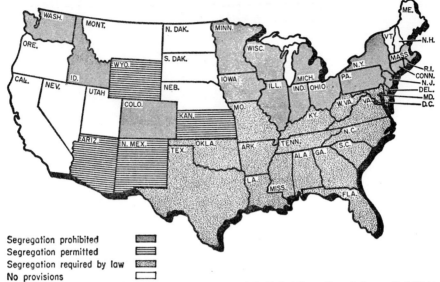

Segregation prohibited
Segregation permitted
Segregation required by law
No provisions

Report of the United States Commission on Civil Rights

STATUS OF SEGREGATION, MAY 1954 At the time of the Supreme Court decision against segregation in 1954, some seventeen states and the District of Columbia legally required the separation of negroes and whites in the schools.

assists from the Court, the lax interpretation of the Fourteenth Amendment generally prevailed until the thirties.

Equality in education. Near the end of the fourth decade of the present century, the first of a series of decisions was handed down which gave "equality" a new meaning. The states were told in 1939 that if there were no state schools for training Negro law students, these students must be admitted to the same state schools that trained the white students.[70] A decade later the Court reaffirmed this ruling.[71] Next, the states were told that, if under the earlier rulings Negroes were admitted to the universities, there could not then be discrimination in facilities offered.[72] At the same time the Court stated that Texas could not claim that a newly created law school with fewer teachers, books, and other necessary items for teaching was a satisfactory substitute for admitting a qualified Negro student to the Texas Law School.[73]

These preliminary steps still seemed to be within the general framework of the Plessy decision, but the states had to demonstrate that "equal facilities" were indeed equal or Negroes must be allowed to use the same facilities the whites used. In 1954, however, a unanimous Supreme Court

[70] *Missouri ex rel Gaines* v. *Canada,* 305 U. S. 337 (1938).
[71] *Sipuel* v. *University of Oklahoma,* 332 U. S. 631 (1948).
[72] *McLaurin* v. *Oklahoma State Regents,* 339 U. S. 637 (1950).
[73] *Sweatt* v. *Painter* 339 U. S. 629 (1950).

PUBLIC SCHOOL DESEGREGATION[a]

	School Districts with Negroes and Whites		Enrollment		In Desegregated Districts		Negroes in Schools with Whites	
Total	Total	Deseg.	White	Negro	White	Negro	No.	%‡
Alabama	114	114	4	539,996†	287,414*	106,199†	70,896†	21	.007
Arkansas	415	228	13	328,023†	112,012†	66,752	18,643	366	.327
Florida	67	67	16	964,241*	237,871*	669,375	130,667	3,650	1.53
Georgia	197	181	4	689,323	337,534	95,731	77,599	177	.052
Louisiana	67	67	2	460,589†	301,433†	68,700	79,077	1,814	.602
Mississippi	150	150	0	304,226†	295,971†	0	0	0	0
North Carolina	171	171	40	820,900*	347,063*	367,764*	133,164*	1,865	.537
South Carolina	108	108	1	368,496*	258,955*	3,108	9,539	10	.004
Tennessee	154	143	45	687,902*	164,940*	380,321	120,447	4,486	2.72
Texas	1,421	899	263	2,045,499	326,409*	1,300,000*	200,000*	18,000*	5.52
Virginia	130	128	55	710,176	228,961	486,231	145,658	3,721	1.63
South	2,994	2,256	443	7,919,371	2,894,563	3,544,181	985,690	34,110	1.18
Delaware	86	86	86	78,730	18,066	68,321	13,976	10,209	56.5
District of Columbia	1	1	1	19,803	117,915	19,803	117,915	98,813	83.8
Kentucky	204	165	163	611,126*	54,874*	492,701*	54,874*	29,855	54.4
Maryland	24	23	23	540,667	160,546	535,691	160,946	76,906	47.8
Missouri	1,597	212*	203*	793,000*	95,000*	NA	90,000*	40,000*	42.1
Oklahoma	1,160	241	197	541,125*	43,875*	324,023*	35,596*	12,289*	28.0
West Virginia	55	44	44	417,595*	23,449*	417,595*	23,449	13,659*	58.2
Border	3,127	772	717	3,002,046	514,125	1,858,134¶	496,756	281,731	54.8
Region	6,121	3,028	1,160	10,921,417	3,408,688	5,402,315¶	1,482,446	315,841	9.3

* Estimated. † 1962–63. ‡ No. of Negroes in schools with whites, compared to total Negro enrollment. ¶ Missouri not included. ªSource: Southern Education Reporting Service, May, 1964.

took a larger step when it ruled that segregation was itself an act of discrimination. The mere fact of forcing children of one race to attend schools different from those attended by children of another race created "a sense of inferiority" for the children restricted to separate schools. The Court recognized that its decision in this case would affect schools in many states and therefore allowed a full year for the consideration of the manner of its enforcement.[74] The following year, after lengthy arguments before it, the Court sent the case back to the district courts with instructions to move forward with integration as rapidly as possible while taking into account the special problems of the area. Public officials were required to indicate what plans there were for desegregation, to provide a time schedule, and to get started on integration as quickly as possible.[75]

Enforcement of the decisions. The District of Columbia, West Virginia, and sections of other border states immediately complied with the ruling. In the Deep South a very different development took place. There, where the problems of integration were clearly the most difficult, delay followed delay. When integration of schools was ordered by the district courts, violence sometimes accompanied the action. Little Rock was the center of the major violence during the first years of desegregation, but violence also occurred in Tennessee and other states. Seven years after the second Court decision, some of the states of the Deep South still had not desegregated schools in even a token manner. North Carolina, Virginia, and Arkansas had begun desegregating in a few cities by permitting a small number of Negro students to register in previously all-white schools. To avoid integration, some states resorted to a number of devices which delayed or prevented the fullfillment of the Court orders. Some public schools were closed, and parents paid to send their children to makeshift private schools. The states cannot, however, allow the use of public buildings nor in any way assist in financing these private ventures without running afoul of the prohibition against discrimination.

The attempt of Prince Edward County in Virginia to avoid desegregation of its schools by closing the public schools was ordered stopped by the Supreme Court in 1964. In its ruling the Court stated that there might be occasions when a state could constitutionally allow one county to close its schools while others remained open. However, this was not acceptable when the clear reason for closing the schools was undeniably to avoid integration.[75a]

The staff report to the Commission on Civil Rights for 1963 noted the increasing problems of at least *de facto* segregation in the schools of some northern cities. It also showed that by 1963-64 Mississippi still had

---

[74] *Brown* v. *Board of Education of Topeka,* 347 U. S. 483 (1954) and *Bolling* v. *Sharpe,* 347 U. S. 497 (1954).

[75] Same cases 349 U. S. 294 (1955).

[75a] *Griffin* v. *County School Bd. of Prince Edward County,* 377 U. S. 218 (1964).

no desegregated schools, while Alabama, Georgia, Louisiana, and South Carolina had four or fewer desegregated school districts.

Several generalizations can be made concerning the integration of the schools since the Court decisions of 1954 and 1955. First, the process of desegregation in the areas where the largest number of Negroes live has been slowest and probably will not be completed for more than a decade. Second, the most rapid integration has occurred in the border states and the District of Columbia. Worry about the desegregation of the races has not been widespread nor deepseated in these areas. Third, the urban areas have, on the whole, been more willing to accept desegregation than have the rural areas. The rural areas in the South have the highest ratio of Negroes to whites, while the large cities have the lowest ratio. In the cities, the presence of institutions of higher education, the attitudes of some trade unions, and the fact of greater cosmopolitanism have been factors in this greater willingness of the urban areas to cooperate in carrying out the Court's decisions.

Housing and race. For many years one of the sore points of discrimination has been the restriction of Negroes and other minorities to particular areas or subdivisions of a city. As early as 1917 the Supreme Court ruled that cities could not prohibit Negroes from living in any area of the city. Such legislation, said the Court, violated the due process of law provision of the Fourteenth Amendment.[76] For a period, however, the Court upheld the right of private citizens to agree to "restrictive covenants" under which the buyer of a house agreed not to sell his home to any person excluded by the covenant.[77] The same question was raised again in 1948 under both the Fifth and Fourteenth Amendments. This time the Court ruled that private persons were free to make restrictive covenants among themselves, but that the state and federal courts could not enforce the provisions. Even if the suits were civil suits, said the Court, the enforcement of the contract amounted to a denial of due process by the state or federal government.[78]

Miscellaneous areas of discrimination. In addition to the major areas of racial discrimination discussed above, the struggle of Negroes to secure equality has extended to many other areas. The Court upheld a District of Columbia law that forbade discrimination in restaurants because of race or color. In areas of the South Negroes have fought not the law but the practice of most eating places to exclude patrons on the basis of color. Parks, beaches, swimming pools, theaters, and many other public businesses have excluded persons because of race. Where state or municipal governments have been responsible for the discrimination they can be and have been successfully challenged in the Court. Where private groups or persons are involved, minorities are confined to demonstrations and boycotts to

---

[76] *Buchanan* v. *Warley,* 245 U. S. 60 (1917).

[77] *Corrigan* v. *Buckley,* 271 U. S. 323 (1926).

[78] *Shelley* v. *Kraemer,* 333 U. S. 1 (1948) and *Hurd* v. *Hodge,* 334 U. S. 24 (1948).

seek their ends. Sometimes these methods have been successful and some-times they have fallen short of the goal. In 1960, both major political parties endorsed "sit-in" strikes to protest discrimination in restaurants in southern states.

More will be said about the three major civil rights acts in the next chapter, but it is worth noting here that Congress in 1964 provided against discrimination in hiring in many situations and also for the first time pro-hibited discrimination in public accommodations declared to be in inter-state commerce. In the meantime the federal courts have also expanded the areas of desegregation wherever it could be pointed out that a state has authority even though the particular facilities on the state property may be privately owned.

SUMMARY

The protection of individual rights and freedoms was first written into the Constitution to protect persons against action by the national and state governments. In the Bill of Rights which was added shortly after the adop-tion of the Constitution the national government was forbidden to legislate to deprive persons of their freedom of speech, press, and assembly. The same first eight amendments provided that the national government must assure the accused of certain minimum procedural protections. After the Civil War, the Fourteenth Amendment was adopted to provide certain protections for the individual against state government action. The extent of the protections of the Fourteenth Amendment has not been made clear, but it is clear that the amendment protects the individual against state action depriving him of speech, press, assembly, or freedom of religion. It is also clear that the Supreme Court interprets the amendment to mean that the state must provide a fair trial for those accused of violating state laws.

The meaning of the various provisions of the Constitution and the Bill of Rights has sometimes changed over the years. Speech and writing that are legitimate at one time may lose legitimacy in other periods. The Supreme Court has modified some of its earlier decisions as well as taken into account the changes in times. Other provisions of the Bill of Rights and the Fourteenth Amendment are still subject to interpretation as new situations develop. The development of devices which can invade a person's privacy without his consent has created new problems for the Supreme Court in its interpretation of the prohibition against unreasonable searches and seizures. The "due process" and "equal protection" clauses in the Fourteenth Amendment have been slowly expanded to limit action by the states in the area of civil liberties and civil rights.

These decisions of the Court to expand the protection of citizens from action by either the state or national government in the area of civil liberties are a development primarily of the last forty years. During that period the Court has shifted its interest from overseeing government regulation of the economic order to the expansion of civil liberties. Most of the important decisions today are in the field of civil liberties.

The plight of racial minorities was largely ignored by the Supreme Court and the other branches of government for eighty years, after some initial action by the national government during the days of Reconstruction. With rare exceptions the Supreme Court paid no special attention to the protection of Negroes from 1880 to 1935. During the last quarter of a century, however, the Negro has received some assistance from all branches of the national government and from a few state governments. As a result, the Negro's right to vote is better protected today than it has been at any time since Reconstruction. Schools are being desegregated in the Border States and a beginning has been made in some of the states of the Old South. State and local governments can no longer expect the national courts to ignore discrimination against persons because of race. Negroes are by no means treated equally with whites everywhere and on all occasions, but they are receiving help from all branches of the national government in their struggle for equality.

BIBLIOGRAPHIC NOTE

Lawmakers and judges are less concerned about freedom of speech and press at a time when the nation seems to be endangered. Writers about civil liberties, however, are more likely to devote their efforts to producing books in times of crisis because they have become more aware of the difficulties faced by the dissenters when the national security is threatened.

The student interested in the many problems of civil liberties should read one of the books describing American constitutional development. The stress in such books is on the decisions of the Supreme Court, but there is usually a discussion of the actions of the executive and the legislative branches of the government. The student should also become acquainted with at least a couple of case books used in courses in Constitutional Law. Dozens of these case books exist. For the undergraduate, Robert E. Cushman, *Leading Constitutional Decisions* (12th ed., New York: Appleton-Century-Crofts, 1963) and Rocco J. Tresolini, *American Constitutional Law* (New York: The Macmillan Company, 1959) are both excellent books. Other case books provide the undergraduate with sufficient material to give him at least a general picture of the problems of civil liberties.

C. Herman Pritchett, *Civil Liberties and the Vinson Court* (Chicago: University of Chicago Press, 1954) gives a good picture of the importance of the Chief Justice and the other members of the Supreme Court in the development of particular patterns of court decisions. Two books by men passionately devoted to their maintenance give us a full discussion of the problems of civil liberties. Robert E. Cushman, *Civil Liberties in the United States* (Ithaca, New York: Cornell University Press, 1956) and George W. Spicer, *The Supreme Court and Fundamental Freedoms* (New York: Appleton-Century-Crofts, 1959) both describe in detail the difficulties faced by the individual in today's world. Professor Cushman's book includes an excellent bibliography at the conclusion of each of his chapters.

Two books with almost identical titles contain analyses of one of the most difficult problems of our era. They are Harold D. Lasswell's *National Security and Individual Liberty* (New York: McGraw-Hill Book Company, 1950) and John Lord O'Brian's *National Security and Individual Freedom* (Cambridge, Mass.: Harvard University Press, 1955). Closely related to the general problem discussed in these books is the question of the refusal of witnesses to testify on communist activities before congressional committees. Two books state succinctly the two major positions that the average citizen may reasonably take upon hearing that someone has refused to testify concerning previous communist activities on the ground that he might incriminate himself. These two books are Sidney Hook's *Common Sense and The Fifth Amendment* (New York: Criterion Books, 1951) and Erwin N. Griswold's *The Fifth Amendment Today* (Cambridge, Mass.: Harvard University Press, 1955). Professor Hook has also written another interesting book dealing with the freedom which may be allowed communists in a democratic society. He calls this book *Heresy, Yes; Conspiracy, No!* (New York: The John Day Company, 1953).

Most writers on civil liberties think of the courts as the major defenders of the rights of individuals. They sometimes doubt the wisdom of elected representatives in the state and national legislatures. Learned Hand, for many years a leading judge in the court of appeals, presents a cogent argument that Supreme Court judges normally ought not to substitute their own views for those of the legislators even in matters of civil liberties. He states this view vigorously in his little book, *The Bill of Rights* (Cambridge, Mass.: Harvard University Press, 1958).

In the years following World War II, the struggle between the communist and free worlds has reached a new peak. The communists were so successful in their aggressive activities in the first decade after the war that many Americans became seriously concerned about their espionage activities within the national government. Some former communists have written books about these activities. Perhaps the most useful of these books is Whitaker Chambers' *Witness* (New York: Random House, 1952). The exposure of communist operations led to the creation of security programs within the federal bureaucracy and to intensive investigations by congressional committees. Eleanor Bontecou's *The Federal Loyalty-Security Program* (Ithaca, New York: Cornell University Press, 1952) presents a critical evaluation of the security programs of the government.

Samuel A. Stouffer, in *Communism, Conformity, and Civil Liberties: A Cross-Section of the Nation Speaks Its Mind* (New York: Doubleday and Company, 1955) tells of the views of Americans concerning the dangers of communism and the feeling of citizens about the need to restrict communist activities.

Several new books have appeared dealing with the history of civil liberties in the United States. Two have been written by Leonard W. Levy—*Legacy of Suppression* (Cambridge: Harvard University Press, 1960) and *Jefferson and Civil Liberties: The Darker Side* (Cambridge: Harvard University Press, 1964). An interesting and useful collection of documents is found in Richard L. Perry (ed.), *Sources of Our Liberties: English and American Documents from Magna Carta to the Bill of Rights* (New York: McGraw-Hill, 1964). In another area of civil liberties, Sidney Hook has provided us with an excellent re-examination of some of the problems of civil liberties faced by modern liberalism in his *The Paradoxes of Freedom* (Berkeley: University of California Press, 1962).

Few fields have seen so many books arise in the last few years as the area of Negro rights. Any listing must be partial. Two helpful books are Jack Greenberg, *Race Relations and American Law* (New York: Columbia University Press, 1959) and Louis E. Lomax, *The Negro Revolt* (New York: The New American Library, 1963). Of special value in the study of these problems are the reports of the Commission on Civil Rights which began to appear in 1959.

7

The Voter

T HE right of every citizen to vote in free elections for candidates offered by independent parties or factions is one of the basic rights of a democratic society. Most democratic nations of the world have arrived at universal suffrage by slow and halting steps. The United States has been no exception to this rule. At the time of the adoption of the Constitution, perhaps no more than one-sixth of the persons over twenty-one voted. Women and non-white males were not considered as even potential electors. White males could vote if they met certain property or tax requirements, which in some states was easy to do.

Today, substantially all white adults, male and female, are eligible to vote. Persons of other races vote without restriction in most areas of the United States. In the South an increasing number of Negroes are registered and vote. Congress and the Supreme Court have intermittently applied pressure on the southern states to remove the remaining legal and administrative restrictions on universal suffrage. If universal suffrage is still not a fact in the United States, the movement in that direction is clear. Unless some unforeseen catastrophe develops, the future of suffrage for all adults regardless of race is bright.

The shift from very limited suffrage to universal suffrage is the result of at least two factors. First, the theoretical basis of our society, like that of other democratic societies, has provided the basic arguments for extending the franchise to all persons who have reached a specified age and who are citizens of the country. Second, the quest for electoral support by the major parties has encouraged party leaders to grant the franchise to more and more non-voters. The parties expect that their efforts to give the vote to those previously excluded will be rewarded with the support from the new voters and their friends. In other words, a combination of theoretical and moral considerations with purely practical political considerations has been the reason for the consistent extension of the franchise to more and more segments of the community.

DEMOCRACY AND THE SUFFRAGE

The right of all citizens to participate in making the decisions of their government is essential in a democratic society. To be meaningful, however, this right demands two prior conditions. Each citizen must have access to information about the candidates and issues on which he is to vote and he must have a real choice among competing candidates. Furthermore, the vote of each man must be considered of equal value. A rich man or poor man of any race or creed is entitled to cast his ballot and to have that ballot counted along with all others.

"The right of voting for persons charged with the execution of the laws that govern society is inherent in the word Liberty, and constitutes equality of personal rights," said Thomas Paine more than 170 years ago. If the right to vote is dependent upon such things as property or taxes, "the dignity of the suffrage is thus lowered . . . in placing it with an inferior thing. . . ." Age alone is a legitimate requirement for voting since "nothing but dying before that time can take it away." [1]

In one form or another every democratic theorist has stated essentially the same argument. At the time of the founding of our government, most such men agreed with Paine that voting was a "natural right" derived from the fact that men were created equal in the sight of God.

This view of the nature of man and of his right to the suffrage was not shared by all who wrote the Constitution nor by a majority of those who wrote the state voting laws of the period. Nevertheless, the idea was present in the discussions of the period and provided a rationale for those who wished to extend the franchise to all white males.

The political basis for extending the franchise. Political theory alone would not have secured the vote for all men. Politicians are responsible for laws and constitutions. They are influenced by political theories, but they are also concerned with their own election and re-election. Their reasons for allowing more and more persons to vote during the course of our history may sometimes have been more closely related to their desire to continue in public office than to their commitment to the democratic creed.

A leading authority on political parties, E. E. Schattschneider, suggests that political parties are always interested in getting the most votes for the least effort.[2] Therefore, when most legally eligible voters are either committed to one or the other of the parties or to not voting at all, the best source of new party support is to be found among those who do not yet possess the vote. The party in power, therefore, changes the voting require-

---

[1] Quoted in Howard Penniman, "Thomas Paine—Democrat," *American Political Science Review*, Volume 37, pp. 244-262, April, 1943.

[2] *Party Government* (New York: Rinehart and Co., 1942).

ments to allow more persons to participate. The party that eases the legal requirements naturally hopes that the new voters will gratefully support its candidates.

If some members of a particular group can vote while other members cannot, it is normally politically expedient to advocate the enfranchisement of the remaining members of the group. At least once in our history we saw the granting of the ballot for such reasons of expediency dramatically illustrated. For years women in America had sought the endorsement of the presidential candidates of both parties for woman suffrage. For years neither party had given more than lukewarm support to the movement. Suddenly after New York, with the largest block of electoral votes in the country, granted women the right to vote in 1917—leaders of both parties rushed to get on the bandwagon. Neither party dared to antagonize the women of New York and risk the loss of that state's electoral votes in the 1920 presidential election.

The desire of both parties for the large Negro vote in the industrial areas of the North may have been at least as important as their democratic faith in moving their members in Congress to support the passage of the 1957, 1960, and 1964 Civil Rights Acts.

The judges of the Supreme Court, who have helped to extend the franchise, were more clearly motivated by ideology than by obvious political advantage. In 1944, for example, they reversed a series of earlier decisions to ban the "white primaries" in the South and thus removed one of the major barriers to effective political action in the area.

HISTORY OF THE SUFFRAGE

White manhood suffrage. In five of the original colonies a man had to own at least fifty acres of land in order to vote. Virginia required that a voter own fifty acres or twenty-five acres and a house twelve feet square. Two colonies expected a man to own 100 acres in order to vote. The remaining five colonies were more concerned about the value of the property rather than its size.

After the Revolution few states made any major changes in their voting laws. One state, Massachusetts, actually increased the value of the land required for voting. Others reduced slightly the amount of land required or allowed the substitution of personal property for real estate as long as the value was comparable. The Constitution is silent on the question of national voting qualifications except to provide that "the electors in each State shall have the qualifications requisite for electors of the most numerous branch of the state legislature." When the Constitution went into operation in 1789 the rules for the suffrage were essentially identical with the old colonial rules.

In the East suffrage requirements changed slowly. It was not until after

Andrew Jackson went to the White House, following the election of 1828, that the move toward universal white manhood suffrage shifted into high gear. Some eastern states had by this time substituted tax-paying for property qualifications, but non-taxpayers remained voteless until well into the Jackson era. Men of substance often fought bitterly against the egalitarian suffrage movement on the ground that the poor, being more numerous

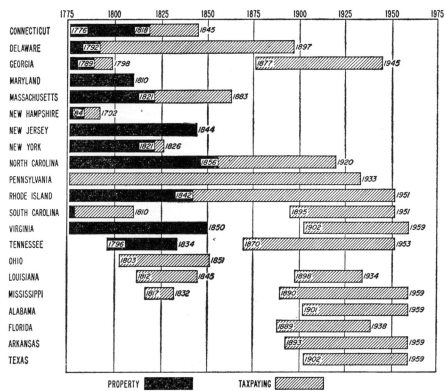

Report of the United States Commission on Civil Rights

DURATION OF PROPERTY AND TAXPAYING QUALIFICATIONS FOR VOTING. Note that this chart still shows five states with tax requirements in 1959. The poll tax actually continued in those states until the adoption of the Twenty-fourth Amendment in 1964. Except for Ohio, tax and property tests were to be found only in the East and South. Frontier conditions made such taxes foolish elsewhere.

would inevitably oppress the holders of property, end the protection of property, and ultimately destroy a free society.

The attitude toward universal suffrage was quite different west of the Appalachians. In the area which is now the Middle West there were few men of wealth. Anyone could own land simply by taking and clearing it. The governments of the towns and the states had few functions, so taxes were minimal. Property and tax requirements, such as those of the older and more established sections of the country, were meaningless in frontier states. All the new states from this area except Ohio placed no restrictions on voting by white men. Ohio required a tax payment before voting.

Voting equality in the Middle West soon worked its way back to the eastern states where the newly developing working groups were demanding the vote. In most states of the East there were prolonged debates but no serious incidents along the road to white manhood suffrage. In Rhode Island, however, the established government continued to refuse to modify the suffrage rules. A rump constitutional convention was therefore called by opponents of the existing government. A new constitution, which provided for universal suffrage, was announced. Thomas W. Dorr was elected governor of the state under this second constitution in 1841. For a brief period civil war seemed probable, since the existing government recognized neither Dorr nor his constitution. The danger receded when Dorr's followers faded away at the sight of the state militia. The pressures created by Dorr's efforts, however, were probably responsible for the constitutional changes which, three years later, granted the vote to all native American white males who paid a dollar tax.

By the middle of the nineteenth century, ownership of property was no longer required for voting in any state except North Carolina. Four other states still retained some taxpaying requirement.

The literacy requirement for voting developed only after the great influx of immigrants to this country near the end of the nineteenth century. States where immigration was heaviest required the passage of a literacy test before permitting a man to vote. The tests were not difficult, but they assured that, if the laws were fairly administered, the voters knew at least some English. In most states the prospective voter merely had to read a few lines from the state constitution or perhaps write his name. New York developed a more sophisticated test. The voter was given materials to read and was examined on those materials. The test required roughly the same knowledge as was required for tests in the fourth grade of elementary school. With the rise of education and the reduction in the number of immigrants, the literacy tests have lost much of their significance. Problems still arise in New York because of the large number of Puerto Ricans who have moved into the state. In the South the literacy tests were intended for the special purpose of excluding Negroes from voting. The 1964 Civil Rights Act states that a sixth-grade education is sufficient proof of literacy.

WOMAN'S SUFFRAGE

The democratization of the suffrage for white male citizens was largely completed by the middle of the nineteenth century. Women and Negroes remained voteless. Indeed, women were legally without any independence from their husbands in most states. They could own no property. No more than a handful of extremists had even considered the possibility that some day women ought to have equal voting rights with men. The great majority of both men and women felt that the latter were naturally inferior to men and should therefore remain subordinate to them.

A few women organized an abolitionist society as early as 1833. Fifteen years later, at a meeting of some women in upper New York, the need for a new legal status for women was mentioned. In the 1850's a temperance society was established. Many of the abolitionists and temperance women later joined together in a campaign for suffrage for women. They used much the same kind of argument to justify their right to the vote that they had earlier used to demand the abolition of slavery.

Four years after the Civil War, the first territorial legislature of Wyoming extended the suffrage to women. Before the end of the century, Idaho, Utah, and Colorado had granted women the vote. Few states followed their lead, and women lost an appeal to the Supreme Court to grant them the vote under the Fourteenth Amendment.[3] Outside of the populist dominated areas of the West, the suffragist movement was notable primarily for its failures. By 1915 eleven states west of the Mississippi had granted woman suffrage; but, of all the states east of the river, only Illinois even allowed women to vote in presidential elections.

In 1917 a major break for the suffragists developed in New York when Tammany Hall took a neutral position in the fight, and the state acceded to the concerted efforts of the suffragist organizations. After New York had granted the vote the rest was easy.

As long ago as 1878, an amendment to the national constitution had been proposed providing that the right of a citizen to vote should "not be denied or abridged by the United States or by any state on account of sex." The amendment made no headway before Congress, in spite of hunger strikes and highly publicized demonstrations, until after New York had granted woman suffrage. President Wilson had refused to endorse the proposal, and the Republican leadership had given the suffragists only slightly more encouragement. After the New York action both parties hastily reversed their positions and insisted upon the passage of the Nineteenth Amendment. The Amendment passed Congress in the summer of 1919 and was submitted to the states for ratification. By autumn of the following year the necessary thirty-six states had ratified the amendment. Women voted throughout the country in the presidential election of 1920.

NEGRO SUFFRAGE

Negroes constitute the only significant group in America which, having once acquired the right to vote, later lost that right. In the years immediately following the Civil War Negroes, with the aid of military occupation, gained

---

[3] *Minor* v. *Happersett,* 21 Wallace 162 (1875).

the vote in the South. As a matter of fact, they gained the vote during this period for the first time in many northern states. Forty years later very few Negroes were allowed to vote in the southern states in spite of the Fourteenth and Fifteenth Amendments which had been adopted to insure equality of political rights for citizens regardless of color. Now in the second half of the twentieth century Negroes are just regaining the voting rights which once seemed so clearly guaranteed in the Constitution.

Before the Civil War, Negroes rarely voted in the North and never in the South. New York was one of four northern states to allow Negro voting before 1860, but even in New York only Negroes who paid taxes were granted suffrage.[4] By the close of the war, seven northern states had provided for Negro suffrage.

The Fifteenth Amendment, proposed by a Republican Congress while Federal troops were still in the South, was ratified in 1870. It provided that no one should be denied the vote because of "race, color, or previous condition of servitude." The amendment did not give Negroes the suffrage, but merely provided that they could not be discriminated against because of race.

The Supreme Court largely nullified the Fifteenth Amendment in a series of decisions from 1876 to 1903. The Court held that the amendment did not give the vote to Negroes and that no person could be convicted for a wrongful act unless he had discriminated against Negroes because of their race. Later the Court stated that the amendment applied only to states not to individuals. Furthermore, said the Court, it must be proved that any action taken by a state was taken with the intention to discriminate.[5] The fact that a law which in practice hurt only Negroes was phrased in a manner which made it appear to apply equally to persons of both races was enough for the Court to uphold the law as non-discriminatory within the meaning of the amendment. The judges did not consider the administration of the law which was frequently highly discriminatory on racial grounds.

Congress, which had authority under both the Fourteenth and Fifteenth Amendments to intervene in states practicing discrimination, ceased to have any serious interest in the affairs of Negroes in the South. The attitude of Congress and the decisions of the Supreme Court coincided with the return to power of the white Democrats in most southern states. The new state leaders, taking advantage of the narrow interpretation of the Court and the indifference of Congress, enacted legislation that apparently applied equally to persons of all races but actually restricted only Negroes.

By 1900 most of the southern states had adopted constitutional provisions or legislation which required residence of two years in a voting district

---

[4] This tax restriction on Negro voting lasted until 1874, long after tax paying had been abolished as a requirement for white citizens.

[5] *United States* v. *Reese*, 92 U. S. 214 (1876); *James* v. *Bowman*, 190 U. S. 127 (1903); and *United States* v. *Cruikshank*, 92 U. S. 542 (1876).

at a time when Negroes were frequently moving from area to area, a poll tax, an educational test or property tax, and the absence of a criminal background. The crimes which banned voting included those which many whites thought were the ones most frequently committed by Negroes. Far more important than the provisions of the laws and constitutions, however, was the fact that white sheriffs and election officials administered the laws. The wide discretion offered to administrators made possible a discrimination that excluded Negroes from voting without restricting whites.

The grandfather clause. The most openly discriminatory device of the period was probably the "grandfather clause." Constitutions or laws stated that anyone who had voted prior to a fixed date could be exempt from other provisions such as those requiring literacy or an ability to understand and interpret the Constitution. Since obviously no Negroes could have voted in the southern states prior to the established date, none could benefit from the "grandfather clause." When a case questioning the constitutionality of these clauses finally reached the Supreme Court in 1915, the judges stated that the clauses obviously made it easier for whites than for Negroes to qualify for voting, and that therefore the clauses violated the provisions of the Fifteenth Amendment.[6]

White primaries. The Democratic Party controlled the politics of the South by the end of the nineteenth century. The Republican Party had been discredited in the area because of its handling of reconstruction following the Civil War. By the time the direct primary was introduced in the South early in the twentieth century, the Democratic Party control was so overwhelming that the party's primary became the only significant election in all but one or two congressional districts in the entire region. The winner of the Democratic primary nomination was automatically also the winner of the election the following November.

The Texas legislature in 1923 prohibited Negroes from participating in Democratic Party primaries. The Supreme Court nullified the act a few years later on the ground that the law violated the anti-discrimination provision of the Fifteenth Amendment.[7] Next the state legislature authorized the state central committee to bar Negroes from the party primaries. Again the Supreme Court ruled that an action of the state government was involved and that the law was therefore contrary to the provisions of the Fifteenth Amendment.[8] At this point the Texas leadership finally understood its problem. Without further action by the legislature, the state Democratic convention adopted a rule that forbade Negro participation in the internal elections of the Democratic Party. This time the Supreme Court refused to throw out the regulation because, said the Court, parties are like any other private group and have the authority to determine their own

---

[6] *Guinn* v. *United States*, 238 U. S. 347 (1915).

[7] *Nixon* v. *Herndon*, 273 U. S. 536 (1927).

[8] *Nixon* v. *Condon*, 286 U. S. 73 (1932).

membership. The Fifteenth Amendment applies to state action and cannot be used to restrict the actions of private organizations.[9]

Six years after this decision, the Supreme Court once more examined the nature of the primaries. This time the case involved not Negro voting but an alleged fraud in the conduct of the Democratic primary in Louisiana. The Court held that federal corrupt practices legislation applied in primary elections in which members of Congress were being nominated. Primaries, according to this more realistic decision, are an integral part of the election process. They were public not private affairs and the states— in this instance Louisiana—recognized this fact by financing and regulating the primaries.[10]

It was only a matter of time until the "white primaries" would again be tested. In 1944 the Supreme Court had its next opportunity to rule on the validity of restrictions on Negro voting in the Texas Democratic Party primaries. This time the Court flatly reversed its earlier decisions. If primaries are an integral part of the election process then the state is responsible and any rules discriminating against the participation of Negroes are clearly unconstitutional.[11]

For a period after the last cited Court decision some of the southern states sought to find ways of keeping Negroes from voting in the Democratic Party primaries. South Carolina repealed all legislation dealing with primaries and argued that the Democratic nominations were then really private matters beyond the reach of the provisions of the Fourteenth and Fifteenth Amendments. The Supreme Court, however, upheld a district court ruling that, even when the state had divorced itself from the financing and regulation of the primaries, this nomination procedure was still an integral part of the election process and limited therefore by the Constitution.[12] A county in Texas resorted to a pre-primary convention at which the all-white Jaybird Democratic Association selected the nominees whose names appeared on the party's primary ballot and were later officially nominated in the primary election; the Supreme Court said that this effort to circumvent the 1944 decision was also unconstitutional.[13]

The Civil Rights Act of 1957. The Democratic Party in its 1948 platform for the first time took a strong stand for equality of peoples of all races politically, socially, and economically. This action by the national convention signified the beginning of a new era in presidential politics. The issue of civil rights is now always a major question in the quadrennial elections. It receives special emphasis because of the large Negro vote in the major industrial states with their large electoral vote. No issue has received greater

---

9 *Grovey* v. *Townsend,* 295 U. S. 45 (1935).
10 *United States* v. *Classic,* 313 U. S. 299 (1941).
11 *Smith* v. *Allwright,* 321 U. S. 649 (1944).
12 *Rice* v. *Elmore,* 333 U. S. 875 (1948).
13 *Terry* v. *Adams,* 345 U. S. 461 (1953).

attention in peacetime elections and in Congress since 1948.[14] It is, after all, an issue upon which the outcome of presidential elections may turn. Both parties are therefore anxious to appear in the forefront of the move to equalize opportunities for persons of all races.

No legislation developed until 1957. Congressional leadership had remained rather consistently in the hands of Southerners. Controversial matters that can be postponed frequently are postponed. When the issues can no longer be avoided, there is an institutional urge to compromise. Both of these things have happened in the case of civil rights legislation. It is probable that a majority of Congress favored some kind of civil rights action during at least part of the nine years after the 1948 declaration during which time there was no legislation. It is also true that this congressional majority, if it existed, did not feel so strongly on the civil rights issue that it wished to endanger normal working conditions in Congress in order to pass the needed legislation. By 1957 there was enough of a scramble between the two parties both in and out of Congress for the Negro vote that a bi-partisan majority developed which insisted that there be no further postponement of action on civil rights. At this point the compromises between various factions were worked out.

The civil rights measure that first passed the House of Representatives in 1957 gave broad powers to the Attorney General to enforce all types of civil rights measures before the federal courts. This strong measure was unacceptable to the southern delegates who recognized that some legislation was inevitable but who felt certain that they could block extreme measures. In the Senate, where the Judiciary Committee was by-passed, a moderate bill was passed which curbed the powers of the Attorney General. The Senate version also provided for jury trial in contempt cases.

A conference committee of the two houses then hammered out a measure that was acceptable to both houses. The final version provided for:

> (1) a civil rights commission which would investigate charges of denial of voting rights because of race or color and would also study all aspects of the matter of "equal protection" as provided for in the Fourteenth Amendment.
> (2) a civil rights division in the Department of Justice to be headed by an Assistant Attorney General.[15]
> (3) authority for the Attorney General to seek a court order to enforce those sections of the act forbidding any attempt to interfere with an individual's right to vote.
> (4) a fine of $1000 and six months imprisonment for violation of the act. If the fine levied were $300 or less and the jail sentence 45 days or less the judge could take action by himself. If the sentence were greater than the above figures then the defendant could demand a new trial before

---

14 See Chapter 11 for a further analysis of the importance of civil rights as an issue in presidential politics.

15 A civil rights division had been created earlier by President Franklin D. Roosevelt, but this new division had congressional authorization.

a jury. Furthermore, anyone who was 21 years old, a citizen, capable of reading, writing and understanding English, who was not barred because of a conviction for a crime, and who was not mentally deficient must be allowed to serve on juries in such cases.

Report of the Civil Rights Commission. The Civil Rights Commission, which was composed of three northern and three southern leaders, heard complaints of attempted discrimination against voters because of race. It also examined the problems of education and housing. In September 1959 the Commission issued a long report describing its findings and making recommendations for new legislation. The Commission divided three to three on a proposed amendment which would have prevented states from restricting voting of any citizen on any grounds other than age, residence, or imprisonment at the time of registration. The three southern members refused to support the proposal saying that the Constitution already includes enough authority "to deal with denials of the right to vote by reason of race, color, religion or national origin." Five members of the Commission proposed legislation which would authorize the President to name temporary federal registrars to register voters for congressional and presidential elections in those areas where it had been proved that citizens were regularly barred because of race or color. John S. Battle, a former governor of Virginia, was the lone dissenter on this issue.[16]

The Commission's study suggested that the fairness of the registrars of voters in the South has determined to a large extent the degree of racial equality allowed in a particular area. The registrars themselves have tended to reflect the views of the majority of the white leaders of the local community.[17] Roughly twenty-five per cent of the Negro citizens of the South vote in national elections, but this group is not evenly distributed throughout that section. The heaviest Negro registration and voting is in the larger urban areas. It is heavier where northerners have moved in large numbers. In a state like Louisiana the heaviest Negro voting is in the southern, French-Catholic sections and the lightest Negro voting is in the rural, northern non-Catholic sections of the state.[18] In several southern states the registrars were instructed to purge their voting lists of persons who failed to meet even minor technical requirements of the law. Actually, as the Supreme Court was to imply in throwing out Louisiana and Georgia action, the instructions to check on violations of the law were really instructions to discriminate against Negroes who could, fairly or unfairly, be excluded from voting.

---

16 The five proponents of this proposal were: John A. Hannah, President of Michigan State University; the Rev. Theodore M. Hesburgh, President of Notre Dame University; George M. Johnson, former dean of the Howard University Law School; Robert G. Storey, former dean of Southern Methodist University Law School; and Doyle E. Carlton, former governor of Florida.

17 *Report of the Civil Rights Commission,* p. 88, 1959.

18 See the interesting essay by John H. Fenton and Kenneth N. Vines "Negro Registration in Louisiana," *American Political Science Review,* Vol. LI, pp. 704-713, Sept. 1957.

Official figures of Negro registration and voting are not completely up-to-date nor completely accurate. According to the Civil Rights Commission, however, "Racial disparities in voting appear to be wider in Mississippi than in any other state." Unofficial figures for Mississippi show that less than four per cent of the total Negro population of voting age is registered. By contrast, in six southern states—Arkansas, Florida, Georgia, Louisiana, North Carolina and Texas—more than 25 per cent is registered. In Florida and Texas nearly 40 per cent is registered.[19]

THE 1960 CIVIL RIGHTS ACT

The 1960 measure authorized the federal courts to name voting referees who could register Negroes in those districts in which discrimination against them had been proven. Prior to the appointment of the referees, the Department of Justice must have sued under the Civil Rights Act of 1957 for a court order to require the registration of persons who had been disqualified by voting officials on grounds of race. Next, the Justice Department must ask for a finding by the court of a "pattern or practice" of discrimination against Negro voting. After this finding the federal judge may appoint the referee who has authority to register for voting not only the Negroes whose cases began the suit but all of those in the area who are qualified to vote under state law but who were refused the opportunity to register after the court's finding of discrimination. A second provision required that all registration and voting records in elections of national officials must be kept for 22 months. This latter provision was necessitated by the failure of some registrars to produce records for the Civil Rights Commission under the 1957 law. The other provisions of the law are not related to voting. The 1960 act is more cumbersome than the proposal made by the Commission, but it was perhaps all that could have been secured at the time.

THE POLL TAX AMENDMENT AND THE 1964 CIVIL RIGHTS ACT

Early in 1964 South Dakota became the thirty-eighth state to ratify the Twenty-fourth Amendment to the Constitution. The amendment bars the payment of any tax as a prerequisite for voting. At the time of passage only five states still had a poll tax requirement: Alabama, Arkansas, Mississippi, Texas, and Virginia. The rate of voting in Texas and Virginia was among the highest in the South, so the repeal may have been primarily a symbol of national support of democracy. Other action was needed to actually increase the Negro vote.

An important part of that action was taken when Congress passed the

---

19 The Commission found no discrimination in Arkansas, Texas, Oklahoma, and Virginia.

Civil Rights Act of 1964. On the voting side, the act provided that there could be no unequal application of registration procedures or any rejection of registrations simply because of minor errors. The law states that the fact of a sixth-grade education shall be considered to meet any literacy requirements for voting. Further, it requires that such tests be in writing and that the tests given to any person and his answers shall be made available on request. The Attorney-General may enter the case on behalf of the potential voter.

The law further provides that the Census Bureau is to compile registration and voting statistics based on race, color, and national origin if the Civil Rights Commission so requests. The Bureau may not ask questions about political affiliation. A possible, but unlikely, use of such material would be to reduce representation from discriminating states as allowed under the Fourteenth Amendment.

The Civil Rights Act, which was passed through the efforts of northern Democrats and Republicans, included in the nonvoting sections two important items. Public accommodations such as restaurants and hotels must be open to the public without discrimination. The other major addition was the provision against discrimination in employment. This prohibition, however, applies only to industries with substantial numbers of workers.

THE VOTING AGE

During the early days of World War II there was much agitation for lowering the voting age to include those who were eligible to be drafted. Various slogans were coined to suggest that those who were old enough to fight were also old enough to vote. Georgia actually did lower the voting age in 1943 to include persons who were eighteen years of age.[20] Kentucky has since joined Georgia in reducing the age requirement to eighteen. Alaska demands that the potential voter be nineteen years old. President Eisenhower twice proposed a constitutional amendment which would give the vote to eighteen-year-olds, but Congress failed to act on the White House suggestion.

NON-VOTING

Much effort has been given to extending the suffrage so that voting will be the right of every adult American. Still, it has been stated that Americans are less interested in voting than the peoples of any other democratic nation. Only about 66 per cent of the persons of voting age cast votes in the 1960 presidential election. In other words, just over 69,000,000 of an estimated 104,000,000 adult citizens voted in that year. The figure of 66 per

---

[20] Franklin L. Burdette, "Lowering the Voting Age in Georgia," *South Atlantic Quarterly*, XLIV, 300-307, July 1945.

cent compares most unfavorably with the figures for the democratic countries of western Europe and elsewhere.

The American Heritage Foundation, however, asserts that these figures
are grossly misleading. Election laws in this country are state laws. A citizen
loses his opportunity to vote if he moves from one state to another during
an election year. That is, he gives up his voting right in one state by moving, but he has not lived long enough in the second state to acquire citizenship there. Those who live in the District of Columbia were without the vote.
The Foundation believed that more than 19,500,000 adults were excluded
from voting in 1960 for various legal reasons. The number of eligible voters,
then, was really only about 84,000,000 instead of the announced 104,000,000.
This means that roughly 81 per cent, not 66 per cent, of the eligible voters
turned out to vote for major party candidates.[21] This figure is below the
percentage in many countries but it is not nearly so bad as the one normally
listed.

Why do eligible voters stay at home on election day? The reasons are
varied. Some feel there is no difference between the two major parties and
so there is no point in making an artificial choice. Others feel that one vote
out of 69,000,000 makes no difference. Still others are apparently satisfied
with the way in which the government is being run and therefore see no
need to cast a ballot.

While noting other causes, The Report of the President's Commission
on Registration and Voting Participation, issued in 1963, emphasized the
importance of legal and administrative causes of low voter turnout. The
Commission, headed by Richard M. Scammon, pointed to registration
systems and residence requirements as among the culprits.

SUMMARY

The extension of the franchise in the United States from fewer than
half of the white male population to most persons of all races has been
the result of at least two significant factors. The ideals of democracy provided a context within which to argue the need for expanding the suffrage.
At the same time there has been a continuing awareness of the political
consequences of this expansion. Today the interest of politicians in extending the suffrage to Negroes in the South grows out of the belief of politicians
that all adult citizens regardless of sex or race should have an equal right to
vote. Politicians are equally conscious of the great interest of Negroes everywhere in the country in the extension of voting rights to the southern Negro.
The politicians are also aware of the strategic voting power of the Negroes
in the major industrial states with the largest electoral votes. The votes of

21 The American Heritage Foundation figures are quoted in Brendan Byrne, *Let's
Modernize Our Horse-and-Buggy Election Laws!* (Washington, Conn.: The Center for
Information on America, 1961).

urban minorities can easily determine the outcome of presidential elections and neither party wishes to be tagged with a label of racial bias that might destroy the chances of victory in the campaign for the White House. Consequently there is pressure on practical and on theoretical and moral grounds for civil rights legislation that would prevent the states from inhibiting or blocking Negro registration or voting in the South.

The pressure on Congress from the major party leaders outside the South and the commitment of congressmen to democracy led Congress to pass Civil Rights acts in 1957, 1960, and 1964. The first did more to clarify the extent of the problem than it did to give the vote to more of the disfranchised southern Negroes. The 1960 act, based on the findings of the Civil Rights Commission established under the earlier law, provided for a method of federal enforcement of voting rights through the federal court appointed "referees," who could force registration where Negroes proved that the state registrars of voters had discriminated against citizens because of race or color. The 1964 act provides for equal application of registration procedures. It also says that a sixth-grade schooling is proof of literacy.

Non-voting has sometimes been thought of as a serious problem in this country. The percentage of non-voters among Americans who are 21 or older is higher than the percentage in many other democratic countries. Recent research suggests that this non-voting, while perhaps partially the result of indifference, is in part the consequence of state legislation requiring that the voter meet certain technical qualifications before he can cast a ballot. If the various state laws which make voting difficult are taken into account the total number of Americans who participate in a presidential election is respectable although lower than in most other democracies.

BIBLIOGRAPHIC NOTE

Materials on the suffrage are to be found in all of the leading textbooks on political parties. The student who wishes a brief history of the extension of voting rights will find good coverage in V. O. Key, Jr., *Politics, Parties, and Pressure Groups* (4th ed., New York: Thomas Y. Crowell Company, 1958); Howard R. Penniman, *Sait's American Parties and Elections* (5th ed., New York: Appleton-Century-Crofts, Inc., 1952); and William Goodman, *The Two-Party System in the United States* (2nd ed., Princeton: D. Van Nostrand Co., 1960).

Longer histories of the suffrage for those who wish greater detail include: Albert E. McKinley, *The Suffrage Franchise in the Thirteen Colonies in America* (Boston: Ginn and Co., 1905) and Kirk H. Porter, *A History of Suffrage in the United States* (Chicago: University of Chicago Press, 1918). Obviously the latter is dated, but it is still the best volume for the development of voting rights in the United States in the years prior to 1918. A less historical and more analytical work is Dudley O. McGovney, *The American Suffrage Medley* (Chicago: University of Chicago, 1949).

Detailed studies of specific facets of the history of the suffrage movement in the United States are also available. Leaders of the women suffrage movement published, over a period of nearly a quarter of a century, six volumes on the history of the struggle to gain the vote for women.

Efforts to gain complete suffrage equality for Negroes are still being made. A number of studies are to be found which discuss the problems of expanding Negro suffrage, the attempts to prevent that expansion, and the methods used by both the exponents and opponents of Negro suffrage in the South. Among these books are: Paul Lewinson, *Race, Class and Party* (New York: Oxford University Press, 1932); C. S. Magnum, Jr., *The Legal Status of the Negro* (Chapel Hill, N. C.: University of North Carolina Press, 1940); V. O. Key, Jr., *Southern Politics* (New York: Alfred A. Knopf, 1949); and Hugh D. Price, *The Negro in Southern Politics: A Chapter of Florida History* (New York: New York University Press, 1957) are among the most pertinent. Of special value for a recent picture of some of the voting problems of Negroes are the various voting and registration studies of the Commission on Civil Rights. The 1961 report includes a quite complete state-by-state summary.

A full description of the present state laws on voting and registration is in Constance E. Smith, *Voting and Election Laws* (New York: Oceana Publications, Inc., 1960).

Indispensable to the student of politics who needs election statistics for presidential and congressional elections since World War II are the five volumes compiled by Richard M. Scammon, *America Votes*. (The first two volumes were published by The Macmillan Company in 1956 and 1958. The last three volumes were published by the University of Pittsburgh Press in 1960, 1962, and 1964).

Many of the books dealing with voting behavior devote considerable space to the reasons why citizens either come out to vote or stay home. A pioneering work, Charles E. Merriam and Harold F. Gosnell, *Non-Voting* (Chicago: University of Chicago Press, 1924) explored the problem in the Chicago area. Other books have dealt with the question of non-voting in less detail. It is possible here to list only a few: Robert E. Lane, *Political Life* (Glencoe, Ill.: The Free Press, 1959); Heinz Eulau, Samuel J. Eldersveld, and Morris Janowitz, *Political Behavior* (Glencoe, Ill.: The Free Press, 1956); and Angus Campbell, Philip E. Converse, Warren E. Miller, and Donald E. Stokes, *The American Voter* (New York: John Wiley and Sons, 1960).

President Kennedy appointed a Commission on Registration and Voting Participation under the chairmanship of Richard M. Scammon, Director of the Bureau of the Census. The Report of that Commission examines the various legal, political, and social reasons for non-voting and recommends means of increasing participation. The Report of the Commission was published in 1963.

8

Public Opinion and Pressure Groups

Since the time of Aristotle, political theorists have concerned themselves in one way or another with public opinion. Most of them have commented on the power of public opinion in the community. The suggestion that the voice of the people was the voice of God was apparently first put forth during the medieval period. Machiavelli, Hobbes, Hume, and others spoke of its importance.

While many writers mentioned public opinion in their works, few of them stated precisely what it was that they had in mind. Some of them used the term to mean the will of all people on a public issue. Others used it to mean the will of the majority of the citizens of the state. Some thought of public opinion as sovereign in the community, while others spoke of it merely as transitory and illusory. Political thinkers, however, continued to use the term without defining it, apparently thinking that their readers would divine a meaning from the context of their writings.

Detailed studies of public opinion, its content and its formation, have been reserved for the last thirty or forty years. These studies sometimes tell us in elaborate terms what we already know. On other occasions the studies have helped us to understand political and social phenomena better.

Most men agree with the views of those with whom they associate regularly in various formal and informal groups. Certain of the interest groups to which men belong are organized and have headquarters in the capitals of the states and in Washington. These groups seek by various means to influence those aspects of public policy which are of concern to members of their groups. Their ability to affect governmental decisions and the means by which they work to attain their ends are among the most interesting problems studied by political scientists.

PUBLIC OPINION AND INTEREST GROUPS

Definitions. Both words in the phrase "public opinion" need to be defined. "Opinion" is used simply to mean the belief of a person or group of persons on any issue. Early writers in the field often used the word to imply that beliefs were based exclusively upon the reasoning of individuals. Today most students of public opinion understand that many views are based upon rational consideration of a problem, but they also accept the fact that many views on problems may be the result of prejudice, group membership, or mere accident.

The word "public" excludes those things which are private in the sense that the parents' opinions about whether Johnny should play tennis or go swimming are private. What then constitutes a public? Is it the people of a nation, a state, a city, or the world? Or is it as small as membership of the Parent Teachers Association of the local elementary school? The answer seems to be that it may be any of these. For the question of buying new playground equipment at the elementary school the PTA may be the public. For municipal taxes the city may be the public. Some issues have a world wide public.

Public opinion as a phrase is used in several ways. We hear politicians say that they have public opinion behind them. What they mean is that a majority of those who hold views on a particular subject are in agreement with them. Sometimes the words are intended to refer to the views which are held by a majority in the entire society. For this book, however, the word means the aggregate of all the views on any particular subject to be found in whatever audience we are concerned with. Public opinion is expressed most clearly in elections. Public opinion of American voters in 1956 was divided roughly 57 per cent for Eisenhower and 43 per cent for Stevenson. If we included all adult citizens who could have participated in the 1956 election, the percentages would be lower and the percentage of those who didn't care or who failed to vote for some other reason would be quite high. The aggregate of the opinions of all those in the particular public which we are examining constitutes public opinion.

Public opinion in a democracy. Subject to certain relatively minor limitations, citizens in a democracy are free to hold and to express almost any view or opinion on public issues. If the democracy is to remain healthy, however, the vast majority of the citizens of that democracy must be in agreement on certain fundamental characteristics of the society in which they live. A democratic society in which large numbers of citizens question its basic institutions and its fundamental beliefs is a society that is heading toward chaos and possible revolution.

In the United States there is no large group of people with serious doubt about the wisdom of retaining the present three branches of government. Very few question the wisdom of free elections or refuse to accept the results of those elections. The acceptance of these and other basic institutions and beliefs means that there is a consensus on these subjects; and that the democracy of the United States may, consequently, be expected to continue without serious internal threat. Because of the consensus on the most fundamental of issues, the political leaders and others are free to hold widely divergent views on almost all other subjects. Strongly held views on these lesser subjects, which may still be very important matters, do not

A TYPICAL NEW ENGLAND TOWN HALL—BEDFORD, NEW HAMPSHIRE

threaten the foundations of the country because the basic principles of our democracy are accepted by all contestants.

In a democratic society a citizen is encouraged to express his views in certain formal ways. He may take part in town meetings; he may vote in elections to express his views on candidates and issues; and he may appear before legislative committees and administrative boards to urge the adoption of particular courses of governmental action. In a democracy there are also many informal means of indicating one's views. Citizens may organize and speak to the law makers and administrators through the group leaders. They may as individuals go to see members of Congress or write to them. In a pluralistic society a citizen may join literally hundreds of groups to press his views. To a certain extent ordinary citizens may use the mass media of communication for the expression of their views. Political parties welcome any who wish to join and work.

The problem in a democracy is often not one of finding opportunities for expressing one's opinions. Rather, the problem is the failure of citizens to take advantage of the abundance of outlets for their opinions.

Public opinion in totalitarian countries. Public opinion is important even in totalitarian regimes. To the degree that the leadership of a totalitarian country feels that it must have the support of various segments of the public, the leadership will take their desires and opinions into account in making public policies. Communist leaders, for example, have always opposed religions of all kinds. When the Stalinist regime felt that it needed the wholehearted support of the Russian people during the second world war, however, religious freedom was allowed for the first time since the earliest days of the regime.

Totalitarian leaders, while granting some concessions to particular groups, also make it clear to all groups that primary loyalty must be to the dictatorship itself. Because the communists have always been aware of the important role which intellectuals have played in the expansion of the party and Soviet influence, the leadership has sought the support of the artists, scholars, and scientists. Novelists, musicians, scientists, and other groups of intellectuals have had the finest housing and special treatment of many kinds in order to buy their assistance for the regime. At the same time the Communist Party leaders have punished those who have refused to bow completely to the party's will.

STUDYING PUBLIC OPINION

Development of surveys. The scientific study of opinions or attitudes on public issues dates back only a few decades. In earlier days, "straw polls" on public support of candidates were taken by newspapers and magazines. The editors inserted coupons in each issue inviting their readers to send in their "votes" on the competing candidates for various offices. Whether the results of the "straw polls" approximated or failed to approximate the election results was purely a matter of accident because the readers who took the trouble to send in the coupons were not a cross section of the public which later voted in the general election. Some groups in the population did not read the paper or magazine and most of those who read it did not fill out the questionnaire. The "straw polls" sometimes added zest to the campaign, but were of little value in predicting the outcome of the election.[1]

---

[1] For several presidential elections the *Literary Digest* predicted elections fairly accurately on the basis of such straw polls. However, the *Digest* was so wrong in its predictions in 1936 that the magazine was discredited and went out of existence. The *Digest* was wrong because its sample did not include a cross section of the voters.

The present day scientific polls begin with a basic assumption about attitudes and voting behavior. It is assumed that people of similar background, income, religion, sex, and so on divide in roughly the same way on public issues whether the views of 100 or 1,000,000 are checked. If a small group that is fully representative of the larger group can be questioned, the responses indicate the responses that the larger group would give if all of its members were asked the same questions. In actual practice the polling organizations do not expect to be able to get an accurate cross section of the entire adult population by checking with only 500 persons. In order to reduce their margin of error they seek the views of 1500 to 3000 persons. With a group of this size they can average about a two per cent error in estimating elections. That error can still allow the prediction of victory for the losing candidate, but in most elections it means that the polls will correctly name the winner.

Selecting the sample. The interviewing of a *representative* sample of the potential voters is crucial for accurate election predicting. To secure that representative sample the polling organizations select persons in a mathematically random fashion. They draw the names of cities, towns, townships and so on across the country. Within these units, smaller units such as blocks are selected, also in a random fashion. Within a block, houses or apartments are chosen in the same manner. If the houses are really selected at random, the persons interviewed should be a cross section of the total population. If the numbers of his interviewees in each category of income etc. are proportionate to the numbers in these categories for the whole population, as established by the Census Bureau, the study director can be satisfied that his sample was representative. The interviewer attempts to determine the income, education, religion, and occupation as well as the opinions of his interviewees on the subject in question. He can feel confident that his results will be similar to election results if the two are held at the same time.

Time may be an important factor in the accuracy of the polls. Some studies have pointed out, that most people in most elections make up their minds several months in advance. It is not always true of enough people, however, to make a September prediction reliable in November. In 1948, for example, the major polls showed Dewey well ahead of Truman in the presidential race. The polls stopped checking sometime before the election. On election day Truman won by a narrow popular vote margin. Post election studies indicated that a fairly large number of persons changed their positions during the last week or so of the campaign. The post-election studies also indicated that the samples were not fully accurate cross sections of the population. Since 1948 the major polling organizations have refined

---

Millions of workers who supported Franklin D. Roosevelt for re-election were unrepresented among the readers of the magazine, since they did not have telephones and automobiles, they were not included among those polled by the magazine.

their sampling procedures and also conducted their polls later in the campaigns. In fact, one polling organization now conducts its final interviews as late as the Saturday preceding the election.

Influence of polls on elections. There are those who raise serious question about the influence of the polls on the outcome of the elections. These people suggest that, by predicting the victory of one candidate, the polls can start a bandwagon movement toward that candidate on the ground that every one likes to be with a winner. There seems to be no evidence of such an effect on the voters. Indeed, the failure of the polls to predict the outcome in 1948 seems proof enough that they cannot start a bandwagon movement. It could be more easily argued that those supporting the candidate who is behind will redouble their efforts when the polls predict a close election.

In predicting presidential elections the polls may go wrong even with generally excellent samples for at least two reasons. In very close elections the allowable two per cent margin of error can make the difference between victory and defeat in the popular vote. Secondly, the sample is a national sample, but the votes that count in a presidential election are the electoral votes from each state. It is possible that while accurately predicting a popular victory for one candidate the electoral vote may go for the opposition candidate because of the distribution of the popular votes among the states. The Gallup Poll, or the American Institute of Public Opinion, used to predict the electoral vote by predicting the outcome in each state. The Institute no longer predicts by states because that portion of an adequate national sample that is drawn from any given state is much too small to be reliable in predicting state results. To reach the same accuracy at the state level requires almost as large a sample as is used in a national poll. Such an operation would be very costly.

Non-election polling. Polls or surveys are conducted on many questions other than elections. Businesses make surveys to discover the reception of existing or potential products. Parties and public officials seek to discover attitudes on all kinds of public issues. The military forces made surveys of the troops to discover what troop reaction is to existing practices or would be to projected changes in those practices. In some of these matters a high degree of accuracy is needed. In others, even a report that allows a margin of ten per cent for error is useful when the alternative is sheer guess.

The result of a poll on military, or labor, or economic, or farm, or health problems is not a sure guide for the member of Congress who desires to carry out his constituents' will. Quite apart from the question of the degree to which he should be guided by the collective views of the people in the district which he represents, there are problems in interpreting opinion polls. A congressman cannot tell with what intensity a constituent holds a view. A doctor may be against a national health program and a young voter who has yet to pay his first major bill for illness may favor the program. The poll does not indicate what priority the young voter will give the health bill when making up his mind in the ensuing election. Nor can the poll tell the legislator whether those who are for changes in legislation are the so-called public opinion moulders or whether they are the rank-in-file whose opinions are influenced by the views of opinion moulders. Men's attitudes are influenced by the groups to which they belong, but the polls cannot tell the congressmen which of the respondents to a questionnaire are the ones who help form the opinions of the various groups represented in the interviews. The polls are not totally lacking in this type of information, but they do not provide much guidance for a congressman.[2]

Opinion polls on elections deal with people in one of the very few circumstances in which each man acts as an individual and each casts a ballot that has the same effect as every other ballot cast. In matters of policy making men do not act in the same way nor is the effect of their action equal. One man believes that foreign aid should be given in small quantities to those countries that have cooperated with the United States on all anti-communist fronts. He speaks to no one about his views and is more concerned with the cost-of-living problem in this country. A second man believes that we should seek to develop the economies of all non-communist countries regardless of their degree of cooperation with the United States. This man writes books. He speaks to meetings of the Foreign Policy Association. He helps to organize a Committee to Save America by Giving Aid to Under-developed Nations. He writes letters to the editor and he is interviewed on a major television program. In the opinion poll his voice is no different from the voices of others interviewed, but the congressman needs to know that this man may affect his future political career in a fashion very different from that of our first interviewee. This second man can and will organize support for our congressman or for his opponent depending upon how the congressman votes on the foreign legislation.[3]

The polls on issues are followed by people who have the responsibility for making state and national policy. Most congressmen are anxious for more information, however, than the polls can provide on public attitudes. He must get this further information from the letters to his office and from his trips back home to talk with political leaders and with those whom he knows are opinion leaders. The chances are good that he pays more attention, and rightly so, to the politicians, the opinion leaders, and the letters which are written by individuals with strongly held views than he does to the opinion survey results.

---

2 See the article by Herbert Blumer, "The Mass, The Public, and Public Opinion," reprinted in his book, *New Outline of the Principles of Sociology* (1946), in *Reader in Public Opinion and Communication,* edited by Bernard Berelson and Morris Janowitz, (Glencoe, Ill.: Free Press, 1953), pp. 43-49.

3 Blumer, *op. cit.*

MEDIA OF COMMUNICATION

Ideas and opinions are conveyed in many ways. In dictatorial nations the only means of securing information and views other than those of the regime itself is through rumor. We are told that this medium of communication is a great source of difficulty to the ruling clique. This may be true in a run-of-the-mill dictatorship which has not reached the ruthlessness of a totalitarian regime.[4] In the totalitarian regimes which are based on terror and the omnipresent secret police the rumor may have less importance in influencing opinions. The rumors may actually be an instrument of the state to confuse and counter other rumors.

In a free society, the individual is important as a medium of communication; but the major media are the newspapers, radio, and television. The three media influence opinions, but the difference in their nature means that they affect opinion in diverse ways.

Newspapers. The oldest of the major media of communication is the newspaper. Today it is still probably the most important source of news and the greatest influence on opinions about public issues. The newspaper is also probably more important than radio and television in its effect on policy makers in the national and state capitals.

The better newspapers provide full coverage of the major news stories concerned with public issues and party candidates. They provide stories on state and local affairs in considerably greater detail than either television or radio can devote to such news on a continuing basis. In addition to the relatively objective news stories provided by each paper's reporters and the press associations, the newspapers also comment on the news in their editorials. Further comments are written by local and syndicated columnists who frequently have large followings among the readers.

The extent of the influence of the newspapers on public opinions is by no means clear. We know that the great majority of newspapers can oppose a candidate and that he can still win by a tremendous electoral majority. Franklin D. Roosevelt in his greatest victory in 1936 was opposed by more than three-quarters of the nations' press. Huey P. Long was consistently opposed by the newspapers of Louisiana yet he just as consistently won elections. This failure of newspapers to effect the election of a single candidate, however, should not be taken as the sole basis for judging the power of the press over public opinion. At the same time that most newspapers were editorially opposing Roosevelt and Long, they were devoting many columns of news to the activities of the two men. These stories were undoubtedly important in developing majorities opposed to the editorial posi-

---

4 See S. M. Lipset, *Political Man* (Garden City, N. Y.: Doubleday and Company, 1960), Chapter 5 for an interesting and useful discussion of this problem.

tion of the papers. If the papers had subjected either man to the silent treatment, his majority might well have been reduced. Newspaper editors and publishers, however, are sufficiently committed to the full presentation of the news that most of them cannot refuse to report the political news. The reporters on a majority of the major papers are likely to be Democrats and liberals even though most publishers are Republicans.

Perhaps the greatest effect the newspaper has on public opinion is that of strengthening the readers in positions already held. Walter Lippmann is accepted as an oracle by some readers, while others prefer the writings of David Lawrence. Probably only a small percentage of readers regularly look at both columns even when both are available. Lazarsfeld and others have demonstrated fairly conclusively that most politically conscious citizens read the papers, but that most of them are selective in their reading. They read those writers whose views coincide with their own and ignore most of the other writers. The same would hold true of editorials and to a lesser extent of cartoons. The latter are so simple and so quickly observed that most readers of the editorial page also look at the cartoons. They are probably not much influenced by cartoons, although they may be amused if they agree with the views of the cartoonist.

Newspapers and public policy making. The newspapers from home plus two or three of the nation's major papers are regularly read by members of Congress, the White House, and the bureaucracy. In the absence of indications to the contrary, members of government are likely to treat the newspapers as representative of public opinion. Still it is difficult to decide how much influence the papers have. No definitive studies have been made, and it is doubtful that they will be made soon. Certainly there is no simple relation between the officials' reading of papers and their views on issues. On the other hand, except on those matters where the views of the home folks are clear, it is difficult to avoid the belief that the daily reading of a couple of newspapers by almost every member of Congress is not totally without effect on their collective outlook on policy.

Radio and television. Radio and television provide news, but each is primarily an instrument for entertainment. Either medium can give the public news faster than the newspapers. Over the past thirty years the newspaper extras, which once were the sources of spot news, have largely disappeared because radio has already told the basic story. People buy the newspapers for the details, but they no longer buy the papers for the initial story.

Both radio and television can give the consumer more of the personality of the political figure than the newspapers can. The news story or columnist's characterization may be accurate, but there is a middle-man whose views intrude upon the views of the ultimate consumers. Radio, and to a greater extent television, allow the consumer to make his own evaluation of the character of the candidate. However false one's judgment, a man's voice or his facial expressions are more convincing than the descriptions that appear in tomorrow's news columns.

Television is more powerful as a medium of communication than radio. It has several advantages. Television is more demanding than radio. No one can read or do household chores while watching a program on his TV set. He must watch or he may miss the point. What he sees may so interest him that he wishes to read about his experience in the paper just as he wishes to read about the baseball game that he attended the day before. Furthermore, the television program can give the viewer a sense of participation that neither radio nor the newspaper can provide. Much of Kefauver's early attraction to the voters was related to their interest in his televised crime investigation. Radio once gave its followers an alternative to the newspaper's interpretation. Television now gives not only an alternative; it also provides a standard by which the viewer can judge the validity of the newspaper reports. After all, the television camera brings the candidate into the living room of the viewer and it shows him more of a political convention than he is likely to see even if he attends the convention itself. Neither radio nor the newspaper can offer as much.

Television has the same advantages and disadvantages that a photograph has over a painting. It can show the bare factual situation, but it has difficulty portraying the nuances of the total situation. Radio has all of the same difficulties with none of the advantages of television. The newspapers, by contrast, can tell the basic story while at the same time presenting an interpretation of the events which the viewer has seen.

INTEREST GROUPS

Basis of groups. The opinions of most men are not likely to be very different from the opinions of their friends and neighbors or the people they know in the miners' union or the Union League Club. Studies of voting behavior suggest that three-quarters of the voters support the same party their parents supported and that roughly the same proportion of those in a particular economic group support the same party. Seymour Lipset has pointed out that the Democratic Party receives the support of a great majority of organized and unorganized workers. Upper income groups tend to support the Republican Party by approximately the same margin. Lipset notes, however, that enough of the members of each class support the opposition party so that neither can afford to become openly a class party. Since each party must seek to retain its support in the class which primarily backs the other party, each party is more moderate than the articulate dogmatists in their ranks would like. The Republicans cannot slip too far from the center without destroying their current claim on the labor votes. By the same token, the ultra liberals in the Democratic Party cannot dominate the party because the leadership does not wish to drive the middle class members from its ranks. Each party seeks to please the majority of its supporters without alienating the minority within its midst. Both parties seek the aid of the same marginal or independent voters, a fact which again drives the two parties to common ground.[5]

It is probably safe to suggest that in any democratic country with a stable two party system, or even a multi-party system where two parties serve as the core for possible coalition governments, the two major parties are never far apart in their domestic programs. The labels and the myths that surround the British Labour and Conservative parties sometimes lead us to think of them as vastly different in their programs. However observers are coming more and more to see that two parties really offer the voters much the same program. Neither is willing to take the chance of isolating itself from the uncommitted voters or from the uncharacteristic supporters within its ranks. With the decline of dogmatic Marxist views within the social democratic parties on the continent a similar development has taken place, although it has not yet perhaps gone as far as in Great Britain.

Groups and men. In the United States most men are members of many groups which influence their actions and thoughts. Men seek out groups that hold views similar to their own. If a man is part of a group of which the majority differs with his views, he either leaves the group, becomes inactive, or changes his views so that they are more in conformity with the views of the others. Men are individuals who think for themselves, but they prefer to conform with the pattern of those with whom they associate most frequently and most continuously. We find that most families vote together for the same candidates.[6] To do otherwise would create tensions within the family which may be disturbing to one or more of its members. In less intimate groups the pressure for conformity is less demanding but nonetheless very strong. It is an unusual person who is closely bound to a group and at the same time actively and frequently disagrees with the positions held by the rest of the articulate members of that group.

A man may be a member of many groups each of which represents only one small facet of his life or his views. He may join the American Political Science Association to satisfy the requirements of his profession and his own interest in the theoretical and technical problems of government and politics. He is part of a particular church because of his religious beliefs, but he does not look upon the church as the source of guidance on the problems of political thought and organization. He joins a country club to satisfy his wife's longing for society, his children's hope for acceptable dates, and his own wish to play golf on a course that is not crowded. He works for a po-

---

[5] *Ibid.*, Chapter 7.

[6] Herbert McCloskey and Harold E. Dahlgren, "Primary Group Influence on Party Loyalty," *American Political Science Review*, Vol. LII, September 1959, p. 757.

litical party because of his general beliefs on public issues which he may have developed as a result of training by his parents or because of the preferences of professors of an earlier period in his life. He may be a member of five or twenty-five other groups for other purposes. He may be active only in his church or his professional society. He may disagree with the views of the leaders or members of most of the other organizations, but so long as these views do not come in conflict with his views it doesn't much matter. His golf game is no better and no worse for political or economic differences with members of the country club. They simply don't intrude on his game and therefore on his reason for being a member of the club. He cannot be equally active in all groups. The less active he is in a group the less difference it makes to him whether he is in agreement with his fellow members.

Groups and pressure politics. For the student of politics man's reaction to group life is important. More important in understanding the making of public policy, however, are the answers to the other questions. How do groups which seek to make or affect policy operate? To what extent do they represent their membership? How effective are these groups in making governmental decisions? Most of the groups which men join are not consciously and overtly seeking to make public policy; they are concerned with different questions. Thousands of other organizations, however, try to mold policy on a single issue or on a number of issues. The groups that seek to influence policy are the ones of most interest to the political scientist.

How pressure groups operate. Any group which seriously wishes to affect policy must locate the best spot to implement its wishes. The answer may be different for different societies and different kinds of groups within the same society. In a nation in which political parties are dominated by their leaders who are in complete control of the legislative body, an organization must work to influence the party leaders. If parties are loosely organized and policy is made in the legislative body with each member of that body something of a law unto himself, the group is better advised to turn some of its attention to the individual members of the legislature.

Wise leaders of any interest group seeking to affect public policy must assess the group's assets and weaknesses. They must analyze the character of the agencies for the enactment and administration of policy. Having done these things, they must choose the grounds upon which to make their stand and the means by which they hope to accomplish their aims. The leaders of any organization will be successful to the degree that their judgment of the organization's strength and their choice of available avenues for the use of that strength corresponds to reality. Some groups can never hope to find the way to influence public policy. Some, by wise planning and action, can maximize rather limited strength. Some will waste great potential strength in attempting to attack the problem of policy making through the wrong channels.

A POLITICAL MEETING IN A ONE-ROOM SCHOOLHOUSE IN PENNSYLVANIA

Categories of pressure groups. In Washington alone there are more than 5,000 trade associations and other organizations interested in the policies that are formulated and administered by public bodies. In the state capitals, county seats, and municipalities there are thousands more organized interest groups. Each group is in some respects different from all others, but we cannot study or describe thousands of pressure organizations and their operations. We must, therefore, find some means of dividing them into categories. In so doing we must be aware that the categories are not all-inclusive and that they do not take into account the almost infinite variations in the form and operation of the pressure groups being categorized. Any set of categories is to a degree arbitrary in the sense that there are at least a dozen ways that the organizations can be grouped. Whatever method one chooses one must ignore certain aspects of some organizations in order to fit them into one or another of the categories.

For the purposes of this book we will set up categories based on a combination of their available funds and the size of their membership. After discussing various general categories we will discuss the targets of pressure group operations, their methods, and significant aspects of particular organizations that are among the largest or most important of the pressure groups now operating.

Simply stated then there are four categories. First, there are those organizations, like the National Association of Manufacturers (NAM), that have a relatively small membership, but either through the organization or its individual members have a relatively large amount of money that may be used to influence public attitudes and public policies. Second, there are organizations, like the National Association for the Advancement of Colored People (NAACP), which have relatively little money and a relatively large membership. Third, there are groups, which, like the AFL-CIO through its various divisions, have both a large membership and a sizeable amount of money to carry on their work of influencing public policy. And, fourth, there are those groups, like the Federation of Atomic Scientists, which are very small and have relatively little money but rely on the prestige of their membership to influence public policy.

Some groups seem to cut across these categories. For example, the American Medical Association has a fairly large membership and can, at least for particular campaigns, collect a large war chest for a policy battle. More important, the individual doctors who are the members of AMA are held in high esteem by the fellow citizens because of the nature of their expertise.

Targets of pressure group operations. Pressure groups may seek to influence public policy at any or all of at least five levels. First, they may try to influence public opinion by using the various media of communication to get their message out to the reading, listening, or watching public.[7] Second, they may seek to control the outcome of elections by actively participating in campaigns through financial contributions to political groups or by other forms of electioneering. Third, they may try to influence the content of the platforms of political parties by appearing before the platform committees or talking with candidates. Fourth, they may place their major emphasis on influencing legislation by talking with legislators, appearing at committee hearings, or by sending telegrams and letters to congressmen suggesting how they should vote on particular issues. Finally, they may try to affect the administration of laws already passed by working with government administrators or challenging administrative interpretations of the law by taking cases to the courts.

It is very rare that a pressure group confines itself to only one or two of the targets mentioned above. Perhaps in the halcyon days of the trusts and monopolies, a pressure group or even a single corporation might have felt safe in ignoring all groups except the legislatures with the thought that bribery or some other form of illegal or semi-legal action would assure the adoption of the policies they wanted. These cruder forms of influence have been largely eliminated. The pressure groups now normally try to influence public opinion, parties, legislators, and administrators. To leave any aspect of these four untouched is to risk failure in the ultimate policy objectives.

Methods of influencing the target. The methods for influencing the various targets of pressure groups must vary with the nature of the group and

---

[7] *United States* v. *Rumely,* 345 U. S. 41 (1953).

the facilities at its disposal. In order to influence public opinion the Federation of Atomic Scientists produce their own bulletin which, in addition to being read by its members, is perused by columnists and publicists who sympathize with the point of view expressed by the editors. They in turn publicize the arguments. Further, since scientists have a special, almost sacrosanct, standing in the community, the members of the Federation are interviewed by reporters and panels for newspapers and television. In other words, with very little expenditure of funds the Federation can place its arguments before the public on a more or less regular basis.

The National Association of Manufacturers can assume that many small weekly newspapers will accept their public relations handouts. They also know that many of the daily newspaper owners, publishers, and editorial writers will sympathize with and express the NAM's point of view not because of any appeal or request but because this is also the point of view of the owners, publishers and editorial writers of the newspapers. In those papers that have large circulations and perhaps influence but which do not sympathize wholeheartedly with the ideology of the NAM, there is always the possibility of buying advertising space to present a position. The NAM itself may not buy much advertising space in newspapers, but many of the related more specialized industrial associations do. Most of these groups also either publish pamphlets, subsidize books and pamphlets of sympathetic authors, or engage in some combination of the two.

The AFL-CIO and its affiliated unions produce their own papers for union members. The unions send their papers and their press releases to commentators, columnists, and reporters who agree with their outlook on public policy with the frequently justified hope that their views will be reprinted in the daily pres. Their leaders, like George Meany and Walter Reuther, are interviewed on radio and television and by reporters from the daily press. Unions also resort to advertising when the papers editorially support a position contrary to the one supported by the unions.

The National Association for the Advancement of Colored People uses some of the traditional means of presenting its views to the public. They provide speakers for meetings, issue press releases, and talk with newsmen. In addition the NAACP may create the incidents which are themselves news. It encourages negroes in the South to attempt to register to vote in states and counties where they have traditionally been denied the opportunity to vote or they urge negro families to send their children to segregated schools. The public uproar that follows such activities assures a wide discussion of the problem of racial equality. Cases which the NAACP assists in bringing to the courts grow out of these episodes and gain publicity as well as decisions. Other Negro groups work in roughly the same manner.

Administration and pressure groups. Pressure groups are sometimes helpful to legislative committees in detecting weaknesses in proposed legislation and commenting on difficulties growing out of previous laws. The groups may work closely with the administrative officials charged with the enforcement of the laws that affect their interests. Since the administrative officials sometimes want the pressure groups as allies in hearings on legislation or appropriations, they may cooperate with the pressure groups. Even if cooperation is not motivated by a desire for new laws or larger budgets, it is likely to come from the fact that there develops a community of interest between the administrative agencies and the particular private groups with which they deal. The mere fact that the private group works with the administrator creates a situation not unlike that within groups. It is simply easier to cooperate than to do battle constantly, and it may be better to solve a problem out of the courts than to risk defeat after years of effort. None of this is to suggest any conscious or unconscious wrong-doing. There is little evidence that administrators kowtow to special interests groups. Administrators enforce the laws when cases of violation are discovered.

Elections and pressure groups. When working with members of congress or parties and candidates, pressure groups are limited to working with the persons committed to their own views or neutral with respect to them. It is seldom that we can find evidence of pressure being successfully brought upon a man to vote against his strongly held convictions. Politicians, especially in the states where competition is keen, must be flexible but they need not be, and seldom are, spineless.

The greatest pressure that can be brought against a politician or a party is the threat of electoral defeat. This ultimate sanction is implied or explicitly stated by certain powerful and not so powerful interest groups

HOW PEOPLE CLASSIFY THEMSELVES POLITICALLY

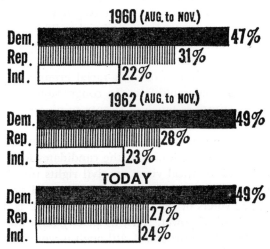

The above graph makes clear how little basic party loyalties are affected by current issues and nominees. The latest figures in the graph are for 1964 (based on Gallup Poll survey data).

when talking with party leaders and members of Congress. But how can they go about accomplishing one or the other? The method used depends upon the strength and nature of the organization. A group with a lot of money but with few members who can be activated to work in a campaign may give or withhold campaign money from the candidates who oppose them while giving it to those who support them. If, as in the case of the AFL-CIO, money can be raised and political workers can be activated, both are granted or withheld depending upon the action of the legislators. The groups with few members and little money can contribute speakers and ideas to their favorites, but otherwise are limited in their campaign work. Weakness does not always insure that the pressure group will not threaten dire consequences at the polls if congressmen vote a particular way. Unless the spokesmen for the little groups, however, can make it appear that they have correctly gauged public opinion, they are likely to have no effect on legislation.

The pressure group that has a relatively large membership but not much money must depend upon electioneering by its members or the group solidarity of its members and the persons whom it claims to represent. Not many groups of any size or wealth can claim group solidarity on most of its issues. Perhaps the outstanding example of solidarity is that between Negroes and the civil rights organizations today. By limiting its efforts primarily to civil rights and racial equality, the NAACP can claim the almost unanimous support of its own members and of the Negro race. In periods of economic depression employment and insecurity may temporarily outweigh racial equality as an issue which determines votes. In periods of prosperity, the NAACP can assert with confidence that whether it actively participates in the campaign or not most Negro voters will be concerned with candidates' views and records on civil rights. This fact may be of little importance in those states where, whatever their numbers, very few Negroes vote. In states where Negroes constitute anywhere from three to fifteen per cent of the total voting population, this racial group solidarity is of great importance to presidential candidates. In congressional districts where the Negro vote may constitute as much as twenty to ninety-five per cent of the total vote, solidarity is crucial and no candidate can today be named by his party in such districts unless his position is unreservedly favorable to strong civil rights legislation. Since, however, the candidates for Congress of both parties then will hold identical views on civil rights the election will actually turn on other matters such as economic and social programs or merely party loyalty of the voters of the district. The NAACP is nearly unique as a group with this kind of power. Even in strictly farm districts there is no such unanimity about farm programs, although it would be a foolish candidate indeed who sought election in a rural Wisconsin district on a platform of more oleomargarine for school children.

Mythical power of pressure groups. The names of a few books on pressure groups—*Government Under Pressure, The Pressure Boys,* and *American Democracy Under Pressure*—suggest how powerful some writers think these groups are and strongly hint that pressure groups are almost by nature bad. Neither is in fact true. Pressure groups may serve good or bad ends. Most of them believe, correctly or mistakenly, that they are seeking the public good. None of them is so powerful that it can control public policy over any wide area of problems or even over a narrow area for a sustained period.[8] Except for groups seeking the most insignificant legislation, no one can hope to present proposals that are unopposed by members of Congress or other pressure groups.

Congressmen are not, as we have already suggested, mere weather vanes whose direction can be changed with each change in the pressure winds. No amount of pressure by the White Citizens Councils can move a Hubert Humphrey to oppose civil rights legislation. His commitment to civil rights is much too deep for such a move. By the same token a Harry Byrd can hardly be expected to support most labor oriented legislation. On most major issues of public policy, the majority of the members of the House and the Senate hold a general position that cannot be changed merely because this or that group suggests that it should be. This is true regardless of the reputation that a group has for power and influence in elections. In the 1959 Congress which was overwhelmingly Democratic and which, it was alleged, had been elected because of the power of the AFL-CIO electoral arm, a large majority of both parties nevertheless voted for a strong bill for the regulation of the internal affairs of trade unions. The bill was opposed by almost every union official in America and certainly by all of those officials who testified before the House and Senate committees. Threats of reprisals at the polls apparently did not significantly influence even the major presidential candidates much less the rank-in-file members of Congress.

It is easy to blame or credit pressure groups with the outcome of congressional votes, but it is a very different thing to prove either that the pressure group actually did influence the votes or that a pressure group could visit reprisals upon recalcitrant congressmen. Establishing a cause and effect relation between the views of a particular pressure group and the votes of members of Congress is extremely difficult. Farm blocs and silver blocs may be as much the result of the convictions of members of Congress as of the pressure of special interests in their home districts. The fact may well be that most people including congressmen from rural Iowa or Wisconsin share the same beliefs about the importance of supporting farm prices.

---

8 There are, of course, a number of serious books and articles dealing with the nature and power of pressure groups. A number of the better books dealing with individual pressure groups are listed in the bibliography at the end of this chapter. Of special value for understanding pressure groups in Washington is Lester W. Milbrath, *The Washington Lobbyist* (Chicago: Rand McNally, 1963). His findings are based on results of interviews with a cross section of lobbyists in Washington.

The critics of pressure groups are not the only source of myths about their power. The legislative representatives in the national offices of the groups claim that they have been effective in the determination of policy. In reporting to the national conventions of their organizations those in the Washington offices claim maximum influence on policy in order to justify their continued existence as legislative representatives. The Washington officers, the permanent bureaucracy of the pressure group, sometimes argue that 90 per cent of the bills which it supported passed and that 92 per cent of the bills which it opposed failed. Those listening to the report are expected to conclude that there is some cause and effect relation between support or opposition and the success or failure of the measures. Usually the assumption is made as expected, though no proof has been offered that precisely the same thing would not have happened had there been no pressure group at all.

Pressure groups and politicians spread the myth of the power of opposition pressure organizations. There is nothing more useful in whipping up the fervor of one's own followers than portraying the opposition as both powerful and evil. The AFL-CIO denounces the power and greed of the National Association of Manufacturers, while the latter depicts the AFL-CIO as a giant labor combine whose power will eventually destroy free enterprise in this country. There is a reason for almost everyone concerned with politics, except the scholar, to exaggerate the power of his own and the opposition's pressure groups.

Power and pressure groups. If we discount the claims of power made by most pressure groups, what can be said of their influence? No research is available to tell us with accuracy precisely how great that power is. Some hypothetical cases and some real cases can help in answering the question.

A bill before Congress may find two roughly equal sets of proponents and opponents, each convinced of the rightness of its general position. In such a case the opposing pressure groups by persuasion or by threats of campaign opposition may actually determine the result. It is also possible that the neutral members will determine the decision; but it is at least equally possible that the neutrals will have their votes determined by their party leaders or by the views of members of Congress whose judgment they trust.

Pressure groups may confine themselves to a single issue or they may spread themselves over a wide field of policy. It seems reasonable to assume that the group which has a large membership and concentrates on one issue is likely to be more effective on that single issue than the group which dissipates its energies over many issues. Pressure groups normally are formed because of the belief of the members in a single issue or a set of closely related issues. The farther afield the pressure group moves from the core problem or problems, the less likely it is that the national office can

A REPRESENTATIVE OF THE AMERICAN INSTITUTE OF PUBLIC OPINION (GALLUP POLL)
CONDUCTING AN INTERVIEW

carry the membership with it on a showdown.[9] The civil rights groups are fine examples of the value of concentrating on a particular set of issues on which not only its own membership, but many related persons are in agreement. Merely making civil rights a public issue assures the NAACP that many of its constituents will act in a manner calculated to help bring about the desired results. If the NAACP should move into other fields, its relations with some of its own members and certainly with some of its peripheral supporters would become less important. Its own membership would become divided and some would question the wisdom of supporting a group that has strayed from its original purposes. The broader the coverage of issues the fewer the number of ardent supporters.

Internal operation and control of pressure groups. The permanent officials of any organization exercise great power in that organization. The executive-secretary or executive director of any group carries on the day to day work of the group.[10] He, rather than its elected officials, knows the details of the operation. Unless the elected officials are unusually vigilant and willing to put in a great amount of time, the permanent staff is almost

[9] In 1940, John L. Lewis, undisputed leader of the United Mine Workers, tried to get the workers to support Wendell Willkie and failed completely.

[10] V. O. Key, *Politics, Parties, and Pressure Groups* (5th ed., New York: Thomas Y. Crowell, 1964), pp. 126-7.

certain to control much of the organization's business. Even in the national government where Congress is in session more than half the year and is extremely jealous of its authority, the permanent bureaucracy exercises great power. In the ordinary pressure group, where the elected official holds office for a limited period during which he is engaged primarily in speech-making and carrying on his regular business, power almost inevitably slips into the hands of the organization's bureaucracy.

A COPE WORKSHOP. Women are phoning to urge union members to register and vote.

The "Washington office" knows what legislation is up for consideration. It talks regularly with members of Congress, committee staffs, and administrators. The headquarters people either testify before committees or prepare the testimony for the elected leaders of the organization. At national conventions the "Washington office" delivers a brief report normally emphasizing the successes of the past and pointing out the need for even greater effort, and therefore, for an even larger budget in the future. No questions are asked. The report is accepted by a grateful convention which believes that without the "Washington office" the dangers to freedom in the society would be unchecked. No one ever really examines to see just how effective the lobbyists have been. Businessmen who are accustomed to taking consumer polls before placing a product on the market and then checking the reasons for its success or failure do not ask for serious evidence of the work of the national office. By the end of the convention a larger appropriation has been made and the "Washington office" continues to operate as in the past.

Regulation of pressure groups. Pressure groups have been regulated since the early days of the Republic. Georgia placed a simple phrase in its constitution early in the 19th century, "Lobbying is a crime." There is no record of the end of lobbying or the prosecution of groups for lobbying in that state. Other states and the national government have regulated the cruder forms of lobbying for many generations. Bribery of public officials has been forbidden. Today, whether because of the law or because of a change in the general mores of the society, bribery is seldom found. Charges of attempted bribery are occasionally made, but successful prosecutions are rare. At the local level it is still possible that some overly-enthusiastic bidder may seek to influence the outcome of the city's selection of a contractor by bribing. At the state level, where politics is sometimes still the major ingredient in the awarding of contracts, bribery of officials is nonetheless rare. A contribution to the party in power may be gratefully accepted, but a personal honorarium for a public official is not.

In more recent years legislatures have turned to another form of regulation as a means of preventing too great power falling into the hands of special interest groups with lots of money. Under the Federal Regulation of Lobbying Act of 1946 persons or organizations seeking to influence legislation are required to register and file regular reports. These reports are filed with clerks of the two houses of Congress. The reports must include the names of those who contributed $500.00 or more to the pressure group and those who received from the organization as much as $10.00.

A House Select Committee was established, under the leadership of the late Frank Buchanan from Pennsylvania, to investigate the operation of lobbyists under the 1946 act and to recommend changes in the law. The committee interviewed lobbyists for labor, businessmen, farmer groups, and others. Seldom has a congressional committee carried out so thorough and so unbiased an inquiry. In its 1950 report, the committee brought to light a few pressure group efforts similar to those disclosed at earlier congressional hearings which involved organized telegram campaigns and some more sophisticated techniques. Mainly, however, the committee described the nature and operation of a variety of lobbying groups. In its recommendations, the committee came up with no startling proposals for change in the existing laws; the emphasis of the report was on publicity rather than regulation. Some of the specific provisions of the 1946 act the committee said should be liberalized to prevent hardship as a result of excessive record keeping and reporting

The position of the Buchanan Committee is generally accepted by most students of the field as sound. Lobbying activities can in large measure be justified under the protection of free speech and the right to petition the government. To try to over-regulate lobbying activities would quickly approach an infringement of these constitutional privileges. To require reporting and publicity does not infringe on the rights of the individual, while at the same time it provides the public with a picture of pressure group power—at least as measured by the expenditure of funds.

SUMMARY

Public opinion has been the concern of students of politics since the time of Aristotle, but the scientific study of the opinions of a society or one of its parts was not undertaken until relatively recently. The concern of most students of opinion in a democracy is not with those items on which there is consensus or agreement. It is rather to discover the views of citizens on issues on which people are divided. Public opinion is the aggregate of the views of all citizens.

Measuring public opinion is now carried out in a more scientific manner than in previous eras. Crucial to an accurate measurement of public opinion is the selection of a cross section of the public being studied. Random sampling, checked against the information gathered by the Bureau of the Census, is the recognized method for securing an accurate sample.

Opinions in the country are influenced by the major media of communication—newspapers, radio, and television. More important on many matters than the influence of the mass media, however, is the influence of the groups to which a citizen belongs.

In the United States thousands of groups are organized to influence legislatures and administrations on matters of importance to those groups. These pressure groups are not as powerful as some writers would suggest. Their power is related to their ability to affect elections and the attitudes of the public officials whom they seek to influence. Liberal pressure groups have little effect on the votes of conservative legislators, for example, but they may affect the votes of those who are already inclined toward a generally liberal position.

Pressure groups may be divided into various categories which are not all encompassing but which make it easier to discuss the roles of the different kinds of groups. For this purpose we have divided pressure groups into four major categories: (1) those, like the National Association of Manufacturers, which have a relatively small membership but a rather large amount of money for use in influencing public and official opinions; (2) those, like the National Association for the Advancement of Colored People, which have a rather large membership but not a great deal of financial backing; (3) those, like the great trade unions, which have both a large membership and a sizeable amount of money to support their positions; and (4) those, like the Federation of Atomic Scientists, which depend upon the expertise and prestige of their members for their influence.

A wise national office of a pressure group will set out to influence public opinion, political parties, members of Congress, or the bureaucracy bearing in mind the strengths and weaknesses of the group which it represents. The nature of the membership and the extent of the financial backing determines what ought to be the target of the group's effort and the means for making that effort most effective.

BIBLIOGRAPHIC NOTE

Much has been written concerning the nature of public opinion. Until relatively recent years, most of the research on public opinion was carried on by social psychologists and by professional polling organizations whose services were purchased by manufacturers, newspapers, and political party organizations. During the last decades more and more political scientists have participated in opinion research and analysis, bringing to their research a knowledge of political institutions and history which frequently has sharpened the product of the research.

Among political scientists A. Lawrence Lowell, *Public Opinion and Popular Government* (New York: Longmans, Green and Co., 1913) was the first to seriously examine public opinion. Beginning about 1930 Harold D. Lasswell began examining many aspects of public opinion and propaganda. In the years since that time, Professor Lasswell has made numerous contributions to the field in both books and articles. He led in the development of "content analysis" as a means for analysing propaganda.

Scholarly research on the development of opinions which are later translated into voting behavior has been carried on by a number of persons and groups for at least two decades. Some of the earliest significant studies of the development of voter attitudes during political campaigns were conducted under the general direction of Paul F. Lazarsfeld. Panels of voters were interviewed several times during a period of roughly six months before and during the campaign of 1940. This research resulted in the book, Paul F. Lazarsfeld, Bernard R. Berelson and Hazel Gaudet, *The People's Choice* (New York: Duell Sloan and Pearce, 1944). Some of the same scholars later studied elections and, in addition to many articles, published Bernard R. Berelson, Paul F. Lazarsfeld, and William M. McPhee, *Voting* (Chicago: University of Chicago Press, 1954).

Major studies of voter attitudes and the factors which caused citizens to support particular parties and candidates in the campaigns since 1948 have been conducted by the Survey Research Center at the University of Michigan. Books growing out of these projects include: Angus Campbell, Gerald Gurin and Warren E. Miller, *The Voter Decides* (Evanston, Illinois: Row Peterson and Company, 1954); Angus Campbell and Homer C. Cooper, *Group Differences in Attitudes and Votes* (Ann Arbor: Survey Research Center, The University of Michigan, 1956). The most sophisticated of the analyses of voter attitudes growing out of the work of the Survey Research Center is Angus Campbell, Philip E. Converse, Warren E. Miller, and Donald E. Stokes, *The American Voter* (New York: John Wiley and Sons, 1960).

Some excellent general books are available on the political attitudes of American voters. Among them are: Herbert Hyman, *Political Socialization* (Glencoe, Illinois: The Free Press, 1959); Seymour M. Lipset, *Political Man* (Garden City, New York: Doubleday and Company, 1960); Eugene Burdick and Arthur J. Brodeck (eds.), *American Voting Behavior* (Glencoe, Illinois: The Free Press, 1959). The last book mentioned contains essays by scholars of almost all of the social sciences and some persons in the humanities as well. Of special interest is the article by V. O. Key and Frank Munger, "Social Determinism and Electoral Decision: The Case of Indiana," p. 296 ff, which questions some of the generalizations of earlier studies which have sometimes neglected purely political issues in discussing men's voting behavior. Two other books of importance are Bernard R. Berelson and Morris Janowitz (eds.), *Reader in Public Opinion and Communication* (Glencoe, Illinois: The Free Press, 1953) and Heinz Eulau, Samuel J. Eldersveld, and Morris Janowitz, *Political Behavior* (Glencoe, Illinois: The Free Press, 1956).

Perhaps the most thorough look at the opinions of the American people has been taken by V. O. Key in *Public Opinion and American Democracy* (New York: Alfred A. Knopf, 1961).

Samuel Lubell holds a special place among those who are concerned with public opinion. A newspaperman, Lubell makes no special effort to conduct a "scientific" poll as we have described it in the text. Instead, he studies previous election returns in order to select areas for interviewing. He then talks with a small number of persons. Based on these interviews and against the background of his analysis of earlier voting records of the area, Lubell writes his works. His method has been criticized by some social scientists, but he has written two very interesting books—*The Future of American Politics* (New York: Harper and Brothers, 1951) and *The Revolt of the Moderates* (New York: Harper and Brothers, 1956).

Some efforts have been made to establish a firm relation between the personality of the citizen and his outlook on politics. These efforts have thus far yielded rather slim results. T. W. Adorno, Else Frenkel-Brunswick, and R. Nevitt Sanford, *The Authoritarian Personality* (New York: Harper and Brothers, 1950) sought to establish a correlation of political orientation and personality structure. Out of the study came the so-called "F Scale" which claimed to provide a guide to the authoritarian character of the respondents. Doubt has been thrown on the validity of the above book in R. Christie and Marie Jahoda (eds.), *Studies in the Scope of Methods of "The Authoritarian Personality"* (Glencoe, Illinois: The Free Press, 1954). This book sharply criticized both the method and the substance of the earlier work.

The psychological reasons for some persons joining particular authoritarian groups are examined in some detail by Gabriel A. Almond, *The Appeals of Communism* (Princeton: Princeton University Press, 1953).

While the books on public opinion and propaganda are numerous and significant, the great body of books dealing with pressure groups have made relatively little contribution to the study of politics and policy making. "Research" has sometimes seemed designed merely to confirm the authors' preconceptions. Some of the notable exceptions to this negative comment are: Peter H. Odegard, *Pressure Politics: The Study of the Anti-Saloon League* (New York: Columbia University Press, 1928); F. W. Riggs, *Pressure on Congress* (New York: King's Crown Press, 1950) which deals with the passage of the Chinese Exclusion Act; Morris Janowitz and Dwaine Marvick, *Competitive Pressure and Democratic Consent* (Michigan Studies Number 32, Institute of Public Administration, The University of Michigan, Ann Arbor, 1956); Arthur A. Maass, *Muddy Waters* (Cambridge: Harvard University Press, 1951); and Vincent Ostrom, *Water and Politics* (Los Angeles, The Haynes Foundation, 1953); Marc Karsons, *American Labor Unions and Politics 1900-1918* (Carbondale, Illinois: South Illinois University Press, 1958); Fay Calkins, *The CIO and the Democratic Party* (Chicago: University of Chicago Press, 1952).

Some recent books of special interest in the public opinion field include Edward C. Banfield, *Political Influence* (Glencoe, Illinois: Free Press, 1961); Raymond A. Bauer, Ithiel de Sola Pool, and Lewis A. Dexter, *American Business and Public Policy: The Politics of Foreign Trade* (New York: Atherton Press, 1963); John H. Fenton, *The Catholic Vote* (New Orleans: Hauser Press, 1960); Harmon Zeigler, *Interest Groups in American Society* (Englewood Cliffs, N. J.: Prentice-Hall, 1964); Lester W. Milbrath, *The Washington Lobbyists* (Chicago: Rand McNally, 1963).

9

Parties and Politics

POLITICAL parties make democracy work. Without parties the millions of citizens of modern democratic states would be helpless in controlling their government, in selecting their officials, and in making known their views on policies. Without parties the citizens would be an unorganized political mass with no means of implementing their views. No candidates could secure nationwide majorities and few could mobilize majorities even in small districts. Some political organization is essential if a large society is to operate with even a moderate degree of success. Parties provide the only organizations that work throughout the society. Pressure groups may organize a portion of the community, but they are concerned with narrow programs of interest only to limited groups. Parties, by contrast, are concerned with the whole of the society and with the whole of public problems.

In spite of the functions which parties perform in the United States and other democracies, they have been scorned throughout most of history. Parties and the politicians who run them are looked down upon as immoral. Politicians, it is said, compromise rather than fight for principle and indeed they do compromise. They are willing to accept less than the moralists would sometimes demand. It is also true that their very willingness to compromise is a major factor in the preservation of democracy. The clash of unbending parties ends in civil war. The willingness to go slow, to preserve institutions rather than demand full attainment of all party programs, to recognize that men who hold different views are usually also interested in maintaining democratic institutions—all these are part of the thinking of politicians and are necessary to the process that makes it possible for men to accept the decision of the majority. The minority is willing to accept the majority's decision, as interpreted by the politician, because the politicians of the majority will not destroy the opportunities of the politicians of the minority to replace them in power after the next election. The minority also recognizes that the changes that will be made during the years between the elections will not be so drastic as to preclude the enact-

155

ment of programs advocated by minority politicians should they win in later years.

DEFINITION OF PARTY

There is no definition of a political party that will hold for all times and all places. A definition that covers the American parties at, say the national level, has little to do with a party in a totalitarian state like the Soviet Union. Further, the nature of a party differs from democratic country to democratic country. Within the United States the party is one kind of organization when we are talking about either of the two major parties, another kind when we are talking about a third party in a particular state, and still another kind when we are talking about a minor party like the Socialist or Prohibition parties. The Communist Party within a democracy differs from all the others mentioned.

It used to be said that a party was a private voluntary organization of likeminded men seeking to control the offices of government in order to enact into law the views of the members of the organization. It is assumed in this definition that the party is competing freely with similar organizations created by men of different views for the control of government. Such a definition does not fit a totalitarian party like the Communist Party or a fascist party in a country where either controls the government. The totalitarian party is not voluntary in the sense that its members may move in and out of the organization as they desire. Nor does the totalitarian party compete with other parties for control of the office and policies. The totalitarian party brooks no organized opposition. By law and by administrative action all parties except the Communist Party are illegal and barred in communist countries.

American parties. Our American major parties do not fit the definition either, but for different reasons. American parties are so hedged in by state legislation that they are no longer private in the sense that they can completely control their own membership or even the method for the selection of most nominees and officers of the party. State laws say who may be members of political parties and state laws prescribe the method by which candidates shall be nominated and who may participate in the nominating process. Nor can we speak of the major parties as organizations made up of "likeminded" men. The Democratic Party houses at the same time both Senator Eastland of Mississippi and Senator Wayne Morse of Oregon, while the Republican Party has room for Senator Javits of New York and Senator John Tower of Texas. Any likemindedness between the two Democrats or between the two Republicans is certainly slight.

In the United States, then, the two major parties may be described as loose national confederations of state party organizations which are concerned with the nomination and usually the election of the President. The word "usually" must be included in the definition because state Democratic parties in the South have occasionally revolted in recent years against the selection of the Democratic National Convention to support either a regional third party or the candidate of the Republican Party.

The nature of the two major parties at the state level will be discussed in greater detail elsewhere. At this point it is sufficient to say that they are the core of the American party system. Their character and outlook are determined by the state party leadership or by the outlook of those persons in the state who have declared themselves to be either Republicans or Democrats. State parties are frequently more concerned with control of state elective offices, and therefore, state jobs and patronage than they are with broad policies of an economic or social character.

Legal definitions of parties. In the United States parties are defined by statute in each of the fifty states. These definitions usually consist of a statement saying which groups are eligible to participate in the general elections and to have the names of their candidates printed on the official ballot or listed on the voting machine. Groups which received a specified number of votes for their candidates in the preceding election are automatically eligible to have their candidates listed on the ballot. Other groups may gain a place on the ballot for their candidates if they have secured the requisite number of signatures on petitions. The number of signatures varies from an insignificant figure easily secured in some states to a very large figure which almost no group not already one of the major parties could hope to secure.

The states may also regulate the names which a party may use. The American Labor Party, once a powerful third party capable of affecting the outcome of the New York elections, ceased to meet the legal requirements for automatic inclusion on the state ballot. In other words, the ALP received fewer votes than required by New York law for official recognition as a party. The New York legislature then passed an act which now makes it impossible for any party to have the word "American" in its name. The ALP, therefore, can never again regain a spot on the ballot under that name. If its supporters again try to fight for votes, they will have to do so under a different name.

FUNCTIONS OF PARTIES

What do parties actually do? How do they differ from other organizations in the community such as pressure groups? Why are they necessary in a democratic state?

What parties actually do. We know parties best from the activities which we see every four years just before a presidential election. Electioneering for candidates is an important function, but in some respects not the most important activity of parties. Election campaigns are preceded by other actions at least as important. Furthermore, the campaigns themselves serve more functions than merely getting a man elected.

The parties (1) select the candidates, (2) choose the issues which shall be debated during the campaigns, (3) as a corollary, determine what issues shall not be debated during any particular campaign, (4) organize the government so that its work can be accomplished, (5) criticize the government if the party is out of power, and (6) serve as the single most important continuing link between the citizen and his government.

The importance of particular functions varies greatly from one democratic country to another. Their importance may also vary from one era to another within a single democratic nation. In times of crisis there may be a greater emphasis on issues than in times of relative peace, prosperity, and general calm. The selection of nominees, for example, may be cut and dried when the party has a first-term President in office seeking re-election, while it is a mad scramble when no single candidate is the obvious choice of the party. In the United States the function of the party as the link between the electorate and its government during the period between elections is of great significance. In other countries, the party may be relatively insulated from the average citizen except during a campaign.

Selection of candidates. Parties are essential for the selection of candidates in a democratic system. The choice of candidates must be narrowed to a number that can be made relatively well known to all interested persons. This action of selection also reduces the number of persons among whom the votes will be divided. Where two parties dominate the voting as in countries like the United States and Great Britain, the choice is between two serious candidates for each office plus a limited number of lesser candidates whose chances of victory are very slight. This reduction of candidates to two serious contenders means that in most elections the winner has the voting support of a majority or near-majority of the people in his constitutency.

Consider for a moment the problem the voter would face if no organizations presented and supported candidates for the available public offices. His choice would be limited only by the number of persons who met the constitutional requirements for the particular post. In the average congressional district of 400,000 persons almost 200,000 would be eligible. In a state the size of New York perhaps 4,000,000 persons meet the relatively simple constitutional requirements for United States Senator. Probably 30,000,000 persons are technically eligible for the Presidency. Without the organizational efforts of political parties, the voter would be caught up in a selection problem so vast that he would probably refrain from voting at all. If he voted he would have no reason to believe that his choice would receive more than a tiny fraction of the total votes cast by the remaining 68,000,000 voters. Hundreds or even thousands of persons could receive votes. None would be likely to receive more than a tiny fraction of the total votes. If a majority of the votes were required to elect the winner, then no one would be elected. If only a plurality (the greatest number received by any candidate) were required, it is almost certain that the winner would lack the support of the great majority of his constitutents. He would come to power without any mandate for action. He would be joined there by others equally without mandates. The system, if the chaos described above could be called a system, would fall of its own inability to accomplish anything.

Selection of issues. There are many issues available for discussion and action at any time in any country. Some are important and some are unimportant. Some are matters on which almost all the people are agreed while others are issues on which the country may be deeply divided. Out of the myriad of possible issues, the parties select a few that become the overriding issues of a campaign or of a session of Congress.

In a democracy in which two parties dominate there is not ordinarily much difference between the parties on most major issues. In the United States, the Republicans and Democrats are agreed that programs like social security shall be expanded. They differ, if at all, on the rate of expansion and the amounts to be paid to the recipients of old age assistance. Both parties are agreed that their workers shall be free to organize, but they differ on the restrictions that may be placed on labor or management in bargaining for changes in existing arrangements for wages, hours, and working conditions. Both parties agree, in other words, on basic issues but differ on the way in which the policies should be administered or on the urgency with which a policy should be pursued.

While parties select issues, they also refuse to select issues on which there will be a serious struggle. This refusal, in a two party system, to select certain issues for campaigning or for legislation makes possible the continued existence of the democratic institutions themselves. The two parties do not get so far apart on economic issues that either side is willing to fight the other if it loses. They are unwilling to take extreme positions both because of a desire to preserve existing institutions and because they do not wish to isolate themselves from the great mass of the citizens.

The selection, and by implication the exclusion, of issues thus accomplishes several things. First, it gives the voters issues upon which they can express themselves. Secondly, in a two party system the selection process encourages middle-of-the-road programs because neither party wishes to get so far away from the other that it is likely to find itself with only a small minority of the votes. Third, these middle-of-the-road programs of the parties mean that those issues that might create civil war by hopelessly dividing the people are simply ignored by both parties or handled so carefully that neither party is committed to action on the issue.

There are those who believe that all issues should be joined, that each public question should automatically develop sharp differences of party positions in order to give the voters an opportunity to take one extreme position or its opposite.[1] Only once in our history has such a situation existed. In the campaign of 1860 there was, or at least many men thought there was, an opportunity to vote to retain slavery or to abolish it. To many southerners the election of Lincoln meant that slavery would be abolished by the national government. Rather than face this possibility men were prepared to destroy the institutions of government themselves. Civil War was the result. Since that time the parties have not allowed so explosive an issue to become a matter dividing the country. Instead they have ignored or glossed over the problems that could have such dire consequences. How much of this glossing over has been the result of a conscious effort to prevent civil disturbance and how much merely to retain a full share of confidence of the voter one cannot say, but moderate major parties have been part of our post-Reconstruction heritage.

Organize the government. Once men are elected to office it is essential that a sufficient number of them work together in producing laws and governing the country to keep the nation operating successfully. Again it is the parties that do the job. Members of the parties in Congress name the members of committees, the leaders of both houses, and the policy directors of the Congress. They determine the priority for bringing issues before the membership for a vote and which issues will not come up for a vote at all.

The President usually names his cabinet members from his party. They are responsible to him as the party spokesman. Though the party structure he deals with the congressional leaders of his own party. If the White House and Congress are controlled by different parties, the leaders of the opposition party in Congress are still the channel through which compromises are worked out, sometimes privately and sometimes publicly, to allow legislation to pass.

Link between the citizen and government. It is estimated that as much as eighty per cent of a congressman's time is spent representing his constituents not as a lawmaker but in providing information and aid in their dealings with the government. In no other country in the world does the legislator give so much time and effort to handling essentially private problems of the voters. No congressman will reduce his work in this field however irrelevant it may seem to be for his constitutional duties. He knows that favors for constitutents, whether of his party or of the opposition party, are expected and may pay dividends in the form of votes in later elections.

---

[1] See, for example, E. E. Schattschneider, *Party Government* (New York: Farrar and Rinehart Inc., 1942) and *Toward a More Responsible Two Party System* (New York: Rinehart and Co., 1950), a report of the Committee on Political Parties of The American Political Science Association for moderate statements favoring the division of parties more along the line of issues. For the opposite position, see E. P. Herring, *The Politics of Democracy* (New York: W. W. Norton & Co., 1940).

Most citizens look on the government as a large, confused, and incomprehensible organization. They don't know what part of the bureaucracy handles their problem. They turn to the one man who will take their "case" and advise them what to do and how. When a son has gone AWOL from the army and been sentenced by a court martial, the parents seek the congressman's aid in reducing the sentence because of alleged mitigating circumstances. When a man needs a loan for his small business he asks the congressman to look into the matter. The congressman almost certainly obliges in either case. The congressman does not undertake to subvert the law; he tries to humanize it and the impersonal bureaucracy. The wise bureaucrat understands the congressman's role and reviews the case. Normally the congressman asks no special favors and expects none. He merely expects an honest re-examination of the case and an explanation of the bureaucracy's action. Sometimes this second look brings a reversal or modification of the earlier action. More frequently no change in the first decision is forthcoming, but the constituent feels that at least he has had an opportunity to appeal and that the congressman has made the appeal possible. The congressman certainly hopes that the constituent is thus satisfied.

The party also represents the citizen to the local government. This time it is the precinct captain or the ward leader who intervenes with the police or the magistrate to explain why a young man or woman should be given another chance. For the immigrant, the members of a minority group, or the poor, the party leader may be the only contact with the government. He knows not the ways of the law and doubts the value of the lawyer or has no money to retain one. The party worker is his alternative.

At all levels of government the party and the party workers assist the citizen in his negotiations with the government. This work of the electoral official with the average citizen has long amazed those who come here from abroad—especially those who come from countries where the politician is looked upon as a remote and powerful person unconcerned with the personal problems of the constituents. This activity of American party workers may not make for greater efficiency of government; indeed, it diverts the elected official from his constitutional task of making laws, but it creates a sense of confidence in government and in the parties. This confidence is one of the reasons for the continuance of a democratic system. Further, it is one of the reasons that a congressman can be elected and re-elected for a generation without making an outstanding record in Congress. His claim to office, however, is that he has served his constituents.

How parties and pressure groups differ. Parties and pressure groups, while both deeply interested in politics and issues, differ in several significant ways. Parties nominate candidates for public office who must compete with the candidates of other parties. Pressure groups, representing almost by definition a minority in the community, do not put forth candidates. They may seek to influence the nominations of the parties and certainly try to affect the programs of the parties, but because of their minority status they dare not name candidates for office. The parties advocate an array of policies of interest to various segments of the community in order to gain the support of a majority of the voters in the community. Pressure groups advocate, in most instances, a limited number of policies which are the primary concern of the members of the group or persons closely associated with it. Parties enact legislation upon which they can be judged and held accountable by their constituents. Pressure groups are seldom held responsible for governmental actions by their own members, and there is no obvious way for the voters to hold them directly responsible for the actions which they advocate.

DEVELOPMENT OF PARTIES

Early organization. No attempt will be made to give a detailed history of American parties. It is worth our while, however, as persons interested in political science and government to look briefly at the manner in which parties have developed in the United States.

The Constitution makes no mention of political parties, but several of its provisions make the operation of parties difficult. At one time the separation of powers and the selection of the President by means of the cumbersome electoral college system both seemed to make party develop- ment difficult if not impossible. The authors of *The Federalist Papers* in- veighed against parties (factions) and felt that the existence of a large federated republic made their growth unlikely. President Washington, the outstanding national hero of the time, warned against parties in his farewell address to the people.

In spite of this opposition, however, parties developed so rapidly that by 1800 the electoral college in its original form had become obsolete and the Twelfth Amendment had to be added to the Constitution to take the political change into account. Two of the authors of *The Federalist Papers* had become powerful party leaders on opposite sides of the ideologi- cal fence by the time President Washington gave his warning to the people. The separation of powers had been in part nullified by the time the third President, Thomas Jefferson, had held office for a single term.

Why did parties develop so rapidly in spite of the apparent general opposition of most of the national leaders of the time? Why did many of the leaders who had spoken and written against parties find themselves among the first drawn into the party battles?

The answer to both questions is simple. Parties had to develop and leaders had to be drawn into the new parties or create still other parties even though they had earlier quite honestly professed to fear and dislike political organizations. The idealized picture of rational men selecting other rational men to hold public office and dispassionately working out the laws of the land simply was not in accord with the facts of even a body as small as the Senate with its 26 members or the House of Representatives with its initial membership of 65. Nor did the picture fit the needs of a country covering the whole eastern seaboard with a population of 3,000,000 persons.

No sooner had the new government begun its work than Alexander Hamilton, an author of *The Federalist Papers,* was called upon to propose legislation in the field of fiscal policy. Hamilton, in order to gain maximum support for his proposals, consulted with friendly members of Congress prior to submitting his proposals to the whole membership. What he did was a perfectly normal, natural thing which men had been doing for hundreds of years whenever they wished to gain acceptance for their ideas and programs. Hamilton may not have thought of his activities as a step in creating a party, but the fact that he was drawing together some members in order to defeat his opponents almost immediately forced his opponents to organize. The members of Congress were soon largely associated with two blocs which have been loosely identified as Federalist (the Hamilton faction) and Anti-Federalist (the Jefferson faction). Both leaders were for a period associated with the Washington Administration until it became impossible for so sharply divided a cabinet to continue.

The next development was equally inevitable. If a faction was to win its position in Congress it had to elect a majority of its people to that body. The only way to assure the election of a majority of its people was to go back to the "grass-roots" and organize the voters—explaining why one faction must be elected rather than another. Thus need brought about the beginnings of the public party as opposed to merely a parliamentary party which had first come into existence in Congress.[2]

The election of 1800. By 1800 it had become apparent to the Jeffersonians that the original scheme of independent electors meeting together in each state to name their favorite for the Presidency and Vice-Presidency was not satisfactory. Therefore, various arrangements were made from state to state to assure that men would be more or less openly pledged to support a Jefferson-Burr ticket for the nation's two top offices. Burr's own New York organization was one of the important local political groups involved in planning and arranging for the prior commitment of electors. Burr and Jefferson, having the support of the same people, received the same electoral vote. Since there was no differentiation between President and Vice-President in the voting arrangements under the original provisions of the Constitution, they were not elected as a team. Instead, they were

---

2 For the best discussion of the development of the parliamentary and the extra-governmental party see Austin Ranney and Willmoore Kendall, *Democracy and the American Party System* (New York: Harcourt, Brace and Co., 1956).

tied for the election to the Presidency. The tie was eventually broken in Congress in favor of Jefferson. Burr became Vice-President. The Twelfth Amendment was soon added providing that electors should vote for President and Vice-President on separate ballots rather than writing both names on a single ballot. Parties were now free to name their men for the two top posts without fear of repeating the confusion of 1800.

The Jeffersonians worked hard at organizing the state and local political groups while the Federalists neglected this part of the process. Needless to say, the Federalists quickly lost their position of equality. They had been out-organized by the men who first clearly recognized that parties or factions needed a base beyond the legislature. The Federalists never recovered even when they belatedly set about creating their own extra-parliamentary organization.

The party system as we now know it received its greatest impetus during the Jackson era. By that time all practicing politicians knew the value of organization and worked at creating a winning alliance among the parties in each state. There have been changes in party names and parties have risen and fallen since the days of Jackson; but except for the Civil War years, the pattern developed during that period has remained largely unchanged.

THE ORGANIZATION OF PARTIES

Parties work both inside and outside the government. Although organization of the national parties began in Congress, they are today stronger outside than they are inside that body.

Party organization in Congress. Parties in Congress work as united groups for certain purposes; for other purposes they easily become fragmented. On organizational and personnel issues a solid Republican Party faces an equally united Democratic Party. No self-respecting Republican who hopes to get a good committee assignment breaks ranks to support a Democrat for the position of Speaker. The Democrats are equally firm in their opposition to Republican candidates for congressional offices.

Issues of public policy find no such unity within either of the major party groups in Congress. A majority of the Democratic congressmen who are from northern constituencies may desire a strong civil rights law, but the southern Democrats in Congress can be counted upon to oppose the measure. The southern members are not going to support a bill which will almost certainly mean their defeat in the following election. Nothing which the congressional leadership, or the President, or any other part of the national party can produce will defeat or re-elect the southern Democrat so he feels no obligation to the national leaders. The civil rights struggles within the Democratic Party are perhaps the most dramatic but lesser struggles and division occur in both parties over other matters of policy.

In state legislatures. The extent of the division within parties at the state level varies considerably. In those states which are dominated by a single party, discipline and unity are not maintained. The presence of factions within the dominant party helps to make up for the lack of a second party thus allowing the voters some choice in elections. In states where the two major parties are almost equally powerful, the legislatures are much more likely to be divided between two rather well disciplined groups. Frequently, in such states, the Republican Party is identified with rural counties while the Democrats get most of their support from the industrial urban centers. One party may control the upper house of the legislature while the other party controls the lower house. Compromises have to be made between the two houses or the leadership of the two parties.

Extra-governmental organization of parties. The formal structure of the two major parties looks very much like a pyramid with a mass of precinct committeemen at the base. Above them are the ward leaders, the city chairmen, the district leaders, the state chairmen, and at the top is the national committee and the national chairman. During the presidential election years, when the party is campaigning for its candidates, there may be some reality to the pyramidal picture. In the intervening period, if the pyramid suggests that the power is at the top and rests on the base of the local and state organizations, the picture is at best a distorted one. Power in the major parties is not at the national level for political and constitutional reasons.

The Constitution vests the control of elections in the state governments, although Congress may exercise power in this field if it so desires. In most matters Congress does not desire to interfere because congressmen themselves are closely tied to the state parties. In practice control of elections has meant control over the parties. The national government has traditionally enacted only legislation aimed at preventing corrupt practices; only recently has Congress intervened in the area of equal voting. The states provide the legal definition of parties. They lay down the rules for party members and describe the manner in which candidates shall be named by the parties in the states and in the congressional districts. They may even describe how the state leaders of the party shall be chosen. The courts of the states refuse to recognize the existence of a national party with control over the activities of the state organizations. If the state parties choose to support the national candidates of the parties bearing their names, they do so. If they choose to oppose these candidates, they also do so. Nothing that the national organization can do will change the situation if the state organization is united and adamant.

When the South split over the platform and the candidates of the Democratic national convention of 1948, the Democratic parties in some of the southern states simply stated that their candidate was not Harry S. Truman who had been nominated by the national convention, but Strom

Thurmond who was without convention support. No one in the national organization could retaliate in the campaign. In effect the Democratic parties in South Carolina, Virginia, Mississippi, and Alabama declared that Truman was the candidate of some alien organization and not of *their* Democratic Party.

Members of each party elected to Congress are responsible either to the state or district organizations or to the voters in their particular districts. Some congressmen, to be sure, are elected only because of landslide votes for the presidential candidate, but these coattail victories are less important than many would like to believe. More and more the voters seem willing to support a presidential candidate of the opposition party while retaining their party loyalty for local, state, and congressional candidates. The nomination of congressional candidates is largely unaffected by the activities or efforts of either the President or the national organization. It may even happen that the state or district organizations cannot, because of the direct primaries, control the nominations within the states and districts. In such instances the successful candidate feels a loyalty only to the voters who made his nomination and election possible.

The national leadership, whether the President or the party leaders in Congress, can provide only a little patronage. The President may be able to give the congressman or senator a few jobs for his faithful supporters at home. The leader in the Senate or the House of Representatives may give him a good, or a mediocre, or a poor committee assignment. Very little more can be given to the newly elected congressmen save perhaps more public attention. Some congressmen find the patronage useful and desirable. Others feel that their status at home may be improved by refusing the help of the leadership. Senator Proxmire, Democrat of Wisconsin, clearly jeopardized his status in the Senate hierarchy when he denounced the stewardship of Senator Johnson, Democratic leader in the upper house. Whatever Senator Proxmire's motives in criticizing the Senator from Texas, his political future in Wisconsin was probably improved because the voters of that state apparently like to have as their representative a man who is willing to challenge the mighty. A better committee position was a small sacrifice for the Wisconsin senator to make for increased prestige among the Democratic and independent voters of his state.

There was a time thirty years and more ago when patronage in the form of jobs for the party faithful was a presidential prerogative. The President who distributed patronage with care might influence votes at least for the first term of his regime. That day is past. The number of jobs at the disposal of the Chief Executive is so limited that it cannot be expected to sway many votes on issues that are important in a senator's state or a congressman's district.

Leaders in Congress and the White House cannot persuade congressmen from the South to vote for civil rights legislation, or farm congressmen to vote for lowering the level of farm price supports, or labor congressmen to vote for legislation restricting the power of unions. Nothing that the national leadership has to offer is worth the risk of losing state or local support.

If it is true that the President and congressional leaders have, at best, limited control over the elected officials, it is even more true of the national chairman and the national committees. The latter are, as we have seen, federated bodies. The former is either an agent of the President or powerless to control patronage if his party is out of power. In any case the chairman can neither grant favors nor influence in any significant way the outcome of state elections. His lack of power on both counts makes him impotent on most policy matters.

Party structure. The smallest unit of the major parties is the precinct organization. The roughly 100,000 precincts are geographical areas of varying size depending upon the population of the area. In the city the precinct may cover only a few square blocks. In rural areas it may cover a number of square miles. The number of voters in a precinct also varies from urban to rural areas. The rural precinct, though large, may include only fifty or a hundred voters. The urban precinct usually includes three hundred to a thousand voters, although precincts sometimes have as many as five or six thousand voters.

The precinct committeeman. The party official at the lowest level of the party is usually called either "precinct committeeman" or "precinct captain." He may be elected in a primary or at a precinct caucus or he may be appointed by persons above him in the party. He is the one on whose shoulders falls much of the organizational and electoral work of the party. He is also the first contact of the average citizen with the party organization. In the crowded cities he is the man to whom the citizen ordinarily turns for legal or political advice. His work may be full-time or part-time, although the latter is rapidly becoming the norm. In a few of our largest cities the precinct worker is still kept on the city payroll by the boss or leader of the party and is expected to spend most of his time dealing with the problems of his precinct.

In the period before election the precinct committeeman, with such help as he can secure from his subordinates, attempts to speak to every sympathizer in the precinct to remind him of the up-coming election. In the case of the primary election he tells them which slate or candidate to support. On election day he is responsible for seeing that the party voters show up at the polls. If he fails to do his job, the party loses votes.

We are now accustomed to thinking of television and radio as the means of reaching the voters. Presidential candidates, it is true, must rely heavily on the modern means of communication. The election of lesser officials still depends primarily on the work of the precinct organization and its leader, the precinct committeeman. If he fails to see that the party sympathizers are registered, no candidate, however appealing, can win their votes. Within the party only the precinct organization can go to the homes and apartments and get voters out to register. Only the precinct organization can get voters to the polls on election day. In local elections, when issues are not particularly controversial, it is the precinct committeeman whose pre-electoral work pays off. He can get his friends and those whom he has helped to come to the polls and vote for his party because he is trusted and has aided them.

Television and radio may have modified some forms of campaigning, but the precinct worker or his equivalent, the worker for an independent political group, is still of great importance to the party's success. When we hear it said that the Democratic Party has done well in congressional elections across the country because it is better organized than the Republican Party, we know that the speaker is saying that the Democratic precinct workers did a better job than the Republican workers in getting voters registered and then getting them to the polls on election day.

The ward. Wards are city sub-divisions. The party in most cities breaks down its organization according to these legal sub-divisions. At the head of the ward organization is the ward leader, ostensibly chosen by the precinct committeemen of the ward. Actually, the ward leader may really be the choice of the boss or city leader. In any case he is selected because he can produce results on election day. Both the boss and the precinct committeemen understand the need for success if they are to enjoy the fruits of their activities. In the larger cities the ward leader helps the precinct committeemen with their political work. He gets jobs for voters on request of the committeemen and he acts for the committeemen in cases that require contact at levels higher than the committeemen can normally go.

City and county organizations. The city or, in the rural areas, the county organizations are of major importance in the party. Frequently, the leaders of this segment of the party are unchallenged by anyone above them in the formal hierarchy of the party. The county or city chairman of the party is chosen by primary or by convention, but he may be merely a titular leader. The real leader, sometimes called the boss, may prefer not to hold the formal position. Traditionally, patronage has been found in greatest quantity at this level of party. Even today many cities and more counties still have not adopted a thoroughgoing merit system. The party organization, therefore, dispenses the jobs to the loyal workers. The organization can also dispense contracts for many kinds of services. Unless state law or city charters provide otherwise, the organization usually grants the contracts to persons who have contributed to the party coffers.

Working with the chairman are a number of other officers of the party. The precinct committeemen or the ward or township leaders normally constitute the city or county committee. The chairman appoints or the committee elects a secretary and a treasurer. When the committee is large, an executive committee is sometimes appointed to decide policy between meetings of the full committee.

State party organization. Committees may exist in the congressional districts, but these committees in most states are not part of the hierarchical organization. The lines of organization usually run directly from the county or city organizations to the state committee. The state committee of the party is based on the party units just below the state level. If the committee has importance, as it may have in states which do not closely regulate the party, members of the state committee may be the most powerful figures in the city and county committees. These leaders want to be in a position to exert maximum influence in the selection of state candidates and in the dispensing of state patronage. At the same time they wish to be able to prevent "undesirable" incursions by the state organization into their own local bailiwicks.

The method of selecting members of the state committee varies from state to state. In some states the law requires that they be selected in primary elections. In others the city or county chairman is automatically a member of the state committee. In still others a convention may select the members to represent the cities and counties. The number of members of the state committee may be less than a hundred or it may be as many as 600 as is the case in California. Clearly, the larger committees are not serious policy or organizational groups.

The state chairman is usually the choice of the governor if the party is in power. When the party is not in power, he probably is the choice of the more powerful members of the state committee. The chairman of the party in power has patronage which he divides among the leaders of the county and city organizations. If a particulary bitter division has occurred in the fight for the gubernatorial nomination, the state chairman may either reduce the amount of patronage offered to the leaders who opposed the governor or he may seek to consolidate the governor's position by granting favors to the opposition in hopes of minimizing the antagonisms of the primary struggle.

The national committee. The national committees of the two major parties are ostensibly selected by the national conventions every four years. In fact, the conventions merely ratify the choices of the states. The state selections may be made in a number of different ways depending upon the law or the party rules in each state.

Both of the national committees include at least one man and one woman from each state. The Republicans, since the 1952 national convention, have provided for bonus members based upon the election of Republican candidates at the state and congressional district levels. This bonus arrangement was decided upon because the southern states which rarely voted Republican in presidential elections and almost never in state and local elections were relatively over-represented on the committee as long as all states were allowed the same number of members.

The national chairman. The presidential nominee of the party is free to choose the national chairman although he usually consults with other party leaders before announcing his choice. Frequently, the chairman is the man who conducted the presidential candidate's campaign for the nomination. During the years when the party controls the White House, the national chairman is the patronage and organizational agent of the President. If the chairman resigns, his successor is chosen by the President although the formal election is by the national committee.

The national chairman does not normally engage much in policy discussions aside from periodic broadsides against the opposition. He is, as Professor Key suggests, "a technician, a specialist in campaign management and machine tending." [3]

When the party is out of power, the post of national chairman is filled by the national committee. Under these circumstances a struggle for the position is almost certainly closely related to the efforts of various presidential hopefuls to gain some advantage at the next national convention.

The chairman's job between campaigns is to raise money, dispense patronage, and carry on other organizational activities. The chairman whose party is in the White House has relatively much greater power than the chairman of the "out" party. In neither case can the chairman issue orders to lower levels of the party. He can request or encourage certain actions, but the state and local organizations are largely free to determine whether they will act as the national chairman wishes or in some other manner.

National advisory committees. From time to time the national organizations of the two major parties have attempted to provide statements of policy which could serve as foundations for national platforms and publicity with the general public.[4] The most recent and most ambitious of these attempts have come since the 1956 elections. In 1957 Democratic National Chairman Paul Butler established a National Advisory Committee consisting of 25 persons who were either members of the national committee or high in the councils of the party. The chairman of the party invited the congressional leaders to participate as members of the committee, but both

---

3 V. O. Key, *Politics, Parties, and Pressure Groups* (4th ed., New York: Thomas Y. Crowell, 1958) p. 352. Paul Butler who was first selected Democratic National Chairman in 1954 deviated some from position of strict organizational work to advocate policies with respect to civil rights and other matters. He was often roundly denounced by some southerners and congressmen for his incursions into the policy field.

4 Both parties issue magazines to keep members of the party informed about policies of their elected officials and reasons for objecting to the policies of the opposition. The emphasis is on the criticism of the opposition. *The Democratic Digest* and *Battle Line* are the names of the Democratic and Republican magazines.

Senator Lyndon Johnson and Speaker Sam Rayburn declined. In their view party policy is made in Congress where the legislation must actually be written.

Early in 1959 the Republican National Committee created a much larger committee consisting of many different types of party members to work out statements of position on a number of issues. This committee made little effort to handle immediate problems, but set about writing more general, long-term policy statements in the major areas of policy making.

Neither of the advisory committees is part of the regular organizational machinery. The role of such committees, if any, in the future of the parties cannot now be predicted. Each, but especially the Democratic committee, speaks for the presidential wing of the party except when merely criticizing the opposition. The role of such groups must obviously be different when the party controls the White House than when it is out of power. The President cannot tolerate a competing source of policy statements in his own wing of the party. He may encourage such a group to publicize his programs or he may want it to stick to long range statements of a general character. He may even arrange for the abolition of the committee entirely. President Kennedy has followed the latter course.

THIRD AND MINOR PARTIES

Definitions. Periodically during the last century new parties have arisen seeking to dislodge one of the two major parties. Only rarely has a new party been able to secure any electoral college votes for its presidential candidate. Somewhat more frequently it has captured a few seats in Congress and perhaps even controlled a state legislature.

These lesser parties are of two sorts. There are those with a sectional base, growing up because of some unmet needs or demands within the region. These parties are frequently without any stated ideological base. They were created to solve a specific problem or set of problems. Their founders were usually at least second or third generation American. We shall call these third parties because, at least within a single region, they competed as equals with the Democratic and Republican Parties.

Minor parties, as we shall use the term, are usually organized nationally but have never developed the voter support which makes them real competitors with the two major parties. Frequently, these minor parties have been socialist with a Marxian ideological base. One of the most persistent of the minor parties has been the Prohibition Party. It has never received more than a handful of votes in any election.

Development of the parties. Most of the third parties of the last century developed in the region from Wisconsin westward to the Rocky Mountains. They sometimes have controlled state governments as did the Progressive Party of Wisconsin and the Farmer-Labor Party of Minnesota.

Sometimes they were significant forces even in presidential elections and of importance throughout a region. The Populist Party won victories in various states of the West and won electoral votes for its presidential candidate in the 1892 election. Thirty years later, the Progressive Party, under Robert M. La Follette, captured the electoral votes of one state and ran second to the Republicans in a majority of the states between the Mississippi and the Pacific. Since that time the only third party to develop was the States Rights Party which was created in the South in 1948 to protest the platform and the candidate of the Democratic Party. Talk of reviving the States Rights Party has come to nothing in the succeeding years.

Minor parties of significance rose during the last decade of the nineteenth century. The Socialist Labor Party and later the Socialist Party, both dominated by German immigrants, sought the vote of workers and others. The Socialist Party reached its greatest strength in 1912 when Eugene V. Debs, its presidential candidate, won almost six per cent of the total votes cast. In later years the party secured a few more votes but it never again won the same percentage of the total vote. The Socialist Party slipped rapidly after the rise of Communism in the Soviet Union. Most of the foreign language sections of the party broke away to join the American communist movement which was dominated by the Russian party. The Communist Party never attained any significant electoral strength in this country. Even when the communists helped create and run the Wallace Progressive Party of 1948 they were unable to attract two per cent of the national vote.

Decline of the third and minor parties. The electoral strength of the minor and third parties is insignificant today. It is possible, though unlikely, that at some future date new parties will arise to challenge the major parties. The third parties have declined in part because the direct primaries made it possible for dissatisfied groups to seek and gain the control of one of the major parties in thus securing their goals with much less effort. The Non-Partisan League created at the close of World War I was perhaps the most obviously successful of these efforts to capture a major party. In the New Deal period many of those who were prepared to set up third parties moved into the Democratic Party making it, for the first time, a serious and continuing threat to Republican supremacy in the Mid-West and Great Plains area.

The minor parties declined for somewhat different reasons. Many members and supporters found that the dogma which had once seemed to describe their European world had little relationship to American problems. Indeed it could be said that the very success of the American system destroyed the appeals of the dissenters of the left. Furthermore, as the number of immigrants was reduced so was the size of the one audience which seemed to listen to the Marxist appeal. The second and third generations were assimilated into the culture so thoroughly that the programs which had appealed to their parents no longer appeared either feasible or desirable.

SUMMARY

Political parties are essential in democratic societies. The nature and organization of parties may differ in different societies, but in all of them the parties perform basic functions of organization and communication. In the United States the two major parties carry out the following functions: (1) select the candidate, (2) choose the issues which shall be debated during the campaigns, (3) determine which issues shall not be debated in a campaign, (4) organize the government so that there is the necessary cooperation among the various branches, (5) criticize the programs of the party in power, and (6) serve as the continuing link between the citizens and the government.

Control of political parties in the United States is dispersed. The state governments control the election process and by extension have come to control the organization of the parties. The states each provide legal definitions of a party. This definition is cast largely in terms of the number of votes which the party's candidates received in the last election. Each state party is free from the control of national leaders whether in Congress, the White House, or on the national committees. So little control is there that in 1948 leaders of four state Democratic parties endorsed a presidential candidate other than the one nominated by the National Convention of the Democratic Party.

The extent of party unity and discipline that is desirable in political parties has been the subject of sharp debate among political scientists. One group maintains that parties should be reorganized in order that the national leadership of the two major parties could make certain that members of the party in Congress and throughout the country supported the measures proposed by the leaders. The other group argues that it is a good thing that discipline cannot be maintained, because freedom is more secure when there is no enforced unity within either major party. This group also argues that it would be undesirable for the parties to differ sharply on major issues because such differences can lead to civil war in a country in which important regional differences have prevented the development of a fully homogeneous society. Whatever the merits of the two positions the domination of the parties at the state level effectively prevents any shift to disciplined parties in the immediate future.

The smallest, but a very important, unit of the party is the precinct committee. It is this unit which maintains continuing contact with the voters and serves as a channel of communication between the voter and the party. Above the precinct committee are the ward, and the city, county, state, and national committees. It is not always possible to say where the power in a party lies in any particular state, but it is probable that organization power is either at the state or county and city level.

Recent developments in party organization, such as the Democratic

National Advisory Committee, have had some publicity value but no in-fluence on the structure of power within the parties.

BIBLIOGRAPHIC NOTE

Most of the earlier political works denounced parties and proposed various means for replacing these apparently evil organizations. The best known of these books, M. Ostrogorski, *Democracy and the Organizations of Political Parties*, Vol. II (New York: Macmillan Company, 1908) was the first thorough description of American parties. Woodrow Wilson had discussed the role of parties in Congress in 1884, but his *Congressional Government* (New York: Meridian Edition, 1956) did not attempt to describe the organization and operation of our parties.

Textbooks can provide the reader with a good description of the organization and activities of parties in this country. Some of these which the student may find especially useful are: William Goodman, *The Two-Party System in the United States (Princeton,* N. J.: D. Van Nostrand Company, 1960); Ivan Hinderaker, *Party Politics* (New York: Henry Holt and Company, 1956); V. O. Key, *Politics, Parties, and Pressure Groups* (5th ed., New York: Thomas Y. Crowell Company, 1964); Avery Leiserson, *Parties and Politics* (New York: Alfred A. Knopf, 1958). A history of American party politics is available in Wilfred E. Binkley, *American Political Parties: Their Natural History* (New York: Alfred A. Knopf, 1959). In a somewhat different category is Austin Ranney and Willmoore Kendall, *Democracy and the American Party System* (New York: Harcourt, Brace and Company, 1956). This book is a textbook, but it gives more space to the analysis of the nature of the parties and their relation to majority rule democracy rather than to a description of party organization and activities.

During the latter part of the nineteenth century several novels were written about parties and party leaders. Some of these novels were really condemnations of the existing party system. They were intended to show that party leaders were corrupt and they did so. These novels gave no indication of the role which the parties had to play to keep the machine of democracy in motion. Half a century later Edwin O'Connor wrote *The Last Hurrah* (Boston: Little, Brown, and Co., 1956) to tell his readers that prior to the development of social security politics under the New Deal and the rise of public relations experts that the political machines played a major role in making the people of the big cities relatively happy. He also helped to show us that until the national government took over the problems of unemployment and social security that the machines had to supply certain of the basic needs of the community.

During the last two decades there have been many criticisms of the nature of American parties. The recent critics, unlike those who wrote at the turn of the century, have insisted that American parties are too loosely organized, that the parties in America should be committed to programs, and that both should be advocating clear cut programs from which the voters could choose. The leading writer of this position has been E. E. Schattschneider whose book, *Party Government* (New York: Farrar and Rinehart Inc., 1952), was to play an important role in the thinking of students of politics in this country. The position of Professor Schattschneider was amplified and somewhat modified by the report of the Committee on Political Parties of the American Political Science Association in its Report, *Toward a More Responsible Two-Party System* (New York: Rinehart and Co., 1950). Taking a different position was E. Pendleton Herring, *The Politics of Democracy* (New York: Rinehart and Co., 1940). Herring is more optimistic about the present American political parties fulfilling the needs of American society.

In recent years commentators from both of the major parties have given their statements concerning the reasons for their affiliations with one or the other of the major parties. Dean Acheson wrote a book, *A Democrat Looks at His Party* (New York: Harper and Brothers, 1955). After former Secretary of State Acheson had witten his statement of reasons for supporting the Democratic Party, Arthur Larson wrote a similar book to indicate why one would support the Republican Party. His book is called *A Republican Looks at His Party* (New York: Harper and Brothers, 1956).

Histories of the two American parties are not numerous. The best of the existing books are Frank R. Kent, *History of the Democratic Party* (New York: Century, 1928) and Malcolm C. Moos, *The Republicans* (New York: Random House, 1956).

For a picture of what the parties stand for there are two books which have collected statements of the party conventions and the party leaders which are now available. Franklin L. Burdette edited *Readings for Republicans* (New York: Oceana Publications, 1960) and Edward Reed edited *Readings for Democrats* (New York: Oceana Publications, 1960).

In a very different category is the excellent book by Robert A. Dahl, *Who Governs?* (New Haven: Yale University Press, 1961). Dahl examines the role of party leaders as well as the role of other segments of the community in making several kinds of community decisions in New Haven.

While third and minor parties have never played a very important role in the election of congressional majorities or of presidential candidates, these parties have been important in the overall American political scene at least during the period from 1890 to 1948. Some of the most important of the parties were the Marxists or socialist and communist parties. A simple presentation of the left wing and third party groups is to be found in William B. Hesseltine, *The Rise and Fall of Third Parties* (Washington, D. C.: Public Affairs Press, 1948). The story of the communist and socialist parties is to be found in a series of books published with the support of the Fund for the Republic. The Communist Party is described in books by Theodore Draper, *The Roots of American Communism* (New York: The Viking Press, 1957) and his second book, *American Communism and Soviet Russia* (New York: The Viking Press, 1960). David A. Shannon has written both of the Socialist Party and of the latter days of the Communist Party. His books are: *The Decline of American Communism* (New York: Harcourt, Brace and Company, 1959) and *The Socialist Party of America: a History* (New York: Macmillan Co., 1955).

A recent book proposing to reform the American party system attracted more than the usual attention because the author was a friend and biographer of President Kennedy—James MacGregor Burns, *The Deadlock of Democracy: Four-Party Politics in America* (Englewood Cliffs, N. J.: Prentice-Hall, 1963).

Smaller books describing American parties and politics have been published by a number of houses recently. Some of them are Lewis A. Froman, *People and Politics: An Analysis of the American Political System* (Englewood Cliffs, N. J.: Prentice-Hall, 1962); Fred I. Greenstein, *The American Party System and the American People* (Engleood Cliffs, N. J.: Prentice-Hall, 1963); and Howard Penniman, *The American Political Process* (Princeton: Van Nostrand, 1962).

For an interesting story of Massachusetts politics, see Murry B. Levin and George Blackwood, *The Compleat Politician* (Indianapolis: Bobbs Merrill, 1962).

10

Nominations and Elections

I$_\text{T}$ is not enough that a man has the right to vote; it is essential that he can cast his vote with the assurance that it will be counted equally with all other votes. He must be certain that no party or person will have special advantage in the political contest because of corrupt administration of the elections. A sense that the election is fairly run is essential to the well being of the democratic process.

In this country the voter participates in two elections in the process of selecting public officials. The first, the primary, determines the candidates of the two major parties. The second, the general election, determines which of the parties will control the offices of government.

Both the states and the national government are concerned with establishing and enforcing the rules of the political game in the elections, but the heavier responsibility falls upon the states. It is the states that set up the electoral machinery, conduct the elections, and assist in preventing corruption. The states also determine the qualification of voters within the limits set by national laws and by the Fourteenth, Fifteenth, Nineteenth, and Twenty-fourth Amendments. The most important legislation by Congress is to be found in the three Civil Rights Acts passed since 1957 and discussed in an earlier chapter. In addition to the effort of the national government to assure Negroes an opportunity to vote, Congress has enacted legislation dealing with the problems of corrupt practices in congressional and presidential elections. This national effort still leaves the primary authority in the field to the state governments.

REGISTRATION

In all but four states today, before a voter can cast his ballot in either the nomination or election process his name must be recorded in the files of the voting district in order that he may be identified for the elections.[1] Massachusetts first provided for the registration of prospective voters at the

---

[1] The presentation of a poll tax receipt was required in Texas. This receipt replaced any other registration arrangement.

beginning of the nineteenth century. A few other states adopted registration requirements during the first half of that century, but voter identification became significant only with the rise of the great cities toward the end of the century. Identification of voters has never been a serious problem in rural areas where the population remains relatively stable and where the number of persons is sufficiently small that watchers at the polls can easily recognize a stranger or a repeater.

In the large cities registration is necessary if there is to be any assurance that there will be no fraudulence in voting. Prior to the development of registration requirements, members of city political machines sometimes voted two, three, or even a dozen times in the same district or in several districts. The possibility for fraud was great where the watchers at the polls were unable to recognize most of the voters. Dishonesty on the part of one or two election officials could make these frauds possible.

State legislatures have sometimes taken into account the differences between the problems of the rural and urban sections of a state by insisting that city voters be required to register while allowing the identification of rural voters by the local election officials on election day.

The registration of prospective voters is important to assure that there are no fraudulent activities in the general election, but it may also be important for primary elections. In the states which have a closed primary system only members of a particular party can participate in the selection of candidates for that party. It is necessary the voter somehow be identified with his party. In practice this means that when the prospective voter gives his name and address to the local registration officials he also indicates whether he wishes to be listed as a member of the Democratic or the Republican Party. In the primary election he may vote only in the primary of the party of which he is a member. If he has not specified a preference for either party he cannot participate in closed primary elections at all. He is then limited to voting in the general election—choosing between the candidates nominated by the members of the major parties.

Types of registration. Registration of two types is to be found in the United States. A small number of states require annual registration of voters. In most states, however, some kind of permanent registration is provided for. Under annual registration laws, each year that an election is to be held the voter is required to go to the offices of the registrar of voters to have his name, address, and voting district recorded.

The permanent registration system is far more common today. Under this system each person must provide at least his name, address, and district to those who maintain the lists of qualified voters before he can vote. He need not register again unless he has moved to a new location or for some other reason has had his name removed from the voting lists.

Some states have no arrangements for removing a name from the lists once the voter has registered. Most states, however, either provide that a name shall be dropped if the voter fails to vote in two or more consecutive elections. Others provide for a periodic check to make certain that persons whose names appear on the lists are still alive and eligible to vote. Where no check is made, the lists soon become hopelessly out of date, cluttered with names of persons long since dead or who have moved to other districts.

The system of permanent registration accompanied by an efficient method for the removal of ineligible names is, in the view of most qualified observers, the best system. Permanent registration has helped reduce fraud without placing a major burden on the voters and without great expense to the taxpayer.

NOMINATIONS

The registered voter in America participates directly in the selections of party candidates. In this respect parties in the United States differ greatly from their counterparts in the democratic countries elsewhere in the world. In the democracies of Europe the selection of party candidates is quite simple. The parties themselves determine how the nominations shall be made. In some countries nominations are controlled by the national party leadership, while in others the district party organization may control the nominations. The Netherlands is an example of the former and Sweden of the latter.

In the United States the parties only partially control the selection of their own nominees. The method of selection is determined by the state governments. The direct primary system established by the states for the selection of candidates has in turn had a significant effect upon the nature of the internal organization and control of the parties. The process of nominating presidential candidates differs from the process used for the selection of lesser state and local officials and will, therefore, be dealt with in a later chapter.

History of the nominating process. The first method for nominating candidates in America was the "caucus" which operated during the colonial period. Caucuses were meetings of a few leading patriots in the New England towns to decide what policies and which candidates should be backed for the local elective offices. After the Revolutionary War similar groups could be found in most of the new states. Men of standing in the community met together to decide who were best qualified to represent the general views of those present on public issues.

Later a caucus in Congress decided whom the Jeffersonian Republicans would support for the Presidency. The results of the congressional caucus were made known to the Republicans in each state who expected their presidential electors to support the candidates of the caucus. Legislative caucuses also developed in some states for the nomination of party candidates.

The convention. "King Caucus" reigned for roughly a quarter of a century. It broke down when the congressional caucus in 1824 failed to name the popular candidate, Andrew Jackson. By 1836 the convention system which, it was claimed, would democratize the parties by turning control over to delegates elected by the rank-in-file members, became the dominant method for selecting the candidates of the major parties. The convention, however, was never an instrument of the people. Rather, it was the instrument of the party leaders. Whether it was a convention to name candidates for the town council or a national convention to name the presidential candidates, it was the political leaders who dominated the show. In the earliest conventions there sometimes was no special connection between the population of a district and the number of its delegates at the convention. Travel being difficult, the delegates were frequently either those in the neighborhood or those who planned to be in the convention area on the day it met.

Corruption in the convention. Stories of the corruption of conventions, especially at the state and local level, were well known by the last years of the nineteenth century. In the cities, the party machine used various devices to insure the selection of its favorites. Meetings were called with little notice so that only the machine members were present. They were called for one hour but were started earlier and the hall was packed by the regular organization representatives before the opposition could arrive. The machine sometimes resorted to strong arm tactics to prevent affective opposition, beating or throwing out those who would suggest men and programs contrary to the desires of the bosses.

In the area where populism was dominant—the great farming region which stretched from Wisconsin out through Montana and down through Colorado, Nebraska, and Kansas—the farmers and the people of small towns looked upon the conventions as agents not only of the machines, but of the railroads, the banks, and eastern corporate wealth. The states in this area were dominated by the Republican Party. After the failure of third party movements the only hope for relief was to capture control of the Republican machinery or devise a means of defeating the leadership. Wisconsin rebels, under the leadership of Robert M. La Follette, found a way to defeat the Wisconsin leadership by establishing the first state-wide direct primary system in 1903.

The history of the direct primary. The adoption of the primary in Wisconsin was quickly followed by its adoption in most of the other states of the Middle West and Great Plains areas. The struggle in these states was for the control of the Republican Party nominating process in order to replace conservative legislators with liberal populist legislators.

During the last decades of the nineteenth century the Democratic Party secured its hold on the states of the old Confederacy. So strong was the Democratic position in the South that any competition for public office had

SAMPLE BALLOT OF
REPUBLICAN PARTY
PRIMARY ELECTION MAY 10, 1960

TO VOTE FOR A CANDIDATE MAKE AN X IN THE SQUARE OPPOSITE TO AND TO THE LEFT OF HIS OR HER NAME

National Ticket	State Ticket	County Ticket	Wellsburg District

National Ticket

For UNITED STATES SENATOR
(vote for one)
☐ CECIL H. UNDERWOOD
Sistersville, W. Va.

FOR CONGRESSMAN
(First District)
(vote for one)
☐ ARCH A. MOORE, JR.
Glen Dale, W. Va.

**FOR DELEGATE AT LARGE
TO NATIONAL CONVENTION**
(Vote for Ten)
☐ CECIL H. UNDERWOOD
Sistersville, W. Va.

☐ THOMAS SWEENEY
Wheeling, W. Va.

☐ HOUSTON G. YOUNG
Charleston, W. Va.

☐ MRS. FREDERICK P. BECKER
(VIE BECKER)
Fairmont, W. Va.

☐ REX KEITH BUMGARDNER
Clarksburg, W. Va.

☐ CARL L. COEN
Moundsville, W. Va.

☐ HOWARD V. CORCORAN
Wheeling, W. Va.

☐ WALTER S. HALLANAN
Charleston, W. Va.

☐ ARTHUR M. HILL
Lewisburg, W. Va.

☐ JOHN D. HOBLITZELL, JR.
Ravenswood, W. Va.

☐ B. F. HOWARD
Welch, W. Va.

☐ EUGENE F. IMBROGNO
Charlton Heights, W. Va.

☐ CLEO S. JONES
Charleston, W. Va.

☐ OWEN R. LEWIS
Philippi, W. Va.

☐ DANIEL L. LOUCHERY
Clarksburg, W. Va.

☐ T. WILLIAM MARLOW
Charles Town, W. Va.

☐ JUDSON D. McCORMICK
Red House, W. Va.

☐ GEORGE H. SEIBERT, JR.
Wheeling, W. Va.

**FOR DELEGATE TO NATIONAL
CONVENTION**
First Congressional District
(Vote for Two)
☐ FRANCIS J. LOVE
Wheeling, W. Va.

☐ MARTHA MOORE MYERS
Wheeling, W. Va.

☐ FRANK A. O'BRIEN, JR.
Wheeling, W. Va.

☐ R. PAUL HUTCHINSON
Fairmont, W. Va.

☐ LOUIS LEVENDORF
Weirton, W. Va.

State Ticket

FOR GOVERNOR
(Vote for One)
☐ HAROLD E. NEELY
Hinton, W. Va.

☐ CHAPMAN REVERCOMB
Charleston, W. Va.

FOR SECRETARY OF STATE
(Vote for One)
☐ CARL E. WEIMER
Maysville, W. Va.

☐ MRS. E. K. STEVENS
(VIRGINIA)
Charleston, W. Va.

FOR AUDITOR
(Vote for One)
☐ LITZ ("Cuz") McGUIRE
Logan, W. Va.

FOR TREASURER
(Vote for One)
☐ MARTIN V. CHAPMAN
Huntington, W. Va.

FOR ATTORNEY GENERAL
(Vote for One)
☐ ELMER H. DODSON
Charleston, W. Va.

☐ GEORGE F. BENEKE
Elm Grove, W. Va.

**FOR COMMISSIONER OF
AGRICULTURE**
(Vote for One)
☐ HOWARD PERINE
Mill Creek, W. Va.

**FOR JUDGE OF THE
SUPREME COURT OF APPEALS**
(Vote for Two)
☐ DAYTON STEMPLE
Philippi, W. Va.

☐ E. FRANKLIN PAULEY
Charleston, W. Va.

**FOR JUDGE
FIRST JUDICIAL CIRCUIT**
(Vote for Two)
☐ WILLIAM T. FAHEY
Weirton, W. Va.

☐ JAMES G. McCLURE
Triadelphia, W. Va.

☐ WILLIAM C. PIPER
Wheeling, W. Va.

☐ J. H. BRENNAN
Wheeling, W. Va.

FOR STATE SENATOR
First Senatorial District
(Vote for One)
☐ MRS. RUTH COX TURNER
Chester, W. Va.

**FOR MEMBER STATE
EXECUTIVE COMMITTEE**
First Senatorial District
(Male)
(Vote for Two)
☐ CHARLES F. BACHMANN
Wheeling, W. Va.

☐ RUSSELL G. NESBITT
Wheeling, W. Va.

☐ S. G. "JACK" WELLS
Wellsburg. W. Va.

(Female)
(Vote for Two)
☐ SARALOU L. (Sally) THOMAS
Weirton, W. Va.

☐ MRS. GEORGE F. BENEKE
Wheeling, W. Va.

County Ticket

FOR SHERIFF
(Vote for One)
☐ THOMAS E. BOYD
Wellsburg, W. Va.

☐ JOHN MAZEIKA
Follansbee, W. Va.

☐ GEORGE C. McGOWAN
R.D. 3, Wellsburg, W. Va.

FOR PROSECUTING ATTORNEY
(Vote for One)
☐

FOR COUNTY COMMISSIONER
Wellsburg District
(Vote for One)
☐ WILLIAM O. VANHORN
Wellsburg, W. Va.

FOR HOUSE OF DELEGATES
(Vote for One)
☐ MARGARET I. BRUMMAGE
R.D. 2, Wellsburg, W. Va.

☐ PAUL L. CONAWAY
Wellsburg, W. Va.

☐ CHARLES R. CORBIN
R.D. 1, Wellsburg, W. Va.

FOR ASSESSOR
(Vote for One)
☐

**FOR MEMBER JUDICIAL
CIRCUIT EXECUTIVE
COMMITTEE**
First Judicial Circuit
(Male)
☐ CHARLES GLAZEWSKI
Weirton, W. Va.

(Female)
(Vote for One)
☐ MRS. THEODORE (JESSIE)
BACKEL
Weirton, W. Va.

Wellsburg District

FOR JUSTICE OF THE PEACE
(Vote for Two)
☐ BESSIE HUMMEL ROSS
Wellsburg, W. Va.

☐ EUGENE J. ELCESSER
Wellsburg, W. Va.

FOR CONSTABLE
(Vote for One)
☐ WARREN A. WALLACE
Wellsburg, W. Va.

☐ RALPH HUNTER, SR.
Wellsburg, W. Va.

**FOR MEMBER COUNTY
EXECUTIVE COMMITTEE**
(Male)
(Vote for One)
☐ FRANK FINELL
Wellsburg, W. Va.

☐ THOMAS F. WHITE
Wellsburg, W. Va.

**FOR MEMBER COUNTY
EXECUTIVE COMMITTEE**
(Female)
(Vote for One)
☐ JANE M. DUNCAN
Wellsburg, W. Va.

SAMPLE BALLOT OF REPUBLICAN PARTY West Virginia primaries are "closed" primaries. In order to get a ballot the voter must have indicated his party preference at the time he registered to vote. On the day of the primary he may ask for and receive only the ballot of his party.

to come through the direct primary which would at least allow for a struggle between the factions within the party. South Carolina first introduced the primary as a party rather than a legal provision. "Pitch Fork" Ben Tillman, representing the populist wing of the Democratic Party in South Carolina, pushed through the primary arrangements in that state. Other southern states, like most other states throughout the country, adopted the direct primary during the first two decades of the twentieth century. Since its establishment, the primary has been the major election in the South. With rare exceptions the winner of the Democratic primary has faced little or no opposition in the general election.

NATURE OF THE DIRECT PRIMARIES

The closed primary. Under state law the closed primary is restricted to registered members of each party. At the time of registration or subsequent to the registration, the voter may indicate which party he prefers. His statement of preference may include a further statement that he generally supports the policies of candidates of the party. He is then eligible to vote in the primary of the party of his choice. Most states now use the closed primary, but in a few the rules for changing party affiliation are so lenient that the voter may switch parties almost at will. Raiding of the opposition party's primary is a relatively simple matter. A number of states, however, require that a change of party by the voter makes him ineligible to vote in the primary of any party for at least one election. The latter arrangement makes raiding difficult and tends to discourage frivolous transfers from one party to another.

The open primary. Wisconsin and a half dozen other states employ the "open" primary for the selection of party candidates. Under the open system the voter makes no prior statement about his party. At the time he votes he is given either the ballots of all parties which have qualified under state law as political parties or a ballot with columns for each qualified party. In the former instance he votes to name candidates of one party and discards the ballots of other parties. In the latter case the voter may cast his votes in one of the party columns only. If he votes for candidates in two or more party columns, his ballot is invalidated. Under either system the voter's choice of party is secret. There is nothing to prevent normally Republican or Democratic voters from casting their votes for the opposition aspirants rather than for those seeking their own party's nominations. This kind of raiding of one party by supporters of the other party has often been charged in open primary states. There is fairly conclusive evidence that such raiding actually has taken place on a number of occasions. It is especially prevalent in those states where one party is predominant. Members of the opposition party, feeling that their candidates are unlikely to win in the general election, seek to influence the nominations of the dominant party. For many

Sample Ballot
Consolidated Primary Election Ballot

SEPTEMBER 13, 1960

Walter H. Bergen

County Auditor, St. Louis County, Minnesota.

Democratic-Farmer-Labor Party Ticket	Republican Party Ticket
You cannot split your ballot. If you vote for candidates of more than one party, your ballot will be rejected.	You cannot split your ballot. If you vote for candidates of more than one party, your ballot will be rejected.

Democratic-Farmer-Labor Party Ticket

▼ Put an (x) opposite the name of each candidate you wish to vote for, in the square indicated by the arrow.

UNITED STATES SENATOR IN CONGRESS
VOTE FOR ONE

| | HUBERT H. HUMPHREY |

REPRESENTATIVE IN CONGRESS
8TH DISTRICT
VOTE FOR ONE

| | JOHN A. BLATNIK |

GOVERNOR
VOTE FOR ONE

| | ORVILLE L. FREEMAN |
| | BELMONT TUDISCO |

LIEUTENANT GOVERNOR
VOTE FOR ONE

| | KARL F. ROLVAAG |

SECRETARY OF STATE
VOTE FOR ONE

| | JOSEPH L. DONOVAN |

STATE TREASURER
VOTE FOR ONE

| | CONRAD H. HAMMAR |
| | BILL O. KJELDAHL |

ATTORNEY GENERAL
VOTE FOR ONE

| | WALTER F. MONDALE |

RAILROAD & WAREHOUSE COMMISSIONER
VOTE FOR ONE

| | JOHN A. (JACK) HENDERSON |
| | HJALMAR PETERSEN |

Republican Party Ticket

▼ Put an (x) opposite the name of each candidate you wish to vote for, in the square indicated by the arrow.

UNITED STATES SENATOR IN CONGRESS
VOTE FOR ONE

| | P. KENNETH (P. K.) PETERSON |
| | JAMES MALCOLM WILLIAMS |

REPRESENTATIVE IN CONGRESS
8TH DISTRICT
VOTE FOR ONE

| | JERRY H. KETOLA |

GOVERNOR
VOTE FOR ONE

| | ELMER L. ANDERSEN |

LIEUTENANT GOVERNOR
VOTE FOR ONE

	HURSEL O, (DOC) KALLESTAD
	ART OGLE
	JOHN C. PETERSON
	G. HOWARD SPAETH
	RUSSELL H. UNDERDAHL

SECRETARY OF STATE
VOTE FOR ONE

| | KENNETH O'BRIEN JOYCE |

STATE TREASURER
VOTE FOR ONE

| | VAL BJORNSON |

ATTORNEY GENERAL
VOTE FOR ONE

| | GAYLORD A. SAETRE |

RAILROAD & WAREHOUSE COMMISSIONER
VOTE FOR ONE

	BERNARD E. ERICSSON
	A. L. FREEBERG
	ROBERT M. (BOB) JOHNSON

SAMPLE BALLOT OF CONSOLIDATED PRIMARY ELECTION BALLOT   Minnesota law called for an open primary for the nomination of candidates. With candidates of both parties on the same ballot, the voter clearly does not need to commit himself publicly to either party before casting his ballot. This type of ballot simplifies raiding of one party's primary by the supporters of the opposition party.

years, Democrats were so weak in Wisconsin that they felt their own candidates had little or no chance to win in the general elections. Indeed, the Democratic Party was so weak during the first decades of the present century that there was seldom a contest for the party nominations. Rather, men had to be prevailed upon to run for state and national office out of loyalty to the party or in the hope of receiving patronage appointments on those occasions when a Democrat captured the White House. Since the Democratic candidates were unlikely to win and since there seldom were contests for those nominations, the Democrats of Wisconsin were free to raid the Republican primaries. During these years Democrats cast ballots for the elder Robert M. La Follette in the Republican primary and then voted against him in the general election. They preferred, in other words, to have La Follette rather than the "Stalwart" Republican if they could not elect one of their own candidates. There may well have been occasions during those years when raiding Democrats held the balance of power in the Republican Party primary.

Cross filing. Several variations on the party primaries exist. The most famous of these is the arrangement for the "cross filing" of candidates. Where cross filing existed, a candidate sought the nomination of more than one party. If he secured the nomination of the two major parties he was automatically the winner of the election. Some states required that a candidate must have the permission of his own declared party before his name could be placed on the ballot of another party. In other instances he had to win in the primary of the party of his choice or his name could not appear on the general election ballot regardless of his success in any other party. In New York it has been customary for each Democratic candidate for state office and for New York City offices to seek the endorsement of both the Democratic Party and the Liberal Party. If he secured that endorsement, his name appeared under both party labels in the general election. On other occasions in New York and elsewhere the major parties have named the same candidate in order to prevent the election of a third party candidate.

The most widely known of the cross filing arrangements was in California. Until the election of 1954 a candidate was able to file for nominations in both the Republican and Democratic primaries. Although the Democrats out-registered the Republicans by a wide margin in California for more than twenty years, Republican candidates who held congressional and state-wide offices frequently were able to win both Democratic and Republican nominations against lesser known opponents within the Democratic party. Prior to the change in the law in 1954 incumbents, a majority of them Republicans, won as many as half of the congressional seats with the primary election endorsement of both major parties.

California modified its primary election arrangements in 1954 to require candidates to list their party affiliations at least in abbreviated form on the primary ballots.[2] Almost immediately the number of persons winning the nomination of both parties dropped precipitously. Apparently when Democratic voters saw that one candidate was a Democrat and one a declared Republican, they were much more likely to vote for the Democrat than for the Republican even if the name of the latter was more prominent. Since the Democratic Party of California, through the Democratic Clubs and by state pre-primary convention, was making a stronger bid to its party members, it is not possible to say that all credit for the shift from bi-party nominations to single party nominations was entirely due to the identification of the candidates' politics, but it was certainly the major factor. In 1959 the state legislature of California abolished all cross filing. Today, candidates may file only in the primary of the party with which they are affiliated.

Who is on the primary ballot? The answer to this question is not simple. Allowing for local variations, however, the names of candidates usually appear on the primary ballots as a result of a specified number of signatures on a petition requesting that the names appear. The number of signatures required is usually easily within the reach of any person seriously desiring to have his named entered. A candidate for city council may need less than a hundred and the candidate for governor is not required to have so many names as to discourage his candidacy. In Texas, where the party bears the cost of the primary election, candidates are required to pay a fee which will help defray the election costs. Although the fee is substantial for statewide offices, there has seldom been a dearth of candidates for these positions. Fees for lesser offices are proportionately smaller.

The legal requirements for getting one's name on the ballot are more or less clearly defined in each state. The question of political practice is a very different matter. Local custom is controlling in each area. Generally speaking, any man or woman who has decided he would like "to get into politics" can round up the necessary signatures from among his friends and acquaintances to get his name on the primary ballot as candidate for the state legislature or city council or county attorney or some other comparable office. He or she may take the initiative in getting on the ballot and subsequently in securing the support needed to gain the nomination. In areas where the prospective candidate's party is hopelessly in the minority, the party leadership will probably request the individual to allow his name to be entered by the party in the primary. In such a case there is unlikely to be any competition. In the case of a dominant party where the winner of the primary is likely to be the winner of the election, competition for the nomination is keen because the anticipated rewards are greater. The leadership of the dominant party or factions within the party may endorse and

---

2 It was claimed by some that the abbreviations still helped Republican candidates since the "Rep." might suggest to voters that the Republican candidates were incumbent representatives.

put up candidates for nomination. These leaders may talk with a number of prospective candidates or they may choose from persons who, on their own initiative, have already entered their names in the contest.

For the lesser offices at the town or county level the contestants are usually the ones who have made the move to become candidates. For reasons of ambition, public service, or advancement in their regular professions these young people have decided to have a go at politics. Their names get on the ballot because of their own efforts to get signatures or to secure the support of party or factional leaders.

For national or statewide offices much the same arrangement is true except that party or factional leaders sometimes seek to prevail upon men of standing, whether in public office or in the community, to accept party support for nomination. A successful congressman who comes from a safe district may be asked to run for the Senate or for the governorship. A successful and philanthropic business man may be urged to run for mayor or for a statewide office. These cases, however, are exceptional. Individual initiative is still the normal route to the primary election ballot and to public office.

Pre-primary conventions. Some states by law and more of them by rapidly developing custom allow a pre-primary convention of the parties for the purpose of endorsing a slate of candidates for state offices. This slate may receive preferential position on the ballot, but in any case it will presumably have the advantage of organized support from party leaders prior to the primary election. Candidates with pre-primary convention support are normally favored to win and usually receive the support of the party voters. An occasional dramatic defeat of the convention's endorsee does come about. Senator Alexander Wiley, Republican, of Wisconsin, defeated the convention endorsed candidate in 1956, but such defeats are rare.

Connecticut, the last state to adopt a primary election system, has a unique version of the primary and convention arrangement. The parties in that state meet in state conventions to nominate candidates for the statewide races. If a defeated candidate polls as much as 20 per cent of the convention votes, he may demand a primary. The law has been in effect since 1954 and thus far no primary has been held.

Iowa has a second variation on the primary-convention relationship. In that state, a convention is held after the primary elections to select candidates if no candidate in the primary secured as much as 35 per cent of the total votes cast in the party's primary. This post-primary convention enables a choice among leading candidates when votes are badly divided in the primary election without requiring the expensive "run-off" which is so widely used in the one-party states of the South.

"Run-off" primaries. In the South where the winner of the Democratic primary is almost certainly the winner of the election, the states provide that if no candidate receives a majority of the votes cast in the primary for a particular position then the two candidates receiving the most votes may fight it out in a second or "run-off" primary. The second primary is not required if the runner-up in the first primary may decide that the chances of victory are so remote that it is not worth the time, effort, and money required to make the second race. Unless the margin between the two top candidates is very great, however, a run-off primary is usually needed to determine the nominee.

Contested primaries. Contests in primary elections vary in frequency with the significance of the primaries themselves. In those states in which the second party is of little or no significance in the final election decision, there is seldom a contest for its nomination. In the same states nomination contests within the dominant party are frequently bitterly waged even when an incumbent congressman or senator is seeking re-nomination and re-election. In states where parties are evenly matched a still different picture appears. The incumbent is not usually challenged within his party for the nomination, while a contest is almost certain to develop in the out party. In other words, tradition in those close states calls for the incumbent to have a second or third or fourth try at the office which he has successfully won for his party. The challengers, however, must each time make clear their qualifications in terms of electoral support in order to be their party's entry in the final campaign. The nature of the contest between the parties clearly affects the character of the nomination struggle within each party.[3]

General evaluation of primaries. Primary elections have neither eliminated corruption in politics nor have they destroyed boss rule, although they have made boss rule more difficult. They have made it possible for opponents to challenge the decisions of party leaders with the party members making the final decision. The fact of this higher forum has probably modified the nature of the candidates whom the bosses have supported. The primaries may have hastened a decline of bossism in America, but the decline has also been promoted by the changing role of government. The merit system has reduced the number of appointments available to politicians. State and national governments have more recently taken over many of the welfare functions which were previously administered by the political machines. Old age insurance and other welfare programs which are now administered by the state or national government have considerably reduced the area within which the machines can work to secure loyal supporters. The primary elections have been one more check on the party leaders who once dominated American political life.

If the boss has been weakened, it does not follow that either a state or a national party organization has been strengthened. The federal character of our election system prevents national party control. Primary elections make state control difficult. The decentralization of the parties seems to

---

[3] V. O. Key, Jr., *Politics, Parties, and Pressure Groups* (5th ed., New York: Thomas Y. Crowell Company, 1964), Chapter 16.

have been strengthened. Even powerful local leaders, or bosses, are unable to control more than a very few members of Congress. No one seems to control the position taken by all of the members of Congress from a state— no one controls the congressman except the voters in the primaries in the particular districts from which the member comes.

Those persons who would like to see the development of a disciplined party system, i.e., one in which Republicans always vote with the Republican leadership and Democrats always vote with the Democratic leadership, find the system of direct primaries is frustrating. The federalized nature of the parties has always been a barrier to disciplined national parties. But parties thoroughly controlled at the state level could at least work out compromises and agreements with other state organizations. A party system in which the party leaders are not even certain that their choices will be nominated in the primaries can hardly claim that they will deliver the victorious office holder's votes when delivery is requested by the party leaders in Washington. A congressman, while independent of his party leaders, may be, as Schattschneider has suggested, more subservient to local and parochial pressure groups. So long as there are primaries, the individual candidate in most states knows that his fate is at least as dependent upon the voters as it is upon the party leadership. His loyalties are therefore loyalties not to the party organizations but to the people who participate in the primary elections. Disciplined national, or for that matter state, parties are difficult to develop when the local citizens are the ultimate sources of power.

ELECTIONS

In the United States, unlike many other democratic countries, elections are held at regular intervals as required by the national and state constitutions. Moreover, there are many more elections in this country than in most other nations. England, for example, holds elections to the national legislature only when the Parliament is dissolved, although an election must be held at least every five years.

In the United States, by contrast, there are elections for offices at some level of government every year. By constitutional provision, presidential elections must take place every four years, elections to the lower house of Congress every two years, and senate elections every six years. In addition, local elections are usually held at least biennially. If the local elections fall in odd years voters cast ballots at least once a year. In addition to the general elections, there are primary elections for the selection of candidates for most offices earlier in the same year in which the general elections are held. Finally, special elections may occur at still other times.

All elections for national offices are now held on the first Tuesday after the first Monday in November. This uniformity is in contrast to the earlier variations in the times of even national elections. Maine, for example, changed to the November election of representatives and senators only very recently. Primary elections in the various states are still held at different times, ranging from February to December in the case of some state offices.

Voting districts. For the purpose of administering the elections, the states are divided into voting districts, called precincts. The size of the precincts is determined by law and takes into account the concentration of population in the area as well as the means of casting the vote. Rural precincts may be large areas with relatively few voters, while city precincts are much smaller and may have many more voters. If voting machines are used, the number of persons who may conveniently cast ballots during the hours of an election is, of course, greater than it is in those districts which still use paper ballots. Given the different problems that must be taken into account, it is no wonder that the number of voters in a district varies from less than 100 voters to more than 1000. The voting population of the average district probably falls between 300 and 3000. The elections are usually held in public buildings such as school buildings which are used for other purposes during the remainder of the year. Churches and stores are among the other possible sites that may be used for elections.

Officials. Voting on election days is under the supervision of three or more officials selected solely for that purpose. Laws in most states require that these officials be drawn from the two major parties, which means that the local party leaders usually make the choice of the precinct officers for the area. The majority party expects to receive the majority of the posts. The task of the officials is to check the voters' names against the registration lists, hand out the ballots or supervise the machines, watch the ballot boxes and count the ballots after the polls have closed. The count at each precinct is certified to a central office where the final results are made public. In addition to the publicly appointed officials, each party is allowed to have a designated number of "watchers" present who may challenge the right of prospective voters to vote and make certain that the opposition party indulges in no skulduggery. At a specified distance from the polling place more party workers are busy handing out party lists and making last minute attempts to persuade voters to cast ballots for their party's candidates. The government pays the expenses only of the publicly appointed polling officials. The pay is low, but it has been a traditional bit of patronage for the party organizations to pass out to the party faithful.

Ballots. During the first century of American government, voting was largely unregulated by either the state or national government. Ballots, if the election was not by voice vote, were printed by the parties and handed out by them. With the increasing population and widespread evidence of corruption, the Australian ballot was introduced in most states. The "Australian ballot" merely means that the ballots are printed at state expense, that they are uniform, and that the voter casts his ballot in secrecy. The uniformity of ballots does not extend from state to state. There is great variation in the symbols, if any, which designate the major parties in the different states. The size of the ballot necessarily varies with the number of offices to be filled. Further, the color of the paper and the number of separate ballots which may be given a voter in each election differs under the laws of the various states. These variations have little meaning for the voter. The one significant difference in the ballots is the way in which the names of the candidates for office are listed.

Party-column type. The party-column type, sometimes called the Indiana ballot, is the most widely used; some thirty states now employ it. On this ballot the candidates' names are arranged in party columns. The first column, which is supposed to give the party an advantage with undiscriminating voters, is reserved for the party which won the preceding election. Candidates are listed within each of the party columns in order of the importance of the office sought. In some states a party emblem appears at the top of the column. Just below the emblem is a circle or a square which the voter may check indicating that he wishes to vote a "straight" ticket, i.e., support all of the candidates of the party of his choice. For those who do not wish to cast a "straight" ticket circles or squares are placed opposite the names of each candidate. The voter may, if he wishes, cast a vote for some candidates of one party and some of another party by checking, in the manner prescribed by law, the appropriate squares or circles in the different columns.

Massachusetts type. The ballot used in the remaining states clusters the candidates of all the parties around the office for which each is running. All candidates, regardless of party, for governor will have their names and their party designation listed in a section for gubernatorial candidates. The same will be true for all the candidates for Secretary of State, and so on for each of the other offices. Ballots arranged in this manner are called "Massachusetts ballots." In nonpartisan elections the "Massachusetts ballot" is used and no party designation is placed beside the names of the candidates for the various positions.

Voting machines. Four-fifths of the states now provide for the use of voting machines in both general and primary elections. Machines are used exclusively in New Jersey and in almost every precinct of five or six other states. The machines have served at least two purposes especially in the heavily populated city precincts. They have helped to speed up the whole voting process, including both the casting of the ballots and the counting of the votes. They have also made fraudulent or merely inaccurate counts more difficult if not impossible. The machines cannot, of course, prevent collusion among election officials to allow repeaters and unqualified persons to vote. Nor can they prevent misstatement of the results by crooked officials. Machine voting allows the use of the mechanical equivalent of the "Indiana" or the "Massachusetts" ballots. For the former there is a large lever which permits the voter to cast a ballot for an entire party slate. Small levers are next to the names of the individual candidates should the voter desire to "split" his ticket. For the "Massachusetts" ballot states no provision is made for straight ticket voting. The voter must pull a separate lever for each office.

A BALLOT BOX AND A VOTING MACHINE

Absentee voting. The problem of the voter who is sick or is unable to be in his voting district on election day has bothered officials for many years. Today some provision for absentee voting is made in every state, but the rules are not uniform. Generally anyone seeking the privilege of using an absentee ballot must apply in person or by mail to the appropriate city or county official for an absentee ballot. He must fill out and return the marked ballot several days before the actual election. The absentee ballots must be sent by registered mail and the ballot must indicate that a notary public or some public official has observed the voter fill out the ballot. Absentee ballots are normally checked after the regular ballots have been counted.

Soldier voting. Special provisions have sometimes been made for the hundreds of thousands of persons in the armed services to vote while they are absent from their homes or even from the country. In World War II efforts were made to encourage soldier voting by preparing simplified ballots for the men overseas. Since the war, pressure for some permanent arrangement for absentee voting by military personnel has continued.

CAMPAIGN FINANCING

In the United States money for campaigns, whether for the presidency or for the local coroner, comes from private donations. Neither of the major parties follows the practice of some other countries of exacting dues from party members. Both the state and the national governments regulate these contributions.

Corporations and trade unions are prohibited from directly contributing to the election of any person to public office. The laws, as now written, however, do not prevent corporation executives from contributing to the election of those whom the corporation may favor. Nor do the laws prohibit the unions from collecting funds on a voluntary basis from union members for campaigns. Further, both unions and corporations, under the loosely written laws, are in a position to contribute to the success of their favorite party or candidates by so-called "educational" activities such as encouraging the registration of potential voters who are likely to be supporters of the corporation's or the union's candidates.

National legislation relating to presidential campaigns will be discussed in the next chapter. Here, we will deal with legislation concerning lesser offices.

Corrupt-practices legislation. State governments have much more detailed legislation with respect to the expenditure of funds than the national government. The latter restricts its legislation to cover only the election of national officials—congressmen, senators, the President, and Vice President. The state and the national governments in corrupt practices legislation are concerned not only with expenditures, but with various kinds of pressures and fraud which can be perpetrated in an election. The Hatch Act, for example, provides that persons who hold positions financed by national funds, except purely political positions, may not hold office in political organizations nor participate in most kinds of political activities. Political parties may not solicit funds from such federally paid employees.

Nationally chartered corporations may not contribute to any political organizations. Corporations, whether nationally chartered or not, may not contribute to the campaign funds of senatorial, congressional, presidential, or vice-presidential candidates. Individual officers in corporations are, of course, as free as anyone else to contribute. Expenditures for senatorial and congressional campaigns are restricted, under the Corrupt Practices Act of 1925, to sums of $10,000 and $2,500 respectively. If state maximums are smaller than those of the federal government they are controlling. Candidates in the more heavily populated states are allowed a certain leeway. They may spend up to three cents per voter—the number of voters being that number which voted for all candidates for senator or representative in the last campaign. Even under this modified ruling no senatorial candidate may spend more than $25,000 nor may a congressional candidate spend more than $5,000. Actually, in the heavily populated states where campaigns are vigorously contested, money in excess of these figures is almost certainly spent, but the expenditures are divided among different campaign committees so as to prevent violation of the law. Further, these limitations on expenditures do not apply to primary campaigns.

Periodically movements develop to change the limitations on campaign expenditures and election practices. In campaign years these changes are likely to be more severe and to appear under the heading of "clean election" laws. Such a move was made in the Senate in the early days of the 1960 session. The bill which passed that body, but which did not pass the House provided for a number of restrictive changes in the laws. In non-campaign years, the proposed legislation may be more realistic and more in line with current thinking about campaign financing. In 1957, when no elections were imminent, the Senate proposed legislation which would emphasize publicity concerning contributions and expenditures rather than the limitations on expenditures. Limits of $15,000 for gifts by individuals and $5,000 to any particular candidate were included in the 1957 proposal, but the stress was on publicity. This approach seems more realistic than the more pious proposals for limited, but largely unenforceable ceilings on campaign expenditures.

SUMMARY

Control of both the nomination and election processes is largely in the hands of the state governments. The national government restricts itself to enactment of civil rights legislation to protect Negro voting in some southern states and corrupt practices legislation to prevent fraud in elections to national offices.

Selection of party candidates in the United States is more complicated than in most other countries where the parties privately decide on their nominees. Every state in this country provides for some form of citizen participation in the nominating process. Whatever the form of the direct primary the fact of popular participation limits the power of party leaders to control the action of elected representatives. The primary elections were established during the present century as a reaction against abuses of the convention system as a device for selecting candidates. The states have adopted different types of primaries to handle the nominating process. The two major types are the "open" and "closed" primaries.

Primary elections assume greatest importance in states which have a single strong party. Winning the Democratic primary in the South is the equivalent of election in all except a half dozen congressional districts. The same kind of situation is true in a few areas of the north which are Republican strongholds.

There are variations in the efforts of the states to assure honest elections. All states have some form of registration, print the official ballots, and regulate expenditures. Limits are put on the amount of money which can be spent by individual candidates and by parties, but the major reliance for control of expenditures is a requirement for publicity concerning the sources of funds and purposes of expenditures. In spite of efforts to control expenses it is probable that in many instances campaign receipts and expenditures exceed the amounts contemplated in the law.

BIBLIOGRAPHIC NOTE

Many articles but very few books have been written on voter registration in the United States. The one book which deals with the matter on a nationwide basis, Joseph P. Harris, *Registration of Voters in the United States* (Washington, D. C.: Brookings Institution, 1929) is old but still very useful. Professor Harris has also written *Model Voter Registration System* (rev. ed., New York: National Municipal League, 1957).

Several books on state registration laws and administration are available. Two which are especially interesting deal with registration in southern states, Donald S. Strong, *Registration of Voters in Alabama* (University, Alabama: Bureau of Public Administration, 1956) and O. H. Shadgett, *Voter Registration in Georgia* (Athens: University of Georgia Press, 1956). Both books give some attention to the special problems of Negro registration in the South.

The bibliography for the next chapter will indicate a number of books concerned with the national party conventions. Less material is to be found on state and local nominating conventions. M. Ostrogorski, *Democracy and the Organization of Political Parties*, Vol. II (New York: The Macmillan Co., 1908) discusses the character of the conventions at the turn of the century. Other books describing the development of the direct primary provide some historical materials on the conventions.

Books on primary elections for the nomination of candidates for public office include Charles E. Merriam and Louise Overacker, *Primary Elections* (Chicago: University of Chicago Press, 1928) and Cortez A. C. Ewing, *Primary Elections in the South* (Norman, Okla.: University of Oklahoma Press, 1953). Joseph P. Harris has prepared *A Model Primary Election System* (New York: National Municipal League, 1951).

Professor Harris is responsible for the one book on the whole election process in the nation. His book, *Election Administration in the United States* (Washington, D. C.: Brookings Institution, 1934) is a valuable guide for any student. Constance E. Smith, *Voting and Election Laws* (New York: Oceana Publications, 1960) provides a good coverage of the election and voting laws in fifty states. For an historical background of present day voting arrangements there is E. C. Evans, *A History of the Australian System in the United States* (Chicago: University of Chicago Press, 1917).

Studies of state and local election administration are rewarding for the student of politics. Among the studies that are of interest are Franklin L. Burdette, *Election Practices in Maryland* (College Park, Md.: University of Maryland, 1950) and Judith N. Jamison, *Local Election Administration in California* (Los Angeles: Bureau of Government Research, University of California, 1952).

Special problems in election administration are dealt with in S. J. Eldersveld and A. A. Applegate, *Michigan Recounts for Governor, 1950 and 1952: A Systematic Analysis of Election Error* (Ann Arbor, Mich.: University of Michigan Press, 1954) and D. S. Hecock and H. M. Bains, Jr., *The Arrangement of Names on the Ballot and Its Effect on the Voter's Choice* (Detroit: Wayne University Press, 1956).

The standard textbooks on political parties also provide at least a section on the questions of the administration of both primary and general elections.

Much has been written on the financing of party campaigns and the control of campaign expenditures. The recent study by Alexander Heard, *The Costs of Democracy* (Chapel Hill, N. C.: University of North Carolina Press, 1960) is the most thorough of these books. For a shorter, interesting discussion of campaign financing see, Jasper Shannon, *Money and Politics* (New York: Random House, 1958).

11

Choosing the President

N₀ PART of the American political process has been more discussed or more criticized than our method of nominating and electing the man to fill the highest office in the land. For more than a century foreign observers have entertained us and their fellow-countrymen with descriptions of our national conventions and the oddities of our electoral college system.[1] American writers have been no less critical of the nomination and election procedure.[2] In spite of all the criticisms and the apparent short-comings of the system, however, the national conventions are now about the oldest existing political institutions in this country and, with possible slight modifications, seem destined to continue as the official method for nominating candidates for both major parties. The electoral college, provided for in the Constitution, has remained unchanged in form and largely in practice since the addition of the 12th Amendment in 1804. Changing laws and new methods of communication have modified the nature of the campaigns of the candidates for the presidency, but the institutions which name the candidates and select the ultimate winner have remained the same.

The convention system for nominating party candidates for President and Vice-President is unique. In some states a somewhat similar arrangement is followed for the selection of certain statewide party candidates, but these conventions are pale replicas of what has frequently been called the "greatest political show on earth." The state conventions do not have the importance, the variety, the drama, nor the press and television coverage of national conventions.

The national conventions are the highest official organizations of the two major parties. These conventions make the final decisions for the party on matters of organization. They also formulate general policies—at least to the extent that policies are enunciated by the executive wing of the party.

---

[1] One of the most vigorous criticisms was made by Ostrogorski in *Democracy and the Organization of Political Parties* (2 vols., New York: The Macmillan Co., 1902), Vol. II, p. 248 ff.

[2] *Toward a More Responsible Two Party System*, Committee on Political Parties of The American Political Science Association (New York: Rinehart & Company, 1950).

The conventions offer the one certain opportunity for the leaders of the state and local party groups to meet together in a single place. Some of the leaders may meet as members of the National Committee, but the latter is not as fully representative of a party as is the national convention. The conventions provide the one time when the party, as a party, acts as a national organization.

THE CONVENTION

History. The conventions came into being after the congressional caucus had failed to name the most popular candidate in 1824. The followers of Andrew Jackson were convinced that the congressional caucus was the means of preventing the selection of their hero and set about finding a more satisfactory method for creating popular control of the nominating process. Jackson was nominated in 1828 by various devices in the individual states. In 1832 he was re-nominated by a national convention. By 1840 the convention system was used by both major parties. Some modifications in the method of selecting delegates and in the operation of the conventions occurred during the next decade or so, but by 1856 the organization and operation of the conventions were stabilized and they have remained largely unchanged. Given the federal character of our parties and the separation of powers between the President and Congress, the convention system with all of its inadequacies is likely to remain more or less unchanged for the foreseeable future.

Size of the convention. From the beginning, the size of the convention has been based on the number of each state's electoral vote. In other words, state delegations have been at least as large as the total number of senators and representatives to which a state is entitled in Congress. The Republican Party was the first to modify the principle that the electoral vote of the states should be the sole basis for representation at the convention. The Republican Party, created in part by the slavery issue, was long a regional party with no more than token strength in the South. That area contributed few electoral votes to Republican presidential candidates between 1876 and 1928, yet for most of that period these states sent two delegates to the Republican conventions for each electoral vote of the state. Pro-Republican states in the North were allowed no greater representation at the conventions. In 1916 the northern delegates put through a significant change. Any district which cast fewer than 7,500 votes for the Republican presidential candidate was deprived of one of its two delegates. The power of the largely paper Republican organizations in the South was reduced still further in 1924 when the minimum for two delegates was raised to 10,000. Still later Republicans provided that congressional districts would not be entitled to any convention delegate unless 1,000 votes had been cast for the Republican presidential candidate in the preceding election. In 1956 that figure was raised to 2,000 votes. By this last date, however, the new figure made little difference because defections from the Democratic candidates in recent presidential elections made it possible for almost every southern district to meet the minimum for one delegate. A number of southern state delegations continue to have their size reduced by the requirement of 10,000 votes to justify two delegates from a district.

In addition to limiting the representation of states with few Republican votes a bonus system has been developed to increase the convention strength of the strongly Republican states. Either a senatorial or a gubernatorial victory in non-presidential election years or the casting of the state's electoral votes for Republican presidential and vice-presidential candidates entitles a state to a bonus of six convention delegates. The combination of deprivations and bonuses meant a total of 1,331 delegate votes were allotted for the 1960 convention.

The size of Democratic conventions. The modification of the allotment of delegates to the Democratic convention came first in 1936. The South, which had furnished electoral support to the party in both good and bad years, was given an opportunity to gain bonus delegates in return for the loss of its veto power by the repeal of the two-thirds rule. Bonus convention votes were first given to states casting their electoral votes for the party's presidential candidate. By 1964 the bonus system helped some southern states, but reduced the relative importance of those southern states that failed to give their electoral votes to Senator Kennedy in 1960. The present system gives extra votes for each 100,000 popular votes cast for the Democratic ticket in the state in 1960. In addition 10 bonus votes are given to any state carried by the Democratic candidate. Votes were also given to each member of the party's national committee. The total vote in 1964 amounted to 2,316.

Effect of the bonus system. The cumulative bonus system in the Democratic Party has had the odd effect of greatly increasing the proportional power of some of the small states. A state which, for example, is entitled to nine votes because of the original allowance of three votes for each of the state's three electors (five such states exist) may wind up after the bonuses with as many as 22 votes—two for the national committee members, one for the minimum granted for total votes cast for the ticket, and ten for having carried the state for the party in 1960. Nevada did just that. She received more bonus votes than she received regular votes. Obviously, this arrangement gives proportionately greater strength to the small states than to the large ones. If we look at the Democratic vote in Nevada and New York in 1960 and their representation at the 1964 convention in Atlantic City we can see how much greater is the relative gain of a small state. Each Nevada delegate in 1964 represented 1,440 Democratic voters in the preceding election while each New York convention vote represented 21,074 ballots cast by the citizens of New York for the Kennedy-Johnson ticket. Some analysts have expressed considerable alarm at this over-representation of the less populated states at the Democratic conventions.[3] Actually, this note of alarm can probably be exaggerated. No one can doubt that the real power at most conventions, Democratic or Republican, is certain to lie in the big states. After all New York not only had 177 votes at Atlantic City, but it also has the largest electoral vote for the November election and therefore is the most prized state of all for any presidential candidate.

Who are the delegates? Delegations have traditionally included most of the party organizational leaders, but until recently neither party had officially decreed that they must be delegates. For the 1964 convention, the Democratic Party provided that both national committee members of each state should be delegates to the convention and each one should have a full vote. In most states, even some with presidential preference primaries, state party conventions select some of the at-large delegates from the state and these delegates also are normally chosen from among the top party leaders. Factional divisions within the party, however, may prevent the selection of all of the top leaders.

The bulk of the delegates from most states, whether there is a primary or not, are lesser lights in the party. In many states the rank-and-file delegates are the party faithful with sufficient cash to pay their way to the convention. They are "the deserving ones" who are allowed by their "betters" to go to the convention because of their work for the party in the past and their anticipated contributions in the future. The next convention will see some of the old timers, but the majority of the delegates at the next convention will probably be other deserving ones who have not attended a convention in recent years.

Methods of selection of delegates. In general there are two methods for selecting delegates to national conventions. They may be selected by state or district party conventions or by primary elections. Various combinations of these two devices are to be found in some states. State or local party leaders may in fact name the persons who will appear on a primary ballot as candidates for the national convention delegation. Members of state conventions may be selected by primary elections and the state conventions then select some or all of the delegates to the national convention. In more than half of the states, however, the selection is made without reference to any public primary. The candidates are selected by party meetings or conventions called solely, or primarily, for the purpose of selecting delegates to the national convention. These party meetings are arranged for under the rules of the party in the state or in the district which the delegates are to represent.

Presidential preference primaries. One of the most controversial reforms

---

[3] Paul T. David, Ralph M. Goldman, Richard C. Bain, *The Politics of National Party Conventions* (Washington, D. C.: The Brookings Institution, 1960), pp. 180-181.

of the last half century has been the presidential preference primary. Some writers have seen the preference primaries as the answer to the alleged corruption and weaknesses of the national convention system. They have become so committed to the virtues of the direct primary that they have proposed the creation of a national preference primary. By contrast, the preference primaries have been described by former President Harry S. Truman as "eyewash." Those who join President Truman in his criticism of the primaries point out the great variety in the primaries, the fact that the outcome in some states is not binding on the delegates, that most candidates are not in most of the primaries, that favorite sons destroy the purpose of the public voting, and that raiding in some states by the opposition party makes the decision worse than meaningless.

Today there remain but fifteen states which use the presidential primary either to elect delegates to the national convention or to name the voters' preference for President. The number has fluctuated over the last forty-five years. In 1916, twenty-two states elected delegates to the national conventions under a preference primary law. That number has never been exceeded although it was freely predicted at the time that primaries would replace the state and district conventions as a means of selecting convention delegates. In 1956 some form of primary was held in nineteen states, Alaska, and the District of Columbia. Three of the states and Alaska merely expressed a preference among those whose names had been entered as presidential possibilities. Since 1956 Montana and Minnesota have repealed their presidential primary laws.[4]

Types of presidential primaries. V. O. Key has divided the presidential primaries into four groups.[5] He also makes clear that the importance of the state presidential primaries in the determination of the outcome of the work of the national conventions is affected by the nature of the questions upon which the voters are asked to express themselves. Some of these questions are determined by law, for example, the nature of the ballot itself. Other questions are determined by the action of the candidates in entering or refusing to enter particular primaries. Briefly, the four types of primaries are:

> 1. Those in which the voters express only a preference for candidates, but do not select delegates to the national conventions. The latter task is carried out by state conventions.
> 2. Those in which the voters express a preference among presidential aspirants and at the same time elect delegates pledged to support that candidate.
> 3. Those in which the voters select delegates and express a preference among the candidates. There may or may not be an indication of which candidates the delegates will support.
> 4. Those in which no preference is expressed among candidates, and

---

4 The above material was drawn from David, Goldman, and Bain, *op. cit.*, pp. 218-246.
5 V. O. Key, *op. cit.*, p. 199.

delegates are listed without any indication of their preference for candidates.

Significance of particular primaries. Clearly, the voters' action is of least importance in those states in which unpledged delegates are selected and in which no preference among candidates is stated. In several of the states using this type of primary—New York, Pennsylvania, and Illinois, for example—the parties actually make up the slates of delegates and no competing slates appear to give the voters a choice even among delegates. By contrast, in those states in which there are pledged delegates whose names are clearly connected with one of the candidates there is a clear choice placed before the voter.

Unfortunately, the legal provisions for the ballot do not always play a significant role in the outcome of the primary. For one reason or another in 1960 very few of the presidential primaries allowed voters any real choice. Those states with small populations seldom have any significant contests in the party primaries. There is almost no reason why several candidates should waste their valuable time in an uncertain scramble that offers so few delegates as a reward for considerable effort. These states usually go more or less by default to some local political figure or to one of the major candidates with fairly close connections with the states' political leadership.

The presence of "favorite sons" on the ballot in states holding preference primaries usually precludes the campaigning of the serious national candidates who have no desire to rule out later arrangements with the local leader by competing with him on his home grounds. In 1960, California, Florida, and New Jersey were among the states avoided by the five major candidates because of the entry of local leaders seeking favorite son status.[6]

Particular candidates may have special advantages in particular states thus preventing the entry of competing candidates who do not wish to be beaten in early primaries. Senator John F. Kennedy was the sole entrant in the New Hampshire primary in 1960 because none of the other candidates felt that he could successfully compete with Kennedy in one of his neighboring states. The fact that only one person appeared in the primary minimized its importance as a guide to the convention delegates from other states.

Other problems arise in other states. Wisconsin's primary can be of some significance in forecasting the popularity of the candidates with the party voters. However, when one party has no contest, as was the case in 1960, the open primary allows raiding which may minimize the importance of the election. Oregon, which requires that every candidate appear on the ballot, forces an artificial election in which perhaps only one or two of the candidates really campaign.

In most election campaigns, some of the candidates can avoid the pri-

---

[6] In Ohio in 1960 while the major candidates stayed out, the favorite son Governor DiSalle pledged his slate to Senator John F. Kennedy.

OFFICIAL BALLOT OF THE DEMOCRATIC PARTY MAY 10, 1960

OFFICIAL BALLOT OF
THE DEMOCRATIC PARTY

Primary Election   **May 10, 1960**

To vote for a candidate make an X in the square opposite to and at the left of his name.

NATIONAL TICKET	STATE TICKET	COUNTY TICKET	DISTRICT TICKET
For President (Vote for one)	**For Governor** (Vote for one)	**For Judge of the Circuit Court** **10th Judicial Circuit** (Vote for one)	**SHADY SPRINGS DISTRICT** **For Justice of the Peace** (Vote for two)
HUBERT H. HUMPHREY Waverly, Minnesota	OREL J. SKEEN Ripley, W. Va.	NORMAN KNAPP Beckley, W. Va.	ROY L. CHILDS Glen Morgan, W. Va.
JOHN F. KENNEDY Boston, Massachusetts	HULETT C. SMITH Beckley, W. Va.	**For Sheriff** (Vote for one)	J. E. "LEFTY" MAYS Beaver, W. Va.
For United States Senator (Vote for one)	WILLIAM WALLACE BARRON Elkins, W. Va.	TONEY KARANTONIS Colcord, W. Va.	T. H. "HERB" WILLS Beaver, W. Va.
JENNINGS RANDOLPH Elkins, W. Va.	**For Secretary of State** (Vote for one)	C. A. "SLIM" THOMPSON Beckley, W. Va.	**For Constable** (Vote for two)
For Congressman Sixth District (Vote for one)	WILLIAM E. BURCHETT Huntington, W. Va.	HARRY E. ANDERSON Beckley, W. Va.	LAKE WHITE Beaver, W. Va.
JOHN M. SLACK, JR. Charleston, W. Va.	JOE F. BURDETT Point Pleasant, W. Va.	EDGAR S. "ED" HALSTEAD Beckley, W. Va.	L. A. "SMOKEY" WICKLINE Beaver, W. Va.
For Delegate at Large to National Convention (Vote for Twelve)	**For Auditor** (Vote for one)	**For County Commissioner** (Vote for one)	CHARLES S. COLE Beaver, W. Va.
C. W. HARRISON Huntington, W. Va.	L. W. (LANCE) FOLEY Mt. Nebo, W. Va.	CHARLES T. BURDISS Coal City, W. Va.	BILL E. CRAWFORD Cool Ridge, W. Va.
MRS. BEATRICE BURNS HARVEY Lewisburg, W. Va.	EDGAR B. SIMS South Charleston, W. Va.	H. DALE COVEY Glen Daniel, W. Va.	JOHN PATE Beaver, W. Va.
HARRY W. HILL Williamson, W. Va.	**For Treasurer** (Vote for one)	H. G. FARMER Bolt, W. Va.	**For Member County Executive Committee** (Male)
WM. BRUCE HOFF Parkersburg, W. Va.	JACK A. NUCKOLS Beckley, W. Va.	**For Prosecuting Attorney** (Vote for one)	(Vote for one)
E. L. JAMES Institute, W. Va.	GEORGE E. (ERNIE) BAKER Clarksburg, W. Va.	THOMAS CANTERBURY Bolt, W. Va.	ROBERT SWEENEY Cool Ridge, W. Va.
CLAUDE R. LINGER Burnsville, W. Va.	JOHN H. KELLY Charleston, W. Va.	ANTHONY J. SPARACINO Beckley, W. Va.	WILSON WOOD Beaver, W. Va.
CHARLES M. LOVE Charleston, W. Va.	HUGH N. MILLS Ravenswood, W. Va.	**For Assessor** (Vote for one)	WELTON "CALAWAY" LILLY Shady Springs, W. Va.
C. LANCE MARSHALL Blue Creek, W. Va.	**For Attorney General** (Vote for one)	COTTON WHITE Beckley, W. Va.	JAMES H. REDDEN, JR. Shady Springs, W. Va.
ROBERT H. MOLLOHAN Fairmont, W. Va.	C. DONALD ROBERTSON Clarksburg, W. Va.	IRA WHITLOCK Beckley, W. Va.	WILEY SHEPHERD Beaver, W. Va.
HOMER A. MOSS Hurricane, W. Va.	HAROLD A. BANGERT Charleston, W. Va.	**For House of Delegates** (Vote for four)	(Female)
J. HOWARD MYERS Martinsburg, W. Va.	WADE H. BRONSON, JR. Williamson, W. Va.	MRS. W. W. "JACKIE" WITHROW Sophia, W. Va.	(Vote for one)
ROBERT E. McCORD Wellsburg, W. Va.	LEE M. KENNA Charleston, W. Va.	H. BEURAN ATKINSON, JR. Beckley, W. Va.	INA LUSK Shady Springs, W. Va.
SAM J. ROMANO Clarksburg, W. Va.	**For Commissioner of Agriculture** (Vote for one)	T. E. BAZZARRE Beckley, W. Va.	MRS. JOHN McGINNIS Shady Springs, W. Va.
BURL A. SAWYERS Charleston, W. Va.	CHARLES M. VAUGHAN South Charleston, W. Va.	WILLIAM A. "BILL" BUCHANAN	MRS. ARDITH BOLT Shady Sr
WALTON SHEPHERD Charleston, W. Va.	WILLIAM B. (BILL) FOX Huntington, W. Va.		
JOHN M. SLACK, JR. Charleston, W. Va.			
THOMAS P. SNELSON Huttonsville, W. Va.			
JAMES			

The choice of presidential nominees in upper left of ballot with dozens of nominees for other offices.

maries without jeopardizing their status at the convention. In 1960 only Senators Hubert H. Humphrey and John F. Kennedy did any extensive campaigning in the primaries. The other candidates contented themselves with negotiating with the political leaders in those states which still select delegates through conventions. Except in the odd Oregon primary, neither of these men ever faced Senator Lyndon Johnson or Senator Stuart Symington. In 1960 Senator Kennedy's victories were undoubtedly important in his first-ballot victory at Los Angeles. The primary losses eliminated Senator Humphrey. The failure of Senators Johnson and Symington to enter the contests at all certainly did not help their chances of nomination.

If all candidates cannot be forced into contests, why do any of the candidates find it worthwhile. The reasons vary, but perhaps the most valid answer is that some candidates have so little organizational support that they feel they cannot compete with the other candidates in political horse-trading. They feel that their one hope of winning the nomination is tied up with their ability to demonstrate to the delegates at the national convention that they can draw votes. Such a position was clearly Senator Humphrey's in 1960 and to a large extent Senator Kennedy's as well. Each man faced possible elimination by competing in the primaries, but each felt he had no chance unless he entered the primaries. Senator Goldwater's victory in California drew other necessary delegates.

Defeat in the primaries. Victories in the primaries may not insure victory at a national convention, but serious defeat in a primary may force a candidate out of contention. Wendell Willkie withdrew from the race in 1944 after being badly beaten in the Wisconsin primary. Harold Stassen was eliminated from the Republican contest in 1948 by his defeat in Oregon. Kefauver, who had gained prominence in 1952 and 1956 by winning primaries—even uncontested primaries—was beaten so badly in California in 1956 by Adlai Stevenson that he was no longer a serious contender. Governor Rockefeller ceased to be a contender in 1964 after his California defeat.

Perhaps the major importance of the primaries may be summarized then as follows. They allow candidates to rise who lack organizational support to negotiate with state party leaders. These contenders may not win the nomination, but they at least make certain that their names are before the convention. The second significance of the primary is its capacity for eliminating candidates who have campaigned, but have been badly beaten.

ORGANIZATION OF THE CONVENTION

The call for the convention. The national conventions always authorize the national committee of the party to issue the call for the next convention. The national chairman and the national committee are responsible for the selection of the time and place for the convention. Their decisions are usually made late in the year preceding the election although the official call for the convention may not be issued until January or February of the election year. The committee in making its choice is concerned with a number of problems. They must have a building large enough to seat not only the numerous delegates and their alternates, but also large enough to allow a reasonable number of spectators to watch the proceedings. They must consider the effect of the location of the convention upon the probable candidates. Some candidates will almost certainly be favorably or unfavorably affected by the location. Their "representatives" on the national committee are always alert to promoting or defending their favorite's interests. The committee is also concerned with the amount of money that the cities are willing to put up in order to attract the convention and the facilities for the housing of the delegates and visitors. In recent years, Chicago and Philadelphia have been the favorite convention cities, although the Republicans in 1956 and 1964 and the Democrats in 1960 journeyed to California for their meetings. The 1964 Democratic meeting was in Atlantic City.

Officers of the convention. Three officers play a powerful role at the conventions. The national chairman of the party serves as chairman of the convention until such time as the temporary chairman is selected. The latter serves until the permanent chairman is elected. Each has considerable influence during his period of tenure as chairman of the convention; but obviously, the permanent chairman is in the position of greatest influence.

DEMONSTRATING AT A NATIONAL CONVENTION

It is he who recognizes speakers, or, what is equally important, refuses to recognize them. It is he who rules on the outcome of voice votes, a matter of considerable importance and great difficulty in conventions of their size.

The permanent chairman in recent years has been the speaker or minority leader of the House of Representatives. Speakers Sam Rayburn and Joseph Martin chaired the conventions for a number of years until

Rayburn refused the honor in 1960 because of his close relation to Senator Lyndon Johnson, a leading contender for the nomination in that year. Congressman Martin was defeated for minority leadership of the House of Representatives in 1959 and subsequently was replaced by Charles Halleck as permanent chairman of the Republican 1960 convention. Republicans in 1964 chose a former national chairman, Senator Thruston Morton, while Democrats chose Speaker John McCormack. The frequent choice by both parties of the Speaker or a former Speaker of the House of Representatives as chairman is a tribute to the standing of these men within their party and to their devotion to party unity. It is hard to overstress the importance of a chairman committed to party unity, particularly when one considers the sharp divisions that now exist in both major parties.

Convention committees. Four committees are selected for each of the conventions. These committees are: credentials; platform and resolutions: permanent organization; and rules and order of business. A committee has a member from each state delegation and they are really selected by the state delegations and merely ratified by the convention. Except under unusual circumstances, the two most important committees are the credentials committee and the committee on platform and resolutions. The former is sometimes crucial in the seating of delegations. In close contests the seating of a delegation may determine the outcome of the nomination. In the Republican Party contests have occurred in almost every convention during the last half century over the seating of southern delegations. In southern states where the Republican Party has been small and largely inactive it has often been difficult to say with certainty which delegation represented the "real" party organization in a particular state. The contests, then, have been between delegations claiming to represent the state party, but in fact have been delegations supporting particular leading candidates. The struggle between the candidates and their southern supporters is quickly transferred to the credentials committee where again there is a test of strength between the supporters of the candidates on the committee. The results of the credentials committee rulings in the Republican conventions of 1912 and 1952 played a major role in determining the convention's selection of William Howard Taft and Dwight D. Eisenhower over Theodore Roosevelt and Robert Taft in the respective conventions. In states where party organizations are more stable and more clearly recognizable there are seldom serious disputes between competing groups claiming to be the legitimate delegates from a particular state. No disputes have arisen over the delegates selected by presidential primaries.

The platform and resolutions committee. The platform committee has sometimes been of little importance while on the other occasions it has been the crucial committee of the convention. When no serious issues divide the convention the report of the platform and resolutions committee is adopted by a voice vote almost without consideration. The committee has, in such a case, listened to and attempted to please all who asked for special planks. It has sought to provide something for almost every minority group in the country while at the same attempting not to offend any other minority group. Occasionally, the committee finds it impossible to ignore a major issue which sharply divides the party. When this happens the struggle for control of the committee is brisk and the debate on the report of the committee may be very heated. In recent years the hottest debates on the reports of the platform and resolutions committee have taken place in the Democratic convention and have been concerned with civil rights. In 1948, the committee attempted to please both the northern and southern wings of the party. It failed to satisfy either. Each side offered amendments to the report on the floor of the convention. Ultimately, the Humphrey-Biemiller Resolution which favored a strong civil rights position was adopted causing several southern delegations to walk out of the convention. Similar fights have been threatened on other occasions in both parties, but no comparable struggle has taken place on the floor of the convention in recent years. In 1964 the major struggle was inside the Republican platform committee over a series of domestic issues.

The other committees. The committee on permanent organization recommends the permanent officers of the convention. Over the past century some serious fights have occurred within the committee and on its reports because it was recognized that the selection of the permanent chairman could give one candidate an advantage over his opponents. In recent years, the permanent chairman has usually been a man so dedicated to maintaining party unity that no faction could claim that he had seriously influenced the outcome of the nomination and therefore there has been little effort to beat down the decisions of the committee.

The committee on rules and order of business usually proposes to the convention that it adopt the rules of the preceding convention. It also proposes the apportionment of delegates for the next convention. The Democratic Convention of 1936 delegated this latter task to the National Committee asking it to come up with a solution to the problem of how to recompense the southern states for the loss of the two-thirds rule. The Democrats seldom have any controversy over the report of this committee, in part because in each of the last few conventions each state has been allotted all the delegates to which it had been entitled in the previous convention plus the possibility of a number of bonus delegates. The Republican conventions have at least heard mutterings from southern delegations as the committee recommended restrictions on the number of delegates allowed in districts which produced fewer than a specified number of votes for the party's candidates in the preceding election.

Voting arrangements at the conventions. The two parties today cast their votes at the convention in roughly the same manner, i.e., one delegate equals one vote, but there are still vestiges of an earlier era to be found in the Democratic Party practice. In the first Democratic convention in 1831 the party provided for a requirement of two-thirds support for the nomination of the candidate for Vice-President. At the next convention the rule was extended to include both the presidential and vice-presidential candidates. That rule continued for just over a century before being repealed at the 1936 convention. At the time of the adoption of the rules at each convention it could have been repealed by simple majority action, but, in spite of discussion of the need to repeal the two-thirds rule, nothing happened. The two-thirds rule prevented the nomination of the man with a majority of the votes in some of the earlier conventions before the Civil War. Then followed a long period during which the first one to gain a majority later went on to win the necessary two-thirds support. During the present century the two-thirds rule once more operated to defeat some candidates who had majority support in the early balloting.[7]

The presence of the two-thirds rule gave the southerners, who for many years were the party's major strength in Congress but who could not select one of their own men for the presidential post, a veto over the convention's selection. The end of the rule and with it the end of the South's veto power over the nomination opened the way to the selection of men whose views on civil rights were vastly different from the views held by most southern delegates. Not only could the South no longer control nominations, but as we shall see, it often could not affect the outcome of the elections themselves.

The unit rule. The provision that the state delegations would be bound to vote as a unit for the candidate supported by a majority of the delegation was once firmly established in the Democratic Party. The unit rule had the effect of bolstering the power of the states when the two-thirds rule was also in operation. Unless state conventions and later state primary laws provided to the contrary, state delegations at the Democratic conventions were bound to vote as a unit. In more recent years a number of states have abandoned the rule, but it continues in effect in some state delegations to the Democratic conventions even today.[8] The unit rule gives state delegation leaders greater authority when trading or jockeying for position at the convention.

Republican conventions have adamantly refused throughout their history to support the unit rule. Even in those instances where state conventions have instructed the entire delegation to abide by the decision of the majority of the delegation, the convention has ruled that each man must vote as an individual and that decisions by state organizations are not binding upon the national convention. There may be occasions when a delegation allows itself to be bound by the unit rule. However, if any

---

[7] David, Goldman, and Bain, *op. cit.,* 208-212.
[8] *Ibid.,* 199-202.

member of the delegation should appeal to the chair there is little doubt that he would be freed from an obligation to abide by the decision of the majority of his delegation.

THE CANDIDATES

Presidential candidates. Some years ago it was the custom of political commentators to state who could and who could not be expected to receive the nomination of the respective conventions.[9] One man laid down some 15 qualifications or restrictions on the character of the persons who could be expected to seek the nominations successfully. Some of the "rules" undoubtedly still apply, but the leading contenders for the Republican and Democratic nominations in 1960 indicate that some of the previously accepted "laws" no longer hold true. In part because of changes in the electorate and in part because of changes in the character of the problems facing the country, new types of candidates seem to be arising and their characteristics may continue to change as the country and its problems change.

Generally speaking, until 1960 it was assumed that a candidate must be white, Protestant, middle-aged, preferably with a background as governor of a large state although a military hero could be substituted if available, and, of course, male. By the same token certain persons were considered as definitely eliminated from consideration. Senators, southerners, men from small states (unless they had succeeded to the Presidency from the Vice-Presidency), those identified with special economic interests whether labor or big business, those who had held the Vice-Presidency but not succeeded to the Presidency, and all twice defeated candidates. While there had been exceptions to some of these limitations during the early decades of the present century, it was not until 1960 that we were faced with the fact that perhaps none of these limitations was particularly important. As a matter of fact, all of the leading Democratic and Republican presidential hopefuls in 1960 would have been unavailable for the nomination if all the limiting factors had been controlling. Senator Kennedy and Vice-President Nixon would have been unlikely to win according to earlier estimates. By old standards, Goldwater's nomination was unlikely in 1964.

Vice-presidential candidates. Traditionally, the vice-presidential candidate has come from a different area of the country than the head of the ticket. Usually the second man has represented a different point of view or a faction of the party different from the one represented by the presidential candidate. A "balanced ticket" was the aim of the leaders of the convention. The vice-presidential candidate might or might not be chosen by the presidential nominee, but the latter probably at least cleared the

---

9 Sidney Hyman, *The American President* (New York: Harper and Bros., 1954), pp. 231-232.

choice for the second position before the convention acted. In any case, it made little difference unless the President died since the Vice-President largely disappeared from public view immediately after taking the oath of office.

In recent years, the Vice-President has taken on more and more tasks. Under Franklin Roosevelt, John Nance Garner assisted with congressional liaison work and Henry A. Wallace headed various wartime boards and commissions. President Truman called on Alben Barkley for many services. The Vice-Presidency has taken on its greatest importance, however, during the two Eisenhower terms. The President sent Vice-President Nixon on a number of trips overseas as his representative. He asked Nixon to attend cabinet and National Security Council meetings; in his absence, Nixon chaired the meetings. In addition, Nixon handled much of the campaigning and political work for the President.

With the change in the character of the office has come a change in the requirements for the incumbent. The "balanced ticket" can no longer be the ideal. The Vice-President must be of much the same mind as the President, since he must act on behalf of the Chief Executive on more and more public matters. If the President is to take the Vice-President fully into his confidence and into the highest councils, the President must think of him as a cooperative ally, not as a man with different views who holds his job simply because he could attract voters who would not have supported the candidacy of the President himself. Both Eisenhower and Kennedy expressed themselves strongly on the Vice-President's having a similarity in outlook and willingness to cooperate fully with the President. It is likely that the future will see a continuing development along these lines and an end to the naming of candidates with significantly differing economic and social points of view.

THE CAMPAIGNS

Several months or even several years may go in to the struggle for the nomination. Three or at most four months are left after the conventions to campaign against the opposition party. This amount of time may be more than is necessary to develop the issues and allow the voters to make up their minds. The British allow but three weeks for a campaign, and they are apparently able to make the issues at least as clear as the American candidates do with their much longer period of speaking. Most voting studies tell us that the great majority of the voters have actually made up their minds months before the campaign is over and that a majority have made their decisions before the candidates are actually nominated.[10] There are, of course, exceptions to this rule. Assuming that the polls were accurate in

---

[10] Paul Lazarsfeld first made this point, and other students of voting behavior have since confirmed it.

the spring and summer of 1948, enough Americans either made up their minds or changed their minds during the last weeks and days of the campaign to bring Truman to victory. Nevertheless, it is at least possible that, had a decision been forced earlier, most of the changes of position would have taken place in time to have brought about the same results.

Changing campaign practices. The campaign methods of the incumbent as compared with the outsider are bound to differ. The incumbent, or the candidate of the party controlling the White House, must defend the actions of the previous four or eight years. The candidate of the "out" party is freer to criticize and to make promises. These basic conditions of campaigns are essentially the same today as they were a hundred years ago.

The job of campaigning, however, in other respects is very different from an earlier era. The task is both easier and more difficult. A century or even a half a century ago, the candidates spoke to a few thousand or a few hundred thousand persons at rallies and from the platform of observation cars on the "Presidential Specials." Speeches could stress one or two subjects throughout the campaign, and the emphasis might be varied slightly to fit the special conditions of the area in which the candidate found himself. He traveled much, but did not need to cover many topics in his talks.

Today the candidate reaches millions of voters in each of his nationally televised speeches. Viewers can make judgments not only about his program but about the nature and character of the speaker. The candidate can cover hundreds of thousands of miles by plane instead of a few thousand miles by train. He can be certain that all who are interested have seen and heard him speak or read his speeches. This opportunity to reach the mass of the citizens is an advantage, but it also means that his speeches cannot be confined to two or three topics nor exclusively to generalities. The very fact that many can hear him every time he makes a pronouncement also means that he must talk on all or most of the major issues of the day and develop his position on each of the questions. The sheer speech writing problem is much greater. No man, even the most talented of writers, can any longer be the full author of his speeches. He may control the content and put on the finishing touches, but he cannot write every line. He certainly cannot do the research needed for the speeches by himself.

Electoral college and campaign issues. Parties and candidates adjust their actions and their campaigns to the nature of the problems which confront them. The presidential candidates and the presidential wing of both parties are faced with certain hard political facts of our constitutional and political arrangements. Victory goes to the candidate who secures a majority of the electoral votes. In other words it becomes necessary to win a popular voting majority in most states which have a large electoral vote. Today those votes are to be found in the major industrial states like New York, Pennsylvania, Illinois, Ohio, California, Indiana, and Michigan. As the country becomes more and more homogeneous and the problems of the workers and minorities in the East become more like the problems of these same groups in the Middle West and the Far West, the candidates and their supporters feel that the campaigns must be directed toward those groups which may well determine the fate of the electoral votes of the large states and therefore the outcome of the elections.

U. S. VOTER PARTICIPATION FIGURES, 1920–1962[10a]

Turnout in elections for President and House of Representatives. *Vote is indicated as a percentage of the civilian population of voting age.*

Year	President	Representatives
1962	—	48.9
1960	63.8	59.4
1958	—	43.4
1956	60.1	56.6
1954	—	42.2
1952	62.0	58.2
1950	—	41.6
1948	51.5	48.6
1946	—	37.6
1944	56.3	53.0
1942	—	32.7
1940	59.7	56.2
1938	—	44.5
1936	57.5	54.0
1934	—	41.8
1932	52.9	50.2
1930	—	34.1
1928	52.3	48.2
1926	—	30.1
1924	44.3	41.0
1922	—	32.4
1920	44.2	41.4

Electoral arrangements. Electors for each state, according to the Constitution as amended in 1804, are to equal the number of senators and representatives to which a state is entitled in Congress.[11] Further, each elector shall vote for a presidential and a vice-presidential candidate. If no candidate for the Presidency receives a majority of the electoral votes the contest shall be transferred to the House of Representatives and the choice be made from among the top three candidates with each state delegation casting one vote. As a matter of custom, since 1796 the electors have cast their votes in accordance with the decision of the voters in each state. In the years from 1832 to 1960 only five of a total of 18,978 electors have voted contrary to the popular decision within a state. Nothing in the Constitution requires electors to cast their votes for the leading vote getter in a state, but custom has decreed several significant rules. First, each party presenting candidates also presents a slate of electors who are pledged to support those candidates. The slate presented to the voters is on a statewide rather than a local or district basis. This means that all the electors of one party are elected

---

10a Source: U. S. Bureau of the Census, *Statistical Abstract of the U. S.: 1962*, eighty-third edition, Washington, D. C., 1962.

11 The Twelfth Amendment, see appendix.

THE RISING COSTS OF PRESIDENTIAL CAMPAIGNS

**Combined Democratic-Republican
Expenditures at the National Level**

(in millions of dollars)

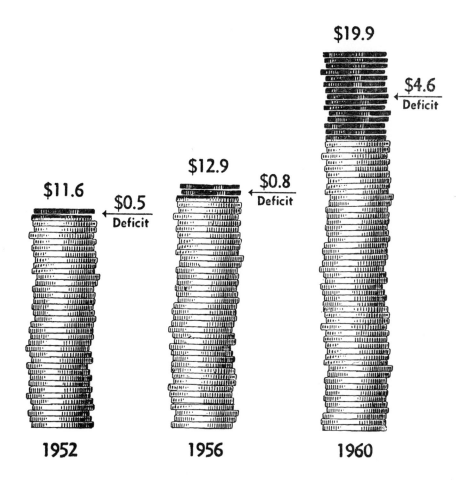

Note: This was money actually spent by committees operating in more than one state, not including money transferred to other organizations.

SAMPLE
OFFICIAL BALLOT
STATE OF MISSISSIPPI
REGULAR ELECTION
NOVEMBER 8, 1960

FOR
PRESIDENTIAL ELECTORS
(VOTE FOR EIGHT)
Nominees of the
Democratic Party of the State
of Mississippi
Pledged to Vote for
John F. Kennedy
for President
and
Lyndon B. Johnson
for Vice-President
of the United States of America

Frank K. Hughes .... ( )
David E. Guyton .... ( )
Will M. Whittington .... ( )
Frank E. Shanahan, Jr. .... ( )
Martin V. B. Miller .... ( )
Edward H. Stevens .... ( )
Curtis H. Mullen .... ( )
Mrs. Lovie Gore .... ( )
.... ( )

Nominees as
Unpledged Electors of The
Democratic Party of the
State of Mississippi
for President
and
Vice-President
of the United States of America

Henry Harris .... ( )
George Payne Cossar ...... ( )
Charles L. Sullivan .... ( )
Clay B. Tucker .... ( )
Earl Evans, Jr. .... ( )
Robert R. (Bob) Buntin .... ( )
Dr. D. M. Nelson .... ( )
Lawrence Y. Foote .... ( )
.... ( )

Nominees of the
Mississippi Republican Party
Pledged to Vote for
Richard M. Nixon
for President
and
Henry Cabot Lodge
for Vice-President
of the United States of America.

John M. Kaye .... ( )
Ralph O. White .... ( )
J. H. Snyder .... ( )
J. J. Newman .... ( )
George W. Shaw .... ( )
C. E. Tolar .... ( )
Dr. Noel Womack, Jr. ...... ( )
J. B. Snider .... ( )
.... ( )

Note that the electors are listed with the names of the candidates to whom they are pledged. The unpledged Democratic slate carried a plurality of the state's votes.

whether the party wins by one vote or one million votes.[12] All minority votes in a state are completely wasted in the sense that they have no bearing on the vote of the electors who cast the officially deciding ballots for President and Vice-President.

The fact that each state casts a unanimous electoral ballot for one ticket places a premium on the large states with the large electoral votes. Anyone who receives the electoral votes of the seven states listed above needs only another fifty votes to assure his election. Since there is a high degree of similarity among industrial and metropolitan areas regardless of geographic location, the candidates are certain to pay particular attention to the desires and wishes of the citizens of these metropolitan areas. Presidential candidates, then, seek always to appeal to the large minorities which may swing the big and usually doubtful states in the party column. In so doing they may alienate less urbanized and less industrialized states.

In the last few campaigns this trend toward appealing to urban minorities has been particularly apparent. The largest single minority has been the Negro voters in the big cities of the North. Even the Democrats, who have traditionally received the support of the southern states, have come more and more to appeal to the Negro minority in the big cities. The candidates are willing to sacrifice southern support if taking a strong stand on civil rights legislation is the only means of assuring Negro support in the North. The candidates are aware that with two exceptions the winning candidate would have won without any southern electoral votes in every election since 1920. Even in 1948, President Truman lost four southern states but still managed to win the election because he carried enough of the large northern states. Had it not been for the diversion of some probable Democratic votes to the Wallace Progressives he would have picked up still more northern electors. The South, therefore, on the issue which is crucial both to them and to the Negro minority in the northern cities, is disregarded in favor of the Negro minority which may determine the outcome of the election in the industrial states. In 1960 Senator Kennedy won in spite of losing four southern states. Again the big northern states were crucial to his election.

The Republican campaign in 1964 seemed to fall outside the recent pattern as described above. The national convention nominated Senator Goldwater, who had voted against the 1964 Civil Rights Act on the grounds that two sections were unconstitutional. He pledged to enforce the law if elected, but otherwise gave no indication of seeking out the urban Negro vote. Instead, he appeared to be the candidate of the middle class voters who preferred to make relatively few changes in existing economic, political, and social institutions of the country.

The Election of 1964. The presidential election of 1964 upset patterns that had characterized American presidential politics for the preceding half

---

12 Alabama Democrats divided the electoral vote in 1960.

century. Unlike campaigns of the recent past which witnessed a high degree of agreement on fundamentals between Republican and Democratic opponents, the 1964 campaign presented distinct alternatives to the electorate. The Republican campaign, in fact, took as its theme the notion that Senator Goldwater offered "a choice instead of an echo" to the policies of incumbent President Lyndon B. Johnson.

This theme reflected the displeasure felt by conservative elements in the Republican Party who resented the fact that since 1940 Republican presidential nominations had been dominated by the Eastern and moderate wing of the party—a wing that accepted most of the domestic and foreign policies of the Democrats but promised to do a better job administering these policies.

The results of the campaign were a staggering setback to these conservative forces. Senator Goldwater and the Republican Party suffered the worst popular defeat in history as President Johnson captured 61.3 percent of the votes cast. Electorally, Johnson won 486 electoral votes to 52 for Goldwater.[13]

Of particular interest was the geographic composition of the election results. Reflecting the salience of civil rights and Senator Goldwater's refusal to vote for the Civil Rights Act of 1964, the Republican candidate's base of electoral support was virtually confined to the Deep South. Goldwater took the electoral votes in Alabama, Georgia, Louisiana, Mississippi, and South Carolina. He also carried his home state of Arizona by a narrow margin. Johnson won every other state, including such traditional Republican strongholds as Maine, Vermont, New Hampshire, Kansas, and Nebraska.

The magnitude of the Johnson landslide carried a number of Democratic congressional and senatorial candidates into office. In the House the Democratic margin rose to 295 to 140 and the party emerged from the election with a 68 to 32 majority in the Senate. Thus, Lyndon B. Johnson began his first full term as President with the most favorable party balance in Congress since the New Deal days of Franklin D. Roosevelt.

Two constituencies. A word should be said about the two election constituencies. The President, as we have noted, feels he is dependent upon the northern industrial states for his election. He must, if a choice has to be made, choose their support rather than the support of the more rural south with its special minority problems. By contrast, the congressional party which is elected from districts in each state and which depends as much on the southern congressmen as on any other for its majority cannot ignore the supporters from that area. In addition, the rural areas are over-represented in Congress in terms of their population. The result is that the Congress is more conscious of southern and rural problems than the President can afford to be.

Given these differences in constituents it is not surprising that the ideological center of gravity of the two parties in Congress is somewhat more conservative than the position taken by the presidential candidate of either

---

[13] The total electoral vote of 538 included the three votes allotted to the District of Columbia, which participated in a Presidential election for the first time in 1964.

party. Seymour Martin Lipset has suggested that a Republican President, despite the more conservative orientation of the Republican Party, is not very far away from a Democratic Congress in his outlook.[14] Congressional Democrats as a group are more conservative than their own presidential candidates but they are more liberal than their Republican colleagues in Congress.

Presidential candidates of the two major parties compete for the same marginal voters during the campaign. The Republican candidate is reasonably certain of a majority of business and professional groups. The Democratic candidate is equally certain of a majority of labor votes. The candidates of the two parties do not expect to receive all of the votes from their major sources of support, but over the years they have received a substantial majority of the votes from these groups. Both candidates need to appeal to the marginal voters if they are to win a majority of the popular and electoral votes. Both must appeal to minority groups in the major cities. Under conditions of declining farm income, both must appeal to farm groups. Since both candidates are bidding for the same support, both candidates are likely to make more or less the same promises. These promises probably coincide with the promises of the congressional representative of the districts with the marginal voters, but the promises may be much more extreme than the congressmen from other types of districts are willing to enact into law. Curiously, both candidates in 1964 represented the center of their respective parties. As was noted earlier, this meant that Senator Goldwater did not appeal to urban liberal voters who traditionally have been the source of candidate strength.

Proposed changes in the electoral arrangements. In part because the electoral system emphasizes the differences between the constituencies of Congress and the President and in part for other reasons, attempts have been made to change the method of electing the President almost since the beginning of our government. Today, there are three types of proposals which are more or less continuously before Congress for changing the electoral system.

The three proposals may be summarized briefly. The simplest and most sweeping proposal would do away with electors completely. The candidate receiving a majority of the national popular vote would be the victor. The second proposal would retain the present voting strength of each state in the electoral college, but would abolish electors as such. Instead of all electoral votes of a particular state going to the candidate receiving the largest number of popular votes in that state, the electoral vote of each state would be divided in proportion to the popular vote cast for each candidate. The third proposal would retain the electoral college, elect two electors at large in each state, but elect the remaining electors by

---

14 S. M. Lipset, *Political Man* (Garden City, N. Y.: Doubleday & Co., 1960), p. 306.

districts which more or less coincided with existing congressional district lines.

Each of the three proposed changes in the electoral system would significantly modify the nature of our party system. Either of the first two proposals would place a premium on increasing the number of voters participating in the elections in all states. Further, they would add to the need for both parties to organize and campaign in states which hitherto have been considered safe states for the opposition. If each vote counted, Republicans would be compelled to work in the deep South, and Democrats would be expected to work harder in Republican strongholds in other regions. Neither party is anxious to create circumstances that would increase its opposition in states where it predominates. The third proposal, under which most electors would be selected by districts, would have the effect of reducing the importance of the large states and the importance of minority groups which are concentrated in a relatively small number of urban districts. In fact, under the third suggestion, the presidential constituency would come to look very much like the congressional constituency. No large state and no minority that now benefits from the present arrangement is interested in seeing its power reduced by the changes proposed.

An ideological argument may be made for any of the three proposed changes in the electoral system. Each proposal has a significant number of supporters. The extraordinary majorities needed in Congress and the states, however, make any change in the electoral system very unlikely. So many groups and state parties would be affected adversely by each of the proposed changes that the necessary two-thirds majority has never been mustered in both houses of Congress. Even if that hurdle is ever surmounted it remains doubtful whether the necessary three-fourths of the states could be prevailed upon to ratify one of the proposals.

Campaign financing. In the United States the funds which make the very expensive national campaigns possible are provided by contributions from private individuals and private organizations. There have been proposals that contributions to the campaigns be made by government appropriations. California and Minnesota now allow a deduction of some political contributions in figuring state income taxes. No other state has made such a move although the suggestion has been made in other legislatures.

Those who contribute to campaigns may do so because of strong ideological or personal commitments to the candidates or the parties. The largest contributions, however, are probably made by persons or groups which have special interests which they believe will be furthered by the election of a particular candidate. Some of the best financed of the special interest groups contribute money to both sides in order that the elected candidates will at least be neutralized when in office. This theory of the neutralization of elected officials through campaign contributions is frequently not borne out in practice, but it does not prevent contributors from acting on the belief.

National and state governments have enacted legislation over the years aimed at preventing excessive campaign expenditures and therefore possible control by any particular individual or group. These regulations have sought to cover four aspects of campaign financing. The laws state (1) who may make contributions, (2) how large the contributions may be, (3) the amount which any political group may spend during the campaign, and (4) what reporting of contributions and expenditures is required.

The best known national legislation on the matter of campaign expenditures is the Hatch Act of 1939. Under this law no person or organization may make a contribution of more than $5,000 to any political organization or presidential candidate during any single campaign year. The law, however, makes no effort to prevent anyone from contributing to a dozen political organizations all having the same purpose. Nor does the law prevent every member of a family from making contributions of $5,000 to each of these political organizations.

The law limits the amount that each political group can spend during a campaign to $3,000,000 in a presidential campaign. Again the law is silent on how many political organizations may spend that amount of money. Estimates on the cost of campaigns in presidential election years run as high as $80,000,000. Nevertheless, no one is prosecuted for over spending, because it is so easy to live within the law and still spend vast sums on the campaigns. There are fifty state committees spending money for each party. There are independent committees for each candidate. There are Republicans organized to support the Democratic candidates and Democrats to support the Republican candidates. There are national committees of four or five kinds supporting each of the major party tickets in addition to the Republican and Democratic National Committees which exist to support the party candidates. Each of these groups can spend to the legally prescribed limit. The only limitation, which means none at all, upon the expenditure of funds for a presidential candidate is the limit of the ingenuity of the candidate's supporters in thinking up new groups to create for their favorites. If $200,000,000 were contributed there would be no serious legal barrier to its expenditure during a campaign.

Expenditures in 1960 "on behalf of all candidates for all offices in the United States probably reached $165 to $175 million. . . . While the share of this total spent on behalf of presidential and vice-presidential candidates cannot be estimated with precision, the two major parties reported expenditures of almost $20 million in their national campaigns alone: the corresponding totals in 1952 and 1956 were $11.6 million and 12.9 million, respectively. Both parties ended the campaigns of 1956 and 1960 in debt." [15]

---

[15] *Financing Presidential Campaigns,* Report of the President's Commission on Campaign Costs (Washington, D. C.: Government Printing Office, 1962), p. 9.

These figures do not include expenditures by non-party groups such as the Committee of Political Education (COPE) and others. Nor does it include the expenditures by any state party committees. Since presidential primaries are conducted on a state basis by individual candidates we have no figures of any real value in this field.

President Kennedy appointed a commission soon after taking office to look into the problems of campaign financing, which both he and President Eisenhower had noted were too important to be left merely to those who could afford to put up very large sums of money. The Commission, headed by Professor Alexander Heard and including in its membership a number of other prominent political scientists and politicians, urged the abolition of limits on contributions while asking for effective disclosure of sources of funds. It also proposed the prohibition of partisan campaign contributions by corporations and labor unions. It recommended that the government finance the costs of the transition to a new administration. Perhaps the most interesting suggestion was that contributions by individual citizens to the party of their choice be tax deductible up to $1,000. As an alternative they would allow a tax credit of $10.00 for a contribution to a party. Congress has not acted on the proposals of the Commission.

SUMMARY

Presidential candidates are selected by the national conventions of the parties. These conventions are made up of delegates who are selected in primary elections or by state and district conventions.

The presidential preference primaries are of four types: (1) those in which the voters express only a preference for candidates, but do not select delegates to the national conventions; (2) those in which the voters express a preference among presidential aspirants and at the same time elect delegates pledged to support the candidate; (3) those in which the voters select unpledged delegates and express a preference among candidates; and (4) those in which the voters express no preference of the candidates whom they intend to support.

The work of the national conventions, aside from the actual nomination of the candidates, is carried out through four committees—credentials, platform and resolutions, permanent organization, and rules and order of business. Each state is represented on all the committees. Committee decisions are reported to the full convention for final action, but the convention seldom questions the work of the committees. Occasionally the platform and resolutions committee will have particular planks modified. In the case of a close fight between candidates, there may be a questioning of the report of the credentials committee since the matter of seating state delegations might determine the outcome of a convention.

The political qualifications of candidates for both the Presidency and

Vice-Presidency have been changing rapidly during the last few decades. No longer is the choice made from among Protestant governors of the large states in the North. At least in 1960, all the leading Democratic aspirants failed to meet some of the traditional tests. On the Republican side, the nomination of an incumbent Vice-President marked another departure from custom. In the selection of nominees for the Vice-Presidency more and more attention is being given to his serious qualifications rather than simply his availability for "balancing the ticket." As the office of Vice-President has taken on added stature since the early days of Franklin Roosevelt's Presidency a greater effort has been made to find men of ability who are in substantial agreement with the presidential candidate on policy issues.

Campaign methods have changed considerably with the advent of radio and television. The candidates gain a much larger audience. At the same time, they have been forced to prepare speeches with great care on more subjects.

The electoral arrangements established in the Constitution and modified by the Twelfth Amendment have remained unchanged since 1804. Today the candidate winning a plurality of the popular vote in a state automatically wins all the electoral votes. Changes have been proposed in the system, but the vested interests of states or minority groups in the present system makes any change unlikely.

The cost of presidential campaigns has continued to rise over the years. It has been estimated that the campaign of 1956 cost as much as $80,000,000. Existing laws regulating the expenditure of campaign funds are so loosely drawn that there is almost no limit on the amount which can be spent on behalf of a candidate. Publicity has been the chief weapon provided to keep expenditures at a reasonable level.

BIBLIOGRAPHIC NOTE

Books abound on various aspects of the choosing of a President. Covering the history of the elections are: W. Dean Burnham, *Presidential Ballots, 1836-1892* (Baltimore: Johns Hopkins Press, 1955); E. E. Robinson, *The Presidential Vote, 1896-1932* (Stanford: Stanford University Press, 1934); E. H. Roseboom, *A History of Presidential Elections* (New York: Macmillan Company, 1957).

For proposed changes in the electoral college system the best information can be found in a report of a congressional committee: *Nomination and Election of President and Vice President,* Hearings before a Subcommittee of the Committee on the Judiciary, U. S. Senate, 84th Congress, 1st session, March and April, 1955.

The choosing of delegates may be, as we have seen, either by primary elections or by other means. A statement of the various means used in the fifty states can be found in R. D. Still, Jr., *Manner of Selecting Delegates to the National Political Conventions and the Nomination and Elections of Presidential Elections* (Washington, D. C.: Government Printing Office, 1955). For a full discussion of the presidential preference primaries which once seemed to hold out much hope to reformers, see Louise Overacker, *The Presidential Primary* (New York: The Macmillan Company, 1926). Miss Overacker's book was written at a time when it still seemed possible that more states might adopt presidential primaries or that even a national presidential preference primary might be feasible.

The major textbooks all deal at some length with the whole of presidential campaigns. They present basic information on the selection of delegates, the nature and operation of the national conventions, and the campaign and election. Among the texts which provide this kind of information are William Goodman, *The Two-Party System in the United States* (Princeton: D. Van Nostrand Company, 1960); Ivan Hinderaker, *Party Politics* (New York: Henry Holt and Company, 1956); V. O. Key, *Politics, Parties, and Pressure Groups* (5th ed., New York: Thomas Y. Crowell Company, 1964); Avery Leiserson, *Parties and Politics* (New York: Alfred A. Knopf, 1958). Somewhat dated but still useful on the party conventions is Howard R. Penniman, *Sait's American Parties and Elections* (New York: Appleton, Century, Crofts, 1952).

In recent years the Brookings Institution, sometimes aided by funds from the Edgar Stern Family Funds, has made a series of careful studies of the national party conventions—their composition, their operation, and an evaluation of their worth. First Brookings gathered detailed information from each of the states on the selection of delegates and their actions at the 1952 conventions in Paul T. David, Malcolm Moos, and Ralph M. Goldman, *Presidential Nominating Politics in 1952*, (five volumes, Baltimore: Johns Hopkins Press, 1952). The story of the selection of convention delegates in various states sometimes appeared in local publications as well as in the more complete volumes. In 1960 Brookings Institution published another major work on the conventions, Paul T. David, Ralph M. Goldman, and Richard C. Bain, *The Politics of National Party Conventions* (Washington, D. C.: Brookings Institution, 1960). In addition to describing all aspects of the national conventions this work also includes suggestions of various areas for continuing research on the problem.

For studies of particular developments in presidential politics we can look with profit at such books as H. Bradford Westerfield, *Foreign Policy and Party Politics* (New Haven: Yale University Press, 1955); Charles A. H. Thomson, *Television and Presidential Politics* (Washington: The Brookings Institution, 1956); Paul Lazarsfeld and Frank Stanton, *Radio Research 1941* (New York: Duell, Sloan and Pearce, 1941).

A rather large number of books has been written which describe the reaction of voters to presidential campaigns. These books seek to tell us why voters make up their minds, when they decide for one or another of the candidates and the various influences which are brought to bear upon their decisions. These books vary in the manner of securing the data for their studies and they are written at different levels of sophistication, but all contribute in some manner to the better understanding of voter motivation. Some of the better known of these books are: Paul F. Lazarsfeld, Bernard Berelson, and Hazel Gaudet, *The People's Choice* (New York: Duell, Sloan and Pearce, 1944); Bernard Berelson, Paul F. Lazarsfeld, and W. N. McPhee, *Voting* (Chicago: Chicago University Press, 1954); Angus Campbell, Gerald Gurin, and Warren E. Miller, *The Voter Decides* (Evanston, Illinois: Row, Peterson, 1954). A recent excellent book by the men at the Michigan Survey Research Center provides us with probably the best available discussion of voters' attitudes in presidential elections. This book is Angus Campbell, Philip E. Converse, Warren E. Miller, and Donald E. Stokes, *The American Voter* (New York: John Wiley and Sons, Inc., 1960).

Former presidents have written memoirs which sometimes are useful in understanding the problems of electing a president. Biographies of former presidents are also frequently helpful. Of much less value are the laudatory biographies of candidates during the campaign years. These biographies normally picture their subjects as all-American boys who find themselves pushed to the front to serve their country. As self-sacrificing and patriotic men they are all willing to give up the quiet home life which they prefer to accept, like Cincinnatus, the greater cause of country. A study of these campaign biographies has been made by W. Burlie Brown, *The People's Choice* (University, Louisiana: Louisiana State University Press, 1960).

Several studies have been made of the problems of financing campaigns and of the regulation of campaign expenditures. The first major study was by Alexander Heard, *The Costs of Democracy* (Chapel Hill, N. C.: University of North Carolina Press, 1960). Herbert E. Alexander wrote *Financing the 1960 Election* (Princeton: Citizens' Research Foundation, 1962). Finally, there is *Financing Presidential Campaigns*, Report of the President's Commission on Campaign Costs (Washington, D. C.: Government Printing Office, 1962).

Several books on the 1960 election are of interest. Paul T. David (ed.), *The Presidential Election and Transition 1960-1961* (Washington, D. C.: The Brookings Institution, 1961); Theodore H. White, *The Making of the President, 1960* (New York: Atheneum Publishers, 1961); Lucy S. Dawidowicz and Leon J. Goldstein, *Politics in a Pluralist Democracy: Studies of Voting in the 1960 Election* (New York: Institute of Human Relations Press, 1963); Sidney Kraus (ed.), *The Great Debates: Background, Perspectives, Effects* (Bloomington: Indiana University Press, 1962).

Two general books on presidential elections worth noting are Nelson W. Polsby and Aaron B. Wildavsky, *Presidential Elections: Strategies of American Electoral Politics* (New York: Scribner's, 1964) and Gerald Pomper, *Nominating the President: The Politics of Convention Choice* (Evanston: Northwestern University Press, 1963).

12

The Presidency

_____

THE Constitution provided the basis for a fairly strong executive, but the presidency has developed powers far beyond those envisioned by the constitutional fathers. The same is true of the judicial and legislative branches, yet the Office of the President has outstripped the other two coordinate organs in the accretion of power.

No two Presidents have attended the most powerful office in the land in the same fashion. Each President's past experience is different, as are the problems and personalities with which he must deal. Nevertheless, the American people, Congress, and subordinates in the executive departments hold great expectations for any occupant of the White House. The opportunity for leadership is literally thrust upon the President. His every word and deed command attention. One of the most significant developments of the past quarter of a century has been the creation of staff aids to the Chief Executive—a vital requirement if the President is to have the information requisite to the hundreds of policy decisions which he must make in the course of a year. This latter evolution is a part of what is often referred to as the "institutionalization" of the Presidency. The truly strong executive will shape the institution of the Presidency rather than bend to a precise pattern set by his predecessors in the office.

THE OFFICE OF PRESIDENT

There was agreement at the Philadelphia Convention that the Constitution should provide for—in the words of the Virginia Plan—"a national executive." But this was only a starting point for discussion. Should there be a single or collegiate executive? What of the method of selection and the term of office? And what of the powers of the office? These and other questions relating to the Presidency appeared time and time again throughout the entire life of the convention.

Election by the legislature was agreed upon until late in the summer when the electoral college method of selection was substituted. A majority of the delegates believed that choice by the national legislature would be incompatible with the separation of powers principle. Devotion to the latter principle also resulted in the Chief Executive being granted powers in his own right rather than only at the whim of the legislative body.

Qualifications. The formal qualifications which are established by the original Constitution are neither numerous nor particularly onerous. A minimum age of thirty-five years is expected, along with natural-born citizenship in the United States. Moreover, candidates are required to have resided in the United States for at least fourteen years, although such residence does not necessarily have to be consecutive.[1]

Qualifications imposed by custom are more numerous and perhaps more burdensome. "Availability" of a presidential candidate often takes into account geography, experience, occupation, religion, and ability among other factors. It may be added that convention has also ordained a more advanced age than the thirty-five years stipulated by the Constitution itself —men under fifty have rarely been nominated. Although women are equally eligible, tradition has placed a very weighty obstacle in their path to that office; as yet, it has not been surmounted.

Term. There was a good deal of sentiment in the Convention of 1787 in favor of a presidential term of seven years with a bar against re-election. As a matter of fact, such a provision was included in an earlier draft of the Constitution. Finally, it was decided to provide a four-year term and to permit re-election. Nothing was said as to how many terms a single incumbent might be allowed, but Washington and Jefferson established a precedent of limiting the terms to two. Several Presidents during the succeeding century and a half felt that conditions justified breaking the two-term tradition in their own cases, and U. S. Grant and Theodore Roosevelt took practical steps to let down custom's bars. It remained for Franklin D. Roosevelt to demonstrate that the two-term tradition, which many citizens supposed was as firmly rooted in the political system of the United States as the Constitution itself, could be ignored under circumstances of national emergency and world chaos. However, in 1951 the Twenty-second Amendment was added to the Constitution. It provides that no person shall be elected to the Presidency more than twice, and that no person who has held the office for more than two years of a term to which some other person was elected shall be elected more than once.

Perquisites. The President originally received a yearly salary of $25,000. It was increased over the years until, in 1949, Congress set it at $100,000 plus a $50,000 tax-exempt expense account. In 1953, at the request of the President, the tax exemption was removed from the expense account. Of course, the funds for such items as travel allowance, upkeep of the White

---

[1] The question was raised by opponents to Herbert Hoover. He had not been a resident for fourteen consecutive years immediately prior to his election, but had resided in the United States considerably more than fourteen years altogether.

House, Secret Service protection, and the maintenance of various means of transportation are provided in addition to the annual salary.[2]

Immunities. The courts have ruled that the President is, except in the case of impeachment, immune from actions directed against him by other branches of the government. He cannot, therefore, be required to appear in court as a defendant or a witness, although he may consent to serve in the latter capacity. Writs of mandamus or injunction which name him cannot be issued by the courts.[3] Contempt-of-court charges are never aimed at the Chief Executive. Even in criminal cases it would be out of the question to call him before other than an impeachment court; against the wielder of the pardon power, no penalty decreed by a court would stand.[4] For similar reasons, his presence may not be demanded by any congressional committee.

GROWTH OF PRESIDENTIAL POWERS

A reading of the Constitution will convey some idea of what a modern President is expected to do, but the potency of the office today dwarfs that which is described in the fundamental law. Certainly an outstanding feature of the American constitutional development has been the growth of the power and prestige of the Presidency.

Presidential conceptions of the office. Of course, the men occupying the office have assessed their own constitutional powers with varying conclusions, but two general views may be distinguished. Theodore Roosevelt expressed, in his "stewardship" theory, what might be termed the broad view of presidential powers. According to this theory, the President, as steward for the people, was duty bound to do anything the national welfare required, unless it was expressly prohibited by the Constitution or statutes. Thus, Lincoln asserted the right, in an emergency, to take measures which would otherwise have been illegal, subject to the risk of having his actions disallowed by Congress. Congress allowed them. Again, Franklin D. Roosevelt, in a message to Congress in 1942, requested repeal of certain provisions of the Emergency Control Act. He advised that in the event of congressional inaction, "I shall accept the responsibility, and I shall act." Congress acted.

President Taft summarized what might be labeled the limited view of presidential powers. His view was that the President could exercise only those powers which could be reasonably traced to some express constitu-

---

[2] A former President is provided a monetary allowance of $25,000 a year, as well as an office staff to consist of persons selected by him and at rates of compensation fixed by him, which in the aggregate shall not exceed $50,000 a year. He is also furnished with suitable office space and is granted the free use of the mails.

The widow of a former President is entitled to a pension at the rate of $10,000 a year.

[3] See *Mississippi* v. *Johnson*, 4 Wallace 475 (1867).

[4] See *Kendall* v. *United States*, 12 Peters 524 (1838).

tional or statutory grant, or implied from them as necessary and proper to their execution.

Presidential exponents of the broad view of executive powers have been responsible for significant additions to the aggregate powers of the office. Even if a particular President holds to the limited view of presidential powers, as expressed by Taft, the precedents established by supporters of the broader concept remain as possible guideposts for future holders of the office.

Congressional contributions. Not only has Congress often consented to or ratified assertions of presidential authority; it has also made positive contributions toward increasing the powers of the office. Indeed, through the delegation of legislative powers during economic and wartime crises, Congress has fused the powers of government in presidential hands almost as though he were an absolute monarch. Yet, delegation of legislative authority is an established feature of our system, operating at all times. For example, the Budget and Accounting Act of 1921 makes the President responsible for the preparation and submission of the budget to Congress. Or, to take another example, since the Reciprocal Trade Agreements Act of 1934, Congress has largely relinquished its historic tariff-fixing role in favor of the Chief Executive.

Judicial decisions. Decisions of the Supreme Court have often strengthened the Presidency. The doctrine that the federal government has inherent, as distinguished from delegated, powers in the field of foreign affairs[5] has magnified the President's role as chief spokesman for the nation in this critical area. The refusal of the Supreme Court to take jurisdiction in certain cases on the ground that political questions were involved, i.e., questions belonging to the sphere of the President or Congress,[6] has given increased latitude to the President in interpreting his constitutional position in both domestic and foreign fields.

Other factors. Wars, internal crises, the complexities of modern government, and the rise of the United States to a commanding position in world affairs—these, and many more situations contributed to the growth of the Presidency. A few comments on certain other specific factors appear appropriate here.

The President, unlike members of Congress, is accountable to a national constituency, and so he is the logical focal point of national leadership. To many individuals, the President personifies the federal government.

The President is the leader of his party. To many party men, this fact alone would make the President the most important man in the country.

---

[5] See *United States* v. *Curtiss-Wright Export Corporation,* 299 U. S. 304 (1936). See also p. 271.

[6] For example, see *Luther* v. *Borden,* 7 Howard 1 (1849).

PRESIDENT JOHNSON HOLDING AN INFORMAL PRESS CONFERENCE AT THE WHITE HOUSE

More important to the public-at-large is the way the President uses his position as party leader to influence legislation and affect the administration of programs.

The modern President plays a very positive role in initiating legislation.[7]

THE POWERS AND DUTIES OF THE PRESIDENT

The powers that the President now exercises can be divided into two broad categories—those chiefly or exclusively executive in character and those arising out of the legislative process. Among the executive functions are:

(1) duties as Chief of State,
(2) enforcement of the laws of the United States, including the general maintenance of order,
(3) appointment and removal of federal officials, both civil and military,
(4) granting of pardons, reprieves, and amnesties,
(5) overseeing the conduct of foreign relations,
(6) acting as commander-in-chief of the armed forces of the United States and as coordinator of national defense efforts, and
(7) supervision over the administrative agencies of the federal government.

The legislative functions will be discussed in the next chapter.

---

[7] This development is discussed in some detail in Chapter 13.

Chief of State. The President is the ceremonial head of the government. Many states of the world have a titular head of state (as the Queen in Great Britain or the President of the Italian Republic) and a real executive (as the Prime Minister and cabinet in Britain) that formulates policy. But in the United States, the President undertakes both of these roles.

Representative activities of the President in his role as Chief of State include: greeting foreign dignitaries; welcoming the leaders of civic organizations to the nation's capital; bestowing medals and other honors; acting as host at state dinners; giving his blessing (and perhaps his money) to various fund drives; and lending his presence to the inauguration of some event, whether it be a public power project or the first home game of the Washington baseball team. The President as Chief of State blends with the symbol of the President as national leader. Particularly in times of crisis, the people turn to the President as the leader who speaks with authority.

Enforcement of the laws. The Constitution commands the President to "take care that the laws be faithfully executed," [8] and, as if fearing that a mere command, however plainly stated, would not suffice, it also prescribes that he swear when taking office that he will "protect and defend the Constitution of the United States," [9] which lays down the order. On the basis of such emphasis, it might be supposed that the President has a very active part in law enforcement. Actually, this particular duty occasions a President some worry at times, but it does not occupy any major portion of his attention. The responsibility for enforcing the laws of the United States rests primarily upon the Department of Justice, the federal district attorneys, the United States marshals, and the federal courts. Yet if circumstances demand it, the President may use any means at his command to assure compliance with federal law. In recent times, both Presidents Eisenhower (in 1957 in Little Rock) and Kennedy (in Oxford and Birmingham) utilized federal troops to guarantee that federal court orders dealing with integration were complied with.

How much discretion does the President have in enforcing or not enforcing the law? To put the question differently, must the President enforce the law if he does not agree with it? Undoubtedly, whether the President likes or dislikes the law should not be the determining factor in its execution, and no President has ever made a firm stand solely on this basis. In practice, however, the attitude of the Chief Executive toward the law is very important with respect to the vigor with which his agents attend to its enforcement. The Justice Department, acting on orders from the President, may, for example, fail to carry through on a particular indictment.

Maintenance of order. In dealing with the responsibilities which the national government owes to the states, it was pointed out that internal

---

8 Art. II, sec. 3.
9 Art. II, sec. 1.

disorders are to be the occasion of federal intervention if the states desire that assistance. These requests are lodged with the President either by a state legislature or by the state governor if the legislature is not in session. It is then obligatory for the President to send in federal military or police forces, although there is no way to compel him to act unless he sees fit. The federal government may send troops to protect federal property or a federal function without awaiting a request from state authorities.

The power of appointment and removal. The Constitution states that the President "by and with the advice and consent of the Senate, shall appoint ambassadors, other public ministers and consuls, judges of the Supreme Court, and all other officers of the United States, whose appointments are not herein otherwise provided for, and which shall be established by law; but the Congress may by law vest the appointment of such inferior officers, as they think proper, in the President alone, in the courts of law, or in the heads of the departments." [10] It is evident from this clause that the power to appoint is at least nominally quite extensive, although it is qualified by the stipulation that major appointments must receive the approval of the Senate, and minor positions may be removed from the presidential area altogether. The Constitution has little to say about the removal power beyond specifying that judges shall hold office during their good behavior.[11]

A classification of federal positions. Federal appointments have traditionally been listed under two categories: (1) major positions which require the consent of the Senate and (2) "inferior" jobs which are now, for the most part, filled under the rules and regulations of the merit system. Actually, some of the so-called "major" places are in reality distinctly less important than certain of the "inferior" jobs, at least on any basis more substantial than political activity. For example, federal marshals and postmasters fall under the first category, although their work is for the most part routine. On the other hand, the principal permanent administrative officers in Washington, the bureau chiefs, and the technicians are generally under the second class, despite the fact that their responsibilities are far greater and even their compensation exceeds that of many in the first category.

Frequency of personal appointments. Approximately twenty-five thousand officials are subject to the direct appointive power of the President. However, very few of these appointments are in any sense personal ones. The several thousand postmasterships are filled by the senators and representatives of the majority party after the Civil Service Commission has rated applicants on the basis of an examination. The numerous collectors of customs, federal district attorneys, and United States marshals are so far

---

10 Art. II, sec. 2.
11 Art. III, sec. 1.

removed from the President's path that they rarely receive even cursory attention from him. Ambassadorial and ministerial appointments have often been made with a view toward taking care of party favorites, and lower federal court judgeships may be subject to the rule of "senatorial courtesy."

Role of the senators. "The custom of senatorial courtesy is the sanction by which a majority of the Senate may require the President to nominate the candidate proposed by the senator or senators from the state in which the office is situated, provided they belong to the same party as that of the President." [12] A fairly recent example of this practice occurred in 1951 when Senator Paul Douglas of Illinois opposed President Truman's nominees for federal judgeships in his state. The Senate rejected the President's nominations.

Cabinet choices of the President are generally approved by the Senate as a matter of course, although in 1959 the Senate rejected President Eisenhower's selection of Lewis L. Strauss as Secretary of Commerce.[13] Contests emerge more frequently with respect to important administrative posts, Supreme Court justices, and diplomatic officials; but even in these cases the President ordinarily has his way. The power to make nominations in the last analysis confers on the President much political influence, and a politically oriented Chief Executive may utilize such patronage as a lever in dealing with congressional and party leaders.

The removal power. Federal judges are specifically exempted from the removal power of the President, even in those instances in which they have clearly demonstrated their incompetence in the position. Only one method, that of impeachment, is set forth by the Constitution. In the case of the other holders of federal positions, no formal provision beyond the cumbersome impeachment process is made for removal and for almost a century and a half the question remained unsettled as to exactly what authority the President had. In general, it was the consensus that removals at times had to be made and that the President was the logical person to act.

It was not until 1926 that the Supreme Court carefully examined the authority of the Chief Executive relating to removals.[14] The Postmaster General, acting under the direction of President Wilson, removed Myers, a first-class postmaster, disregarding an 1876 law requiring the Senate's approval for such removals. The Supreme Court upheld the President in an opinion which seemed to say that the Constitution endowed the President with an illimitable power to remove all officers in whose appointment he had participated, with the exception of the federal judges. However, the

---

[12] Joseph P. Harris, *The Advice and Consent of the Senate* (Berkeley and Los Angeles: University of California Press, 1953), p. 217.

[13] Mr. Strauss was the eighth cabinet nominee in history and the first since 1925 to be rejected by the Senate.

[14] *Myers* v. *United States,* 272 U. S. 52 (1926).

sweeping principle of the Myers case was modified in the 1935 Humphrey case.[15] Congress, in creating the Federal Trade Commission, had laid down the conditions under which the President could remove the commissioners. When President Roosevelt removed Commissioner Humphrey, not in accordance with these conditions but because of their divergent views on public policy, Humphrey sued for his salary. In distinguishing the Myers case, the Court pointed out that a postmaster was an executive officer restricted to the performance of executive functions. But Congress could create quasi-legislative or quasi-judicial agencies and require them to discharge their duties independently of executive control, and in doing so limit their removal for cause.

The Humphrey case left unresolved the status of members of quasi-judicial agencies with respect to which Congress had said nothing about removal. This question came before the Supreme Court in 1958 as a result of the President removing a member of the War Claims Commission, a strictly adjudicatory agency. The Court held the President's act invalid because of the nature of the office involved, saying: "We are compelled to conclude that no such power is given to the President directly by the Constitution, and none is impliedly conferred upon him by statute simply because Congress said nothing about it." [16]

Congress may restrict the powers of removal with regard to inferior officers. But in the absence of specific legislation to the contrary, the President may remove at his discretion an inferior officer whose term is limited by statute. The President may remove military officers by nominating to the Senate the officer's successor, provided the Senate approves the nomination.[17]

Pardons, reprieves, and amnesties. The framers followed the time-honored tradition of conferring the pardoning power on the executive; the Constitution succinctly states that the President "shall have power to grant reprieves and pardons for offenses against the United States, except in cases of impeachment." [18] The accused may be pardoned before conviction, immediately after conviction, or during the period while he is serving a prison sentence. At one time the Court ruled that a person did not have to accept a pardon, but now it appears that he has no choice if the President insists.[19] The legal guilt and blot of a prison record can be expunged at least in part by the issuing of a pardon after a convicted person has finished his prison term.[20]

---

15 *Humphrey's Executor (Rathbun)* v. *United States,* 295 U. S. 602 (1935).
16 *Wiener* v. *United States,* 357 U. S. 349.
17 *Wallace* v. *United States,* 257 U. S. 541 (1922).
18 Art. II, sec. 2.
19 *Biddle* v. *Perovich,* 274 U. S. 480 (1927).
20 In *Ex parte Garland,* 4 Wallace 333 (1867), the Supreme Court held that "if granted after conviction, it removes the penalties and disabilities, and restores him all his civil rights; it makes him, as it were, a new man, and gives him a new credit

The President's power to pardon for criminal contempt of court has been upheld.[21] It remains doubtful that the pardoning power may reach civil contempt of court. The Court has not passed on whether the President may pardon for contempt of Congress. A *reprieve* may be granted which will delay the execution of a sentence. Or the President may decide to *commute* a sentence, substituting life imprisonment for the death penalty or reducing a prison sentence from, say, twenty to ten years. In case of a civil war or general rebellion, the pardoning power permits the President to grant an amnesty to the participants in so far as that seems wise after the hostilities have ceased, but Congress by law may also grant amnesties.

Actual exercise of the pardon power. Although the governors of some of the states actively exercise the pardoning power which is conferred on them, the President finds it prudent to delegate his responsibility to a large extent to the Department of Justice. He has so many other matters to engage his attention that it is deemed best to charge the Department of Justice with receiving applications, investigating claims, and drafting recommendations. Personal pleas from relatives drew heavily on the time and particularly the emotions of some of the earlier Presidents, notably Abraham Lincoln. The current practice of delegating the actual administration of the preliminaries to the Department of Justice seems very wise. After the Department of Justice has gone over the application, considered the evidence presented, communicated with the trial judge and prosecutor, and made up its mind as to what should be done, the President has only to go through the routine of following its recommendation.

Foreign relations. The Constitution clearly gives the national government exclusive control in the foreign relations field, but the delegated powers with respect to this area are divided among the President, Congress, and Senate. Thus, the President is authorized to appoint ambassadors, public ministers, and consuls, make treaties, and receive ambassadors and other public ministers. Congress is given power to regulate foreign commerce and declare war; the Senate shares the appointive and treaty-making provisions with the Chief Executive.

The President, however, now dominates the foreign affairs field. The Supreme Court has given powerful support to the President's position by

---

and capacity." However, in *Carlesi* v. *New York,* 233 U. S. 251 (1914), the Court modified that statement in one particular. Carlesi had been convicted and pardoned of a federal offense. When he was tried on another offense in New York courts, evidence was produced to the effect that he was an habitual criminal on the basis of the federal conviction. On appeal his attorneys argued that his pardon had, as was said in an earlier case, "blotted out the existence of guilt, so that in the eyes of the law the offender is as innocent as if he had never committed the offense" and that hence the fact of his previous conviction could not be used as evidence against him. The Supreme Court rejected the argument. Therefore, one cannot say that a pardon absolutely "blots out the fact of guilt," even though it does restore civil rights.

21 *Ex parte Grossman,* 267 U. S. 387 (1925).

holding that he has authority to speak as the sole organ of the national government in international affairs.[22]

Actual conduct of foreign relations. The Department of State and its representatives abroad actually carry most of the responsibility for managing the relations of the United States with foreign countries.[23] Nevertheless, the President must make important decisions with respect to the appointment of our diplomatic representatives abroad. In some instances, he accepts the recommendations of political leaders; in other cases, he decides to elevate officers of the foreign service. The President usually receives and welcomes the ambassadors and ministers of foreign governments, not only when they arrive and present credentials but also at state functions. If important treaties are to be negotiated, the President must decide, either on his own initiative or upon the advice of the State Department, who the representatives of the United States shall be to the conference which handles such tasks. Sometimes the President, himself, attends "summit" conferences.[24]

For example, in July, 1955, President Eisenhower met with the leaders of Britain, France, and Russia at Geneva. In June, 1961, President Kennedy traveled to Vienna, Austria, for a two-day meeting with Premier Nikita S. Khrushchev of the Soviet Union to discuss the Berlin question. On the same trip the President talked with President Charles de Gaulle of France and Prime Minister Harold Macmillan of Great Britain. President Johnson has likewise found it important to maintain direct contact with other world leaders as part of his job of directing the foreign policy of the United States during a period of international tension.

The power of recognition. The Constitution is silent on the subject, but it is now accepted that as a consequence of the President's power to receive and dispatch diplomatic agents, he possesses the power to recognize or not to recognize foreign governments. That this power may be a weapon in our conduct of foreign policy has been demonstrated many times. President Wilson, by refusing to recognize the Huerta regime in Mexico, contributed to the downfall of Huerta's government. Speedy recognition of the Republic of Panama in 1903 by President Theodore Roosevelt made possible the construction of the Panama Canal. The possible political effect, both at home and abroad, of not extending recognition to Communist China has been the subject of much speculation in the United States during the past decade.

Treaties and executive agreements. The Constitution grants the President power to make treaties with the advice and consent of the Senate, provided two-thirds of the senators present concur. In practice, the role of the Senate consists of accepting, rejecting, or modifying the instruments

---

22 *United States* v. *Curtiss-Wright Export Corporation,* 299 U. S. 304 (1936).
23 See chap. 28.
24 For a comprehensive discussion of this point, see Elmer Plischke, *Summit Diplomacy* (College Park, Md.: Bureau of Governmental Research, University of Maryland, 1958).

transmitted by the Chief Executive. For major treaties, however, the President may find it politically wise to include a bipartisan group of senators in the American delegation negotiating the treaty. Once ratified, a treaty becomes the supreme law of the land even as the Constitution or laws of Congress. The Supreme Court, in *Missouri* v. *Holland*,[25] upheld the proposition that Congress can pass laws to give effect to a treaty, which, without the treaty, it would not have the power to enact.

Presidents have made increasing use of the executive agreement which does not impose the formal procedural restraints required in the case of treaties, but which is nevertheless the supreme law of the land.[26] Congress may authorize specific types of executive agreements in advance, or the President may enter into agreements, which may or may not come before Congress as a whole, depending upon whether legislation is necessary to give them effect. Examples in the former category are reciprocal trade agreements and the 1941 Lend-Lease Act. Many matters of a routine nature may be included in the latter category such as minor territorial adjustments and private pecuniary claims against another government. However, major policy matters also come under the latter listing as exemplified by the "Open Door" Policy, the Hull-Lothian Agreement,[27] and the Yalta Agreement of 1943.

Following World War II, considerable public and congressional criticism was expressed as to the potential scope of the treaty and executive agreement powers. Senator John W. Bricker, of Ohio, proposed a constitutional amendment which provided that a treaty should become effective as internal law in the United States only through legislation which would be valid in the absence of a treaty, and that Congress be empowered to regulate all executive agreements. A modified version of the "Bricker" Amendment was defeated in the Senate in 1954, when it fell one short of receiving the required two-thirds majority. Both the Truman and Eisenhower administrations strongly opposed the concept embodied in the proposed amendment, and its defeat upholds the freedom of action accorded to the President in the foreign affairs field.

Military affairs. The Constitution designates the Chief Executive as Commander-in-Chief of the armed forces and hence places grave responsibility on his shoulders for national defense. In tranquil times the power is primarily one of supervising the internal management of the military services and of appointing and dismissing officers. In time of war all the applicable powers of the national government are focused upon the one objective of victory through the person and office of the Commander-in-Chief. The

---

25 252 U. S. 416 (1920).

26 *United States* v. *Pink*, 315 U. S. 203 (1942).

27 Entered into on September 2, 1940, whereby our government handed over to the British Government fifty overage destroyers in return for ninety-nine year leases for naval bases in the Western Atlantic.

war powers of the President, complemented in large measure by delegations of authority from Congress, find expression in the control of industrial production, rationing, prices, and a multitude of other areas.

During World War II President Roosevelt seized numerous industrial facilities, beset with labor-management problems, which were engaged in production of materials necessary for the war effort. Before Congress authorized such seizures in 1943, the Chief Executive had acted under his general authority as President and Commander-in-Chief. The original executive order which permitted the military authorities to exclude persons of Japanese ancestry from certain designated areas along the West Coast in order to prevent espionage and sabotage illustrates another facet of the Commander-in-Chief power in times of national emergency. The fact that Congress later backed up the executive order by legislation no doubt made the action more palatable to the Supreme Court, but the initiator of the policy was the President not Congress.

The right to proclaim a state of martial law would appear to flow logically from the Commander-in-Chief powers, and it is associated with these powers; but the Constitution itself beclouds this point somewhat. Martial law involves military assumption of normal civil law enforcement functions; effective martial law requires suspension of the writ of habeas corpus—thus permitting military authorities to hold persons indefinitely without placing charges against them. Article I, section 9 provides: "The privilege of the writ of habeas corpus shall not be suspended, unless when in cases of rebellion or invasion the public safety may require it." This clause appears in the Legislative Article so it would seem that the founders intended Congress to determine when the public safety demanded suspension of the writ. However, President Lincoln suspended the writ on his own authority several times in the early years of the Civil War. Again Congress acted to back up the President by authorizing the President to suspend the writ of habeas corpus "during the present rebellion."

President Lincoln coupled suspension of the writ of habeas corpus with an order that persons guilty of disloyal practices should be liable to trial and punishment by military commissions. In the famous case of *Ex parte Milligan*,[28] decided after the war, the Supreme Court unanimously ruled that the President had no power to order civilians to be tried by military courts in areas where the regular courts were open and functioning. The Court, however, upheld the President's power to appoint a military commission to try the eight Nazi saboteurs who were landed in the United States from submarines during World War II.[29]

The Supreme Court has almost always backed the President in his ex-

---

[28] 4 Wallace 2 (1866).
[29] *Ex parte Quirin*, 317 U. S. 1 (1942).

ercise of the Commander-in-Chief and related powers.[30] A recent exception to the rule, however, was the opinion in the Steel Seizure case. President Truman, acting under his Commander-in-Chief and general "executive" powers, ordered the seizure to avert a threatened strike which he felt would jeopardize the national defense effort during the Korean hostilities. A divided Court held that the President was exercising legislative authority, which the Constitution vests in the Congress alone.[31] Nevertheless, history appears to point to the fact that the primary check on the Commander-in-Chief powers in time of war, particularly if supported by a sympathetic Congress, is the judgment of the President himself.

By his deployment of the military forces, the President has made armed conflict inevitable. President Polk ordered American troops into disputed territory in 1846, thus setting off the war with Mexico. In 1950 President Truman ordered American military action in Korea before receiving congressional and United Nations sanctions. Congressional debate over the commitment of troops within the framework of the NATO Agreement indicated growing congressional discontent with the potential presidential prerogative concerning military undertakings. In 1955 President Eisenhower asked for and received a congressional resolution authorizing the President to employ armed forces for the protection of Formosa. Early in 1957 the President requested that Congress arm him with emergency powers to act in the explosive Middle East area. Congress responded with a joint resolution authorizing the President to give economic and military assistance to Middle East nations. President Kennedy's policy in October of 1962 with respect to the removal of Russian-furnished offensive weapons in Cuba was in accord with a joint resolution passed by Congress a few weeks earlier. The resolution expressed the determination of the United States to prevent the "Marxist-Leninist" regime in Cuba from extending by force or threat of force its aggressive activities to any part of "this hemisphere."

Supervision over the administrative agencies. While the tasks of the legislative and the judicial branches of government have, of course, grown heavier during recent years, it is in the administrative field that the greatest elaboration of function has taken place. From a comparatively simple system with a handful of departments and a few hundred employees, we have moved to a position where we find ourselves with numerous separate administrative agencies manned by over two million public employees. Such a Gargantuan setup cannot of itself be particularly cohesive. Unless some

---

[30] For a detailed account of the Supreme Court's opinions concerning the powers of the President, see Glendon A. Schubert, Jr., *The Presidency in the Courts* (Minneapolis: University of Minnesota Press, 1957).

[31] *Youngstown Co.* v. *Sawyer,* 343 U. S. 579 (1953).

provision is made for coordinating its efforts, there will not only be waste and duplication but distinct inefficiency. The framers of the Constitution did not in their wildest dreams foresee such an administrative system as is now operative in the United States. Indeed so little did they envision a complex administrative machinery of any character that they made little or no direct provision for its structure or supervision. Congress has assumed the power of deciding the structure and extent of the authority of the administrative departments, although at times it has granted to the President limited right to reconstruct and even assign tasks. Under the constitutional stipulation that he shall generally exercise the appointing power, and faithfully execute the laws, under the permission to "require the opinion, in writing, of the principal officer in each of the executive departments, upon any subject relating to the duties of their respective offices," [32] and under the judicial ruling that he shall be permitted to exercise the removal power except in a few restricted areas, the President has claimed the right to supervise administration.

Actual exercise of supervision. Although it has long been agreed that the President should supervise the administrative agencies, this power has not always been vigorously exercised. Presidents, even before the present generation, have been busy men with all sorts of demands on their time and energy. Any far-reaching supervision of federal administration requires much more than merely a passive desire on the part of the President to coordinate. Moreover, it necessitates some integrated system of organization, and, at least, certain machinery within the executive office itself. Even in the case of the departments, which are reasonably well integrated with the executive office through their secretaries, the President has not always found it easy to demand adherence to certain standards and policies. If it is difficult to bring the regular departments into line, it is a much more Herculean task to achieve any large measure of control over the independent establishments which have been created over the years.

Recent efforts toward improvement. Within the past twenty years, legislative enactments have markedly increased the President's organizational authority with respect to the administrative agencies, subject to congressional review. Under the Reorganization Act of 1939, President Roosevelt initiated several organizational changes, the most significant being the creation of the Executive Office of the President. The 1939 statute provided for only a two-year grant of authority and exempted many agencies from the scope of the authorization. The First War Powers Act of 1941, the Reorganization Act of 1945, and the Reorganization Act of 1949 as extended maintained the principle of presidential responsibility for administrative reorganization; but certain exemptions and possibilities of congressional vetoes were provided.

---

[32] Art. II, sec. 2.

The creation of the two Hoover Commissions,[33] under the chairman-ship of former President Herbert Hoover in 1947 and 1953, to undertake comprehensive studies of the organization and functions of the executive branch, indicate Congress' awareness of the desirability for a continuing study of administrative practices. It is estimated that over 70 per cent of the first Hoover Commission's recommendations have been put into operation, including significant creations such as the Department of Health, Education, and Welfare, and the General Services Administration. The second Hoover Commission's reports were more controversial since they dealt with matters of public policy (for example, government competition with private enter-prise) as well as administrative problems. The over-all effect of these studies is not yet discernible.

Executive orders. The broad structure and powers of administrative departments are outlined in congressional enactments, but there are numer-ous details which can scarcely be provided for by law. Even if Congress saw fit to spend the time necessary to specify every minute subdivision and regulation, it is probable that there would be areas requiring administrative discretion which only time and experience could bring to light. Increas-ingly, it has been the practice to leave the details of organization and op-eration to be filled in by executive orders or administrative regulations. These are ordinarily prepared by experts in the department concerned, submitted to the administrative head, and promulgated either by him or by the President. Thus it is apparent that executive orders originate for the most part in and embody the ideas of staff members of the administrative agencies. Nevertheless, if they are promulgated in the name of the President, there is a certain measure of responsibility incident thereto. Moreover, the President may be sufficiently interested and informed to submit the pro-posed executive orders to his advisers who will recommend changes to be incorporated before the orders are actually put into force. With as adequate a staff as a President now has, the initiative in certain cases may be taken by the executive office itself rather than by an agency.

In 1936 the realization of the need for a publication and record of ex-ecutive and administrative orders led to the establishment of the *Federal Register*. It is a daily compilation of presidential proclamations and execu-tive orders, of proclamations, notices of hearings, and rules issued by admin-istrative departments or agencies, and orders and decisions of departments or quasi-judicial agencies.

THE CABINET AND PRESIDENTIAL STAFF

A president, prime minister, or dictator cannot make rational policy decisions without counsel from political and technical advisers. Historically,

---

[33] In each case the official name being Commission on Organization of the Executive Branch of the Government.

the President's cabinet developed as an institution always available for a discussion of political problems. The over-all impact of the cabinet's influence on presidential decisions has diminished particularly since the 1930's with the mushrooming of a number of staff services working directly in the Executive Office of the President. The cabinet remains available for advisory consultation, but it may well be that the problem selected and the orientation of the discussion has been determined by specialists within the Executive Office or other administrative agencies.

The President's cabinet. Beginnings of the cabinet. Shortly after taking office President Washington found it necessary to talk over certain questions with the principal officers of the government. By 1791 he had come to the point where he called regular conferences of key officials for the consideration of difficult problems; the label "cabinet" seems to have first been applied to these group discussions in the year 1793. The informal practice was more or less solidified by the treatment which the President was accorded by the two other branches of government. To start out, Washington seems to have expected that the Senate would serve substantially the same purpose that upper houses in colonial legislatures filled; that is, it would be an advisory council with as much executive as legislative responsibility. The Constitution more or less implied this might be the case when it specified the "advice and consent" of the Senate in making appointments and treaties; but, when President Washington sought such assistance in connection with Indian affairs, he was displeased with the results. Relying on the precedent of English and colonial courts, the President even asked the Supreme Court to render opinions of an advisory nature, but here again he was rebuffed. After such experiences he proceeded to set up an informal group of advisers, despite the criticism occasionally aimed at the "cabinet conclave," which the militant ex-revolutionists thought might take on too much authority.[34]

The cabinet continues as a political institution without benefit of statutory authority. Its importance in history has varied with the use which Presidents have chosen to make of it. Some Presidents have relied more upon personal advisers for counsel, and indeed, President Jackson dispensed with cabinet meetings altogether, though he subsequently resumed the practice of holding them.

Traditionally, the cabinet is composed of the heads of the executive departments. Although not all Vice-Presidents have attended cabinet meetings, events of the past quarter of a century seem to indicate their permanent inclusion. President Eisenhower added to vice-presidential prestige in the matter of cabinet attendance by formally making Mr. Nixon the chairman of the group in his absence. President Franklin D. Roosevelt initiated

---

[34] The early development of the cabinet is carefully traced in H. B. Learned, *The President's Cabinet* (New Haven: Yale University Press, 1912).

the procedure of inviting nondepartmental agency heads to meet with the cabinet, a practice continued by President Eisenhower.

Although Washington included both Thomas Jefferson and Alexander Hamilton in his cabinet, he discovered that two such divergent influences led to difficulties. Since the days of Washington, it has been the general practice to limit cabinet choices to members of the President's own political party.[35] Sometimes cabinet members are selected to give representation to the different wings of the party, as when Wilson named William Jennings Bryan, the leader of the "free silver" element of the party, as Secretary of State.

Often members are named to the cabinet so as to give representation to various geographical regions of the country. For example, President Eisenhower's original cabinet included two members each from Michigan and New York, and one each from Illinois, Massachusetts, Ohio, Texas, and Utah.

While the cabinet as a whole has never been selected on the basis of the members' expertness in handling administrative tasks, some attention is often paid that consideration.[36] The Secretary of Commerce will, more likely than not, be a man who has had considerable experience in business affairs. The Secretary of Agriculture is almost always a man who has been directly or indirectly interested in agriculture. The Attorney General is always a lawyer, although he may have had little to do with public affairs before taking office. There are several instances where Secretaries of State and of the Treasury have had at least fairly extensive experience in the fields of world affairs and public finance.[37]

General nature of cabinet business. The cabinet usually meets once a week. In 1954 President Eisenhower appointed a Secretary to the Cabinet whose duties include preparation of an agenda, keeping a record of proceedings, and checking on the implementation of decisions reached. Although not too much is known about what goes on in the secrecy of cabinet meetings, and there is undoubtedly considerable variation from administration to administration, it is generally understood that two types of business are transacted. In the first place, the broad policies of the governments are examined, canvassed, and dissected. Matters of detail are discussed by the higher officials within a department or by the President and a department head, but they do not as a rule occupy the time of the cabinet as a body. But the President may frequently consult the cabinet on questions of what

---

35 There have been numerous exceptions to the rule, the most recent being the naming by Kennedy of two Republicans to his cabinet in 1961 and their continuation by President Johnson.

36 For a discussion of other factors involved in the choice of cabinet members, see Richard F. Fenno, Jr., *The President's Cabinet* (Cambridge: Harvard University Press, 1959), Chap. 2.

37 Secretaries of State Stimson, Hughes, Hull, Dulles, Herter, and Rusk may be mentioned; in the Treasury Department, Hamilton, Gallatin, McAdoo, Mellon, and Dillon.

attitude the United States shall take on some international situation, of what shall be done to reduce unemployment, or of what the government can do to control labor disputes. Thus, its chief function is in helping to formulate the policies of the United States on far-reaching public questions. How great the cabinet's contribution will be in policy-making depends in large measure on the President himself, and, of course, upon the other influences bearing on the Chief Executive—as within his own Executive Office —but no one can doubt its important role over a period of a century and a half.

The second type of business is somewhat more routine. If there is a question about which department is to handle a certain problem, if several departments are in conflict over an issue, if some common approach to the exercise of specific authority shared among several departments seems desirable, then the President may ask the cabinet to attempt coordination. Needless to say, in a government as complicated and gigantic as ours, misunderstandings may arise and conflicting policies may be followed. When these are ironed out important benefits accrue.

The Executive Office of the President. The first Presidents had no need for elaborate office organizations; a handful of secretaries and clerks could easily care for the correspondence and business which had to be dealt with. As the office has become more commanding, its routine as well as its important duties have expanded until an elaborate organization is required.

The President's Committee on Administrative Management in 1937 pleaded, "The President needs help." Based upon the recommendations of this committee, and pursuant to the Reorganization Act of 1939, the Executive Office of the President came into existence. With its creation a new center of power has developed within the federal administration. The institutionalization of the presidency is accented. Certain of the components of this office are discussed below.

In the words of the *Government Organizational Manual,* the *White House Office* serves the President in the performance of the many detailed activities incident to his immediate office. But what latitude is permitted under this phraseology! Under President Eisenhower the White House Staff reached a level of influence far beyond its attainment under his predecessors.[38] Here approximately four hundred persons perform an infinite number of routine, personal, political, and public relations tasks necessitated by the nature of the modern presidency. The names of certain staff officials, as the Assistant to the President, or the Press Secretary, are well publicized. However, the majority of the battery of staff aides—whether they be classified as secretaries, special assistants, special consultants, administrative assistants, military aides, or by some other title—work at their assigned duties with relatively little public attention directed toward them.

---

[38] See Marian D. Irish, "The Organization Man in the Presidency," *Journal of Politics,* XX, 259-277, May, 1958.

EXECUTIVE OFFICE OF THE PRESIDENT

THE PRESIDENT
BUREAU OF THE BUDGET
THE WHITE HOUSE OFFICE
NATIONAL SECURITY COUNCIL
NATIONAL AERONAUTICS AND SPACE COUNCIL
OFFICE OF EMERGENCY PLANNING
OFFICE OF SCIENCE AND TECHNOLOGY
COUNCIL OF ECONOMIC ADVISERS

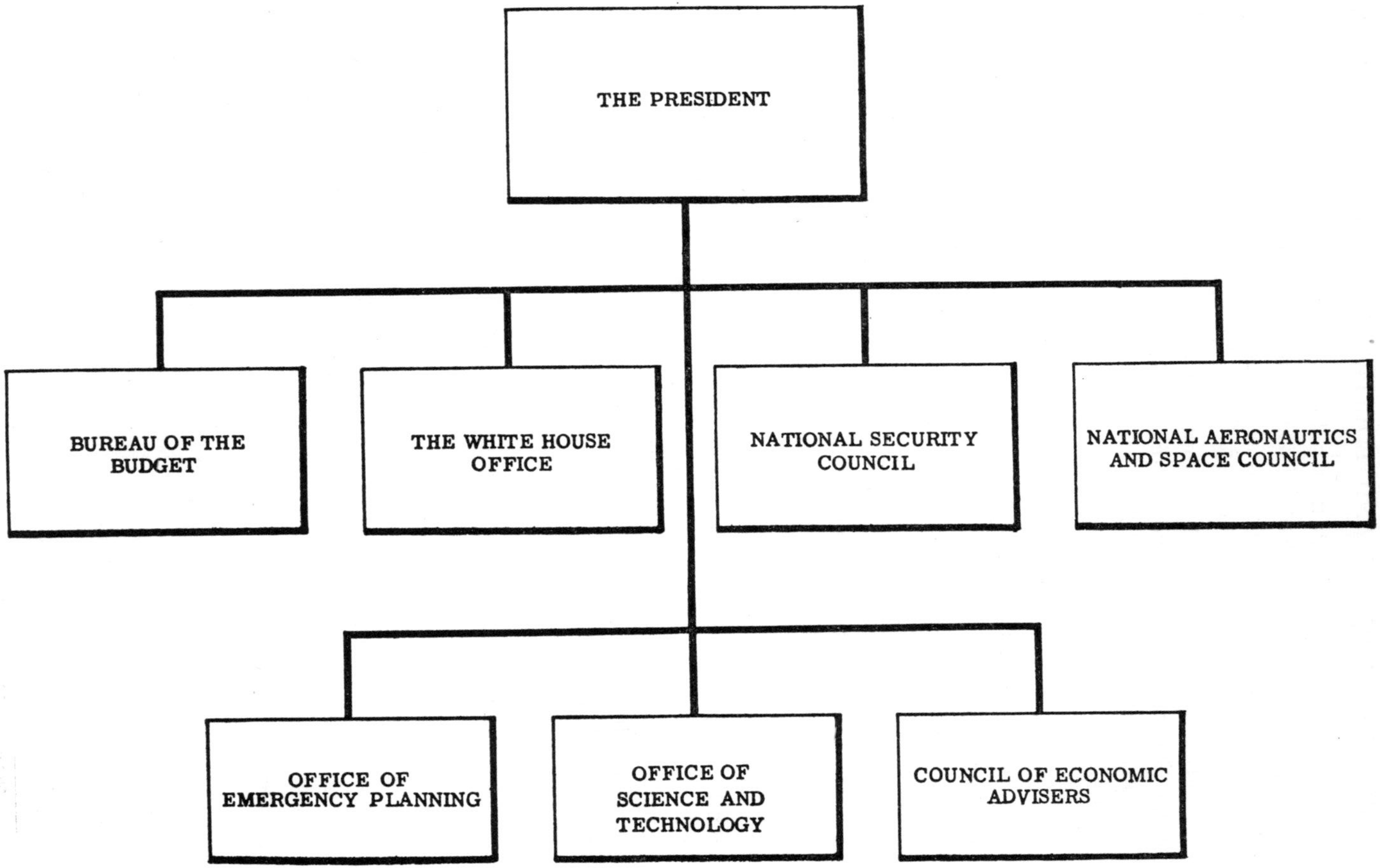

Among the more important political functions performed by the staff are (1) keeping the President informed on matters of public policy, (2) coordination and liaison activities with both the legislative and executive branches of government, (3) advising the President in personnel matters, and (4) preparing the multitudinous variety and number of communications (including presidential addresses) emitting from the President's office.

From its creation in 1921 until 1939, the *Bureau of the Budget* was located in the Treasury Department. In the latter year the Bureau was transferred to the Executive Office of the President, where it has developed into the key staff agency in the executive branch.

The preparation of the budget document lies with the Bureau, as well as the function of controlling the administration of the budget following legislative enactment. Budget preparation cannot be divorced from policy determination. Although the President establishes general guide lines within which the Bureau of the Budget will evaluate agency requests for funds, the Bureau itself, in translating the general concepts into specific recommendations, makes policy decisions which will not be overridden by the President as a rule.

A number of other functions are charged to the Bureau. It makes recommendations to improve administrative management throughout the executive branch; it coordinates legislative proposals initiated by the departments and agencies; it plans and coordinates federal statistical services; it assists the President in the preparation of executive orders and veto messages; and it serves to keep the President informed on an over-all basis as to the progress of the work programs carried out by the administrative agencies.

Created by the Employment Act of 1946, the *Council of Economic Advisers* consists of three members appointed by the President by and with the advice and consent of the Senate. As watchdog of the national economy, the Council advises the President on economic development, appraises the economic programs and policies of the national government, and recommends to the Chief Executive policies for economic growth and stability. It prepares an annual economic report which the President is required by law to transmit to the Congress.

A number of other units within the Executive Office of the President are expected to perform important advisory and/or coordinating functions. These include the *National Security Council,* the *National Aeronautics and Space Council,*[39] the *Office of Science and Technology,* and the *Office of Emergency Planning.* Changes in the organization of the Executive Office of the President are rather frequent as each President seeks to improve the effectiveness of his advisory staff.

---

[39] See p. 563 for a discussion of the National Security Council, and p. 572 for a discussion of the National Aeronautics and Space Council.

THE VICE-PRESIDENCY

The framers of the Constitution were not very enthusiastic about providing for a Vice-President and, had they authorized Congress to choose the President, they might have omitted the office altogether. Under the scheme finally accepted for selecting a chief executive, it was essential that someone be designated to act for the President in case of death or disability. So the office of Vice-President was created with qualifications similar to those laid down for the President.

Duties. The Constitution provides that the Vice-President shall preside over the sessions of the Senate, with a vote only in case of a tie. In this constitutional role, Vice-Presidents have contributed little to the legislative process. However, in recent years the stature of the office has been elevated considerably through statutory and extra-legal means.[40] Since 1949 the Vice-President has been a member of the National Security Council. Garner, Truman, Barkley, and Nixon proved helpful to their chiefs in congressional, particularly senatorial, liaison matters. Certainly one factor in the selection of Lyndon Johnson as vice-presidential candidate was the fact that he had been a successful majority leader in the Senate. Mr. Nixon traveled abroad on "goodwill" missions for the Eisenhower Administration and Vice-President Johnson continued this practice in behalf of President Kennedy before the latter's tragic assassination elevated Johnson to the Presidency.

Succession to the presidency. Eight Presidents have died during their terms, and their Vice-Presidents have taken over the office. The Constitution does not state that a Vice-President in such an event shall assume the presidency—it merely orders that the duties of the Chief Executive "shall devolve upon the Vice-President." Actually, every one of the eight has taken the title "President" and for all practical purposes not differentiated himself from a regularly elected holder of the office.

The Constitution authorizes Congress to provide by law for the case of removal, death, resignation, or inability, both of the President and Vice-President. At present, the order of succession is governed by a 1947 law which places the Speaker of the House immediately after the Vice-President, then the President *pro tempore* of the Senate, and then the heads of the executive departments in order of their establishment.[41]

President Eisenhower's disability on two separate occasions served to

---

40 See Irving G. Williams, *The American Vice-Presidency: New Look* (Garden City, N. Y.: Doubleday & Co., 1954).

41 Presidential succession had been dealt with before in 1792 and 1886. The 1886 law fixed the succession to follow the heads of the executive departments in their established order of State, Treasury, War, Justice, Post Office, Navy, and Interior. Under the present law, Defense displaces War, Navy is eliminated, and Agriculture, Commerce, Labor, and Health, Education, and Welfare are added.

focus attention once again on the "inability" aspect of presidential succession. The crux of the matter is that neither in the Constitution nor statute is provision made as to who shall decide whether the President is unable to discharge the responsibilities of his office.

Early in 1957 President Eisenhower recommended to Congress a constitutional amendment providing two ways for the Vice-President to take over presidential duties on a temporary basis. The President, himself, could inform the Vice-President in writing that he was disabled; or, if the President were unwilling or unable to do so, the cabinet by a majority vote could make the decision. Many members of Congress, without commenting on the substance of the President's proposal, expressed the opinion that a constitutional amendment was unnecessary since Congress by statute could remedy the uncertainty. So far, however, Congress has not acted to clarify the situation.

SUMMARY

The formal, specific powers conferred upon the President in the Constitution clearly indicate that the framers intended the Chief Executive to exercise considerable influence on governmental policies. However, one must look for additional factors to explain the outstanding position which the President now commands in our system of government. Most of the specific constitutional powers granted to the President are stated in broad terms, thus allowing the Chief Executive to place his own interpretation upon their exercise. For example, the President is to "take care that the laws be faithfully executed"; under the separation of powers principle, the President is the judge as to exactly how this clause is to be carried out.

Judicial decisions have seldom circumscribed the actions of the President. As a matter of practice, the courts are usually presented with a *fait accompli* with respect to cases involving presidential decisions.

"Big" government requires an ever-increasing delegation of legislative power to the executive branch. This development places responsibility in the hands of the President for the initiation as well as the implementation of policy. The President's role in the budgetary process is an excellent example of this fact.

Certainly one of the most significant and obvious magnifications of presidential power has occurred in the foreign relations field. In time of war the Commander-in-Chief role, supported by appropriate legislation, admits almost dictatorial proportions.

Underlying all of the manifestations of presidential power is the simple fact that a democracy, just as any other type of government, must have a focal point of leadership. The presidency fulfills this requirement in our system of government.

See *Bibliographic Note* at end of Chapter 13.

13

The President and Congress

AN EMINENT British political scientist once wrote that the difference between a good Congress and a bad one is largely the difference between a Congress that accepts the President's leadership and one that seeks to refuse the initiative the Chief Executive tries to communicate.[1] One might reverse the emphasis of the value judgment by suggesting that the difference between a strong President and one not so strong turns upon the President's ability to persuade Congress to follow his lead. No matter from which end of Pennsylvania Avenue one views the question, there are compelling reasons for the modern President's assuming leadership in legislative matters; in earlier periods of our history this would not have been necessary. With federal expenditures approaching $100 billion annually, with comprehensive economic and social programs under govern-mental guidance becoming commonplace occurrences, with the specialist and technician epitomizing progress, with atomic war hovering ever in the background, it is to the President that the public and Congress look for the enunciation of the unity of purpose which justifies the nation's public poli-cies.

No future President will be permitted to play the negative role in leg-islative matters assumed by some of the former holders of the office. The institutional growth of the presidential office will guarantee that this will not happen. The bureaucrats in the Executive Office of the President and in other key policy-determining spots give continuity to the office of the Presidency as a political institution. Their precise relations to the President, and the President's utilization of his formal and informal powers with re-spect to Congress, will vary with the time, circumstance, and personalities involved. But modern democratic governments, in order to survive, require executive leadership which in our system can be provided only by the Pres-ident.

---

[1] Harold J. Laski, *The American Democracy* (New York: The Viking Press, 1948), p. 73.

A STUDY IN CONTRASTS

Cabinet government. In the world today there are two principal types of democratic government in actual operation—cabinet and presidential. Cabinet and presidential governments vary in their methods of procedure from country to country, but the British model is perhaps best suited to demonstrate the contrast between the cabinet type and the presidential type of the United States in so far as their respective relations to the lawmaking branch are concerned.

The cabinet, which is the most important element of the executive in Britain, is chosen from among the leaders of the dominant political party in the House of Commons. The cabinet drafts a program, which is summarized in the message of the king or queen to Parliament, and it then proceeds step-by-step to carry that program into effect. Although private members of the legislative branch may introduce bills of their own, there is very slight chance of their passage. Furthermore, all proposals to spend public funds can originate only from the cabinet. The House of Commons may debate the various bills which the cabinet has prepared and in minor particulars may go so far as to amend them. However, if the House of Commons refuses to accept the general provisions of any bill or if major changes not acceptable to the cabinet are made, the cabinet must then follow one of two courses. It may resign at once and clear the way for a new cabinet which will receive the support of the House of Commons. Or, hoping that the voters will favor its policy, it may call for new elections with the appeal to the electorate to choose "M.P.'s" who will uphold the cabinet's position. If the new membership of the House does act favorably on the controversial legislation, the cabinet is regarded as triumphant and consequently remains in office. If the voters re-elect the same members, however, the cabinet has no alternative but to resign. The cabinet system goes far in guaranteeing harmonious relations between the executive and the legislative branches—if there is lack of unity, changes are made to restore the equilibrium.

Presidential government. Presidential government, on the other hand, is a contribution which the United States has made to democratic institutions. In framing their constitutions many countries have examined the presidential form, but except for certain Latin-American countries, few of them have seen fit to adopt it.[2] This form of democracy separates the executive and legislative branches, assigning to each a major role in the government. No machinery is provided for integrating the two—indeed the basic concept seems to be that the two will check each other. Of course, there is no absolute separation of powers, for under the complex social con-

---

[2] As suggested in Chapter 1, the new French constitution provides for what might be considered a semi-presidential type.

ditions that now prevail such a relation would produce chaos and possibly even the breakdown of the governmental system. The men of 1787 saw fit to supplement separation of powers with the doctrine of checks and balances. Thus they gave the President the veto power, authorized the Senate to confirm presidential appointments and approve treaties, gave Congress fiscal control over administration, and permitted the legislative branch under extreme circumstances to remove a chief executive through impeachment proceedings.

Experience of the United States with presidential government. The flexibility and development character of our constitutional system is nowhere better illustrated than in the area of executive-legislative relations. Some provisions of the written Constitution prescribe formal contacts between the President and Congress; these provisions have not changed since the adoption of the Constitution. Vast changes have occurred, however, in the meaning, intent, and application of these formal requirements by Presidents and Congresses. Complementing the application of the constitutional contacts between the executive and legislative branches have been informal, extralegal, and customary procedures which have considerably modified the rigidity of the separation of power principle. The Presidency has gained more power and prestige through these developments than has Congress. Congress may be credited with many specific contributions toward an enhancement of the President's position vis-à-vis itself. The ever increasing delegation of authority to the executive branch is a case in point. Conflicts between the President and Congress have arisen throughout our nation's history and will certainly continue to occur.

FORMAL RELATIONSHIPS BETWEEN THE PRESIDENT AND CONGRESS

The Constitution specifically refers to several areas of presidential-congressional relations. Some of these references are mandatory in nature, others permissive; but in either category the President is left with wide discretion in the actual usage.

Sessions of Congress. There are countries which permit the executive to call the legislative body into session and dismiss it at its pleasure. The framers of the Constitution had no disposition to confer this authority on the American President, for they had experienced the arrogant and dictatorial practices of the colonial governors who sometimes ruled without legislatures. However, they anticipated occasions when the two houses of Congress might not be able to agree on a date of adjournment and hence empowered the President to act.[3] The opening date for congressional sessions

---

3 Art. II, sec. 3. This anticipation has not been realized in practice, for Congress decides on a date of adjournment without too much difficulty. In October, 1914, however, Woodrow Wilson was urged to, but did not, use his power to act; see *New York Times*, October 24, 1914.

is fixed by the Constitution, but the time of adjournment is left to the discretion of Congress itself. By insisting upon the disposal of certain business before adjournment upon threat of calling the members back into special session, the President has something to say about how long Congress will meet. This, however, does not involve fixing an exact date of adjournment.

Special sessions. An important formal control which the President may exercise is his right to call special sessions. In the language of the Constitution, he may "on extraordinary occasions, convene both houses, or either of them." [4] But the President is the sole judge of what constitutes an "extraordinary occasion." As a matter of fact, there have been truly extraordinary occasions when the President did not summon Congress, as was the case with Lincoln upon the outbreak of the Civil War. In a majority of the states, legislatures called into special session may deal only with the specific problems presented to them by the governor. In contrast to this, once Congress is convened in special session there are no limitations upon what it considers or how long it remains in session.

Before the Twentieth (Lame Duck) Amendment provided that Congress assemble in regular session shortly before the President himself took office, it was a common practice for new Presidents to call special sessions soon after they were inaugurated in March. They wanted the Senate to confirm appointments and perhaps preferred to have attention given to general legislative business at once rather than after some nine months had elapsed. Inasmuch as Congress now starts a regular session just before a President is inaugurated, there is far less reason for special sessions than there was before.

Initiation of legislation. Comprehensive presidential programs as a basis of legislative action are largely a product of the twentieth century; although from the beginning of the federal government, suggestions for legislation have to some degree emanated from the executive branch. The President is required by the Constitution to "give to the Congress information of the state of the Union, and recommend to their consideration such measures as he shall judge necessary and expedient." [5] But note the amount of discretion permitted the Chief Executive by these provisions. It assumes that the President will transmit messages to the legislative branch but as to when, how many, and on what specific subjects—other than the general statement concerning information on the state of the union—the decision remains with the President.

All of the Presidents have presented an annual state of the union message and other communications to Congress. However, Woodrow Wilson is to be credited with interpreting his responsibility in this respect as a *power*

---

[4] Art. II., sec. 3.
[5] Art. II, sec. 3.

rather than a *duty*. He "brought to the Presidency the matured theory of a would-be prime minister." [6] Wilson resurrected the defunct custom of presenting important messages in person to a joint session of Congress. He used his position as party leader to guide his majority toward the legislative goals set forth in presidential messages.

Since the time of Wilson the message power has assumed even more significance. Congress has enlarged the potentiality of message power as a presidential technique of leadership by requiring an annual budget message[7] and an economic report.[8] But developments within the presidential office itself have been even more important. With the nation reeling under the impact of the most disastrous economic depression ever experienced, the President's role as the initiator of governmental programs reached heights heretofore unsought by Chief Executives or unacceptable to Congress. Even in Franklin D. Roosevelt's Administrations the annual messages were apt to mention legislative objectives in rather general terms, with more specific proposals following in spasmodic although often dramatic fashion. The Truman Era saw the transformation of annual messages from imprecise and unelaborated presentations into relatively defined and detailed bills of particulars.[9] The Eisenhower Administration followed the Truman pattern, but the mechanics for drawing the President's program together and the method of its presentation became more formalized and institutionalized. Departments and agencies were requested to suggest specific legislative proposals. There was already in existence a division in the Bureau of the Budget for the purpose of coordinating proposed legislation, but under President Eisenhower the cabinet and the National Security Council also reviewed and coordinated proposals. The precise way in which future Presidents use the staff agencies available to them for the preparation of "their" legislative programs will no doubt vary with the occupants of the White House. But the bureaucrats, the public, and Congress have come to depend upon the President to furnish concrete proposals for the consideration of the legislative branch. It is understandable why the President is often referred to as the "Chief Legislator."

The executive branch not only drafts specific bills to be introduced into Congress by friendly members; it is often called upon to review bills which individual members have themselves initiated. The specialists in the administrative agencies may very well point out complications and inconsistencies which have escaped the original draftsman. Little is lost and

---

6 W. E. Binkley, "The President as Chief Legislator," *Annals*, CCCVII, 95. See also Marshall E. Dimock, "Woodrow Wilson as a Legislative Leader," *Journal of Politics*, XIX, 3-19, February, 1957.

7 Required by the Budget and Accounting Act of 1921.

8 Required by the Full Employment Act of 1946.

9 Richard E. Neustadt, "Presidency and Legislation: Planning the President's Program," *The American Political Science Review*, XLIX, 1000, December, 1955.

much may be gained by such procedures. If the administration supports the bill, the sponsor's hand is strengthened in Congress. If the bill is opposed by the administration, it may still be introduced.

The veto power. Another function which the Chief Executive exercises in the field of legislation is so important that it requires a rather detailed examination. The veto power is accorded one of the longest sections of the Constitution[10] in contrast to other important matters which receive no mention at all or are disposed of in a few words.

General character of the veto power. The Constitution stipulates that every "bill, resolution, or vote to which the concurrence of the Senate and House of Representatives may be necessary (except on a question of adjournment) shall be presented to the President of the United States." It adds: "and before the same shall take effect, shall be approved by him, or being disapproved by him, shall be repassed by two-thirds of the Senate and House of Representatives." It has been held that this does not apply to proposed amendments of the Constitution[11] nor to concurrent resolutions which merely express the sentiment of Congress without having any force of law behind them. Except for votes on adjournment, which are specifically exempted by the Constitution, all other acts of Congress are subject to the presidential veto. But it should be emphasized that the veto is definitely not of the absolute type, for Congress may override this presidential barrier by casting a two-thirds vote in favor of a vetoed measure.

Presidential handling of bills and resolutions. After the presiding officers of the Senate and House of Representatives have duly signed a bill or joint resolution, attesting that it has been passed by the necessary majority in their respective houses, a messenger delivers this bill or resolution to the office of the President. The Chief Executive may proceed to sign the bill— if it is of outstanding interest, he sometimes signs it in the presence of its sponsors in the Senate and House of Representatives.[12] In many cases the President is not particularly enthusiastic about a bill or joint resolution and wishes to take no personal responsibility for it. If he is not so opposed to it that he wishes to veto it, he may allow the bill to remain on his desk without any action for ten days. If Congress has not in the meantime adjourned, the bill becomes law without his signature. In both of these cases the President then transmits the bill or resolution to the General Services Administration for promulgation and publication in the *Statutes of the United States.* If he deems a bill or resolution distinctly objectionable, he

---

10 Art. I, sec. 7.

11 The first ten amendments were not submitted to the President for his signature. In *Hollingsworth* v. *Virginia,* 3 Dallas 378 (1798) the Supreme Court remarked, although it did not directly rule, that the President's signature to proposed amendments is not necessary.

12 A colorful ceremony sometimes takes place with newspaper photographers present to take photographs. The pens which the President uses to sign may be presented to the sponsors as a memento.

can make direct use of the veto power. In this event the President refuses to sign and returns the bill or resolution to the house of Congress in which it originated within ten days, usually with a statement of reasons why he refused to approve.

"Pocket vetoes." Toward the end of a session numerous bills and resolutions are passed by Congress in an effort to clean up accumulated business. These go to the President in batches. If Congress adjourns within ten days after the President receives these bills and resolutions, and he takes no action, it is said that the measures have been "pocket vetoed." A considerable number of these last-minute actions fail to become laws as a result of the inaction of the President; the Chief Executive may not be particularly opposed to them, but he does not want to take the responsibility of giving his positive approval, perhaps because he has not had the time to investigate them. A period of ten days is not very long in which to decide what to do about a multitude of congressional proposals,[13] and it is sometimes expedient for a President to use the "pocket veto" generously. Unlike the situation in some states, where the legislature has a chance to override vetoed bills when it convenes in its next session, Congress must carry a measure which has been "pocket vetoed" through the complete legislative cycle and send it to the President as a new bill if it is ever to become the law of the land.

The ten-day provision. For more than a century it was believed that no bills could be signed by the President after the adjournment of Congress, but in 1920 Woodrow Wilson successfully attempted to overthrow that precedent by signing several bills within the ten-day period specified by the Constitution.[14] The extension of time, which was upheld by the Supreme Court by unanimous vote,[15] is of considerable advantage in that it affords the President additional time to decide what action to take. Ten days is none too long at best—indeed some states sometimes permit their governors two or three times that period in which to dispose of their legislative work.

Use of the veto power. The pocket veto has been used quite frequently, but the early holders of the office used the direct veto very sparingly. It was not until Andrew Jackson assumed office that any considerable disposition to employ this control was evident—and even including his vetoes there

---

[13] See the case of *Okanogan Indians* v. *United States,* 279 U. S. 655 (1920). The Court held that ten days does not include Sundays, that calendar rather than legislative days are intended, and that adjournment means the adjournment at the end of a session rather than the final adjournment of a Congress which takes place only every two years.

[14] President Wilson received bills when he was in Europe in connection with the peace terms. It was held that ten days did not include the period elapsing between the dispatch of the bill to the office of the President and his receiving of the bill in Europe. In other words, he was allowed ten days in which to take action after he received the bill in Europe.

[15] See *Edwards* v. *United States,* 286 U. S. 482 (1932).

were just over fifty presidential vetoes from the establishment of the republic down to the Civil War. Recent Presidents have a more impressive record although there has been little if any tendency to abuse the power. In comparison with state governors, the Presidents have had records of striking restraint, for the former frequently veto as many as ten to fifteen per cent of all bills and resolutions received and occasionally as many as one-fourth or more. Even the most vigorous President has not approached a veto record of one per cent. In the two years and ten months of his term of office, President Kennedy vetoed 21 bills. In no case did the Congress attempt to override Kennedy's use of the veto power.

Presidents, until the time of Andrew Jackson, based their few vetoes on an apparent conflict with the Constitution or on technical defects in the wording. Modern Presidents have found the veto power to be a most potent weapon in influencing the direction of public policy. In other words, measures are apt to be vetoed not because the President believes them to be unconstitutional, but because he disagrees with the policy involved or the method suggested for solving a particular problem. President Eisenhower was particularly adept at focusing public attention on controversial issues through the use of the veto. He frequently employed the power in politically explosive areas such as education, housing, and agriculture. The threat of a presidential veto proved to be one of Eisenhower's most important techniques in dealing with a Congress which was controlled by the Democrats in six of the eight years he held office. Advance warning that a particular bill faces a presidential veto may achieve a modification more to the President's liking while the measure is still before the legislative branch. Or, of course, after the President has vetoed a bill and Congress cannot muster the necessary majority to override, a second bill on the same subject may be tailored to meet the Chief Executive's objections. In both of these categories, President Eisenhower achieved remarkable success in shaping public policy.

Overriding of vetoes. When the President returns a vetoed measure to the house of Congress in which it originated, there may be enough support to repass it by a two-thirds vote in both houses, thus overriding the veto. That this is the exception rather than the rule is indicated by the fact that over the last fifty years less than three per cent of the presidential vetoes have been overridden by Congress. President Eisenhower did not have a law passed over his veto until he had been in office for six and one-half years. Finally Congress acted to spoil this record when it passed a billion dollar public works appropriation measure providing funds for rivers, harbors, flood control, and reclamation projects—a traditional "pork barrel" device.

The item veto. Some states permit their governors to exercise the item veto in connection with appropriation measures. It has been suggested that this power should be extended to the President. The main argument in favor of this proposal is to permit the President to veto parts of appropriation bills which he opposes. Sometimes "riders" have been attached to general appropriation bills which are not germane to the contents, but which the President can do nothing about unless he is willing to veto the whole bill. At other times, the President may oppose certain sections which are germane, but which he believes are contrary to public interest. It would require a constitutional amendment to grant the President the item veto, and Congress has not seen fit to initiate the suggestion.

OTHER EXECUTIVE INFLUENCES OVER CONGRESS

Every President has the same specific powers granted in the Constitution relating to his formal contacts with Congress in so far as legislative matters are concerned, but Presidents have interpreted and applied these provisions differently. Similarly many of the informal contacts available to the President are as old as the Constitution but are not necessarily employed by the various Chief Executives in the same way.

Personal contacts. A President may be able to persuade members of Congress to support his proposals by talking with them directly. This technique is not necessarily confined to members of the President's own party. It is not unusual, particularly with respect to legislation in the field of foreign affairs, for the President to invite opposition party leaders to conferences. President Kennedy regularly scheduled conferences with his party leaders. In his first year in office he also held separate meetings for all standing-committee chairmen. President Johnson on occasion has invited the entire membership of certain committees to confer with him at the White House.

Patronage. No one can dispute the significance of patronage as a legislative control in past history. Its importance has decreased in recent years because the number of patronage jobs has declined. Yet members of Congress still have supporters who ache for appointments; and the President still has some patronage plums at his disposal; *ergo,* the members of Congress agree to meet the wishes of the President in return for concessions which he grants in the way of offices. Often a member of the President's party, who has been defeated in a congressional race, can be kept in the public eye by appointment to office. This, in turn, may be a stepping stone for a return to Congress in a future election.

National leadership. The role of the President in American life confers on the Presidency very great influence in all sorts of matters. Not the least of these is the legislative process.

Many Presidents have sparked the imagination of the American people for programs and projects in a way impossible for an individual member of the legislature or for Congress as a whole to emulate. Jackson was the first President to appeal to the people for support of his policies over the head of Congress. Most of the twentieth century Presidents have employed this technique but with varying degrees of success.

President Franklin Roosevelt introduced his "fireside chat" to explain his policies to the people. Now television permits the President to "come into living rooms" all over the United States. President Eisenhower rather frequently explained his proposals or his reasons for making a particular decision to the public at large. He went before the people in May, 1957 to explain his budget upon which Congress was hacking away. The precise effect of his speeches upon the final budget remains unmeasured. There were sizable cuts, but who can say the decreases would not have been greater had the appeal not been made. A portion of one of the two speeches made on the subject of the budget was, in a manner, a justification for the President's appeal for popular support.

> To this office—to the President, whoever he may be, there comes every day from all parts of the land and from all parts of the world a steady flow of dispatches, reports and visitors. They tell of the needs, the successes and the disappointments of our people in their efforts to achieve peace with justice in the world. They tell, too, of the progress and difficulties in building a sturdy, prosperous, and just society here at home.
>
> On the basis of this information, decisions, affecting all of us, have to be made every day. Because your President, aside from the Vice-President, is the only government official chosen by a vote of all the people, he must make his decisions on the basis of what he thinks is best for all of the people. He cannot consider only a district, state or region in developing solutions to problems. He must always use the yardstick of the national interest.

Party leadership. Many of the executive-legislative relations already mentioned are obviously associated with the fact that the President is leader of the party. Yet his status as party chief affects his congressional political followers in other ways. Presidents have sometimes thrown their support to a particular candidate in the party primary, although this technique is used infrequently since it might be resented by the voters. The role of the President in the general election is another matter. If the President is running for re-election, he is, of course, actually campaigning for all of his party candidates. In the mid-term election the President has more discretion as to when, where, and how often he shall speak, and otherwise engage in campaign activities. Here his personal (and political) regard for the individual concerned may well determine whether the President gives the candidate a perfunctory pat on the back or whether he goes out and makes a fighting speech in the candidate's district.

Effect of the Twenty-second Amendment. Resolutions have been introduced in Congress to repeal the Twenty-second Amendment. One argument made in favor of its repeal is that since the members of the President's party know that he cannot run again following reelection to a second term, his effectiveness is diminished vis-à-vis these members, particularly in the last two years of his administration. This thesis assumes that the influence of the patronage factor is lessened as the end of the second term approaches. It is also suggested that party leaders who are interested in securing the party's presidential nomination will seek to draw public attention to themselves. They may wish to define party issues in their own right.

Former President Truman testified in favor of repeal of the amendment, saying: "You do not have to be smart to know that an officeholder who is not eligible for re-election loses a lot of influence. So, what have you done? You have taken a man and put him in the hardest job in the world, and sent him out to fight with one hand tied behind his back, because everyone knows he cannot run for re-election." [16]

President Eisenhower was not as positive in his stand concerning the possible repeal of the amendment as was Mr. Truman. At one point he seemed to favor repeal, but, in other comments, he appeared to believe that a longer period of experience with the amendment was desirable before a final decision should be made. In response to a question as to whether he felt that he had one hand tied behind his back, he replied: "Well, I haven't sensed that particular feeling. I find this: That it seems to me that I am more bombarded with requests for help of all kinds, whether it be administrative, altruistic and charitable, or political, than I ever had in my prior years in the Presidency." [17]

The truth of the matter is that it has been impossible to establish a cause and effect relation between the two-term limit and the influence of President Eisenhower in the last two years of his administration. In many ways his influence was even greater than in his first term of office. This does not mean that the situation might not be different in the case of a future President.

THE FUTURE OF EXECUTIVE-LEGISLATIVE RELATIONSHIPS

A frequent and obvious criticism of our constitutional system is that it makes possible a state of affairs where one party controls the executive branch while the opposite party secures a majority in one or both branches of Congress. Many Presidents have found themselves confronted with the opposition party in control of Congress for the last two years of their administrations as a result of shifting party tides in the congressional mid-term elections. President Eisenhower, however, is the only President who has experienced this situation for the last six years of his tenure in office. Deadlock and delay is certainly encouraged by such a division of party control over the branches of government, but the relations between President Eisenhower and the Democratic controlled Congress would seem to in-

---

16 "Presidential Terms of Office," *Hearings Before a Subcommittee of the Committee on the Judiciary United States Senate,* Eighty-Sixth Congress, First Session, Part 1, p. 7.
17 At a press conference on May 5, 1959.

dicate that a reasonable degree of cooperation may be achieved. This does not mean, of course, that such would always be the case. Rather it proves that divided government does not necessarily lead to a perilous legislative stalemate. One observer has commented:

> The Democratic party had two alternative types of opposition party roles which it could play while Eisenhower occupied the White House. One would have been to oppose him on most occasions in an attempt to positively discredit the Republican administration; the other, to support him whenever possible and take the chance that the administration would make mistakes and at least in part discredit itself. The latter policy, no less politically motivated than the former, was the one chosen. Its chief architects were Senate Democratic Floor Leader Johnson and House Speaker Rayburn. Because the Democratic party is still the majority party, it is in an advantageous position to win more Congressional and Presidential elections than the Republican party until the power balance between the two major parties shifts. Should Democrats aggressively and by every means oppose the administration, they would run the risk of creating new issues, including opposition as an issue in itself, which might upset their long-term advantage.[18]

Suggestions for modifying present patterns of executive-legislative relationships. History proves that a degree of conflict between the President and Congress is inevitable even though the same party controls both the executive and legislative branches of government. The separation of power principle may be modified, but it is never shelved completely even when one party has the Presidency and majorities in both houses of Congress. Many Presidents have had more difficulty getting along with a Congress run by their own party than Mr. Eisenhower had with the legislative branch controlled by the Democrats. The following suggestions are not confined necessarily to attempting to assure that the same party will be in charge of the Presidency and Congress.

The introduction of *cabinet government* has been advocated. A fair-minded observer sees much in that system as used in Great Britain that is impressive. However, American traditions have run along somewhat different lines. Moreover, this change would require a drastic revamping of our constitutional system, which as a matter of practicality appears to rule out the suggestion.

It has been suggested that the majority party leaders in the Senate and House of Representatives be associated with the President and certain members of his cabinet in a *joint executive-legislative council*. This group would meet at regular intervals, collaborating in the formulation of national policy, and in the procedures necessary for putting policies into operation. Advocates of this proposal believe that the formalizing of execu-

---

18 Jack W. Peltason (ed.), *American Government Annual, 1959-1960* (New York: Holt, Rinehart and Winston, Inc., 1959), p. 89.

tive-legislative relations in this fashion would strengthen both branches of government. This suggestion could be implemented by means of a joint resolution and executive order. This recommendation already has limited application in the device of the presidential conference with legislative leaders. It certainly has merit if the President and the legislative leaders are of the same party. However, excepting a crisis, it is difficult to imagine opposition party leaders giving full support to this recommendation if they have majorities in Congress.

A multitude of *additional proposals* have been made on the subject of executive-legislative cooperation. Among these are: creation of congressional advisory councils at the departmental level in particular functional fields; presidential resignation or a general national election following adoption by a two-thirds vote of both houses of a concurrent resolution of "no confidence" in the President; the synchronization of national elections to avoid deadlock between the two branches; and giving cabinet members the privilege of the floor in Congress in order to explain the administration's policies.

Even the most modest formal modifications of the separation of power principle in so far as it applies to executive-legislative relations seems out of the question for some time to come. In the first place, many of the *proposals* assume a degree of party responsibility with respect to members and discipline which do not exist. Unless there occurred a revamping of our party system with an emphasis on these latter points, one could argue that no amount of tampering with the separation of power credo is going to drastically alter the legislative process. In the second place, the American people remain to be convinced that any basic changes are needed in the present system. No doubt the pattern of executive-legislative relations will see further changes, but these, as in the past, will in all probability be of the extralegal, informal type rather than of the formal, legal variety.

SUMMARY

It is now customary to refer to the President as the "Chief Legislator." This title does not signify a dictatorial President making laws without congressional consent; it suggests the role played by the President in initiating legislation and in shaping public policy generally in cooperation with Congress.

From the first days of a legislative session until adjournment, the Chief Executive's recommendations are received and debated in Congress. In rapid succession headlines proclaim the fact that the *President's* State of the Union Message, the *President's* Budget Message, and the *President's* Economic Report has been transmitted to Congress. Later in the session due notice is given the public that the *administration's* bill on a particular matter is being debated, that the *President* is sending a special message to Congress requesting specific legislation in some field, that the *President* is threatening to veto or has vetoed a bill.

The significance of all of these activities is that to a large degree the initiative rests with the President in focusing the attention of Congress and the public upon the issues confronting the nation. This pattern is observed even if the President is faced with opposition party majorities in the houses of Congress.

The actuality of separation of powers is almost certain to lead to some conflict between the executive and legislative branches even when the same party is in control of both branches. Divided government, meaning that the same party is not in command of the executive and legislative departments, undoubtedly puts more strain on executive-legislative relationships. Yet the last six years of the Eisenhower Administration demonstrated that a reasonable amount of cooperation and compromise is possible even in such situations. The danger remains, however, that divided government will encourage a contest between the President and Congress in which the primary objective becomes the creation of election issues rather than co-operative legislative enactments.

Many suggestions have been made as to how the gap between the White House and Capitol Hill may be bridged or at least narrowed. Any drastic, formal changes in this direction seem not likely to occur any time soon. Informal techniques affecting executive-legislative relationships will continue to develop in accordance with the necessities, the personalities, and the pressures of the times.

BIBLIOGRAPHIC NOTE

The most comprehensive discussion of the development of the constitutional and legal powers of the President is found in Edward S. Corwin, *The President: Office and Powers* (4th ed., New York: New York University Press, 1957). The late Harold J. Laski, distinguished British political scientist, saw the presidency as the focal point of American democracy in *The American Presidency* (New York: Harper & Brothers, Publishers, 1940). Wilfred E. Binkley traces the historical development of the presidency in his *The Man in the White House* (Baltimore: Johns Hopkins University Press, 1958). Among the other significant books on the presidency are Edward S. Corwin and Louis W. Koenig, *The Presidency Today* (New York: New York University Press, 1956); George Fort Milton, *The Use of Presidential Power, 1789-1943* (Boston: Little, Brown & Company, 1944); W. E. Binkley, *The Powers of the President* (New York: Doubleday & Company, 1937); James Hart, *The American Presidency in Action* (New York: The Macmillan Company, 1948); Sidney Hyman, *The American President* (New York: Harper & Brothers, 1954); Clinton Rossiter, *The American Presidency* (New York: Harcourt, Brace and Company, 1956); and Louis Brownlow, *The President and the Presidency* (Chicago: Public Administration Service, 1949).

William Howard Taft stresses the legalistic approach to the presidency in his

Our Chief Magistrate and His Powers (New York: Columbia University Press, 1916).

For the use of presidential powers in times of emergency, see Clinton Rossiter, *Constitutional Dictatorship* (Princeton, N. J.: Princeton University Press, 1948) and B. M. Rich, *The Presidents and Civil Disorder* (Washington, D. C.: The Brookings Institution, 1941).

Most of the above works listed include a discussion of the President's role in foreign affairs and as Commander-in-Chief. For more detailed examinations of these topics one may consult Elmer Plischke, *Summit Diplomacy: Personal Diplomacy of the President of the United States* (College Park, Md.: Bureau of Governmental Research, University of Maryland, 1960); W. M. McClure, *International Executive Agreements* (New York: Columbia University Press, 1941); Elbert M. Byrd, *Treaties and Executive Agreements in the United States* (The Hague: Martinus Nijhoff, 1960); and the U. S. House of Representatives, *The Powers of the President as Commander in Chief of the Army and Navy of the United States* (H. Doc. 443, 84th Cong., 2d Sess., 1956).

For a discussion of other specific aspects of presidential power, see W. H. Humbert, *The Pardoning Power of the President* (Washington, D. C.: American Council on Public Affairs, 1941); John D. Larkin, *The President's Control Over the Tariff* (Cambridge, Mass.: Harvard University Press, 1936). For an exhaustive study on the relations of the President and the Senate with respect to making appointments, see J. P. Harris, *The Advice and Consent of the Senate* (Berkeley, Calif.: University of California Press, 1953). A popular novel covering this same topic is Allen Drury's *Advise and Consent* (Garden City, N. Y.: Doubleday & Company, 1959).

Richard E. Neustadt's *Presidential Power: The Politics of Leadership* (New York: John Wiley and Sons, Inc., 1960) is a study of the presidency in terms of operational problems, particularly emphasizing the Truman and Eisenhower administrations. L. H. Chamberlain's *The President, Congress, and Legislation* (New York: Columbia University Press, 1946) examines some 90 legislative enactments in evaluating the role of the President and Congress in initiating legislation. Other works dealing with executive-congressional relations are Wilfred E. Binkley, *President and Congress*, 3rd rev. ed. (New York: Vintage Books, 1962); E. P. Herring, *Presidential Leadership* (New York: Farrar & Rinehart, Inc., 1940); and Marvin Jones and others, *Legislative-Executive Relationships in the Government of the United States* (U. S. Department of Agriculture, Graduate School, 1956).

For an excellent description of the origin and operation of the Executive Office of the President, see E. H. Hobbs, *Behind the President* (Washington, D. C.: Public Affairs Press, 1956). A discussion of the formal and informal relations between the executive and legislative branches is found in J. Leiper Freeman, *The Political Process: Executive Bureau-Legislative Committee Relations* (New York: Random House, 1955).

Malcolm Moos' *Politics, Presidents, and Coattails* (Baltimore: The Johns Hopkins University Press, 1952) examines the influence of the President in congressional elections.

There are excellent biographical studies of most of the Presidents. No attempt is made here to present a comprehensive listing of titles in this category, but four recent studies of interest include: Marquis W. Childs, *Eisenhower: Captive Hero* (New York: Harcourt, Brace & Company, 1958); Robert J. Donovon, *Eisenhower: The Inside Story* (New York: Harper Brothers, Publishers, 1956); James M. Burns, *Roosevelt: The Lion and the Fox* (New York: Harcourt, Brace & Company, 1956); and Rexford G. Tugwell, *The Democratic Roosevelt* (New York: Doubleday & Company, 1957).

For an historical account of the development of the cabinet, see H. B. Learned, *The President's Cabinet* (New Haven, Conn.: Yale University Press, 1912). For a more analytical study of the cabinet as a political institution, see Richard F. Fenno, Jr., *The President's Cabinet* (Cambridge, Mass.: Harvard University Press, 1959). See also Stephen Horn's *The Cabinet and Congress* (New York: Columbia University Press, 1961).

Two interesting views of the Kennedy impact on the White House are provided by Theodore C. Sorenson, the late President's close adviser, in *Decision Making in the White House: The Olive Branch or the Arrows* (New York: Columbia University Press, 1963) and by Grant McConnell's *Steel and the Presidency* (New York: Norton, 1962) which deals with Kennedy's fight with the major steel companies.

Ruth C. Silva's *Presidential Succession* (Ann Arbor, Mich.: University of Michigan Press, 1951) is the most thorough discussion of that topic.

On the vice-presidency, consult Irvin G. Williams, *The American Vice-Presidency: New Look* (New York: Doubleday & Company, 1954) and E. W. Waugh, *The Second Consul: The Vice Presidency* (Indianapolis, Ind.: Bobbs-Merrill Company, 1956).

14

The Powers of Congress—An Over-all View

T HE work of Congress may be characterized as both legislative (lawmaking) and non-legislative (non-lawmaking). To be sure, the genesis of a law (statute) may depend upon a non-legislative factor, but a clear differentiation between the lawmaking and non-lawmaking powers of Congress is necessary in order for one to comprehend the national legislative process.

Eight non-legislative powers or functions are discussed in this chapter. A significant development of the twentieth century has been the emphasis placed by Congress upon two of these powers, i.e., (1) supervision of the administration, and (2) the investigatory function.

The latter part of this chapter explains the scope of the legislative powers of Congress. The concept that Congress may exercise only those powers delegated to it in the Constitution is basic to our plan of federal government. Delegated powers consist of two types—enumerated and implied. Emerging from the subtleties of constitutional interpretation is the central fact that Congress, when faced with a national problem, will discover the legislative means to deal with it.

NON-LEGISLATIVE POWERS OF CONGRESS

Housekeeping function. Congress must provide for a number of auxiliary services necessary to its functioning as a legislative body. A variety of administrative and technical services have been developed over the years with practically no attempt being made to co-ordinate them. Each house maintains its own separate fiscal, personnel, and procurement systems. Although Congress in recent years has insisted that the executive branch improve its administrative management procedures, many of its own procedures in this area are of nineteenth century vintage. The Library of

Congress, as indicated by its name, was established for the benefit of the members of Congress. Now a specialized division of the library, the Legislative Reference Service, is set up to render service to congressional committees and individual members in a number of ways.

The Legislative Reorganization Act of 1946 provided for an increase in committee staff personnel and at least encouraged a movement toward professionalization, but the hiring and releasing of committee staff is still dominated in many instances by the committee chairmen. Many other specific types of housekeeping activities are undertaken such as property management, publication, and records-keeping.

Executive function. As a part of the check and balance system within the framework of the separation of powers principle, the Constitution permits the Senate a share in the executive functions of appointment and treaty-making. Thousands of nominations submitted by the President, such as military appointments and minor positions in the federal service, are confirmed without hearings and *en bloc*. Top level nominations to civilian posts are referred to the appropriate committee, hearings are held, and the committee reports to the parent body. It takes only a simple majority, a quorum being present, to confirm. Treaties are first considered by the Foreign Relations Committee. A two-thirds majority is required for senatorial acceptance of treaties.

Representation function. The average member in Congress would seldom be re-elected if he spent all of his time in the role of lawmaker. In a very real sense, he is the representative of his constituents in a multitude of ways. Although each member is elected as a partisan of a political party, he is aware that in theory, and of practical necessity, his duties encompass obligations to the *public* not just the *party*. He spends a considerable amount of time greeting the "folks" from his home district; he writes letters of recommendation; he sets up interviews for his constituents with high government officials. Almost every member's office operates what amounts to an information bureau for the people of his state or district. Perhaps a farmer wants to know the best fertilizer for use on a particular type of soil; he is likely to receive from his congressional representative a number of pamphlets on the subject, published by the Department of Agriculture. If a pension check has not been delivered on schedule, a telephone call from a member of Congress to the appropriate bureau will bring a speedy explanation. Again and again, members of Congress are requested to check into what a constituent considers an unreasonable or discriminatory ruling by an administrative agency.

More important to the formation of public policy than the specific representative functions performed for individuals is the broader role of congressmen in articulating the various social and economic interests in his district. One may speak for the business man; another for the wheat farmer, another for the cattleman, another for the steelworkers, another for retired government workers, and so on. But public policy results from the reconciliation of these often conflicting and competing interests.

Constituent function. Congressional participation in the amending process is termed the constituent power. In some of the states which use the initiative, it is possible for the people to take steps which may produce formal changes in the state constitutions. But no provision is made for popular action leading toward amendment of the federal Constitution. Proposals to amend must be made by a two-thirds vote of Congress or by a national convention convened by Congress at the request of two-thirds of the states. The latter alternative has never been used nor is it likely to be. In the first place, if the pressure from the states were such that two-thirds of the legislatures petitioned Congress within a two- or three-year period to call a national convention, the same pressures would have been felt in Congress. In such a circumstance, Congress would almost certainly initiate the proposed amendments in the usual way. Moreover, there is no way to make Congress call a national convention no matter how many state legislatures petition for one. It is hard to conceive of Congress establishing a national convention when by doing so it would lose the initiative in the amending process.

Electoral function. Perhaps the very routineness of the duties of Congress in connection with the election of the President and a Vice-President blind one to their existence. No one can get very excited about the canvass which the two houses of Congress, meeting together, make of the electoral votes for it has been known for some two months who the President and Vice-President will be. However, when the electoral college system was first established, it was thought that the Congress would end up choosing the President and the Vice-President most of the time. The rise of political parties upset the contemplated method of selection, for the electoral votes came to reflect party affiliation rather than the personal choice of electors. The House chose the President after elections in 1800 and 1824.

As long as the two party system continues to operate effectively in the United States, it is highly unlikely that the presidential selection will be thrown into the lower house of Congress. However, if as many as three political parties received a considerable number of electoral votes, the possibility of House selection would be evident.[1] In such a circumstance, the states in the House of Representatives would vote as units with equal weight, choosing from among the three candidates with the highest number of electoral votes, a majority of state votes being necessary for election. If no person received a majority of the electoral votes for the vice presidency, the Senate voting as individuals would choose the vice-president from among the two candidates having the most electoral votes.

In the famous "disputed" election of 1876 between Hayes and Tilden,

---

[1] It is this possibility that makes the Southern strategy of "independent" electors more than an idle threat.

Congress appointed a commission to determine which of the electoral votes in dispute should be counted. Congress then accepted the verdict of the commission, so this was not a question of the House of Representatives choosing the President, but of Congress making a determination as to the validity of votes.

The Constitution also empowers each house of Congress to be the judge of the elections, returns, and qualifications of its own members.[2] Almost every election finds one house or the other being called upon to decide a contested election case.

Administrative supervision. With the astonishing growth of administrative activities, oversight of the administration has developed into one of the most significant congressional functions. To begin with, the administrative agencies are almost entirely the work of Congress. Not a single one is provided for in any detail by the Constitution itself, and only the temporary ones or minor ones are the result of executive action. The form, the organization, and the powers to be exercised by the administrative departments are in most instances specified by an act of Congress. Moreover, the fuel that runs these agencies comes only from congressional drafts on the Treasury, for no money can be paid out by any department except on the authority of Congress.

One section of the Legislative Reorganization Act of 1946 charges the standing legislative committees with continuous scrutiny of the agencies exercising functions within the committees' jurisdiction. Periodic or annual reports are frequently required of executive agencies. The work of the appropriation committees is outstanding in supervising the administrative machinery. In hearings before these groups, the administration not only must justify requested funds, but also must satisfy committee members that monies appropriated in the past have been utilized to full advantage and in the way which Congress intended. The auditing of agency accounts is the responsibility of the Comptroller General, who is responsible to the legislative not the executive branch of government.[3]

Investigatory function. The power to conduct investigations is not specifically granted to Congress in the Constitution, but the Supreme Court has held that the investigatory function is an essential and appropriate auxiliary to the legislative power. The first congressional investigation occurred in 1792 when a House committee inquired into the disastrous St. Clair expedition against the Indians. The investigatory power encompasses inquiries concerning the administration of existing laws as well as proposed or possibly needed laws. Within such broad scope it has touched innumerable facets of our social, economic, and political systems. However, the power is not unlimited. In a recent case the Supreme

---

2 For a fuller discussion of this point, see p. 282.
3 For a discussion of legislative oversight, see p. 388.

Court reaffirmed this conclusion when it declared that Congress has no general authority to expose the private affairs of individuals without justification in terms of the functions of Congress. "No inquiry is an end in itself; it must be related to and in furtherance of a legitimate task of Congress." [4] This line of reasoning imposes some limitation on the specific questions which an individual may be required to answer in a particular hearing, but it obviously does not weaken the general power of Congress to pursue inquiries which are related to any of the enumerated or implied powers possessed by the legislative branch of government.

Witnesses may be compelled to attend, produce books and papers, and testify before congressional committees. In testifying, witnesses are accorded certain protections as in a judicial proceeding, such as the right to refuse to answer questions on the basis of possible self-incrimination, i.e., on the ground that their statements may be used against them in future judicial proceedings. The general public has often been puzzled when a witness "takes" the Fifth Amendment following what appears to be a routine question. One reason for claiming the protection of the Fifth Amendment at such an early stage in the proceedings is because the courts have ruled that a witness may be assumed to have waived the self-incrimination immunity if he answers certain types of questions bearing on facts of possible incriminating activities. Naturally, many witnesses refuse to answer questions early, fearing that by answering a number of questions they may have passed the point of no return as far as the protection of the Fifth Amendment is concerned. A lesser number of witnesses have refused to answer inquiries on the grounds that the committee is exceeding its authority in asking them or that the question is not pertinent to the matter being investigated. In general the courts have upheld very few witnesses in these latter contentions.

Refusal to answer what the committee deems a proper question may become the basis for a federal court trial to determine whether the witness is to be adjudged in contempt of Congress. Until 1857 Congress punished persons judged in contempt by imprisonment enforced by the two houses' own sergeant-at-arms. Since that date, however, persons cited for contempt of Congress are subject to indictment and punishment by the regular courts. Recent legislation has made possible a procedure whereby the witness before a congressional committee may be granted immunity from prosecution based on self-incriminating statements. In such a case, one may not refuse to answer a question on the grounds of possible self-incrimination without being cited for contempt of Congress.

For many years investigations were frequently conducted by special committees created for the particular task at hand. Since the Legislative Reorganization Act of 1946, most of the legislative inquiries have been managed by the regular standing committees or their subcommittees.

4 *Watkins* v. *United States*, 354 U. S. 178 (1957).

Particularly since World War II, considerable criticism has been directed at the investigatory process as conducted by some committees. One criticism which is undoubtedly justified is that the investigations are often politically inspired. It is probable that this difficulty will never be overcome, since the results of any inquiry of interest to any large segment of the public will almost certainly be used to advance the political fortunes of individuals or political parties. Not only that, the opponents of the investigation will always charge political motivation, no matter what the actual circumstances happen to be. The line between political motivation and concern for the public welfare is often impossible to draw. Statutes, party platforms, and administrative rulings are frequently politically inspired, but this appears to be inevitable in a democratic society and may well be one of the basic strengths of the system.

Another criticism levied at committee investigations concerns their operating processes. Sometimes a committee member has taken testimony in a closed session without other members being present. Defamatory testimony has been released to the press before the affected persons have had a chance to testify. Some witnesses have not been permitted to read prepared statements or to have benefit of legal counsel. Witnesses have objected in vain to televised hearings at which they were to appear. Transcripts of previous testimony have not always been available for study by witnesses. These practices would certainly be among those designated as undesirable procedures.

Recently, it would appear that the actual conduct of hearings has improved. Some legislative committees have adopted codes of procedure, but a general code of fair procedure for all committees has not been accepted by either house of Congress.

An unanswered question is how far Congress may go in compelling records and testimony from executive branch officials. Congress has investigated many administrative activities without the cooperation of the President, but the records in such cases are apt to be incomplete. The principle that the President himself cannot be compelled to testify before a congressional committee or a court is clearly established. Jefferson refused to honor Marshall's subpoena in the trial of Aaron Burr, and the court did not attempt to challenge his decision. The House Un-American Activities Committee issued a subpoena for former President Truman to testify concerning certain matters which had occurred during his Administration. The former President declined, stating: "It must be obvious to you that if the doctrine of separation of powers and the independence of the Presidency is to have any validity at all, it must be equally applicable to a President after his term of office has expired when he is sought to be examined with respect to any acts occurring while he is President."

Frequently, a conflict has developed between Congress and the President over a presidential refusal to submit data or documents, or over a presidential order to lesser officials not to make executive files available to legislative committees. In the latter category, Congress has often asserted the claim, but so far has never cited for contempt any official who refused on the President's order to honor a subpoena or to turn over the records of his office. Presidents have usually justified their refusal to permit Congress to examine certain papers on the basis that such a course would not be "in the public interest," or that the nature of the documents sought fell within the category of a personal communication between the President and members of his Administration. Just as Congress may sometimes abuse its investigatory power, it is clear that the President could abuse the right to withhold information from Congress. The practical and constitutional considerations in this area of presidential-legislative relations are such that self-restraint is required by all concerned. For the most part, this has indeed been the case. It would appear that both Congress and the President are content to let the constitutional question involved remain unresolved, and indeed a judicial decision in this area might well be ignored anyway.

Judicial function. Congress, of course, has important duties with respect to the functioning of the court system. All of the courts below the Supreme Court have been created by Congress, and even though the highest tribunal is specified in the Constitution, Congress has provided for its composition, organization, and appellate jurisdiction. At one time Congress made the rules under which the courts operate and even now it has the authority to do this, although it currently prefers to delegate that task to the courts themselves. The money to run the courts is appropriated by Congress; the laws which they assist in enforcing are passed by Congress; and the judges who constitute their benches have to be confirmed by the Senate. Finally, Congress itself is charged with the direct exercise of judicial power in connection with the impeachment process.

Nature of impeachment. The impeachment of public officials has been established in those countries which modeled their political institutions after those of England. It must not be confused with the ordinary procedure by which those accused of criminal offenses are tried. Although in many respects it resembles that procedure, it does not take its place; that is, impeachment does not prevent ordinary judicial trial on the same charge.

Who may be impeached. The Constitution is not entirely clear as to what officers of the federal government are subject to impeachment. The Constitution merely reads that "the President, Vice-President, and all civil officers of the United States shall be removed from office on impeachment for, and conviction of, treason, bribery, or other high crimes and misdemeanors." [5] Military and naval officers are obviously not included, being subject to courtmartial. The question early arose as to whether "civil officers" is intended to include members of the legislative branch. While

---

[5] Art. II, sec. 4.

there may be some doubt as to the exact status of congressmen in connection with impeachment charges, in 1798 it was decided for all practical purposes that members of Congress are not subject to the process.[6] In addition to the President and Vice-President, it is at present understood that cabinet members, federal judges, and other high administrative officials are subject to impeachment. Although lower officers might in theory be impeached, the fact that they can be removed from office and prosecuted in the regular courts would scarcely justify the use of the cumbersome impeachment machinery. The United States has been relatively fortunate in its experience with its public officers—only a dozen cases of impeachment have been necessary in more than a century and a half, and of those no more than four have resulted in conviction. The best known of all of the impeachment trials was that of President Andrew Johnson, whose conviction failed by one vote.

Basis of impeachment. The Constitution is clear enough when it sets down treason and bribery as the basis for impeachment; it is not so clear when it adds "other high crimes and misdemeanors." In general, it is understood that only serious offenses of a criminal nature can be made the basis of impeachment proceedings. But what of the case in which the Senate found Judge Ritter not guilty on eight specific charges involving splitting of bankruptcy fees, the acceptance of free accommodations from bankrupt hotels in Florida, and so forth, and then convicted him on a final omnibus charge which detailed the earlier counts and alleged that his conduct had been unbecoming to the bench? Judge Ritter attempted to have the Supreme Court intervene on his behalf on the ground that conduct unbecoming a judge was not a valid charge on which to base articles of impeachment, but he was refused a hearing. It would appear, then, that the earlier concept of an adequate basis has been somewhat expanded.

Steps in impeachment proceedings. The House of Representatives is given the first responsibility for impeachment proceedings, for charges must be brought on its floor and articles of impeachment must be voted by it before a trial can be conducted in the Senate. Notwithstanding the very small number of impeachment cases, it is not at all uncommon for representatives to make charges against judges and administrative officials from the floor of the House. Indeed members have been known to press charges against the same official repeatedly. If the House decides the charges are worthy of investigation, it sets up a special committee to consider the case and make a report. This report is read in the House, discussed, and if adopted by a majority, results in voting of articles of impeachment which

---

6 In 1798 in the case of William Blount, a Senator from Tennessee, such a precedent was established. Blount, having been charged with conspiracy to provoke Louisiana and Florida to revolt against Spain and to turn themselves over to Great Britain, was then expelled from the Senate. When the House passed articles of impeachment, the Senate refused to try Blount on the ground that, having expelled him, it no longer had jurisdiction.

specify the charges against the accused. These articles are sent to the Senate, which is in turn obliged to fix a date for itself to sit as a court to examine charges. Ordinarily several weeks or months are permitted to intervene before the trial is begun, which gives the accused and the managers appointed by the House to be prosecutors an opportunity to prepare their arguments and evidence. Furthermore, it saves many trials for most of those who see ruin staring them in the face resign after articles of impeachment have been voted.

If the accused does not resign, the Senate at the date fixed starts to hear the case. The presiding officer of the Senate acts as judge, but if the President is being tried, the Chief Justice of the United States occupies the chair. Senators take an oath to give due consideration to the evidence; managers from the House of Representatives present the case for the government; and the counsel for the accused attempts to rebut these charges. After these proceedings, the senators retire to deliberate as a jury. If two-thirds of their number agree that the accused is guilty, it is said that a conviction has resulted; otherwise the charges are dropped.

Penalty in impeachment cases. Whenever impeachment charges result in conviction, the accused is removed at once from the public office which he holds. If the Senate stipulates, the accused may in addition be prevented from holding "any office of honor, trust or profit under the United States" in the future. The President cannot pardon those convicted under this procedure. Subsequent trial in an ordinary court may be resorted to in cases in which imprisonment seems to be necessary in addition to the disgrace of removal from office.

LEGISLATIVE POWERS

"The powers not delegated to the United States by the Constitution, nor prohibited by it to the States, are reserved to the States respectively, or to the people." In this succinct manner, the Tenth Amendment describes the distribution of power principle of our federal system. The Tenth Amendment did not *create* the distribution of power principle; this was the product of the original Constitution, but the amendment stated explicitly the principle which was implicit in the newly-formed federal system. The legislative powers delegated to Congress may either be enumerated or implied.

Enumerated powers. Article I, Section 8, is the primary reservoir of general legislative powers expressly granted Congress. Herein is listed an imposing array of permissive powers, many of which were denied to Congress under the Articles of Confederation. In this section specific mention is made of the power to tax, coin money, regulate commerce, declare war, borrow money, raise armies, provide a navy, establish post offices and post roads, as well as certain others. Other specific grants of power to Congress are scattered throughout the original Constitution and also in some of the amendments.

Implied powers. As imposing as the list of enumerated powers is, it is doubtful that the Constitution could have endured, certainly not without frequent amendment, if the implied power doctrine had not developed.

The last clause in Article I, Section 8, grants to Congress the power "to make all laws which shall be necessary and proper for carrying into execution the foregoing powers, and all other powers vested by this Constitution in the government of the United States, or in any department or officer thereof." This clause, sometimes called "the elastic clause," is the basis for the implied powers exercised by Congress, which in turn has given the Constitution the flexibility necessary to answer the needs of succeeding generations in our society. Chief Justice Marshall's opinion in *McCulloch* v. *Maryland,*[7] in which the Supreme Court upheld the power of Congress to establish a national bank even though no express constitutional provision granted such authority, remains the classic justification for the doctrine of implied powers. In examining the "necessary and proper" clause, Marshall noted that it was placed among the powers of Congress, not among the limitations on these powers; its terms purported to enlarge, not to diminish the powers vested in the government. The Chief Justice went on to write:

> We admit, as all must admit, that the powers of the government are limited, and that its limits are not to be transcended. But we think the sound construction of the constitution must allow to the national legislature that discretion, with respect to the means by which the powers it confers are to be carried into execution, which will enable that body to perform the high duties assigned to it, in the manner most beneficial to the people. Let the end be legitimate, let it be within the scope of the constitution, and all means which are appropriate, which are plainly adapted to that end, which are not prohibited, but consist with the letter and spirit of the constitution, are constitutional. . . .

In some cases it is easy, even for the ordinary citizen, to see the connection between a law based on this doctrine and a specific enumerated power. Thus, since Congress may raise armies, it requires little imagination to understand why laws drafting men for the armed forces have been held constitutional. However, in many instances where laws of Congress have been upheld by the Supreme Court, much more subtle reasoning is required. For example, consider the case of the Ohio farmer who had been alloted a quota of 11.1 acres for wheat production. The quota allotment system had been upheld under the power of Congress to control the flow of agricultural commodities produced for sale in interstate commerce. But farmer Filburn sowed twenty-three acres in wheat, claiming that the excess wheat was produced for use on his own farm rather than for shipment into the stream of interstate commerce. He refused to pay an assessed penalty

---

[7] 4 Wheaton 316 (1819).

for producing the extra wheat and finally the case came before the Supreme Court. The Court upheld the penalty assessment saying in part:

> It is well established by decisions of this Court that the power to regulate commerce includes the power to regulate the prices at which commodities in that commerce are dealt in and practices affecting such prices. One of the primary purposes of the Act in question was to increase the market price of wheat, and to that end to limit the volume thereof that could affect the market. It can hardly be denied that a factor of such volume and variability as home-consumed wheat would have a substantial influence on price and market conditions. This may arise because being in marketable condition such wheat overhangs the market and, if induced by rising prices, tends to flow into the market and check price increases. But if we assume that it is never marketed, it supplies a need of the man who grew it which would otherwise be reflected by purchases in the open market. Home-grown wheat in this sense competes with wheat in commerce. The stimulation of commerce is a use of the regulatory function quite as definitely as prohibitions or restrictions thereon. This record leaves us in no doubt that Congress may properly have considered that wheat consumed on the farm where grown, if wholly outside the scheme of regulation, would have a substantial effect in defeating and obstructing its purpose to stimulate trade therein at increased prices.[8]

It is now clear that the implied powers of Congress may be derived not only from a single delegated power but also from a combination of such powers taken together. This doctrine is sometimes labeled the theory of "resulting powers."

Inherent powers. It is sometimes maintained that Congress has inherent authority (as opposed to delegated) to enact legislation. In the area of domestic legislation this thesis finds little if any judicial support. But the Supreme Court has said: "The broad statement that the federal government can exercise no powers except those specifically enumerated in the Constitution, and such implied powers as are necessary and proper to carry into effect the enumerated power, is categorically true *only*[9] in respect of our internal affairs." [10] In legislation affecting certain aspects of foreign relations, then, the inherent power doctrine appears on firmer ground. Specifically, the Court mentioned that the powers to declare and wage war, to conclude peace, to make treaties, and to maintain diplomatic relations with other states could have been exercised by the national government even if they had not been granted in the Constitution. It is true that this list includes those areas generally dominated by the executive branch, but nevertheless Congress has a part to play in the effective exercise of all of them.

Federal police power. The police power, which authorizes legislation for the general welfare, public health, public safety, and public morals, has long been associated with the reserved powers of the states. The federal

---

8 *Wickard, Secretary of Agriculture, et al.* v. *Filburn,* 317 U. S. 111 (1942).
9 Italics added.
10 *United States* v. *Curtiss-Wright Export Corporation,* 299 U. S. 304 (1936).

government has often passed laws which affect all of these subjects; but in the last thirty years, federal legislation of this type has multiplied to the degree that the police power, as a specific grant of power, is sometimes thought to reside with the federal government. Strictly speaking, Congress does not possess the "police power" in the sense that it may pass any law for the protection of the health, safety, and morals of the people. And the general welfare clause of the federal Constitution is tied to the taxing and spending powers.[11] However, Congress does pass laws to protect the public in countless ways, but the legislation is based on a specific or implied grant of authority. Congress does not by law prohibit the publication of obscene novels, but it does prohibit their shipment in interstate commerce or through postal channels. It is not violating a federal law to play a slot machine, but it is against federal law to ship many types of slot machines or their parts in interstate commerce. If a person steals an automobile, in most cases he will not have violated a federal law; but if he transports the vehicle across a state line, a federal statute has been violated. The use of many habit-forming drugs is not contrary to federal law, but strict licensing and tax measures passed by the federal government cut down on the ease with which distributors may evade state laws on the subject. Gambling as such is not a federal crime, but "bookies" who take bets must pay an annual occupational tax of fifty dollars. In other words, such persons who are operating in violation of state laws have the choice of paying the federal tax, and thus publicizing their activities to state authorities or face the possibility of being indicted by the federal government. The examples given are but a few among many to illustrate how the federal government legislates in the "police power" field.

Exclusive and concurrent powers. Certain powers are exclusively within the authority of the national government. The most obvious example here is where the states are specifically forbidden to take certain actions, but where Congress is allowed to legislate in the same areas using enumerated or implied powers. Thus Article I, Section 10 prohibits the states from entering into any treaty, alliance, or confederation, from coining money, emitting bills of credit, making anything but gold and silver legal tender, or passing any laws impairing the obligation of contracts. These prohibitions do not apply to laws of Congress.

The Constitution also forbids certain types of activities by the state unless with the consent of Congress. Examples of this category would include the passing of comprehensive import or export tax laws or tonnage duties in regard to ships, the keeping of troops or ships of war in time of peace, and the entering into compacts with another state or foreign power.

Other types of powers remain exclusively with the national government because of their character, i.e., only the national government is competent to exercise them within the letter and spirit of the Constitution. Many as-

---

11 See p. 424.

pects of foreign relations would fall into this classification, even though the states might not be specifically forbidden in the Constitution from legislating thereon. Finally, certain powers may be exercised by the states until such time as Congress decides to enter the same field, as is discussed below.

Concurrent powers describe powers conferred upon the national government by the Constitution, but that may also be exercised by the states. The doctrine of concurrent power is far from a static concept and has been the subject of considerable interpretation by the courts. Thus, from time to time, the states have controlled bankruptcy proceedings; today, federal bankruptcy laws, where applicable, displace state regulations. Or to take another example—Pennsylvania in 1939 passed a statute having to do with the registration of aliens in that state; but Congress passed its own alien registration act and the Supreme Court ruled the Pennsylvania law void on the ground that it had been superseded by the federal law.

The Supreme Court has indicated at least three criteria which it may look to in determining whether the states have been precluded from passing laws in the areas of concurrent jurisdiction. These are: (1) where Congress has occupied the field to the exclusion of parallel state legislation, (2) where the dominant interest of the federal government precludes state intervention, and (3) where the administration of state acts would conflict with the operation of the federal plan.[12]

Congress at times has given the states permission to act in a particular area otherwise exclusively national. State courts have been granted the power to naturalize aliens. Congress has given up control over certain objects shipped into the states in interstate commerce, where such shipment, if sold in the state, would be in violation of state law. A specific example here would be national legislation allowing states to treat convict-made goods shipped in interstate commerce, upon arrival and delivery within their borders, as though it was purely local commerce.

Finally, certain traditional functions of the states such as taxation and borrowing are plainly concurrent powers. A state tax that interfered with a federal function would no doubt be declared void. On the other hand, if the federal system is to survive, it is plain that Congress could not cripple the states' taxing or borrowing powers so as to make them incapable of carrying out their own governmental functions.

Delegation of legislative powers. The first section of Article I proclaims that all legislative powers herein granted shall be vested in a Congress of the United States. May Congress delegate powers to agencies of the executive branch? The answer here is an emphatic yes! Statute after statute assigns quasi-legislative duties to the President, administrative agencies, and regulatory commissions. What are the limitations surrounding congressional delegation of legislative authority? The Supreme Court has experienced

12 See *Pennsylvania* v. *Nelson,* 350 U. S. 497 (1956).

some difficulty in applying consistent standards to this problem. The Court has said that Congress may enact general provisions and let the agency fill in the details. The general law must fix standards of legal obligations to which administrative action must conform.

The National Industrial Recovery Act was declared unconstitutional on the basis that Congress, instead of prescribing rules of conduct, had authorized the President to make codes which prescribed the rules of conduct.[13] On the other hand, "fair and reasonable" is an acceptable standard in legislation permitting the Interstate Commerce Commission to fix railroad rates. The Court has upheld a tariff law which permitted the President to modify tariff schedules within limits, when he found that certain conditions specified by Congress had come into existence. Moreover, in legislation in the field of international affairs, the Court has said that Congress may grant the President a degree of discretion and freedom from statutory restrictions which would not be permissible in domestic affairs.[14]

SUMMARY

Congress spends an inordinate amount of time on activities which may be designated as non-legislative functions. The authority for the constituent, electoral, executive, and judicial functions stems directly from the Constitution and is exercised much in the manner which a reader of the Constitution could forecast. The Constitution also provides for the *system* of representation, but the *function* of representation entails tasks, both frivolous and significant, which may not be devined from a study of the constitutional text. The role of Congress with respect to supervising the administration, although not spelled out in the Constitution, was acknowledged by the founding fathers, the paramount position of the legislative branch in financial matters standing as a reminder of this fact. However, the *degree* and the refinement of congressional techniques in this area is a more recent development. The investigatory function, complementary to all other congressional powers, legislative and non-legislative, has been upheld by the Supreme Court as a necessary concomitant to the legislative process.

The outstanding principle of American federalism in its origin was the doctrine that the national government possessed only those powers which were delegated to it in the Constitution. This general principle remains firm, but the concept of *implied* powers (a type of delegated power to be contrasted with *enumerated* powers) has enabled Congress to legislate whenever a *national* problem has arisen.

See *Bibliographic Note* at end of Chapter 16.

---

[13] *A. L. A. Schechter Poultry Corporation et al.* v. *United States,* 295 U. S. 495 (1935).
[14] *United States* v. *Curtiss-Wright Export Corporation,* 299 U. S. 304 (1936).

15

Congress—Membership and Organization

THE separation of powers principle remains a basic feature of the national governmental system. Neither the ofttimes dramatic role of the President, nor the potent judicial review function of the Supreme Court should obscure the fact that in the final analysis, the policies accepted by or formulated by Congress determine the public weal or woe.

Congressional elections are the most obvious link between the hopes and aspirations of the voters and declared governmental policy. Members of Congress are, after all, the only national officials chosen directly by the people. Here is the quintessence of a representative democracy; free elec-tions in which the people choose the delegates to a national assembly which is expected to translate the multiform voice of the people into the voice of the government.

Our electoral system is not designed to mirror in Congress an exact reflection of the strength of the various parties who sponsor political can-didates. The system, however, invariably produces a working majority for one political party in one or both houses of Congress. The most im-mediate and perhaps the most important result of a working majority in either house of Congress is the organization of the houses along party lines with the officers and committee chairmen all of the dominant party.

It has long been a favorite national pastime to lampoon the American Congress. To some degree, in the case of Congress, shortcomings as well as virtures, have their own rewards. What some people label as deficiencies in Congress may be counted as blessings by others. The choosing of committee chairmen by the seniority system is an example in point. Undoubtedly, Congress as a going political institution has its faults; but year in year out, its timing on policy decisions closely approximates that nebulous something called public opinion.

COMPOSITION OF THE TWO HOUSES

The Connecticut Compromise resulted in Congress being constituted as a bicameral body. In accordance with this formula, each state is guaranteed two senators, while a state's representation in the House of Representatives is proportional to its population. However, each state must have at least one representative in the lower house.

Apportionment in the House of Representatives. Inasmuch as the House of Representatives is based on population, its size is not specified by the Constitution beyond the point of stipulating that there shall not be more than one member for every 30,000 people. Based on the present population it would be possible theoretically for the House membership today to exceed 5,000. The first House of Representatives had only 65 members, but that number increased gradually by law until following the 1910 census the membership had reached 435. The Constitution requires that the membership of the House be reapportioned in accordance with the population after each census. Nevertheless, after the census of 1920, Congress, reluctant to further enlarge the number of Representatives or to diminish the representation of a number of states, failed to enact the necessary legislation, thereby continuing the apportionment of the 1911 figures. In 1929 Congress felt impelled to take steps that would prevent a continued disregard of the Constitution. It was agreed that the size of the House of Representatives should be fixed at 435, unless subsequent legislation changed that number. In 1959 when Alaska and Hawaii were admitted as states, the total membership was raised to 437 temporarily in order that each of the new states might have one representative. In 1963, however, the number of seats reverted to the old figure, 435.

Legislation passed in 1941 specified the particular mathematical formula which the Bureau of the Census is to use in computing the seats to be assigned to the various states. Under the 1951 apportionment act, nine states lost from one to three seats each, while seven states gained from one to seven seats.[1] The 1960 census resulted in significant apportionment changes. California gained a total of eight additional seats; her 38 representatives place her second only to New York in House membership. Sixteen states lost seats, nine states gained additional members to the House of Representatives.[2]

---

[1] The states losing seats were: Arkansas 1, Illinois 1, Kentucky 1, Mississippi 1, Missouri 2, New York 2, Oklahoma 2, Pennsylvania 3, and Tennessee 1. Those gaining seats were: California 7, Florida 2, Maryland 1, Michigan 1, Texas 1, Virginia 1, and Washington 1.

[2] California led with an increase of 8, followed by Florida 4, Arizona, Hawaii, New Jersey, Maryland, Michigan, Ohio, and Texas 1 each. Pennsylvania lost 3 seats and New York 2. Proportionately, Arkansas suffered the greatest loss—a third of its previous membership of 6. Massachusetts lost 2 seats, with Alabama, Illinois, Iowa, Kansas, Kentucky, Maine, Minnesota, Mississippi, Missouri, Nebraska, North Carolina, and West Virginia losing 1 representative each.

The single-member district. If a state has more than one representative in the lower house of Congress, the state legislature normally divides the state into districts, with one house member being elected from each district. Thus is created the traditional "single-member" district. This system often results in a state having membership in the House of Representatives from both major parties. Both parties rely upon some "safe" or sure districts throughout the country. Even when a party's congressional candidates poll an overwhelming majority of the votes in the country as a whole, the losing party elects a considerable number of its candidates. On the other hand, the single-member district method of election is apt to magnify the majority party's representation in the House as compared to its numerical majority in total votes. For example, in 1958 the Democratic Party polled approximately 55 per cent of the popular vote for members of the House of Representatives, yet it controlled 65 per cent of the elected membership. It may be argued that this magnification of the party's representation in the House serves a good purpose, since it makes it more likely that a party will have a safe working majority for the consideration of legislative matters.

A few states elect representatives from the state-at-large rather than according to the district system. Of course, if a state has only one member, an at-large election is automatic. However, two states—New Mexico and North Dakota—elect their two representatives from the state-at-large, while two or three states may elect one member from the state-at-large and the remainder from districts.

Present election law assumes that the single-member district system exists where a state has more than one representative, but even when Congress made this fact clear by a law in 1842 a few states successfully defied the requirement. As matters now stand, a state is required to elect all of its members from the state-at-large if its allotment of representatives is decreased and the state legislature fails to redistrict the state. If a state has an increase in House membership, and the legislature fails to redistrict, the old districts are to continue to elect one member each, with the additional representatives elected at-large. If there is no change in the number of representatives due a state, the members shall be elected from the districts required by the law of such state, and if any of them are elected from the state-at-large, they shall continue to be so elected. It would appear then that Congress is willing for those states which have more than one representative and elect one or more at-large to continue to elect them in this manner so long as their allotment does not change.

Gerrymandering. Gerrymandering is the practice of drawing district lines for partisan advantage.[3] Originally, the prime manifestation of gerry-

---

[3] The word gerrymander was coined by an editor following a redistricting scheme sponsored by Elbridge Gerry, a famous Massachusetts politician in the early years of the Republic. Someone remarked that a particular district resembled a salamander in shape. The reply was that it was less a salamander than a "gerrymander."

mandering occurred when the majority party in the state legislature arranged the congressional district lines in the state to work to its advantage. Senator Paul Douglas was referring to this type of gerrymander when he said:

> We all know, or should know, of the extraordinary district which the New York Legislature carved out in Brooklyn. The legislature went all over Brooklyn to find areas where Republican majorities existed, so that one Republican district could be created in Brooklyn. Apparently, there had not been such a district for some time; but the New York Legislature accomplished that job.[4]

Today the most obvious cases of gerrymandering with respect to congressional elections are shown by comparing the population of metropolitan districts with rural-small town districts. Since the rural and small-town delegates continue to dominate most state legislatures, metropolitan areas are generally under-represented in Congress. The following examples, based on 1960 Census figures, illustrate this point. The population of Arizona's First District (Phoenix) was 663,510; of the Third District (8 rural counties), 198,236. In Michigan the Sixteenth District's population (part of Detroit and Dearborn) was 802,994, the Twelfth's (upper peninsula), 177,431. In Texas the Fifth District's population (Dallas) was 951,527, while the Fourth (7 counties) had only 216,371 inhabitants.

Congress has the power to require the states to put into operation more equitable apportionment systems. For a number of years before the 1929 Apportionment Act, Congress had required that districts be composed of contiguous, compact territory with substantially equal populations. The latter act and subsequent apportionment acts have failed to include such directions.

Until recently the Supreme Court had refused to give relief to citizens in gerrymandered districts, treating apportionment as a political question beyond the reach of judicial authority. The appropriate remedy, said the Court, was to secure state legislators who would apportion properly, or for Congress to invoke its powers.

In 1962, however, the Supreme Court began to veer away from its view that apportionment was strictly a *political question*. In *Baker* v. *Carr*[5] the Court ordered a federal district court to decide whether citizens in Tennessee were being denied equal protection of the law because of malapportionment in the state legislature. In *Wesberry* v. *Sanders*,[6] the wide variation in the size of districts in the national House of Representatives was attacked and, while recognizing that "it may not be possible to draw congressional districts with mathematical precision," the Court held that this was "no excuse for ignoring our Constitution's plain objective of mak-

---

4 *Congressional Record,* Vol. 102, p. 5547.
5 369 U. S. 186 (1962).
6 376 U. S. 1 (1964).

ing equal representation for equal numbers of people the fundamental goal for the House of Representatives."

While *Baker* v. *Carr* seemed to indicate that at least one house of a state legislature must reflect population, the Court moved beyond this point in 1964. On June 15, 1964, in cases involving the apportionment of the upper houses of six state legislatures (Alabama, New York, Maryland, Virginia, Delaware, and Colorado) the Supreme Court held that each state make an "honest . . . effort to construct districts, *in both houses of its legislature, as nearly of equal population as is practicable."* [7] Thus, it would appear that rural domination of state legislatures, and hence, of congressional districting, will be materially reduced during the next decade.

Equal representation in the Senate. It is not possible to overemphasize the importance of the equal representation of the states in the Senate. The size is determined on the basis of the number of states rather than population, and the psychology manifested by the Senate is accounted for to a large extent by this equality of representation. The original principle of federalism has undergone a drastic revision in the allocation of power between the state and national government, but the provision for equal representation, which was derived from it, is still a very real and living force in determining the attitude and conduct of the United States Senate.

Until 1913 senators were chosen by the state legislatures, a fact tending to suggest a status akin to that of ambassadorial representatives. The Seventeenth Amendment provided for their direct election by the people, but sometimes senators appear to think of themselves as spokesmen for sovereign states rather than as lawmakers of the United States.

Despite the fact that equal representation is so basic a factor in the composition of the Senate, there has been a considerable amount of criticism directed toward the principle. For example, on the basis of the 1960 census returns, the twenty-five smallest states contained about 15.4 per cent of the total population, yet controlled 50 per cent of the Senate's membership. If the states with few people "ganged up" against the thickly settled areas, there might be intolerable conflict and selfishness. Fortunately, that happens so rarely that it scarcely constitutes a serious problem. Regional economic interests are more important than the populations of the states in influencing the votes of their representatives.

Qualifications of members. The formal qualifications for members of Congress are specified in two brief sections of the Constitution. "No person shall be a representative who shall not have attained to the age of twenty-five years, and have been seven years a citizen of the United States, and who shall not, when elected, be an inhabitant of that State in which he shall be chosen." "No person shall be a senator who shall not have attained the age of thirty years, and been nine years a citizen of the United States, and who shall not, when elected, be an inhabitant of that State for

---

[7] Italics added.

which he shall be chosen." (See Article I, Section 2.2 and Section 3.3.)

A state may not add to these constitutional qualifications for senators or congressmen. The House once seated a member whose election was contested on the ground that he had not resided in the district the number of months required by state law. Both the House and Senate have seated members elected during their term of office as state judges, notwithstanding the provisions of state constitutions barring the election of judges to any federal office during such term.

Questions have arisen as to when elected members must meet the age or term of citizenship requirements—at the time of election or at some later period. Apparently, it is now established in both the House and the Senate that it is sufficient if the requirements are met when the oath is administered.

Although there have been a few exceptions, custom decrees that a representative be a resident of the district from which he is elected. This requirement is in marked contrast to the practice in Britain where voters often choose as their representative in the House of Commons a person whose residence may be in a district in another section of the country. These divergent electoral practices can be explained by the difference in the party systems of the United States and Britain and the differing concepts as to what the relations of the representative to his constituents should be. In general the member of the House of Commons thinks of himself as a representative of the *nation* to a greater extent than individual members in the House of Representatives who are more apt to think of themselves as *district* representatives. A few years ago Dr. George Galloway wrote:

> The typical Congressman is primarily a Washington representative for his district, not a national legislator. He is responsible to a local, not a national electorate. His chief objective is reelection so as to gain power and political advancement. To this end, he spends his time mostly promoting the interests of his district and running errands for the folks back home.[8]

Obviously, the constitutional qualifications for membership within the United States Congress are met by literally millions of citizens. Just as obvious is the fact that additional informal requirements may be necessary for the successful candidates. Merely being "an inhabitant of that state in which he shall be chosen" is not a very adequate recommendation in the case of most candidates, for there is a psychology in many political circles which causes newcomers to be regarded with suspicion and considers residence of fifteen or twenty years in a locality temporary sojournment. Of course, political prominence is virtually a *sine qua non,* although occasionally relatives of deceased politicians may be given the mantles of their departed, and political machines may designate puppets who have never before been in the public eye. But these and a few other exceptions only go to prove the

---

[8] George B. Galloway, *The Legislative Process in Congress* (New York: Crowell Company, 1935), p. 375.

rule that successful candidates are those who have long taken an active part in state and local politics. Occupational, racial, social, and religious qualifications may or may not be expected, depending upon the time and the place.

For many years, even after the passage of the woman suffrage amendment, few women were successful congressional candidates. Miss Jeannette Rankin of Montana was the first woman to be elected to Congress, serving in the House from 1917 to 1919. Mrs. Hattie Caraway of Arkansas was the first woman elected to the Senate (1932), but ten years earlier a woman had been appointed to fill the vacancy in the Senate caused by the death of Senator Watson of Georgia. In the 1962 elections for the House of Representatives, eighteen women were elected to membership. Senator Margaret Chase Smith was the sole woman serving in the Senate until 1960, when she was joined by Maurine Neuberger, who was elected to the Senate seat formerly held by her deceased husband.

The legal profession continues to furnish a high percentage of the total congressional membership. In the 86th Congress, 62 per cent of the senators and 52 per cent of the representatives were attorneys. In this same Congress, the average age of the senators was 57.1 years, the oldest member being 91 and the youngest 34. In the House the average age was 51.7 years, ranging from 84 to 30 years. In the Senate 62 per cent of the members were veterans of the armed forces, while the percentage of veterans in the House stood at 59 per cent.[9]

Congressional elections. Several sections of the Constitution serve as authorizations for Congress to pass laws bearing on the general subject of congressional elections. Article I, Section 4 permits Congress to regulate the times, places, and manner of holding elections for senators and representatives. In Section 5, each House is empowered to be the judge of the elections, returns, and qualifications of its own members. Congress is specifically given the power to enforce by appropriate legislation three amendments (Fourteenth, Fifteenth, and Nineteenth) dealing with the right of citizens of the United States to vote.

Considering the potential scope of the above constitutional sections, it is somewhat surprising that relatively few statutes have been enacted pertaining to congressional elections. This inactivity is probably explained by the traditional attitude, prevalent at the constitutional convention and in large measure even today, that the responsibility for election procedures should rest by and large with the states.

Attention has already been drawn to the efforts of Congress to fix the principle of electing House members from single-member districts. Members to both the House and the Senate must be selected through the use of

---

[9] For a discussion bearing on veterans in the House of Representatives, see Albert Somit and Joseph Tanenhaus, "The Veteran in the Electoral Process: The House of Representatives," *The Journal of Politics*, XIX, 184-201, May, 1957.

secret ballots, the first Tuesday after the first Monday in November of even years.[10] Bribery, intimidation, or threats to prevent or influence votes are illegal. An important Supreme Court decision in 1884 established the doctrine that when a person is eligible to vote by the statutory provisions covering state elections, he has a constitutional right to vote for members of Congress.[11] Legislation relative to campaign financing has already been discussed.[12]

Following a Supreme Court decision in 1921,[13] there was considerable doubt as to whether various election laws could be applied to *nominating primaries*. One practical effect of such a restrictive interpretation was to exclude the election process in many Southern States from federal controls since the real contests were in the Democratic primaries, with the winner there being assured of victory in the subsequent November election. However, in 1941, the Supreme Court removed any doubts on this point. In a significant decision, the Court held that Congress possessed the authority to regulate primary elections involving members of Congress.[14] Despite this decision, Congress has been slow to bring the nominating process within the scope of its regulatory powers, but precedents have been established. The Taft-Hartley Act of 1947 prohibited corporations and labor unions from making contributions or expenditures in connection with any primary election, political convention, or caucus held to select candidates for Congress. The 1957 Civil Rights Act, which empowered the Attorney General to secure injunctions to protect the right to vote in any federal election, is made applicable to primaries.

The power that each house possesses to judge "the elections, returns, and qualifications of its own members" makes each house the final judge in cases of disputed elections. Election to seats in Congress has been challenged on various grounds among which are fraud, bribery, and excessive expenditures. If a seat is contested for irregularity, the house concerned may defer giving the oath of office to the member-elect until an investigation has been completed. The Senate in 1928 refused to seat Frank L. Smith, of Illinois, and William S. Vare, of Pennsylvania, because of excessive campaign expenditures. The House refused a seat to Brigham H. Roberts, of Utah, in 1900 on the ground that he was a polygamist. The power of Congress to judge the qualifications of its members has the effect of permitting either house to add to the constitutional qualifications of its membership.

If a senator dies or resigns during his term, a successor may be ap-

---

10 In September, 1957, Maine ratified a constitutional amendment discarding her traditional September congressional election in favor of the November date observed by the other states.

11 *Ex parte Yarbrough,* 110 U. S. 651.

12 See page 191.

13 *Newberry* v. *United States,* 256 U. S. 232.

14 *United States* v. *Classic,* 313 U. S. 299.

pointed by the governor of his state to serve until the next general election, at which time a successor is elected for the balance of the former senator's term. In case of the death or resignation of a representative during his term, the governor of his state may call a special election for the purpose of selecting a successor to serve for the unexpired portion of the term.

Term of office. Representatives are elected for two years, senators for six years, with a third of the senators being elected every two years. The two-year term for members of the House was intended to keep congressmen closely in touch with public sentiment and thus lead to more representative government. The short term has been criticized because as soon as a representative is elected he must spend an inordinate amount of time and energy building up political fences and campaigning for re-election. Two-year terms may play a part in bringing about deadlocks in which the President is on one side of the political fence and Congress on the other. The voters rarely elect a President of one party and at the same time send to Washington a majority of representatives of the opposition.[15]

In the off-year elections, when a President is not elected, the balance of power in Congress may swing to the party which has been in the minority, leaving the executive branch in the hands of the formerly dominant party. Within the last thirty years, this situation has occurred in the administrations of Hoover, Truman, and Eisenhower. Such a state of affairs may increase the possibility of division, delay, and deadlock. The charge will almost certainly be made by both parties that some policy decisions are made not in the interest of the general welfare but for the purpose of creating a politically embarrassing situation for the opposite party. Such charges, no doubt, are often close to the truth, but because of the nature of our unregimented party system and the frequent inter-party legislative coalitions—which form, dissolve, and reform—it is possible that divided control of the legislative process does not affect the final product to the extent some critics have suggested. From 1952 to 1960, the President's party enjoyed a majority in Congress for only two years, but our governmental processes have continued to be, in general, responsive to the demands of the times.

It has often been suggested that a four-year term for representatives, coinciding with that of the President, would be a more desirable arrangement. Since this would require a constitutional amendment, however, it does not seem likely that any change will ensue unless the general public becomes much more critical of the two-year term than it now appears to be.

Salary and perquisites. The salary of senators and representatives is fixed at a uniform rate by their own action. They now receive $30,000 per year, of which $3,000 is exempt from taxes for members who maintain two

---

[15] This did happen for the first time in a century, in 1956, when the Democrats controlled Congress despite the Eisenhower landslide.

homes. In addition, there are a number of perquisites which supplement the salaries. Travel allowance is granted at twenty cents per mile for one round trip annually from their homes. Free telegraph and telephone service, though limited, are also very helpful. Likewise, the franking privilege permits the sending of official mail without the payment of postage. An allowance is made for stationery, which may be collected in cash when it is not used up in office supplies. Both senators and representatives are permitted to use office space in federal buildings in their home states at a place of their own designation, or to receive up to $1,200 annually for rentals elsewhere.[16]

Retirement and insurance benefits. Members of Congress may, if they choose, join the Civil Service Retirement System, but under more favorable provisions than applicable to executive civil service employees. For those who elect to join the system, a seven and one-half per cent deduction is withheld each month from their salaries. The legislative branch pays into the fund an amount equal to the deductions of members of Congress. Members are entitled to receive a retirement allowance, after the age of sixty-two and a minimum of five years service, of two and one-half per cent of their annual salary multiplied by their years of service. No member may receive an annuity greater than 80 per cent of the final salary received as a member of Congress.

All members of Congress are automatically covered under the Federal Employees' Group Life Insurance Act unless coverage is waived or cancelled. Payment of double indemnity is made for accidental death. No premium is due after age 65. Life insurance is provided after retirement following 15 years of service or because of disability. The insurance continues in effect for 31 days after termination from Congress, during which an individual policy may be purchased at standard rates without a medical examination. Members under age 65 are covered for $20,000. The insurance of a member over age 65 is reduced by two per cent for each month he is over 65 until a reduction of 75 per cent is reached. The remaining 25 per cent stays in effect.

Staff assistance. All representatives are allowed basic amounts of $17,500 per year for clerk hire, with the allowance being increased to $20,000 for members whose constituency is 500,000 or more. In general, gross salary allowances for clerk hire are considerably in excess of the basic rates. It has been estimated that the average representative gets about $37,000 per year for office help.

Senators are allotted funds for clerk hire under an even more complex system than applies to House members, depending among other factors upon the population of their states. Some senators receive as much as $130,-

---

16 The Speaker of the House and the Vice-President receive annual salaries of $43,000, with an additional annual $10,000 expense allowance.

000 per year for office employees.[17] The 1946 Legislative Reorganization Act authorized each senator to employ an administrative assistant, who, it was hoped, would be able to relieve individual senators from many of the details associated with the office, such as talking with some of the many individuals who seek positions, contacts in business or government, or other favors. The administrative assistants in general have probably not had as much success in this respect as some had hoped, because visitors to senators' offices often insist that they must talk to their elected representative in person. Nevertheless, the talents of administrative assistants are used in many other ways, and the position as such has much to recommend it. Certain of the senatorial aides have gone on to become members of Congress in their own right. The House of Representatives has not authorized a similar post in the offices of its members, although bills allowing for this are introduced in each session of Congress.

Members of Congress have been criticized, particularly from sources outside of Congress, for putting relatives on their office payrolls. It is difficult to pinpoint the precise extent of nepotism since no records are kept on this basis, so a person seeking to ferret out examples of nepotism has to check through office payrolls name by name. An associated press survey in 1959 revealed that at least 62 representatives and 14 senators had relatives on their office staffs. To make matters worse, it developed that in some cases high salaries were paid to relatives who were still in college, or who also were employed elsewhere. The use of public funds under these conditions appears inexcusable. A law prohibiting the hiring of any relatives is probably not the answer. Perhaps a requirement for full disclosure of the number of relatives on the payroll of each member would be a start in the right direction. On this basis the electorate would be the final judge of the propriety involved in each case.

Privileges and immunities of members. Members of Congress have no criminal immunity of importance, since they are liable to arrest for treason, felonies, and the breaking of the peace. On the other hand, their immunity in civil cases is fairly broad. They cannot be arrested in connection with civil matters while coming to, attending, or going from a session of Congress, nor can they be subpoenaed as witnesses in civil cases.

Senators and representatives cannot be held liable in court for what they say on the floor or in committee sessions. This immunity is sometimes abused by individual members who take advantage of their freedom of speech and make sensational and unfounded charges against citizens or organizations, which, of course, have no legal remedy for redress. On the other hand, one can readily see the necessity of leaving members free to voice their opinions, without fear of perpetual harassment in the form of court suits.

---

[17] A ceiling of $16,300 per year is placed on the salary any one employee of a senator may receive.

Congress has the power to discipline its own members. The mildest rebuke is being "called to order" by the presiding officer. More severe is the vote of censure, following charges and committee investigation. In 1954 the Senate used this type of disciplinary measure toward the late Senator Joseph McCarthy, although the word "condemn" was substituted for "censure." Finally, either house may expel a member by a two-thirds vote.[18]

THE ORGANIZATION OF CONGRESS

Inasmuch as all the representatives are elected for two-year terms which begin and end at the same time, it is necessary for the House of Representatives to organize every other year. Unless there has been a change in the majority control, the Senate has comparatively few organizational problems, but it at least goes through the motions of organizing.

Sessions. For many years Congress convened every year in December. In the even years a so-called "short" session was begun which had to terminate not later than the fourth day of the following March. In the odd years a "long" session continued until late spring, summer, or even fall, depending upon the pressure of business. The first of these sessions was characterized as a "lame-duck" session because some of the members who sat had already been notified by the voters at the November election that their office-holding would not be continued. Members of Congress who had been named to succeed them would, under this odd arrangement, not actually sit for approximately thirteen months after election. It was obviously not particularly rational to have defeated members make laws and vote appropriations while the members-elect were cooling their heels. The Twentieth Amendment took cognizance of the evils inherent in this situation by fixing January 3 of the odd years as the date when the new terms should begin and by specifying that Congress should assemble on that date unless other provisions were made by law.

Party caucus. Although party factionalism and dissension is often apparent in the national legislative process, the organization of Congress is always achieved strictly according to party lines. Shortly before the official opening of a new Congress, the party members gather in their respective caucuses. The party caucus or conference is the ultimate source of authority in organizing Congress. All Republican members in the House are members of the House Republican conference, and all Democratic members in the House belong to the House Democratic caucus; all Republicans in the Senate meet with the Senate Republican conference, and all Democrats in the Senate are members of the Democratic Senate conference. The majority party caucus in each case will nominate individuals who will become the duly elected officers of the two houses; the minority party caucuses will nom-

---

[18] Members in Congress from the Confederate States were expelled at the beginning of the Civil War.

UNITED STATES HOUSE OF REPRESENTATIVES

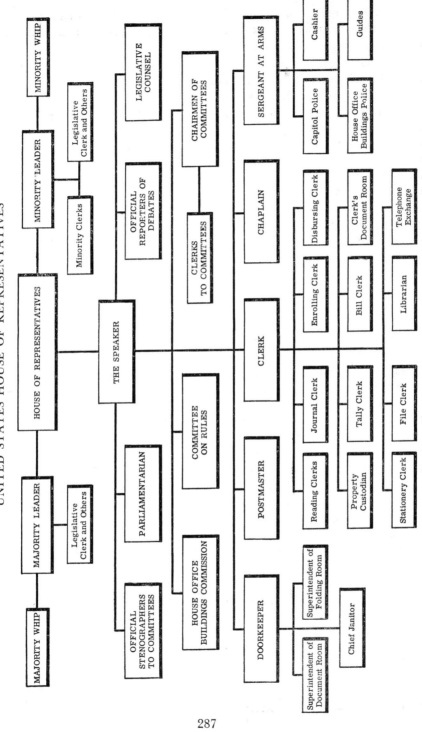

inate slates of officers, even though their nominees have no chance of election. Each caucus will either select certain party leaders and committees directly or delegate the authority to select them.

Formal organization of the House. When the House of Representatives assembles early in January of the odd years, it must go through certain preliminaries before it can begin its other duties. The clerk of the preceding House calls the roll of members, prepared on the basis of certificates of election which members-elect present as evidence of their claim to the seats. Only the persons whose names appear on this roll may participate in the election of the Speaker. As soon as the Speaker is elected and sworn in, the victorious candidate being the choice of the majority party caucus, he administers the oath of office *en masse* to the other members, whose names now constitute the permanent roll of the House. Shortly thereafter, the chamber ratifies the choices of the majority party for other House officers, i.e., clerk, sergeant at arms, doorkeeper, postmaster, and chaplain. These officers, unlike the Speaker, are not elected members to Congress.[19] The rules of the last session are adopted. The House, after conferring with the Senate, then notifies the President that it is ready to receive any communication which he may desire to make.

Formal organization of the Senate. Organizing the Senate at the start of a new Congress is ordinarily a relatively simple procedure. The Senate does not have a temporary roll, since two-thirds of its members are holdovers from the preceding Congress. It does not choose its presiding officer, since the Vice-President serves in that capacity. The Senate continues under its old rules without pausing to adopt the rules of the preceding session.[20] On the opening day the credentials of the senators-elect are presented. Each newly elected member is escorted by the senior senator from his state to the desk where the new senator takes the oath of office. The Senate proceeds with the election of its officers including the president *pro tempore,* secretary of the senate, sergeant at arms and doorkeeper, chaplain, secretary to the majority, and secretary to the minority. As in the House, these choices have been determined in the majority party caucus (with the exception of the secretary to the minority). The president *pro tempore* is the only one of the group who is an elected member of the Senate. Following conferral

---

[19] Constitutionally, the Speaker does not have to be an elected member, but he has been in every instance.

[20] Some senators have argued that the Senate is not a continuing body and that it should adopt its rules at the beginning of each Congress. This question was renewed when a motion was made to consider the adoption of rules for the Senate at the start of the Eighty-fifth Congress. The motion was tabled, so the old rules continued in effect, but in the course of the debate the Vice-President gave as his opinion: ". . . the right of a current majority of the Senate at the beginning of a new Congress to adopt its own rules, stemming as it does from the Constitution itself, cannot be restricted or limited by rules adopted by a majority of the Senate in a previous Congress." At the opening of the Eighty-sixth Congress a motion to "open up" the rules of the Senate for revision every two years was tabled by the lopsided vote of 60 to 36.

UNITED STATES SENATE

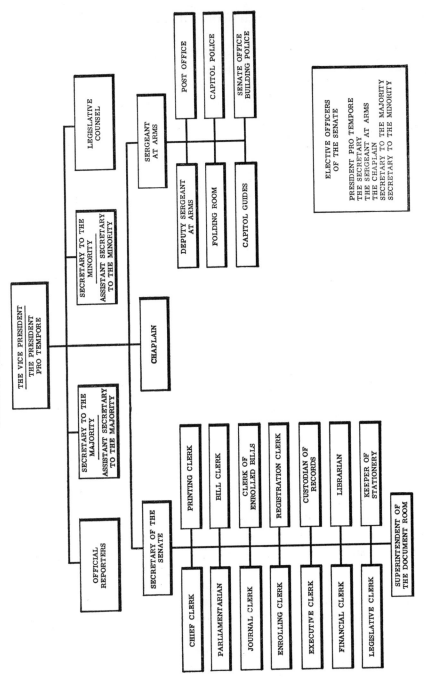

THE VICE PRESIDENT
THE PRESIDENT
PRO TEMPORE

OFFICIAL
REPORTERS

SECRETARY TO THE
MAJORITY
ASSISTANT SECRETARY
TO THE MAJORITY

CHAPLAIN

SECRETARY TO THE
MINORITY
ASSISTANT SECRETARY
TO THE MINORITY

LEGISLATIVE
COUNSEL

SERGEANT
AT ARMS

POST OFFICE

CAPITOL POLICE

SENATE OFFICE
BUILDING POLICE

DEPUTY SERGEANT
AT ARMS

FOLDING ROOM

CAPITOL GUIDES

ELECTIVE OFFICERS
OF THE SENATE

PRESIDENT PRO TEMPORE
THE SECRETARY
THE SERGEANT AT ARMS
THE CHAPLAIN
SECRETARY TO THE MAJORITY
SECRETARY TO THE MINORITY

SECRETARY OF THE
SENATE

PRINTING CLERK

BILL CLERK

CLERK OF
ENROLLED BILLS

REGISTRATION CLERK

CUSTODIAN OF
RECORDS

LIBRARIAN

KEEPER OF
STATIONERY

CHIEF CLERK

PARLIAMENTARIAN

JOURNAL CLERK

ENROLLING CLERK

EXECUTIVE CLERK

FINANCIAL CLERK

LEGISLATIVE CLERK

SUPERINTENDENT OF
THE DOCUMENT ROOM

with the House, the President is notified that the Senate is ready to proceed to do business.

Rules. The rules of the House of Representatives have grown up over a lengthy period and are at present so complicated that they are quite confusing to laymen; and it is not certain that they are ever clear to all members of the House. Some of the rules have come down from the English Parliament and are hoary with age; others have been set by the Constitution. The House itself has from time to time drawn up regulations which seemed wise; speakers and chairmen of the committee of the whole have made numerous rulings on controversial questions. Finally, the House has adopted the *Manual of Parliamentary Practice,* drafted by Thomas Jefferson, to apply to those cases not otherwise provided for. The basic rules alone, leaving out the *Manual,* the constitutional provisions, and the rulings of Speakers and chairmen of the committee of the whole, run to more than two hundred printed pages. The rulings of Speakers and chairmen have been assembled in eleven printed volumes of large size.[21] It is no wonder that not even the Speaker himself, despite his lengthy service in the House, can always trust himself to declare what the rules are on a given point. Consequently, the House employs two experts in parliamentary procedure, one of whom is invariably in attendance at the arm of the Speaker during sessions. Members gradually become acquainted with the fundamental rules and can make their influence felt, but it usually requires at least four years to acquire even reasonable familiarity.

In general, the Senate rules are distinctly less complicated than those of the House. Jefferson's *Manual,* prepared for that purpose, continues as the general basis for senatorial rules. Over the years the Senate has adopted forty rules which cover sixty-one printed pages. The rulings of the presiding officers have been collected and serve to guide procedure.[22] The smaller size of the Senate permits an informality which could not well be associated with the larger House of Representatives. More than that, the Senate stresses the role of the individual to a far greater extent than does the House.

It is said that the House of Representatives operates under the most complicated rules of procedure known to any legislative body. Newer members may suffer considerable disadvantage because of their unfamiliarity with the procedure; but once they master the rules in fair degree, they are not apt to push for major changes. Under the system, control of the House is centralized in the hands of a relatively small group, who view the rules, not as a barrier to be surmounted, but as necessary tools facilitating the

---

[21] Eight of these volumes were prepared by Asher C. Hinds under the title *Parliamentary Precedents of the House of Representatives* (Washington, D. C.: Government Printing Office, 1899). A supplement of three volumes was edited by Clarence Cannon and published in 1935.

[22] An excellent guide to Senate procedure was published as Senate Document No. 93, 85th Congress, 2d Session. See Charles L. Watkins, and Floyd M. Riddick, *Senate Procedure: Precedents and Practices* (Government Printing Office, Washington, 1958).

work of an unwieldy legislative body, while at the same time protecting the rights of the minority party.

At times it may appear that the individual member of the House of Representatives stands helpless before the onrush of the majority. On the other hand, one of the chief criticisms of Senate procedure is that privileges accorded individual members may in fact block majority action.

Presiding officers. Prior to the "revolution" of 1910-1911, which was directed at the Speaker of the House, the holder of that office could almost claim to be monarch of all he surveyed. Indeed, his authority was so extensive that one well-known speaker was dubbed "Czar." [23] The Speaker would recognize only those members who conferred with him beforehand and convinced him that their views were sound. Committee appointments, which he dispensed, went to those who could be depended upon to follow his wishes. The Rules Committee, of which he was chairman, would give a place on the order of business only to those measures which the Speaker desired enacted and would bring amendments to the rules only in so far as they were approved by that worthy. In 1910-1911 insurgent Republicans joined forces with a powerful Democratic minority to strip from the Speaker his position on the Rules Committee and his power to appoint members to standing committees.

At present the Speaker exercises three principal formal functions: (1) the power to recognize, (2) the power to apply the rules, and (3) the power of appointment. In addition, he is the number one man of the majority party and as such occupies a very prominent place in the councils of that party as they relate to the business of the House of Representatives. In order to speak, make motions, or offer amendments, representatives must secure the floor and that requires recognition by the presiding officer. Although the rules of the House make some stipulations as to who shall be given the floor, a considerable amount of leeway remains to the Speaker. If he is favorably disposed toward a representative, it is probable that recognition will be readily accorded; if he is hostile, the member may find it difficult to obtain the floor at all. In extending recognition the Speaker, of course, favors his own party.

Although no longer chairman or even a member of the Committee on Rules, the Speaker applies the great accumulation of rules already established. If there is any doubt as to what a rule requires, the Speaker has the authority to interpret. Thus, Speaker Reed ruled that in determining whether or not a quorum was present not only those who answered the roll call but those physically present in the chamber might be counted. There was violent objection at the time by minority members who sought to keep the House from transacting business by preventing a quorum, but it has for long years been regarded as a sensible interpretation with a bene-

---

[23] Thomas B. Reed was frequently referred to as "Czar" Reed.

ficial effect. A majority of the House may overrule the interpretation placed on a rule by the Speaker, but this prerogative is one that is very rarely invoked or exercised.

As leader of the dominant party the Speaker confers at frequent intervals with the little group of party leaders which has so much to say about what shall be done in the House. He is, of course, active in the party caucus. Not infrequently he is called to the White House to go over legislative matters. The Speaker has the right to refer bills to committees—a power which in the past has sometimes been distinctly important. At present most bills are more or less automatically sent to committees by the clerk on the basis of their subject matter but when there is a question as to what committee shall receive a certain bill, the Speaker still decides.

The Speaker has retained a certain amount of appointive power. He selects the chairmen of the committee of the whole house; he may appoint speakers *pro tempore* for not over three days; he appoints members to various special committees; he appoints house conferees when a bill is sent to a conference committee; and he generally chooses house members for other joint committees and commissions created by law.

The Vice-President of the United States is assigned the task of presiding over the sessions of the Senate. His power as presiding officer or as party leader is much less than that of the Speaker. His power of recognition is severely limited under Senate rules, which require that he recognize the first senator who rises.[24] He interprets and applies the rules, but the Senate overrides its presiding officer somewhat more frequently than is true in the House. He makes appointments to various committees in much the same manner as the Speaker. Although he is not to be compared to the Speaker as a congressional party leader, certain Vice-Presidents have been effective liaison agents between the President and party leaders in the Senate.

The Senate chooses a president *pro tempore* to preside in the absence of the Vice-President. This post is generally given to the member of the majority party who has served longest in the Senate.

CONGRESSIONAL COMMITTEES

It is impossible to understand the legislative process unless one grasps the vital role committees play in the operation of Congress. The number, type, and functions of committees may seem at first glance to complicate rather than facilitate the work of Congress; but in fact each type of committee fills a specific need which long experience has proved necessary. At this point, the types of committees whose membership is composed of representatives of both parties are discussed. A discussion of party committees is reserved for a later chapter.

---

[24] A rule further modified by the Senate custom calling for immediate recognition of the majority leader when he seeks the floor.

Standing committees. All parliamentary bodies find it necessary to use some type of committee system to facilitate the handling of legislative matters. Two important principles underlie the utilization of the permanent or standing committees that continue from Congress to Congress in each house. The first principle is that of division of labor. With literally thousands of bills and resolutions introduced each session, it is utterly impossible for every member to give initial or careful consideration to a fraction of these bills. By making committees responsible for screening measures according to fairly definite subject matter areas, more bills can be given consideration than if the whole house performs this function. The second principle involved is that of specialization. For example, the Senate Committee on Labor and Public Welfare will be assigned all bills falling in this area. It is assumed that members of this committee, through experience, will be able to analyze the problems and the legislative needs in this particular sphere more readily than an *ad hoc* group. Not all parliamentary bodies make this latter assumption; in the British House of Commons, for example, there are four general committees, designated as A, B, C, and D, with the Speaker assigning measures to them indiscriminately.

In spite of the attempt of the Legislative Reorganization Act of 1946 to clarify jurisdictional lines of the standing committees, conflicts continue to arise, especially in the Senate. It is easy to understand, for example, how the Committees on Foreign Relations, Armed Services, Government Operations, and Appropriations would all be concerned with the various aspects of our foreign relations. Sometimes the progress of a bill in the legislative process depends in considerable degree upon the referral to a committee favorably disposed toward the subject matter. If the decision of the presiding officer of either house is questioned, as to which committee should receive a bill, a majority vote of the membership decides the issue.

An outstanding authority on Congress has written: "The real locus of the legislative power is not in the House or Senate as such; it is in their standing committees." [25] All legislation, with occasional exceptions, must clear through these committees before it reaches the floor of either house. Neither house of Congress passes, by any means, all of the measures reported by its standing committees; on the other hand, almost without exception, neither house *considers* a proposal unless a standing committee has reported favorably upon it. Before the Legislative Reorganization Act of 1946, the number of standing committees in the House was forty-eight and in the Senate thirty-three. The number now is twenty in the House and sixteen in the Senate. At present, a senator normally serves on two standing committees (sometimes three); representatives usually serve on one standing committee (sometimes two).

Membership is divided between the majority and minority parties on the basis of a gentleman's agreement arrived at by the leaders of the two

---

[25] Galloway, *op. cit.,* p. 649.

parties. In general, the division depends upon the respective strength of the parties in each house. The majority party in each house maintains a majority of its members on every committee, no matter how slender its over-all margin happens to be. The House and the Senate formally elect their committee members, but the actual selection has been made by a committee on committees in each party caucus. This job would be harder than it actually is were all committee assignments shuffled every two years. Once a member of Congress lands a committee he deems desirable, however, he usually wishes to remain there. His service to his constituency is often intimately associated with the committee upon which he serves; thus a member from a farming region may find it advantageous to serve on the Agricultural Committee. Perhaps more important is the fact that seniority on a committee brings power and prestige and is the road to a possible chairmanship.

The selection committees stick closely to the seniority principle in making assignments. If the party loses control of a chamber and thereby has fewer seats on a committee, the member with the least seniority will be dropped first, and so on down the line. Members who have been re-elected to Congress have priority in their choices of committees, if they wish to change, over newly elected members. The freshmen members are given their posts after these other assignments have been made.

STANDING COMMITTEES OF CONGRESS
(EIGHTY-EIGHTH CONGRESS, 2D SESSION)

House	Members	Senate	Members
Agriculture	36*	Aeronautical and Space Sciences.	15
Appropriations	50	Agriculture and Forestry	17
Armed Services	38*	Appropriations	27
Banking and Currency	33	Armed Services	17
District of Columbia	25	Banking and Currency	15
Education and Labor	31	District of Columbia	7
Foreign Affairs	33	Finance	17
Government Operations	31	Foreign Relations	17
House Administration	25	Government Operations	15
Interior and Insular Affairs	34*	Interior and Insular Affairs	17
Interstate and Foreign Commerce	33	Interstate and Foreign Commerce	17
Judiciary	35	Judiciary	15
Merchant Marine and Fisheries	31	Labor and Public Welfare	15
Post Office and Civil Service	25	Post Office and Civil Service	9
Public Works	34	Public Works	17
Rules	15	Rules and Administration	9
Science and Astronautics	31		
Un-American Activities	9	* Includes participating but non-voting	
Veterans Affairs	25	Resident Commissioner from Puerto Rico.	
Ways and Means	25		

Committee chairmen. Chairmen are always members of the majority party. They are formally chosen by a vote of the House or Senate, but with rare exceptions, the posts go to the majority member of longest continuous service on the committee. The selection of chairmen by means of the seniority system has frequently been condemned. It is argued that selection solely on this basis is contrary to democratic principles; that seniority and competency do not necessarily go hand-in-hand; that members from competitive two-party districts are at a disadvantage since their chances of continuous re-election are much less than are those of members campaigning in constituencies dominated by one party. Proponents of the present system point to the guarantee that an experienced legislator will be chosen. They assert that the selection process, as it now stands, is a very impersonal and objective way of handling a problem which could lead to manipulation, intense personal rivalry, and party splits. One author has written:

> The significant effect of the seniority system is that it tends to concentrate political power in the hands of members from "safe and solid" areas of the country, areas where there is very little real competition between the two major parties. This tends to insulate committee chairmanships from the real meanings and mandates of national electoral conflicts. It tends to undermine the ability of party leaders to carry out campaign pledges. Above all, it tends to bring a greater number of conservatives than of liberals into committee chairmanships. . . .[26]

A look at the chairmanships of the standing committees in the Eighty-eighth Congress shows the concentration of Southerners in these positions when the Democratic party controls Congress. In the House of Representatives, the South (the eleven states which composed the Confederacy) furnished eleven out of twenty committee chairmen; in the Senate this region controlled ten out of sixteen chairmanships.

A mere listing of specific functions of a committee chairman fails to convey the aggregate power attached to the position. He is an agent of Congress and of his party, but chairmen have often thwarted what appeared to be the wishes of both. Most of his decisions may in theory be over-ridden by a majority of the committee, but in fact this is seldom the case. The power to appoint subcommittee chairmen is a potent weapon, since a member's future career may be influenced greatly by his actions in this capacity. Chairmen arrange the agenda for committee meetings, appoint subcommittees, and refer bills to them. They usually determine when the committee shall meet, whether there shall be public hearings, and who shall be heard. They handle reported bills on the floor and participate as principal managers in conference committees.

Conference committees. When the two houses of Congress are unable to agree on the details of a bill, although they favor its general character, it is the practice to set up a conference committee, composed of members from both houses, to settle the differences. The "managers," representing the House and the Senate, are appointed by their respective presiding officers usually on the recommendation of the chairmen of the committees

---

[26] Bertram M. Gross, *The Legislative Struggle* (New York: McGraw-Hill Book Co., 1953), p. 278.

handling the legislation. Both parties are represented among the conferees from each house, and usually come from the committees handling the bill. The number from each chamber varies from three to nine, but the number of conferees from the Senate and the House of Representatives is not necessarily equal. The members from each house vote as a unit so difference in numbers does not affect the final decision.

The conferees meet in closed sessions, with no records kept of the deliberations. In theory the committee's jurisdiction extends only to those sections of the bills which are in conflict. However, it is not unusual for substantive amendments to be offered at this stage. Unless questioned under a point of order procedure in one of the houses, they become a part of the legislation if the conference report is accepted. Sometimes one or the other house will instruct its representatives not to give way on a certain point, but generally the members have considerable latitude in deciding how far to go in order to meet the objections of the other chamber. Although conference recommendations may be turned down by either house, the bulk of their recommendations are accepted with little discussion and without a roll-call vote. Conference committees have been criticized because of the secrecy surrounding their sessions and for exceeding their jurisdiction in some of their recommendations. Overall, however, it appears that these committees serve a useful purpose. Some of the fiercest battling of the legislative process probably occurs at this point. Accommodations are necessary on the part of the members of both houses, and accommodations free from the eyes of the public and pressure groups may well be possible here; from a practical view they may be impossible for many members in open session. For the individual member, supporting a conference committee report is a far different matter from supporting or failing to support legislation on the floor.

Special committees. Special committees may be appointed to handle matters which are not recurring in nature and are discharged when they complete their assignments. They may be created to investigate specific subjects which seem to require attention, or they may be named to represent their respective house on certain ceremonial matters.

The original La Follette-Monroney Committee, from whose recommendations came the Legislative Reorganization Act of 1946, suggested that the practice of creating special investigating committees be abandoned, on the ground that they lack legislative authority, and that the jurisdiction of the standing committees could be so defined in the new rules as to cover every conceivable subject of legislation.[27] The Senate version of the 1946 act prohibited special committees, but the House would not accept this provision. It is true, however, that the number of special investigative committees since 1946 has diminished considerably.

---

[27] Galloway, *op. cit.,* p. 574.

Some special committees continue from year to year until they are practically accepted as permanent additions. For example, the Senate's Select Committee on Small Business has been in operation every year since 1950. It is entirely possible that this committee will eventually be converted into a permanent standing committee. Many times in the past special committees have stolen the headlines from the regular standing committees. A case in point in recent years is the Senate's Select Committee to Investigate Improper Activities in Labor-Management Relations. It should, however, be emphasized that special committees usually do not have the same powers as regular standing committees in respect to recommending legislation. Recommendations from special committees must normally be referred to the appropriate standing committee to be handled as any other bill.

Joint committees. Joint committees may be established by concurrent resolutions or by statute. If by the latter method, they are usually for the purpose of making continuing studies of particular subjects, or working with certain administrative units in an advisory capacity. The Joint Committee on Atomic Energy is a good example of a statutory joint committee. It is the only one of the present joint committees which is authorized to report on legislative matters in the same manner as a standing legislative committee.

Committee of the whole. A great deal of the business of the House is transacted by the committee of the whole. This committee is to be distinguished from the House itself only with some difficulty. It meets in the same chamber, has the same members, and goes through some of the same motions, but it is presided over by a chairman other than the Speaker, uses much less burdensome rules than the House, and is particularly advantageous because it expedites matters. The quorum of the committee of the whole is 100 instead of a simple majority of the membership. Debate is limited to five minutes in the case of a single person on one bill, whereas in the formal sessions of the House an hour may be permitted. So the House meets as a committee of the whole to carry on most of its debates and to consider amendments to pending bills; then it adjourns to meet as a House to pass the bill. One of the greatest advantages of the committee of the whole is that the time-consuming roll-call vote is not used.

Since 1930 the Senate has not made use of the committee of the whole for the consideration of bills and resolutions. It is used in the upper house for the consideration of treaties.

SUMMARY

The Constitution sets forth in broad outline certain primary requirements relative to the membership and organization of Congress. The vast majority of the delegates at the Constitutional Convention of 1787 favored a bicameral legislature. Some undoubtedly favored this system because each house would act as a restraint upon the other. More significant, however, was the fact that a two-chambered arrangement permitted an essential compromise in which the *states* retained *equality* of representation in the Senate, while *population* was to determine representation in the House of Representatives.

The Constitution, as interpreted by the Supreme Court, grants Congress ample power to restrain what might be termed undemocratic practices in the states such as gerrymandering and discriminatory suffrage provisions in primary and general elections. Since 1929 Congress has given the states no guidelines in the matter of drawing congressional district lines. Voting rights and what Congress should do to guarantee them have been acute issues from time to time since the Civil War. The 1957 and 1964 Civil Rights Acts reached down to the primary in seeking to give some measure of protection to persons who believed their right of suffrage denied illegally.

Other provisions in the Constitution deal with the members' qualifications, their terms of office, and their privileges and immunities.

One of the outstanding characteristics of the Constitution is the fact that it stresses broad principles rather than enumerating details. Thus each house of Congress is left free for the most part to establish rules of procedure; salaries and other perquisites of membership are fixed by law.

But constitutional provisions, laws, and resolutions of Congress are not the only important elements affecting the membership and organization of Congress. Custom, attitudes of the public, and the development of political parties are particularly significant in this respect. The almost absolute requirement that a member of the House live in the district he represents is a good example of how custom influences membership. How does one explain the preponderance of lawyers in the Congress? Part of the explanation stems from an attitude held by many individuals that legal training and experience equip one to serve better in Congress than other types of education and vocations.

The importance of the political party in nominating and electing members to Congress is quite obvious, but just as significant is the role of the party in organizing Congress. With the exception of the presiding officer of the Senate (the Vice-President), the majority party picks the officers of Congress, selects the chairmen of all committees, and assures itself of a majority membership on each committee.

The standing committees, more so than any other institution in Congress, determine the character of legislation. Their chairmen, chosen almost automatically through a seniority system, over-shadow in power and prestige the rank-and-file member. The roles played by the conference committee, other joint committees, special committees, and the committee of the whole are, on the whole, complementary to the work of the standing committees.

See *Bibliographic Note* at end of Chapter 16.

16

Congress in Action

THE formal passage of a bill into law
is the operation of the government most frequently observed by the general
public. Although the procedural maze through which most bills must pass
is at times mystifying, an ordinary citizen with a little practice can follow
the published legislative history of a measure with confidence. However,
one would have gained only the most superficial knowledge of the complexity of the legislative process. The realities involved in the passage of a
major legislative measure often escape even the most experienced observers
of the Capitol Hill scene.

In a frequently quoted passage of *Federalist Paper* Number X, James
Madison wrote: "A landed interest, a manufacturing interest, a mercantile
interest, a moneyed interest, with many lesser interests, grow up of necessity
in civilised nations, and divide them into different classes, actuated by
different sentiments and views. The regulation of these various and in-
terfering interests forms the principal task of modern legislation, and involves the spirit of party and faction in the necessary and ordinary operations of the government."

A well-known textbook on the national legislative process is entitled
The Legislative Struggle: A Study in Social Combat.[1] Professor Roland
Young writes: "The activity involved in adjusting interests, modifying or
mollifying expectations, and altering the existing pattern of order lies at
the heart of the legislative process." [2]

The emphasis on conflict among groups, though obviously important.
fails to tell the whole story with respect to the nature of lawmaking. Conflict without compromise spells chaos. It is equally important to stress the
cooperative aspects of congressional legislation. All societies have group
conflicts but their parliamentary bodies have not always been able to resolve
the difficulties. If one agrees that politics is the "art of the possible," then

---

[1] Bertram M. Gross (New York: McGraw-Hill Book Company, Inc., 1953).
[2] *The American Congress* (New York: Harper & Bros., New York, 1958), p. 5.

one must credit Congress with being a remarkably successful political institution.

INSTRUMENTS OF PARTY CONTROL

Most measures enacted by Congress are not decided strictly according to party lines. Even if the parties have taken definite stands on issues in their platforms, or the President as a party leader pushes some program, the local interest of the individual member may outweigh the pull of party loyalty or party pressure. This is not meant to imply that party affiliation is unimportant in the passage of legislation, for a fairly high degree of party cohesion may be observed on certain measures in nearly every session of Congress. Yet party machinery is much more in evidence throughout the legislative process in matters not directly related to the way an individual member votes.

Party leadership is diffused rather than centralized. It stems from action taken or authorized by the party caucus.

In the House. *The Speaker* of the House is the acknowledged leader of the majority party although he shares the leadership with other party instrumentalities.[3] As presiding officer he acts, subject to certain parliamentary restrictions, to aid his party whenever possible, and he is one of the principal advisers in determining party strategy.

Second in importance to the Speaker as party agent is the *majority floor leader* who is chosen in party caucus. He represents the majority on the floor and gives the party's view on proposed legislation. Through consultation with committee chairmen, with other of his own party leaders, and with the minority party leadership, he has a great deal to do with scheduling measures for floor discussion. He is the chief manager of his party's legislative efforts. The *majority whip* is the right-hand man of the floor leader. One of the whip's principal duties is to maintain a communications system so that he can contact party members upon short notice at all times. The whip and his assistants are important links between the leadership and the rank and file membership. They canvass members as to how they stand on various issues; and they keep members informed as to the probable program for the following week.

A *majority steering committee*[4] composed of members from various geographical regions, plus a number of *ex officio* personnel such as the Speaker, floor leader, whip, and the chairmen of certain standing committees was proposed for each party by the Legislative Reorganization Act of 1946. The Democrats have never utilized this possible mechanism of party leadership. The Republicans have tended to use it largely as an advisory body to the regular party leadership.

---

[3] See p. 291 for a description of the powers of the Speaker.

[4] The Republicans in the House of Representatives designate this group as the policy committee.

The Rules Committee, a regular standing committee, is a potent instrument of the majority party leadership. Through its power to recommend special rules, which if accepted by a House majority become effective, it is the most important agency in the House of Representatives for scheduling floor debate. By failing to recommend a special rule, it has an effective veto over bills, which without its support will never come up for a vote in the chamber. A majority of members may discharge the Committee from further consideration of any resolution providing for a special rule, but this is rarely accomplished. The committee holds hearings on requests for special rules in the same way that other standing committees hold hearings on legislative proposals. It may require changes in the substance of bills as the price for reporting special rules. Special rules set the time permitted for debate, and determine whether any amendments may be offered in the course of debate. The power of the Rules Committee is such that its chairman is generally conceded to be one of the most powerful figures in the House of Representatives.

The Rules Committee has often been severely criticized for bottling up proposed legislation considered desirable by many groups. The committee, under Democratic or Republican majorities, has, since 1938, been classed as conservative in its attitude toward social and economic legislation. However, it should be remembered that, when enough House members really want to, they may override the Rules Committee. That the committee continues to operate as it does, in spite of criticism, would seem to indicate that the House of Representatives finds its services more valuable than unbearable. The conservative nature of the Rules Committee was modified in 1961. In that year the committee's size was increased from twelve to fifteen and two moderate Democrats were appointed. This action was reaffirmed in 1963.

The *standing committee chairmen* round out the principal instruments of majority party control. These various controls do not always work in harmony, because in our system party leaders frequently disagree. It is not unusual for a committee chairman to block a bill which the majority leadership favors, or for the Rules Committee to refuse a special rule for a proposal endorsed by other party stalwarts.

Minority party leadership is similar in organization to that of the majority party, but its scope of operation is restricted by the very fact that it is in the minority. The minority party chooses a *minority leader, minority whip,* and a *steering committee,* and, of course, is represented on all standing committees, including the Rules Committee. The ranking minority member on each committee stands ready to assume the chairmanship if his party wins a majority of the seats, and if he, himself, is re-elected. The minority party leadership works to achieve a united front against those policies of the majority party upon which it differs. It makes sure that the minority party's views are heard even if not acted upon. Moreover, it cooperates in many ways with the majority leadership, particularly with respect to matters of procedure.

In the Senate. Each party in the Senate as in the House uses the party caucus (called conference by both parties in the Senate) to name party leaders and establish party machinery. Yet there are significant variations from House practices. The Vice-President, made the presiding officer by the Constitution, is beyond the reach of the caucus. However, the majority party nominates the president *pro tempore,* whose selection is confirmed by Senate vote. The Democrats concentrate considerable power in the person of their *floor leader,* who serves as chairman of the conference and the policy committee. The Republicans bestow these positions upon different individuals.

The *policy committees*[5] in the Senate differ from their counterparts in the House since they have been authorized by law since 1946. They receive an appropriation for staff assistance. The Democratic policy committee is made up of nine members, three of them *ex officio* (floor leader, whip, and secretary of the conference), the remaining members being appointed by the floor leader. The Republican policy committee has ranged in numbers from nine to twenty-three (at present it is composed of fourteen senators). The chairman is named by the conference. The chairman of the conference, the secretary of the conference, the floor leader, and the whip serve as *ex officio* members; the remainder are nominated by the chairman of the conference and ratified by the conference membership.

The general idea behind the creation of policy committees was to encourage the parties to formulate over-all legislative policies. This purpose has been served only to a limited degree, however. The policy committee of the majority party has come to be the primary agency for setting the legislative schedule for the consideration of measures on the Senate floor.

The floor leaders and the whips of their respective parties serve in much the same way as their opposite numbers in the House. Their power of direction over the course of specific legislation is limited by the Senate rules more so than it is in the House. The Senate prides itself on permitting the individual member a wide range of participation in its procedures.

The Rules Committee in the Senate does not enjoy the power to affect the course of legislation in the manner of the House Rules Committee. As in the House, however, the chairmen of the Senate standing committees are an important element in the over-all majority leadership.

FORMS OF CONGRESSIONAL ENACTMENTS

Bills are the form used for most legislation, whether permanent or temporary, general or specific. A *private bill* is for the individual benefit

---

[5] See Hugh A. Bone, "An Introduction to Senate Policy Committees," *American Political Science Review,* L, 339-359, June, 1956.

of a person or several specified persons, corporations, or institutions. *Public bills* relate to matters of general application or deal with classes of individuals. A *joint resolution* goes through the same parliamentary procedure as a bill; it must be signed by the President,[6] and has the force of law. Generally, joint resolutions are legislative proposals involving a single matter rather than a comprehensive piece of legislation. Certain matters, such as a declaration of war, ordinarily call for a joint resolution, but there is no hard and fast rule differentiating joint resolutions from ordinary legislative acts. "A *concurrent resolution*[7] expresses facts, principles, opinions, and purposes of the two houses." [8] It is not signed by the President and does not have the force of law. In recent years Congress has sometimes used the concurrent resolution to repeal existing law where this provision was incorporated in the original legislation. There is some doubt as to the constitutionality of this procedure. A matter concerning the operations of either house alone is initiated by a *simple resolution.*

DRAFTING AND INTRODUCTION OF BILLS

Where bills originate. There is a widespread belief that proposals to enact laws originate among the senators and representatives themselves, as indeed some of them do. However, for every bill which is solely the idea of a member of Congress there are scores which have their inception in the office of the President, in the multiplicity of administrative agencies, in the councils of pressure groups, and in the minds of private citizens. One author writes: "It is a wise child, the saying goes, who knows his own father. In the case of a bill, wisdom is not always enough to identify the real parents. Sometimes nothing short of omniscience will do." [9] Even if the drafter of the original bill is known, by the time it goes through the additions, deletions, substitutions, and amendments of two standing committees (one in each house) and changes on the floor of both chambers, possibly plus modifications in a conference committee, the original author might be hard put to pick out his own contributions.

In general, the senators and representatives act as sponsors rather than as originators in the making of laws. In the Senate several senators may be co-sponsors of the same bill. House rules prohibit co-sponsorship, but it is not unusual for several members of the lower house to sponsor identical bills. Getting the right person to act as sponsor for proposed legislation is one of the first bits of strategy considered by those interested in a bill's passage. If the chairman of the committee to which the proposal will be referred can be persuaded to attach his name to the measure so much the

---

6 With the exception of joint resolutions proposing constitutional amendments.

7 Italics added.

8 George B. Galloway, *The Legislative Process in Congress* (New York: Crowell Company, 1935), p. 50.

9 Gross, *op. cit.,* p. 181.

better. Generally speaking, it is more advantageous, for obvious reasons, to have a member of the majority party give his name to a bill. On the other hand, a name alone is not going to guarantee passage. Therefore, if the choice is between a "name" sponsor who is not really interested in pushing the legislation and a lesser light who is genuinely concerned with the subject matter, it is probably better to select the latter person.

Bill-drafting assistance. Drafting legislation requires a specialized knowledge and skill not possessed by the average person. The very form and technical requirements are such that even one who is competent to write articles, books, and business reports as a professional can scarcely make headway in drafting a bill. Lawyers sometimes take a hand at preparing bills and, of course, have the advantage of being familiar with legal terminology. Pressure groups, administrative agencies, and congressional committees develop specialists in bill-drafting. But what of the individual member or the committee that does not have such talent available? Each house of Congress maintains a bill-drafting agency known as "The Office of Legislative Counsel." The office is staffed by experts who steer clear of partisanship in their work.

Number of bills. No legislative body in the world can begin to equal the record of the Congress of the United States in multiplicity of bills. In many countries only a hundred or so bills are brought to a national legislature in the course of an entire year. Where a cabinet form of representative government prevails, bills are entrusted to the leaders who head the government. Hence, there are not numerous bills relating to the same subject, or to pet projects of pressure groups, or individual members. In the Eighty-fourth Congress a total of 19,039 bills and resolutions were introduced— 11,914 originating in the House and 7,125 in the Senate.[10] Of this number 1,921 were enacted into law.

Introduction. Only members of Congress may actually introduce bills. Even if the drafting occurred in the President's office, some member must add his name to the measure and start it on its way through the formal procedural process. There are any number of reasons for members introducing bills. It is generally good strategy for a member of Congress to inform his constituents of the number of bills that he has initiated even though the number that actually become law is small. Bills are often for the purpose of drawing attention to a particular problem, even when the legislative climate of opinion is not favorable toward passage. The prospect of raising a campaign issue may be behind an introduction. Campaign promises may be involved, as when a candidate has assured the voters in his district that if elected, he will sponsor a particular bit of legislation.

Timing may be an important consideration. For example, bills in-

---

[10] See Floyd M. Riddick, "The Eighty-Fourth Congress, Second Session," *Western Political Quarterly*, X, 64, March, 1957.

creasing taxes are not frequent in an election year; yet bills increasing social security benefits are often passed in those same years. Is it better to start a measure early in the session or near its termination point? By introducing it early there will be more time for public and committee discussion; on the other hand, opponents of the measure will also have more time to mobilize opposition pressures.

A member of the House may introduce a bill by placing it in the "hopper" provided for that purpose at the side of the clerk's desk any time while the House is in session.[11] A representative may insert the words "by request" after his name to indicate that the introduction of the measure is in compliance with the suggestion of some other person. The "first reading" of the bill is accomplished by entering the title in the *Journal* and printing the title in the *Congressional Record.*

The procedure is more formal in the Senate. At the time reserved for the purpose, a senator who wishes to introduce a measure rises and states that he offers a bill for introduction and sends it by page to the secretary's desk. The bill is read by title for the *first* and *second* reading.

Two thousand or more bills have been introduced under this simple procedure during a single day! Tax bills by constitutional mandate and general appropriation bills by custom start in the House of Representatives. Other measures may be introduced in either house with equal facility. The larger size of the House of Representatives and the comparative nearness of the representatives to the "grass roots" does, however, result in more bills originating there. As soon as possible, the employees of the House or Senate give each bill a number.

THE COMMITTEE STAGE

Reference to a standing committee. Shortly after a bill has been introduced in either the House of Representatives or the Senate, it is referred to a standing committee for consideration. In the great majority of cases there is little question as to what committee will receive a bill, for the title of the bill usually indicates what particular standing committee should receive it.[12] Formerly, Speakers of the House frequently used their power to refer as a very potent device for controlling the course of legislation. If a certain committee were known to be unfavorable to a bill, the Speaker could see that a bill which he opposed went to that committee, whether or not it was the logical committee to receive the bill. Again, if the Speaker favored a bill and discovered that the regular standing committee in that field opposed the measure, it was customary for the Speaker to assign the bill to some other favorable committee. The Speaker still decides to which

11 For a concise discussion of the introduction of bills, see Charles J. Zinn, *How Our Laws Are Made* (House Document No. 451, 84th Congress, 2nd Session).
12 See p. 293 for a discussion on this point.

committee a bill shall be referred in those exceptional cases in which there is some question as to the province involved, but both he and the President of the Senate, who has the same power, may be overruled by a majority vote.

Printing. After the bill has been referred to a standing committee, it is ordered printed, without regard to whether it has any merit or support. Copies are furnished the members of the committee and to senators and representatives and may usually be obtained by interested citizens.

Committee consideration. There are several courses open to a committee with respect to any bill which has been referred to it. It may:

(1) Report the bill for floor consideration without change;
(2) Report the bill for floor consideration with amendments;
(3) Substitute a bill for the original one;
(4) Report unfavorably upon the bill; or
(5) "Pigeonhole," i.e., file the bill away without taking any action on it.

From 50 to 75 per cent of all bills introduced are pigeonholed. It is a rare occasion when an unfavorable report is submitted by the committee. Thus bills which have any real chance for further consideration by either of the houses will be handled in one of the first three ways mentioned above.

Most committees find it convenient or necessary to subdivide into smaller groups for the actual consideration of measures before them. A large committee such as the House Appropriations Committee may break down into twelve or thirteen subcommittees, smaller committees into three or four. These subcommittees act very much like regular committees, sorting the wheat from the chaff, deciding what changes should be recommended in a certain bill, and otherwise preparing to dispose of the business entrusted to them. Subcommittee decisions are subject to review by the full committee, but since they become specialists in the subject matter areas referred to them their recommendations are apt to be accepted by the parent group. The procedure the committees follow depends quite largely upon their own inclination, for the rules of the Senate and the House of Representatives do not regulate them in any detail. Inasmuch as the formal sessions of the two houses are held in the afternoon, the committees do most of their work in the morning although any committee by special leave may hold meetings while its own house is in session.

A common procedure is for the committee to request comments upon the bill from any interested agencies of the executive branch. Normally, other interested individuals or groups will be given an opportunity to testify on the proposal in due time.

Hearings. Hearings will be called for most major and for many minor controversial bills. There is often more to a hearing than meets the eye. One observer describes the uses of committee hearings as fivefold:

1. To make policy decisions as rational as possible, on the basis of facts.

2. As a political sounding-board for legislative policy makers—to ascertain what power groups support or oppose a certain legislative proposal, to assess their strength of conviction and relative power.

3. As an instrument for calculating the political advantages and disadvantages of casting a "yea" or "nay" vote if and when the bill reaches the floor.

4. As a method by which those already committed to a legislative policy can give it an aura of well-reasoned respectability, by making it appear that the decision was arrived at on rational grounds.

5. As a device to suppress facts whose exposure might lend support to a policy which those who control the committee machinery do not wish to be enacted into law.[13]

On the latter point, the following example has been given:

Sixteen Senate bills to liberalize the Displaced Persons Act were introduced during the first session of the 81st Congress and referred to the Judiciary Committee. These bills were designed to correct inadequacies of existing laws as they affected European victims of the last war. No public hearings were held on any of these bills until July 26. On that date Senator McCarran announced that the hearings would not be concerned with European displaced persons, but with the Pakistanis, Arabs, Greeks, Chinese, and others. As a result, those who were concerned with the European situation, even the members of the commission that was [sic] administering the act, were long denied the opportunity to appear before the committee.[14]

Most persons outside of Congress would no doubt consider the first reason listed as the only proper use of committee hearings. However, even the formality of going through the hearings has its advantages. The supporters and the opponents of proposed legislation are revealed; their motives may be assessed, and the testimony given may influence members of Congress who were not on the committee.

Hearings may extend over a number of days. Government officials, interest group representatives, academicians, and other interested persons may be invited or request permission to testify. Generally, witnesses read from prepared statements before any of the committee members ask questions.

PROCEDURE IN THE HOUSE

Calendars. When a committee is prepared to report a bill to the House of Representatives, it notifies the clerk of that readiness and returns the bill. When first reported, bills go on one of three calendars: (1) the Calendar of the Whole House on the State of the Union, commonly referred to as the "Union Calendar," for bills raising revenue, general appropriation bills,

---

13 Julius Cohen, "Toward Realism in Legisprudence," *Yale Law Journal*, April, 1950. Cited in Galloway, *op. cit.*, p. 301.

14 Galloway, *op. cit.*, p. 301.

and bills of a public character directly or indirectly appropriating money or property; (2) the House Calendar for public bills not raising revenue nor directly or indirectly appropriating money or property; and (3) the Private Calendar, for private bills. If a measure pending on either the Union or House Calendar is of a noncontroversial nature, it may be placed on a fourth list, the Consent Calendar, upon petition by any member. In this case, the bill continues to be listed on its original calendar. A fifth calendar, the Discharge Calendar, may be used to list bills discharged from committees.

Selection of bills for consideration. Despite the apparent ruthlessness of the standing committees in pigeonholing bills, the calendars become congested. This, of course, means that the House rarely has sufficient time to consider all bills that are listed. Bills on the calendars are carried over from the first to succeeding sessions of the same Congress; but at the beginning of each new Congress, the calendars start anew. Thus bills that "die on the calendars" must be reintroduced if they are to be considered.

The calendared order has almost nothing to do with the order in which a bill is discussed. Various devices are used by the House to select those bills to be considered from the mass of bills listed. Certain measures, i.e., general appropriation bills and revenue bills, have privileged status and may be called up for consideration at almost any time. The majority leadership, working closely with the Rules Committee, may have special rules introduced calling up specific measures. Bills may be brought before the House without objection under the unanimous consent procedure.

Additional flexibility for the scheduling is provided by reserving special times for specific types of measures and procedures. These include Calendar Wednesday (every Wednesday), District of Columbia Day (second and fourth Mondays), Suspension of Rules (first and third Mondays), Consent Calendar business (first and third Tuesdays), Private Calendar business (first and third Tuesdays), and Discharge Calendar business (second and fourth Mondays). These special procedures may or may not be used.

Under Calendar Wednesday procedure, committee chairmen are given the chance to call bills under their jurisdiction from the House or Union lists for consideration. Actually, this procedure is seldom employed.

In addition to its legislative responsibilities to the country at large, Congress must legislate for the District of Columbia. The House uses District of Columbia Day to facilitate its handling of District matters.

On the days specified above, and during the last six days of the session, the Speaker may entertain a motion to suspend the rules with respect to a particular bill. The motion must be seconded by a majority of the members present and then passed by a two-thirds vote. If this is accomplished, the measure is considered passed by the action of two-thirds of the House agreeing to the original motion.

On Consent Calendar days and Private Calendar days, bills are passed as they are called from the calendars provided no objections are raised. To prevent abuse of the system, each party designates three "official objectors" for each of these calendars, who are supposed to see to it that undesirable bills are killed.

House consideration. When the time fixed for bringing a bill to the floor of the House of Representatives has arrived, the House ordinarily meets as a committee of the whole. Bills from the Union Calendar must be considered in such fashion. The time for general debate is usually fixed by a special rule. The control of the time is divided between the chairman and ranking minority committeeman of the committee that reported the bill. Members wishing to speak for or against the bill usually arrange in advance with the person in control of the time on their respective side to be allowed a certain amount of time during the debate. Others may ask the member speaking at the time to yield to them for a question or a brief statement. Often permission is granted a congressman by unanimous consent to extend his remarks in the *Congressional Record* if sufficient time to make a lengthy oral statement is not available during the actual debate.

At the expiration of the time allotted for general debate, the "second reading" of the bill begins, section by section. At this time amendments are in order to each section unless a "gag" rule is in operation. No member is permitted to speak more than once or for longer than five minutes regarding a proposed amendment. Each amendment is voted upon by the committee of the whole. The process of offering, discussing, and voting upon amendments brings forth some of the most skillful parliamentary maneuvering observable. Sometimes an amendment is offered for the purpose of splitting the bill's supporters or for raising a new issue that the committee has not considered. Also:

> A floor amendment provides a member of Congress with a good opportunity to attract attention and build up his record. A member who offers an amendment to an important bill can sometimes move much more into the limelight than by introducing a score of bills that are never acted upon. From the strategic viewpoint, moreover, floor amendments provide ideal instruments for consuming time and postponing final decision on a bill. Amendments that succeed in narrowing the support enjoyed by a measure are an ideal way of building up a final coup de grace. Both sides in a contest find that a vote on even a minor amendment may provide an ideal method of testing the strength of opposing forces and of serving as a guide to subsequent floor strategy.[15]

At the conclusion of the second reading, the committee of the whole "rises" and reports the bill as agreed upon to the House. Ordinarily, the House immediately votes on amendments which have been reported by the committee of the whole in the sequence in which they were drawn. Following completion of voting on amendments, the House votes upon the passage of

15 Gross, *op. cit.,* pp. 353-354.

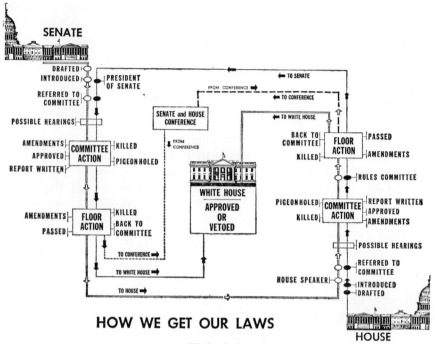

HOW WE GET OUR LAWS

"Under the Dome," *published by the Chamber of Commerce of the United States of America*

HOW WE GET OUR LAWS

the bill. The Speaker puts the question: "Shall the bill be engrossed [16] and read a third time?" An affirmative vote on this question is usually automatic, almost always by title only, and presages the final passage of the measure.

If a bill is considered by the House rather than in the committee of the whole, it is read a second time in full after which it is open to debate and amendment. General debate may be limited under a special rule; amendments are offered under the "hour" rather than the "five-minute" rule. The procedure from that point is similar to that outlined above.

PROCEDURE IN THE SENATE

Bills that have passed the House are sent to the Senate and referred to appropriate committees in the Senate as though they were introduced in that chamber.[17] Following consideration by the standing committees, legis-

---

[16] An engrossed bill is a true copy of the bill decided upon including amendments.

[17] An unusual event occurred in the first session of the Eighty-fifth Congress when the Senate voted to put on its calendar the Civil Rights Bill passed by the House, without referral to the Judiciary Committee, which normally would have considered the bill first. This action was prompted by the knowledge that the chairman of the Judiciary Committee was opposed to the bill and might delay the bill so long in committee that the Senate would not get a chance to act upon it during the session.

lative matters are placed on the Calendar of Business; matters relating to nominations and treaties are placed on the Executive Calendar. The Senate Rules Committee plays no part in determining when bills are to be discussed. Neither does the Senate use the device of setting aside special days to facilitate the consideration of pending bills.

At the time a bill is reported, a Senator may ask unanimous consent for its immediate consideration. If there is no objection and the bill is noncontroversial, it may pass with little or no discussion. At certain times, the Senate proceeds to the consideration of the calendar of bills. Bills that are not objected to are taken up for discussion. At other specified times, a senator may move to take up any bill out of its regular order on the calendar. Majority support for this motion is necessary to put it into operation. As a matter of fact, most controversial bills are taken up in the Senate upon the recommendation of the majority floor leader backed by his party majority.

The Senate does not use the committee of the whole except for the consideration of treaties. The actual consideration of a measure is on the third reading, since the first two readings were accomplished upon referral to committee. The bill is read in full, amendments may be offered, and the final passage voted upon about as in the House.

Filibustering in the Senate. A striking difference in Senate and House procedure is the freedom permitted individual senators to debate bills or motions to take up bills. This may lead to the practice known as filibustering. According to one authority on the subject, filibustering ". . . is a device to delay business in order to defeat legislation or to force unwilling adoption as a price for time to consider other and perhaps much more important matters. Whether the underlying purpose is positive or negative, the technique is designed to consume time." [18]

The Senate rules provide that "no one is to speak impertinently, or beside the question," but this has not prevented senators from reading the Bible, giving their favorite cooking recipes, refreshing the memories of their few hearers with the dictionary, or otherwise consuming time.

Throughout the years frequent attempts have been made to limit debate in the Senate, but it was not until 1917 that a cloture[19] rule was adopted. In that year, following a denunciation by President Wilson after a Senate filibuster had resulted in the defeat of a bill to arm merchant ships, Rule 22 was adopted. It made possible the closing of debate upon "a pending measure" if two-thirds of the senators present and voting so decided. As subsequent events proved, this was a rather ineffectual way of shutting off debate because arguments over motions to "bring up" measures could go

---

[18] Franklin L. Burdette, *Filibustering in the Senate* (Princeton, N. J.: Princeton University Press, 1940), p. 5.

[19] Meaning the same as closure or a method of ending debate and receiving an immediate vote upon a measure before a legislative body.

on endlessly. In 1949 the rule was modified, following an extended filibuster. In some ways the modification made the cloture procedure even more difficult to apply. For example, a two-thirds majority of the entire membership was necessary to bring a filibuster to a close. However, the procedure could be applied to motions to consider bills as well as to pending measures, with the exception that a motion or resolution to change Rule 22 was not subject to closure.

There was mounting dissatisfaction with Rule 22 in the 1950's among many senators from outside the South. Pressure to adopt a stronger anti-filibuster measure was tied in with increasing demands to enact legislation in the civil rights field, a trend resisted by many southern senators. In 1964, after more than 57 days of debate, the Senate invoked cloture as a prelude to passing the Civil Rights Act of that year. This was the first time that debate had been cut off on a civil rights proposal.

The strategy of those favoring revision of the cloture procedure was shaped by the fact that the Senate does not re-adopt its rules at the beginning of each new Congress, since historically it has been considered as a continuing body with two-thirds of its members holdovers from the previous Congress. The effect of this theory was that the 1949 cloture rule could not be applied to stop a filibuster aimed at preventing a change in Rule 22, even at the beginning of a new Congress. Those who wanted to modify the rule argued that a simple majority of senators at the opening of a new Congress could adopt new rules without being bound by the old rules. In the first session of the Eighty-fifth Congress, an opinion by the Vice-President upheld this view, but a motion to accomplish this purpose was tabled.

At the opening session of the Eighty-sixth Congress, lines were once more drawn for a battle over Rule 22. Once more a strong coalition of Democrats and Republicans prepared to offer a motion that the Senate proceed to adopt new rules. In the meantime, Senator Lyndon Johnson, majority floor leader, was busy lining up support for a compromise measure more palatable to the southern senators. As it turned out, Senator Johnson had the votes to pass his measure. Eventually the Senate tabled the motion that the Senate adopt new rules and passed a modified Rule 22. The new rule makes it possible for cloture to be invoked by a two-thirds vote of those present; it may be applied to end debate on all measures, including motions to amend Senate rules. One section was added which stipulates: "The rules of the Senate shall continue from one Congress to the next Congress unless they are changed as provided in these rules." Whether the present rule remains in operation probably depends upon tactics of those in the Senate who oppose an extension of civil rights guarantees by the national government. If the filibuster is used frequently to block such proposals, there will undoubtedly be a determined effort to further modify the cloture rule so as to make it easier to shut off debate.

Critics of the present cloture rule maintain that it is an absurd situation when a majority of members in a parliamentary body must stand helplessly by while a minority obstructs the legislative process. But supporters of the present rule stoutly insist that extensive debate is necessary to guarantee the minority the right to explain its views and to protect what it believes to be its vital interests. In any case, there appears little support for any proposition to limit debate in the Senate to the degree practiced in the House.

METHODS OF VOTING IN CONGRESS

There are four methods of voting used in the two houses of Congress. The most prevalent is the familiar *viva voce,* or voice vote. If there is a fairly even split, and it is difficult to ascertain how the voice vote has gone, a rising[20] vote may be ordered. A third method, which may be demanded by one-fifth of a quorum, requires that congressmen file past tellers to be counted.[21] Finally, there is the formal roll-call vote,[22] upon the demand of one-fifth of those present (not quorum), which is used in the final passage of most important bills. The clerk calls the roll of the members alphabetically, and each one answers "yea" or "nay" to be permanently recorded in the journal. A single roll call in the House of Representatives consumes something like thirty-five minutes[23] which, considering the generous use made of this method of voting, presents a serious problem. During a single year the lower house may have the roll called more than two hundred times which is the equivalent of at least a month of sessions. Considering the popularity which gadgets enjoy in the United States, it would seem that the House of Representatives, particularly, might install one of the electrical voting systems which various state legislatures now employ. But Congress seems satisfied to get along with its present facilities, despite the fact that many bills cannot be given a hearing for lack of time.

When congressmen are absent from Washington or ill, they sometimes arrange to have their votes "paired" with those of absent colleagues who stand on the other side of a question. In this way they do not lose their voice entirely despite their absence from the chamber. In contrast to these members who want their votes counted, there are always those who are very reluctant to have their votes recorded at all on certain measures. Party pressure may compel them to vote finally, but it is not uncommon to find them slipping away before a vote is taken or even refusing to answer when their names are called.

---

20 Those in favor stand and are counted, then those opposed stand and are counted.
21 Not used in the Senate.
22 Not used in the committee of the whole.
23 The time consumed by a roll-call vote gives members time to come from their offices or committee rooms, thus obviating the necessity of continuous presence on the floor.

FINAL STEPS IN THE PASSAGE OF A BILL

Bills which have passed both House and Senate may be sent to a conference committee.[24] At any rate, once the two houses pass the measure in identical form, an engrossed copy is signed by the two presiding officers, and it is sent to the White House. The President's role at this point has already been discussed.[25] All of the bills and resolutions from a session are held until Congress has adjourned; then they are published in a series of volumes known as *Statutes at Large of the United States*.[26]

CASE HISTORY OF THE 1959 LABOR LAW

A summary of the procedural aspects involved in the passage of a bill fails to reveal the drama, the clash of personalities and interests, and the backstage maneuvering associated with the enactment of a controversial statute. For the purpose of stressing some of these points, a brief case history of the 1959 Labor Law follows.

Before the 1959 law, no major labor legislation had been enacted by Congress since the Taft-Hartley Act of 1947. President Truman had advocated repeal of the latter law in 1949, but his suggestion went unheeded. In 1954, 1955, and 1956, President Eisenhower had made recommendations looking to certain changes in labor legislation but nothing came of his proposals. Beginning in 1957 a Senate Select Committee on Improper Activities in Labor-Management Relations, under the chairmanship of Senator McClellan of Arkansas, had been looking into the affairs of some of the major unions such as the International Brotherhood of Teamsters, headed by James R. Hoffa. The committee uncovered instances in some unions of misappropriation of pension and welfare funds, collusion between union officers and management, the use of picketing and boycott techniques to extort money from employers, undemocratic one-man rule, and the hiring of former felons in positions of responsibility.

The climate of opinion appeared ripe for the enactment of some type of labor legislation, especially since both union and management leaders went on record as favoring some changes.

In 1958 the Senate Labor and Public Welfare Committee, working closely with Senator McClellan, reported out a bill sponsored by Senator Kennedy (Democrat) and Senator Ives (Republican). In general the bill did not look to a sweeping revision of the Taft-Hartley Law, but was designed to curb most of the malpractices revealed by the McClellan

---

[24] See p. 295.

[25] See p. 250.

[26] Before the large volumes appear, individual acts are printed as "slip-laws." Two volumes of the statutes are prepared: one containing public acts and resolutions; a second, private acts, concurrent resolutions, treaties, and presidential proclamations.

Committee. As originally reported, it had at least the nominal support of much of organized labor, including the AFL-CIO. On the other hand, the bill was opposed by President Eisenhower, by Secretary of Labor Mitchell, and by many business groups as a "half-way" measure which, if passed, would provide an excuse for failure to pass a more comprehensive law within a reasonable time. The Kennedy-Ives Bill was eventually approved by the Senate by an 88 to 1 vote.

The Eisenhower Administration continued to oppose the act as being too mild; the President threatened a veto unless the House added additional restrictions on certain union activities. When the bill was being debated on the House floor, Representative Judd (Republican) announced that Labor Secretary Mitchell had authorized him to say that the proposal was "a bad bill." The House failed to pass the Kennedy-Ives measure, thus setting the stage for a renewal of the battle in the opening session of the Eighty-sixth Congress.

In April, 1959, the Senate began debate on the Kennedy-Ervin Bill, a measure which closely paralleled the Kennedy-Ives Bill passed by the upper house in 1958. Minority Leader Everett Dirksen offered a substitute amendment which included many of the provisions backed by the Administration. This move was defeated with almost all of the Southern Democrats joining Northern Democrats and eleven Republicans in voting against it. Senator McClellan offered an amendment labeled as a "labor bill of rights." It provided specific guarantees which the Arkansas Senator said would protect union members from coercion and arbitrary action by union leaders. By a 47-46 vote the McClellan amendment was accepted, Vice-President Nixon casting the deciding vote. With passage of the so-called bill of rights section, however, any hope of labor support for the bill vanished. After a considerable round of private conferences, a bi-partisan coalition led by Republican Senator Kuchel wrote a new section into the bill toning down the parts objected to by organized labor which passed by a 77 to 14 vote. After 55 votes on amendments, the Kennedy-Ervin Bill passed the Senate by a 90 to 1 roll-call vote. Some additional restrictions on unions had been added on the floor, but the measure was not the "strong" one which the Administration had hoped for.

The Senate bill was referred to the House Education and Labor Committee. Following weeks of hearings on labor reform proposals, the committee met in executive session for a month to write its bill. In July the committee voted 16 to 14 to send a measure to the floor which became known as the Elliott Bill, after its sponsor Carl Elliott of Alabama. Basically, it was the same bill, somewhat refined, which had passed the Senate. Of the ten Republicans on the committee, six voted to report the proposal, while the Democrats on the committee split 10-10 on the report.

Two committee members, Representative Landrum of Georgia (Democrat) and Representative Griffin of Michigan (Republican), offered a substitute for the Elliott Bill. It was identical in many ways with the latter bill, but it also included the strong Taft-Hartley changes favored by the President. Another substitute for the Elliott measure was offered by Representative Shelly of California (Democrat), supported by a caucus of 43 Democrats. Generally, this bill was similar to the original Kennedy-Ervin Bill before amended in the Senate.

Speaker Sam Rayburn endorsed the Elliott Bill in a nationwide radio broadcast; President Eisenhower, in a TV-radio speech, urged the House to accept the Landrum-Griffin version; and AFL-CIO President George Meany came out for the Shelly proposal. Senator Kennedy favored the Elliott Bill, while Senator McClellan threw his support to the Landrum-Griffin substitute.

Meanwhile, labor and business groups, which had been extremely busy throughout the battle, stepped up their lobbying activities. House members said that they were getting veiled threats from labor and management representatives indicating that members' political futures depended upon how they voted on the labor reform issue. Many representatives said that they had never been caught in such intense crossfire from rival pressure groups.

The first measure voted upon was the Shelly Bill. It was rejected by a 245 to 132 vote. Practically all votes for the AFL-CIO endorsed proposal came from Northern Democrats. The following day the Landrum-Griffin Bill was substituted for the Elliott measure by a 229 to 201 vote. The vote was hailed as a defeat for House Democratic leaders and the leaders of organized labor; it was heralded as a personal victory for President Eisenhower. The substitution was made possible by a coalition of Southern Democrats and Republicans. Eighty-five of the 95 Democrats who supported the Landrum-Griffin Bill came from Southern states. Only ten Northern Democrats voted for the bill, 160 voted against it. Republicans supported the Landrum-Griffin substitute 134 to 17.

President Eisenhower commented: "With, I am sure, millions of Americans, I applaud the House of Representatives for its vote today in support of the Landrum-Griffin labor reform bill which would deal effectively with the abuses disclosed by the McClellan Committee."

On the other side of the fence, AFL-CIO President Meany labeled it "a victory for the anti-labor forces—the National Association of Manufacturers and the Chamber of Commerce." He continued: "It was not a vote on the issue of corruption. It was a vote to punish honest labor. Twelve years of anti-labor propaganda and politicking have paid off for the anti-union forces determined to make Taft-Hartley even worse."

The vote on the final passage of the labor reform bill was 303 to 125, despite overnight efforts by labor lobbyists to keep the margin of victory as slim as possible in the hopes the bill would be watered down by House-Senate conferees.

The conference committee considered the House version and the Senate version of the labor bill for twelve days. Senator Kennedy, chairman of the conference committee, worked to move the House bill more in the direction of the Senate version, but he was generally unsuccessful. The bill reported out of conference was largely the House passed act. The conference committee report was accepted by the House of Representatives 352 to 52, by the Senate 96 to 2. When President Eisenhower signed the bill, the first major labor law since the 1947 Taft-Hartley Act had cleared through the legislative process.

TOWARD THE MODERNIZATION OF CONGRESS

Criticism of Congress. During the decade preceding 1946 there was a rising tide of criticism of the system under which Congress operated. It was alleged that the President and the administrative departments were organized in such a way as to give effective attention to present-day problems, whereas Congress continued to work under a system drawn up in the last century when the public business was far less in both volume and complication. To begin with, the members of Congress tended to ignore these complaints as unfounded, but in 1944 a Special House Committee of Executive Agencies recognized their basis by recommending that action be taken to "modernize" Congress. Shortly thereafter, a Joint Committee on the Organization of Congress was set up under the chairmanship of Senator Robert La Follette. Groups, such as the American Political Science Association and the National Planning Association, had also given consideration to the problem of the organization of Congress and made public certain recommendations as to specific changes.

The Legislative Reorganization Act of 1946. Congress by no means accepted all of the recommendations of its Joint Committee, but the Legislative Reorganization Act of 1946 contained several provisions designed to overcome certain alleged congressional weaknesses. The streamlining of committees was certainly a significant contribution.[27] An attempt was made to clarify committee duties so as to avoid jurisdictional disputes.[28] The formation of Senate policy committees stemmed from the act.[29] Certain types of private bills were barred from the legislative program.[30] Congressional staff aids were improved by enlarging the staffs of the Legislative Reference Service, of standing committees,[31] and of the individual members. Another main objective of the Act was to provide closer cooperation between the legislative and executive branches. Standing committees were to exercise

[27] See p. 293.
[28] See p. 293.
[29] See p. 302.
[30] For example, private pension bills and certain financial claims against the government.
[31] Supposedly on a professional rather than a political basis.

"continuous watchfulness" over the execution of the laws by administrative agencies under their respective jurisdictions.

Results from other provisions of the Act have been somewhat less positive than those mentioned above. The lobbyist registration feature might be mentioned in this connection. This section was so phrased that its specific applicability was difficult to determine, and its enforcement almost impossible.[32]

The Act sought to coordinate the procedure for handling the taxing and spending powers of Congress by providing that a Joint Budget Committee (composed of all members from the two committees in each house dealing with revenue and appropriations) recommend a legislative budget for the guidance of Congress. After experimenting with this procedure for a short time, Congress gave up in its efforts to coordinate financial planning in this manner.

CONGRESSIONAL PUBLICATIONS

For students of government several publications of Congress are valuable sources of information in connection with the process of lawmaking. The *Congressional Record* is published every day during sessions of Congress and often for several weeks after adjournment. It does not, however, contain the texts of bills, the detailed reports of committees, or the proceedings of the Senate during executive session. Moreover, members of Congress are permitted to revise statements which they have made on the floor before publication, or the houses themselves may order remarks stricken from the record. Undelivered speeches of members of Congress are inserted in the *Record* under "leave to print," even to the spurious (Applause) and (Extended Applause) parentheses. Nevertheless, the *Record* affords reasonable assistance to a serious student of the legislative process. If the *Record,* with its twenty to thirty thousand double-columned pages each two years, may be regarded as so voluminous that it is padded, the *Journals* published by the two houses are so abbreviated that they seem skeletal in form. The *Journals* are worth consulting for formal action, but they contain so little on their bones that they give only a fragmentary notion of what has taken place. The *Congressional Directory* is a convenient annual handbook which includes much pertinent information regarding committees, committee members, biographical records of senators and representatives, and so forth. Committee reports are unfortunately not so easily available as these three publications, but they are frequently more important as sources of information than the *Record.* They are often published as *House* or *Senate Documents* and may be obtained under that guise, although some of them are brought out in limited numbers and after a few years are almost unobtainable.

---

[32] See p. 332.

SUMMARY

The constitutional requirements for passing statutes are formidable in their own right. When the pressures of our pluralistic society, the nature of our party system, the fact of our federalism, the diffusion of the leadership function in the legislative process, and the roadblocks that may be raised by various procedural devices are added, one generally must concede that Congress performs its lawmaking function in an acceptable fashion. This does not mean that the operation of Congress may not be improved even within this frame of reference, as indeed was demonstrated by the Legislative Reorganization Act of 1946. The subsequent operation of certain parts of this legislation, however, shows that old patterns often continue in spite of reform measures designed to cancel or redirect them.

Congress is frequently criticized by various individuals and groups who blame antiquated procedures and over-concern for tradition and minority rights in Congress for stalling legislative action on some particular proposal. Almost invariably these same critics applaud the use of the self-same tactics when they are used to defeat "undesirable" legislation. One thing about congressional procedure is clear. With the possible exception of the filibuster—and it is no longer so potent a force as it once was—when a simple majority of either house *really* wants to take action, it can do so with dispatch. The same reasoning may be applied to other areas of suggested congressional reform. For example, the House Rules Committee remains a power because a majority in the House of Representatives is convinced that it serves a useful function; the same might be said for the seniority system in the selection of committee chairmen. The point is that Congress *is* responsive to public pressure; when the American public—or to be more accurate *publics*—generate enough support behind any specific procedural reform proposal, a congressional majority will be for it.

BIBLIOGRAPHIC NOTE

Robert Luce, a former representative, wrote a detailed, four-volume analysis of legislatures in America as well as abroad. See *Legislative Procedure* (Boston: Houghton Mifflin Company, 1922); and published by the same company, *Legislative Assemblies,* 1924, *Legislative Principles,* 1930, and *Legislative Problems,* 1935.

A number of books, designed as texts for courses on legislatures and legislation, contain valuable information on Congress and the state legislatures. For example, see Harvey Walker, *The Legislative Process: Lawmaking in the United States* (New York: The Ronald Press Company, 1948); and Joseph P. Chamberlain, *Legislative Processes: National and State* (New York: D. Appleton-Century Company, 1936).

Many excellent general works on Congress have been published. George B. Galloway, who was staff director of the joint committee which produced the Legislative Reorganization Act of 1946, drew upon a decade of experience on Capitol Hill in writing *The Legislative Process in Congress* (New York: Thomas

Y. Crowell Company, 1953). Bertram M. Gross in *The Legislative Struggle* (New York: McGraw-Hill Book Company, Inc., 1953), stresses the "realistic" approach in studying Congress, centering his discussion on group dynamics. James M. Burns decries the parochialism of Congressmen in *Congress on Trial* (New York: Harper & Brothers, 1949). Ernest S. Griffith, former head of the Legislative Reference Service, finds many areas in which to praise our national legislature in *Congress: Its Contemporary Role* (3rd ed., New York: New York University Press, 1961). Roland Young's *The American Congress* (New York: Harper & Brothers, 1958) seeks to develop a theoretical framework within which the functions of Congress may be better evaluated. James Burnham argues that Congress is no longer an effective "coordinate branch," having given so much ground to the executive branch. See his *Congress and the American Tradition* (Chicago: Henry Regnery Company, 1959). Dean Acheson's *A Citizen Looks at Congress* (New York: Harper & Brothers, 1957) is a brief but acute evaluation of the role of Congress in the American governmental process.

An historical account of the development of American representation is presented in Alfred de Grazia, *Public and Republic: Political Representation in America* (New York: Alfred A. Knopf, Inc., 1951).

On the problem of apportionment, see L. F. Schmeckebier, *Congressional Apportionment* (Washington, D. C.: Brookings Institution, 1941) and "Legislative Apportionment," *Laws and Contemporary Problems*, Spring, 1952.

An excellent guide on the organization of Congress is Floyd M. Riddick's *The United States Congress: Organization and Procedure* (Manassas, Virginia: National Capitol Publishers, Inc., 1949).

William S. White's *Citadel: The Story of the Senate* (New York: Harper & Brothers, 1957) emphasizes the importance of tradition in that chamber. The most thorough treatment of the Senate remains the two volume work of G. H. Haynes, *The Senate of the United States* (Boston: Houghton Mifflin Company, 1938).

On congressional elections, see H. C. Remick, *The Power of Congress in Respect to Membership and Elections* (Princeton, N. J.: Princeton University Press, 1929) and Cortez A. M. Ewing, *Congressional Elections, 1896-1944* (Norman, Okla.: University of Oklahoma Press, 1947).

Studies dealing with specific standing committees of Congress include E. E. Dennison, *The Senate Foreign Relations Committee* (Stanford, Calif.: Stanford University Press, 1942); A. C. F. Westphal, *The House Committee on Foreign Affairs* (New York: Columbia University Press, 1942); and Robert K. Carr, *The House Un-American Activities Committee* (Ithaca, N. Y.: Cornell University Press, 1952). An old but valuable general work on the committee system is that of L. G. McConachie, *Congressional Committees* (New York: Thomas Y. Crowell Company, 1898).

The role of the conference committee is examined in Ada C. McCown's *The Congressional Conference Committee* (New York: Columbia University Press, 1927) and Gilbert Y. Steiner's *The Congressional Conference Committee* (Urbana, Ill.: University of Illinois Press, 1951).

Several books consider the role of parties in the national legislative process. Woodrow Wilson's classic *Congressional Government* (Boston: Houghton Mifflin Company, 1885) has a great deal to say about the powers of the legislative committees; P. D. Hasbrouck's *Party Government in the House of Representatives* (New York: The Macmillan Co., 1927) is particularly good for the period covered. A recent book by David B. Truman, *The Congressional Party* (New York: John Wiley and Sons, Inc., 1959) covers the range of activities in the Eighty-first Congress, analyzing the voting behavior of senators and representatives in developing a theory of the legislative party. The pressures on members from party and constituencies are detailed in Julius Turner, *Party and Constituency* (Baltimore: The Johns Hopkins University Press, 1952).

A fascinating account of the origin and passage of the Employment Act of 1946 is presented in Stephen K. Bailey, *Congress Makes A Law* (New York: Columbia University Press, 1950). For a case history approach to many of the problems facing individual members of Congress, see Stephen K. Bailey and Howard D. Samuel, *Congress at Work* (New York: Henry Holt and Company, 1952). For a revealing study of the actualities of the national legislative process, see Roland Young's *Congressional Politics in the Second World War* (New York: Columbia University Press, 1956).

A collection of articles bringing together the institutional and behavioral approach to the study of both state and national legislative processes is found in John C. Wahlke and H. Eulau (eds.), *Legislative Behavior* (Glencoe, Ill.: The Free Press, 1959).

The most authoritative account of the filibuster is found in Franklin L. Burdette's *Filibustering in the Senate* (Princeton, N. J.: Princeton University Press, 1940).

Among the many works on the investigatory power and practice, see Telford Taylor, *Grand Inquest* (New York: Simon and Schuster, 1955); Alan Barth, *Government by Investigation* (New York: The Viking Press, 1955); and N. M. McGeary, *The Development of Congressional Investigatory Power* (New York: Columbia University Press, 1940).

Among the several books dealing with the need for improving congressional procedures, one may consult Robert Heller, *Strengthening the Congress* (Washington, D. C.: National Planning Association, 1945); James M. Burns, *Congress on Trial* (New York: Harper & Bros., Publishers, 1949); and Thomas K. Finletter, *Can Representative Government Do the Job?* (New York: Reynal & Hitchcock, 1945).

For an assessment of the operation of the Legislative Reorganization Act of 1946, see George B. Galloway, *Congressional Reorganization Revisited* (College Park, Md.: Bureau of Governmental Research, University of Maryland, 1956).

The title indicates clearly the nature of Gladys M. Kammerer's *The Staffing of Congress* (Lexington, Ky.: University of Kentucky Press, 1949).

Recent noteworthy publications are David N. Farnsworth, *The Senate Committee on Foreign Relations* (Urbana: University of Illinois Press, 1961); George B. Galloway, *History of The House of Representatives* (New York: Thomas Y. Crowell, 1961); Donald R. Matthews, *U. S. Senators and Their World* (Chapel Hill: University of North Carolina Press, 1960); Robert A. Wallace, *Congressional Control of Federal Spending* (Detroit: Wayne State University Press, 1960); Robert Bendiner, *Obstacle Course on Capitol Hill* (New York: McGraw-Hill, 1964); James A. Robinson, *The House Rules Committee* (New York: Bobbs-Merrill, 1963); and Robert L. Peabody and Nelson W. Polsby (eds.), *New Perspectives on the House of Representatives* (Chicago: Rand McNally, 1963).

Of particular interest for capturing the flavor of Congress are the letters of the late Congressman Clem Miller, written during his freshman year. See Clem Miller, *Member of the House: Letters of a Congressman,* edited by John W. Baker (New York: Scribner's, 1962).

A storehouse of information on the work of Congress is presented in a weekly publication by a private group in the *Congressional Quarterly,* Congressional Quarterly Incorporated, Washington, D. C. The *Congressional Quarterly Almanac* is an annual publication which brings together summary information on many aspects of the national legislative process.

17

Law and the Judicial Process

THROUGHOUT the course of history, law has generally been regarded as an indispensable condition of a moral and civilized life. There have been exceptions to this thesis, as in the writings of Plato where he considers the most desirable government one in which a "philosopher king" rules without relying upon laws but upon his wisdom and sense of justice. Aristotle rejected Plato's ideal, reasoning that the wisest ruler cannot dispense with the law for the impersonal quality of the law is beyond the reach of a personal sovereign.

Justice under the law is a phrase not uncommon in democratic and despotic communities. In both cases law is the instrument for obtaining justice, but what is justice? Generalizing from two well-known opposing views of the Greek philosophers, one might say that in a despotic society justice is conceived to be "the interest of the stronger;" under a constitutional regime it might be described as "giving to every man his due." In a democracy the intricate political process determines what every citizen is due.

In the United States the judicial process is the culmination of the search for justice. In interpreting and applying the law, and especially in judging the constitutionality of statutes, abstract concepts of justice held by individual judges may influence the decision. However, these would be the exceptional cases, and even then ideals of justice would be only one of a multitude of considerations affecting the disposition of the case. Furthermore, in our governmental system any judicial decision is subject to recall by the political process as illustrated by the passage of a statute or the adoption of a constitutional amendment.

THE NATURE OF LAW

Law in the broadest sense is observable regularity in the behavior of persons or things. The discussion in this chapter deals with law as it affects persons in society, not objects subject to certain laws of physics or mechanics.

322

Any society or group within a society depends upon certain rules of conduct to maintain order, to define relations between persons in their social and economic activities, and to settle conflicting claims. In primitive societies custom or folklaw served these purposes well. In more complex societies, composed of many different groups with diverse occupations and interests, the uniformity of custom breaks down. If individuals in these diverse groups are to maintain orderly relations with one another, there must be rules which are binding upon all. For thousands of years governments have been the established agencies for enforcing systems of rules throughout rather definite territory. The existence of governmental rules does not eradicate the labyrinth of customs, understandings, group regulations, and folkways present in all communities. These non-governmental prescriptions are essential to any community and continue to regulate innumerable aspects of everyday life.

The basic distinction between governmental and non-governmental regulations is the coercive nature and general applicability of the governmental type. For example, if one does not abide by the bylaws of a social club, he may be expelled from club membership; if one does not obey traffic regulations, he may pay a fine or go to jail.

There are many definitions of law, some of which are used in a very specialized sense, or within a particular sociological, historical, or psychological context. Law as used in the discussion which follows means those rules of human conduct which are enforceable by the authority of the state.

WRITTEN LAW

Laws in modern states may be either written or unwritten. Written laws assume many forms; but in any case, there will be in existence a document which may be referred to as the source of authority.

Constitutions. Constitutions are regarded as the basic, fundamental rules under which governments operate. They delineate the general structures, powers, and inter-relations of the legislative, executive, and judicial branches of the government. They usually contain a section enumerating certain political and civil rights of individuals in the state. If the state is federal in form, there will be statements concerning the distribution of powers between the central government and its constituent units.

Statutes. Statutes consist of laws enacted by legislatures. The United States Congress probably enacts more statutes than any legislative body in the world. Some of these are so significant that they rank close to the Constitution itself in circumscribing or expanding the power of the state. Others may affect the welfare of only one citizen. It has often been said that statutes reflect the views of the dominant group in a given society. This statement may be misleading if taken at face value insofar as it applies to the American scene. The pluralistic feature of American society, with many powerful political, economic, social, and religious groups, along with thousands of lesser organizations vying for power, promotes legislative compromise rather than legislative extremes.

Administrative rules and regulations. Administrative rules and regulations mount in importance as the functions of government expand, as the need for specialized knowledge increases, and as the pressure is felt on the legislative body to confine itself more and more to broad matters of policy. The main direction which administrative regulations shall take is set by statutes. On the other hand, there are important areas of policy left to administrative discretion and interpretation in which directives from the administrative body concerned are enforceable as law. Certain executive orders of the President may be based on powers conferred on the executive in the Constitution, and therefore not subject to legislative review at any stage.

UNWRITTEN LAW

Common law. Common law is said to be unwritten law but one needs to be careful of the connotation suggested. Common law is unwritten in the sense that there has been no definite, deliberate act of a legislative or administrative body which may be quoted as the source of authority. Common law is judge-made law; its rulings have evolved through centuries based on court decisions. It does not embrace the general body of customs of a community but is a body of very technical rules relating to particular legal questions.

Common law is one of the significant contributions of England to the modern world. It has been developing there for at least a thousand years and has been so highly regarded that it has been adopted as a legal basis by many other countries. The core of the system evolved during the first three centuries after the Norman Conquest when it became the established practice to send out royal justices to hear legal controversies throughout the kingdom. Without the benefit of any significant body of written law, these royal representatives rendered decisions on the basis of what appeared to be the customs of the community. As new and different cases arose, the judges looked to former judicial decisions for guidance. Gradually, there developed a body of judge-made law *common* to the whole realm.

The colonists brought the English common law with them to the new world, and it became the basic civil law in all the states but Louisiana, which because of its French antecedents chose the *Code Napoleon*.[1] Inasmuch as local conditions have varied from state to state and the common law is developing rather than static, there are state common law systems rather than a single body of common law in the United States. That is not to say that there are great differences from one state to another, but the de-

---

[1] Even in Louisiana common law has influenced the legal system.

tails have been influenced by local problems and psychology enough to have a good deal of variation.

This presents difficulties to the federal courts which must decide cases where the common law is the only guide. The rule has long been that a court would apply the common law of the state in which it operated, but diverse citizenship[2] has made that difficult at times, because there would be two common laws involved. For some years, the federal district courts used the accepted common law where there was no conflict between the common law of the states of the parties to the case. Where there was a contradiction, the federal judges used their own judgment in working out a compromise. The decisions in these cases were gradually building up a system which some predicted might become a system of federal common law. In the 1930's the Supreme Court of the United States put an end to this process when it held that a federal district court must apply the common law of the state in which the act complained of took place.

Equity. Equity proceedings are closely related to common law but are actually supplementary to the body of common law. Equity commences where common law or statutes end. It permits a judge to issue an order to prevent an injustice when there is no legal remedy under law which would suffice.

Equity and the common law developed side by side in Great Britain. In those cases in which common law could not be applied without injustice, it became the practice in England for those affected adversely to ask the king for assistance. Kings, not caring to be bothered personally with such petitions, charged their chancellors with receiving and deciding the pleas. Inasmuch as there was an increasingly large number of these cases, the ministers of the king drew up rules which might be uniformly applied. From this early beginning, there developed over several centuries an elaborate body of rules known as "equity."

In equity cases courts proceed by issuing writs, such as those of specific performance and injunction, the first of which orders a positive action while the latter prohibits a certain action. For example, suppose the superintendent of an orphanage had contracted the services of a popular singer to lead the children in the singing of Christmas carols on Christmas Eve. Further suppose that three days before the appointed time, the singer decided that he had rather appear on a national television show. Now the ordinary remedy at law would be for the superintendent to sue the singer for breach of contract *after* Christmas. But, obviously, the head of the orphanage wants the singer to appear, because the children have been looking forward to the occasion; he is not interested in any monetary damages under common law procedures. In such a circumstance, an equity decree might order the singer to fulfill his original contract. This would be an example of a spe-

---

[2] Where a resident of one state is suing a resident of another state.

cific performance (no pun intended) decree, and failure to heed the court order could be punished by holding the singer in contempt of court.

Even more common in equity proceedings is the prohibitory injunction. For example, even today injunctions are sometimes issued by courts to prevent mass picketing, where the employer has convinced the court that mass picketing will probably lead to violence and to the destruction of the employer's property. From these examples, one can understand why equity is referred to sometimes as "preventive justice."

Although in England separate courts originally administered equity rules, both common law and equity decrees are now applied by the same federal courts in the United States. Some of the individual states, however, maintain separate equity courts. Equity makes little or no use of juries, depends more upon written arguments and evidence than upon public sessions, and is preventive in its aim rather than punitive.

CIVIL AND CRIMINAL CASES

When seeking to understand the nature of law and the judicial process, one must keep in mind the distinction between civil and criminal cases.

Civil cases. Normally, a civil case is between private persons and/or private organizations although the government may be involved in civil suits. Unless the government happens to be a party to the action, it assumes a neutral role in civil cases. The government establishes the judicial framework within which parties may seek redress of personal injuries. There may be statutes defining procedures and possible remedies, although common law or equity will be relied upon in the absence of such statutes. If a parked car is demolished because of the reckless handling by the driver of another automobile, the government does not step in and make the driver pay for the damage inflicted. Perhaps the driver or his insurance company will pay without any question. On the other hand, the owner of the parked vehicle may have to institute a civil case in order to collect damages. If a court decides in favor of the owner of the parked automobile, the authority of government is on his side in case the damage claim is not paid.

Criminal cases. In a criminal case the state is always the plaintiff and the accused person the defendant. The government in criminal cases is acting as the protector of society. Violators of laws of the state will be tried and subject to the punishment which the government has previously determined to be appropriate to the type of criminal action involved. The distinction between civil and criminal cases is not, as some persons mistakenly believe, the difference in going to jail or paying a fine. As the result of a verdict in a criminal case, an indivdual may be required to go to jail and/or pay a fine. On the other hand, the loser in a civil case may find himself in jail if he refuses to abide by the court's decision.

In the example of the parked car, the negligent driver might find that the state has charged him with reckless driving. He has no choice here, as he did in his relation with the owner of the parked car. He must appear in court and answer the government's charge.

THE NATURE OF THE JUDICIAL PROCESS

It is probable that the judicial process is the oldest function of government. Organized society has always required a satisfactory means of settling conflicts which inevitably arise among individuals. In primitive or near primitive societies, the demand for or an understanding of legislative enactments was lacking, but the need for a regularized method of settling disputes was very real.

Even in modern states disputes are settled in many ways outside the purview of government. Our concern here, however, is with the process of adjudication in which a regularly constituted continuing tribunal seeks to settle a conflict by ascertaining the facts and applying rules (usually preexisting) to effect a correct settlement.

Broadly speaking, American courts in the adjudicative process perform three functions. They determine the facts of the case; they determine what the law is; they apply the law to the particular case at hand.

The late Jerome Frank, who was a distinguished federal court of appeals judge, described the trial process by means of the following simple formula: $R \times F = D$, in which R is the legal rule (law), F represents the facts of the case, and D stands for the court's decision.[3] Obviously, if R and F are known, then D may be almost mechanically obtained. Unfortunately, R and F are not easy to find, and this is a gross understatement. On the continent of Europe, where the civil law system is utilized (not to be confused with civil law in the Anglo-American sense), the R factor is easier to ascertain since the courts must rely upon codified statutes and not upon judicial precedents to find what the law is. On the other hand, in the jurisdictions using the common law system (often referred to as the Anglo-American system), the judges may seek the law in sources other than written codes, as for example in previous court opinions. Thus the determination of R assumes much more importance in an American court than in a French court.

Determination of the facts (F). In the United States the trial courts (courts of original jurisdiction) make the initial determination of facts. In a relatively few civil cases, there may be no question of facts since both parties may agree as to what they are. In these circumstances the court proceeds to find R and pronounce D. Normally, this is not the way of litigation, so the facts must be dealt with. Fact-finding embraces the complete panorama of the courtroom battle—the questions and summations of the opposing lawyers, the testimony of the parties to the case, the testimony

---

[3] *Courts on Trial* (Princeton, N. J.: Princeton University Press, 1949), p. 14.

of expert and not so expert witnesses, and the roles played by the presiding judge and jury. Ultimately, it remains for the judge, the jury, or these two combined to decide what the facts are.

Historically, the primary purpose of the jury was to determine facts. However, in the federal courts and in many states, the judge has a veto over the facts as determined by the jury if he is convinced that the weight of the evidence does not support the jury finding. It is to be emphasized that most judges are rather slow to exercise this power. Perhaps, in most cases where the judge might have found otherwise than the jury, the evidence has not been so overwhelming in one direction that reasonable men might not disagree on the facts of the case. Also, and this is important to the judge, his action in overruling the jury may become grounds for an appeal.

It is also possible in the federal courts and in some state courts for the judge to direct a verdict of acquittal, but again this power is used rather sparingly.

If the court does not direct an acquittal, the jury retires for its deliberation. Before retiring, the jurymen receive from the judge his instructions or "charge." The instructions will define the elements of the crime charged against the accused in the indictment. The judge's charge explains the legal rules involved. In addition to instructing the jury on the law, federal court practice as well as that in a number of states, permits the judge to comment upon the evidence.

There has been much criticism of the role of the jury in determining the facts within the framework of the legal rules in which it has been instructed by the court. It appears naive to expect the members of the jury, as laymen in the law, to grasp the subtleties and distinctions of the rules read to them by the judge. The "general verdict," which is the type of verdict returned by most juries, dodges this problem completely. Thus the general verdict returned might be, "We find for the defendant." In other words, the jury does not report the facts it found. There is no way for the court to determine what factors or what process of reasoning was instrumental in guiding the jury to its decision. There is no guarantee that the jury understood or paid any attention whatever to the rules of law as explained to them by the judge.

Federal rules and some state rules permit, at the discretion of the judge, a call for a "special" rather than a "general" verdict. Here the jury merely gives responses to questions of fact which have been formulated by the judge. However, the formulation of the questions may be difficult even for the judge, and it may raise the possibility of reversibility in a higher court. Actually, the special verdict is used less frequently than one might suppose.

In the American judicial system the trial courts overshadow appellate courts in determining the F factor. In theory the appellate courts leave undisturbed the finding of facts as decided by the trial court. However, where trial judges are given the power to set aside the verdict of the jury, the appellate court possesses like power. Therefore, a certain proportion of cases will be reversed or returned because the appellate court re-examines the findings of fact.

Determination of the law (R). American courts are often faced with a variety of alternatives in fixing the R factor in cases before them. These alternatives may not be clear-cut but rather of degrees, but at any rate, they lodge considerable discretionary powers with the judges. From a bewildering maze of constitutional, statutory, administrative, and common law principles, the court is expected to select "R."

Judge-made law, as distinguished from codified law, is intimately associated with the principle of *stare decisis* (to stand by the decision). In other words, the precedents established by previous decisions in like cases will be followed by the court. Thus is built up a body of case law which represents the accumulated experience of the judges settling disputes. *Stare decisis* understandably promotes the stability and certainty of the law. It also encourages courts to adopt conservative approaches in deciding what the law is. There often develops a time lag between rules based on *stare decisis* and the changing attitudes and demands of a dynamic society. If the doctrine were immutable, irreconcilable cleavages would develop between the courts and the people or other branches of government. But the doctrine is not absolute. If it were, there would be no feasible way for judge-made law to keep abreast of the times.

In the first place, there is nothing in the rule of *stare decisis* which requires the courts of one state to follow the precedents established by the courts of another state, or of comparable or inferior courts in the same state. Thus, in applying this reasoning to the federal courts, a judge in a federal district court would follow a principle laid down by the Supreme Court, but he would not be bound, although perhaps influenced, by what had been decided in another federal district court.

Courts also distinguish cases. In other words, a case which apparently is similar to previous cases, and in which the precedents of the earlier cases would seem to be binding, is decided in another way on the grounds that certain important facets of the immediate controversy distinguish it from the older ones.

The technique of distinguishing cases preserves the tradition and stability of the *stare decisis* doctrine but adds flexibility to its application. It is easy to see that when a number of cases have been distinguished in a particular area of law, a body of alternative precedents develops. A judge may refer to the older doctrine, but he may also cite as precedents to his ruling the cases which have been distinguished. One should not gain the idea that in the application of *stare decisis* there is a list of cases labeled "distinguished" and another list labeled "undistinguished." The fact is that all of the cases are inextricably mixed which increases the alternatives for the court.

Not infrequently, courts do not mince words but directly overrule precedents which have been followed for years. Even where a particular case or precedent is overruled by name, the change is probably not as abrupt as one might imagine. Usually there have been advance indications that a particular rule or case's force is ebbing. Take as an example the "separate but equal" doctrine which permitted states to maintain compulsory segregated public facilities for Negroes and whites in schools, transportation systems, parks, and other places. The doctrine originated in an 1896 case and was not overruled in so far as public schools were concerned until 1954.[4] But long before 1954, at least as far back as the 1930's, the Supreme Court had made significant inroads into the doctrine. Even in the field of education, the Court since 1939 had been more and more restrictive in permitting segregation at the graduate and professional school level. It was clearly only a matter of time before the original 1896 ruling would lose its meaning.

The courts themselves may or may not adhere to the principles of *stare decisis,* but the courts are not the only influences affecting the law as developed through *stare decisis.* If judge-made law is too far remote from the temper of the times, the legislature is apt to be heard from. Statutory law is superior to common law. Statutes may be passed which nullify the rulings of judges based on common law principles. It is not feasible for the legislature to pass an act purging from the law every "out-of-date" decision of the courts. The important point is that if certain common law principles no longer serve the needs of the community, the people through their representatives in the legislature can do something toward remedying the situation.

Construing the law. Just because a law is written does not guarantee that its meaning and applicability is crystal clear. As a matter of fact, many statutes are purposely couched in vague and uncertain terms as the price for securing support from various groups in the legislative process. Even with the best of intentions, a legislature cannot foresee all of the justiciable questions which will arise as a result of the law. Ultimately, the courts must determine the meaning of the law as contests evolve from its application. Interpreting or construing the law is another facet of the courts' search for the "R" factor. In performing this often highly discretionary function, the judges not only pore over the meaning of words and phrases, but delve behind the face of the statute into an even more misty area called "the intent" of the legislature. Frequently, members of the legislature are surprised to learn their true intent!

A few examples will serve to illustrate the powers of the court in interpreting statutes. The Sherman Antitrust Act, passed by Congress in 1890, made illegal every contract, combination, or conspiracy in restraint of trade or commerce in the interstate or foreign field. But what was meant by com-

---

4 See pp. 107-108.

bination or by restraint of trade? Was a striking labor union to be considered a combination in restraint of interstate commerce or did the act apply only to business organizations? Congress did not specifically answer these points so eventually the courts had to spell them out. Five years after the passage of the act, a case was before the Supreme Court involving the American Sugar Refining Company which controlled a near monopoly over the manufacture of refined sugar in the United States.[5] Was this monopoly illegal under the Sherman Act? The Court said no because it refused to include the manufacturing process within the meaning of commerce. Note that the Court could have decided in favor of the government and ruled that a monopoly or near monopoly in the manufacture of a product was illegal under the Sherman Act. Today, after the passage of many more congressional statutes and after many more Supreme Court opinions on the subject, manufacturing of goods for interstate commerce is considered subject to the regulatory power of Congress.

Consider the field of civil rights and the role of the Court in interpreting the application of statutes. One of the most perplexing tasks of the judiciary has been in connection with deciding whether certain individual actions have fallen within the purview of various statutes prohibiting conspiracy to violate the laws. One criterion used by the Supreme Court in making this determination was the now famous "clear and present danger test" first expressed by Justice Holmes. Justice Holmes wrote: "The question in every case is whether the words are used in such circumstances and are of such a nature as to create a clear and present danger that they will bring about the substantive evil that Congress has a right to prevent. It is a question of proximity and degree." [6] Note that in this particular case Congress had not specifically outlawed the conduct which was admitted to by the defendant. The Court had to decide whether the conduct fell under the general prohibitions established by statute.

The courts judge the intent of Congress in many other types of cases, sometimes with rather confusing results. On the latter point, consider the 1953 case of *Toolson* v. *New York Yankees, Inc.*,[7] in which the Supreme Court refused to apply the antitrust laws to major league baseball, stating "that Congress had no *intention* of including the business of baseball within the scope of the federal antitrust laws." But in 1955 professional boxing[8] received no such exemption, nor did professional football in 1957.[9] In the latter two cases, there were no congressional antitrust statutes which specifically mentioned boxing or football any more than there were antitrust statutes which covered baseball.

---

[5] *United States* v. *E. C. Knight Co.*, 156 U. S. 1 (1895).
[6] *Schenck* v. *United States*, 249 U. S. 47 (1919). See p. 102.
[7] 346 U. S. 356.
[8] *United States* v. *International Boxing Club of New York*, 348 U. S. 236.
[9] *Radovich* v. *National Football League*, 352 U. S. 445.

Title III of the Legislative Reorganization Act of 1946 is known as the Federal Regulation of Lobbying Act. Among other provisions, the act required registration and disclosure of money spent by persons who sought to accomplish: (1) the passage or defeat of any legislation by the Congress of the United States, and (2) to influence, directly or indirectly, the passage or defeat of any legislation by the Congress of the United States. The Supreme Court upheld the power of Congress to pass such an act but in doing so narrowly construed the intent of Congress as to the activities covered. The language of the law as indicated above would seem to be applicable to persons who used most any technique to influence the defeat or passage of a bill before Congress. Actually, the Court declared that the intent of Congress was to apply the law only to those who sought to influence legislation through direct communication with members of Congress.[10]

The examples cited are not intended as criticism of the Court. Their purpose is to illustrate another process which courts utilize in searching for "R."

Judicial review. The most unique development in American jurisprudence is the function of the courts known as judicial review. In essence this is the power of the courts to judge whether statutes or administrative rules and regulations, including executive orders, conform to the Constitution. State and federal courts exercise this power, but the emphasis of the following discussion is on the role of the Supreme Court in wielding the judicial veto over written laws.

Judicial review has been praised and condemned in the United States, but the average American probably associates the practice with the concept of democratic government. The fact is, however, that judicial review is certainly not essential to a democratic type of government. Great Britain, for example, is admittedly a democratic type state, but the courts are not empowered to rule acts of Parliament unconstitutional. In other words, the fact that the British Parliament passes a statute makes it constitutional. If the law is so far afield from customary practice as to raise a volume of protest, then the fact of its passage will become an issue in the next election. One argument against judicial review in our national governmental system is that it is anti-democratic, since it permits non-elected judges to overrule decisions of popularly elected officials. This argument loses much of its validity if one recognizes that in the American system the judicial veto can only be suspensive or temporary if the democratic power of the people determines otherwise through the constitutional amending process. As a matter of fact, the history of judicial review in the American system demonstrates how, in the long run, the Court itself accommodates the expression of continuing popular will, particularly as reflected in acts of Congress, by distinguishing or reversing its previous rulings. The doctrine of judicial

---

[10] *United States* v. *Harriss,* 347 U. S. 612 (1954). See also p. 318.

review is not provided for specifically in the Constitution. It is a power assumed by the courts which has become an accepted fundamental feature of our governmental system. The doctrine did not originate in the mind of Chief Justice John Marshall in the famous case of *Marbury* v. *Madison*.[11] Marshall's application of the doctrine had antecedents in the statements of English jurists, in the powers exercised by the English Privy Council in reviewing and annulling acts of the colonial legislatures, and in the opinions of state courts and lower federal courts declaring acts of state legislatures null and void. The *Marbury* v. *Madison* case is particularly noteworthy in the development of judicial review, because for the first time an act of Congress was declared unconstitutional, and because of Marshall's justification or reasoning as to the power of the Court to so declare. On the latter point, Marshall had this to say:

> It is emphatically the province and duty of the judicial department to say what the law is. Those who apply the rule to particular cases, must of necessity expound and interpret that rule. If two laws conflict with each other, the courts must decide on the operation of each.
>
> So if a law be in opposition to the Constitution; if both the law and the Constitution apply to a particular case, so that the court must either decide that case conformably to the law, disregarding the Constitution; or conformably to the Constitution, disregarding the law; the court must determine which of these conflicting rules governs the case. This is of the very essence of judicial duty.
>
> If, then, the courts are to regard the Constitution, and the Constitution is superior to any ordinary act of the legislature, the Constitution, and not such ordinary act, must govern the case to which they both apply.[12]

This is a very convincing argument, but it is more convincing to Americans than to many other peoples because it has been a part of our governmental doctrine for over one hundred and fifty years.

Justice Gibson, of the Pennsylvania Supreme Court, some twenty years later, presented a strong argument against the doctrine of judicial review. He wrote:

> The Constitution and the right of the legislature to pass the act, may be in collision. But is that a legitimate subject for judicial determination? If it be, the judiciary must be a peculiar organ, to revise the proceedings of the legislature, and to correct its mistakes; and in what part of the Constitution are we to look for this proud pre-eminence? Viewing the matter in the opposite direction, what would be thought of an act of assembly in which it should be declared that the Supreme Court had, in a particular case, put a wrong construction on the Constitution of the United States, and that the judgment should therefore be reversed? It would doubtless be thought a usurpation of judicial power. But it is by no means clear, that to declare a law void which has been enacted according to the forms prescribed in the Constitution, is not a usurpation

---

[11] See p. 39.

[12] *Marbury* v. *Madison,* 1 Cranch 137 (1803).

of legislative power. It is an act of sovereignty; and sovereignty and legislative power are said by Sir William Blackstone to be convertible terms.[13]

It is useless to speculate as to what the nature of our political system would have been without judicial review. It is as much a part of the larger constitutional system as the original Constitution itself.

The impact of the doctrine cannot be measured by a cataloguing of the eighty-odd laws of Congress which have been declared unconstitutional. Some of these decisions dealt with rather insignificant policies, while others involved fundamental issues which rocked American society. Undoubtedly, the power of judicial review has acted as a deterrent to the passage of numerous statutes. There is still another aspect of judicial review which has not been specifically alluded to, but which is perhaps the most important of all to the American federal system. This is the power of the courts, and more importantly of the Supreme Court, to declare laws of the state and local assemblies null and void as violative of the national Constitution. On this point Justice Holmes said: "I do not think the United States would come to an end if we lost our power to declare an act of Congress void. I do think the Union would be imperiled if we could not make that declaration as to the laws of the several states."

The power of the Supreme Court to declare state and local laws contrary to the federal Constitution is not only imperative in order to guarantee the supremacy of the Constitution, but also it is essential in assuring uniformity of interpretation of constitutional law. Without judicial review by the Supreme Court, laws of one state might be considered valid under the federal Constitution by its courts while the reverse might be true in the courts of other states.

Applying the law (D). Having determined the facts (F) and the rule of law (R) to be followed, the D factor should be easy to establish. The difficulty of predicting the decision in a particular law case normally arises out of a court's interpretation of F and/or R. Applying the law or giving a decision is not always uncomplicated, but that aspect of litigation is more mechanical than deciding the facts or fixing upon the correct rule.

Suppose a statute prohibits banks from charging more than eight per cent per annum for a certain type of loan. Mr. X negotiated a loan, but after making his first payment to the bank, claims that he is being charged more than eight per cent. Eventually, he takes the case to court. The facts of this case should not present any particular difficulty. Deciding what the law was would be more difficult. Among the factors to be considered would be: Did the legislature have the constitutional power to limit the amount banks could charge for loans? If so, did the law apply to the particular type of loan negotiated by Mr. X? Assuming the facts were as stated by Mr. X

---

[13] *Eakin* v. *Raub,* 12 S. & R. 330 (Pa. 1825).

and an affirmative answer was given by the court to the questions asked above, then the decision would be that Mr. X did not have to pay the overcharge levied by the bank. Note that the decision has to do with the particular question at hand. Mr. Y is not automatically protected by the decision in Mr. X's case. Indirectly, Mr. Y is aided because other banks and other courts may be aware of the decision in the first case. But if Mr. Y negotiates a loan and thinks that he is being overcharged, it is up to him to go into court to prove his point.

FACTORS INFLUENCING JUDGES' DECISIONS

The fact that alternatives are often available to the judges in the ascertainment of the rule of law to be followed, frequently evokes debate as to whether judges "make" or "find" the law. Saying that judges "find" the law is in keeping with the idea nurtured in the doctrine of natural law of the existence of immutable standards of justice, which may be discovered by the application of "right reason." Positivism, in which the law becomes the expression of the sovereign authority within a state, elevates the legislature's role in pronouncing law, but standards of values or ways of looking at problems in the natural law context long colored the American judicial process and to some extent still do.

Characterizing the work of judges as "finding" rather than "making" law also fits the customary view that the judiciary is the non-political branch of government. The life tenure of federal judges, their divorcement from active party politics, and their reticence if not absolute refusal, to comment upon burning political issues, all sharpen the image of the judge as a non-participant in policy-making. There is, however, a growing tendency to identify the role of the judges in the formulation of public policy; in other words, the emphasis of this trend would be on the "law making" aspects of the judicial process. Over a hundred years ago Alexis de Tocqueville wrote: "Scarcely any political question arises in the United States that is not resolved sooner or later into a judicial question." Jeremiah Smith, while a teacher in Harvard Law School following a career on the New Hampshire Supreme Court, is supposed to have remarked: "Do judges make law? 'Course they do. Made some myself."

But if one accepts the notion that judges make law, does it follow that a judge's decisions are a reflection of his personal subjective predilections? A categorical answer to this question is impossible, but comments concerning the issue raised appear appropriate.

In the first place it should be remembered that the members of the federal judiciary are political appointments. That is to say that in the vast majority of cases the persons selected as judges are members of the same political party as the President who names them to the bench. Theodore Roosevelt appointed 72 new federal judges of whom 69 were Republicans.

President Harding selected 43 Republicans and one Democrat as his choices to the federal courts. Franklin D. Roosevelt appointed 106 Democrats and two independents. With few exceptions, President Eisenhower has followed the established pattern of naming members of his party to the federal judiciary.

Particularly in the filling of federal district court judgeships, the President himself may not be aware of the background or the social or economic philosophy of the man he appoints. Traditionally, this is a patronage appointment upon the recommendation of local political leaders, especially United States senators if they are of the same party as the President. On the other hand, a President is more apt to examine carefully the credentials of those who are suggested for the Supreme Court. If the Chief Executive considers himself a "conservative," he is not likely to nominate an outstanding "liberal" to the highest tribunal.

Noting the past political associations of judges is certainly not a reliable method of predicting their decisions. The social and economic philosophies of our two major political parties are not so clearly distinguishable that partisan judges, even if they tried, could scarcely consistently hand down "Republican" or "Democratic" opinions. Moreover, there are many examples in the history of the Supreme Court where "conservative" lawyers became noted for their "liberal" decisions and vice-versa. Also decisions in most complicated controversies do not lend themselves to being tied into neat packages with either a "liberal" or a "conservative" tag attached.

The foregoing discussion is not meant to imply that past political associations might not influence a judge's decision, but so might innumerable other past associations and experiences. An individual, upon becoming a judge, cannot suffocate his past opinions, philosophies, or personality by donning judicial robes. He is, however, by reason of being a judge, cast in a new role, probably impelled by changed motives, and called upon to adhere to rather traditional methods of logic and procedure in disposing of cases. If he is on the Supreme Court, he is subject to the informal and formal (as in dissenting opinions) constraints of his brethren on the bench.

Mr. Justice Frankfurter once wrote:

> It is a cynical belief in too many quarters, though I believe this cult of cynicism is receding, that it is at best a self-delusion for judges to profess to pursue disinterestedness. It is asked with sophomoric brightness, does a man cease to be himself when he becomes a Justice? Does he change his character by putting on a gown? No, he does not change his character. He brings his whole experience, his training, his outlook, his social, intellectual, and moral environment with him when he takes a seat on the supreme bench. But a judge worth his salt is in the grip of his function. The intellectual habits of self-discipline which govern his mind are as much a part of him as the influence of the interest he may have represented at the bar, often much more so. For example, Mr. Justice Bradley was a "corporation lawyer" par excellence when he went on the Court. But

his decisions on matters affecting corporate control in the years following the Civil War were strikingly free of bias in favor of corporate power.[14]

Another quotation, this one from the pen of Mr. Justice Cardozo, deals with another aspect of the general problem, that is, the approach of the judges in deciding cases.

> The directive force of a principle may be exerted along the line of logical progression; this I will call the rule of analogy or the method of philosophy; along the line of historical development; this I will call the method of evolution; along the line of the customs of the community; this I will call the method of tradition; along the lines of justice, morals and social welfare, the *mores* of the day; and this I will call the method of sociology.[15]

Although it is extremely doubtful that most judges consciously apply the precise principles as explained by Justice Cardozo, it remains a classic summation of the workings of one judicial mind in its search for the correct rule of law.

Judicial self-restraint. Under the separation of powers principle and the check and balance system incorporated in the federal and state constitutions, the courts are subject to certain checks by both the executive and legislative departments of government. Federal judges are appointed by the President with the advice and consent of the Senate. Congress must establish all federal inferior courts, only the Supreme Court being provided for in the Constitution, and even the Supreme Court's appellate jurisdiction is fixed by law. Federal judges are subject to the impeachment process just as all civil officials of the executive branch are.

As a matter of practice, the scope of the judicial process is restricted to an important degree by action of the courts themselves. The various techniques of judicial self-restraint have not always been imposed with the object of directly limiting the judicial power, but often for the sake of a more orderly and consistent procedure, and perhaps as a defensive maneuver to avoid head-on conflict with the executive or legislative branches. Judicial self-restraint should not be conceived as a sign of weakness or lack of courage on the part of the courts. It gives flexibility to the judicial process and, viewed in historical perspective, strengthens the judicial system.

The courts do not seek cases. There must be an actual controversy brought before the court in a regularized manner. The Supreme Court set the precedent of refusing to give an advisory opinion on a constitutional question as early as 1793, when it refused to advise the President on certain questions arising as a result of the war in Europe. In 1934 Congress passed the Federal Declaratory Judgment Act authorizing the federal courts to

---

14 Quoted in Felix Frankfurter, *Of Law and Men* edited by Philip Elman (New York: Harcourt, Brace and Co., 1956).

15 *The Nature of the Judicial Process* (New Haven: Yale University Press, 1921), pp. 30-31.

declare rights and other legal relations in cases of actual controversies. But this is not an advisory opinion; it has the force and effect of a final decree.

Article III of the Constitution mentions that the federal court jurisdiction shall extend to certain types of cases or controversies. The case or controversy stipulation has been interpreted by the Supreme Court to require: actual adversary suits as distinguished from collusive suits; the threat to a claimed legal right must be real rather than speculative; the dispute must be of such a nature that the granting of relief to the injured party is within the remedial capacity of the court; the decision of the court must not be subject to direct review by the legislative or executive branches of the government.

Particularly important with respect to judicial review is the rule requiring one who challenges the constitutionality of a law to have standing to bring the suit into court. In practice this means that one who seeks to challenge a particular statute must have been personally injured or be threatened with injury by the application of the statute. Mr. X cannot challenge the constitutionality of a statute which may injure Mr. Y but does not affect Mr. X adversely.

A rule of long standing is that the Supreme Court presumes the constitutionality of statutes. "Saving the statute" sometimes forces the Court to construe it in such a manner that the legislature is no doubt puzzled by the interpretation.

The doctrine of "political questions" is an important self-restraining influence. Upon certain questions the Supreme Court will not essay opinions, because the issues have been decided or should be decided by the political branches of the government, i.e., Congress or the President. What constitutes a "political question" is only for the Court to say. Professor Corwin lists the more common classifications of political questions as:

(1) those which raise the issue of what proof is required that a statute has been enacted, or a constitutional amendment ratified;
(2) questions arising out of the conduct of foreign relations;
(3) the termination of wars, or rebellions; the questions of what constitutes a republican form of government, and the right of a state to protection against invasion or domestic violence; questions arising out of political actions of states in determining the mode of choosing presidential electors, state officials, and reapportionment of districts for congressional representation; and suits brought by states to test their political and so-called sovereign rights.[16]

The lawyer's role. The emphasis frequently given to the relation between lawyer and client somewhat obscures the role of the legal profession in shaping the direction of judicial decisions in broad matters of constitutional law. A lawyer's contemporary reputation may well be based on his won and lost record in litigation, but his more enduring contribution to

---

16 Edward S. Corwin (ed.), *The Constitution of the United States of America* (Washington, D. C.: United States Government Printing Office, 1953), p. 547. It should be noted that since the publication of Corwin's book the Courts *have* taken a more active interest in election and reapportionment matters.

"the law" may be the part he played in aiding the courts in enunciating the rule in important cases.

In the first place the judicial power is not self-invoked. Cases must reach the courts through established procedures and channels. Lawyers guide the litigation from inception to conclusion. Many of the historic cases decided by the Supreme Court bear the names of individuals who themselves were scarcely aware of the impact of their particular case on the course of constitutional law. Perhaps one or a number of interest groups had been advised by legal counsel that this specific case was an excellent one to test in the courts. The individual alone could never have financed extended litigation, but because of the nature and timing of his case, others are willing to provide the resources necessary for the controversy to be pushed as far as possible in the judicial hierarchy.

Government lawyers as well as private counsels use discretion in the cases which they wish to advance. Sometimes the strategies of opposing counsels become as involved and as complicated as the constitutional question eventually passed upon.

Should issues be presented narrowly or broadly? Should more than one case involving substantially similar questions be pushed in different jurisdictions? Should the case be brought in a state or federal court when either avenue is available? What is the surest way to achieve standing before the courts? What are the most effective arguments and precedents that should be used?

The impact of the counsel's argument or brief upon the judges' decision is not always easy to discern, but there have been some notable claims as to its effectiveness. It has often been remarked that huge segments of Daniel Webster's arguments became a part of John Marshall's opinions. Mr. Brandeis, before becoming a Justice of the Supreme Court, left his name to a form of brief (the Brandeis brief), in which he included non-legal materials such as committee reports, books, articles, expert testimony, and various other types of data, intended to impress the judges with the factual matter which the legislature used in determining the necessity for social and economic legislation. This is an excellent example of the counsel furnishing sociological, psychological, and historical data, in addition to legal precedents, which the Court may draw upon in reaching its decision.

SUMMARY

Law has been defined in this chapter as those rules of human conduct which are enforceable by the authority of the state. The context of American law is the result of legislative, executive, administrative, and judicial contributions within permissive or circumscribed areas outlined in written constitutions.

American law is written or unwritten. The former category includes constitutions, statutes, executive orders, and administrative rules and regulations; the latter classification encompasses common law principles and equity proceedings. The distinguishing feature of the unwritten law is that it is judge-made on the basis of precedents established in previous cases.

Another method of classifying law is whether it is civil or criminal. A civil case is normally between individuals and/or organizations. In criminal cases the government is always the prosecutor with the defendant being accused of a crime against the state.

The judicial process seeks to establish the facts, determine the governing rule of law, and then to apply the rule to the facts. American judges are allowed considerable latitude in fixing the applicable law. This fact is obvious where unwritten law is involved, not so obvious in cases dependent upon written law. However, in interpreting the precise meaning of the law or the intent of the lawmaker, the line between making and applying rules by the judges is blurred.

American courts, but particularly the Supreme Court of the United States, enjoy pre-eminence through the exercise of judicial review, i.e., the determination of whether laws are constitutional. In this performance, as well as its function of interpreting laws, the Supreme Court may have checked temporarily what appeared to have been community will, but withal the Court has a rather remarkable record in "keeping abreast of the times."

Since alternatives are often available to the courts in rendering decisions, much discussion has ensued concerning the factors impelling judges to decide cases as they do. That the past experience of a judge including social, economic, political, educational, and religious factors is bound to leave their imprint on his judicial attitudes cannot be denied. On the other hand, the environment of the court, its traditions, personnel, and established procedures become immediate influences upon a new appointee. To put it mildly, predicting judicial decisions on the basis of the background of the judge prior to his donning the robe is far from being an infallible method.

See *Bibliographic Note* at the end of Chapter 18.

The Federal Court System

T_{HE} existence of two distinct types of court systems functioning in the United States—one organized by the national government, the other under the control of the several states—understandably proves confusing to the casual observer. The confusion may be compounded because, although the state systems are not inferior to or appendages of the national system, certain types of cases may be initiated in either state or national courts. Other cases originally heard in the state courts may be carried on appeal into the national courts, provided they fall within the jurisdiction granted the national judiciary under Article III of the Constitution and are authorized by congressional statutes.

The organization of the federal court system is a model of simplicity. With the exception of the Supreme Court, which is provided for in the Constitution, the remaining structure is based on legislative enactments.

The general public is perhaps less informed concerning the role of the Supreme Court in the American constitutional system than on any other major political institution. This is not to imply that the present or past criticism of the Court would never have arisen if the public were fully informed as to its rule. As a matter of fact, the most severe critics of particular decisions are often among the best informed in political and legal circles as to the ways of the Supreme Court.

BASIS OF A SEPARATE FEDERAL COURT SYSTEM

The two separate systems of courts—the federal courts and the state courts—to some extent at least parallel each other. Under a unitary form of government, there would be no justification for two separate judicial organizations. Under the federal plan of government, however, either separate judicial hierarchies must be established or it must be decided which of the governments is to have the courts. If a national court structure were adopted, the states, although they are the bases of the federal form, would be ignored. On the other hand, if the central government had to depend entirely upon state governments to enforce its laws, there would be friction. The delegates, remembering the experience under the Articles of Confederation, recognized the danger and wisely decided to authorize the establishment of a complete system of federal courts alongside the state courts.

JURISDICTION OF THE FEDERAL JUDICIARY

Inasmuch as there had been no national courts under the government set up by the Articles of Confederation, the framers had to blaze a trail in outlining the jurisdiction of the federal courts. The disputes that had arisen under the confederation gave them some guidance; moreover, there were certain fields that were clearly national rather than local in character. On the other hand, other types of cases belonged to a borderland shared by the two governments. Since the Constitution attempted a specific enumeration of the powers of the central government, it was necessary to take great pains in listing the cases that might be brought to federal courts in order that only stipulated cases could be assumed by these tribunals. Two broad categories of cases were finally brought under federal jurisdiction: (1) those which involved certain subject matter, and (2) those which involved specified parties.

Subject matter. *Cases arising under the Constitution, federal laws, and treaties* compose the broadest jurisdictional grant given the federal courts. Cases arising under this clause are said to involve a *federal question*. Often one reads that an attempt will be made to appeal a particular case to the Supreme Court because a "federal question" is involved. Perhaps an individual believes that some state law has deprived him of a legal right which he thinks is guaranteed to him by the federal Constitution, laws, or treaties. If the highest state court decides against this contention, the fact that a federal question has been raised forms the basis of an appeal to the Supreme Court of the United States. For example, suppose an individual is arrested by local authorities, indicted by a grand jury the same day, tried the following day without benefit of legal counsel, found guilty and sentenced to die in the electric chair. This procedure would undoubtedly conflict with that part of the Fourteenth Amendment which says that no state shall deprive a person of life, liberty, or property without *due process of law*. The individual concerned would first exhaust his appellate rights within the state court system; but failing here, he might petition the Supreme Court to hear his case on the grounds that the state had violated his constitutional right to be tried according to due process of law.

One of the arguments in favor of a separate and complete system of federal courts emphasized the lack of uniformity that would attend interpretations of federal laws, treaties, and the Constitution itself if this function were entrusted to the state courts. Therefore, when it was decided to provide for a separate hierarchy of federal courts, it was only natural that the framers should specify certain fields based on subject matter that belonged under the jurisdiction of those courts. Anyone will appreciate the importance of having federal laws applied and interpreted by federal courts. Treaties are also the expression of the will of the national government. While some treaties are not likely to require interpretation and enforcement by the courts of law, it is not uncommon to encounter those that do. Courts of any grade, state or national, may interpret the federal Constitution; but there must be some method of checking inferior courts so that eventually there will be a single authoritative statement of what a clause of the Constitution means. Only the federal Supreme Court can act in this capacity.

Admiralty and maritime jurisdiction covers two general classes of cases. The first has to do with acts committed on the high seas and other navigable waters including torts,[1] injuries, and crimes, as well as prize and forfeiture cases. The second class relates to contracts and various other transactions concerned with shipping. The Supreme Court at first confined its admiralty jurisdiction to tidal waters, but eventually extended it to include all navigable waters in the United States.

Nature of parties. Cases may come to the federal courts in several categories based upon the nature of the parties involved.

The *United States* must be allowed to bring suits *as party plaintiff* in the federal courts, but the United States cannot be sued without its consent. Congress by law can and has given permission for the government to be sued under certain conditions. Since 1855 the government has been suable on contracts in the Court of Claims, but it was not until the passage of the Federal Tort Claims Act of 1946 that the United States could be sued in torts. Generally speaking, United States government corporations may sue and be sued in the same way as any other corporation.

An important function of the Supreme Court is rendering decisions in *disputes involving two or more states*. No other federal court is given jurisdiction in such disputes, and since no state is going to permit itself to be brought into the courts of a sister state, the Supreme Court is the only court passing upon state versus state conflicts. The Court has heard suits to restrain pollution of air or water within a state, to prohibit the diversion of water from an interstate stream, numerous boundary disputes, and many other types of conflicts. A state may not sue another state on behalf of an individual in order to evade the Eleventh Amendment, but under the doctrine of *parens patriae* may bring suit against another state to protect the welfare of its people as a whole.

The Eleventh Amendment prohibits *suits against states by citizens of another state* when the state is the *defendant* party. If the state is the party *plaintiff*, i.e., if the state institutes legal action against a citizen of another state, the federal courts may accept jurisdiction on appeal. Also

---

[1] A tort is defined as any wrongful act not involving a breach of contract for which a civil action will lie.

suits against state officials acting either in excess of their statutory authority
or in pursuance of an unconstitutional statute are suits against the state
officer in his individual capacity and are not considered prohibited by the
Eleventh Amendment.

Litigation in *controversies between citizens of different states* is generally
referred to as "diversity of citizenship" cases. Mr. A in Alabama may wish
to bring suit against Mr. B in Tennessee. He may institute proceedings in
the Tennessee court system against Mr. B. However, since Mr. A lives in
a different state he has the alternative of bringing his suit in the federal
court system. Corporations may also have access to the federal courts under
the diversity of citizenship clause. In the case of corporations, the Supreme
Court has, for convenience sake, adopted the rule that all the stockholders
of a corporation are citizens of the state of incorporation. Recently, Congress by statute has also deemed a corporation a citizen for diversity jurisdictional purposes of the state in which its principal business is located.
Until 1958 the amount in controversy in diversity of citizenship cases had
to be at least $3,000, but in that year the amount was raised to $10,000.

*In controversies between a state, or citizens of a state, and a foreign
government or its citizens or subjects,* there are certain limitations which
are not apparent. Under international law foreign states cannot be sued
in American courts by individuals or American states without the consent
of the foreign state. Neither may foreign states sue American states in the
federal courts. However, an American state can sue foreign citizens or a
foreign state may sue American citizens, and suits between American citizens
and foreigners are possible in the federal courts.

The Supreme Court has jurisdiction over *cases affecting ambassadors,
other public ministers, and consuls.* The Court has interpreted this clause
as applying to diplomatic personnel accredited by foreign states to the
United States, not to American diplomatic personnel. Representatives of
foreign powers in the United States are exempt from jurisdiction of
American courts under international law, so the principal effect of this
category is in permitting foreign diplomats to sue private individuals in
the federal courts. Consuls, unless protected by specific treaty rights, do not
enjoy the same immunity as do ambassadors and public ministers.

The federal court system has jurisdiction in *controversies between
citizens of the same state claiming lands under grants of different states,*
but this provision has become obsolete with the settlement of boundary
disputes between states and the passing of land grants by the states.

Exclusive and concurrent jurisdiction. It is not to be supposed that the
cases placed under the jurisdiction of the federal courts by the Constitution
must invariably be brought to those courts. Although the Judiciary Act
of 1789 provided for a complete set of lower federal courts, state courts were
permitted to exercise jurisdiction concurrently with the federal courts in
many types of cases. The specific areas of concurrent jurisdiction have

varied from time-to-time according to congressional statutes, but the general principle of concurrency of jurisdiction is very much a part of the American court system. The most important area of concurrent jurisdiction is in connection with diversity of citizenship cases.

On the other hand, Congress has designated many categories of cases as falling exclusively to the federal courts. Among these are crimes against the United States, admiralty and maritime, bankruptcy, patent, and copyright cases, and also cases involving ambassadors, ministers, and consuls.

Original, removal, and appellate jurisdiction. Cases may be brought to a federal court in three different ways: (1) they may be started there, (2) they may be removed from a state court, and (3) they may be appealed from a state court. The majority of federal court cases come under the first category. Indeed in the federal district courts, which handle the vast majority of cases, there are only the first two possibilities for these courts have no appellate jurisdiction. It is not uncommon to have a defendant in a case of diverse citizenship ask to have a case removed to a federal court, because he is not satisfied that the state court of the plaintiff will give a fair trial; but most of the cases found on the docket of a federal district court were brought there without recourse to any other court. When cases · are removed from a state court, the removal must take place before the decision and ordinarily will occur early in the proceedings. Appeals may be taken under certain circumstances from state tribunals, although never from a lower state court to a lower federal court. Only after a state supreme court[2] has decided a point relating to the federal Constitution, a federal law, or a treaty in a manner which is questionable or has denied a right claimed under the federal Constitution can an appeal be lodged with the Supreme Court of the United States.

Civil cases. The civil cases which are entered on the dockets of federal courts are of three general varieties: (1) cases in law, (2) cases in equity, and (3) admiralty cases.

When persons or corporations of diverse citizenship resort to the federal courts, they usually have *cases in law*. At least $10,000 must be at stake and much larger sums are ordinarily involved—even hundreds of thousands or millions of dollars. Civil wrongs, designated "torts," may provoke the dispute; contracts entered into expressly or made by implication may be the basis. These cases all seek monetary damages and are based to a considerable extent upon the common law.

The nature of *cases in equity* has already been discussed. The federal courts get a variety of types of conflicts under equity jurisdiction but by far the majority relate to bankruptcy proceedings. Congress has enacted elabo-

---

2 If state procedure does not permit certain cases to be heard by the state supreme court, then an appeal may be lodged with the Supreme Court of the United States following a decision by the highest court in the state which is permitted to hear the case.

AMOUNTS OBLIGATED FOR
UNITED STATES COURTS and the ADMINISTRATIVE OFFICE*

FISCAL YEAR 1964

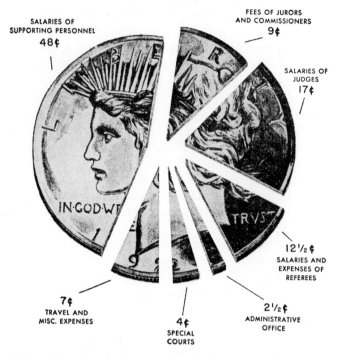

SALARIES OF
SUPPORTING PERSONNEL
48¢

FEES OF JURORS
AND COMMISSIONERS
9¢

SALARIES OF
JUDGES
17¢

12½¢
SALARIES AND
EXPENSES OF
REFEREES

7¢
TRAVEL AND
MISC. EXPENSES

4¢
SPECIAL
COURTS

2½¢
ADMINISTRATIVE
OFFICE

*Exclusive of the Supreme Court

Administrative Office of the United States Court

HOW FEDERAL FUNDS FOR THE ADMINISTRATION OF JUSTICE ARE SPENT

rate laws relating to bankruptcy and has charged the federal district courts with administering them. Therefore, when an individual or corporation, either on its own initiative or upon the petition of creditors, is thrown into bankruptcy, a federal district court not only must authorize the bankruptcy to begin with but also must supervise the subsequent steps. In individual cases it is common to liquidate the assets and pay off the creditors, in so far as assets will permit under the eye of the court. However, great corporations, particularly railroads and holding companies, often cannot be dealt with so simply. The federal district court appoints receivers who take over the property and attempt to manage it efficiently enough to restore a condition of solvency. In 1959 over 100,000 bankruptcy proceedings were commenced in the federal courts.

The third type of civil case over which federal district courts take jurisdiction—*admiralty cases*—is far less commonplace than the other two. Federal district courts located in the hinterland of the United States are

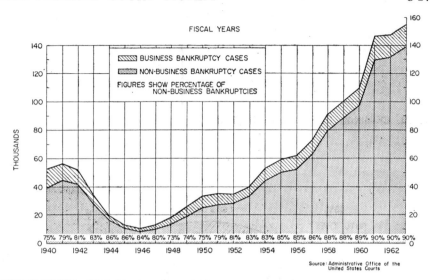

FISCAL YEARS

BUSINESS BANKRUPTCY CASES

NON-BUSINESS BANKRUPTCY CASES

FIGURES SHOW PERCENTAGE OF NON-BUSINESS BANKRUPTCIES

THOUSANDS

Source: Administrative Office of the United States Courts

DISTRICT COURTS—BUSINESS AND NON-BUSINESS BANKRUPTCY CASES COMMENCED ANNUALLY, 1940 TO 1963

seldom called upon to decide cases in which two ships have collided, a shipper maintains that freight has been ruined, or a master and a crew find it impossible to agree. However, in the district courts located in important shipping centers—New York, Boston, New Orleans, Los Angeles, San Francisco, Houston, and Seattle—these cases are constantly arising. Special admiralty and maritime rules have grown up over a period of more than two thousand years. They may be modified by Congress or interpreted by the courts, but they are more international than national in character.

Criminal cases. Most cases in the criminal field are occupied by the states; hence homicides, burglaries, and other serious offenses ordinarily are tried by state courts. However, Congress has the authority to enact statutes which deal with the protection of federal property, the postal system, and interstate commerce. Other statutes relate to the safeguarding of the currency and banking systems, treason, offenses against international law, and offenses committed on the high seas, in the District of Columbia, on federal property, or in a territory. Some of these categories, treason for example, involve few offenses and hence do not bring many cases each year.

The transportation across state lines of stolen automobiles, women for immoral purposes, loot obtained from a bank, and kidnapped persons now carry heavy penalties. Counterfeiting of metal or paper money is also one of the more serious offenses against the federal government. The robbing of national or federal reserve banks either by employees or outside criminals is a federal offense. Smugglers, bootleggers of untaxed liquor, dope peddlers, violators of the pure food laws, and related offenders account for many of the cases which fill the dockets of federal courts. There are the many cases involving the misuse of the mails or violations of the immigration statutes.

The court *procedure in criminal cases* is regulated both by provisions of the Constitution and by rules which the Supreme Court has drafted as authorized by Congress in order to establish uniform practice in all federal district courts. A trial by a jury made up of one's peers must be accorded in

TOTAL CRIMINAL DEFENDANTS 34,845

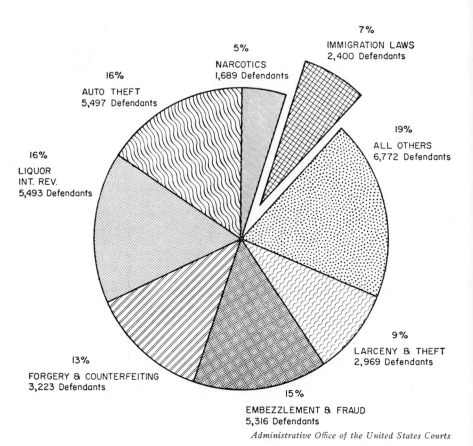

Administrative Office of the United States Courts

DISTRICT COURTS—DEFENDANTS IN CRIMINAL PROCEEDINGS COMMENCED DURING FISCAL YEAR 1963

serious cases, although accused persons may waive the jury trial in favor of a trial by the presiding judge. Counsel must be furnished to those who are unable to hire their own; opportunity must be given to consult counsel; and public assistance must be forthcoming for the summoning of witnesses. The accused must be confronted with witnesses against him, cannot be compelled to take the witness stand, and must be given a speedy and fair trial. Reasonable bail must be permitted except for the most serious crimes, while cruel and unusual punishment is banned.

Enforcing federal court decisions. Normally, court decisions are accepted by the parties concerned as a matter of course. Actually, the courts themselves, with only a few federal marshals at their disposal, are not in a strong position to guarantee that their decisions are carried out. Therefore, the judicial branch looks to Congress and the President to take appropriate actions to see that court decisions are obeyed. A striking example of executive action to enforce a court decision occurred in 1957 when President Eisenhower dispatched troops to Little Rock, Arkansas, to assure compliance with a court decree ordering integration of certain Negro pupils into a formerly all-white public school.

The Judiciary Act of 1789 conferred upon federal courts the power to punish by fine or imprisonment at the discretion of the courts all contempts of authority in any case or hearing before them. Contempts may be either civil or criminal. If a party to a civil suit refuses to abide by a decree, he may be found in civil contempt of court. Obedience to the court order usually removes the penalty which the court has set in a civil contempt action. Criminal contempt is more serious in that it is intended as a punishment to vindicate the authority of the court. Subsequent action on the part of the individual concerned does not necessarily purge the original punishment.

Summary contempt means that the judge exercises the contempt power without any procedural protections afforded the offender. Summary contempt is now authorized only when the judge sees or hears the conduct constituting grounds for contempt. Other contempts can be effected only after notice with representation by counsel, if desired, and trial by jury if provided for by an act of Congress.

Constitutional and legislative courts. A traditional two-fold classification of federal courts divides them into constitutional courts and legislative courts; although this classification breaks down in so far as the District of Columbia courts are concerned.

Generally, it is said that constitutional courts exercise their jurisdiction based on the cases and controversies provision mentioned in Article III of the Constitution. On the other hand, legislative courts are given specific, specialized jurisdiction under the statutes which create them. Another practical distinction between the two types of courts relates to the tenure of their judges. Judges on constitutional courts hold their office "during good behavior" and can be removed from office only by impeachment and conviction. Legislative court judges are appointed for a definite term of years.

Specialized and legislative courts. In addition to the tribunals which constitute what the man in the street considers the federal court system, it has been necessary from time-to-time to set up other courts for special purposes. These are usually known as "legislative" courts, because they have resulted entirely from congressional action and may be regulated by Congress without regard to any restrictions on matters of tenure and salary reductions that apply to the judges in "constitutional" courts. The establishment of these courts is interpreted to be within the power of Congress because of authority implied from the taxing, patent, appropriation, commerce, and other powers specifically granted by the Constitution.

Perhaps the most important of these special courts is the *Court of Claims* which was created by Congress as early as 1855 although the Court of Claims was made a constitutional court by congressional action in 1953. The United States as a sovereign power cannot be sued without its consent; yet, as a matter of fairness, some provisions must be made for considering the claims of those who allege that they have suffered injury as a result of governmental action. The Court of Claims has jurisdiction to render judgment upon any claim against the United States founded upon the Constitution, upon any act of Congress, upon any regulation of an executive department, or upon any express or implied contract with the United States. Since the Federal Tort Claims Act of 1946, the Court is also empowered to review on appeal judgments of the federal district courts.

The complete authority given Congress over the *District of Columbia* by the Constitution has been utilized to establish there *a federal district court and a court of appeals.* For a long while these courts were considered as legislative courts since Congress assigned them certain types of cases not based on the jurisdiction accorded to federal courts in Article III. Over a period of years and after a number of cases, the Supreme Court has come to its present rule regarding the nature of the District of Columbia courts. It is that "as regards their organization and the tenure and compensation of their judges, they are constitutional courts controlled by Article III, but as regards their jurisdiction and powers they are both legislative and constitutional courts, and so can be vested with nonjudicial powers while sharing the judicial power of the United States." [3]

A *United States Customs Court* has been set up to pass on controversies arising out of duties to be paid by importers.[4] A *Court of Customs and Patent Appeals* hears cases which are carried to it from the Customs Court and from the Commissioner of Patents. In 1950 a United States *Court of Military Appeals* came into being, authorized to review courts-martial. The *Tax Court* of the United States, which reviews tax decisions of the Internal Revenue Service, is not really a court, but a part of the executive branch of the government.

---

[3] C. Herman Pritchett, *The American Constitution* (New York: McGraw-Hill Book Company, Inc., 1959), p. 113.

[4] Made a constitutional court by congressional statute in 1956 (70 Stat. 532).

THE HIERARCHY OF CONSTITUTIONAL COURTS

Three levels of courts—district, court of appeals, and Supreme Court—constitute the heart of the federal court system. Of these, only the Supreme Court is provided for in the Constitution. The pertinent section of Article III relating to this point reads: "The judicial power of the United States shall be vested in one Supreme Court, and in such inferior courts as the Congress may from time to time ordain and establish." [5]

Federal district courts. The bottom rung of the constitutional court system is composed of ninety-one district courts throughout the states, territories, and the District of Columbia. Every state has at least a single district; the more populous states have more than one, with New York and Texas each having four. These courts have single-judge benches except when injunctions are sought to prevent the enforcement of federal or state laws alleged to be unconstitutional. In such a case, a panel of three judges may be used, and an appeal as a matter of right goes directly to the Supreme Court.

In those districts in which large cities are situated, the amount of work which comes to the district courts is large. Consequently, it becomes necessary to assign more than one judge and to have several sessions of the court going on simultaneously. In the Southern District of New York, covering New York City, as many as eighteen judges have been assigned to hear cases. The district judges numbered 287 as of 1962, but this number is far from excessive considering the volume of work confronting the district courts.

The great bulk of cases which come under federal jurisdiction are dealt with by federal district courts which have original jurisdiction only. Between 1940 and 1955, the number of civil cases alone increased by 55 per cent. In addition, there is an increasing number of cases due to the enlargement of federal criminal law. It is no wonder that backlogs develop on the dockets of many district courts. In the Southern District of New York it takes an average of almost four years to dispose of a civil case.

As the trial courts in the federal judicial system, the district courts employ grand juries and trial juries. All final decisions of the district courts are subject to review by the courts of appeal, but only a relatively small percentage of the cases is actually carried to the appeal courts.

Courts of Appeal. Immediately above the district courts in the judicial hierarchy stand the courts of appeal. The courts of appeal were created by Congress in 1891 and were known until 1948 as circuit courts of appeal. These courts were organized primarily to relieve the Supreme Court of some of its appellate work. They have only appellate jurisdiction.

---

[5] Art. III, sec. 1.

A FEDERAL GRAND JURY AT SEATTLE WITH WITNESSES, ATTORNEYS, AND COURT ASSISTANTS

The United States and its territories are divided into ten areas over each of which is placed a court of appeals. Some of these areas—for example, the Rocky Mountain states—cover tremendous territories, stretching for hundreds and even thousands of miles; while others, such as New England, are compact in size. There is an unnumbered circuit in the District of Columbia with a Court of Appeals which handles a large volume of cases arising from the activities of various federal administrative agencies. These courts are multiple-bench courts, having from three to nine judges assigned to them, depending upon the volume of business. At least two judges must sit in a single case though three is the normal number.

The courts of appeal hear appeals from the district courts and from quasi-judicial administrative agencies under certain conditions. They are courts of final appeal for most cases, since only a few of the cases heard there are eventually carried on to the Supreme Court.

The Supreme Court. Although the Supreme Court is the only federal court specifically mentioned in the Constitution, its structure is not outlined in any detail in that document. One of the first statutes enacted by the new Congress in 1789 was the monumental Judiciary Act which set up a number of federal courts and defined their powers. This act specified that the Supreme Court should consist of a Chief Justice and five associate justices, who in addition to their duties in connection with the highest tribunal in the court system, should participate in the work of the lower federal courts by going on circuit through the various parts of the country.

THE UNITED STATES COURT SYSTEM

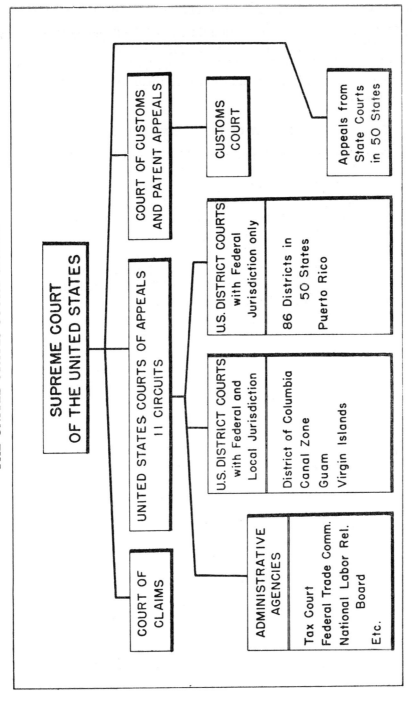

In 1801 Congress saw fit to decrease the size of the Supreme Court to five; in 1807 it was enlarged to seven; in 1837 provision was made for nine seats; in 1863 its size reached a high-water mark of ten; in 1866 there was a drastic cut to seven justices; and since 1869 there have been nine members of the Court.

HISTORY OF THE SUPREME COURT

Very shortly after Congress provided for the organization of the Supreme Court, President Washington in 1789 appointed John Jay and five associate justices to the bench. During the early years there was little for them to do. Only a modicum of prestige was attached to the Court during this period, and justices were known to surrender their seats to accept positions in state courts. In 1795 John Jay resigned to undertake diplomatic service for the United States. He was followed as Chief Justice by John Rutledge who, borne down by ill-health, served only during 1795-1796 and was never confirmed by the Senate. Then Oliver Ellsworth assumed the post, presiding over the Court until 1800.

The appointment of Marshall. Shortly before the Federalists reluctantly turned the government over to their Republican opponents, President Adams, in 1801, appointed John Marshall as Chief Justice. At the time, this action on the part of a retiring Federalist seemed unlikely to add to the general strength of the Supreme Court, for it was regarded by President Jefferson and his associates as little short of an insult. The size of the Court was reduced to five and impeachment proceedings were started against Justice Samuel Chase. Had these succeeded, they doubtlessly would have been extended to include other members of the Court. Finally, President Jefferson and his fellow officers let it be generally known that they held the Supreme Court almost (if not absolutely) unworthy of respect. For a period of something like a year, the Court did not meet at all, and then it convened only to face the open hostility of the executive and legislative branches of the government.

Contributions of Marshall. John Marshall had served in the Revolutionary Army, in the Government of Virginia, and as the Secretary of State under President Adams. He had achieved a more than local reputation as a shrewd attorney, but there was comparatively little in his record to indicate that he would rescue the Supreme Court from its position of obscurity and even jeopardy and transform it into an agency of commanding effectiveness and influence. Yet that is what he managed to achieve during the almost thirty-five years of his chief justiceship. He is particularly important because he laid down the broad outlines of a constitutional system which has continued with modifications to this day. Despite his attachment to his native state of Virginia, the basic premise of Marshall's credo was that the national government must be given adequate authority. He wanted a strong government hampered neither by the petty jealousies of the states nor by a strict, literal interpretation of the Constitution.

The persuasive logic of Marshall in setting forth the arguments for judicial review have already been mentioned.[6] He frequently took the occasion in judicial opinions to refute the argument that the Constitution was drawn by the states. "The government of the Union, then . . . ," wrote Marshall, "is, emphatically, and truly, a government of the people. In form and substance it emanates from them. Its powers are granted by them, and are to be exercised directly on them, and for their benefit." [7] Marshall's contribution to the concept of implied powers is probably more significant even than his justification for judicial review.[8] Chief Justice Marshall's statements on the power of Congress to regulate commerce were cited again and again by other Supreme Court justices in the late 1930's and early 1940's in upholding governmental programs grounded on the commerce power which were being contested in the highest federal Court. "What is this power?" Marshall had asked. "It is the power to regulate; that is, to prescribe the rule by which commerce is to be governed. This power, like all others vested in Congress, is complete in itself, may be exercisd to its utmost extent, and acknowledges no limitations, other than are prescribed in the Constitution." [9] If any one sentence, from the thousands of words left to posterity in the opinions of the renowned Marshall, epitomizes his judicial attitude it must be this one: ". . . we must never forget that it is a *constitution* we are expounding." [10]

Roger B. Taney. Marshall was succeeded as Chief Justice by Roger B. Taney, who served during the years 1836-1864. Perhaps largely because of his association with the Dred Scott case, it was long the accepted belief that, despite his lengthy service, he did little in the way of adding to the brilliant achievements of his predecessor. However, the careful investigations more recently completed by reputable scholars indicate that Justice Taney has been a most underrated and misunderstood Chief Justice.[11] His contribution to American constitutional development followed along the general lines which Marshall had laid down but carried those principles forward quite materially. By the end of his career on the Court, the doctrine of judicial supremacy had been pretty firmly established as an integral part of the constitutional system of the United States.

The years 1864-1910. During the years from the Civil War to the present century, the role of the Supreme Court was important, but the developments were in general less spectacular than they had been during the earlier period

---

6 See p. 333.

7 *McCulloch* v. *Maryland,* 4 Wheaton 316 (1819).

8 See p. 270.

9 *Gibbons* v. *Ogden,* 9 Wheaton 1 (1824).

10 *McCulloch* v. *Maryland,* 4 Wheaton 316 (1819).

11 See Carl B. Swisher, *Roger B. Taney* (New York: The Macmillan Company, 1935).

of Marshall and Taney. Salmon P. Chase, Morrison R. Waite, and Melville W. Fuller presided over the Court during the period 1864-1910 with reasonable competence, but few would place them in the Marshall-Taney class. One of the most important developments in this period was the flowering of the concept of substantive due process of law. Before this era due process of law had been considered almost solely in its procedural sense, i.e., as applying to the *methods* whereby the national and state governments restricted life, liberty, or property unreasonably. By the turn of the century, the Supreme Court was applying the concept of substantive due process, i.e., judging whether the *content* or *subject matter* of a law was arbitrary or unreasonable. During its early application substantive due process proved to be a conservative doctrine protecting the interests of property owners against many forms of state legislative regulation.

Developments during 1910-1936. It is perhaps fair to state that the Supreme Court reached its zenith during the second and third decades of the twentieth century. Its role as guardian of the Constitution was not seriously challenged. It was during this period that Chief Justice Taft put through the important reforms that made it possible for the Supreme Court to dispose of its business with a minimum of delay. These were the years characterized by such distinguished justices as Oliver W. Holmes, Louis D. Brandeis, Benjamin N. Cardozo, William H. Taft, and Charles E. Hughes. The substantive due process of law concept was enlarged to cover certain areas of personal liberty. For example, some laws unduly restricting freedom of speech or press were declared unconstitutional as violating due process of law in its substantive meaning.

When Congress under the leadership of President Franklin Roosevelt sought to have the national government cope with the problems of agricultural adjustment, industrial recovery, and business regulation incident to the depression, the Supreme Court declared their efforts to be in conflict with the Constitution and hence null and void. Although the Court had its defenders, the President was caustic in his denunciation of the rulings and criticism aimed at the Court from many quarters became intense and bitter. It was argued that the Supreme Court was dominated by the vested interests, that it prevented the government from meeting the crying needs of the 1930's, that its justices were "nine old men" who were senile, infirm, and generally incapable of performing their duties.

The Reorganization Bill of 1937. Early in 1937, after he had been overwhelmingly re-elected, President Franklin D. Roosevelt without warning sent to Congress a bill which would have brought about important changes in the Supreme Court as well as in the entire federal judiciary. The most controversial section of the bill involved the addition of a new judgeship for every judge who did not retire within six months after reaching the age of seventy years; in the case of the Supreme Court a maximum size of fifteen justices was set. The Senate Judiciary Committee finally voted to report adversely on the bill by a margin of ten to eight.

The Compromise Act. In August, 1937 a bill was signed by the President, which, although not enlarging the personnel of the federal courts, expedited appeals on constitutional questions. Under this act the Department of Justice may appear in the lower courts to defend congressional statutes, the district and appeal-court hearings of cases involving important constitutional questions may be combined, and injunctions intended to hold up the application of federal laws were safeguarded.

Events from 1937 to 1953. With respect to his "court packing" proposal, it has been said that President Roosevelt lost the battle but won the war. Even while the controversy raged over the court reorganization plan, the Supreme Court, without a change in personnel, upheld the constitutionality of key New Deal statutes including the Wagner Labor Relations Act and the Social Security measure. Wags labeled this change of direction by the Court as "the switch in time, that saved nine." One leading authority on American constitutional law has written: "It is probable . . . that the change in interpretation was due largely to coercion in the form of the movement to reorganize the Supreme Court, backed by popular sentiment which strongly favored the substantive program of the New Deal even if it did not include enthusiasm for direct interference with the Supreme Court." [12] Moreover, by 1941 only two members of the "old Court" remained on the bench. No national statutes dealing with broad economic policies have been declared unconstitutional since 1937. The comprehensive powers of the national government within the federal structure particularly with reference to the commerce, taxing, spending, foreign relations, and so-called "war" powers appeared to be almost unchallengeable in the courts. More and more the thorniest and most emotion-packed issues related to matters of personal liberty—to the procedural and substantive aspects of due process of law and to the meaning of equal protection of the law.

The Warren Court—1953 to the present. Upon the death of Chief Justice Vinson, President Eisenhower named Earl Warren, former Governor of California, to the chief justiceship. By 1959 only four appointees of the Roosevelt-Truman era remained on the Supreme Court. The most crucial issues confronting the Court, however, remained the same—those dealing with individual rights. In the first five years following the Warren appointment, the Court handed down a series of opinions which appeared to buttress concepts of individual liberty at the expense of existing governmental laws and procedures. In a historic decision in 1954, a unanimous court struck down the "separate but equal" doctrine which permitted segre-

---

[12] Carl B. Swisher, *American Constitutional Development* (2nd ed., New York: Houghton Mifflin Company, 1954), p. 954.

gation by races in public schools.[13] A barrage of criticism from the Southern States ensued, a constant theme advanced being that the Court was guided by psychological and sociological hypotheses rather than by legal principles. Succeeding decisions struck sensitive areas of individual and group opinion throughout the United States including elected officials at both national and state levels, bar associations, veterans and patriotic organizations, and law enforcement societies to name but a few.

Examples of specific cases in which the decisions resulted in heaped criticism of the Court were:

(1) The *Jencks* decision holding that F.B.I. and other government agency reports must be made available to defendants in criminal trials if the persons who made the report were called as witnesses;[14]

(2) The *Watkins* decision which appeared to curtail somewhat the power of congressional committees in making investigations and requiring witnesses to testify;[15]

(3) The *Yates* decision which made it more difficult for the government to convict for the crime of conspiring to overthrow established governments;[16]

(4) The *Sweezy* decision which limited the individual states' power to require witnesses to testify in state authorized investigations;[17]

(5) The decisions in *Backer* v. *Carr* and subsequent cases in which the Supreme Court reversed its earlier position and entered into the problem of districting in state legislative seats and the national House of Representatives;[18]

(6) The *Nelson* decision in which it was held that a state could not convict a person for the crime of sedition against the United States;[19]

(7) The *Mallory* decision declaring inadmissible in the trial a voluntary confession made between arrest and a delayed arraignment before a federal commissioner.[20]

Criticism of the Supreme Court in the late 1950's equalled if it did not surpass, in bitterness and volume the strictures of the mid-1930's. The Court was not without its defenders, but the source of leadership in attacking and defending was rather different from the battle of a generation earlier. Members of Congress, rather than the President, initiated proposals to "curb" the Court. While the supreme tribunal was the "darling" of many "conservatives" in the 1930's, conservative groups in the 1950's generally spoke of the Court in less endearing terms.

The Constitution plainly empowers Congress to fix the appellate jurisdiction of the Supreme Court. A bill was introduced in the Senate in 1958 (the Butler-Jenner Bill) which would have limited the Court's appellate

---

13 *Brown* v. *Board of Education,* 347 U. S. 483 (1954).
14 353 U. S. 657 (1957).
15 354 U. S. 178 (1957).
16 354 U. S. 298 (1957).
17 354 U. S. 234 (1957).
18 369 U. S. 186 (1962).
19 350 U. S. 497 (1956).
20 352 U. S. 449 (1957).

jurisdiction in many specific types of civil rights cases. Among these were controversies arising from investigations by congressional committees, and cases involving statutes regulating subversive activities in the states. The bill was defeated by the rather narrow margin of 49 to 41. An obvious defect in the Butler-Jenner type bill is the confusion which would result under our existing court structure if the Supreme Court were not able to give a constitutional interpretation which would be uniformly applied by the lower courts throughout the land. Lacking the finality of Supreme Court review, it would be possible for the eleven courts of appeal to differ widely in their interpretation, thus creating a situation where a law might be constitutional in one section of the country but unconstitutional in another. Other bills have been introduced in Congress, generally less drastic than the Butler-Jenner Bill, aimed at either modifying a particular decision of the Supreme Court or of limiting its present jurisdiction.

Meanwhile, some observers believe that the Court, in a few recent decisions, showed signs of retreating from certain of its advanced positions. The conviction of a recalcitrant witness before the House Un-American Activities Committee was upheld, and the Court's 5-4 decision went far to give constitutional sanction to the Committee's operation. The Court also explicitly approved the right of New Hampshire to enact laws prescribing state sedition. If the outcome of past Court crises is repeated, the Supreme Court will continue to reassess the balance between individual rights and the authority of government even though in doing so, it must weather an occasional storm.

Present composition. The Supreme Court is now made up of a Chief Justice and eight associate justices who are appointed by the President with the consent of the Senate for an indefinite term. There are no constitutional or statutory qualifications for Supreme Court justices. All of the justices have been lawyers, but of the 92 men who served on the Court from 1789 through 1958, 38 had had no previous bench experience. Included in the group without prior judicial experience are such people as Marshall, Story, Taney, Hughes, Brandeis, and Warren.

Retirement on full pay is permitted at seventy if a justice has served ten years. The Chief Justice is paid an annual salary of $40,000 and the associate justices $500 less. The Chief Justice is in a position to exert a considerable degree of leadership chiefly from his role as presiding officer at the frequent conferences of the justices and from his power in assigning the writing of opinions.

Sessions. The Supreme Court ordinarily begins its formal sessions in October and adjourns for the summer in May or June, thus setting aside a period of some four months when it does not convene at all. Even during the fall and winter months it takes periodic recesses for the preparation of opinions. As of 1962 ten o'clock rather than noon was fixed for a sitting to begin. The lengthy summer period, the numerous recesses during the remainder of the year, and the late hour of opening the Court, lead some people to conclude that the Supreme Court has very little to do or at least carries on its work with a maximum of leisure. In reality it is not possible to measure the industry of the Court in terms of formal sessions, for much, probably most, of the work is carried on outside of these formal sittings. During the time when it is not recessing, the Supreme Court meets in formal session Monday through Thursday of every week. Monday is known as "decision day" because the Court ordinarily announces its decisions and reads its orders on that day.

A formal sitting. Promptly at 10:00 A.M. the justices of the Court in their somber black silk gowns, led by the Chief Justice, file into the courtroom through their private entrance and take their places at the bench which dominates the chamber. The justices sit in strict order according to seniority, with the Chief Justice in the center and eight associate justices arranged four on either side—the two newest members occupying the seats at the extreme right and left. After preliminaries have been disposed of, including the admittance of new members to the bar of the Court, the Court proceeds promptly to the consideration of the cases which it has agreed to hear. In contrast to the rank and file of courts in the United States, this Court does not permit long drawn-out arguments from attorneys, the introduction of irrelevant material, or eloquent oratory. Counsel have been informed beforehand as to how much time will be permitted for argument, and they are expected to confine themselves strictly to that period. Inasmuch as most of the material is included in the printed record which has to be submitted to the Court before the case can come up for hearing, the oral arguments are less comprehensive and detailed than they might be. Attorneys take the opportunity of summarizing the points which they consider significant while the justices use this as the occasion for putting questions to the attorneys in regard to aspects of the case which are not entirely clear. The Court halts the proceedings for a half-hour lunch recess and a mid-afternoon adjournment for the day is the rule.

Conference. Friday is conference day, at which time the justices meet behind closed doors for the purpose of discussing the cases argued earlier in the week. The Chief Justice, as presiding officer, presents each case along with his views as to how it should be decided. Then each associate justice in order of seniority is given the opportunity to discuss the case. When the time comes to vote, the order of seniority is reversed, with the Chief Justice voting last. If the Chief Justice is in the majority, he assigns either himself or one of the associate justices to write the majority opinion. If the Chief Justice is of the minority, the senior associate justice of the majority assumes the assignment role. After the majority opinion has been written, it is circulated to all members of the Court for comment and criticism. Actually, the original opinion may be rather much changed as a result of these comments; if serious differences develop, an additional conference may be held on the case. To a degree which many persons ignore, the final majority opinion represents much more than the individual conclusions of the writer. Concurring opinions are frequently written by a member of the majority who accepts the specific decision but does not agree with the reasoning of the majority opinion. The senior member of the minority may assign a justice to write a dissenting opinion, or any member of the minority is free to write his own dissent.

Decisions, opinions, and reports. The Supreme Court arrives at decisions by a simple majority vote with a minimum of six justices required as a quorum.[21] This requirement leads to the five-to-four splits of the Court which have occasioned not a little concern to some observers, who point out that not much confidence can be put in a decision when the judges themselves are so evenly divided. Prior to 1934 there had been comparatively few instances of such a split in the Court—only about a dozen altogether which involved important points of law or an average of less than one every ten years. Then in a brief period in the 1930's, the Court handed down a number of important decisions by five-to-four votes. Sharply divided decisions have been rather frequent during the past twenty years, while dissents in general have reached an all-time high.

The Supreme Court not only decides cases but it prepares opinions which explain why it has decided exactly as it has. Over a period of years these opinions may be regarded as of greater importance than the decisions themselves. Decisions have to do with questions which are often of immediate rather than long-range import, whereas the opinions may be so closely reasoned and cover such ground that they will be referred to again and again by the Court in future cases. Moreover, the opinions frequently include *obiter dicta* or supplementary statements on legal points which may be made the basis for subsequent action by the Court. While not written for popular consumption and couched in words that may seem technical to those not familiar with legal terms, the opinions of Chief Justice Marshall, Justice Holmes, Justice Cardozo, and certain other judges are striking examples of fine writing, impressive clarity, and logical organization. Eventually, the opinions are published in volumes known as *United States Reports* which appear at the rate of two or three each year from the Government Printing Office and are to be found on file in various libraries.[22]

Original jurisdiction. In two types of cases the Supreme Court receives original jurisdiction from the Constitution and hence may consider cases

---

21 On those occasions when there is a tie because of the lack of a full bench, the case will be reargued, or if there is no re-hearing, the decision of the lower court will be upheld.

22 Before 1882 the reports of the Supreme Court were published by the clerks of the Court and bore their names; thus there were four volumes of Dallas, nine of Cranch, twelve of Wheaton, sixteen of Peters, twenty-four of Howard, and so forth.

which have not been appealed from lower federal or from state supreme courts. One of these categories involves cases which have to do with the ministers and ambassadors of foreign countries in the United States. Inasmuch as these officials are not subject to the jurisdiction of American courts under international law and diplomatic usage, few cases of this sort ever arise. The second type case is that to which a state is a party. Even though the Supreme Court has original jurisdiction in the instances mentioned above, Congress by law may grant inferior courts *concurrent* jurisdiction. For example, Congress has given the Supreme Court exclusive jurisdiction in controversies between two or more states, but permits lower federal court concurrent jurisdiction with the Supreme Court in other cases in which a state is a party.

Appellate jurisdiction. The great majority of cases that come to the Supreme Court are appealed to that Court from the highest state courts or from lower federal courts. Congress has permitted the Court wide discretion in exercising its appellate jurisdiction. Mandatory right of appeal occurs in only two types of cases, these being: (1) where the validity of a treaty or statute of the United States is questioned and a state court has held it invalid; (2) where the validity of a state law has been questioned on the ground that it contravenes the Constitution, treaties, or laws of the United States and a state court sustains its validity. In a number of other instances, the right of appeal exists, but the Supreme Court may or may not review the cases. Examples in this latter category would include appeals from federal courts of appeal in which a federal law or treaty is held unconstitutional, or where a state law or constitutional provision is declared invalid as contravening a federal law, treaty, or the Constitution. Also in this category are included appeals from federal district courts where a federal criminal statute is found unconstitutional, where a judgment has been rendered in a suit to enforce the antitrust laws, the Interstate Commerce Act, and certain provisions of the Federal Communications Act, where a three-judge court grants or denies an injunction in suits to restrain enforcement of state or federal statutes, or orders of certain federal agencies.

Usually, 70 to 80 per cent of Supreme Court cases are not heard as a right of appeal, but from the granting of *writs of certiorari* by the Court. Parties desiring the Court to review their cases petition for writs of certiorari which, if granted, direct the lower court to send up the record in the case to the Supreme Court. The reviewing of these petitions by the justices represents a considerable workload as it is not unusual for them to consider fourteen or fifteen thousand a year. If as many as four justices agree that the case merits consideration, the petition is granted. It is to be emphasized that the granting of the petition is completely at the discretion of the Court. Generally, less than 20 per cent of the petitions for writs of certiorari are granted.

JUDICIAL ADMINISTRATION

The Judiciary Act of 1789, with only slight modification, has stood the test of time in so far as it created a sound judicial structure. However, it was not until 1922 that the Congress passed legislation bearing on the managerial aspects of handling the business of the courts. In that year, thanks largely to the work of Chief Justice Taft, Congress established the Judicial Conference of Senior Circuit Judges.

The Judicial Conference of the United States. Originally, the Judicial Conference was composed only of the Chief Justice and the chief judges of the circuit courts of appeal. Subsequent legislation enlarged the conference to include the Chief Judge of the Court of Claims and a district judge from each of the circuits to be selected by the judges of the circuit. The Judicial Conference of the United States is charged, among other things, with making comprehensive surveys of the conditions of business in the courts; with preparing plans for assignment of judges to or from circuits or districts when necessary; and with submitting suggestions to the various courts in the interest of uniformity and expedition of business.[23] It has been said that the Conference is in effect a board of directors for the judicial branch of the government with the Chief Justice as its chairman. Also there is a judicial conference for each of the circuits consisting of all the district and courts of appeal judges.

Judicial councils. Each circuit has a judicial council consisting of the judges of the courts of appeal. The creating statute empowers the council to make all necessary orders for the effective and expeditious administration of the business of the courts within its circuit. The district judges are charged with promptly carrying into effect all orders of the councils. In order to expedite court business the councils have power to take such steps, including particularly the assignment of judges, as may be necessary to dispose properly of the volume of cases in each district.

Administrative Office of the United States Courts. For the judicial conferences and councils to function effectively, Congress recognized that there must be some additional agency to keep the records, dig out the facts, and provide the information generally required by policy-makers. So it was that the Administrative Office of the United States Courts was established in 1939. It prepares the budget for the courts; supervises with the judges, the clerks, probation officers, referees in bankruptcy, reporters, and other officers; collects and compiles statistics on the volume of business in the courts; audits and disburses through the United States' marshals money for the

---

23 See "Administration in the Judicial Branch of the Federal Government," an address before the State Bar of Arizona by Warren Olney, III, Director, Administrative Office of the United States Courts, April 11, 1958.

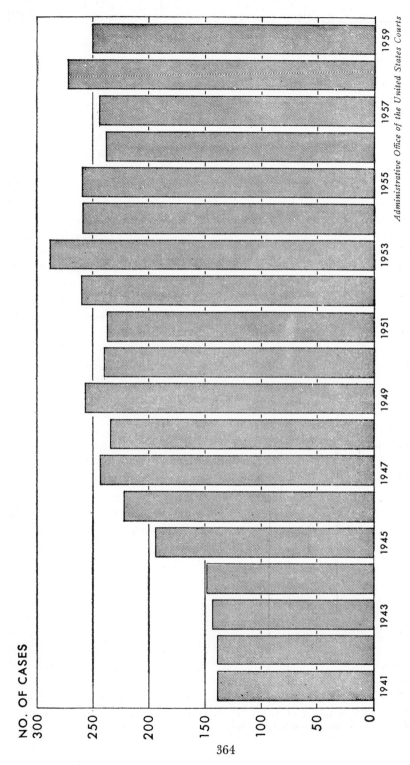

NO. OF CASES

EIGHTY-SIX DISTRICT COURTS HAVING ONLY FEDERAL JURISDICTION—CIVIL CASES PENDING PER
JUDGESHIP, AT THE END OF FISCAL YEARS 1941-1959

Administrative Office of the United States Courts

operation of the courts; and performs such other functions as may be as, signed by the Judicial Conference of the United States.

Congestion of district court dockets. The increasing emphasis on judicial administration in recent years as evidenced by congressional statutes is due in large part to the mounting congestion of the court dockets, particularly of the district courts. In January of 1961 there were pending on the dockets of the United States district courts more than 71,000 cases. If the disposition of cases continued at its present rate, it would take the district courts sixteen years to dispose of the present backlog. From 1941 to 1957 the backlog increased 126 per cent. In over 38 per cent of all civil cases in the federal courts, there is a delay from one to five years between the date of issue and the time of trial. During 1941 each district judge terminated an average of 169 cases; by 1958 the average had risen to 236 civil cases— an increase in productivity of 40 per cent. However, for the same period the average pending workload per judge rose more than 82 per cent.

Improvements have come in some areas. The backlog of criminal cases in the federal courts reached a high of 10,487 cases in June of 1954. By June, 1961 that backlog was cut to 7,691 cases which was the second smallest total since 1889.

Changes in the diversity of citizenship jurisdiction of the federal courts by a 1958 law reduced by 9,000 the number of new civil actions as compared to the previous year. Legislation passed in 1962 which increased the number of federal judges. But as Chief Justice Warren pointed out: "Our strength [the judiciary] must come mainly from improved methods of adjusting caseloads, dispatching litigation for hearing, resolving complicated issues, eliminating non-essential ones, increasing court room efficiency, and through dispatch in decision making and appeal. *These things Congress cannot do for us. We must do them ourselves.*" [24]

THE DEPARTMENT OF JUSTICE

The Department of Justice is, of course, not a court but an administrative department. However, many of its functions relate to the various federal courts and to the administration of federal justice. From the very beginning the United States had an Attorney General, but it was not until 1870 that a Department of Justice was finally provided to handle the increasingly large volume of governmental legal business.

General organization. The Department of Justice has at its head the Attorney General who was a member of the President's cabinet even before the establishment of the department. In addition to generally overseeing the Department of Justice, the Attorney General gives advice and opinions to the President and to the heads of the executive departments of the gov-

---

[24] From an address by Chief Justice Warren at the Assembly Session, 81st Annual Meeting, American Bar Association, Los Angeles, California, August 25, 1958.

DEPARTMENT OF JUSTICE

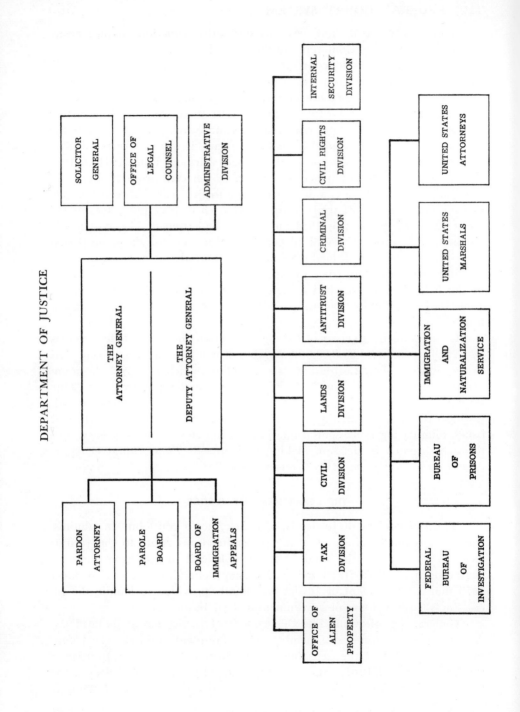

ernment upon request. In cases of extreme importance, he may represent the government before the United States Supreme Court. The Deputy Attorney General is chief liaison officer of the Department for Congress and other governmental departments and agencies.

Subdivisions. Attached to the Department of Justice is the office of the Solicitor General, which is primarily concerned with representing the federal government in the Supreme Court. Although this office may permit the legal counsel of the several departments to prepare and present cases involving their departments before the Supreme Court, frequently the actual presentation is handled by the Solicitor General himself or by his assistants.

A Civil Rights Division, headed by an Assistant Attorney General, was established in 1957. It has the responsibility for the enforcement of all federal statutes affecting civil rights—election laws, corrupt practice acts, and the laws relating to illegal deprivation of rights of citizens, including the rights of citizens to vote in federal elections.

Of outstanding significance is the criminal division which has responsibility for and supervision over the enforcement of federal criminal laws generally, including laws relating to criminal practice and procedure. A very importannt function of this division flows from the fact that it has general direction and supervision over the United States attorneys in the federal district court areas with respect to the conduct of criminal prosecutions involving violations of federal criminal statutes.

The much publicized Federal Bureau of Investigation is within the Justice Department. In general the F.B.I. has charge of the investigation of all violations of federal laws except those assigned to other agencies.

In 1964 an Office of Criminal Justice was established to insure both the fairness and effectiveness of federal law enforcement.

SUMMARY

Article III of the Constitution lists the types of cases and controversies to which the judicial power of the United States shall extend. Outside of the specific types of cases in which the Supreme Court is granted original jurisdiction, the judicial power in its original and appellate exercise is entirely dependent upon Congress for structuring the inferior courts and delineating their jurisdiction. Congress may not enlarge or diminish the original jurisdiction of the Supreme Court, but it may grant lower courts concurrent jurisdiction even in this regard. More important, Congress may by statute completely control the appellate jurisdiction of the highest court. In practice Congress permits the Supreme Court almost, but not quite, complete freedom to choose the cases which it wishes to hear on appeal. The few exceptions, where appeal is a matter of right, involve cases in which the constitutionality of national or state statutes is in doubt. These mandatory appeals emphasize the desirability of having one final interpretation on controversial statutes by the Supreme Court which is binding on all of the lower courts.

Recently, rather bitter criticism by individuals and groups of specific decisions announced by the Supreme Court, many of which involved individual rights, has led to proposals to "curb" the powers of the Court. History is replete with similar examples. In the past the genius of the Court has eventually reflected the persistent, dominant opinions of the times. Whether this is so by virtue of its leadership in creating a favorable climate of opinion, or by its accommodation to public pressure, or a combination of both factors, is impossible to determine.

In addition to its almost absolute power over Article III or "constitutional" courts, Congress may establish specialized "legislative" courts for almost any purpose associated with its enumerated or implied powers.

Probably the gravest problem facing the federal court system today is the tremendous backlog of civil cases building up on the district court dockets. Delay in litigation breeds a distrustful attitude toward the judicial process. Improving judicial administration has become a necessity and will assuredly command more attention from Congress, the bench, and the bar.

BIBLIOGRAPHIC NOTE

Two small volumes by Benjamin N. Cardozo, written before he came to the Supreme Court, are still considered classics on the nature of law and the judicial process although one wonders if certain sections would have remained the same if written after his Supreme Court experience. See *The Nature of the Judicial Process* (New Haven, Conn.: Yale University Press, 1921) and *The Growth of the Law* (same publisher, 1924). For an outstanding contribution on the development and nature of the Anglo-American system of law, consult Roscoe Pound's *The Spirit of the Common Law* (Boston: Marshall Jones Company, 1931). For a brief comparison of the Anglo-American system of law with the civil law system of the European continent, see Henry J. Abraham, *Courts & Judges* (New York: Oxford University Press, 1959). For a penetrating and often critical analysis of the American legal system, attention is directed to Jerome Frank's *Law and the Modern Mind* (New York: Brentano's Inc., 1930) and *Courts on Trial* (Princeton, N. J.: Princeton University Press, 1950). James W. Hurst in *Law and the Condition of Freedom in the Nineteenth Century United States* (Madison, Wis.: University of Wisconsin Press, 1956) analyzes the interaction of government and law with private economic groups. William Hurst's *The Growth of American Law* (Boston: Little, Brown and Company, 1950) discusses the varied roles of lawyers, judges, legislators, and bureaucrats in the development of law. For a more specific analysis on the role of lawyers, see Benjamin P. Twiss, *Lawyers and the Constitution: How Laissez-Faire Came to the Supreme Court* (Princeton, N. J.: Princeton University Press, 1942).

A number of books deal with the organization and procedure of American courts. Lewis Mayers, *The American Legal System* (New York: Harper & Brothers, Publishers, 1955) is one of the most comprehensive works of this type. Other important publications dealing with various aspects of this subject include: Charles W. Bunn, *A Brief Survey of the Jurisdiction and Practice of the Courts of the United States* (St. Paul, Minn.: West Publishing Company, 1939); Robert

J. Harris, *The Judicial Power of the United States* (Baton Rouge, La.: Louisiana University Press, 1940); Henry M. Hart and Herbert Wechsler, *The Federal Courts and the Federal System* (Brooklyn: The Foundation Press, 1953); Lester R. Orfield, *Criminal Procedure From Arrest to Appeal* (New York: New York University Press, 1947).

The best general history of the Supreme Court is Charles Warren's *The Supreme Court in United States History* (2 vols., Boston: Little, Brown and Company, 1922). Briefer and more critical is Louis B. Boudin's *Government by Judiciary* (New York: William Godwin, Inc., 1932). Alpheus T. Mason's *The Supreme Court from Taft to Warren* (Baton Rouge, La.: Louisiana University Press, 1958) discusses specific aspects of the Court's work in the past quarter of a century. For two excellent chronological studies on the Supreme Court's interpretation of the Constitution, see Carl B. Swisher, *American Constitutional Development* (2nd ed., New York: Houghton Mifflin Company, 1954) and Alfred H. Kelly and Winifred A. Harbison, *The American Constitution: Its Origin and Development* (rev. ed., New York: W. W. Norton & Company, Inc., 1955). For a topical analysis of the Court's interpretation of the Constitution, see C. Herman Pritchett, *The American Constitution* (New York: McGraw-Hill Book Company, Inc., 1959). For a detailed analysis of the Court's role before the Civil War, consult Charles G. Haines, *The Role of the Supreme Court in American Government and Politics, 1789-1835* (Berkeley, Calif.: University of California Press, 1944) and Charles G. Haines and F. H. Sherwood, *The Role of the Supreme Court in American Government and Politics, 1835-1864* (same publisher, 1957).

Judicial review is the subject of several works including Charles G. Haines, *The American Doctrine of Judicial Supremacy* (Berkeley, Calif.: University of California Press, 1932); Robert K. Carr, *The Supreme Court and Judicial Review* (New York: Rinehart & Company, 1942); Edmond Cahn, *Supreme Court and Supreme Law* (Bloomington, Ind.: Indiana University Press, 1954); and Charles P. Curtis, Jr., *Lions Under the Throne* (Boston: Houghton Mifflin Company, 1947).

The intermixture of law and politics in the judicial process is stressed in Victor G. Rosenblum, *Law as a Political Instrument* (New York: Random House, 1955) and Jack W. Peltason, *Federal Courts in the Political Process* (same publisher, 1955).

An ambitious attempt at analyzing the behavior of Supreme Court justices is found in Glendon A. Schubert's *Constitutional Politics* (New York: Holt, Rinehart, and Winston, Inc., 1960). C. Herman Pritchett's *The Roosevelt Court: A Study in Judicial Politics and Values, 1937-1947* (New York: The Macmillan Company, 1948) analyzes justices' behavior using mathematical equations. Fred V. Cahill in his *Judicial Legislation* (New York: The Ronald Press, 1952) gives a critique of the judicial function with particular reference to the standards of judgment and the scope of judicial discretion.

A number of Supreme Court Justices have written about the Court's work, but none of these studies pretend to give any "inside" information which is not available elsewhere. Robert H. Jackson's *The Supreme Court in the American System of Government* (Cambridge, Mass.: Harvard University Press, 1955) discusses the Supreme Court as a unit of government, as a law court, and as a political institution; Charles E. Hughes' *The Supreme Court of the United States* (New York: Columbia University Press, 1928) was written between the author's two periods of service on the Court; Felix Frankfurter's *Law and Politics* (New York: Harcourt, Brace and Co., 1939), and *Of Law and Men* (same publisher, 1956) consist of papers and addresses of Justice Frankfurter from 1913 to 1956 and contain some extremely interesting comments concerning justices known by the author.

A number of books have been written in recent years analyzing the role of the

Supreme Court in our system of government. Among these are: A. T. Mason and W. M. Beaney, *The Supreme Court In a Free Society* (Englewood Cliffs, N. J.: Prentice-Hall, Inc., 1959); Bernard Schwartz, *The Supreme Court: Constitutional Revolution in Retrospect* (New York: The Ronald Press, 1957); John P. Frank, *Marble Palace* (New York: Alfred A. Knopf, 1958); Paul A. Freund, *On Understanding the Supreme Court* (Boston: Little, Brown and Company, 1949); Carl B. Swisher, *The Supreme Court in Modern Role* (New York: New York University Press, 1958).

Alan F. Westin in his *The Anatomy of a Constitutional Law Case* (New York: The Macmillan Co., 1958) traces the "Steel Seizure" case from its entrance to its completion in the federal court system.

Biographies of Supreme Court justices reveal much about the nature of the judicial process that is not revealed elsewhere. No attempt is made here to list all of the many excellent studies of this type but among the wider-known biographies are: Albert J. Beveridge, *The Life of John Marshall* (4 vols., Boston: Houghton Mifflin Company, 1916-1919); Alpheus T. Mason, *Brandeis: A Free Man's Life* (New York: The Viking Press, 1946), and *Harlan Fiske Stone: Pillar of the Law* (same publisher, 1956); Merlo J. Pusey, *Charles Evans Hughes* (New York: The Macmillan Company, 1951); Catherine D. Bowen, *Yankee From Olympus* (Justice Holmes) (Boston: Little, Brown & Company, 1944); and Carl B. Swisher, *Roger B. Taney* (New York: The Macmillan Company, 1935).

Two excellent recent books dealing with the American courts are John P. Roche, *Courts and Rights: The American Judiciary in Action* (New York, Random House, 1961), and Walter F. Murphy, and C. Herman Pritchett, *Courts, Judges, and Politics* (New York: Random House, 1961).

The opinions of the Supreme Court may be found in *United States Reports* published each year.

19

National Administration

THE size, complexity, and the powers of the national administrative structure are such as to strain the credulity of the ordinary citizen. Often persons employed in a huge administrative unit know little of the work of the agency beyond the day-to-day operations in their own offices. Some members of Congress vote for vast expenditures year after year without fully understanding the purpose behind the request for funds. Citizens are quick to criticize the "red tape" of governmental administration without the faintest notion as to the requirements of an adequate reporting and reviewing system.

Many of the complications of the national administrative system exist because it was conceived within the give and take of democratic policy-making. Much of the continuing controversy with respect to administrative organization and procedures is a reflection of group struggle in a dynamic, democratic society. These points should be borne in mind as one reads the following sections on the national administration.

THE NATURE OF THE ADMINISTRATIVE PROCESS

There is a story concerning a grasshopper who asked the advice of an ant on how to keep from freezing in the winter time.

"That is easy," replied the ant, "turn into an ant."

"But how am I to do this?" puzzled the grasshopper.

"Oh, keep quiet," snapped the ant. "I only make policy around here; I don't carry it out."

Obviously, what was needed in this instance was an administrator to carry out the policy once it was made.

A well-known rhyme by Alexander Pope runs:

> "For forms of government let fools contest,
> Whate'er is best administer'd is best."

To which Professor Herman Finer has replied:

> "But what is best must free men still decide,
> Lest leaders gull them, and officials ride." [1]

---

[1] *Theory and Practice of Modern Government* (rev. ed., New York: Henry Holt and Co., 1949), p. 8.

Taken together these verses furnish a kernel around which comments concerning the nature of administration may be wrapped. Governmental policy, no matter how noble or how base, is not self-executing. The end product of political decision-making is achieved through administration. Upon admitting this, one is faced with the premise of Professor Finer's verse. The determination of what policies are to be administered lies within the province of the elected representatives of the people—in the national government, with Congress the President. Such a black and white distinction between policy-making and administration is a convenient working hypothesis, but it must be immediately qualified. For example, it does not allow for the impact and influence of administrative organizations on *what* is to be done (policy), or conversely the deference shown Congress by administrators in *how* something is done (administration).

Consider the budget as an example of the intermixture of policy-making and administration. To begin with, it is a congressional statute which charges the President with the responsibility for preparing the budget estimates. But administrative agencies must make policy decisions concerning the continuation of old programs or the institution of new ones as a basis of their budgetary requests. True enough, Congress in the budget authorization stage may modify or deny the administrative requests. But if this is done in wholesale disregard of the suggestions from the adminstrative branch, the logic of the executive budget is destroyed. Although the legislative branch will probably insist upon certain deletions, additions, and modifications, the core of the budgetary requests is apt to be granted. Further suppose, however, that a particular program is going to require the establishment of a number of field offices throughout the United States. A chairman of a congressional committee, perhaps one of the appropriations committees, may demand that field offices be created in his state or district. This may not be what the administrator for the program had in mind, but in the interest of keeping on good terms with a powerful member of Congress, he may accede to the legislator's wishes.

For a long time Congress has delegated legislative authority to administrative agencies and agents. The most obvious example of delegation, but not the most prevalent, can be seen when Congress sets up an independent regulatory commission "which does legislative, judicial, and executive acts, only softened by a quasi." [2] The rules and regulations of many agents and agencies, including but not confined to regulatory commissions, have the force of law behind them. To be sure, they have the broad policy objectives outlined by statutes, but the interpretation and application of these involves discretion at every turn.

Nevertheless, the administrative apparatus is a distinct instrumentality

---

[2] The phrase is that of Justice Holmes in a dissenting opinion. See *Springer* v. *Philippine Islands,* 277 U. S. 189 (1928).

of government. It is often referred to as the national administration, or the federal bureaucracy. In this usage it does not include those persons employed by the legislative or judicial branches of government. A realistic concept of "the administration" must not fail to perceive of it in terms of both *organizations* and *people*. People make up the organization, but sometimes the organization makes over the people. Decision-making in an administrative agency is done by finite people but for infinite reasons. The organization, its structure, its customs, and its mission leaves some imprint upon those who administer its programs. And, of course, administrators may have much to do with shaping the organization toward the accomplishment of its objectives.

ADMINISTRATION AND THE CONSTITUTION

The Constitution has very little to say about administration as such, and what gleanings are obtained from that document on the subject are indirect ones. The constitutional fathers undoubtedly assumed a bureaucracy of sorts would be required, but they wisely left its primary structural determination to time and the political organs of the government.

In Article II there are hints relating to the establishment of administrative offices. Of the President the Constitution says, "He may require the opinion, in writing, of the principal officer in each of the executive departments, upon any subject relating to the duties of their respective offices." Also ". . . and he shall nominate, and, by and with the consent of the Senate, shall appoint ambassadors, other public ministers and consuls, judges of the Supreme Court, and all other officers of the United States whose appointments are not herein otherwise provided for, and which shall be established by law; but the Congress may by law vest the appointment of such inferior officers, as they think proper, in the President alone, in the courts of law, or in the heads of departments."

Under Article I, the legislative article, there is no provision specifically suggesting that Congress may create administrative agencies. But a portion of Article II, quoted above, speaks of Congress being able by law to vest the power to appoint "inferior officers." But in the legislative article there appears a clause which permits Congress "to make all laws which shall be necessary and proper for carrying into execution the foregoing legislative powers, and all other powers vested by this Constitution in the government of the United States, or in any department or officer thereof." It was the creation of an administrative agency, the second Bank of the United States, which eventually called forth Marshall's ringing endorsement of the implied power doctrine, based on the "necessary and proper" clause, and upholding the power of Congress to incorporate the bank. Certainly since this historic decision in 1819, it is accepted doctrine that Congress may create the neces-

EXECUTIVE BRANCH OF THE GOVERNMENT

JANUARY 1, 1964

THE PRESIDENT OF THE UNITED STATES

EXECUTIVE OFFICE OF THE PRESIDENT

THE WHITE HOUSE OFFICE
BUREAU OF THE BUDGET
COUNCIL OF ECONOMIC ADVISERS
NATIONAL AERONAUTICS AND SPACE COUNCIL
NATIONAL SECURITY COUNCIL
OFFICE OF EMERGENCY PLANNING
OFFICE OF SCIENCE AND TECHNOLOGY
SPECIAL REPRESENTATIVE FOR TRADE NEGOTIATIONS

DEPARTMENTS

DEPT. OF STATE — Secretary
DEPT. OF THE TREASURY — Secretary
DEPT. OF DEFENSE — Secretary
DEPT. OF JUSTICE — Attorney General
POST OFFICE DEPT. — Postmaster General
DEPT. OF THE INTERIOR — Secretary
DEPT. OF AGRICULTURE — Secretary
DEPT. OF COMMERCE — Secretary
DEPT. OF LABOR — Secretary
DEPT. OF HEALTH, EDUCATION, AND WELFARE — Secretary

AGENCIES, BOARDS AND COMMISSIONS

GENERAL SERVICES ADMINISTRATION — Administrator
HOUSING AND HOME FINANCE AGENCY — Administrator
INDIAN CLAIMS COMMISSION — 3 Commissioners
INTERSTATE COMMERCE COMMISSION — 11 Commissioners
NATIONAL AERONAUTICS AND SPACE ADMINISTRATION — Administrator
NATIONAL CAPITAL HOUSING AUTHORITY — 5 Members
NATIONAL CAPITAL PLANNING COMMISSION — 12 Members
NATIONAL CAPITAL TRANSPORTATION AGENCY — Administrator
NATIONAL LABOR RELATIONS BOARD — 5 Members
NATIONAL MEDIATION BOARD — 3 Members
NATIONAL SCIENCE FOUNDATION — 25 Members
PANAMA CANAL COMPANY — 9-13 Directors
RAILROAD RETIREMENT BOARD — 3 Members
RENEGOTIATION BOARD — 5 Members
ST. LAWRENCE SEAWAY DEVELOPMENT CORPORATION — Administrator
SECURITIES AND EXCHANGE COMMISSION — 5 Commissioners
SELECTIVE SERVICE SYSTEM — Director
SMALL BUSINESS ADMINISTRATION — Administrator
SMITHSONIAN INSTITUTION — 11
SUBVERSIVE ACTIVITIES CONTROL BOARD — 5 Members
TAX COURT OF THE UNITED STATES — 16 Judges
TENNESSEE VALLEY AUTHORITY — 3 Directors
U.S. ARMS CONTROL AND DISARMAMENT AGENCY — Director
U.S. CIVIL SERVICE COMMISSION — 3 Commissioners
UNITED STATES INFORMATION AGENCY — Director
UNITED STATES TARIFF COMMISSION — 6 Commissioners
VETERANS ADMINISTRATION — Administrator
VIRGIN ISLANDS CORPORATION — 7 Directors
FOREIGN CLAIMS SETTLEMENT COMMISSION — 3 Members
FEDERAL TRADE COMMISSION — 5 Commissioners
BOARD OF GOVERNORS OF THE FED. RESERVE SYSTEM — 7 Members
FEDERAL POWER COMMISSION — 5 Commissioners
FEDERAL MEDIATION AND CONCILIATION SERVICE — Director
FEDERAL MARITIME COMMISSION — 5 Commissioners
FEDERAL HOME LOAN BANK BOARD — 3 Members
FEDERAL DEPOSIT INSURANCE CORPORATION — 3 Members
FEDERAL COMMUNICATIONS COMMISSION — 7 Members
FEDERAL COAL MINE SAFETY BOARD OF REVIEW — 3 Members
FEDERAL AVIATION AGENCY — Administrator
FARM CREDIT ADMINISTRATION — 13 Members
EXPORT-IMPORT BANK OF WASHINGTON — 5 Directors
DISTRICT OF COLUMBIA — 3 Commissioners
COMMISSION OF FINE ARTS — 7 Commissioners
CIVIL AERONAUTICS BOARD — 5 Members
CENTRAL INTELLIGENCE AGENCY — Director
CANAL ZONE GOVERNMENT — Governor
ATOMIC ENERGY COMMISSION — 5 Commissioners
AMERICAN BATTLE MONUMENTS COMMISSION — 11 Commissioners
ADVISORY COMMISSION ON INTER-GOVERNMENTAL RELATIONS — 26 Members

EXECUTIVE OFFICE OF THE PRESIDENT • BUREAU OF THE BUDGET

sary administrative apparatus to carry out the policies warranted under the enumerated and implied powers of the national government in the Constitution.

THE GROWTH OF NATIONAL ADMINISTRATION

A few employment statistics will indicate the emergence of "big" government in the United States. In 1801 approximately 3,000 persons were employed by the executive branch of the national government. A hundred years later the number was about 300,000. In 1916, on the eve of World War I, executive civil servants numbered 480,000, but by 1939 that figure had expanded to 900,000. Twenty-five years later the figure stood at slightly more than 2,500,000. Another way of looking at the tremendous growth of the national administration is to compare its growth with the total population increase. On this basis, in 1801 one out of every 1,769 people in the United States was employed by the national administration; in 1964 one out of every 73 people was so employed.

One of the concepts of administration, dear to the hearts of Jacksonian Democrats, was the notion that any average citizen was capable of performing efficiently in most, if not all, administrative positions. No one argues this point today, with the government requiring thousands of specialists in scientific, technical, administrative, and other areas. The reasons for the increase in governmental personnel and for the necessity for specialists are not difficult to discern. The industrial revolution may be taken as a starting point. As more and more individuals become wage earners in an industrial society, certain traditional values are subject to strain. The problem of economic security may be cited as an example. In a society fundamentally agricultural, unemployment does not assume the significance it does when a majority of the population must depend upon wages for its food.

In a sense, at least until recent times, people living on farms took pride in a considerable degree of self-sufficiency with respect to the necessities of food, clothing, and shelter. Industrial workers were caught on a somewhat mysterious conveyor, the industrial system, whose speed-ups and slow-downs, complexities and immensity, have led to increasing demands that government intervene to soften the rigors of the impersonal system. In the late nineteenth and early twentieth centuries, governmental agencies were created to regulate various aspects of business organization and practices. The establishment of the Interstate Commerce Commission (1887) and the Federal Trade Commission (1915) are examples in point.

Increasing urbanization, following on the heels of the industrial revolution, fostered new issues whose resolutions seemed to demand additional governmental machinery. For instance, the nature of public health and welfare problems was vastly different in urban as compared to rural communities. Closely related to the industrial revolution and urbanization was

THE GOVERNMENT OF THE UNITED STATES

THE CONSTITUTION

This chart seeks to show only the more important agencies of the Government. See text for other agencies.

LEGISLATIVE

THE CONGRESS

Senate   House

Architect of the Capitol
General Accounting Office
Government Printing Office
Library of Congress
United States Botanic Garden

EXECUTIVE

THE PRESIDENT

Executive Office of the President
The White House Office
Bureau of the Budget
Council of Economic Advisers
National Aeronautics and Space Council
National Security Council
Office of Emergency Planning
Office of Science and Technology

JUDICIAL

The Supreme Court of the United States
Circuit Courts of Appeals of the United States
District Courts of the United States
United States Court of Claims
United States Court of Customs and Patent Appeals
United States Customs Court
Territorial Courts

DEPARTMENT OF STATE

DEPARTMENT OF THE TREASURY

DEPARTMENT OF DEFENSE

DEPARTMENT OF JUSTICE

POST OFFICE DEPARTMENT

DEPARTMENT OF THE INTERIOR

DEPARTMENT OF AGRICULTURE

DEPARTMENT OF COMMERCE

DEPARTMENT OF LABOR

DEPARTMENT OF HEALTH, EDUCATION, AND WELFARE

INDEPENDENT OFFICES AND ESTABLISHMENTS

Atomic Energy Commission
Civil Aeronautics Board
District of Columbia
Export-Import Bank of Washington
Farm Credit Administration
Federal Aviation Agency
Federal Communications Commission
Federal Deposit Insurance Corporation
Federal Home Loan Bank Board
Federal Mediation and Conciliation Service
Federal Power Commission
Federal Reserve System, Board of Governors of the
Federal Trade Commission
General Services Administration
Housing and Home Finance Agency
Interstate Commerce Commission
National Aeronautics and Space Administration
National Labor Relations Board
National Mediation Board
National Science Foundation
Railroad Retirement Board
Securities and Exchange Commission
Selective Service System
Small Business Administration
Smithsonian Institution
Tax Court of the United States
Tennessee Valley Authority
United States Civil Service Commission
United States Information Agency
United States Tariff Commission
Veterans Administration

the impact caused by technological advances. Think of the expansion of the grant-in-aid programs and administrative machinery necessary for highway construction as a result of the automobile. Increasing efficiency in transportation and communications gave rise to more problems in interstate commerce which only the national government could hope to solve.

The great depression of the 1930's saw the national government undertaking a multitude of programs which either had not been performed before at all or had been left to the states. Partly because of the depression and partly because the preachments of decades of "reformers," who had demanded more positive governmental action in social and economic matters, the "New Deal" of Franklin D. Roosevelt received overwhelming support in three presidential elections. At present, the American public has seemingly committed both major political parties to the concept of the service state, even though the term "welfare" state remains unpopular.

PATTERNS OF ADMINISTRATIVE ORGANIZATION

The department. Under the Constitution, Congress created single-headed departments for administrative purposes. The first Congress established the Departments of Foreign Affairs (State), War, and Treasury; the offices of Attorney General and Postmaster General were provided for with the former being outside of any department, but with the latter within the Treasury Department. Soon, a Department of the Navy was added. There followed the creation of the Post Office Department in 1829, the Department of the Interior in 1849, and a Department of Justice in 1870. In 1889 there was established the first of the so-called "clientele" departments as a Department of Agriculture was organized. Here for the first time was a department created for the benefit of a particular segment of the nation, i.e., the farmer. Other "clientele" departments followed with the Department of Commerce and Labor being created in 1903, but then split into separate departments in 1913. To complete the departmental story, the Defense Department dates from 1949 and the Department of Health, Education, and Welfare from 1953. In 1962 President Kennedy's proposal for a new Department of Urban Affairs was defeated in the House.

Independent commissions. Prior to 1882 new administrative functions were added to existing departments. This sometimes resulted in a department being charged with a number of unrelated functions. The Department of Interior, for example, was at one time or another assigned duties relating to education, hospitals and eleemosynary institutions, labor, railroad accounts, and interstate commerce. Occasionally, a group would become influential enough in Congress to demand a regrouping of related functions into a new department. This is what happened with respect to the Departments of Agriculture, Commerce, and Labor.

In 1883 a different technique in national administrative organization was instituted, with the creation of the Civil Service Commission. Here was introduced the plural-headed agency, with a requirement that no more than two of the three commissioners could be members of the same political party. The Civil Service Commission was a management arm of the President through which, it was hoped, the civil service would be improved. Even more significant as an administrative device was the establishment of the Interstate Commerce Commission in 1887 as the first independent regulatory body in the national administrative structure.

At present, there are nine independent regulatory commissions; three are concerned with carriers, two with public utilities, two with finance and credit, and two with aspects of trade and industry.[3] A distinctive feature of the national regulatory commissions is their virtual independence from presidential control. The commissioners are appointed by the President with senatorial confirmation, but for overlapping terms; representation from both political parties is required, and the removal of members is restricted to causes set forth in statutes. The purpose of such independence is to assure impartiality and to shield the commissioners from political domination or control.

One of the chief functions of regulatory commissions is to establish standards and rules to govern the conduct of groups falling within their jurisdiction, and also to enforce these rules in specific cases. Thus it is common to speak of the commissions as carrying out quasi-legislative (rule-making) and quasi-judicial (adjudicative) functions in addition to administrative duties.

The work of the independent regulatory agencies has not escaped criticism. It has sometimes been charged that certain commissions have been captured by the very groups which they are supposed to regulate in the public interest. As far back as 1937, the President's Committee on Administrative Management advocated a partial integration of independent regulatory agencies by placing them within the executive departments. It was suggested that the regulatory functions be separated from the administrative duties by transferring the latter activities to an existing bureau while leaving the judicial function to the commissions. This principle was followed with respect to civil aviation matters. The Civil Aeronautics Act of 1938 established a Civil Aeronautics Authority within the Commerce Department. Subsequent reorganization plans left the rule-making and adjudicatory functions in a Civil Aeronautics Board, with independent status within the Department, but with certain administrative activities being carried out by the Civil Aeronautics Administration. Also in 1950 the United States Maritime

---

3 Carriers: Interstate Commerce Commission, Federal Maritime Board, and Civil Aeronautics Board; Utilities: Federal Power Commission and Federal Communications Commission; Finance and Credit: Securities and Exchange Commission and Federal Reserve Board; Fields of Industry: Federal Trade Commission and National Labor Relations Board.

Commission was abolished, its functions being transferred to two agencies within the Commerce Department—the Federal Maritime Board and the Maritime Administration.

An even more drastic reorganization with respect to the regulatory function was proposed by the second Hoover Commission. This plan would have transferred all of the adjudicative functions of regulatory commissions to a separate trade court presided over by judges. No concrete changes have as yet evolved from this recommendation, but the proposal itself and the concept behind it has the support of the American Bar Association and influential individuals. For example, in 1959 when Louis J. Hector resigned as a member of the Civil Aeronautics Board, he submitted a report to President Eisenhower suggesting a "basic and radical" reorganization of functions carried on by federal regulatory agencies. He recommended that policy-making and administrative duties be transferred to an appropriate executive department, judicial and appellate functions to an administrative court, and investigative and prosecution activities to the Justice Department. Mr. Hector said that he was disturbed at the inability of the commissions to give a true judicial hearing to parties who came before them. He reiterated an often-voiced complaint that the policies and plans of the regulatory agencies were not coordinated with those of other agencies of the government and that they were not responsive to the general policies of the President.

It is probable that the "basic and radical" reorganization suggested by Mr. Hector and others will be slow to materialize. The idea of independence from presidential control has strong support in Congress. The various groups subject to regulation have powerful allies on Capitol Hill. It is probable that many such groups prefer a continuation of the present system, or at least they do not desire to revamp the system completely.

A more traditional approach to the solution of many problems associated with the work of the regulatory agencies is exemplified by the investigations undertaken by a special subcommittee of the House of Representatives' Committee on Interstate and Foreign Commerce in 1959. Six regulatory agencies were examined, with others scheduled for future examinations, to determine (1) whether the law has been and is being faithfully executed by the agency in the public interest, and (2) whether the law and the statutory standards it contains have been and are being interpreted by rule, or internal procedures, to enlarge the area of regulation beyond that intended, and to administer it through procedures not intended by the Congress.[4] After extensive hearings in which some sensational charges were made by several witnesses concerning improper pressures being exerted on commissioners by interested parties from industry, and the executive and legislative branches of government, the subcommittee made several broad recommendations. Among these were:

---

[4] *Independent Regulatory Commissions*, House Report No. 2711, 85th Congress, 2d Session.

(1) Establishment of a code of ethics governing the conduct of commissioners, commission employees, practitioners, and others who appear before the commissions;

(2) Representations or communications, written or unwritten, not authorized by statute made to any commissioner or commission employee for the purpose of influencing the decision in any proceeding should be prohibited by law providing both civil sanctions and criminal penalties;

(3) Written communications received by any commissioner or commission employee from any member of the United States Congress or from any person in the executive branch pertaining to any proceeding should be made a part of the public record, and the substance of unwritten communications from similar individuals would also be included in the public record;

(4) Commissioners or employees of commissions should be prohibited from making unauthorized disclosure of any vote, opinion, or recommendation or information in the commission pertaining to any proceeding, or projected proceeding. Other recommendations had to do with prohibiting various types of direct and indirect techniques aimed at influencing commission decisions. Still another proposal recognized that the internal procedures of commissions might have to be revised so that they could effectively enforce the statutes involved and their own rules and regulations.

It is possible that other recommendations on the subject will be forthcoming as a result of subsequent investigations. Additional legislation dealing with regulatory commissions appears very probable within the next year or two. It seems likely that it will take the direction indicated by the subcommittee's report rather than the more extreme course advocated in some quarters.

The government corporation. The government corporation in the federal structure is used primarily when the government undertakes a business-type activity. This type of administrative unit was created in considerable numbers during the World War I period and has been on the increase ever since. The theory of the "authentic" government corporation requires a board of directors free to manage its own affairs; freedom of financial action, including power to borrow money and the right to retain earnings for working capital; freedom to develop its own auditing and accounting procedures; and freedom to construct its own personnel system. Actually, over the last twenty years the trend has been to limit government corporations in many of these areas. Even those government corporations, which at one time possessed most of the above powers, have been brought under the provisions of the Government Corporation Control Act of 1945. This act requires that all such corporations created after 1945 must be federally incorporated (some had been incorporated previously under state law); the General Accounting Office must audit corporation accounts annually; each corporation must present an annual budget to the Bureau of the Budget and to Congress; controls are imposed on other types of financial activities such as the power to borrow money.

There are a variety of corporate or quasi-corporate type agencies throughout the government. The second Hoover Commission found eighty-one credit agencies in the federal structure subject to the Corporation Control Act, although all of these were not listed as being government corporations per se. Originally corporations were generally established outside the regular agencies. In 1939 all existing government corporations, with the exception of the Tennessee Valley Authority and the Federal Deposit Insurance Corporation, were put within established agencies of government.[5]

The newest pattern of organization to emerge is one in which both government and industry are represented. In 1962, Congress passed legislation establishing the Communication Satellite Corporation in which three directors would be named by the President—with the consent of the Senate—six would be named by the communications industry and six by other investors. The new corporation's major activity was operation of the communications satellite (COMSAT) which has both commercial (television and telephone) aspects as well as national defense implications. The bill was passed only after cloture had been applied to a group of liberals who opposed the proposal and it is too early to decide whether COMSAT represents a future pattern or merely a unique experiment.

Other types of organizations. In addition to the types of organizations already alluded to, the federal administrative structure presents a large number of units which defy ready classification. For example, there is the Veterans Administration, headed by an administrator, charged with carrying out laws authorizing benefits for former members of the Armed Forces and their dependents, employing more persons than a majority of the executive departments. There is also the General Services Administration, performing certain housekeeping functions for most federal agencies; and there are various organizations performing specialized tasks which do not fall under regulatory or business-type functions.

Internal organization. Though there is some divergence among the normal administrative establishments in internal organization, the uniformity seems to be greater than in the broad outline of structure. There are subdivisions which are designated "bureaus," "services," "offices," and "divisions," headed by chiefs, commissioners, directors, comptrollers, and so forth; but there is actually often less difference among them than the titles would imply. In other words a "bureau" in one department may be very similar in form and functions to a "division" in another department; an "office" may differ only in minor details from a "service." All of the departments and establishments of any consequence are subdivided into sections which carry on the duties entrusted to them. These are headed by single

---

5 TVA, though chartered under federal jurisdiction, maintains its own personnel system.

officers who, although sometimes appointed on a political basis, tend to be professional in background and continue to hold the position more or less permanently. Bureau chiefs may be merit system appointees within the civil service system or political appointees without permanent tenure. The secretaries, undersecretaries, assistant secretaries, administrators, directors, and commissioners, who are in general charge of the administrative agencies, are almost invariably political appointees. They go out of office when a new President is inducted or at least as soon as their terms, as prescribed by law, have expired.

Line, staff, and auxiliary functions. Often the line, staff, and auxiliary functions of administration tend to become blurred as to separability, but their general differentiation is plain enough. Line personnel perform the primary services for which an agency was created. They issue licenses, inspect food, build roads, lend money, establish quotas, deliver mail, inoculate people, show farmers how to conserve soil, and build dams. But the line personnel have common needs necessary for them to perform their functions. They need money, paychecks, desks, automobiles, janitorial services, and pensions. *Auxiliary* organizations concerned with payrolls, budgeting, purchasing, and so forth, exist to satisfy these necessities. An integrated organization requires *staff* personnel for over-all planning, direction, control, and supervision.

Most governmental organizations have certain units within their structure primarily concerned with one of these types of functions. On the other hand, some organizations are created to perform staff or auxiliary services for many different agencies. The Budget Bureau is an example of a staff agency vis-à-vis other governmental agencies. The General Services Administration is an auxiliary agency serving throughout the administrative structure.

Field organization. About 90 per cent of all national government employees are located outside of Washington, D. C. Some agencies have much more elaborate field organizations than others, but in any case, most central offices are faced with about the same type of problems with respect to their field units. Despite the magic of modern technology, communications constitute a problem. All instructions can not be given by telephone or in face-to-face conversation. Written instructions are subject to varying interpretation. How much authority must the field unit possess to make on-the-spot decisions without advance permission from Washington? A common complaint in the field is that "those administrators" in Washington really do not understand the problem. A common complaint in Washington is that the people in the field are not abiding by the regulations. Sometimes a conflict arises in the field between loyalty to the administrative organization or to the needs of the clientele being served.

The first Hoover Commission was critical of many aspects of field operations. There appeared to be too many separately organized field offices representing departments and bureaus. Many examples of inadequate reporting from the field to the central office and of poor inspection procedures by the central office were found. Many federal field offices in the same area would be engaging in similar activities but with little or no cooperation. The Commission recommended greater standardization of regional boundaries, improved reporting and inspection procedures, and increased utilization of pooled administrative services. Perhaps the greatest improvement has come in the latter two areas, but even here the development is uneven.

An over-all view of the administrative structure. Looking at the national administrative structure as a whole, the following generalizations may be made. At the top of the pyramid is the President, drawing certain authority from the Constitution and additional authority from legislative enactments. He is assisted by what may be termed a policy staff, made up of such institutions as his cabinet, and such units as the White House Office, the National Security Council, and the Council of Economic Advisers. Central staff agencies, such as the Bureau of the Budget, the Civil Service Commission, and the General Services Administration, perform their respective duties throughout the administrative structure. Then come the operating agencies. These have been classified into four different types.[6] To begin with, there are the ten great executive departments. Secondly, a score of separate administrative agencies may be mentioned such as the Veterans Administration, Housing and Home Finance Agency, a number of government corporations, and certain other agencies. Thirdly, one finds the regulatory commissions. And, finally, there is a miscellaneous group of boards and agencies including the Smithsonian Institution, the National Gallery of Art, the National Mediation Board, and five or six additional organizations.

ADMINISTRATIVE PROCEDURES

The following discussion deals with administrative procedures in the areas covering the functions of rule-making, adjudication, and licensing. All modern governments at every level have found it necessary to rely more and more upon administrative discretion in translating broad public policy pronouncements into social action.

Rule-making. Administrative legislation (quasi-legislation) refers to the issuance of administrative rules and regulations having the force of law. The legal basis for this function stems from statutes, which, after having determined a particular policy, permit a specific agency to "establish regulations suitable and necessary for carrying this act into effect." The first Congress under the Constitution adopted this practice to a limited extent, but its widespread use and tremendous impact on the administrative process and

---

[6] John D. Millett, *Government and Public Administration* (New York: McGraw-Hill Book Company, Inc., 1959), pp. 114-115.

the rights of individuals is a product of the late nineteenth and twentieth century.

Rule making involves a delegation of legislative power by Congress to administrative organizations or agents. For a brief period in the 1930's, the Supreme Court in at least three instances declared laws unconstitutional on the grounds that Congress had gone too far in delegating its power to the administrative branch. However, in the last twenty-five years no laws have been declared void on this basis. As long as Congress establishes fairly definite standards within which the administrative authority is to be exercised, the Court appears to be satisfied. The rationale behind delegation of authority includes the recognition that administrative officials are more expert in dealing with technical problems than Congress; that Congress does not have the time, even if it had the skill, to decide the details of policy administration; and that flexibility in the administration of laws must be achieved by administrative rather than congressional action.

Rule-making is often associated in the popular mind with the work of the independent regulatory commissions. All types of administrative agencies, and sometimes particular officers, are granted this power.

A few examples will serve to illustrate the nature of the rule-making function. Congress does not set the maximum rates of interest on deposits in Federal Reserve Banks, but the Board of Governors of the Federal Reserve System does. Congress does not determine the standard of purity required in foods and drugs, but the Food and Drug Administration does. Congress does not fix the rules and standards of service for telephone companies, but the Federal Communications Commission does. Congress does not set the minimum wage for persons employed on merchant ships receiving federal subsidies, but the Maritime Administration does. In World War II Congress did not determine the prices at which thousands of commodities were to be retailed, but the Office of Price Administration did. Once the administrative agency made its decision, however, it was as though Congress had made the determination in so far as the legal effect upon the individual was concerned.

Administrative adjudication. Administrative adjudication is a somewhat more precise term used to describe the quasi-judicial activities of administrative agencies. Administrative adjudication is the process whereby administrative officials settle controversies involving legal rights and duties in specific instances arising from the application of laws. This function is carried out by a myriad number of agencies such as departments, bureaus, offices, commissions, and special types of so-called administrative courts—as, for example, the Tax Court. Many cases adjudicated by administrative agencies involve millions of dollars worth of property and may result in economic and social consequences far removed from the decision at hand. Suppose a public utility contests a decision of a regulatory agency involving rate-fixing. The outcome of this controversy not only affects the specific public utility in question, but the possible outcome of similar cases and also the thousands of citizens who are served by the utility.

Legislative justification for the expanded use of administrative adjudicative procedures follow the same line of reasoning as mentioned with respect to rule-making. An additional reason, particularly compelling, is that administrative officials utilize informal proceedings which are not available to judicial tribunals, thus saving much time and expense. As a matter of fact, comparatively few controversies reach the point at which the formal adjudicative process is invoked. But where it is invoked there is a fairly standardized procedure. The aggrieved party files a request for a hearing. A hearing examiner then takes testimony and evidence upon which the ultimate decision will be based. Finally, the commission, board, or officer as the case may be, renders a decision. In certain cases, depending upon a number of factors, this decision may be subject to review by the regular courts.

Licensing power. Administrative agencies at the national, state, and local levels have been delegated the licensing power. This power includes both the issuance and revocation of licenses. One authority classifies licensing according to: (1) the expense incurred by the licensee, (2) the personal privilege involved, and (3) the effect upon public morals or safety of the exploitation of the license.[7] Examples in the first category would be the floating of a sale of securities, selling a product under a patent, or conducting a taxicab business. The second class would include such a "right" as driving an automobile; the third classification may be illustrated by licenses to operate dance halls, liquor stores or pool halls.

The power to license is perhaps subject to more abuse through discrimination than almost any other administrative procedure. Legislative standards may offer certain guide lines, but experience has shown that under any standard the administrator must still be allowed discretion in interpreting and applying the standards.

A well-known licensing operation of the federal government is that performed by the Federal Communications Commission in granting radio and television stations broadcast licenses. Obtaining permission to operate a television station requires much more than meeting certain standards. There are a limited number of permits available in a particular area, so the Commission often has to make a choice between competitors. It is apt to be charged with discrimination or favoritism even if it acts with the purest of motives in mind.

The Department of Agriculture, the Department of Commerce, the Federal Power Commission, the Securities and Exchange Commission, and the Atomic Energy Commission are a few of the federal agencies involved in licensing.

---

[7] James C. Charlesworth, *Governmental Administration* (New York: Harper & Bros., 1951), p. 131.

Administrative Procedure Act. In the 1930's a number of groups, particularly the American Bar Association, advocated legislation aimed at correcting "administrative lawlessness." In general, these groups felt that administrative procedures were not sufficiently uniform, formalized, and publicized. Thus the historic "rule of law," according to this view, was becoming "the rule of men." A bill dealing with administrative procedure was passed in 1940 but was vetoed by President Roosevelt. In the meantime, the Attorney General had appointed a committee to make a complete study of the subject; but in a final report, the committee split in its recommendations, with a majority opposing the enactment of a general code of administrative procedure. After World War II, another drive, sparked by the American Bar Association, resulted in the enactment of the Administrative Procedure Act of 1946. This legislation was very similar to the proposals in the minority report of the Attorney General's Committee of 1941. This bill was given unanimous approval by both Houses of Congress and was signed by President Truman.

As is usually the case, the extreme results predicted by proponents and opponents of the act have failed to materialize. The law has not solved all of the problems associated with administrative procedure, but neither has it placed insurmountable obstacles in the paths of administrators. Professor Hart has written: . . . "The fact remains that Congress has imposed a code which is at the worst less objectionable than the thundering of the traditionalists might have led one to expect, and which is unlikely to *wreck* federal administration." [8] Judicial interpretation of the law has been less upsetting to administrators than many imagined it might be.

The stated purpose of the Administrative Procedure Act is "to improve the administration of justice by prescribing fair administrative procedure." There follows a section devoted to defining such terms as agency, rule-making, order, adjudication, and sanction. Another section requires agencies to publish in the *Federal Register* information pertaining to the nature and requirements of all formal or informal procedures available and substantive rules adopted as authorized by law.

Subsequent sections deal with what might be considered as normal procedure in rule-making and adjudication. Stress is laid on the traditional concept of procedural due process of law in the matter of notice, hearing, impartiality, and review. A number of provisions bear on the impartiality aspect of the adjudicative process. For example, agency employees engaging in the performance of investigation or prosecuting functions may not participate in the agency decision. Certain provisions are intended to give the hearing examiner a status free from agency or outside pressures. The review guarantee extends to types of review within the administrative agency and also to judicial review of administrative decisions. This latter point

---

[8] James Hart, *An Introduction to Administrative Law* (2nd ed., New York: Appleton-Century-Crofts, Inc., 1950), p. 628.

was deemed of particular importance by the law's sponsors. Allowing for certain exceptions the statute permits "any person suffering legal wrong because of any agency action, or adversely affected or aggrieved by such action within the meaning of any relevant statute, shall be entitled to judicial review thereof."

One of the most troublesome problems confronting the courts in reviewing administrative decisions is the question of the finality to be accorded administrative findings of fact. The law permits judicial review of agency findings "unsupported by substantial evidence." The question then becomes what is "substantial evidence"? Although there is no easy solution to the whole matter of finality, the courts have developed a somewhat pragmatic approach to the problem. In general, the courts have insisted on their *right* to examine the facts, particularly with reference to whether they are supported by substantial evidence. However, in practice they are prone to exercise the right rather sparingly.

ADMINISTRATIVE ACCOUNTABILITY

Democratic theory assumes that elected government officials will be held accountable for their actions or inactions through the electoral process. But what of the administrators? They originate many of the policies which they later administer. They are the experts which the President, Congress, and the Court respect for their special knowledge and skills. Who is to say when a law is not being administered in accordance with congressional intent? What controls exist to assure that the administrators adhere to the letter and spirit of statutes and of the Constitution itself? Many students of government view the problems raised by these and related questions as one of the most important issues governments (particularly democratic governments) face today.

Judicial control. An historic and hallowed doctrine is that at least certain types of administrative decisions are subject to judicial scrutiny and control. The Administrative Procedure Act bolsters the already established principle of judicial review of agency actions. Perhaps the review extends to a consideration as to whether the statute being administered is constitutional. Or perhaps an individual takes a case into the court system questioning the method by which the law has been applied. He may contend that the administrator has violated due process of law. Again courts may assess penalties against administrators who act outside the law, perhaps as a result of a damage suit instituted by an aggrieved party. Such suits would be against the official as an individual rather than as a governmental agent.

There is no question that judicial control is extremely important, but it suffers serious limitations. In the first place, it relates to actions taken by administrators, almost never to their failure to act. The Attorney

General's Committee on Administrative Management pointed out that in addition to constitutional limitations forbidding the use of judicial power to correct under-enforcement, ". . . the courts cannot, as a practical matter, be effectively used for that purpose without being assimilated into the administrative structure and losing their independent organization." [9]

Judicial intervention can be only spasmodic. It must await institution by persons affected by particular administrative decisions. And most important, litigation is expensive. Ordinarily, the aggrieved party must "exhaust his administrative remedy" before the courts will consider the case. The average person simply does not have the patience, time, or money to depend upon a possible judicial finding in his favor.

Another difficulty has been alluded to in a previous section relating to the scope of judicial review. Is the administrative finding of fact to be binding upon the Court? If not, are the judges competent to pass upon admittedly highly technical questions relating to the facts?

Legislative controls. Both theory and practice emphasize the role of Congress in holding administrative officials accountable for their procedural and policy decisions. In theory it is quite clear that the policy goals of the administrative process are set by statute. Even in the exercise of quasi-legislative and quasi-judicial powers, the public purpose to be served by such powers is defined in law. The problem of accountability remains, of course. What techniques are available to Congress to assure itself that the administration is acting in accordance with its declared wishes? Here it should be stated that Congress at times purposely leaves its intent foggy, preferring to gauge the political effect of a particular administrative program with the benefit of hindsight.

The most obvious technique of congressional control lies in the appropriation process. Congress not only determines the *amount* of money an agency is to spend, but also the *purpose* for which it is spent. A legislative agency, the General Accounting Office, passes upon the legality of expenditures.

Another technique of legislative control is often labeled "legislative oversight" of administration. "In essence, the power of legislative oversight involves simply the authority to require administrative officers to explain their actions." [10] This may be accomplished by asking an official to testify before a congressional committee, by a requirement of formal reports, and most importantly—through congressional investigations.

In specific instances, Congress has not been content with mere "oversight," but has provided for a degree of legislative participation in administering programs. For example, the Atomic Energy Act included provisions

9 *Administrative Procedure in Government Agencies,* Senate Document No. 8, 77th Cong., p. 76.
10 Millett, *op. cit.,* p. 195.

for non-military use of fissionable material under license from the Atomic Energy Commission. But no such license was to be issued unless a report was submitted to Congress which was to remain before that body for ninety days. This procedure allowed Congress to pass modifying legislation *before* the administrative policy became effective.

Congress also possesses great powers with respect to the selection of administrative personnel. Statutes may require senatorial confirmation of administrative officials; they may vest the head of the agency with the appointing power; or they may fix the appointive power within the framework of the competitive civil service regulations.

So far, the various controls mentioned have been formal and easily identified in practice. Actually, a number of informal procedures are constantly in operation, although they are not so easy to spot. Even if the top administrator is vested with appointive power, he may find it expedient to clear his choices with key members of Congress. There are instances where the administrator has bowed to pressure from members of Congress— even to the point of choosing a person as a subordinate who was not sympathetic with the agency's program. Many types of administrative decisions may be cleared with appropriate committees although there are no formal requirements to that end.

There is no question about the power of Congress in the matter of administrative accountability. However, the fact of the power does not guarantee its effective or wise use. One can understand that the investigatory technique might be used sparingly if the Presidency and Congress are controlled by the same political party. On the other hand, if the Presidency and the congressional majority are not of the same party, the temptation to use the investigatory power as a political weapon is ever present. There always is the possibility that the legislature will run afoul of the separation of power principle and encroach upon the Chief Executive's domain.

The efficacy of budgetary review suffers in many respects, partly because of the deficiencies in congressional procedures on this score and partly because of the technical nature of the substantive programs which the committees review. Another related difficulty is the lack of standards for measuring administrative efficiency, a subject dear to the heart of most legislators. The Post Office Department runs a deficit; is this proof of inefficient administration, or is it an indication that Congress needs to appropriate more money if the department continues to render the services expected of it? To take another example: The legislative branch has determined that the number of federal employees must be reduced. To achieve this result, Congress is apt to use the so-called "meat axe" approach, by requiring a flat percentage reduction of the personnel in all agencies. To the administrator this is a foolish approach. To Congress the decision may appear logical because, in the first place, it is not equipped to judge the precise requirements of every agency; and in the second place, because the political pressure from various interest groups will be less effective where all the agencies have been treated the same.

Internal accountability. There are many degrees of accountability both formal and informal within an administrative organization. In theory the President at the top of the administrative hierarchy has a line of command running through the heads of the department to subordinate units within the administrative structure. One of the points brought out time and again by various reorganization studies is that the theory breaks down at various points. The second Hoover Commission found that the President had direct responsibility in supervising thirty-one different agencies. No President could possibly be personally aware of the problems or the deficiencies in administration in such a span of agencies. The hierarchical principle is also important within a particular department or agency and in theory permits the department or agency head to keep tab on operations through his bureau chiefs, who in turn check on their division chiefs and so on down the line. Thus hierarchical control is an important principle of administrative management even though it does not work as smoothly as an organization chart would lead one to believe. One difficulty arises because some bureau chiefs are protected from arbitrary removal by statutes, so the department head's instructions might not be so carefully considered by such persons, as those who are appointed by and may be removed by their superior. What is more important is the fact that statutes often confer duties specifically on the bureau chief for the administration of a program. His authority then in this particular area may surpass that of the department head.

The Bureau of the Budget, as a staff arm of the President, is the focal point for checking the conformity of agency operations with the standards expected by the President. The Bureau of the Budget is in a powerful position vis-à-vis executive agencies because of its budget review function; but, through its Office of Management and Organization, Office of Statistical Standards, and Office of Accounting, it may also influence the internal procedures of the various agencies.

Informal factors have a very important bearing on the way an organization carries out its duties. One such factor has been called "bureau philosophy," which has been described as "the sum total of the group values, the accepted ways of doing things, that grow up in an administrative unit, and with which the members of the unit identify." [11] Such a philosophy "makes group decisions possible where otherwise anarchy would prevail— each participant attempting to impose his own 'inarticulate major premises' upon the rest. By relating particular decisions to a coherent set of principles, it facilitates their defense. By providing a rule of *stare decisis*, it fills in most of the gaps of discretion left by the formal controls and provides

11 H. A. Simon, D. W. Smithburg, and V. A. Thompson, *Public Administration* (New York: Alfred A. Knopf, 1956), p. 543.

organizational members with safe ways of exercising discretion and making decisions." [12]

The clientele served by the bureau learns to accommodate its plans and operations to the "bureau philosophy." If the accommodation involves too much stress and strain, the affected groups will work through the political process to seek to have formal controls exercised over the bureaucrats.

ADMINISTRATION REORGANIZATION

The two concepts most frequently associated with the term "reorganization" have been economy and efficiency. While economy and efficiency are without question desirable goals in any type of organization, the determination of what is economical and what is efficient with respect to governmental administration is fraught with difficulties unknown to most other types of administration. The vastness of the governmental structure, its coercive characteristics, the unremitting struggle for its control by political parties, the constant group pressures on the formation and administration of policy, and the fact that government services generally—unlike business services—are not predicated on the profit motive underscore some of these difficulties.

Study groups and reorganization authorizations. As early as 1887 the Senate set up the Cockrell Committee to study the "methods of business in the Executive Departments." Theodore Roosevelt created the Keep Commission to study "departmental methods." President Taft sponsored a Commission on Economy and Efficiency, and in 1923 Congress appointed the Joint Committee on the Reorganization of the Government Departments.

The administrative system of the federal government had become so top-heavy by 1930 that widespread alarm was expressed by many citizens and groups. Congress had added a bit here and a bit there, never bothering to overhaul and integrate, until a truly fantastic structure had been erected. Perhaps the most telling of the criticisms was the one which pointed out how utterly impossible it was for any President to keep his eye on so variegated and unintegrated a setup. Under the Constitution the Chief Executive is charged with responsibility for supervising the executive and administrative departments; certainly, it is exceedingly desirable to have someone ultimately responsible for what the departments do. Although the President was nominally at the head of the system, it was humanly impossible for him to do more than keep a weather eye out for abuses. In the second place, such a top-heavy structure was thought to be more or less inefficient. Half a dozen agencies might be working on different phases of the same problem, and no one of them desired or was assigned, final responsibility. One agency repeated what had already been done by another; another attempted to bring about the very opposite end being sought by a fourth. Moreover, boards were charged with handling duties that virtually all experts in public

---

[12] *Ibid.*

administration agree should be placed under a single head, if prompt and decisive action is to be expected. Finally, large numbers of critics waxed eloquent about the economic wastefulness of a system that permitted duplication, red tape, working at cross purposes, and long delay. Extreme enthusiasts believed that huge savings could be realized without decreasing the efficiency of the services rendered if the system were more adequately arranged.

Herbert Hoover, after making a survey of the extent of duplication, persuaded Congress to grant him authority to reconstruct the system subject to congressional approval. Acting under this permission, Hoover undertook an extensive rearrangement and consolidation of administrative agencies, but a Democratic Congress refused to approve any of the changes which he had worked out. Hence, despite all of the interest on the part of the Presidents, the criticism of thousands of citizens, and the proposals looking toward improvement, very little was accomplished toward reorganization until the 1930's. The agencies themselves were not anxious to be regimented; public employees feared their jobs might be swept away by a reorganization; politicians wanted nothing that would make it more difficult to use the government for their own interests; pressure groups had what amounted to a vested interest in certain administrative agencies; the states foresaw an expansion of federal power; and Congress was unable to agree as to what steps would prove advantageous.

The first Roosevelt reorganization. One of the last pieces of legislation signed by President Hoover was a bill which gave Franklin D. Roosevelt power to do what no predecessor had been able to do. For two years the Chief Executive was to have an almost free hand in remodeling the administrative setup, with the provisos that the ten major departments must be retained and that orders carrying out changes should not go into effect until they had rested before Congress for sixty days. Though occupied with the problems presented by the worst depression in American history during the two-year period allowed for this reconstruction, the President found some time to give to reorganization and issued numerous orders which Congress accepted. But while he was with one hand consolidating and integrating, with the other he was, even more rapidly, adding new agencies that could not be fitted into any orderly system. Some important changes were made, but they were not far-reaching enough in character to effect any general reorganization.

The Reorganization Act of 1939. In 1936 President Roosevelt appointed a Committee on Administrative Management to examine the problem of too many agencies and recommend what should be done to deal with it. The President submitted a bill embodying most of the recommendations of the Committee. The Senate rejected the President's proposal and requested the Brookings Institution to prepare another study of needed reorganization. Something of a compromise resulted from the recommendations of these two groups. An act was passed in 1939 authorizing the Chief Executive to "reduce, co-ordinate, consolidate, and reorganize" within defined limits, subject to concurrent resolutions of both houses. One of the most important changes resulting from this authorization was the creation of the Executive Office of the President in which eventually several units were placed so as to improve the staff services available to the Chief Executive.

Reorganization during World War II. Shortly after the entrance of the United States into World War II, Congress authorized the President to make such reorganization of the administrative structure as would contribute to national defense. Authority under the act was to extend for the duration of the war plus six months. President Roosevelt issued a number of orders which brought about some consolidation of administrative agencies. The reorganization did not begin to keep pace with the pressure which the national defense program developed toward setting up of additional agencies.

By 1945 the situation had become so involved that President Truman sent a special message to Congress asking for authority, similar to that given his predecessor in 1939, to abolish, consolidate, and reorganize agencies in the federal administrative system. In this connection, he pointed out that in 1945 there were 1,141 principal component parts of the executive branch of the government as follows: thirteen in the executive office of the President, 499 in the ten departments, 364 in the twenty-three emergency boards, and 265 in twenty-six independent establishments, boards, commissions, and corporations.

The Reorganization Act of 1945. Shortly before recessing for Christmas in 1945, Congress passed an act which authorized the President to make sweeping changes in the federal administrative structure during the years 1946 and 1947. Provision was made that the ten major departments should be retained and that five independent agencies could not be abolished. Especially important was the section which made it possible that changes proposed by the President would become effective unless vetoed by a majority vote of both houses of Congress. Despite limitations imposed by the act, it conferred more sweeping authority on the President to reorganize than had ever been granted previously. But the actual accomplishments under the act were disappointing to many. Most of the changes were of minor significance and left the vast federal administrative structure far from co-ordinated.

The first Hoover Commission. The most significant advance in administrative reorganization in recent years has resulted from the decision by Congress to unify the armed services. Following a recommendation by the President, Congress in 1947 authorized the setting up of a National Military Establishment as one of the major departments with cabinet status. Three departments, i.e., the Army, Air Force, and Navy were provided as constituent parts of the National Military Establishment. Two years later the National Military Establishment became the Department of Defense.

Another step promising possible results of far-reaching importance was also taken by Congress in 1947 when a twelve-member commission was created to investigate the simplification of the national administrative structure. With one third of the members chosen by the Speaker of the House, the President *pro tempore* of the Senate, and the President, respectively, this commission not only received a free hand in considering possible changes, but also, unlike some of the earlier bodies, adequate funds to defray expenses. Former President Hoover was named chairman.

The Commission, working through twenty-four task forces and using the services of hundreds of experts in various administrative fields, uncovered hundreds of instances of duplication, overlapping, and "inefficiency." The Commission proposed many changes designed to eliminate the weaknesses found by its research. Congress accepted the report and enacted legislation allowing the President to submit plans for reorganization. Unless the plans were turned down by a majority of both the Senate and the House of Representatives, they would automatically take effect. It has been estimated that over 70 per cent of the first Hoover Commission's recommendations have been put into operation, including significant creations such as the Department of Health, Education, and Welfare and the General Services Administration. The high percentage figure is misleading, in a sense, because many of the recommendations were completely non-controversial so, of course, were acceptable to Congress and the President. In important controversial areas the Commission's recommendations did not come to pass.

Second Hoover Commission. Following the election of President Eisenhower in 1952, congressional leaders once again called for another full-scale study of federal administrative reorganization. A second Commission on Organization of the Executive Branch of the Government was set up with Herbert C. Hoover as the chairman. The second Hoover Commission was given broader authority than any of its predecessors. Not only could the Commission deal with administrative problems, but it could also make recommendations concerning general policy. In its report submitted in 1955, the Commission recommended a variety of plans for reorganization and also advised that the government stop competing with private enterprise in those instances where business could deal adequately with the problems. There has been little disagreement with the generalization, but much disagreement on the matter of where business can "adequately" deal with the problems. The fact that the Democrats were in control of Congress after 1954 augured ill for some of the Commission's policy proposals. The Commission believed that about fifty of its recommendations could be carried out through presidential reorganization plans; another 145 could be achieved by discretionary action on the part of agency heads; but some 167 proposals would require legislative action. Many of the suggestions have been accepted, including several which required legislation; others are still being considered by Congress. The power of the President under the

Reorganization Act of 1949 expired in 1959, but Congress later renewed the authority through 1962.

The issues of administrative reorganization.[13] Administrative reorganization raises a number of issues which are essentially political in nature and which revolve around group conflict in American society. Ultimately, the political institutions, especially the legislature, must make decisions concerned with resolving the conflicts.

The issue of economy. The justification for reorganization proposals often has been in terms of reducing the cost of government. Actually administrative expenditures are but a small part of the total expense of governmental operations. The more fundamental issue thus becomes the volume and scope of government services. There is no question that many persons and groups feel that many types of activities undertaken by the national government should be curtailed or abolished. But this is a policy question which the elected representatives must decide. There is nothing amiss with any group making recommendations to Congress or the President on basic policy issues, but it appears doubtful that advocates of curtailed governmental activities should seek their ends through the guise of administrative reorganization.

Strengthening the administrative role of the President. Without question, many reorganization plans have had as their chief purpose the strengthening of the administrative authority of the President. The Chief Executive is granted certain constitutional powers with respect to supervising the administration. It is sometimes argued that the President is a more effective avenue for popular control over the bureaucracy than is Congress. It is maintained that two conditions must be met in order for the President to effectively supervise and control the administrative structure. The President's administrative position must be institutionalized, especially by the development of central staff agencies within the executive office. Secondly, federal administrative activities must be brought together under a limited number of executive departments, each headed by an official appointed by and removable by the President.

But as one outstanding authority suggests:

> There are two complications to this line of reasoning, no matter how cogent it may be. The first is that the legislature is often unwilling to accept the major assumption that the chief executive is the only effective avenue for popular control over the bureaucracy. Legislative members are popularly elected. They exercise considerable oversight of administrative activity. They can change policies or programs which are unsatisfactory by law. And such action by law is preferable democratic procedure, so they assert, than executive order. In the second place, the chief executive can enjoy only such institutional assistance as the legislature sees fit to provide him. And if the legislature does not desire to place all administrative ac-

---

13 This section is based primarily on the discussion in Millett, *op. cit.*, pp. 135-140.

tivity in the hands of department heads appointed and removable at will by the chief executive, then there is little the chief executive can do about it. Suppose the regulatory commissions do exercise substantial policy-making authority; suppose they do tend to develop policy on a case-by-case approach arising out of adversary proceedings; suppose they do not take an over-all, long-range view of policy goals; are these conditions necessarily to be deplored? Why assume the chief executive or one of his political lieutenants would necessarily do a better job; that is, a job politically better accepted.[14]

Congress, no doubt, will continue to fear executive aggrandizement. As long as the separation of powers principle remains a basic tenet of the American constitutional system, the national legislature is not apt to abdicate its constitutional powers over the administration to the degree hoped for by some who see the President as the most valid expression of the popular will.

Administrative consolidation. An objective of reorganization proposals with logic solidly in its favor has been to bring about consolidation or integration of activities having some related interest in respect to such factors as clientele, geographical area, function, or technique of operation. Considerable progress has been made in some areas, but many major proposals in this direction immediately run head-on into the political facts of our pluralistic society. Interest groups and bureaucrats develop their own lines of communication and influence with respect to Congress. A President may find that the collective influences against integration proposals far outweigh his own. This may not be, and probably is not, the most desirable state of affairs, but it helps explain the reluctance of various Presidents to push consolidation proposals at every turn.

Procedure in administrative reorganization. Since administrative reorganization is so tinged with political controversy, there has been much disagreement as to how it should be accomplished. For example, instead of Congress authorizing the President permanent powers with respect to initiating reorganization proposals, it has permitted him to act within definite time limits set by statutes. At times, Congress has specified that certain agencies and functions are not to be the subject of reorganization plans. Then again, the President's plans would go into operation unless blocked by a majority vote of both houses of Congress. At other times, an adverse vote by either house was sufficient to kill the Chief Executive's recommendations. Without much doubt, Congress will continue to reserve some sort of legislative veto.

SUMMARY

Policy-making and administration should not be considered as entirely separate processes since they are tied together at every turn. Nevertheless,

---

14 Millett, *op. cit.,* pp. 137-138.

in a democracy the administrative organization must be the servant through which the policies of government are consumated, rather than the master dictating means and ends to the political organs.

The Constitution has little to say about the administrative structure. However, based on the few pertinent constitutional phrases, and on the implied power to create agencies necessary to carry out policy decisions, Congress has structured the national administration to meet the exigencies of the moment. For about a hundred years, the administrative structure retained a semblance of symmetry since new functions were usually assigned to old departments. But over the next fifty years a multitude of pressures, spawned by the bigness and tactics of business, by wars, economic depressions, and the awakening of the social conscience of the nation, forced Congress to create special purpose agencies, boards, regulatory commissions, and government corporations without as well as within existing executive departments. Some of these agencies, such as the regulatory commissions, were deliberately made independent of the President; others were in theory subject to his direction, but in fact were frequently undirected.

The astounding growth of the administrative machine mirrors the trend away from the *laissez faire* concept of the role of government to the acceptance of a positive role requiring governmental action in broad areas dealing with economic and social matters.

As a consequence of these developments, three closely related areas of inquiry have received attention in recent years. Reference here is to (1) the reorganization movement, (2) the concern for fair administrative procedures, and (3) the embracing question of administrative accountability.

BIBLIOGRAPHIC NOTE

There are many textbooks intended as introductions to the study of public administration in the United States. Representative books in this category include: Leonard D. White, *Introduction to the Study of Public Administration* (New York: The Macmillan Company, 1955); John M. Pfiffner and Robert V. Presthus, *Public Administration* (4th ed., New York: The Ronald Press Company, 1960); M. E. Dimock, Gladys O. Dimock, and Louis K. Koenig, *Public Administration* (New York: Rinehart and Company, Inc., 1958); Herbert Simon, Donald W. Smithburg, and Victor A. Thompson, *Public Administration* (New York: Alfred A. Knopf, 1956); and James C. Charlesworth, *Governmental Administration* (New York: Harper & Bros., 1951). For a more detailed treatment of specific areas in public administration than is usually found in introductory textbooks, see Dwight Waldo (ed.), *Ideas and Issues in Public Administration* (New York: McGraw-Hill Book Company, Inc., 1953) and Albert Lepawsky, *Administration: The Art and Science of Organization and Management* (New York: Alfred A. Knopf, 1949).

John D. Millett in his *Management in the Public Service* (New York: McGraw-Hill Book Co., Inc., 1954) is concerned with the mechanics of administrative practices, but in his *Government and Public Administration* (same publisher, 1959) discusses thoroughly the varied roles of the political branches of the government in seeking to assure a "responsible" administrative service. Two excellent studies analyzing the role of the federal bureaucracy are M. E. Dimock's *Administrative*

Vitality (New York: Harper & Bros., 1959) and Charles S. Hyneman, *Bureaucracy in a Democracy* (same publisher, 1950). For a study emphasizing the political philosophy of American public administration, see Dwight Waldo's *The Administrative State* (New York: The Ronald Press Company, 1948).

Herbert A. Simon's *Administrative Behavior* (2nd ed., New York: The Macmillan Company, 1957) deals with the interpersonal factors in the administrative decision-making process. For a more traditional approach to administrative practices, see Catheryn Seckler-Hudson, *Organization and Management: Theory and Practice* (Washington, D. C.: The American University Press, 1955).

For historical approaches to the study of public administration, one should consult L. M. Short, *The Development of the National Administrative Organization in the United States* (Baltimore: The Johns Hopkins University Press, 1923) and a series of studies by Leonard D. White, published by The Macmillan Company, namely *The Federalists* (1948), *The Jeffersonians* (1951), *The Jacksonians* (1954), and *The Republican Era* (1957). For a detailed account of administration in a specific department, see J. M. Gaus and L. O. Walcott, *Public Administration and the United States Department of Agriculture* (Chicago: Public Administrative Service, 1940).

A vast amount of material is available on the subject of administrative reorganization. Particularly worthwhile publications on this topic include: W. Brooke Graves, *Basic Information on the Reorganization of the Executive Branch, 1912-1948* (Public Affairs Bulletin 66, Washington, D. C.: Library of Congress, 1949); H. Emmerich, *Essays on Federal Reorganization* (University, Ala.: University of Alabama Press, 1950); Commission on Organization of the Executive Branch of the Government (First Hoover Commission), 19 reports and 18 task force reports (Washington, D. C.: Government Printing Office, 1949); and Commission on Organization of the Executive Branch of the Government (Second Hoover Commission), 20 reports and 19 task force reports (Washington, D. C.: Government Printing Office, 1954).

All students should be familiar with the *United States Government Organization Manual,* published annually by the General Services Administration, Government Printing Office, Washington.

20

Federal Civil Service

Federal civil servants are drawn from all strata in American society. Even at the upper levels, no particular social class or small group of universities furnishes the bulk of the civil servants. Whatever may be said of the "spoils system," it served to democratize the federal service. The adoption of a merit system did not result in a governing elite based on position or education. As it worked out, the competitive service tended to set minimal entrance requirements within the reach of the "ordinary" citizen.

Particularly between World Wars I and II, the Civil Service Commission was frequently criticized for assuming a rather negative attitude toward personnel problems. The Commission appeared intent upon keeping the service non-political, but beyond that exerted little leadership in solving important personnel problems. Today the Commission views its role with respect to federal personnel management in a much more positive way. Although the agencies themselves play a more active role in the personnel management field than they did twenty years ago, the Civil Service Commission exercises great influence by establishing standards for recruitment, training, classification, and promotion policies, and possesses adequate authority to see that the agencies comply with these standards.

CIVIL SERVICE AND THE MERIT SYSTEM

Meaning of federal civil service. The federal civil service includes all civilians who are employed by the federal government; it does not encompass the elected officials or the judges. Over 98 per cent of the civilian employees are found in the executive branch with the remainder falling within the legislative and judicial branches. The federal government is by far the largest employer in the United States. Its two and one-third million civilian employees represent almost every occupation, skill, and profession that can be found outside the government and many that are found only in government.

Growth of the civil service. The striking expansion of the administrative side of government has had many effects, not the least of which is the accentuation of the problem of finding adequate public personnel. The increase in civil servants is in part due to the population growth; however, more significantly, its expansion is a reflection of changing concepts as to

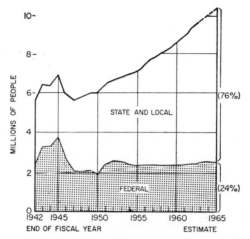

TREND IN GOVERNMENT CIVILIAN EMPLOYMENT, FEDERAL AND STATE AND LOCAL, 1942-1965

the role government should play in American society. The national government started out in 1789 with approximately three hundred civil servants. In the centennial year it gave civil employment to slightly more than 150,000 persons; by 1939 the number approximated one million, but the war sent it soaring above the three million mark. Since 1956 the civilian employment figure has remained around 2.4 million. Over 90 per cent of these employees are out in the field. The state of California has more federal civil servants than the metropolitan area of Washington, D. C.

Civil service and the early Presidents. During the early years of the republic, political parties had not yet become powerful, and the need for patronage was not strongly felt either as a means of advancing party interests or as a means of financial support for the party treasury. The number of federal jobs was quite small, and there was still fairly general acceptance of the theory that federal positions were the property of the government and not of any partisan group. It would not be accurate to say that there was no disposition toward making appointments to federal positions on other than a merit basis, but even so the general record of the first six presidents in securing competent personnel was good.

Washington left an indelible imprint on the civil service. He was practical enough to select principal federal officials from different regions of the country, to staff field offices with local personnel, to make support of the Constitution a factor in determining fitness, and to give occasional preference to officers of the Revolutionary Army.

UNITED STATES CIVIL SERVICE COMMISSION

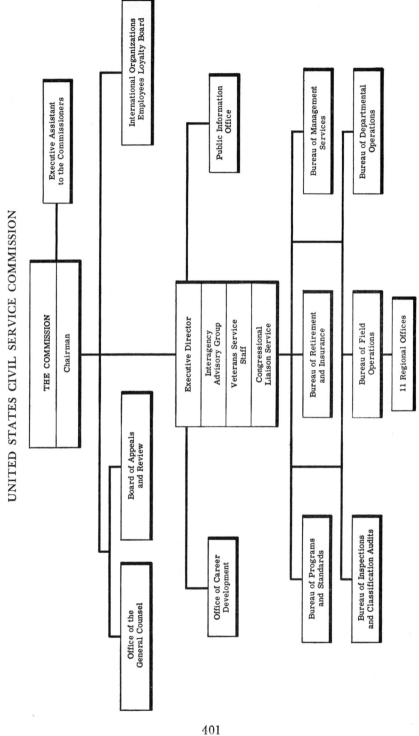

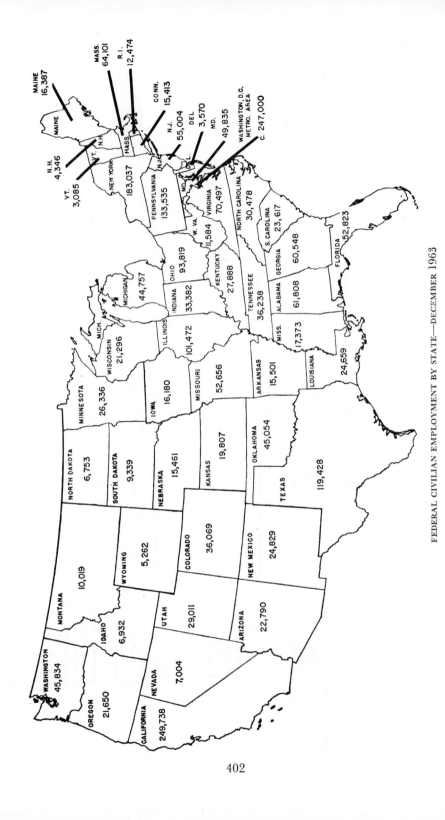

FEDERAL CIVILIAN EMPLOYMENT BY STATE—DECEMBER 1963

John Adams continued Washington's policy of making fitness an essential requirement for federal employment. At the end of his term, he made a number of "midnight appointments," placing deserving Federalist party members in newly created positions.

Following the Republican victory in 1800, President Jefferson set out to restore a proper balance between Federalists and Republicans in the public service. He moved cautiously in removing Federalists, however, and at least attempted to justify each dismissal on legal or moral rather than political grounds. By appointing qualified Republicans, he managed to maintain the high quality of the civil service.

Madison and Monroe, being of the same political faith as Jefferson, found no reason to disturb the established service. John Quincy Adams, although not holding to the political views of his immediate predecessors, refused to pack the service with his own supporters as a matter of principle.

The spoils system. Political patronage is the practice of rewarding one's political supporters with appointments as well as bestowing other favors, such as government contracts, on the same basis. The spoils system, built on the assumption that "to the victor belongs the spoils," stretched political patronage to its farthest extremes.

Andrew Jackson was the first President to introduce the spoils system openly and deliberately into the national government. He removed many appointees in order to provide patronage for party leaders. He also used the patronage technique to strengthen his party and to gain support for his programs. Nevertheless, the introduction of the spoils system was a manifestation of a social and political philosophy cutting deeper than the obvious goal of building party strength. Professor Paul P. Van Riper has written:

> Andrew Jackson's theories of public office came both to symbolize and to support the individualistic and equalitarian spirit of his times as well as the social mobility characteristic of American society. His concept of the spoils system as "reform" also served to dignify and fortify the organizational system of the new Democracy. Democratic politics is considerably more expensive initially than aristocratic politics. In the absence of corporate contributions, the offices furnished that margin of financial and personal incentive which permitted the political machinery of a Martin Van Buren to flourish. The equally important necessity to bridge the gaps within a governmental system based upon both a horizontal and a vertical division of political power, placed a further premium upon any and all devices available for the coordination of public policy now that the unifying forces of the Federalist period were largely gone. But beyond this, the growing size of the executive establishment forced, of necessity, an increasing subletting and delegating of administrative authority, including the appointing power. Thus, the spoils system—and it deserves to be called a system—furnished both a political and an administrative solution to many of the pressing problems of a developing nation.[1]

---

[1] *History of the United States Civil Service* (Evanston, Ill.: Row, Peterson and Company, 1958), p. 535.

Generally speaking, the spoils system flourished between the administrations of Jackson and Lincoln. It has been said of this period that national political campaigns tended to become great lotteries with government jobs as prizes. After every change in the Presidency, the city of Washington was besieged by office-seekers.

Establishment of the Civil Service Commission. Following the Civil War, more and more criticism was directed at the philosophical underpinning of the spoils system as well as its on-the-surface drawbacks. Many reformers believed that the spoils system, while perhaps desirable in its origin as a necessary means of making the bureaucracy more representative of all the people, had outlived its usefulness on this score. In a sense, the majority of the officeholders had themselves become impervious to the needs of the times. As a by-product of the industrial age, there was a growing demand for experts in public as well as private employment; the need for stability in government service loomed more important.

Expressions on the need for civil service reform were incorporated into the platforms of the political parties. Studies and proposals concerning the civil service system were issued by private and congressional groups during the administrations of Presidents Grant and Hayes, but it took a much more dramatic event to generate the public pressure necessary to assure a fundamental change of policy. President Garfield was assassinated by a disappointed office-seeker in 1881. Garfield's death aroused more public indignation over the spoils system than the reformers had been able to stir up over the previous twenty years. Congress responded by passing the Pendleton Act signed by President Arthur in January, 1883.

The Pendleton Act established a Civil Service Commission of three members, no more than two belonging to the same political party, appointed by the President with Senate confirmation. The use of competitive examinations was authorized to determine the fitness of applicants for public service; provisions were included to protect federal employees from forced campaign contributions; a probationary period was to precede a career-type appointment; the President was authorized to establish rules and regulations for carrying out the provisions of the Civil Service Act. In other words, this important legislation was a move toward the creation of a *merit* system for federal employment under the cooperative leadership of the President and the Commission.

Slow growth of the merit system. Foreign students are frequently amazed by the leisurely growth of the merit system in the United States. The Pendleton Act, despite publicity as a drastic reform, covered only 13,780 positions or just ten per cent of the total field. The Civil Service Commission received the most niggardly appropriations and was regarded with extreme suspicion by members of Congress, heads of departments, and the political fraternity in general. Ten years after the new system went into effect just over one-fourth of the federal positions were subject to it; twenty years saw 51 per cent placed under its jurisdiction. By 1914 the proportion had passed the two-thirds mark, and in 1924 it almost reached the three-fourths level. In 1932 a new high of over 81 per cent was achieved, but the impact of the depression—and the return of the Democrats to power after twelve years of Republican administration—pushed the figure back

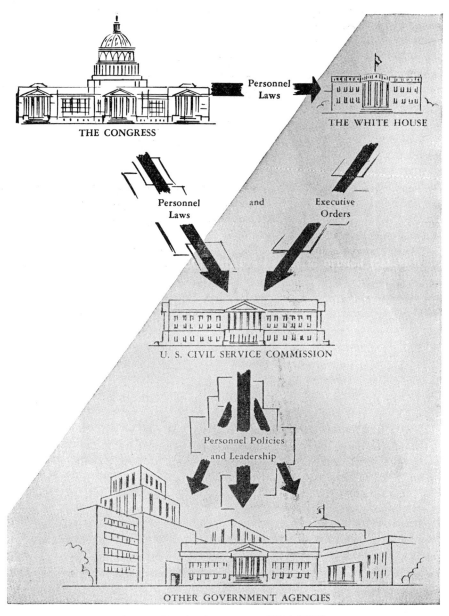

MANAGING THE FEDERAL MERIT SYSTEM

to slightly over 60 per cent in 1937. The Ramspeck Act of 1940 brought the number of employees under merit appointments to approximately 80 per cent. At present, 86 per cent of federal employees are in positions subject to the merit system supervised by the Civil Service Commission.

Excepted positions. The remaining federal positions, some 14 per cent, are excepted from the Commission's merit procedures. Of these, slightly more than a third are excepted by statute and the others by action of the Civil Service Commission. Some people believe that all of these are patronage positions, but actually relatively few are really patronage jobs.

Examples of positions excepted by statute are doctors, dentists, and nurses in the Bureau of Medicine and Surgery of the Veterans Administration, and all positions in the Tennessee Valley Authority, Atomic Energy Commission, and the F.B.I.

Positions excepted by action of the Civil Service Commission are placed in one of three schedules—A, B, or C—after a study has been made by the Commission of relevant factors such as duties, pay, and location of the positions.

Schedule A is for positions for which it is not practicable to hold any examination. Examples are professional and technical experts for temporary consultation purposes, narcotics agents for undercover work, and many positions in foreign countries.

Schedule B covers certain positions for which competitive examinations are impracticable, but for which noncompetitive examinations are given. Examples are positions assigned to Navy communications intelligence activities.

Schedule C is for positions whose occupants serve in a policy-determining capacity to the politically appointed heads of agencies or in a confidential capacity to them and their key officials. This schedule was established to define more clearly the career service by setting apart from it positions properly in the political area. Supposedly positions in this schedule should be filled by the administration in power with persons who fully support its political aims and policies.

No examination is required for appointment to Schedule C jobs. Departments and agencies may recommend to the Commission that a particular position be placed in this category, but the final authority to place positions in Schedule C rests with the Civil Service Commission. Altogether there were some 1,200 positions excepted under this procedure as of 1958.

RECRUITMENT, EXAMINING, AND HIRING

Contrary to the popular notion, the Civil Service Commission is not charged with making appointments to federal positions. The Commission directs recruitment and examination programs, but the agencies do the actual hiring.

Recruitment. No aspect of public personnel administration is more important than recruiting, for unless the basic material is reasonably good, no amount of in-service training, supervision, service rating, classification, or research will be able to provide an adequate staff of public employees. Underlying the entire recruiting problem is the prestige generally attached to public employment. If citizens generally believe that public employment offers satisfactory opportunities and is worthy of the services of the most capable men and women, recruiting is likely to be comparatively simple. On the other hand, if popular prejudice holds that the rewards of public employment are inadequate and that only the below-average can find scope for his talents in that capacity, the greatest effort will be necessary to attract good material. The United States has not been particularly fortunate in the prestige value of public employment, at least until quite recently. Prior to 1933 very few university-trained people seriously thought of public service as a career. That is not to say, of course, that there were no able public employees for, despite the general psychology, a reasonable number of capable people did somehow or other get into the service.

For a long period the Civil Service Commission carried the main burden in recruiting employees for the federal service. Frequently, no special effort was made to get the announcements of examinations to the particular groups of people or institutions who would be most likely to indicate an interest. In recent years there has been a vast improvement in recruitment techniques. Now United States civil service boards of examiners play an integral role in the recruitment and examining of candidates. These boards of examiners are made up of agency personnel who are nominated by the agencies and are subject to Commission approval. The Commission trains the board members in recruiting and examining techniques, directs and supervises their operations, and inspects their work to make sure it conforms to Commission standards. Over 800 boards of examiners are in operation throughout the United States. Some are located in post offices, and many are in other agency field establishments across the country. Contacts are maintained with sources of applicants—especially colleges, universities, and specialized organizations.

The Federal Service Entrance Examination is of particular interest to college students. The examination is especially designed to recruit highly qualified career-minded people who have the potential to become career managers, skilled technicians, and professional administrators. Through 1958 over 157,000 persons had taken the Federal Service Entrance Examination. Of this number, 73,000 passed the examination, and over 12,000 men and women were selected for appointment.

Examinations. Examinations for all kinds of jobs are not open at all times. There must be jobs to fill before an examination is scheduled and applications are accepted. Agencies—not the Commission—decide how many employees to hire and when to fill jobs, subject to appropriations made by

Congress and controls exercised by management in the executive branch.

When an agency has or expects to have vacancies and there is no existing list of eligibles for the jobs, the Commission may be asked, or the agency's civil service board of examiners may request permission to schedule an examination. The Commission conducts examinations for positions which are common to a number of agencies or for which it has been impracticable to set up boards of examiners.

Assembled examinations. The majority of applicants for federal civil service are given assembled examinations. After their applications have been approved, they are notified to present themselves on a scheduled date at a specified examination place. A card bearing each one's name and the examination to which he has been admitted is furnished for identification. Due attention is given to the convenience of the applicants, and consequently examinations are held at numerous centers in every state. The questions are uniform, however, for all of those throughout the country taking the same examination. A time limit is imposed so that stragglers will not take undue advantage.

Unassembled examinations. Although some of the beginning positions calling for technical and professional training are included under assembled examinations, the majority of these posts are in the unassembled category. In other words, candidates for a job which requires professional training and a considerable amount of practical experience are not asked to present themselves at any one place for a written examination. Because training and experience are the most important factors determining ability to fill these positions successfully, the candidate is required to submit a detailed statement of the courses he has taken in specified fields, the degrees he holds, the books and articles he has written, the investigations he has made, and the practical experience he has had in his profession. Transcripts of credits may be required from universities; references from those under whom one has received professional training or employment are necessary; and an essay describing qualifications and pertinent background may be submitted. Examiners draw up a scale of weights by which to rate the education and professional experience and thus arrive at a grade for each candidate. The grading of unassembled examinations is, of course, not a simple matter. A civil service expert and an expert in the field of examination must read every submitted test.

Personal interviews and oral examinations. Either the assembled or the unassembled type of examination may include a personal interview or oral examination, but the latter is much more likely to require this supplementary test. A written examination does not indicate the many personality traits which are important to successful performance. Personnel bureaus may stipulate an oral examination or a personal interview with two or more examiners who have had experience in the field in which the position is classified.

Vocational tests. For a number of positions the primary requisite is actual skill in performance rather than a potential ability to acquire skill. Typists are judged very largely on the typing which they turn out; railway mail clerks are evaluated by their speed and accuracy in sorting mail under somewhat trying circumstances. Inasmuch as it is recognized generally that the best way to test these skills is a practical exercise based on them, the federal civil service now makes wide use of vocational tests.

Eligible lists. As soon as the candidates in an examination have been rated, an eligible list is prepared which contains the names of all who have received a grade of 70 or more, with the highest at the top and those having just 70 at the bottom. From these lists names are drawn as calls come in from various appointing agencies.

Veterans preference. The veterans of former wars have been a potent force in American political life. Veterans feel that they are entitled to special consideration with respect to public jobs and, through organized pressure groups, have managed to secure preferred treatment for themselves. Most personnel experts have long since accepted the political fact of life that veterans preference for public employment is inevitable. However, modifications of certain aspects of veterans preference laws and regulations are possible at times. For example, until 1953, a certain number of points were added to veterans' scores, if the addition would bring the score up to 70; now veterans must receive a passing grade (at least 70 per cent) in order for the extra points to count.

Ten points are added to the earned ratings of those persons who have a service-connected disability, or who are receiving disability retirement benefits, or to the wife or widowed mother if the veteran cannot qualify because of disability, or to the unmarried widows of veterans. In addition, for certain positions, persons receiving the ten-point bonus are placed at the top of the register, ahead of others with higher scores, if they have been certified as having at least a ten per cent disability. Non-disabled veterans have five points added to their scores.

There are many other aspects of veterans preference besides the addition of points to the exam marks. Certain custodial positions, as determined by the President, are open only to veterans; requirements as to age, height, weight, and minimal educational standards may be waived in many cases. Also, once appointed to a position, veterans have advantages over nonveterans with respect to tenure and appeal rights.

The hiring process. In order to facilitate the work of the Civil Service Commission, divisions of personnel supervision and management have been set up in all the important departments and independent establishments since 1938. These are headed by personnel experts whose units handle the relations between the agency and the Civil Service Commission and perform personnel functions for the agencies.

When an agency wants to fill a competitive-service position by hiring someone outside the federal service, it asks the appropriate Commission's office or board of examiners for a *certificate of eligibles.* To fill a single vacancy, the Commission office or board of examiners sends the agency the names of the top three eligibles on the register. The appointing officer may select any one of the three names certified.

If an appointing authority is uncertain about the qualifications of the persons whose names have been certified, he may call them in for personal interviews. Inasmuch as it is scarcely feasible to summon those who live a thousand miles distant, a nearby person may be appointed. If one person is chosen from among the three, the personnel officer of the agency formally notifies the fortunate one, and the remaining names are returned to the Commission or board of examiners where they will again be placed on the register.

Employees may be moved to other positions at the same or higher grades in their own or different agencies without again competing with persons outside the federal service. For such internal shifting, the Commission prescribes standards to assure that the candidate is qualified to do the job for which he is being considered. The standards specify the experience, training, and other requisites persons must have to qualify for the jobs. Agencies have been given authority to determine whether individual employees meet these standards; and they can promote, transfer, or reassign their employees without prior approval of the Commission. However, the Commission inspects the agencies' procedures with respect to such matters, and if violations are found, the agency concerned may have its authority to act revoked.

Types of appointments. The number and kinds of people employed by the federal government at any one time are influenced by many factors, such as the public demand for services and national emergencies. Thus the work force may be smaller or larger one year than it was the year before. Government is no different from private industry in that its personnel needs vary from month to month and year to year. And, like many progressive business establishments, the federal government has developed a well-rounded career plan for those qualified individuals who seek careers in the public service.

Not everyone who enters the federal service intends to spend his entire working life in it, and also, the government may not have continuing jobs for everyone who is employed at any one time, as during war-time expansion. The appointment system takes these and other factors into account by providing different types of appointments, each designed for specific situations. The three types most commonly used are temporary, career-conditional, and career.

When it is known that a particular job is of a temporary nature, the person hired to do that job is given a *temporary* appointment with no promise of continued employment. For example, the thousands of additional postal workers employed during the Christmas mailing rush are hired as temporary employees.

When it is believed that a job is of a continuing nature, the person appointed to it is given a *career-conditional* appointment if he is a new employee. If he satisfactorily completes a probationary period of one year and demonstrates his career intentions by satisfactorily serving two addi-

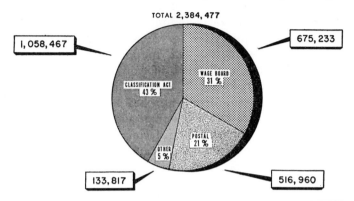

DISTRIBUTION OF FULL-TIME FEDERAL EMPLOYEES BY PAY SYSTEM

tional years, he may be given a *career* appointment. A career appointment does not guarantee a lifetime job. It does, however, make a government career possible by giving the employee the privilege of transferring to other jobs in the civil service without competing with the general public; it puts the employee in a preferred group that is among the last to be reached in the event of layoffs; and it simplifies re-employment in case a person leaves the civil service and decides to return at a later date.

Compensation. In general the salaries in the lower grades for federal government employees are the equal of, or higher than, pay for similar work in private industry. The higher one goes up the pay scale, however, the lower the salaries are when compared with those for similar work in private industry. The head of a federal agency does not get anywhere near the salary paid to the head of a large corporation. The highest salary any employee in the career service can expect to receive is $20,000 a year, the ceiling placed on salaries under present law.

Elaborate classification schemes attempt to guarantee "equal pay for substantially equal work." Men and women are paid the same for the same kind of work and there are safeguards to prevent discrimination as to race, religion, or political beliefs. The Civil Service Commission issues classification standards which indicate the kinds of positions that may be placed in the various classes on the basis of duties, responsibilities, and qualifications required. It also establishes class titles and sets forth the grade for each class. The agencies have the responsibility, using the published standards, of determining the class and grade (and consequently the pay) of individual jobs. If no published standards apply directly, agencies classify positions consistently with similar standards. By periodic on-the-spot audits, the Commission determines whether the agencies are correctly applying the standards. The Civil Service Commission has the authority to revoke or suspend an agency's classification authority if necessary. There are three major pay systems which include around 95 per cent of all civilian employees.

A classification act determines the pay for nearly one million clerical, administrative, fiscal, professional, technical, and most custodial and protective employees. There are eighteen grades, ranging from grade one, which includes positions having the simplest, routine duties, to grade eighteen, which covers positions having the most difficult and responsible duties. The number of positions in grades 16, 17, and 18 is restricted by law.[2] To each grade, except grade eighteen, there is attached a range of several pay rates which include the entrance rate and several additional rates to which employees are advanced on the basis of satisfactory performance and length of service. The Civil Service Commission is authorized to establish entrance rates above the minimum pay rates for positions where the supply of manpower is short and the government is faced with unfavorable competition in getting its fair share of available qualified people.

The Postal Field Service Compensation Act fixes the pay for approximately a half-million clerks, carriers, postmasters, and other employees who receive, transport, and deliver mail. The salaries of these employees are based upon the duties performed and are paid in accordance with salary schedules provided by law.

The wage-board system includes over 700,000 employees in the crafts, trades, and labor occupations, frequently referred to as "blue-collar" workers. The large majority of these employees is in the Department of Defense. The pay of this group is determined by their respective agencies in accordance with local prevailing rates.

The remaining government workers (about five per cent) are paid under various systems that were designed to meet special conditions. For example, such is the case for employees in the Tennessee Valley Authority and the Foreign Service.

TRAINING, RATINGS AND PROMOTIONS

Government employees are given wide opportunity to advance in their organizations. Agency officials realize that they must provide employees with training and career development assistance if management is to have capable personnel to fill key positions in the future.

Training. Training activities vary from one agency to another, but all of them seek to develop employees who show promise and prepare them for positions of increasing responsibility. All agencies have orientation programs in some form or another for new employees. In some cases employees enter training programs which teach the best ways to handle job assignments. Some

---

2 As of 1962, 2,570 of these "super grades" were allowed.

employees may be trained at government expense in non-government training centers such as colleges and universities when it is in the best interests of the federal government to do so. The Civil Service Commission has general responsibilities for co-ordinating training programs and assisting the departments and agencies in employee training matters.

Ratings. The government, like private organizations, attempts to encourage and measure the efficiency of employees. Agencies have experimented with various ways of rating employees' performances. Certain jobs may be rated under a precise unit measurement approach, as for example, the number of pages of routine typing turned out by a typist. Sometimes a "graphic" rating scale has been utilized in which the supervisor checks on a prepared form various facets of the employee's traits and performance. In 1950 Congress enacted a Performance Rating Act which provided for three ratings—unsatisfactory, satisfactory, and outstanding. Many critics have noted that the onerous restrictions placed on supervisors with respect to rating employees in the highest and lowest categories almost automatically pushes employees into the "satisfactory" class. The second Hoover Commission found that approximately 98 per cent of those rated were placed in the "satisfactory" group.

Promotions. In an organization as vast as the federal service, there is always room for and need for the outstanding employee who seriously applies himself to the task of becoming more useful and capable. Of course, the essential problem in any promotion system is to assure that advancement is on the basis of merit rather than on some other criteria. A recent study of promotions in the federal government revealed that the annual rate of promotion is about one out of every four employees. The Civil Service Commission and the agencies have long been concerned with improving promotion policies.

In 1958 the Civil Service Commission announced the institution of "The New Federal Merit Promotion Program." Prior to this, the only absolute promotion requirement was that an employee to be promoted had to meet the minimum requirements for the position. As of January 1, 1959, any promotion programs had to meet the following mandatory requirements:

> (1) Promotions are to be made only under the newly established government-wide promotion program and only under appropriate guidelines and plans established by the agency. These guidelines must embrace such merit features as:
> > (a) areas of consideration which are as broad as practicable,
> > (b) qualification standards which are at least equal to competitive standards,
> > (c) evaluation methods that are reasonable, valid, and applied fairly,
> > (d) selection from among the best qualified,
> > (e) prompt release from former positions of persons selected for promotion.

(2) Agencies shall consult employees in the development and installation of their plans.

(3) Agencies shall make information on promotion plans readily available to employees.

(4) Individual promotion actions shall be documented to show that each selection for promotion was made in accordance with the plans.

(5) The Civil Service Commission through its inspection process will review agency guidelines, plans, and promotion actions to determine their compliance with the new program.

EMPLOYEE RECOGNITION AND WELFARE

For many years the federal service enjoyed a competitive advantage over private employers in many job categories because of the "fringe benefits" available to public servants. In the last twenty years or so, however, many business concerns have offered as attractive or more attractive "benefits" than the federal government. In recent years the federal government has improved its own programs with respect to such matters.

Awards program. An effective means of encouraging and rewarding valuable employee ideas and superior accomplishment is provided by the Government Employees Incentive Awards Act which became effective in 1954. The purpose of the incentive awards program is three-fold; first, to improve government operations through the good ideas and superior performances of federal employees; second, to increase employee satisfaction by recognition of their contributions to improving government operations; and third, to increase the prestige of the federal service by having more people, both in and out of government, informed on the many superior achievements and outstanding ideas of federal employees. During a recent year, well over 100,000 employees shared in awards totaling over nine million dollars. It was estimated that this investment improved government operation to the extent of nearly 170 million dollars. The highest award—$25,000 (the maximum allowed)—went to a navy scientist for his contributions to missile development.

Employee unions. As far back as 1889, the letter carriers found it to their advantage to organize themselves into associations. As the movement spread among other federal workers, the associations took on the characteristics of trade unions although they did not designate themselves as such. In 1912 Congress recognized the right of federal employees to organize and petition Congress, but the Taft-Hartley Act of 1947 banned employee unions which claimed the right to strike against the federal government. Today government workers have several unions which deal with their problems. The largest number of members are found in the various postal employees unions and the regular trade unions for the building trades and printers. White collar workers in the classified service may belong to the

National Federation of Federal Employees or the American Federation of Government Employees. All the unions seek to secure higher wages and better hours and working conditions for government workers. Probably the various postal workers' unions are the most effective in dealing with Congress because union members are to be found in sizable numbers in every congressional district in the country. It is difficult to assess the effectiveness of the unions representing the classified white collar workers, but the unions may be assumed to have had some effect on the increase in salaries and the improvement in working conditions over the years.

Vacation and sick leave. Most federal employees earn annual leave for vacation and other purposes at the rate of thirteen days a year for the first three years and twenty days a year for the next twelve years. After fifteen years, they earn twenty-six days of annual leave each year. Employees also earn thirteen days of sick leave a year which may be used during illness or for medical, optical, or dental attention, and it may be accumulated and carried over from year-to-year without limitation.

Group life insurance. In keeping with modern trends in industry, Congress has provided a fringe benefit in the form of group life insurance which is available to most government employees. This insurance is obtained by the government through private insurance companies. Participation in the plan is voluntary and each employee who joins is insured for an amount which is approximately equal to his yearly salary.

Because of the large number of employees in the group and because record keeping has been reduced to a minimum, the cost to the employee and to the government is very reasonable. Through regular payroll deductions, the employee pays $6.50 a year for each $1,000 of his insurance and the government pays an additional $3.25. There is no cost to an employee after he reaches the age of sixty-five nor to an employee after retirement with at least fifteen years of service or for disability. However, the insurance carried by an employee or retired employee gradually reduces, beginning when he reaches the age of sixty-five until it reaches 25 per cent of the original amount.

Group health insurance. In July of 1960 the federal government initiated the policy of sharing the cost with employees of group health insurance plans. The government's contribution varies from one-third to one-half of the total cost depending upon the particular plan selected by the individual.

Retirement. The federal government has more than a dozen separate retirement systems. The largest of these, embracing over two million civilian employees, is the Civil Service Retirement System. The other plans apply to special groups such as employees of the Tennessee Valley Authority and the Foreign Service.

Employees under the Civil Service Retirement System contribute six and one-half per cent of their basic salaries and employing agencies match employee deductions. These amounts are deposited to a fund which from time-to-time is supplemented by direct appropriations by Congress.

Retirement benefits are computed on the basis of length of service and the highest average annual basic salary earned during any five consecutive years of service. Employees must retire at age seventy after fifteen or more years of service and may retire with full benefits at age sixty with thirty years of service. Employees who become totally disabled after five years or more of service also receive retirement benefits.

DISCIPLINARY AND REMOVAL ACTIONS

Although career employees under the merit system enjoy what is usually designated as "permanent tenure," they are subject to disciplinary action and to removal for cause. Neglect of duty, regular tardiness, and infractions of rules and regulations may be penalized by a reprimand, a reduction in rank, or suspension for a period of time with loss of pay.

The decision to fire incompetent or undesirable employees belongs to the departments and agencies. If the decision of the agency is sound and based on satisfactory evidence of an employee's incompetence or unsuitability, neither law nor the Civil Service Commission's regulations interfere with removal action. On the other hand, officials have often complained that the procedural protections afforded employees are so time consuming for the agency that in many cases persons are retained despite their incompetence. Nevertheless, thousands of government employees are removed for cause each year. Generally, an employee serving the probationary or trial period of one year may be removed merely upon written notice giving the reasons and has no appeal to higher authority. A mere written notice is sufficient for employees with purely temporary appointments and for almost all non-veterans in positions excepted from the competitive civil service. However, the majority of federal employees are covered by the Lloyd-La Follette Act, the Veterans' Preference Act of 1944, or procedures prescribed in Commission regulations.

If he has completed the probation period and has other than a temporary job in the competitive service, a non-veteran removed for cause may ask the Civil Service Commission to review the action only on the grounds that the proper procedure was not used, or that he was removed for political reasons or discriminated against because of marital status or physical handicap.

Veterans are given greater appeal rights under the Veterans' Preference Act. They may appeal to the Commission for a review of the basis for the removal action as well as the procedure used.

LOYALTY-SECURITY PROGRAM

Since 1939 employees of the national government have been asked to sign an oath stating that they are loyal to the United States and not members of any organization advocating the violent overthrow of our constitutional system. A demand for a more stringent check to ensure that government workers were loyal led to an executive order by President Truman in 1947, under which an employee could be removed if reasonable doubt of his loyalty were found. A second executive order in 1951 was still more strict in its provisions. The Civil Service Commission created a Loyalty Review Board to handle cases arising under the executive orders. In 1953 President Eisenhower abolished the board, and placed the final responsibility for dismissing employees as security risks in the hands of department and agency heads.

The Supreme Court has not dealt kindly with a number of actions of the government in carrying out its loyalty-security program. After first saying that an employee need not be confronted by his accusers,[3] the Court has since been less generous to the government. The judges have now ruled that the security program applies only to persons working for "sensitive" agencies.[4] The Court has also held that no person can be removed from his job unless agency procedures are followed in the removal process.

Congress established a Commission on Government Security in 1955 to make a study of existing security programs and to make recommendations for improvements. The Commission, reporting in 1957, recommended that there should be a "loyalty program applicable to all positions and a suitability program within the framework of civil service regulations." The Commission stated that any person about whose loyalty there is reasonable doubt should be dismissed from the federal service regardless of whether he is in a position classified sensitive or nonsensitive. On the other hand, if the employee is found to be a "security risk" but loyal, he should be transferred to a nonsensitive position or be dismissed under normal civil service procedures. Although these recommendations have not been enacted into law, they have been accepted in principle by various governmental agencies.

Civil Service Commission investigations. Since 1948 the Civil Service Commission has been responsible for investigating applicants for federal service positions. Most of the investigations are made to determine the fitness of persons employed or being considered for employment. Depending on the duties of the position involved, the Commission conducts either national agency checks and inquiries or full field investigations.

The national agency check and inquiry is a limited type of investigation

---

3 *Bailey* v. *Richardson,* 341 U. S. 918 (1951).

4 *Cole* v. *Young,* 351 U. S. 536 (1956).

of persons who have been appointed to nonsensitive positions. These are positions with duties that do not affect the national security. Approximately 80 per cent of all government positions are in this group. These investigations consist of checking the files of the major investigative agencies in Washington, and sending written inquiries to previous employers, references, schools, local police departments, etc.

Full field investigations are made of persons to be assigned to sensitive positions. These positions have duties that are critical in terms of national security. Full field investigations include these basic elements: (1) a national agency check; (2) personal interviews with former employers, supervisors, references, neighbors, school authorities, and other associates; and (3) checks of police, credit, and other pertinent records.

SUMMARY

Gone are the days when civil servants were conceived of primarily as clerks handling routine paper work. The functions undertaken by the federal government today call for skilled personnel in technical, professional, managerial, and research fields.

The early Presidents managed to develop a fairly adequate merit system of appointments even though competitive examinations were not part of the process. The "spoils system" no doubt resulted in a general lowering of the capabilities of government employees but did serve to democratize the federal service. Eventually, the concept inherent in the "spoils system" clashed with ideals of efficiency, specialization, and continuity of service which had become accepted as desirable conditions of industrial employment. The assassination of President Garfield by a disappointed office-seeker provided the impetus needed to assure legislative action toward civil service reform.

From the modest beginnings following the creation of the Civil Service Commission, a merit system based on competitive examinations developed slowly. As the twentieth century brought more and more persons into government and as the public service rivaled private industry in the complexity of functions undertaken, the major civil service problem tended to become how to obtain, train, and retain the best persons possible rather than how to keep out the most inept applicants. Within the past quarter of a century, the Civil Service Commission has devoted much of its attention to leading and cooperating with hiring agencies in recruitment, classification, training, and promotion policies.

If the government expects to get its fair share of capable personnel, it must not lag behind industry in the rewards offered government workers. Government salaries in the lower grades are competitive enough but become much less so in the top grades. Probably the government can never hope to compete on the basis of salary alone at these levels. Thus arises the necessity of building attractive career-development programs emphasizing prestige values as well as the more tangible elements such as reasonable promotion possibilities, retirement, insurance and vacation and sick leave plans.

BIBLIOGRAPHIC NOTE

Textbooks on public personnel administration include thorough discussions of the federal civil service. Among the works in this category are Glen O. Stahl, *Public Personnel Administration* (4th ed., New York: Harper & Brothers, 1956); Norman J. Powell, *Personnel Administration in Government* (Englewood Cliffs, N. J.: Prentice-Hall, Inc., 1956); and William G. Torpey, *Public Personnel Management* (Princeton, N. J.: D. Van Nostrand Company, Inc., 1952).

For an excellent analytical history of the federal civil service, one may consult Paul P. Van Riper's *History of the United States Civil Service* (Evanston, Ill.: Row, Peterson and Company, 1958). The struggle of a reform organization to improve federal civil service is detailed in Frank M. Stewart, *The National Civil Service Reform League: History, Activities, and Problems* (Austin: University of Texas Press, 1929). For a particularly enlightening publication number on the modern civil service, see American Assembly, *The Federal Government Service: Its Character, Prestige, and Problems* (New York: Columbia University, Graduate School of Business, 1954).

A number of recent studies stress the importance of the higher civil service executives and the difficulties of keeping them in government. See Paul T. David and Ross Pollock, *Executives for Government* (Washington, D. C.: The Brookings Institution, 1957); Marver H. Bernstein, *The Job of the Federal Executive* (Washington, D. C.: The Brookings Institution, 1958); and John J. Corson, *Executives for the Federal Service: A Program for Action in Time of Crises* (New York: Columbia University Press, 1952).

The loyalty-security issue has produced a number of books. On this subject see R. S. Brown, Jr., *Loyalty and Security* (New Haven, Conn.: Yale University Press, 1958); E. Boutelon, *Federal Loyalty Security Programs* (Ithaca, N. Y.: Cornell University Press, 1953); and Sandra Weinstein, *Personnel Security Programs of the Federal Government* (New York: Fund for the Republic, 1954). Also on this subject, see the *Report* of the Commission of Government Security (Washington, D. C.: Government Printing Office, 1957).

The two Hoover Commissions made many recommendations highlighting the problems and suggesting ways for improving the federal civil service. See U. S. Commission on Organization of the Executive Branch, *Personnel Management* (Washington, D. C.: Government Printing Office, 1949) and U. S. Commission on Organization of the Executive Branch, *Personnel and Civil Service* (Washington, D. C.: Government Printing Office, 1955).

For a discussion of personnel management in a government agency free to develop its own program, see Harry L. Case, *Personnel Policy in a Public Agency: The T.V.A. Experience* (New York: Harper & Brothers, 1955).

The *Annual Report* of the Civil Service Commission includes statistics, highlights the past year's developments in personnel management, and comments upon pending legislation relevant   federal civil service.

21

National Finance

THE financial operation of the national government challenges the understanding of the citizen perhaps more than any other governmental activity. The magnitude of government finance is partly responsible for this fact, but this is no doubt the easiest facet to comprehend. The complications are compounded by various interrelations which often spur the experts to acrimonious debate. It is now generally agreed that monetary and fiscal powers are valuable weapons at the disposal of the government to fight depressions, unemployment, and a slumping national income. But the problem is when to use what weapon or combination of weapons. Coordination of financial policy is extremely difficult with a number of executive agencies such as the Bureau of the Budget, the Treasury Department, and the Federal Reserve System wielding great influence. Finally, Congress zealously guards its constitutional position with respect to the power of the purse. Add a strong mixture of politics to the above technical problems, and the opening sentence of this paragraph makes even more sense.

FISCAL AND MONETARY POLICIES

The fiscal and monetary policies of the national government are directed toward the goal of maintaining high employment levels and promoting continuous economic growth without undue inflation. Fiscal action includes government taxing, spending, borrowing, and debt management; monetary policy is concerned with the volume of money, the availability of credit, and the rate of interest.

Older economic theories held that the normal state of a free economy was always at full-employment levels. Temporary departures (depressions) were recognized as being inherent in the capitalistic system, but so were self-corrective actions. In other words, the stability of the economic system was primarily the business of business—not of government.

When the Federal Reserve System was established in 1913, there was widespread belief in the United States that the monetary system was a primary cause of periodic depressions which appeared invariably to be set off by financial stringency and crisis. It seemed then that there were increasingly frequent and severe mechanical failures in the functioning of the system which was supposed to provide the money to keep the economic system in motion. Supporters of the Federal Reserve Act expected the newly-created banking system to remedy these "mechanical failures" by giving the country an elastic currency, by providing adequate facilities for discounting commercial paper, and through supervision over banking.

The "Great Depression" indicated that monetary policies, as administered by the Federal Reserve System, were not in themselves enough to head off economic chaos. During the administrations of Franklin D. Roosevelt, the government stressed fiscal policies as one proper means of combating the depression. The most obvious manifestations of the new emphasis were the various "pump priming" operations of the government. The total effect of many *ad hoc* programs, each designed to meet a particular need or to assist a particular group, was to expand government expenditures greatly. It was expected that such policies would place more purchasing power in the hands of consumers, thus tending to increase consumer spending with a resultant rise in employment, profits, and prices. World War II pushed into the background the many bitter arguments as to the necessity and efficacy of the New Deal's fiscal measures.

The Employment Act of 1946. The Employment Act of 1946, passed by overwhelming majorities in both houses of Congress, committed the federal government to use all practical means to maintain economic stability and maximum employment. The legislative history of the law was marked by sharp conflict over its wording and precise intention.[1] Administration and labor leaders wished to commit the federal government to the full use of its fiscal powers to guarantee full-employment. Other groups, particularly from the world of business, wished to rely more on the private sector of the economy to provide jobs. These latter groups, although they believed that monetary policy had a useful function to perform, were reluctant to rely too heavily on fiscal measures; they feared that undue concentration on full-employment would lead to higher labor costs, mounting deficits, rising prices, and expanded governmental activity. The final wording was a considerably altered version of the original bill as it had been introduced. Thus the goal of "full-employment" became "maximum employment"; specific commitments to use public works and federal loans to maintain employment were changed in favor of a policy of using "all practical means"; the over-all purpose of the act became to "promote" rather than to "assure" employment.

Impact of Treasury operations. The cash income and outgo of the Treasury directly affect the amount of funds at the disposal of the public, the distribution of their disposable income, and the distribution of the total expenditure.

---

[1] For a detailed account of its passage, see Stephen K. Bailey, *Congress Makes A Law* (New York: Columbia University Press, 1950).

Treasury *receipts,* whether from taxation or the sale of government securities to non-bank holders, shift money and deposits—mostly deposits—from individuals and business firms to the government. Every dollar taken in by the government is taken out of the pocketbook or bank balance of someone. The direct and immediate effect is to reduce the spending power of the public by the same amount that the government's is increased.

About four-fifths of federal revenues come from income taxes on individuals and corporations. The remainder comes from a variety of sources such as inheritance, excise, and social security taxes.

Treasury *expenditures* place additional funds at the disposal of the public. Every dollar paid out by the government gives someone another dollar to spend. In the aggregate, expenditures tend to return funds that Treasury receipts drained away.

Expenditures affect the distribution of total spending just as receipts affect the distribution of income at the disposal of the public. For example, recent federal budgets have resulted in the largest part of total expenditure going into the military, foreign aid, and atomic energy programs. The bulk of this spending goes into hard goods such as aircraft, munitions, machinery, and equipment. The net effect is that a portion of personal and corporate income which otherwise would have gone for other types of products is channeled into a relatively few industries. In this case the distribution of total spending has been altered in favor of the heavy goods industries.

The net impact of Treasury operations depends primarily on the relation between *receipts and expenditures.* Aggregate spending—public and private—may be affected both by changes in the total as well as in the distribution of funds at the disposal of the public.

The effect on total spending depends primarily on whether the Treasury is operating on a cash deficit or surplus. If the government takes in more than it pays out, the tendency is to reduce money balances and spending; on the other hand, if it pays out more than it takes in, the tendency is to increase them. The final effect, however, depends on how the surplus is used or how the deficit is financed.

If the surplus received is held on deposit in the Federal Reserve Banks or is used to retire government securities held by the federal reserve banks and commercial banks, the excess cash intake is not returned to the public and the funds at its disposal are decreased by the amount of the surplus. If surplus cash receipts are used to retire government securities held by non-bank holders, there is no change in the total amount of funds at the disposal of the public. In this case, all receipts are returned to the public by way of Treasury expenditures plus payments to non-bank bond holders.

A cash deficit increases the amount of funds at the disposal of the public only if it is met by borrowing from the banking system. If it is met by selling Treasury securities to non-bank buyers, cash receipts from the public will be as large as payments to the public.

Treasury operations are also likely to effect a shift in the pattern of expenditures. If receipts are drawn mainly from the higher and paid out to the lower income groups, the tendency is likely to be to diminish investment and increase consumer spending; if receipts are drawn mostly from the lower-income groups and are used for investment, the tendency is likely to be the opposite.

Debt management operations may be used so as to enlarge or contract the total supply of spendable funds. Spending powers may be reduced by offering types of securities and terms which are attractive to non-bank investors, thus siphoning funds away from the public and diminishing the total demand for goods and services. To increase spending power and stimulate the demand for goods and services, securities can be offered which are attractive to the banking system. Purchases by the commercial banks give the government funds without reducing money balances held by the public. To the extent that the proceeds of new issues are paid out to the public, privately held balances are increased, and individuals and business firms have more to spend.

Economic stability—no simple problem. Neither fiscal nor monetary policies have yet proved as effective in maintaining economic stability as their more ardent supporters appeared to expect. In the first place, there is certainly no general agreement among the "experts" as to exactly what instruments of monetary and fiscal controls should be exercised in a given circumstance. Proper timing of decisions is extremely important, but this, in turn, depends upon forecasts of economic trends which unfortunately often prove incorrect. A prolonged strike in a major industry, such as the steel strike in 1959, has an impact upon the whole economy, including governmental budgetary estimates.

But how does one predict the duration of such a strike? Coordination of governmental fiscal and monetary policies are difficult to achieve. Federal Reserve operations may well be contradictory to the Treasury policies. Then, too, the separation of powers principle may present a serious hurdle. Congress is not always easily persuaded to use its taxing and spending powers in the way that the President desires. Even if Congress is cooperative, there is almost certain to be a long delay between the President's recommendations and the statutes authorizing action.

The employment of fiscal and monetary instruments toward the goal of economic stability is accepted as a proper function of the federal government. However, their particular use will continue to nurture political controversies.

THE TAXING POWER

The responsibility of finding income to meet governmental expenditures has been entrusted by the Constitution to Congress, the exact authorization being: "The Congress shall have the power to lay and collect taxes, duties, imposts, and excises, to pay the debts and provide for the common defense and general welfare of the United States." [2]

TAX LIMITATIONS

Purpose. The taxing power is limited by the stated purposes for which the funds may be spent. "Debts" and "defense" are fairly definite terms, but wide differences of opinion have been expressed as to the meaning of the "general welfare" provision. It should be noted that the phrase does not stand alone, but is associated with the taxing power. In other words, Congress is not empowered to pass any law for the general welfare, but is authorized to tax and spend for the general welfare. Even within this conceptual framework, two divergent views of the meaning of the clause have been espoused since the creation of the Republic. Madison asserted it amounted to no more than a reference to the other powers enumerated in the subsequent clauses of the same section; that, as the United States was a government of limited and enumerated powers, the grant of the power to tax and spend for the general welfare was confined to the enumerated legislative fields. Hamilton, on the other hand, maintained the clause conferred a power separate and distinct from those later enumerated, was not restricted in meaning by the grant of them, and that Congress consequently had a substantive power to tax and to appropriate, limited only by the requirement that it should be exercised to provide for the general welfare of the country.

The Hamilton interpretation is now the prevailing one. As early as 1896,[3] the Supreme Court inclined toward this view, and in 1936 the Court gave its unqualified endorsement to Hamilton's position with respect to the taxing power.[4]

Uniformity of indirect taxes. The Constitution requires that duties, imposts, and excises shall be uniform throughout the United States. The Court has declared the uniformity requirement is "geographical" not "intrinsic." [5] The subject matter of a levy must be taxed at the same rate wherever found in the United States, but legislative classification for tax purposes is permitted. Thus cigars made from a low-grade tobacco may be taxed at a different rate from cigars manufactured from a high-grade tobacco.

Prohibition of export taxes. The Constitution stipulates that Congress is not to tax articles exported from any state. This clause was insisted upon by the southern state delegations in the constitutional convention. They

---

2 Art. I, sec. 8.

3 *United States* v. *Gettysburg Electric Railway Co.,* 160 U. S. 668.

4 *United States* v. *Butler,* 297 U. S. 1. Hamilton's view of the taxing power was accepted even though the Court declared the taxing provisions of the first Agricultural Adjustment Act unconstitutional on the ground, among others, that the processing tax was in fact a penalty imposed upon one group for the benefit of another group.

5 *Knowlton* v. *Moore,* 178 U. S. 41 (1900).

feared their states might be discriminated against under a system which permitted import taxes on goods brought to them and compelled them to pay export taxes on their agricultural products exported to England.

Apportionment of direct taxes. Another limitation on the taxing power which goes back to the fears and jealousies existing among the original states is that which specifies that direct taxes must be apportioned according to population. The Constitution reads: "No capitation, or other direct, tax shall be laid, unless in proportion to the census or enumeration hereinbefore directed to be taken." [6] Before the end of the eighteenth century, the Supreme Court had interpreted "direct taxes" as meaning poll taxes and taxes on land,[7] leaving various other types of taxes as of the indirect variety which could be levied freely without apportionment. Apportionment does not rule out direct taxes, but it makes them so difficult to administer that they have not been attempted for more than half a century.

In looking about for new sources of revenue to meet the expenses of the Civil War, Congress in 1862 enacted a law providing for the imposition of *income taxes* without apportionment among the states on the basis of population. This law operated for a number of years and was finally repealed after the emergency was over. The hard times of the 1890's again led Congress to impose an income tax without apportionment among the states. Almost immediately an attempt was made to have this tax declared unconstitutional on the ground that a tax on income derived from land amounted to a tax on the land itself. A case involving wealthy New York parties reached the Supreme Court the next year after the law went into effect; and after two hearings and a change in the personnel of the Court, it was finally held by a five-to-four vote that the law was contrary to the Constitution.[8] The Supreme Court did not go so far as to say that all income taxes are direct taxes; but it did rule out the tax on the income from land and state and municipal bonds, at the same time declaring that the entire law would have to fall because of these parts. An amendment to the Constitution was proposed to remove the barrier set up by this decision, and in 1913 the Sixteenth Amendment was proclaimed in effect, providing that "Congress shall have the power to lay and collect taxes on incomes, from whatever source derived, without apportionment among the several states, and without regard to any census or enumeration."

State instrumentalities. The Constitution contains no express limitations on the power of either a state or the national government to tax the other or its instrumentalities. The doctrine that there is an implied limitation in this area stems from the case of *McCulloch* v. *Maryland*,[9] which held a state tax on national bank notes invalid on the basis that the tax impeded

---

6 Art. I, sec. 9.

7 See *Hylton* v. *United States,* 3 Dallas 171 (1796).

8 *Pollock* v. *Farmers' Loan and Trust Co.,* 158 U. S. 601 (1895).

9 Reported in 4 Wheaton 316 (1819).

the national government in the exercise of its power to establish and maintain a national bank. The rule of tax immunity was later applied to state and national governments alike, covering among other subjects, salaries of all government officers and employees, government bonds and their interest, and sales of goods for governmental use. Modification of the absolute doctrine began when the Supreme Court ruled that where a state engages in a business enterprise, in contrast to a function traditionally governmental in nature, it loses its tax immunity in the former case.[10]

In recent years other modifications have followed. For example, both national and state governments now tax the salaries of each other's employees. The Court appears inclined to measure state immunity from federal taxation upon the pragmatic test of actual burden rather than by the theoretical limitation growing out of *McCulloch* v. *Maryland*. There is an important difference to be noted with respect to federal-state taxation immunity. The national government may *permit* a state to tax, let us say, the salaries of federal officials, but on the other hand, it may *prohibit* such taxation if it so desires. But if the federal government determines that state officials' salaries are to be subject to an income tax, the states must accept the national policy.

Regulative versus fiscal purpose. The taxing power is ordinarily associated with the raising of revenue and has in general been employed for that purpose. Yet the Supreme Court has long viewed as irrelevant the fact that Congress imposes a tax with the intent of regulating an activity rather than producing revenue. In 1866 Congress passed an act which, in effect, prevented private banks from issuing bank notes by imposing a ten per cent tax on such issuances.[11] In 1912 Congress made it virtually impossible to manufacture matches in which poisonous phosphorus was used by imposing upon such matches a tax of two cents per hundred. The Supreme Court has upheld the Marihuana Tax Act of 1937,[12] which placed a tax of a hundred dollars per ounce on the transfer of marihuana to an unregistered person. A federal tax upon professional gamblers has also been sustained.[13]

On the other hand, in a few instances the Supreme Court has declared national tax laws unconstitutional. A tax imposed on goods produced by child labor was invalidated on the ground that Congress could not do indirectly through the taxing power what it was not empowered to do directly.[14] During prohibition days, Congress levied a tax upon liquor dealers who operated in violation of state law. The Court held this tax void after the repeal of the Eighteenth Amendment, holding that the federal govern-

10 See *South Carolina* v. *United States,* 199 U. S. 437 (1905).
11 *Veazie Bank* v. *Fenno,* 8 Wallace 533 (1869).
12 *United States* v. *Sanchez,* 340 U. S. 42 (1950).
13 *United States* v. *Kahriger,* 345 U. S. 22 (1953).
14 *Bailey* v. *Drexel Furniture Co.,* 259 U. S. 20 (1922).

ment had no power to impose an additional penalty for infractions of state law.[15]

In summary, three generalizations may be made concerning the use of taxes as regulatory devices. First, a law enacted by Congress as a tax statute is not void merely because it has regulatory effects. Second, Congress may use tax laws to aid in enforcing other delegated legislative powers. Third, if Congress is attempting to achieve by a tax, what it is not authorized to do by the Constitution, there is a possibility that the law may be declared unconstitutional.

THE BUDGET

What is the budget? The budget of the United States is the financial expression of the President's program for the government during the ensuing fiscal year—beginning July 1 and ending June 30. By law, it must be transmitted to the Congress each year within fifteen days of the date Congress convenes. In the budget the President estimates how much money will be received under existing tax laws and how much money will be needed to carry out the government's activities, including whatever new programs he proposes.

Preparing a budget. Preparations begin approximately a year before a budget is to become effective—policies and general investigations may have been given attention much earlier. During the summer the Bureau of the Budget requests the various departments and agencies of the government to provide estimates of their next year's expenditures. Estimates of revenue yields are requested from the Treasury Department, which also is expected to furnish the necessary information in regard to interest on the national debt and amounts which are required for tax refunds, retirement of the indebtedness, and so forth. After these estimates have been prepared by the appropriate agencies, they are transmitted to the Bureau of the Budget early in the fall as a basis for its drafting of the next budget.

After the Bureau of the Budget has canvassed the estimates and obtained a general idea of the requests, it schedules *conferences and hearings* in order to go over the various items, especially those that are increased. General conferences may be arranged between representatives of the bureau and of the particular department involved to discuss the estimates. It is the practice in many instances, however, to designate a staff member of the bureau to hold hearings on departmental requests. On these occasions, representatives of the department appear before the examiner to argue their claims, show reasons why their requests are necessary, and answer the questions that may be put by the latter. The hearings on detailed items may be

---

[15] *United States* v. *Constantine*, 296 U. S. 287 (1935).

very important, for they frequently determine whether requests will be approved. The director of the bureau—and in the last analysis the President himself—has the power to overrule the recommendations of the examiner, but this is not the rule in routine matters.

The approved departmental requests, the revenue estimates, and the recommendations for handling any deficit are *assembled into a budget,* and it in turn is submitted to the President for approval unless he has already given his consent step by step. The document is then rushed to the Government Printing Office so that it can be transmitted to Congress by the President during the last week or so of January. It may be added that a budget usually runs to more than a thousand printed pages.

The budget before Congress. Although the President has the responsibility for formulating the budget, its final form depends upon congressional enactment. Congress is free to ignore, modify, or add to the President's recommendations. The Constitution specifies that all revenue measures originate in the House of Representatives; custom decrees that general appropriation bills originate in the House as well. Once a revenue or appropriation bill is reported out of committee, it goes through the same process previously described for the passage of legislation. Eventually Senate committees, and then the Senate as a whole, will get a chance to review and act upon the budget. It is often necessary for a conference committee to work out differences between House and Senate versions of revenue and appropriations bills. The President has the power of veto over these financial measures although it is seldom used with respect to a general appropriation bill.

The budgetary authorization process in Congress is essentially a disjointed effort. Little over-all consideration of the entire budget picture is provided either by the various committees or by Congress as a whole.

The House of Representatives splits the President's neat budget document apart, with the spending proposals going to the Appropriations Committee and the revenue sections to the Ways and Means Committee. (The same type of division is used in the Senate.) Further fragmentation takes place in the committees with the Appropriations Committee parceling out its share to fourteen subcommittees, and the Ways and Means Committee to three subcommittees. In theory the full committee, in each case, reviews the recommendtions of its subcommittees. However, in practice, particularly with respect to the Appropriations Committee, because of the time pressure and the complexity of the subject matter, the subcommittee evaluations usually are accepted by the parent group.

Actually the House, and later the Senate, votes on some twelve to fourteen appropriation measures over a three or four-month period. Congress does not know precisely how much money it is appropriating until all of the figures are totaled at the end of the session.

Since the revenue aspects of the budget are being considered by a different set of committees, and in an uncoordinated time sequence, there is not necessarily any correlation between the amount of expenditures and the money needed to be raised for the spending programs involved.

The Legislative Reorganization Act of 1946 took cognizance of the difficulties described above by providing for a so-called "legislative budget." The act directed that the Committees on Ways and Means and Appropriations of the House of Representatives and the Committees on Finance and Appropriations of the Senate meet jointly at the beginning of each regular session of Congress. After study and consultation this joint committee was to report to each house a "legislative budget" for the ensuing fiscal year including total receipts and expenditures. This procedure was attempted once or twice, but the recommendations of the joint group were ignored by the standing committees. For over a decade now, the joint review committee has not even convened.

Another approach was experimented with in 1950 when the House of Representatives passed an omnibus appropriation bill, that is, a measure which consolidated all appropriation bills into one act. This procedure proved unwieldy, and some members complained that it gave even less time to consider the whole budget than there had been for the various parts. The next year the House reverted to its old method of handling appropriations.

Administrative officials are required to justify their programs before at least four standing legislative committees. This procedure comes about because two statutes must be passed before money is actually available for spending purposes. One statute must authorize an activity, another must provide for its financing. Programs as such are thus reviewed by the non-appropriation committees of the two houses. Acting on the recommendations of these committees, the two houses of Congress vote on the authorizations for program expenditures before appropriating funds to carry them into effect. It is not unusual for an authorization to carry a higher figure than the appropriations committees suggest for expenditures. Of course, it is possible for Congress to overrule its appropriations committees, but this power is in fact seldom exercised.

An annual expenditure budget? The second Hoover Commission pointed out that there was no direct control over the *annual budget surplus or deficit.* This situation arises because the appropriations which Congress authorizes each year are intended to control not annual expenditures but the levels of obligations which the agencies may incur, sometimes over several years. Therefore, although Congress and the executive branch exercise a control concerning the total level of payments over a period of years, the payments are not effectively controlled annually. For example, the Department of the Air Force could not legally contract for, let us say, 1,000 heavy bombers until funds for this purpose were appropriated by Congress. But such an order would not be filled for at least two or three years. Congress would have to make available an appropriation until the total disbursement was made. Thus funds pyramid in size from year to year and make it difficult to balance income and outgo. The Hoover Commission estimated that out of a total of $62.4 billion to be paid out in fiscal 1956, approximately $24.5 billion arose from prior appropriations.

The commission proposed that Congress adopt a new approach to appropriation funds called the "annual accrued expenditure" budget. Under this procedure for those programs with a long lead time between obligation and disbursement, an agency would submit to Congress its proposed program for a fairly long period. Congress would appropriate only that amount actually needed for disbursement purposes in the next fiscal year. For succeeding years the agency would be permitted "contracting authority" for the entire program. In recent years this procedure has been followed in some areas, and prospects appear bright that the principle will be extended.

Executing the budget. After Congress has voted the funds, the executive branch assumes responsibility for administering and controlling the appropriations. The rate at which these may be obligated by the agencies is controlled by the Bureau of the Budget normally on a quarterly basis. Agencies further subdivide their apportionments into allotments to their own organizational units. The Bureau of the Budget may require agencies to establish reserves and is empowered to review and approve agency regulations governing the administrative control of funds.

This system is designed to prevent an agency from using up its funds before the end of the fiscal year. Rather frequently, for one reason or another, an agency requires additional funds beyond its original appropriation if it is to continue at normal operating efficiency. In such a case, Congress usually obliges by passing a deficiency appropriation measure.

At times the question has arisen as to whether the executive authority *must* spend all of the funds appropriated for a project, or whether the appropriations were merely to be considered a ceiling beyond which the administration could not act. In most instances, Congress would consider it praiseworthy if all of the funds appropriated were not spent, but sometimes the failure to spend may be the result of a major policy decision on the part of the President—the wisdom of which Congress may doubt. For example, in 1948 President Truman impounded funds beyond the amount recommended by him for the procurement build-up of the Air Force. This is the type of constitutional issue which is not apt to be settled by any Supreme Court decision but by the political process. So far Congress has grumbled at times, but has never really forced the issue on the point in question. On the other hand, if a President consistently refused to spend funds which Congress believed should be spent, impeachment would certainly be threatened if not pursued.

The General Accounting Office. The General Accounting Office is an agency of the legislative branch of the federal government. The office is directed by a Comptroller General who is appointed by the President with the advice and consent of the Senate for a term of fifteen years and is removable only by a joint resolution of Congress or by impeachment. The General Accounting Office performs an independent audit of receipts, expenditures, and the use of public funds. A power of the Comptroller General which has been more controversial is the function of "settling accounts." In practice this amounts to passing upon the legality of expenditures by the departments and agencies; if such expenditures are not in accordance with the law as interpreted by the Comptroller General, they may be disallowed. Thus, the Comptroller General has developed what, in essence, is a preaudit function since administrative officers check with the General Accounting Office before making expenditures where there is any question of difference of opinion as to the meaning of the law.

RECEIPTS

Income taxes. For many years income taxes have stood first on the list as the number one producer of federal revenues. For the past several years approximately 80 per cent of budgetary receipts have been derived from this source. Income taxes levied by the national government are of the net

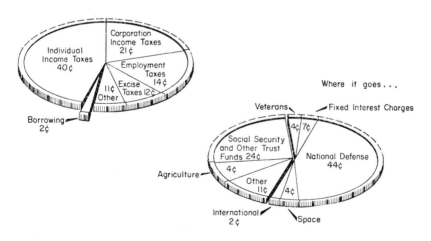

Where it comes from...

Individual Income Taxes 40¢

Corporation Income Taxes 21¢

Employment Taxes 14¢

Excise Taxes 12¢

Other 11¢

Borrowing 2¢

Where it goes...

Veterans 4¢

Fixed Interest Charges 7¢

Social Security and Other Trust Funds 24¢

National Defense 44¢

Agriculture 4¢

Other 11¢

4¢

International 2¢

Space

Fiscal Year 1965 Estimate

THE BUDGET DOLLAR

variety and apply to both individuals and corporations. Since it is based upon ability to pay, the income tax is regarded generally as an equitable tax.

Excise taxes. Excise taxes consistently furnish the second highest amount of the budgetary receipts. Excises are levied on the manufacture or sale of automobiles, tobacco, gasoline, liquor, jewelry, cosmetics, and luggage and on services like air transportation and some entertainment.

Other receipts. Additional receipts are derived from estate and gift taxes, customs, repayments and interest on loans, earnings of certain government enterprises, rents, fees, and sales of timber, power, and surplus property. Of historical interest is the decline in importance of custom duties as a source of income. Once the mainstay of national receipts, responsible for over 90 per cent of all income in the early days of the Republic, the revenue from this source in recent years has amounted to about 1 per cent of the total.

Trust funds. Various funds which the federal government collects are held in trust for later payment to private individuals or to state and local governments. Because these funds are not available for general expenditures, they are not included as ordinary budgetary receipts and expenditures.

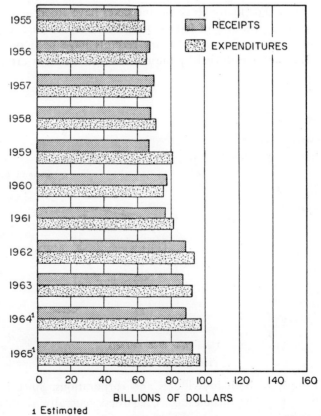

1 Estimated

Source: Chart prepared by Dept. of Commerce, Bureau of the Census.
Data from Executive Office of the President, Bureau of the Budget.

THE MAGNITUDE OF FEDERAL FINANCING: RECEIPTS AND EXPENDITURES FOR FISCAL YEARS
1955 TO 1965

EXPENDITURES

The striking rise of expenditures. It would be impossible for one who had not been in contact with the United States during the last third of a century to conceive of the heights to which public expenditures have risen. Leaving out the war years, federal government spending rose from $521 million in 1900 to about $3 billion a year in the decade following World War I. With the adoption of the antidepression measures in the 1930's, expenditures rose and reached $9.1 billion in 1940. After a spurt in spending caused by World War II, a substantial decline took place, but federal expenditures were still much higher than their prewar levels. Fiscal expenditures for 1950 were more than four times what they had been ten years previously; however, expenditures for national defense, international affairs, veterans services and benefits, and the interest on the national debt were in total amount almost ten times as great as in 1940. With the outbreak of aggression in Korea in June, 1950, expenditures rose again as the United States expanded its military program so that for 1953 the budget exceeded $74 billion. The President recommended expenditures of $92.5 billion for fiscal 1963. Today expenditures for agricultural purposes alone are greater than the total budgetary receipts in 1940.

MONEY AND BANKING

The monetary system. The national government has exclusive control over currency based on the constitutional power of Congress to "coin money, regulate the value thereof, and of foreign coin," [16] and on the constitutional provision forbidding the states to "coin money, emit bills of credit, or make anything but gold and silver coin a tender in payment of debts." [17]

When Congress provided for a uniform system of currency in 1792, the English monetary system of pound, shilling, and pence, was discarded in favor of the less complicated decimal plan of dollars, dimes, and cents. At the same time, a bimetallic monetary system was established, both gold and silver coins being minted with intrinsic values of their own. This system was hard to keep in balance because the relative value of the two metals fluctuated according to the supply and demand curve of each. After trying for over a hundred years to maintain a value ratio between gold and silver by law, Congress in 1900 placed the country on the gold standard. The gold standard was a casualty of the depression, being abandoned by the government in 1933. Today, our monetary system is described as "managed," in which the amount of money in circulation is determined by factors other than the amount of gold held in reserve. Still, gold plays an important role

[16] Art. I, sec. 8.
[17] Art. I, sec. 10.

in our system. Currency is measured in terms of gold even though it is not convertible into gold. Federal reserve notes are based in part on the gold certificates held by the Federal Reserve System. Finally, gold is used to adjust international trade balances.

Federal reserve notes constitute about 85 per cent of the total of currency and coin in circulation today. They are issued by federal reserve banks backed by commercial paper, government bonds, and gold certificates. The composition of currency and coin in circulation has been changed substantially since the turn of the century when gold coins and gold certificates were the principal component. This component maintained its predominant position through 1917, by which time federal reserve notes had taken the lead in relative importance. Since then federal reserve notes have remained the most important segment of currency and coin in circulation although their position declined somewhat from 1924 through 1931 when gold coins and certificates staged a significant comeback. Beginning in 1933, gold coins and certificates were taken from general circulation and the amount now outstanding accounts for one-tenth of one per cent of the total of all currency and coin. National bank notes, which have been in process of retirement since 1935, reached their peak of importance in 1915, accounting for over 25 per cent of the total circulation. Since then they have declined steadily and now make up only two-tenths of one per cent of the total.

The Federal Reserve System. The most important element of the federal banking structure is the Federal Reserve System which was created in 1913. A Federal Reserve Board is composed of seven governors appointed by the President with the consent of the Senate for overlapping fourteen-year terms. Giving assistance to the Board is the Federal Open Market Committee, made up of the governors and five additional members named by federal reserve banks, and the Federal Advisory Council, consisting of twelve members, one from each federal reserve district.

Under the supervision of the Federal Reserve Board are twelve federal reserve banks which are located in key cities of the large districts into which the United States has been divided. All national banks must belong to and hold stock in the federal reserve district bank in the district where they are located; state banks may be members if they meet the requirements. The federal reserve district banks do not carry on a general banking business with corporations and individuals; rather, they act as fiscal agents for the federal government and as banks for local member banks.

Instruments of federal reserve policy. The Federal Reserve has three general means of influencing over-all credit and monetary conditions by affecting the reserve position of member banks—discount operations, open market operations, and changes in reserve requirements. Changes in member bank reserve positions affect the total volume of credit that can be granted by member banks, and thereby the volume of the economy's money without directing the flow of credit and money into particular sectors of the economy. Decisions regarding the use of available funds are left to the banks, their borrowers and other depositors, and the currency-holding public. The Federal Reserve System sets the rate at which federal reserve banks will lend money to member banks on commercial paper offered as security.

Discount operations. Through discounts for and advances to member banks, the Federal Reserve is able to supply individual banks with additional reserve funds. By this means and by raising or lowering reserve bank discount rates, the system can directly influence the availability and cost of bank credit and indirectly influence the availability and cost of non-bank credit. Discounts for proper banking purposes are initiated by individual member banks, subject to reserve bank approval, but changes in the discount rate are made at the discretion of the Federal Reserve after consideration of the need to tighten or ease credit conditions. The volume of member bank discounts has come to be regarded as an important factor in the tightness or ease of the credit market, and changes in reserve bank discount rates are viewed by the business community as an objective index of Federal Reserve policy.

Open market operations. Through purchases of government securities in the open market, the Federal Reserve can take the initiative and offset drains on or expand member bank reserves. Similarly, through sales of such securities, it can extinguish reserves and reduce their total volume. Because government securities play a key role in the credit market and because all financial institutions are affected by changes in yields and prices of such positions, open market operations have direct effects upon credit availability and the climate of business expectations. Actually, open market operations are used flexibly in combination with discount operations to provide an orderly and adequate flow of credit and money.

Changes in reserve requirements. Raising or lowering reserve requirements of member banks has the effect of diminishing or enlarging the volume of funds that member banks have available for lending. Such action also impinges on the liquidity position of banks and so affects the deposit expansion potential of bank reserves. The law sets certain basic requirements for each of three classes of member banks, but empowers the Federal Reserve to increase the requirements up to twice the prescribed basic percentages. The use of this power encounters numerous administrative and technical problems which handicap its frequent and continuous application in affecting the demand for federal reserve credit. For this reason it is used mainly for influencing unusual and large changes in bank reserve positions occasioned by special circumstances. It is not so adaptable to meeting day-to-day changes in credit conditions.

Selective credit regulation. The types of credit to which selective regulation has been applied by the federal reserve authorities are stock market credit, consumer credit, and real estate credit. Stock market credit has been subject to margin requirements since 1934. The other two types of credit have been regulated only temporarily.

By limiting the terms on which a given type of credit may be granted, selective credit regulation affects decisions regarding individual loans in the area to which it is applied. For example, if a person must pay 50 per cent down before he can buy articles on the installment plan, there will be fewer purchases. This type of regulation is a supplement to general credit regulation in that it can be directed to specific problem areas without involving action to influence credit conditions generally.

Federal Deposit Insurance Corporation. Widespread banking failures in the 1930's resulted in the creation of a new federal agency to protect bank depositors. The Federal Deposit Insurance Corporation insures deposits up to a maximum of $10,000 in all banks within the federal reserve system as well as in other banks meeting certain requirements. Currently, the corporation insures deposits in more than 13,000 banks.

THE NATIONAL DEBT

Prior to World War I the United States owed only about one billion dollars which was negligible considering the resources of the country. What seemed at the time an unprecedented pouring out of public funds built this nominal sum up to $25 billion at the close of the war. The government attempted to retire as much of the debt as possible during the 1920's, so that by 1930 the total was only slightly in excess of $16 billion. Expenditures during the depression, plus increased national defense needs, pushed the total to nearly $43 billion in 1940. World War II sent the debt soaring to over $269 billion; and, although it has been less than the latter figure for some of the post-war years, the general movement has been ever upward until an all-time high of nearly $300 billion was reached in 1962.

Congress has from time to time enacted a "permanent" statutory debt limit. At present, this amount is set at $285 billion, but Congress has authorized a temporary increase over the "permanent" ceiling occasionally at the request of the President—currently $308 billion.

Sharp differences of opinion exist regarding the possible effect of the huge national debt on the nation's future. Many individuals view the debt as a major threat to the financial security of the country. Others take comfort in the fact that we "owe the debt" to ourselves. Still others believe that the size of the present debt is not serious when our greatly increased national income is taken into account, and that a sharp reduction would be deflationary—upsetting to the nation's economy.

Types of borrowing. The federal government uses at least two general types of financing—long-term and short-term. The former refers to borrowing money by the sale of bonds with a life period of one to three or more decades. Short-term borrowing is employed to supplement the long-term bonds, sometimes because the market is not favorable to the issuance of long-term bonds, sometimes to provide temporary financing, and again because the amount required is hardly large enough to warrant the issuing of formal bonds. Short-term borrowing uses notes, bills, and certificates of indebtedness which run from thirty to sixty days to a year or two years. When they mature, either more short-term securities or long-term bonds may be issued to provide money for their payment or they may be retired through the use of current revenues. Long-term bonds are retired either by issuing new bonds to replace them or by full payment from sinking funds built up by contributions through the years. Federal bonds are refunded frequently before they mature since they usually contain a provision which permits the government to call them in for payment after a certain date.

THE TREASURY DEPARTMENT

The collection of the revenues of the United States, the custody of funds, and the paying of bills is entrusted to the Treasury Department. Today, it ranks as the fourth largest department, employing approximately 75,000 people.

Collection of revenue. Excise and income tax collections are handled by the Internal Revenue Service. Nine regional commissioners supervise the field office operations within their regions. Sixty-four internal revenue districts are headed by directors with each state having at least one district.

The Bureau of Customs is responsible for the assessment and collection of import duties. Under the direction of a commissioner, the activities of the bureau are performed in fifty-one districts, each headed by a collector of customs.

Custody of funds. Once collected, revenue is deposited to the credit of the United States in the twelve federal reserve banks and in other approved banks. Funds are paid out by these depositories upon presentation of federal checks which are made out by the disbursing section of the Treasury Department on the authorization of the Comptroller General's office. In addition to current funds, the Treasury, of course, has to keep billions of dollars of gold and silver which are owned by the United States. Most of the gold is stored in vaults at Ft. Knox, Kentucky, while storage vaults for silver bullion are located at West Point, New York.

Keeping of records. One of the chief functions of the Treasury Department in Washington is to keep the complicated records of the receipts and disbursements of the United States. Prior to 1940 the Treasury maintained ten divisions which handled various fiscal matters, but these were consolidated into a coordinated Fiscal Service, headed by an assistant secretary. At present, this service is divided into three subdivisions—these being the Office of the Treasurer of the United States, the Bureau of Public Debt, and the Bureau of Accounts. The latter bureau is entrusted with the large amount of work having to do with financial records and accounts. Since the Budget and Accounting Procedures Act of 1950, the Bureau of Accounts is required to cooperate with the General Accounting Office and the Bureau of the Budget in developing a unified accounting system for the federal government.

SUMMARY

Fiscal policy comprehends taxation, spending, borrowing, and debt management; monetary policy is concerned with the volume of money, the availability of credit, and the interest rate. The fiscal and monetary policies of the government today are managed and directed toward achieving economic stability. Up to thirty years ago the government was generally content to let the nation's economy drift in and out of depressions under its own self-regulatory features. However, there remains plenty of room for honest differences of opinion as to when and specifically how the national government should use its newly discovered financial powers.

The taxing power has frequently been used to destroy or circumscribe activities frowned upon by the national government. Although used sparingly, the tax offset technique appears to be a foolproof method for persuading the states to undertake programs which the national government thinks desirable.

It is now established doctrine that Congress may tax and spend for what it considers the general welfare, without specific application to any of the enumerated powers. In effect this means that it is almost impossible to question in court the purpose for which monies are appropriated.

Since 1921 the President has been charged with the responsibility for presenting the budget to Congress. The unified financial plan submitted by the Chief Executive is torn asunder by Congress. Congress has failed to devise procedures which permit it to keep the complete budget in proper perspective while considering and passing individual tax and appropriation measures.

BIBLIOGRAPHIC NOTE

For standard works dealing with public finance, see P. E. Taylor, *Economics of Public Finance* (rev. ed., New York: The Macmillan Company, 1953); W. J. Shultz, *American Public Finance* (6th ed., Englewood Cliffs, N. J.: Prentice-Hall, Inc., 1954); and Harold M. Groves, *Financing Government* (4th ed., New York: Henry Holt and Company, 1954). For a study emphasizing some of the political problems involved in financial policy, see Paul J. Strayer, *Fiscal Policy and Politics* (New York: Harper & Bros., 1958). J. M. Keynes' *The General Theory of Employment, Interest, and Money* (New York: Harcourt, Brace and Company, 1936) has had a significant impact on thinking with respect to the positive employment of governmental fiscal and monetary powers. For a discussion by economists and political scientists exploring the economic, political, and administrative problems in the promotion and maintenance of economic stabilization within the framework of a democratic society, see Max Millikan (ed.), *Income Stabilization for a Developing Democracy* (New Haven, Conn.: Yale University Press, 1953).

The national budgetary process is detailed in Arthur Smithies, *The Budgetary Process in the United States* (New York: McGraw-Hill Book Company, 1955). The budgetary process at all levels of government in the United States is examined in Jesse Burkhead, *Governmental Budgeting* (New York: John Wiley & Sons, Inc., 1956). A brief but enlightening treatment of the national budget is found in V. J. Browne, *The Control of the Public Budget* (Washington, D. C.: Public Affairs Press, 1949). *The Federal Budget in Brief,* published annually by the Bureau of the Budget, is especially designed to give the citizen a concise picture of the President's recommended budget plan.

Randolph Paul's *Taxation in the United States* (Boston: Little, Brown and Company, 1954) describes the national government's tax system from Colonial times to the 1950's; Roy Blough's *The Federal Taxing Process* (Englewood Cliffs, N. J.: Prentice-Hall, Inc., 1952) is an excellent account of the various factors influencing taxation, including the role of the expert and of pressure groups; also see J. P. Crockett, *The Federal Tax System of the United States* (New York: Columbia University Press, 1955). For a discussion of the role of the Economic Advisers in the first years following the Employment Act of 1946, see E. G. Nourse, *Economics in the Public Service: Administrative Aspects of the Employment Act* (New York: Harcourt, Brace and Co., 1953). The impact of tax policies on the nation's economy is treated in A. H. Hansen, *Fiscal Policy and Business Cycles* (New York: W. W. Norton & Company, 1941). For a brief but provocative discussion of federal tax policies, see Herbert Stein and Joseph Pechman, *Essays in Federal Taxation* (New York: Committee for Economic Development, 1959). Concerning the national debt, see Marshall A. Robinson, *The National Debt Ceiling* (Washington, D. C.: The Brookings Institution, 1959) and Charles C. Abbott, *The Federal Debt* (New York: The Twentieth Century Fund, 1953).

A concise, "official" statement on the Federal Reserve System is found in *The Federal Reserve System: Purposes and Functions* (Washington, D. C.: Board of Governors of the Federal Reserve System, 1954). Other valuable government publications in this area include Robert V. Roosa, *Federal Reserve Operations in the Money and Government Securities Markets* (Federal Reserve Bank of New York, 1956) and *The Quest for Stability* (Federal Reserve Bank of Philadelphia, 1954). See also G. L. Bach, *Federal Reserve Policy-Making* (New York: Knopf, 1950).

Elias Huzar's *The Purse and the Sword* (Ithaca, N. Y.: Cornell University Press, 1950) deals with congressional efforts to control appropriations. For another view of this problem, see Harvey Mansfield's *The Comptroller General* (New Haven, Conn.: Yale University Press, 1939). For a description and criticism of governmental accounting practices, see the task force report on *Budget and Accounting in the United States Government* (Washington, D. C.: Commission on Organization of the Executive Branch of the Government (Second Hoover Commission), 1955).

A recent work of particular interest is Aaron Wildarsky's *The Politics of the Budgetary Process* (Boston: Little, Brown, 1964).

22

Government and Business

THE CONSTITUTION was framed in a climate of opinion devoted to the concept of laissez faire capitalism; therefore, it is not surprising that there are no specific clauses in the Constitution concerned with the regulation of business. But a number of provisions such as the commerce clause, the bankruptcy power, and the exclusive control by the national government over monetary matters were designed to lend the weight of national policy against undue interference by the states with many aspects of business matters. As it turned out the power over commerce by the national government became a two-edged sword. The commerce clause has protected business from state and local discrimination; on the other hand, when the public demanded that trusts and monopolies be curbed, it was to the commerce power that the national government turned to effect regulation. Effective application of antitrust legislation was long retarded by the Supreme Court's interpretation of the scope of the commerce power. This factor imposes no real difficulty today, but problems do remain.

THE SCOPE OF THE COMMERCE POWER

The Articles of Confederation did not provide the central government with power over matters of commerce. One of the most compelling arguments in favor of the new Constitution was that by granting to Congress the power to regulate interstate and foreign commerce the destructive and discriminatory commercial practices of the individual states could be halted.

For nearly a century, the decisions of the Supreme Court under the commerce clause rarely dealt with questions of what Congress might do in the exercise of the commerce power. More often the Court's decisions were concerned with the permissibility of state activity which it was claimed discriminated against or burdened interstate commerce. In this period of the Republic's history, there was little occasion for the affirmative exercise of the commerce power, and the influence of the commerce clause on the economy of the United States was a negative one, resulting almost wholly

440

from its operation as a restraint on the powers of the states. The enactment of the Interstate Commerce Act in 1887 marked the beginning of a new era with respect to the positive use of the commerce clause by the national government. Again in 1890 the commerce power was resorted to by Congress when the Sherman Antitrust Act was passed, and thereafter, mainly after 1903, statute after statute has been based on the commerce clause.

Judicial interpretation of the commerce clause. Chief Justice John Marshall's opinion in the case of *Gibbons* v. *Ogden,* in which one of the questions was whether commerce encompassed navigation, provided a noteworthy precedent for construing the meaning of commerce in broad, sweeping terms rather than narrow, restrictive ones. He wrote:

> The subject to be regulated is commerce; and our constitution being, as was aptly said at the bar, one of enumeration, and not of definition, to ascertain the extent of the power it becomes necessary to settle the meaning of the word. The counsel for the appellee would limit it to traffic, to buying and selling, or the interchange of commodities, and do not admit that it comprehends navigation. This would restrict a general term, applicable to many objects, to one of its significations. Commerce, undoubtedly, is traffic, but it is something more; it is intercourse. It describes the commercial intercourse between nations, and parts of nations, in all its branches, and is regulated by prescribing rules for carrying on that intercourse.[1]

Despite the sweeping language of Marshall's opinion, the Supreme Court subsequently adopted a very restrictive interpretation of congressional power under the commerce clause. In an 1895 case the Court made a distinction between production and commerce, saying: "Doubtless the power to control the manufacture of a given thing involves in a certain sense the control of its disposition, but this is a secondary and not the primary sense; and although the exercise of that power may result in bringing the operation into play, it does not control it, and affects it only incidentally and indirectly. Commerce succeeds to manufacture, and is not a part of it." [2]

With only a few exceptions, the doctrine that commerce was essentially transportation persisted for 40 years after the 1895 decision. Mining, contracts for advertising material, insurance policies, and professional baseball were a few of the areas held by the Court to be beyond the reach of the commerce power; but the exceptions to the general rule were important. Thus the Court permitted national regulation of intrastate matters if these activities *directly* burdened interstate commerce. In a significant opinion in 1914, Justice Hughes, writing for the majority, pointed out: "Whenever the interstate and intrastate transactions are so related that the government of the one involves the control of the other, it is Congress, and not the State, that is entitled to prescribe the final and dominant rule, for otherwise Con-

---

[1] 9 Wheaton 1 (1824).
[2] *United States* v. *E. C. Knight,* 156 U. S. 1.

gress would be denied the exercise of its constitutional authority and the State, and not the Nation, would be supreme within the national field." [3]

In the 1930's, the Court began to move away from the concept of "direct effect" as a criteria of the reach of the commerce power over local matters. By the 1940's it had been abandoned completely. "But even if appellant's activity be local and though it may not be regarded as commerce, it may still, whatever its nature, be reached by Congress if it exerts a substantial effect on interstate commerce, irrespective of whether such effect is what might at some earlier time have been defined as 'direct' or 'indirect.' " [4]

Commerce power today. Almost every aspect of the nation's economy is subject now to statutes based on the commerce power. The Supreme Court has reiterated that the power to regulate commerce includes the power to foster, protect, control, and restrain.

The control extends to transportation by rail, motor carriers, inland and coastal carriers, and air carriers; to the communication facilities of the telephone, telegraph, radio and TV; to manufacturing, mining, lumbering, and oil and natural gas production and distribution; to buying and selling of goods and services in interstate commerce; to wages, hours, working conditions, and labor-management relations; to many facets of agriculture and to public accommodations such as hotels and restaurants. Under the commerce power hydro-electric dams have been constructed, bridges built, rivers widened, flood control projects established, and anti-trust laws passed. Congress has prohibited in interstate commerce lotteries, impure food and drugs, white slaves, liquor, and stolen automobiles. And Congress has divested itself of its power over interstate commerce to permit the states to enact regulatory statutes which otherwise would be unconstitutional, as when states seize convict-made goods shipped within their borders.

REGULATION OF GENERAL BUSINESS

Regulation of business has been a concern of the national government since the late nineteenth century. Public policy has differentiated in the treatment accorded public utilities and other industries requiring direct regulation on the one hand and the rest of business on the other. Our concern in this section is with the latter type of business regulation.

The combination movement. Following the Civil War improved transportation facilities, urbanization, and the growing population accentuated the rise of the modern corporation with its mass production and distribution techniques. Paralleling the growth of large-scale enterprise was the combination movement. One of the early devices for combination was the *trust,* where one or more persons secured a majority of the stock of different corporations thus permitting the operation of the separate corporations as

---

[3] *Houston, E. & W. Texas Ry. Co.* v. *United States,* 234 U. S. 342.
[4] *Wickard* v. *Filburn,* 317 U. S. 111 (1942).

a unit. Shortly after the early trust movement, holding companies and mergers became important in the combination movement. *Holding companies* were created to acquire voting control of existing corporations, at least some of which kept their corporate identity. *Mergers* usually referred to the buying and dissolving of one corporation by another. Other types of combinations are less formally structured, but still relatively effective in restricting output or administering prices of commodities. Various types of pools or "gentlemen's agreements" would fall into this category.

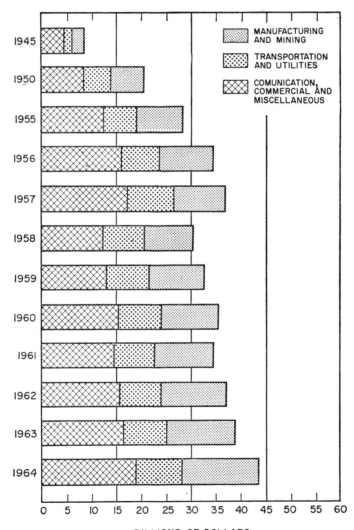

BILLIONS OF DOLLARS

Source: Chart prepared by Dept. of Commerce, Bureau of the Census.
Data from Securities and Exchange Commission and
Dept. of Commerce, Office of Business Economics.

TRENDS IN PRIVATE CAPITAL IMPROVEMENTS, 1945 TO 1964

Often the public thinks of combination as an attempt by a few persons to strangle competition, thus making it probable that the consumer will pay more for the goods and/or services involved. On the other hand, advocates of combination practices assert their success is dependent upon efficiency principles. They point to the desirability of huge capital assets for the purpose of developing new products and industrial techniques. The possibility of controlling a near monopoly, at least in the early stages of a new product or process, is supposed to encourage "risk" investment that otherwise might not be made. Both sides in the controversy are able to point to many specific examples in support of their arguments. However, governmental regulation of business combinations is predicated on the assumption that the advantages of having a relatively large number of competitors in an industry outweighs any benefits which might accrue to society by having relatively few competitors.

Is "big" business increasing its hold over the American economy? Part of the difficulty in answering this question, of course, depends upon one's definition of "big." At times, but not always, a small business in government statistics has been defined as one employing fewer than 500 persons. If a firm had 499 employees, it was small; but 501 employees placed it in the "large" category. Total assets or annual sales volume have also been used as criteria for "bigness." A few years ago general opinion held that concentration was increasing. Since World War II smaller firms have at least held their relative position, aided by positive governmental programs on their behalf and by the rather vigorous enforcement of antitrust laws.

The Sherman Antitrust Act. Congress moved toward federal regulation of trusts and monopolies by passing the Sherman Antitrust Act in 1890. In broad, sweeping terms it made illegal every contract, combination, or conspiracy in restraint of trade or commerce in the interstate or foreign field. It soon became apparent that the legislation as enforced by the executive branch and as interpreted by the courts fell far short of achieving the degree of restriction upon trust and monopolistic activities that many persons and groups believed desirable.

Other than giving the federal courts necessary jurisdiction and district attorneys authority to restrain violations of the law, no specific machinery was established for the enforcement of the Sherman Act. The attitude of the President concerning the enforcement of the law was, of course, very important. For example, Theodore Roosevelt, made a distinction between those combinations in restraint of trade that he considered "bad" and those he believed to be "good."

The members of the Supreme Court became much concerned with the "rule of reason" in interpreting the Sherman Act. The essential problem was whether the law prohibited *all* restraints in trade or only *unreasonable* restraints. Although the Court was far from consistent in the application of this rule, with a majority leaning first one way and then another, the uncertainty of the Court's position had the effect of discouraging institution of suits by the government against various types of combinations. In general in the period from 1911 to 1940, the Supreme Court applied the law to only "unreasonable" combinations. Another significant interpretation of the Court diminishing the effectiveness of the Sherman Act was the holding that manufacturing *per se* did not come within the reach of the commerce power.

Despite these and other difficulties, the government did check some abuses and broke up at least temporarily some of the larger combinations. In the latter category, one might mention the partial victories gained against the Standard Oil Company and the American Tobacco Company. Another important early case which the government won was the application of the Sherman Act to railway combinations.[5]

The Clayton Antitrust Act. The Clayton Act, passed in 1914, sought to strengthen the earlier Sherman Act by specifically forbidding certain practices such as rebates, price-cutting for the purpose of driving out competitors, the acquiring of stock by corporations in competing firms, and interlocking directorates. Furthermore, it provided that officers of corporations should be personally liable for violations of the terms of the act and made it somewhat less difficult for prosecutions to be brought by those suffering from the practices prohibited.

Federal Trade Commission. The Federal Trade Commission was organized as an independent administrative agency in 1915 pursuant to the Federal Trade Commission Act of 1914. The Commission is composed of five members appointed by the President with the consent of the Senate. It is charged with the responsibility of enforcing certain anti-monopolistic practices outlawed by the Clayton Act, as amended, and with preventing unfair methods of competition and unfair or deceptive acts or practices.[6] The Commission has not always enjoyed outstanding success in its endeavors. Part of its difficulties may be traced to inadequate appropriations and to restrictive court decisions. In recent years the courts have permitted wider scope to the Commission's powers, and Congress has been somewhat more generous with funds. On the other hand, a Task Force of the first Hoover Commission was critical of other aspects of the agency's work. It stated:

> The Federal Trade Commission's operations, programs, and administrative methods have often been inadequate. . . . The Commission has

---

[5] *Northern Securities Co.* v. *United States,* 193 U. S. 406 (1904).

[6] The original Federal Trade Commission Act laid down a general prohibition against the use in commerce of unfair methods of competition and unfair or deceptive acts or practices. Subsequent legislation has broadened the Commission's authority. The Wheeler-Lea Act amendments conferred special authority for the control of false advertising of foods, drugs, cosmetics, and curative or corrective devices; the Wool Products Labeling Act and Fur Products Labeling Act requires informative labeling of those products; the Flammable Fabric Act prohibits the marketing of fabrics which the Commission designates as dangerously inflammable; the Lanham Trade Mark Act permits cancellation of certain trade-marks improperly registered or improperly used in competition.

FEDERAL TRADE COMMISSION

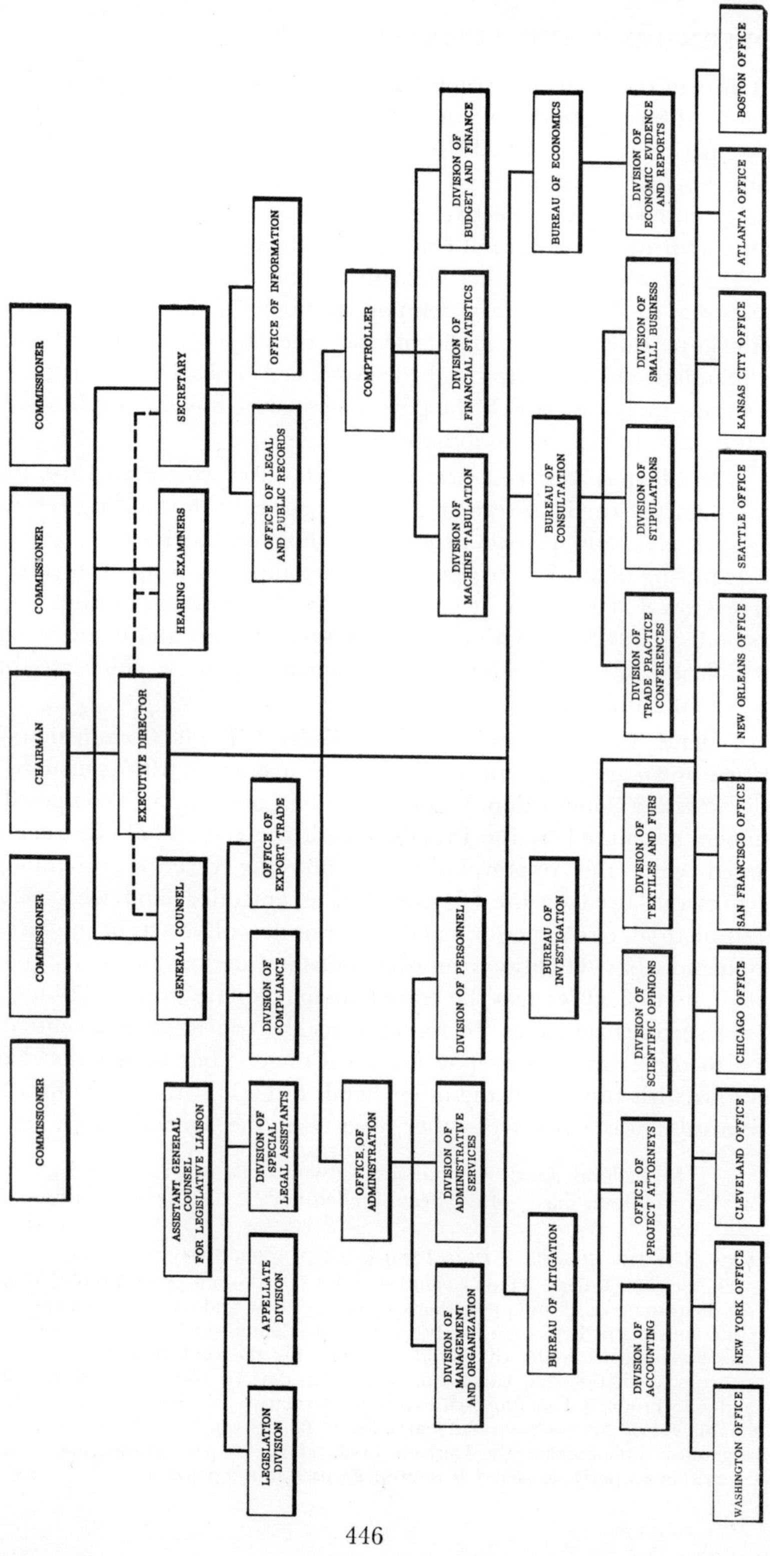

become immersed in a multitude of petty problems; it has not probed into new areas of anticompetitive practices; it has become increasingly bogged down with cumbersome procedures and inordinate delays in disposition of cases. Its economic work—instead of being the backbone of its activities—has been allowed to dwindle almost to none. The Commission has largely become a passive judicial agency, waiting for cases to come up on the docket, under routinized procedures, without active responsibility for achieving the statutory objectives. . . . With notable exceptions, appointments to the Federal Trade Commission have been made with too little interest in the skills and experience pertinent to the problems of competition and monopoly, and too much attention to service to political party.[7]

Within the past few years the Federal Trade Commission has acted with more vigor and imagination. One has to appreciate the enormity of the task facing the Commission in seeking to police the wide and complicated areas of its jurisdiction. The volume of activity for the Commission has more than doubled since 1955.

The Commission's law enforcement work falls into two general categories: (1) enforcement through formal litigation leading to mandatory orders against offenders, and (2) law observance achieved by action of a voluntary and cooperative nature. The formal litigation cases are conducted by procedures similar to those used in ordinary courts. Cases are instituted by the issuance of a formal complaint charging unlawful practices. If the charges are found to be true, a cease and desist order may be issued by the Commission requiring discontinuance of the unlawful practice. Appeals may be taken to the United States Courts of Appeal, but the Commission's findings of fact are final.

The Trade Practice Conference Division assists in obtaining voluntary observance of law on an industry-wide basis by working with members of industry and other interested groups to formulate trade practice rules. These rules define and prescribe business practices that are unfair, deceptive, or otherwise unlawful. Two recent examples may be cited which illustrate the use of trade practice rules: (1) The rules for the nationwide rabbit industry inhibit misrepresentation in the sale and distribution of all types, breeds, varieties, and strains of live domestic rabbits. Among the many different types of deception covered in the rules is the practice by sellers of representing that they will buy back the offspring of the rabbits sold by them when they will not, or that they will pay more for such offspring than is the fact. (2) The building wire and cable rules furnish guidance on prohibited discriminatory prices, rebates, refunds, discounts, credits, etc., which effect unlawful price discrimination. Other subjects include prohibited forms of trade restraints, prohibited sales below costs, inducing breach of contract, consignment distribution, enticing away employees of competitors, and commercial bribery.

7 Commission on Organization of the Executive Branch of the Government, *Task Force Report on Regulatory Commissions* (Washington, D. C.: 1949), pp. 119-125.

Unfair practices in individual cases may be corrected through the stipulation procedure, whereby offenders enter into voluntary agreements, or "stipulations," to discontinue unlawful practices. The Commission has been especially active lately in seeking to protect the public from deceptive advertising. For example, complaints were issued in a recent year challenging advertising that would lead the public to believe the following: that reprinted books under new titles were fresh from an author's pen; that hair growers could restore a luxurious growth in all cases; that watches with one or two jewels contained at least seventeen; that certain contact eyeglasses offered day-long comfort, were unbreakable, and provided eyes with superior ventilation; and that a certain grass sold by mail order multiplied itself fifty times during a summer without weeds.

Many of the investigations conducted by the Commission, initiated by the agency itself or as the result of congressional concurrent resolutions, have paved the way for specific statutes. The Packers and Stockyards Act of 1921 was a direct consequence of Federal Trade Commission reports. Likewise the Public Utility Act of 1935, the Federal Power Act of 1935, and the Natural Gas Act of 1938 emerged from an elaborate utility corporation study by the Commission. One of the most recent economic studies, the effect of which is yet undetermined, dealt with the $330-million-a-year antibiotics industry. Questions were raised in this report whether patent licensing arrangements among manufacturers of the so-called "broad spectrum" antibiotics were illegally monopolistic and resulted in excessively high prices to the public.

Of late the Commission has been rather active in the enforcement of section seven—the antimerger section—of the Clayton Act. As amended in 1950, this part of the Clayton Act prohibits mergers or consolidations of corporations for the purpose of suppressing competition whether brought about by the direct or indirect acquisition of either stock or assets of the acquired corporation. The general purpose of this section is to halt monopolistic combinations in their incipiency and before they have attained the proportions required to justify a Sherman Act proceeding. Under the Commission's premerger clearance procedure, interested parties may request advice of the Commission concerning a proposed merger or acquisition. Facts relating to the proposed transaction may be submitted in writing or in conference. On the basis of these facts, as well as other information available to the examiners, the parties are informed as to whether or not consummation of the merger would likely result in further action by the Commission. There is, however, no legal requirement that the Commission be notified of corporate mergers either before or after the consummation. Except in instances where a complaint about a particular merger is received, or where premerger consideration is requested, the Commission must rely on financial newspapers, trade journals, manuals of investments, and the like for information that a merger has occurred or is contemplated.

The Robinson-Patman Act. The Robinson-Patman Act, passed in 1936, was aimed at practices engaged in by chain stores which, it was claimed, gave them "unfair" advantage over independent retailers and middlemen. It prohibited persons or organizations dealing in interstate commerce from giving or receiving, directly or indirectly, any discrimination in prices or services that substantially lessened competition—unless justified by differences of cost. The act did not apply to goods of different quality. The legislation also authorized the Federal Trade Commission to set the discounts that could be allowed for the size of shipment. In an over-all view, the Robinson-Patman Act has offered some protection to independent retailers and distributors, but not to the extent they had hoped for. The legislation has certainly not checked the growth of the mass distribution industries.

Exemptions from antitrust statutes. A number of statutes permit specific exemptions from antitrust legislation. The Webb-Pomerene Export Trade Act of 1918 allows cooperative agreements among persons engaged in export trade. Statutory exemption is also provided for marketing associations of farmers, dairymen, and other types of agricultural entrepreneurs.

For many years various independent retail associations have attempted to require manufacturers to set and enforce the retail prices at which their products could be sold. This was intended to prevent certain stores from offering "cut-rate" prices on name brands and was aimed particularly at large chain stores. By 1940, primarily because of the leadership provided by the National Association of Retail Druggists, state legislatures of 40 states were persuaded to pass "fair-trade" acts. These laws generally provided that prices fixed in a contract signed by any one distributor with the manufacturer would become binding on all other distributors within the state upon the serving of notice. However, price-fixing for commodities shipped in interstate commerce remained subject to federal antitrust laws. Congress acted to support the state legislatures by passing the Miller-Tydings Act in 1937, authorizing price maintenance for interstate commerce commodities in those states where the "fair-trade" laws had been enacted. But in 1951 the Supreme Court held that the act did not extend to non-signers of specific contracts.[8] The following year Congress passed the McGuire Act which extended the price-maintenance features to non-signers of contracts, thus "recalling" the Court's decision. Since no state agencies check on compliance with "fair-trade" contracts, their influence has varied from state to state depending upon the amount of policing manufacturers and retail groups are willing to undertake. Also a number of state supreme courts have declared state laws on the subject unconstitutional.

Sporadic application of antitrust statutes. Many factors in addition to certain ones already mentioned have added up to sporadic and uneven application of the antitrust statutes. During both world wars almost no atten-

---

[8] *Schwegmann Bros.* v. *Calvert Distillers Corp.,* 341 U. S. 384.

tion was given to trust problems and, as a matter of fact, some war-time statutes appeared to encourage practices which would have been illegal in normal times.

One of President Franklin D. Roosevelt's early New Deal measures, the National Industrial Recovery Act, represented an almost complete about-face in public policy with respect to antitrust matters. The law provided for the establishment of industry codes of "fair competition," subject to the approval of the President. Codes, licensing requirements, and agreements were all to be exempted from the antitrust laws for the duration of the statute (two years). When this legislation was declared unconstitutional in the *Schechter* case,[9] the exemptions also fell.

Antitrust policy today. Generally speaking, with the exception of the war years, antitrust policies have been pursued with vigor by both Republican and Democratic administrations for the past 25 years. Because Congress has been more generous with appropriations, the Justice Department and the Federal Trade Commission have been able to increase their activities in the application of existing antitrust laws. The Presidents in this period have not thrown any obvious roadblocks in the way of strict enforcement procedures. The Supreme Court has largely abandoned its "rule of reason" criterion and has completely reversed the concept that manufacturing is not subject to the commerce power, thereby making it subject to the Sherman and Clayton acts.

An important factor in the revival of antitrust policy in this period has been the willingness of the courts to accept and apply economic concepts of competition. However, the Court is still developing its rationale as to what standards of competition are permissible under the antitrust laws. In some cases within recent years, the Supreme Court has stressed market structure as a criterion of competitiveness. In essence this approach holds that competition becomes "unworkable" if one or a few firms possess so dominant a share of the market that prices may be fixed or competitors excluded. Thus in the American Tobacco Company case the Supreme Court reasoned: ". . . the material consideration in determining whether a monopoly exists is not that prices are raised and that competition actually is excluded but that power exists to raise prices or to exclude competition when it is desired to do so." [10]

On the other hand, some economists have urged the Court's consideration of the "business performance" test as a competitive standard. Does the actual performance of the business in terms of prices, wages, profits, and technical progress indicate monopolistic design? In certain cases the Court has certainly been influenced in its decisions by this type of analysis.

It does not appear likely that any basic statutory changes in approaches to the problem of trusts and monopolies will occur any time soon. No doubt

9 295 U. S. 495 (1935).
10 328 U. S. 781 (1946).

there will be further refinements in the judicial interpretation of the present laws. Many economists have argued that there should be a reassessment of present policies. They point out that "bigness" *per se* is not always undesirable. A thesis that has been given wide publicity, at least among professional economists, is the theory of "countervailing power." Essentially, this theory holds that market power may best be checked, not by antitrust action, but by the organization of countervailing power by those who confront dominant power in the market.

Role of the Department of Justice. The Antitrust Division of the Department of Justice is responsible for the enforcement of the Sherman Act and certain sections of the Clayton Act. A criminal presecution may be instituted by this division in the case of a willful violation of the antitrust laws such as occurred in the electrical equipment manufacturing industry in 1962. For less serious violations the government may seek a federal court injunction to prohibit offenders from continuing the unlawful practice.

Civil suits may be initiated for the purpose of dissolving monopolistic companies. Consent decrees play an important part in the Antitrust Division's work. Under this procedure a business does not necessarily admit that it has been guilty of illegal practices but does agree not to engage in certain specific practices in the future.

The Securities and Exchange Commission. Following the stock market crash of 1929, congressional investigations revealed a shocking tale of speculation, misrepresentation, manipulation, and other malpractices which had prevailed in the operation of the nation's stock exchanges. Of the $50 billions of new securities which were floated in the decade after World War I, fully one-half became worthless. One of the principal contributing factors to the success of the manipulator was the inability of investors and their advisers to obtain accurate financial and other information upon which to evaluate securities. Manipulators were further aided by the dissemination of false and misleading information, tips and rumors which flooded the market place. There was almost no limit to the amount of credit which a broker might extend to a customer. A slight dip in the market price of securities often set off a chain reaction—the customer was sold out in a declining market at a loss because he had insufficient funds to put up additional margin. These sales further accentuated the market decline and caused other margin customers to be sold out; brokers who had over-extended themselves with banks in order to finance excessive speculation frequently became insolvent, thus further endangering the position of other customers.

Reacting to the abuses in stock market transactions, Congress passed the Federal Securities Act in 1933 and created the Securities and Exchange Commission in 1934 to administer the legislation. The Commission is composed of five members, not more than three of whom may be members of the same political party. The members are appointed by the President, with the

SECURITIES-EXCHANGE COMMISSION

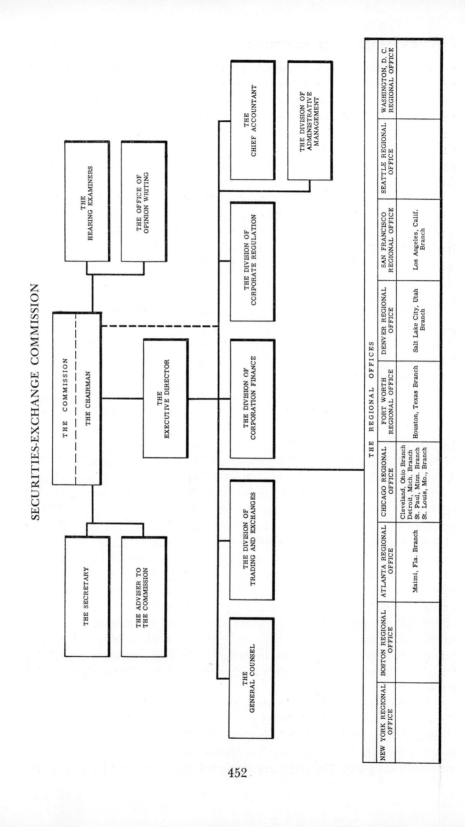

THE REGIONAL OFFICES

NEW YORK REGIONAL OFFICE	BOSTON REGIONAL OFFICE	ATLANTA REGIONAL OFFICE	CHICAGO REGIONAL OFFICE	FORT WORTH REGIONAL OFFICE	DENVER REGIONAL OFFICE	SAN FRANCISCO REGIONAL OFFICE	SEATTLE REGIONAL OFFICE	WASHINGTON, D. C. REGIONAL OFFICE
		Maimi, Fla. Branch	Cleveland, Ohio Branch Detroit, Mich. Branch St. Paul, Minn. Branch St. Louis, Mo., Branch	Houston, Texas Branch	Salt Lake City, Utah Branch	Los Angeles, Calif. Branch		

advice and consent of the Senate, for five-year terms, one term ending each year. The chairman is designated by the President.

The S.E.C. has been given several important duties which relate to the interstate sale of most securities. The function of the Commission is not to guarantee any investments, but to provide the public with essential information concerning securities offered for sale, and to afford protection against misrepresentation. In registering securities, directors and financial officers are required to furnish a prospectus which describes the property upon which the securities are based. If these statements are false or only partially accurate, investors may institute civil suits for recovery. Manipulative and other fraudulent practices in the purchase and sale of securities are prohibited. In order to discourage speculation on a "shoestring," the Federal Reserve Board is instructed to assist S.E.C. by fixing the cash margins required for loans having securities as collateral.

In 1935 Congress extended the authority of the Commission by giving it jurisdiction over gas and electric holding companies which engage in interstate commerce or use the United States mails. The act provided that after January 1, 1938, holding companies coming under the scope of S.E.C. should limit their operations to a single integrated system rather than spread all over the country as several of the giant holding companies had done. The Commission passes upon proposals for reorganization, merger, or consolidation of the companies under its jurisdiction.

Under bankruptcy proceedings, the Commission in certain circumstances has the duty, and in others a discretionary power, to serve as adviser to United States District Courts in connection with the reorganization of debtor corporations. Of primary importance is the Commission's assistance in the formulation of plans of reorganization which will provide fair and equitable treatment to the various creditors and other security holders and which will help to assure that the corporation will emerge from bankruptcy in a sound financial condition and able to carry on without the continued threat of bankruptcy.

SUBSIDIES TO BUSINESS

Where the government subsidizes a particular segment of the economy, invariably the justification is that the policy will contribute to the general welfare of the nation. However, it has often been true that subsidies become so entrenched by statutes that it is extremely difficult to remove them even though the general welfare of the country might best be served by a discontinuance of the program. Also it is a rather common occurrence in Congress for "logrolling" [11] to result in benefits to special interests without any appreciable value flowing to the community-at-large.

_____

11 A combining to assist another in consideration of assistance in return.

The tariff. Historically, the tariff has amounted to a subsidy to the manufacturing interests although some types of agricultural production eventually benefited by import duties. Behind the tariff walls, American industries were guaranteed a domestic market free from foreign competition.

Five distinct periods have been noted in the history of American tariff policy.[12] (1) 1789-1815: Protectionist policy was taking shape but was not yet applied in full force. (2) 1816-1832: There was a considerable rise in tariffs and the system of protection had its first great triumph. (3) 1833-1860: With the exception of a short interruption between 1842 and 1846, protectionist policy was under severe attack and duties were lowered. (4) 1861-1933: With minor interruptions under Cleveland and Wilson, the trend of tariff rates was sharply upward. (5) 1934 to the present: Under the influence of the Reciprocal Trade Agreements program, the trend of tariff duties has been downward.

The creation of the United States Tariff Commission in 1916 was a step toward relieving pressure on Congress in the exercise of its tariff-fixing power. The Tariff Commission does not fix tariffs or exercise any quasi-legislative or quasi-judicial functions. Its primary duty is to investigate and report upon tariff and foreign trade matters as required by statute to the President, Congress, or specific committees in Congress.

With the passage of the Reciprocal Trade Agreements Act of 1934, Congress, in effect, turned over its traditional tariff-making role to the President. The President was empowered to negotiate tariff agreements for three years, subject to certain restrictions, without any further action on the part of Congress. The Trade Agreements Act was an effective political technique for reducing duties. The President, it was felt, would be more concerned with the broad impact of our trade policy, whereas individual congressmen would be more apt to be moved by the particular pressures of their constituencies.

Succeeding Congresses renewed the grant of power to the President for negotiating trade agreements. Various "safeguards" were usually included in the renewals. A "peril" point provision required the President to notify the Tariff Commission of any intention to negotiate a trade agreement and to submit a list of items under consideration. The Commission could then indicate the point at which the tariff rate would permit imports to threaten or injure a domestic producer. The President had to justify his actions to Congress if he fixed rates below the "peril" point.

"Escape" clause provisions enabled any interested parties to request the Tariff Commission to investigate and report to the President whether any reduction in operation was causing or threatening to cause injury to domestic producers. The Commission could recommend adjustment if it

---

[12] Merle Fainsod, Lincoln Gordon, and Joseph C. Palamountain, Jr., *Government and the American Economy* (3rd ed., New York: W. W. Norton & Company, 1959), pp. 97-98.

found the complaint justified. The President could reject the recommendation, but Congress by a two-thirds vote could override the decision of the Chief Executive.

In 1962 Congress passed the most significant trade bill since the 1934 Reciprocal Trade Agreements Act. The 1962 legislation granted the President authority for five years to cut tariffs by 50 per cent. He may also eliminate the tariff on goods of which the United States and the European Common Market and other European countries account for 80 per cent of free world trade. If tariff cuts hurt domestic interests, the President may raise tariffs through the use of "escape clauses" or give federal "trade adjustment" assistance such as increased federal unemployment compensation to workers or loans and technical assistance to injured domestic industries.

The United States subscribes to the General Agreement on Tariffs and Trade (GATT) in which thirty-seven countries participate. This agreement emphasizes negotiation in place of unilateral action in the fixing of tariff rates.

President Kennedy persuaded Congress in 1962 to enact legislation which would permit the President to negotiate agreements with the European Common Market countries on the basis of greatly reduced or complete elimination of tariffs in certain areas. Under this recommendation, peril point provisions would not apply, but the government could render direct financial assistance to injured industries.

Other subsidies. The government has long granted various other types of indirect and direct subsidies to business groups. The effects of such subsidization often result in benefits flowing to groups who do not consider themselves a part of the particular business community subsidized. Federal land grants to railroads in the nineteenth century spurred the phenomenal growth of the railroad industry, but obviously had a tremendous effect upon the entire economic system. River and harbor legislation is a traditional method by which members of Congress bring money into their districts. Subsidies to rail, water, and air carriers for transporting the mail help explain the difficulty the postal service has experienced in paying its own way. Generous grants for the construction of highways and airports stimulate business activities in many related fields.

The federal government is especially interested in maintaining a strong merchant marine. The Maritime Administration, an agency of the Department of Commerce, administers a subsidy program both for the building and operating of merchant ships. Construction and operating differential subsidies are based on the relative cost of construction and operation of ships in the United States and in foreign countries. In addition, Congress has also seen fit to require a certain percentage of goods purchased under the foreign aid program to be transported in American-flag ships.

GOVERNMENT PARTICIPATION IN BUSINESS ACTIVITIES

The national government has always been engaged to some degree in business-type enterprises, the postal service being an example. Considering our nation's devotion to the principles of capitalism, an incredible number of such enterprises have added to the list in the past forty years.[13] The government is apt to create agencies of this type in economic emergencies, in time of war, and for the development of projects which are not adapted to private enterprise because of their nature or their magnitude. The Bureau of the Budget reported in 1956 that the government was engaging in 19,771 commercial and industrial activities producing goods and services for its own though not necessarily its exclusive use.

Within the Defense Department one finds furniture repair shops, coffee-roasting plants, cobbler shops, cement-making plants, paint factories, and sawmills. The Justice Department is responsible for the Office of Alien Property and Federal Prison Industries, Inc. The Department of Interior supervises numerous projects among which are The Alaska Railroad, The Virgin Islands Corporation, and the Bonneville, Southwestern, and Southeastern Power Administrations. The Veterans Administration operates bakeries, laundries, and dry cleaning plants. The Government Printing Office, by its own description, is the "largest and best-equipped complete printing plant in the world."

The Post Office. During its entire existence the government has assumed responsibility for carrying the mails, though it was not until 1874 that the Post Office Department was created. The Postmaster General heads an organization which employs over 500,000 persons, operates some 37,000 local post offices, covers one and a half million miles with rural deliveries and handles over 55 billion pieces of mail in a single year.

The Post Office Department not only carries letters and other first-class matter but also huge quantities of newspapers, magazines, and books. Since 1913 it has transported enormous numbers of parcel post packages which contain almost every conceivable commodity. It operates its own insurance system for the benefit of those who desire protection of their packages against loss or destruction. A registration arrangement provides unusual care in handling valuable letters or packages, while a special delivery service speeds up delivery after mail has reached its destination. The Department also operates a domestic money order and a postal savings system.

The Post Office Department customarily spends more money than it receives. Since 1900 it has shown a profit for only eleven years. Critics often point to the deficits as proof of the inefficiency of governmental bureaucracy. On the other hand, the Department views the deficit problem more as a

---

[13] This section does not include a discussion of the various lending agencies of the government. These are discussed in appropriate places throughout the text. A brief discussion of the newly created Communication Satellite Corporation is found on p. 381.

reflection of public policy than of bad management. It calls attention to various "public service costs" which it is required by statute to bear. These costs include unreimbursed services for other governmental agencies; specific rate subsidies for mailing of second- and third-class mail by certain non-profit organizations, free-in-county second-class mail, classroom publications, and mail for the blind; excess rates paid to foreign air carriers; and custodial services for other government departments and agencies.

A large share of the postal deficit is incurred in handling second- and third-class mail. In effect the government is subsidizing those who mail newspapers, magazines, circulars, and advertising matter. Increased postal rates which went into effect in 1958 will no doubt help the Post Office Department make a better financial showing, but the basic fact that the Department is a service organization, not one designed to make a profit, will probably continue to be reflected in its fiscal record.

Tennessee Valley Authority. The Tennessee Valley Authority is a government corporation created by an act of Congress in 1933. Authority is bestowed upon TVA by statute and executive order to develop the Tennessee River and its tributaries in the interests of navigation, the control of floods, and the generation and disposition of electric power, and for the conservation, development, and use of the resources of the region. TVA is under the administration of a board of three members with overlapping terms of six years, appointed by the President with Senate approval. The backbone of its activities is a system of 22 dams and reservoirs on the Tennessee River and its tributaries. Although the federal government operates many multi-purpose dams, TVA stands unique in the scope of authority granted it for comprehensive regional planning.

Many aspects of the TVA system have been severely criticized over the years; its electrical power operations, which compete with private power companies in the region, have been the focus of much of the criticism. The fact that a governmental corporation sells any of its products in competition with private companies has been protested. A more frequent criticism is that the competition is "unfair" for a number of reasons. TVA pays lower interest rates on borrowed money than private corporations and is not obliged to pay taxes; it is alleged that TVA shows a profit on its power activities by tailoring its accounting methods to hide government subsidies. Defenders of TVA call attention to the thousands of families in the region enjoying electrical power where before they had none; they note the general decrease of private power rates in the area; they cite the contributions to the national defense effort by TVA facilities; they insist TVA accounts accurately reflect generating and distribution costs.

The argument continues. No other valley authority has been established, though often advocated. On the other hand, it appears that TVA will continue to exemplify governmental regional planning at its best or worst according to one's view.

The Atomic Energy Commission. The Atomic Energy Commission was established in 1946. It is composed of five members, one designated as chairman, all appointed by the President with the consent of the Senate.

Upon its creation the Commission was given a monopoly of fissionable material with broad powers over production, research, and utilization in the atomic energy field. In the first decade of its existence, the Atomic Energy Commission created a whole new industry. It now has installations in nearly half of the states. These include plants for the extraction of uranium from ore, for processing feed material, and for the manufacture of weapons. Installations also include a commercial power plant, testing ranges, and other research facilities. Actually the bulk of the work in the atomic energy field is done on a contract basis by private firms.

In the last few years there has been increasing pressure from business groups for the government to relax its control in the atomic energy field. An amendment to the Atomic Energy Act in 1954 was at least a partial victory for this point of view. It permits the private construction, ownership, and operation of atomic power plants and the use of nuclear fuel by private firms, under the licensing control of the Commission. Patents developed under contract with the AEC remain government property, but patent protection in areas of private atomic research is afforded for nonmilitary application. Even in these cases, compulsory licensing for all comers is required for the first five years at royalty rates set by the Commission.

DEPARTMENT OF COMMERCE

Created as a full-fledged department in its own right in 1913, the United States Department of Commerce is responsible for promoting the nation's industry and business, its foreign and domestic commerce, its transportation systems, and its scientific and technical growth.

Business and Defense Services Administration. Created in 1953, the Business and Defense Services Administration is responsible for carrying out the Department's programs relating to current defense production, long-range industrial preparedness, and certain services to business groups. With respect to the first two of these programs, B.D.S.A. develops the priorities and allocations necessary to the accomplishment of current military and atomic energy programs, and under the general guidance of the Office of Civil and Defense Mobilization, develops plans for industrial mobilization in the event of a future emergency. In the area of service to business, 25 Industry Divisions and an Office of Small Business provide for representation of the domestic interests of business and industry in their relations with governmental agencies.

Office of Business Economics. The Office of Business Economics, through its monthly publication, *Survey of Current Business,* furnishes the business community with a concise record of the nation's economic progress. Its analyses cover national income, gross national product, consumer expenditures for goods and services, and expenditures for plant and equipment. They provide basic economic measurements of the state of the national economy.

Area Redevelopment Administration. Mr. Kennedy promised, if elected, to give priority to a program of federal aid to depressed areas. Certain sections of the country were more severely affected by changes in our economy than others. The first major victory of the Kennedy Administration in 1961 was the creation of the Area Redevelopment Administration. The legislation aimed to give relief in areas of persistent unemployment by federal aid—loans for industrial or commercial facilities, loans or grants for public facilities, technical assistance, and related information. Under President Johnson's War on Poverty program these projects will be greatly increased.

Bureau of Public Roads. The Bureau of Public Roads represents the federal government in matters relating to highways over a broad range of engineering, administrative, and research activities. It supervises the expenditures of funds granted to the states for highway improvement and controls road construction in national forests, parks, and parkways. A significant example of the Bureau's responsibility is furnished by the Federal-Aid Highway Act of 1956. This legislation authorizes nearly $25 billion of federal funds for the construction of an interstate highway system over a period of 15 years. Upon completion the system will provide a 41,000-mile network of master roads and expressways throughout the states and linking 90 per cent of the cities of more than 50,000 population.

The National Bureau of Standards. Essential scientific services are provided to the government and the public through the National Bureau of Standards. A staff of chemists, physicists, mathematicians, metallurgists, and other highly trained technicians offers advice to government agencies on technical problems, invents devices and develops techniques to meet the special needs of government, and tests equipment and material for governmental and general use. As custodian of the national standards of physical measurement, the Bureau is the ultimate source in the United States for thousands of standards used in our industrial economy. Its calibration services insure the accuracy of scientific instruments by comparing them with national standards.

Bureau of the Census. Census taking is one of the government's oldest activities. The Constitution provides for a population census every ten years as a basis for determining apportionment of congressional representation among the states. First taken in 1790 the decennial census was broadened to include manufactures in 1810, mineral industries and agriculture in 1840, state and local governments in 1850, irrigation in 1890, drainage in 1920, business in 1930, and housing in 1940.

From 1790 to 1900, the staff for taking the decennial census was recruited and maintained for a temporary period every ten years. Because of the problems and complexities arising from the proportions to which the census job had grown, a permanent census office was established in 1902 although a number of temporary workers are still employed to aid in the population count. The frequency of some of the censuses has been increased and their timing has been changed to distribute the work more evenly over each decade. The censuses of population and housing are conducted every ten years in the year ending with a zero. Other censuses are conducted at five-year intervals—the censuses of business, manufactures, and mineral industries cover the years ending in three and eight; the census of agriculture (including irrigation and drainage) covers the years ending in four and nine; and the census of governments covers the years ending in two and seven.

Between censuses, the Bureau makes current surveys to keep up to date some of the more important population, housing, manufacturing, business, and state and local government statistics. Employment and unemployment data are collected monthly. Monthly estimates of the national population and annual estimates of state population are made. Special censuses are taken at the request and expense of local areas. The Bureau annually compiles the widely used *Statistical Abstract of the United States,* a compendium of information from governmental and recognized private sources.

Coast and Geodetic Survey. The Coast and Geodetic Survey was created in 1878, but some of its present functions date back to legislation passed in 1807. Its present functions include:

(1) Surveying and charting the coasts of the United States, its territories and possessions and the printing of nautical charts to insure safe navigation;

(2) hydrographic and topographic surveying of some inland waters;

(3) the determination of geographic positions and elevations along the coasts and in the interior of the country, to coordinate coastal surveys and to provide a framework for mapping and other engineering work;

(4) the study of tides and currents in order to make annual tide and current forecasts;

(5) the compilation and printing of aeronautical charts for civil aviation;

(6) observations of the earth's magnetism for information essential to the mariner, aviator, land surveyor, radio engineer, and others;

(7) seismological observations and investigations to supply data for designing structures resistant to earthquakes; and,

(8) gravity and astronomic observations to provide basis data for geodetic surveys and studies of the earth's crust.

Weather Bureau. The National Weather Service was established in 1870 under the Signal Corps of the Army. It was transferred to the Department of Agriculture in 1891 and organized as the Weather Bureau. Subsequent legislative and executive action has greatly increased the Bureau's responsibilities, especially in providing weather service for civil aviation. The Bureau became a part of the Department of Commerce in 1940.

The Weather Bureau is responsible for observing, reporting, and forecasting the weather for the public. Storm warnings, flood warnings, weather forecasts, and other meteorological information are made available to the general public by television, radio, telephone, and newspapers. Specialized weather services required for air transportation, agriculture, and shipping are also provided.

From Washington, D. C., the Weather Bureau transmits charts and forecasts information by teletypewriter and facsimile to guide local field offices in issuing forecasts and warnings. Usually forecasts are issued four times a day to cover expected weather developments in the next thirty-six to forty-eight hours. In addition, warnings of severe weather are issued as appears necessary. Five-day forecasts are issued three times a week, and thirty-day outlooks are issued twice a month.

The Patent Office. Congressional statutes have established more generous patent privileges than are permitted in most other countries. Statutes decree that those who invent or discover "any new and useful act, machine, manufacture, or composition of matter, or any new and useful improvement thereof" may be protected in their use during a period of seventeen years. Applications must be made to the Patent Office, and full description of the discovery must be furnished. Patents may be granted to those who develop new plants, and for new, original, and ornamental design for an article of manufacture. However, for patents on ornamental designs the period of protection is for three and one-half, seven, or fourteen years. Trademarks registered with the Patent Office confer protection for twenty years. Since 1790 almost 3,000,000 patents have been granted.

Individuals must protect their patents against infringement since the government does not undertake this obligation. Thus the patentee must himself bring suit to enjoin and to seek damages for the use of his invention without his permission. The defendant may reply with a patent of his own or make the claim that the patent in question is invalid. From 1900 to 1945 the Supreme Court has held as invalid a majority of the patents litigated within its jurisdiction. Since such litigation is expensive, it has often been suggested that large corporations with tremendous financial resources and highly competent legal talent at their disposal have a decided advantage over less affluent individuals or corporations in infringement controversies. Of the patents issued between 1939 and 1955 about 60 per cent went to corporations with 50 firms receiving approximately 20 per cent of the total.

Patents controlled by a single corporation or group of corporations have frequently formed the basis for the domination of an entire industry. In the past twenty years, the Justice Department has brought an increasing number of suits against firms who, the government alleged, were using patent privileges to violate the antitrust laws. For example, the government charged in 1954 that the Radio Corporation of America had used its control of more than ten thousand radio, television, and related patents to monopolize those industries and to hinder individual research and development. A competitor, it was charged, had the choice of accepting RCA control and paying full royalties or attempting to circumvent RCA patents with his own. Eventually, RCA agreed to make all of its radio and black-and-white TV patents available without charge to the whole industry. Its color TV patents would be placed in an open pool available without charge to any other firm joining the pool, and the corporation agreed to license at reasonable royalties all new patents it received for a period of ten years.

New Bureaus Created in 1961. Two new bureaus were established within the Department of Commerce in 1961, both dealing with international commerce. The Bureau of International Business Operations provides expanded services to Americans in the export trade. The Bureau of International Programs provides information and advisory services regarding foreign countries and regions to U. S. business concerns in the conduct of their foreign trade and investment operations.

SMALL BUSINESS ADMINISTRATION

In the past 25 years many statutes have given specific aid to various types of small businesses. However, the Small Business Administration, created in 1953, is the first independent agency in the federal government ever established in peacetime solely to advise and assist small business concerns. The agency's creation involved something deeper than just another example of the government providing largess to a vocal pressure group. The legislation represents another approach to the policy of maintaining competition and discouraging greater concentration of industry in the hands of "big" business.

The Administration's financial specialists counsel with small business concerns on their financial problems and, if borrowing is necessary, help them obtain funds from private lending sources. If a small business concern cannot obtain private financing on reasonable terms, the SBA will consider making a loan to it. Loans may be made for business construction, conversion, or expansion and for the purchase of equipment, facilities, machinery, supplies, or materials. For classification purposes a manufacturing firm is considered small if it employs 250 or fewer persons per year. A wholesale concern is classified as small if its yearly sales are $5,000,000 or less. Most retail and service trade concerns are considered small if their yearly sales or receipts are $1,000,000 or less. The agency also makes disaster loans (floods, storms, droughts, etc.).

SBA also supervises the administration of statutes requiring that a fair proportion of the total purchases and contracts for property and services for the federal government be placed with small business enterprises. In addition many types of advisory services are made available to the small business man.

SUMMARY

Almost all aspects of the nation's economic structure, including business activities, are now subject to congressional regulation through the reach of the commerce power. Decisions by the Supreme Court in the 1930's reversed a ruling of long standing—that manufacturing, i.e., the production of goods, was not subject to controls under the commerce clause. It is well to recall that the power to regulate commerce includes the power to foster, protect, control, and restrain.

The combination movement following the Civil War brought "big business" with the attendant trusts and monopolies to the forefront of the economic life of the country. The general nature of the government's antitrust policies were set by the Sherman Antitrust Act of 1890. Although exemptions from general policy have been made, other legislation relating to general business regulation, including the Clayton Act, have sought to make more specific the generalities of the Sherman Act. The Supreme Court's narrow interpretation of the meaning of commerce, and its application of the "rule of reason" in antitrust suits, long made it difficult to enforce antitrust laws. The renewed vigor of the government in pressing antitrust actions in the last twenty years is due in part to the changed attitude of the Court on these two points.

Historically, the United States' tariff policy particularly benefited the business interests. Since 1934, with the passage of the Reciprocal Trade Agreements Act, Congress has more or less relinquished its tariff-setting function to the executive branch. Lower tariffs have resulted, but Congress has added "peril point" and "escape" clause provisions designed to keep the tariff high enough to give the American manufacturer some advantage over foreign competitors.

The government operates a startling number of business-type enterprises, many for its own specialized needs. No one objects to the postal system being in government hands—particularly as long as it is running a deficit. On the other hand, when a governmental agency such as TVA competes directly with private enterprise in a large scale undertaking, bitter criticism of the policy is bound to arise. It will be interesting to observe the future operation of the Atomic Energy Commission in this respect.

BIBLIOGRAPHIC NOTE

Courses in Government and Business are offered in many colleges and universities by economics departments as well as political science departments. Among the well-known textbooks used in such courses are: M. E. Dimock, *Business and Government* (4th ed., New York: Henry Holt and Co., 1961); Merle Fainsod, Lincoln Gordon, and Joseph C. Palamountain, Jr., *Government and the American*

Economy (3rd ed., New York: W. W. Norton, Inc., 1959); and George A. Steiner, *Government's Role in Economic Life* (New York: McGraw-Hill Book Co., Inc., 1953).

A. A. Berle, Jr., and Gardiner Means in *The Modern Corporation and Private Property* (2nd ed., New York: The Macmillan Company, 1940) develop the thesis of the separation of ownership and control in the modern corporation. Two more recent books by A. A. Berle, Jr., *The Twentieth-Century Capitalist Revolution* (New York: Harcourt, Brace and Company, 1954) and *Power Without Property* (same publisher, 1959) enlarge and elaborate upon this thesis.

For a discussion of the traditional American laissez faire concepts, see Sidney B. Fine, *Laissez Faire and the General Welfare State* (Ann Arbor, Mich.: University of Michigan Press, 1956); Thurman Arnold, *The Folklore of Capitalism* (New Haven, Conn.: Yale University Press, 1937); and J. K. Galbraith, *The Affluent Society* (Boston: Houghton Mifflin Company, 1958).

The dramatic change in governmental policy and philosophy is described by Arthur M. Schlesinger, Jr., in *The Coming of the New Deal* (Boston: Houghton Mifflin Company, 1959). For a statistical analysis of increasing governmental functions, see Solomon Fabricant's *The Trend of Government Activity in the United States Since 1900* (New York: National Bureau of Economic Research, Inc., 1952).

The most thorough investigation ever undertaken on the concentration of economic power in America was in the late 1930's and early 1940's under the direction of the Temporary National Economic Committee. A final report of the committee was published as Senate Doc. 35, 77th Cong., 1st Sess. (1941). Forty-three separate publications, popularly referred to as the TNEC monographs, came out of the investigation. For more recent studies on the same subject, see Edward S. Mason, *Economic Concentration and the Monopoly Problem* (Cambridge, Mass.: Harvard University Press, 1957); and David Lynch, *The Concentration of Economic Power* (New York: Columbia University Press, 1946).

For a comprehensive description and critical analysis of antitrust policies, see H. B. Thorelli's *The Federal Antitrust Policy* (Baltimore: The Johns Hopkins University Press, 1955). S. N. Whitney in his *Anti-trust Policies* (2 vols., New York: Twentieth Century Fund, 1958) uses the case history approach, covering 20 different industries. Clair Wilcox's *Public Policies Toward Business* (Chicago: Richard D. Irwin, Inc., 1955) stresses the policies associated with maintaining and moderating competition. W. A. Adams and Horace M. Gray argue in *Monopoly in America* (New York: The Macmillan Company, 1955) that the government fosters monopolistic practices through failure to pursue vigorous regulatory policies. J. K. Galbraith in *American Capitalism* (Boston: Houghton Mifflin Company, 1952) develops the countervailing power concept as an approach to the maintenance of economic competition. Emmette S. Redford's *Administration of National Economic Control* (New York: The Macmillan Company, 1952) is a critical examination of the administrative process as it relates to regulatory activities.

Edward S. Corwin's *The Commerce Power* v. *States Rights* (Princeton, N. J.: Princeton University Press, 1936) is a painstaking analysis of the development of the commerce power up to the mid-1930's. For a more recent study of one aspect of the commerce power, see Joseph E. Kallenbach's *Federal Cooperation With the States Under the Commerce Clause* (Ann Arbor, Mich.: University of Michigan Press, 1942).

Floyd Vaughan in his *The United States Patent System* (Norman, Okla.: University of Oklahoma Press, 1956) emphasizes the part played by patents in pooling, consolidation, and monopolistic practices.

The *Annual Reports* of the Federal Trade Commission contain considerable information on the work of that agency.

23

Public Utility Regulation

"PUBLIC utilities is a collective name covering diverse industries which it is common practice to group under this designation because certain common characteristics give them unity." [1] Traditionally these common characteristics have included such features as: (1) a business in which property is devoted to an enterprise of a sort which the public itself might appropriately undertake; (2) a business whose owner relies on a public grant or franchise for the right to conduct the business; (3) a business in its nature a monopoly; (4) a business which is bound to serve all who apply. Actually, there is no hard and fast rule today as to what constitutes a public utility, particularly since legislative bodies, both national and state, regulate certain industries as though they were public utilities, even though they might not fall within the traditional designation.

One approach to the classification of public utilities suggests the following categories: (1) services of transportation or the common carrier function (the transporting medium and ancillary services associated with highways, railways, pipeways, waterways and airways); (2) services facilitating communication (postal service, telegraph, telephone, radio, television, etc.); (3) facilities providing power, light, heat, and refrigeration; and (4) facilities providing water, sanitation, flood protection, irrigation, and drainage.[2]

Policies with respect to certain of these services are touched upon in other sections of this book. This chapter will deal with some of the more important aspects of public utility regulation by the national government which have not been treated elsewhere.

In many states of the world public utilities are owned and operated by the government. While at national, state, and local levels in the United States there is considerable governmental *ownership* of public utilities, the primary pattern is governmental *regulation,* frequently by an independent board or commission. State and local governments regulate those considered solely intrastate in their functions, while the federal government assumes regulatory responsibilities for those that are interstate in character. Two

---

[1] Martin G. Glaeser, *Public Utilities in American Capitalism* (New York: The Macmillan Company, 1957), p. 3.

[2] *Ibid.,* p. 9.

general objectives emerge from past national governmental policies in this area. The first is to protect the consumer or user from unreasonable rates and discriminatory treatment; the second, related to the first but not always the same, is to foster competition within and/or between public utility industries. Techniques employed toward the accomplishment of these goals have varied because of the diversity of the interests involved, the varying political strength of the groups concerned, the altered circumstances caused by technological advances, and because of the changing philosophy of the role of government itself. Piecemeal regulation, though probably unavoidable, has nevertheless left many gaps and contradictions in national policy with respect to public utilities.

TRANSPORTATION

Transportation was the first type of enterprise within the broad range of public utilities to be regulated by government in the United States. In many areas of transportation, regulation in the public interest has followed an initial stage in which the government actively promoted the growth of the transportation system by direct subsidies and other favors. Regulation has not necessarily meant the end of subsidization, but it may be interpreted as meaning that a particular transport service has reached a point in its development where considerable numbers of people are dependent upon its services and/or competitors in a regulated sector have convinced legislative bodies that the unregulated industry has too great an advantage over those who are subject to governmental-fixed standards.

The Interstate Commerce Commission. Set up in 1887, the Interstate Commerce Commission was the first of the national regulatory commissions. The Commission was established to administer legislation designed primarily to halt certain abuses which had been practiced by railroads including excessive charges, rebates, special rates, and pooling agreements. Subsequent legislation has strengthened the authority of the Commission and broadened the scope of its jurisdiction. Today, it has broad supervisory powers over facilities under its jurisdiction with respect to rates and services, systems of accounts, records, and reports, financial mergers, issuance of securities, safety of operation and equipment, and other activities. In addition to railroads, the Commission's jurisdiction extends to motor carriers, coastal shipping, intercoastal and inland waters, pipelines (except natural gas and water), freight forwarders, rail-and-water transportation, and sleeping-car companies.

Railroad regulation. During the late nineteenth and early twentieth centuries, national transportation policy was primarily concerned with regulating rates and services of railways and attempting to break up railroad combinations under the Sherman Act. In both of these areas the government experienced considerable frustration as a result of court interpretations of

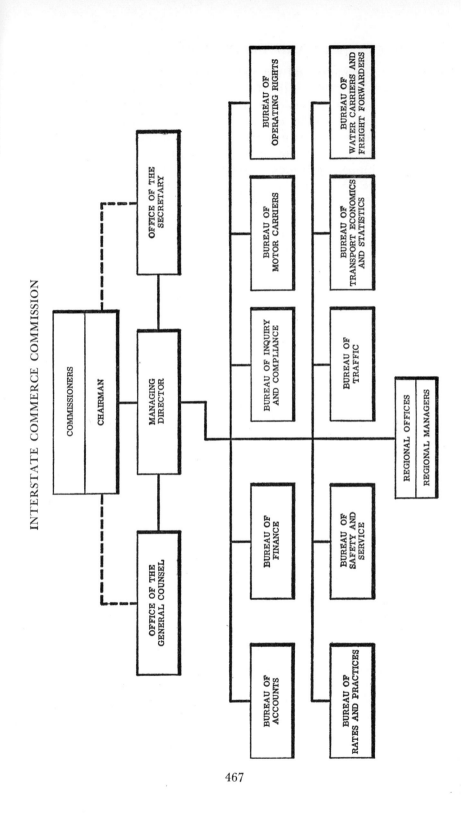

INTERSTATE COMMERCE COMMISSION

COMMISSIONERS
CHAIRMAN

OFFICE OF THE SECRETARY

OFFICE OF THE GENERAL COUNSEL

MANAGING DIRECTOR

BUREAU OF OPERATING RIGHTS

BUREAU OF MOTOR CARRIERS

BUREAU OF INQUIRY AND COMPLIANCE

BUREAU OF WATER CARRIERS AND FREIGHT FORWARDERS

BUREAU OF TRANSPORT ECONOMICS AND STATISTICS

BUREAU OF TRAFFIC

BUREAU OF FINANCE

BUREAU OF ACCOUNTS

BUREAU OF SAFETY AND SERVICE

BUREAU OF RATES AND PRACTICES

REGIONAL OFFICES
REGIONAL MANAGERS

the Interstate Commerce and the Sherman Antitrust Act. It was not until the Hepburn Act of 1906 that the ICC was finally authorized to fix maximum rates for railway carriers. However, the Commission's power before World War I did not extend to other crucial areas of the railway industry. It lacked control over the financial structure of railroads, including the issuance of securities. As one authority states: "A negative, restrictive policy, confined to protecting shippers against extortion, might restrain avarice; it could not ensure adequate service, progressive management, and a development of transportation facilities to meet national needs." [3]

The weakness of railroad transportation as an integrated national system was revealed by the demands of World War I. The national government assumed control over the industry for a twenty-six month period in order to move the men and materials of war more effectively. Although governmental control was criticized as inefficient, the necessity for imposing it in the first place profoundly affected postwar railway policy. Most of the proposals for restoring the lines to private operation contemplated additional public control and the consolidation of existing lines into fewer but stronger systems.

The Transportation Act of 1920 gave the ICC authority to fix minimum as well as maximum rates. The Commission was given control over security issues and other financial operations. A contingent fund, financed by excess profits (over 6 per cent annually on the investment), was to be administered by ICC for the purpose of making loans or for the lease of equipment to carriers. The most significant change in national policy with respect to the railway industry were the provisions encouraging consolidation of systems. The ICC was authorized to prepare a comprehensive consolidation plan, but it was not given specific statutory power to enforce its recommendations. Carriers could themselves initiate certain types of consolidations; pooling agreements, heretofore illegal, were made possible with ICC approval. The Reed-Bulwinkle Act of 1948 granted an exemption from antitrust laws to certain aspects of rate determination where railroads jointly considered rate charges.

The depression, short-sighted management policies, and the increasing competition from other types of carriers compounded the plight of the railway industry. World War II brought a temporary respite from financial difficulties; but shortly thereafter, the trend toward declining profits and actual losses continued—even though by 1957 the ICC had authorized the railroads to almost double their World War II rates. Legislation in 1958 authorized governmental guarantees up to $500 million for private loans, and empowered the ICC to permit the discontinuance, curtailment, or consolidation of unprofitable interstate train service. In 1960 the Secretary of Commerce referred to the railroads as the "sick man" of transportation.

---

[3] Merle Fainsod, Lincoln Gordon, and Joseph C. Palamountain, Jr., *Government and the American Economy* (3rd ed., New York: W. W. Norton & Company, Inc., 1959), p. 266.

Hopefully, the Mass Transit Act of 1964 will help some of the commuter railroads, but the financial plight of most lines remain a critical problem.

The regulation of motor carriers. The Motor Carrier Act of 1935 brought certain motor carriers within the jurisdiction of the Interstate Commerce Commission. This act is an example of the politics involved in extending regulation to an unregulated sector of the economy. Support for the legislation came from the railroads who were feeling the pinch of competition from the trucking interests. The suggestion for regulation received some support from bus operators and big truckers who saw in the legislation a means of stabilizing their industries, by limiting the entry of future highway competitors. The American Trucking Association approved the proposal in its late stages when it was assured that administration of the act would be vested in a separate bureau within the ICC. The exemptions to the act's provisions also bespoke of successful maneuvering by interest groups. Thus the law was not applicable to farm vehicles transporting agricultural products or vehicles distributing newspapers or carrying livestock. School buses and taxicabs were also exempt from its provisions.

Common carriers were most completely regulated by the Motor Carrier Act. Such carriers may operate only under a certificate from the ICC after a finding that they are able to perform and that the proposed service is required by the public convenience and necessity. A so-called "grandfather" clause entitled all carriers who were in operation on June 1, 1935 to receive the certificate of convenience and necessity by virtue of that fact.

Contract carriers are regulated to a lesser degree. They need only a "permit" to operate, and this is subject to less demanding standards than the certificate required of common carriers.

Although there was some fear that the ICC would favor railroads over truckers in administering the act, there is no clear pattern of decisions to indicate that this has occurred. The Commission has frequently ruled that the existence of adequate rail service, or the fact that railroads might be adversely affected, is not sufficient ground for denying a motor carrier permission to initiate or extend its operations. On the other hand, the ICC has substantially lessened competition within the motor-carrier industry itself. This occurs when the Commission refuses to authorize competitive services unless it can be shown that the existing carriers cannot or will not provide satisfactory service.

The regulation of water transportation. Before 1940 regulatory activities with respect to water transportation were confusing to say the least. Since its creation, the ICC had exercised some control over traffic carried jointly by railways and water carriers under common management. In 1916, the United States Shipping Board was created to regulate common carriers by water operating on the Great Lakes and on the high seas. Later this board's functions were assumed by the United States Maritime Commission, which in turn gave way in 1950 to two agencies—the Federal Maritime

Board and the Maritime Administration. The former agency inherited the regulatory functions, while the latter unit has many promotional and planning duties associated with the development of the American merchant marine.

In 1940 the situation was clarified somewhat when the ICC was given jurisdiction over the domestic carriers previously regulated by the Maritime Commission. Also for the first time certain types of water carriers engaged in coastwise, intercoastal, and inland waterways shipping were brought under the jurisdiction of the ICC. Nevertheless, there were many exemptions such as private carriers and contract carriers of bulk cargoes and liquid cargoes (such as oil tankers). It has been estimated that less than one-third of the domestic tonnage was made subject to regulation by the Commission.[4]

A significant milestone with respect to water transportation occurred in 1954 when Congress, after literally decades of debate, passed legislation making possible the construction of the St. Lawrence Seaway.

The Transportation Act of 1940. There was growing recognition in the 1930's that the national government lacked any unified policy with respect to transportation. In 1938 the ICC recommended that the regulation of all forms of interstate and foreign transportation be placed within a single agency, presumably itself. Congress was not willing to go this far, but the Transportation Act of 1940 did confer additional authority upon ICC. Perhaps the most significant feature of the act was its statement of policy.

> It is hereby declared to be the national transportation policy of the Congress to provide for fair and impartial regulation of all modes of transportation subject to the provisions of this Act, so administered as to recognize and preserve the inherent advantages of each; to promote safe, adequate, economical, and efficient service and foster sound economic conditions in transportation and among the several carriers; to encourage the establishment and maintenance of reasonable charges for transportation services, without unjust discriminations, undue preferences or advantages, or unfair or destructive competitive practices; to cooperate with the several States and the duly authorized officials thereof; and to encourage fair wages and equitable working conditions;—all to the end of developing, coordinating, and preserving a national transportation system by water, highway, and rail, as well as other means, adequate to meet the needs of the commerce of the United States, of the Postal Service, and of the national defense. All of the provisions of this Act shall be administered and enforced with a view to carrying out the above declaration of policy.

Thus national policy recognizes the desirability of integrating rail, motor, and domestic water transportation to meet the needs of the American economic system. Unfortunately, the Transportation Act did not confer sufficient authority upon the Interstate Commerce Commission to make the statement of policy effective. The exemptions allowed and the continued reg-

[4] Glaeser, *op. cit.*, p. 144.

ulatory activities of other agencies in the transportation field bear testimony to this fact.

Air transportation. In 1926 the Department of Commerce was authorized to regulate air transportation, to license pilots, develop air navigation facilities, promote flying safety, map airways, and furnish flight information to those who needed it. For a brief period from 1934 to 1938, three separate federal agencies held sway over civil aviation; the Post Office Department awarded mail contracts and established routes; the Interstate Commerce Commission fixed the mail rates which the Post Office Department paid; and a bureau in the Commerce Department carried out several types of functions with respect to aviation.

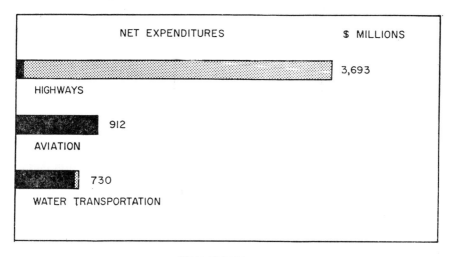

NET EXPENDITURES $ MILLIONS

HIGHWAYS   3,693

AVIATION   912

WATER TRANSPORTATION   730

TRANSPORTATION

Administrative Budget

Trust Funds

FEDERAL EXPENDITURES RELATING TO TRANSPORTATION, FISCAL YEAR 1965

The Civil Aeronautics Act of 1938. By 1938 civil aviation had become big business and the transport of passengers and mail was recognized as a permanent factor in American industry and an adjunct vital to the nation's defense. Under the Civil Aeronautics Act of 1938, the Civil Aeronautics Administration and the Civil Aeronautics Board came into being.

To the Civil Aeronautics Administration was delegated responsibility for the enforcement of safety, air traffic control, operation of airways, aviation communications, and the improvement of airports. The Civil Aeronautics Board was charged with writing civil air regulations, investigating accidents, economic regulation of the industry, awarding of routes, and establishing mail rates.

In 1948 an Air Navigation Development Board was created; its responsibility was the development of new air traffic control tools and air navigation aids and facilities. The Airways Modernization Board absorbed the functions of this agency in 1957.

The Federal Aviation Agency. As early as 1948, the President's Air Coordinating Committee warned that the techniques and tools available for the control of air traffic were marginal even by pre-World War II standards. During the early and middle 1950's, as the federal airways became more and more congested, and larger and faster aircraft appeared in commercial operation, it became increasingly apparent that the existing structure could not provide the traffic management needed by an air industry fast moving into an era of jet speeds and automation.

The Federal Aviation Act of 1958 was passed to establish the governmental authority and machinery necessary to permit more effective promotion and control in aviation matters. With the creation of the Federal Aviation Agency, there came into existence for the first time a single government aviation agency equipped with adequate authority to initiate and execute the policies and programs required for the support and promotion of safe and efficient flight. The new agency incorporated the functions and activities of the Civil Aeronautics Administration, the Airways Modernization Board, and that part of the Civil Aeronautics Board that had the responsibility for determining the rules of air safety. The Federal Aviation Agency began, as of January 1, 1959, to operate on a five-point plan described in the following principles: (1) to regulate air commerce so as to promote its development, safety, and requirements in natonal defense; (2) to control the navigable airspace and to regulate civil and military flight operations in the interest of safety and efficiency; (3) to develop and operate a common system of air traffic control and navigation, for both civilian and military aircraft; (4) to develop a plan for the agency's functions in the event of war; (5) to prescribe minimum standards for design, material, and workmanship in aircraft construction and the construction of other elements of aviation.

Civil Aeronautics Board. The primary function of the Civil Aeronautics Board remained unchanged under the Federal Aviation Act of 1958. It is the agency concerned with the regulation of the economic aspects of air carriers. The Board is responsible for granting authorizations to carriers to engage in interstate and foreign air transportation. It issues permits to foreign air carriers authorizing them to engage in air transportation between the United States and foreign countries, and also authorizes the navigation of foreign civil aircraft in the United States for other purposes.

CAB has jurisdiction over tariff, and the rates and fares charged the public for air transportation; it establishes rates for the carriage of mail by air carriers; and it authorizes and pays subsidies to certain air carriers where required for the development of an adequate air transportation system.

In the interest of maintaining regulated competition, the Board passes on mergers, acquisition of control and interlocking relations involving air carriers, and passes on contracts for cooperative working arrangements between air carriers. CAB also has jurisdiction over unfair competitive practices of air carriers and ticket agents selling air transportaion; it regulates the accounting practices of air carriers and requires them to file regular financial and operating reports.

CAB has pursued a policy of restricting entry into the air commerce field on the basis that existing common carriers should be strengthened, thereby lessening the need for government subsidies. Protection of the certified carriers from competition has resulted in bitter controversies between the Board and the nonscheduled carriers ("non-skeds"). In 1938 CAB granted exemption from its economic regulation to certain operators who made irregular trips and ran charter flights. Following World War II, the number of "non-skeds" multiplied rapidly; some began to offer regularly scheduled services, albeit in violation of the law. They met peak demands on routes that had already been allocated to certified carriers; they introduced some innovations, later adopted by the regular carriers, such as air coach and air cargo. Naturally, the certified carriers protested the activities of these groups. The CAB sided with the regular airlines. In 1947 it withdrew its exemption order. Later the "non-skeds" were prohibited from making more than three flights a month on major routes or eight flights between fixed points. Meanwhile it became apparent that the "non-skeds" had considerable political support in Congress. Since 1956 CAB has modified some of its policies to the advantage of the non-scheduled carriers. It has established a new category, the "supplemental air carrier," which carriers are allowed unlimited charter flights and up to ten flights a month between any two points.

Future transportation policy. National transportation policy will be an important public issue in the years that lie ahead. If past performance is indicative of future action, Congress will move slowly to change the basic statutes that now govern transportation industries.

In March of 1960 the Secretary of Commerce submitted a report on transportation to the President,[5] who in turn passed it on to Congress without any elaboration. It is possible that the report might become the basis of future legislation, but it is mentioned at this point to underscore the concern of responsible government officials with federal transportation policy. The present situation is described in these terms:

> National transportation is presently out of balance. It is less a national system than a loose grouping of individual industries. We have built vast networks of highways, railways, inland waterways and seaports, airways and airports, and pipelines, with little attention to conflict among these expanding networks. Economic regulation has been administered in

---

[5] *Federal Transportation Policy and Program* (Washington, D. C.: U. S. Government Printing Office, 1960).

rigid compartments although many basic problems are common to many areas of transportation. Total capacity is not closely geared to total need.[6]

In stressing a long-range general approach to the problem, the report stated:

> Regulation in the long run should remain only where monopoly or the threat of destructive competition remains. This approach requires greater freedom for the carriers in setting their own rates and determining and developing their routes and services. The tighter regulation that was well adapted to protecting the public under the predominant monopoly of the railroads is no longer well suited to highly competitive transport networks. Common carrier rates of all kinds are rapidly becoming regulated by competition whether the common carriers like it or not—the competition of highly developed private and exempt carriers. And conditions in the transportation industries, once a larger degree of market and cost information becomes available, promise workable results under substantially reduced regulation. Concurrent with this reduction should come reduced exemption from the antitrust laws applicable to the transportation industry in general.[7]

It is probable that many persons oppose the tone of the general approach suggested in the report as favorable to "big business." Much of what is suggested for the transportation industry generally has already been applied to the railroads.

The Secretary of Commerce's report carried several specific recommendations, but one in particular is apt to gain support from most economic and political groups; in several places references were made to the necessity for improving methods of cost analysis.

In 1962 President Kennedy called for legislation to improve the nation's transportation system. The recommendations with respect to urban transportation received wide publicity and in 1964 many of them were incorporated in the Mass Transit Act which Congress passed in that year.

REGULATION OF COMMUNICATIONS

Regulation of interstate electrical communication may be said to date from passage of the Post Roads Act in 1866 which authorized the Postmaster General to fix rates annually for government telegrams. In 1887 Congress gave the Interstate Commerce Commission authority to require telegraph companies to interconnect their lines for more extended public service. Government regulation of the accounting practices of wire communication carriers began with the Mann-Elkins Act of 1910. This act authorized the ICC to establish uniform systems of accounts for telegraph and telephone carriers, to make evaluation studies of certain wire telegraph companies, and to be informed of extensions and improvements in order to keep these evaluation

---

[6] *Ibid.*, p. 3.
[7] *Ibid.*, p. 5.

studies up to date. In this connection, telephone and telegraph carriers were required to file monthly and annual financial reports with ICC.

The first legislation dealing with marine radio was approved by Congress in 1910. Under the administration of the Secretary of Commerce and Labor, the Wireless Ship Act required installation of wireless apparatus and the hiring of operators on large sea-going passenger vessels. The Radio Act of 1912 was the first law for control of domestic radio in general; certain frequencies were set aside for government use, and the Secretary of Commerce and Labor was made responsible for the licensing of wireless stations and operators. A Federal Radio Commission was created in 1927. This legislation recognized the importance of commercial broadcasting, placing broad powers in the Commission with respect to the issuance of radio station licenses, the allocation of frequency bands to various services, assignment of specific frequencies to individual stations, and control of station power.

Federal Communications Commission. At the request of President Roosevelt, the Secretary of Commerce in 1933 appointed an interdepartmental committee to study the whole subject of federal control of communication media. The committee recommended the establishment of a new agency which would regulate all interstate and foreign communication by wire and radio, including telegraph, telephone, and broadcast. The Communications Act, passed by Congress in 1934, coordinated in a Federal Communications Commission broadcast regulatory functions exercised by the Federal Radio Commission, supervision of certain telegraph and telephone operations formerly vested in the ICC, jurisdiction over government telegraph rates which had been under the Post Office Department, and some powers of the Department of State with respect to cables. The act gave to the newly-created Commission additional authority, including supervision of rates of interstate and international common carriers, and domestic administration of international agreements relating to electrical communication generally. The FCC is composed of seven commissioners appointed by the President, subject to confirmation by the Senate. Not more than four commissioners may be members of the same political party. The normal term of a commissioner is for seven years.

Common carrier regulation. Common carrier communication services include telephone and telegraph by means of radio and wire (including submarine cable). Such communication which is purely intrastate in character is not subject to Commission regulation. Provisions of the Communications Act affecting common carriers reflect congressional policy that the public interest in adequate public communications service and reasonable rates is to be protected and promoted by federal regulation.

Among the regulatory provisions of the act is the requirement that every subject common carrier furnish service upon reasonable request and at reasonable charges. No carrier may construct or acquire additional interstate facilities, or curtail or discontinue interstate service, without Commission

FEDERAL COMMUNICATIONS COMMISSION

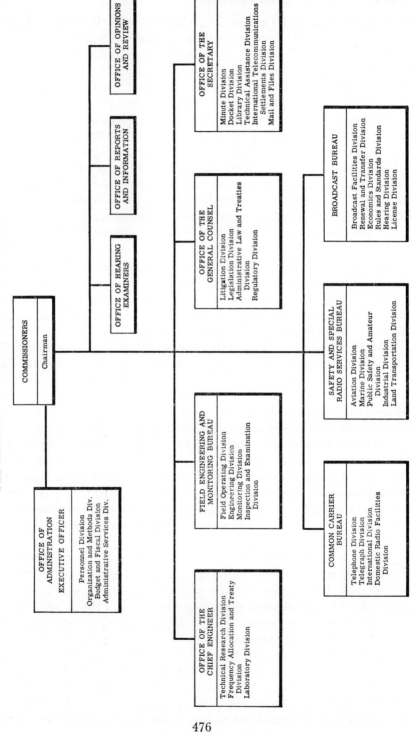

approval. All charges, procedures, classifications, and regulations in connection with interstate and foreign communications service must be just and reasonable and nondiscriminatory. To implement this requirement, the common carriers concerned must file tariff schedules with the Commission, and the rates and regulations set forth in these schedules are subject to review and regulation by the FCC.

Broadcast regulation. Broadcasting is not deemed to be a common carrier by the Federal Communications Act. Hence the FCC has no jurisdiction over charges made by broadcast stations for air time, nor does it maintain surveillance of internal station management, salaries paid performers or technical personnel, or programming except as it may conflict with a few specific prohibitions in congressional statutes. For example, the United States Criminal Code prohibits broadcast of information concerning "any lottery, gift enterprise, or similar scheme," also utterance of obscene, indecent, or profane language.

The most powerful weapon the FCC has at its command with respect to broadcasting is the licensing power. Licenses for operating broadcasting stations, including FM and television, are issued by the Commission, which assigns the wave length to be used, the hours the license covers, and the strength of the broadcasting equipment. Because the channels are limited and are a part of the public domain, it is important that they be entrusted to licensees who have a high sense of public responsibility. In general, applicants must be legally, technically, and financially qualified and show that their proposed operation will be in the public interest. Licenses are for three-year periods so the FCC is in a position to measure station promises against its performance on a periodic basis.

The sensational revelations in 1959 and 1960 of the existence of "fixed" quiz shows and of various types of "payola" once more focused attention on what the FCC can and cannot do. The Commission does not have the power to require specific types of programming. It does not prescribe any percentages of time which should be devoted to particular subjects, such as news, education, religion, music, public issues, etc. However, the Commission does have the power to review the performance of a station, including its programming, when it applies for renewal of its license, to determine whether it has lived up to its obligations and the promises made in obtaining permission to use the public airways. While it does not pass upon the nature or length of commercials on the air, the Commission's review of a station's performance considers deviation from promised service which tends toward over-commercialization. Also under a cooperative arrangement with the Federal Trade Commission, which has jurisdiction over false and misleading advertising on the air, the Commission notifies stations concerned of broadcast advertising cited by FTC so that these stations may take any necessary action consistent with their obligations to operate in the public interest. The FCC does not license networks as such. However, stations owned by or affiliated with networks are subject to certain broadcasting regulations contained in the Commission's rules.

Many critics felt that the FCC and FTC had ample powers to prevent many of the abuses which had come to the public's attention. Attorney General Rogers inclined toward this view, although he recommended that "payola" be made a federal crime, and that the FCC be authorized to suspend licenses where stations failed to discharge their responsibilities correctly. Congress responded by outlawing various types of "payola," but the FCC was not given the power to suspend licenses.

The Communication Act expressly provides: "If any licensee shall permit any person who is a legally qualified candidate for any public office to use a broadcasting station, he shall afford equal opportunities to all other such candidates for that office in the use of such broadcasting station." The station does not, however, have to permit a political broadcast in the first place, and it may charge for the time if it does allow one. If one candidate pays for a political broadcast, the "equal time" provision merely requires that the station permit other candidates to buy equal time; it does not guarantee equal "free" time. Of course, if the station gives free time to any candidate, then all of the candidates for that office are entitled to equal treatment. During the 1960 Presidential campaign, Congress suspended the requirement that broadcasting stations give equal time to Presidential and Vice-Presidential candidates. This facilitated debates between the Presidential candidates of the two major political parties.

The question has arisen as to whether stations may editorialize, giving only one side to controversial questions. A Boston radio station broadcast editorials in support of the election of particular candidates. In the 1941 Mayflower case, the FCC ruled against the station, such ruling having the effect of banning all editorializing on the part of broadcasting stations. However, in 1949 the Commission revised its position concerning editorializing. It introduced the principle that a station may express editorial opinions in broadcasts as long as equal opportunity is given to opposing groups for the purpose of replying. This decision has left some confusion in its wake, as for example, exactly what is editorializing. Obviously, also a station might find that following an editorial on the air, it might be swamped with requests by many relatively small groups for equal time. Bills have been introduced in Congress which seek to clarify this area of uncertainty, but so far none has become law.

ELECTRICAL POWER AND NATURAL GAS

The activities of various national governmental agencies in connection with electric power have already been discussed. Hydroelectric dams are operated by different agencies such as TVA, the Bureau of Reclamation, and the Army Corps of Engineers. TVA markets its own power, while independ-

FEDERAL POWER COMMISSION

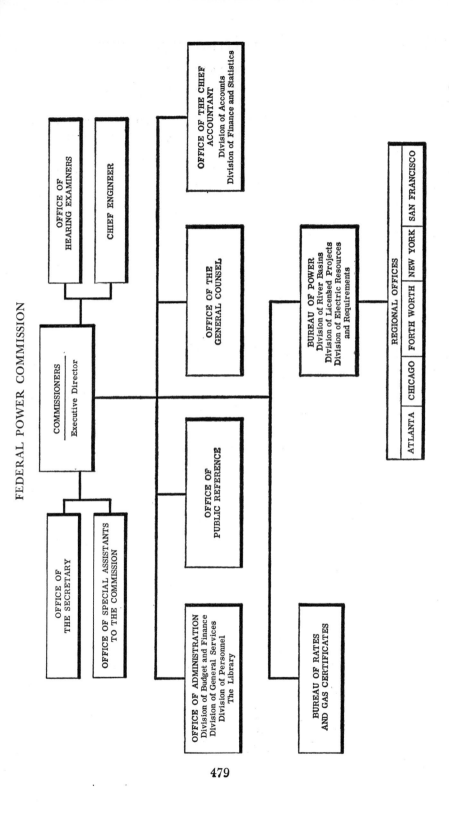

479

ent administrations[8] market most of the surplus power from projects under the jurisdiction of the Bureau of Reclamation and the Army Corps of Engineers.

The Federal Power Commission. The Federal Power Commission was created by the Federal Water Power Act of 1920, but it was not until 1930 that it became a full-fledged independent regulatory commission. FPC is authorized to pass on applications of private utilities which wish to develop the water power in the public domain or the navigable waters of the United States.[9] The Public Utility Act of 1935 placed upon the Commission the responsibility of regulating wholesale rates, services, corporate practices, and financial dealings of private utilities which transmit electricity across state lines.

The Natural Gas Act of 1938 directed the Commission to regulate companies engaged in the transportation or sale of natural gas in interstate commerce, including supervision over rates and services. A number of bills have been introduced in Congress in recent years aimed at diminishing FPC's authority in the area of rate-fixing. President Truman vetoed such a bill in 1950. In 1956 Congress passed a measure which would have prohibited the Commission from fixing the rates charged by independent producers of natural gas sold for distribution in interstate pipe lines. President Eisenhower had been expected to sign the act, but he vetoed it, citing the "arrogant" tactics of lobbyists who worked for its passage.[10]

PROBLEMS OF REGULATION

Many states of the world own and operate the various types of public utility enterprises discussed in this chapter. While the national government operates a limited number of such projects (and, of course, local governments many more), it is almost certain that the main emphasis in the United States will continue to be one of regulation rather than nationalization. But even within this regulatory frame of reference many problems are apparent. In most areas regulation has been piecemeal, authority divided, and unity of purpose often impossible due to the nature of our federal system, the separation of powers principle, and the political power of economic groups in our society. The use of the independent commission as the principal type of regulatory agency has also been questioned,[11] but it does not appear likely that any drastic change away from this form of regulatory agency is likely in the near future. The problems referred to so far are political and must

---

[8] Namely, the Bonneville, Southeastern, and Southwestern Power Administrations.

[9] The Supreme Court in *United States* v. *Appalachian Electric Power Co.*, 311 U. S. 377 (1940), upheld the Commission's power to pass on an application for a power construction on the New River on the ground that the stream was *potentially* navigable.

[10] During the Senate debate on the measure, a senator reported that a representative of the gas interests had contributed $2,500 to his campaign fund.

[11] See p. 378.

be settled by the political process. On the other hand, a continuing problem —which has often carried political implications, but which theoretically should be solvable by objective standards—is that of rate-fixing for services offered the public.

Rate regulation. Congressional and state legislative statutes have often authorized regulatory bodies to fix "just and reasonable" rates for public utility-type services. Courts were brought into the rate-making process when they were requested to review regulatory agencies' determinations as to what constituted a reasonable rate, i.e., a fair return on the fair value of the property being used. If the value of the property is agreed upon, it becomes a rather simple matter to decide what is a reasonable or fair rate of return; the crucial problem becomes one of fixing the base, that is to say the value of the investment.

Many "theories of valuation" have been advanced by rate-fixing authorities and by the public utilities. *Original cost* less depreciation, *cost of reproduction* less depreciation, the *commercial value* of the business, and the *prudent investment* (what a prudent business man would be willing to invest in the property) are among the principal theories which have been used to establish rate bases.

The Supreme Court in the famous *Smyth* v. *Ames*[12] case sought to steer a middle course between rival theories. Justice Harlan wrote: "In order to ascertain that value the original cost of construction, the amount expended in permanent improvements, the amount and market value of its bonds and stock, the present as compared with the original cost of construction, the probable earning capacity of the property under particular rates prescribed by statute, and the sum required to meet operating expenses, are all matters for consideration, and are to be given such weight as may be just and right in each case."

The Court did not indicate what weight any of these factors should be accorded. To further complicate the problem, Justice Harlan added: "We do not say that there may not be other matters to be regarded in estimating the value of property."

Both state and national regulatory agencies tussled with the imprecise standards of the *Smyth* v. *Ames* decision for almost a half-century without receiving a great deal of additional direction from the Supreme Court. One factor would be weighted more at times, then a different one. Rate cases often dragged out over years. Determining reproduction costs proved especially troublesome, if not impossible, with the valuation—at best an estimate —often becoming obsolete by the time drawn-out litigation was terminated. Finally in 1942, the Supreme Court moved far from the *Smyth* v. *Ames* doctrine when it cleared the way for regulatory commissions to use either the original cost or prudent investment theory for rate base determination.[13]

---

[12] 169 U. S. 466 (1898).
[13] *FPC* v. *Natural Gas Pipeline Co.*, 315 U. S. 575.

Today, the Court reserves the right to review rate-fixing cases, but in general leaves regulatory bodies much wider latitude in selecting the most appropriate approach for the determination of the base. Fixing of rates remains an extremely complicated business, to say the least, but regulatory commissions are in a better position to apply pragmatic approaches to the problem than they were twenty years ago.

SUMMARY

Regulation, rather than outright ownership, is the principal technique employed by the national government in dealing with problems associated with public utility type enterprises. The independent board or commission, heralded by the creation of the Interstate Commerce Commission in 1887, continues to be the type of national administrative organ relied upon to protect the public from specific abuses as well as to preserve and/or promote competition within a particular industry.

Regulation of a specific area in the public utility field has been activated by different factors. For example, pressure from the public brought into existence the Interstate Commerce Commission; the railroads were instrumental in having national regulation extended to motor carriers; the government took the initiative in some cases such as communications and airways.

From the beginning of regulation the problem of setting rate bases has been a particularly thorny one. In recent years the Supreme Court has permitted agencies more latitude in making this determination.

The piecemeal approach to the regulation of public utilities and the politics of administration, complicated by the fact that numerous agencies are involved, have prevented the development of a truly national policy in many specific areas; the lack of a national transportation policy is a case in point.

BIBLIOGRAPHIC NOTE

Martin G. Glaeser's *Public Utilities in American Capitalism* (New York: The Macmillan Company, 1957) gives extensive coverage to the whole range of policies and problems, both historical and current, associated with the regulation of public utilities at all levels of government in the United States. All of the national regulatory agencies issue *Annual Reports*. Particularly interesting in this connection is the *First Annual Report of the Federal Aviation Agency* (Washington, D. C.: Government Printing Office, 1959). Merle Fainsod, Lincoln Gordon, and Joseph C. Palamountain, Jr., in *Government and the American Economy* (3rd ed., New York: W. W. Norton, Inc., 1959) have several excellent chapters dealing with the development and current practices of the national government in the public utility area. A number of Ph.D. theses, dealing with the regulatory activities of both the national and state governments in selected areas, are brought together in Emmette S. Redford's (ed.), *Public Administration and Policy Formation: Studies in Oil,*

Gas, Banking, River Development, and Corporate Investigation (Austin, Tex.: University of Texas Press, 1956).

Both the first and second Hoover Commissions published final and task force reports concerned with various facets of government policy toward public-utility type enterprises. See U. S. Commission on Organization of the Executive Branch of the Government, *Federal Business Enterprises* and *Task Force Report on Regulatory Commissions* (Washington, D. C.: Government Printing Office, 1949); *Business Enterprises and Transportation* (Washington, D. C.: Government Printing Office, 1955).

Federal Transportation Policy and Program (Washington, D. C.: Government Printing Office, 1960) gives the views of the Secretary of Commerce as to legislation needed for the development of a truly national transportation policy. For two very useful works on the general subject of transportation, see Philip D. Locklin, *Economics of Transportation* (4th ed., Homewood, Ill.: R. D. Irwin, 1954) and Charles L. Dearing and Wilifred Owen, *National Transportation Policy* (Washington, D. C.: The Brookings Institution, 1949). For more intensive treatments of specific areas of transportation policy, see Gilbert Goodman, *Government Policy Toward Commercial Aviation: Competition and the Regulation of Rates* (New York: King's Crown Press, 1944); Charles A. Taff, *Commercial Motor Transportation* (Chicago: R. D. Irwin, 1950). Earl Latham examines the forces operating to prevent effective coordination of railroad transportation in the early New Deal period in his *The Politics of Railroad Coordination, 1933-1936* (Cambridge, Mass.: Harvard University Press, 1959).

The classic account of the activities of the first federal regulatory agency is Isaiah L. Sharfman, *The Interstate Commerce Commission* (5 vols., New York: Commonwealth Fund, 1931-1937). Two important works that examine national regulatory commission activities are Robert E. Cushman's *The Independent Regulatory Commission* (New York: Oxford University Press, 1941) and Marver H. Bernstein's *Regulating Business by Independent Commission* (Princeton, N. J.: Princeton University Press, 1955). The latter study concludes that commissions have not been satisfactory instruments of government regulation.

For an enumeration of the FCC's functions with respect to radio and television, see Federal Communications Commission, *Radio and Television Broadcast Primer,* Information Bulletin No. 2B, 1959.

A recent work dealing with the variety of problems in the relations between the government and the oil industry is Robert Engler's *The Politics of Oil: A Study of Private Power and Democratic Directions* (New York: Macmillan, 1961).

24

Agriculture and Conservation

SINCE the early 1930's the national government has been committed to a policy of price supports for agricultural commodities. Even though the number of farm families continues to decline, agricultural production generally stays ahead of consumption. It is thus that the problem of surpluses remains unsolved. Farm legislation stands high on the agenda of Congress almost every year; this is testimony not only to the search for a satisfactory solution to the "farm problem" but also to the political strength of the farming regions. To a great degree legislation dealing with agriculture is not decided upon party lines as the farm states have political strength in both political camps.

National legislation affecting conservation is largely a product of the twentieth century—if public land policy is excluded. This chapter includes discussions of conservation measures affecting land and forests, water and electric power, mineral resources including oil and natural gas, and fish and wildlife. Political controversy has accompanied legislation in many of these areas because of the economic stakes involved, because of administrative jurisdictional disputes, and because of frequent disagreement between the legislative and executive branches of government on conservation policies.

CHANGING PATTERN OF AMERICAN AGRICULTURE

Approximately 13 per cent of Americans live on farms. Farm population has declined by 2.9 million since 1950, by 8.4 million since 1940, and by 9.8 million since 1920. The number of individual farms has declined significantly, there being 6.5 million in 1920, but only 4.8 million in 1955. The number of farms of less than ten acres has increased since 1920; farms in the middle-sized category have decreased in number; the very large farms—five hundred acres or more—have increased.

Despite a declining farm population, mechanization and improved technologies have raised total agricultural production. Whereas in 1870 one farm worker produced enough to support only five people, by 1956 the number of persons supported per farm worker had risen to nineteen. In percentages the total farm output has risen faster than the total population of the United States in the past 15 years. Large increases in crop yields have been a major source of the recent upsurge in farm output. The rise in yields per acre of most of our leading crops have ranged from 20 to 75 per cent over the last decade. The yield of corn, which accounts for a fourth of total crop production, increased by more than 35 per cent. On the other hand, the net income of the farm population declined from 13.8 per cent of the net national income in 1935 to 6.6 per cent in 1955. On a per capita basis for the year 1958, farmers received an annual income of slightly more than $1,000 compared to slightly more than $2,000 for non-farm population.

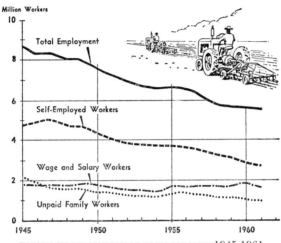

TRENDS IN AGRICULTURAL EMPLOYMENT 1945-1961

A successful farmer today requires much more capital than did his counterpart of even ten years ago. For the whole of the United States the dollar value of farm land in 1959 was up 68 per cent from 1947-1949. Technological progress and shifts in types of farming have stimulated investment in farm machinery and structures.

Farm home furnishings and facilities have improved greatly during the last decade. Electrification of farms has increased from 78 per cent of the total in 1950 to 95 per cent in 1958; for the same period telephones increased from 38 per cent to 60 per cent, television from 3 to 73 per cent.

Important changes are also taking place in the education of people living on farms. A larger proportion of high school and college-age boys and girls from farms are in school than ever before. The proportion of farm residents that are high school graduates is increasing rapidly. Farm people have not yet caught up with city people in education, but they are making good progress in that directon.

The infant mortality rate has dropped in both rural and urban areas since 1950, but it fell more in the rural than the urban districts (about one-fourth and one-eighth, respectively). The most-rural states maintained—even

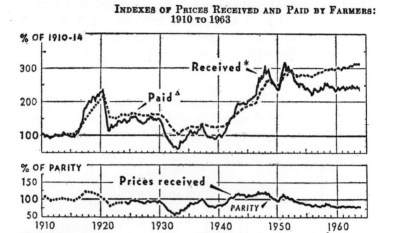

INDEXES OF PRICES RECEIVED AND PAID BY FARMERS: 1910 TO 1963

*Monthly data.
△ Includes interest, taxes, and wage rates. Annual average data, 1910 to 1923; by quarters, 1924 to 1936; by months, 1937 to date.

Source: Dept. of Agriculture, Economic Research Service.

FLUCTUATIONS IN COST OF LIVING FOR FARMERS, 1910-1964

bettered slightly—their physician-population ratio between 1950 and 1958. However, rural states still lag behind urban states in availability of physicians to care for their people. The physician-population ratio is about half as great in the most-rural as in the most-urban states.

POLITICAL POWER OF FARMERS

Agriculture remains the most basic of our industries; not only are foodstuffs necessary for our population, but the raw materials produced on the farms are essential to many segments of our industrial organization. Spokesmen for agriculture consistently maintain that national prosperity is dependent upon farm prosperity.

The political power of the farmer in Congress is disproportionate to the size of the farm population. In the Senate this is true because each state has two senators; one predominantly agricultural state, such as Mississippi, balances off a more industrialized, thickly populated state such as New York. In the House of Representatives the agricultural regions are granted more representatives than their population warrants, because a majority of the state legislatures are controlled by rural members who frequently draw congressional district lines favoring their element of the population.

Finally, the traditional depiction of the farmer, as the backbone of our nation—superior to city-dwellers in morals and manners, frugal, self-reliant and industrious—continues to find support far beyond rural regions.

Farm organizations. In the period between the Civil War and the beginning of the twentieth century the Granger movement, the Farmer's Alli-

PER CENT OF AGE GROUP ENROLLED

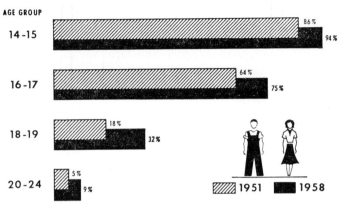

DATA FROM BUREAU OF CENSUS

U. S. DEPARTMENT OF AGRICULTURE   AGRICULTURAL RESEARCH SERVICE

EDUCATION OF FARM PEOPLE SCHOOL ENROLLMENT OF FARM YOUTH IS HIGHER

PER CENT WHO ARE HIGH SCHOOL GRADUATES

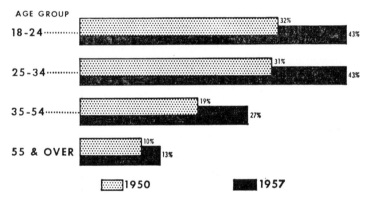

INCLUDES THOSE WITH HIGH SCHOOL OR MORE EDUCATION
DATA FROM BUREAU OF CENSUS; APRIL 1950 DATA BASED ON TOTAL POPULATION,
MARCH 1957 DATA ON CIVILIAN POPULATION

U. S. DEPARTMENT OF AGRICULTURE   AGRICULTURAL RESEARCH SERVICE

MORE FARM PEOPLE ARE HIGH SCHOOL GRADUATES

ance, and the Populist Party all drew heavily upon agricultural regions for
support. Generally, all of these groups sponsored political programs which
had as their objectives a lessening of the power of trusts and monopolies
through antitrust proceedings and governmental regulation of rates charged
by public utility-type enterprises. Since World War I, organized farm groups
have been increasingly concerned with having the national government give
direct support to farm prices and income. There are, however, wide differences of opinion among present-day farm organizations as to the most de-

sirable approach for assisting farmers. The Grange and the American Farm Bureau Federation have been primarily interested in promoting programs that would benefit the more prosperous farmers. The National Farmer's Union, on the other hand, has worked for governmental programs which would aid small farmers, sharecroppers, and farm workers. The latter organization has often been allied with industrial labor organizations in pressing for various social welfare programs; the Grange and the American Farm Bureau Federation often take the same position as the more conservative business groups with respect to social, economic, and labor legislation. Even within a particular organization, certain alignments may be working at cross purposes. Thus the cotton farmers in the AFBF might favor legislation which is opposed by the wheat farmers in the same organization.

The AFBF was particularly influential in the early days of the New Deal and was instrumental in shaping farm policy in the 1930's. Before long, however, the organization was fighting a continuing battle with some units within the Department of Agriculture such as the Soil Conservation Service and the Farm Security Administration, the latter agency being the champion of the small farmer, tenants, and farm laborers. Eventually, the Farm Bureau opposed many of the policies and adminstrative practices of the Department of Agriculture during the Truman Era. In recent years it has been rather closely aligned with the Republican party and has usually supported the policies of Secretary of Agriculture Benson.

The National Farmer's Union has generally found the Democratic party leadership more sympathetic to its objectives than the Republican leaders. During the Eisenhower period it marshaled support for Democratic candidates in congressional elections and this support has continued under Presidents Kennedy and Johnson.

One should be careful not to identify completely any farm organization with a particular political party. For example, the American Farm Bureau Federation has always drawn strength from the Democratic South, while the Farmer's Union is strong in some traditionally Republican states. Farm politics have always cut across party lines and will no doubt continue to do so.

There are literally hundreds of more specialized agricultural organizations which seek and frequently win congressional support for their particular interests. Thus we find the dairy interests, cattlemen associations, beet producers, peanut growers, citrus fruit raisers, etc., all working singly or in combination to influence legislative policy.

THE FEDERAL GOVERNMENT AND AGRICULTURE

The promotion of agriculture is a long standing function of the national government. Much of the controversy concerning public land policy in the early years of the republic turned on whether the public lands should be considered primarily a source of governmental revenue or a means of en-

DEPARTMENT OF AGRICULTURE

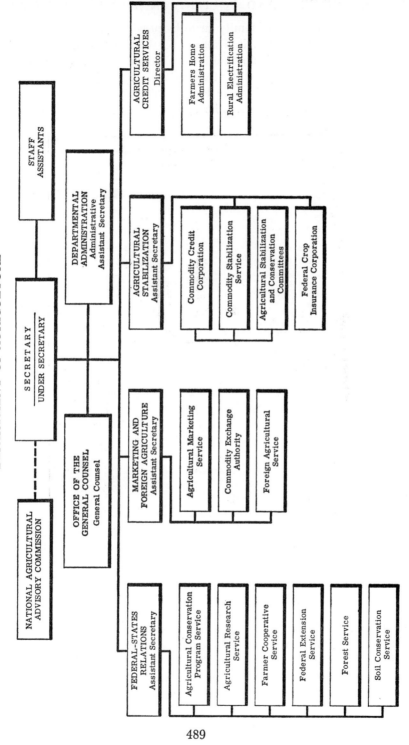

couraging the development of family farms by providing cheap land to those who were willing to cultivate it. Eventually, the Homestead Act of 1862 opened up the western public domain for settlement on the basis of granting 160 acres of free land to any settler after five years of residence.

In 1839 Congress granted to the Patent Office the authority to expend $1,000 for agricultural purposes. The agricultural activities of this office

THE ANIMAL ROOM OF THE PHARMACOLOGY DIVISION OF THE FOOD AND DRUG ADMINIS-TRATION   This branch of the government inspects and analyzes samples of products to detect and direct appropriate action against adulterated or misbranded articles. It maintains sea food inspection service; prevents the importation of products in violation of statutes; and enforces Food and Drug, Tea, Naval Stores, Insecticides, Import Milk, Caustic Poison, and Filled Milk Acts.

gradually expanded, but the farming interests demanded a Department of Agriculture. Such a department was created in 1862, although its head did not achieve full cabinet status until 1889. Many of the present day activities of the Department—such as its cooperation with state agricultural experiment stations, research and advisory functions, crop and marketing reports, and others—were undertaken very early in the organization's history. Most of the policies designed to bolster farm income by a system of government loans, guarantees, and production controls can, however, be traced to the New Deal period.

The Secretary of Agriculture now heads a department employing approximately 85,000 persons. Its personnel operate not only in the continental limits of the United States and the territories but in foreign states as well. The line operations of the Department are supervised by an Assistant Secretary for Federal-State Relations, an Assistant Secretary for Marketing and Stabilization, an Undersecretary for Foreign Agricultural Service, the Director of Agricultural Economics, and the Director of Agricultural Credit.

FEDERAL-STATE RELATIONS

Agricultural Research Service. Research is conducted at a 12,000 acre research center at Beltsville, Maryland and at numerous other locations in the states, territories, and foreign countries. A large part of the research ac-

DIGESTER AND STILL USED BY BUREAU OF AGRICULTURAL ECONOMICS TO DETERMINE NITROGEN CONTENT IN CEREALS   The Bureau studies the economics of production and marketing, farm labor, land economics, and problems of rural life. It collects, interprets and issues data on the production of farm crops and live stock.

tivity is in cooperation with State Agricultural Experiment Stations and other public and private agencies.

Crop research investigations are conducted to develop improved varieties of food, feed, fiber, and other plants. Methods are sought to improve crop production through the control of plant diseases and crop pests. Research projects are carried out on all farm livestock, poultry, and domestic fur animals to develop superior strains and types, to establish nutritive requirements, to determine means of maintaining maximum fertility, and to achieve efficient use of feed in the production of meat, milk, eggs, wool, fur, and other products.

THE COTTON LABORATORY IN THE STANDARDIZATION BUILDING OF THE DEPARTMENT OF AGRICULTURE   Scientific research in the cotton laboratory includes studies of staple length, its preparation for the market, staple classification and standardization, and new uses for cotton.

Farm and land management studies seek to improve fertilizers, soil management, and irrigation practices. The economics of production research deals with efficiency in the use of labor, equipment, land, and water. Home economics studies are made on the composition and nutritive value of foods, as well as on their preparation and preservation. Extensive research is carried out in the field of chemistry and related physical and biological sciences to develop new and improved foods, feeds, drugs, fabrics, and industrial chemicals from agricultural commodities.

The Agricultural Research Service also carries out a variety of regulatory functions, including federal meat inspection, port and border inspection and quarantine services to keep out destructive pests, and cooperative programs for the control and eradication of insects and diseases of crops and livestock.

Federal Extension Service. Extension work in agriculture and home economics is a cooperative affair between the federal government and the states and localities designed to bring advice and assistance to rural people. Research results, technnological advancements, and other facts from the Department of Agriculture and State Agricultural Colleges and Experiment Stations are combined into a unified educational program. County agents, home demonstration agents, 4-H Club agents, and other specialists provide farm families with useful information through practical demonstrations and other means.

Soil Conservation Service. The Soil Conservation Service provides technical assistance to landowners through some 2,700 locally organized soil conservation districts in developing conservation plans and applying soil and water conservation practices. These districts, first organized in 1937, are local units of government which are organized under state laws and are responsible to the landowners in the districts and to the state legislatures. The Service furnishes assistance only upon the request from the district governing authority. Technical personnel composed of agronomists, agricultural, hydraulic, and cartographic engineers; biologists, soil scientists; and other specialists are responsible for making the detailed soil surveys upon which their recommendations are based. The Service gives the landowners technical guidance for putting its suggestions into operation.

The Soil Conservation Service also has important duties in connection with watershed protection, flood prevention programs, and for certain water conservation and utilization projects.

MARKETING AND FOREIGN AGRICULTURE

Agricultural Marketing Service. The main objective of the Agricultural Marketing Service is to provide market operators, farmers, consumers, government officials, and other agencies with reliable research information aimed at (1) expanded outlets for farm and food products, (2) improvements in the efficiency of marketing processes, marketing methods, transportation, storage, and marketing facilities, and (3) reduced costs. The organization engages in numerous activities in pursuance of this goal. It collects, analyzes, and interprets data concerning factors affecting agricultural prices, farm income, the supply and consumption of farm products, and trends in farm population. The crop and livestock estimating service provides basic information relating to acreage, yield, and production of crops; the stock and value of farm commodities; and the number, production, and value of livestock items.

More than twelve hundred daily newspapers carry news based on federal market reports covering information of supply, movement, and price at specific markets for practically all agricultural commodities. The Marketing Service handles the inspection, grading, classing, and standardization of agricultural commodities. This service promotes confidence between buyers and sellers, encourages better preparation of products for market, and furnishes consumers with more definite information as to the quality of the products they buy.

Various statutes make the Marketing Service responsible for the disposal of surplus commodities. The School Lunch Program provides a minor outlet,[1] but a more significant volume of surpluses goes to charitable institutions and to state and local welfare agencies. In a recent year over three and a half million needy persons were certified as eligible to receive surplus foods. Requests for food for distribution abroad are met after all domestic demands have been satisfied; commodities have been sent to over 80 foreign countries.

Foreign Agricultural Service. The Foreign Agricultural Service administers a number of programs for the Department. It provides information essential to the timely and effective marketing of United States products abroad. Agricultural attaches are stationed in more than fifty countries, working toward the development of foreign markets for American agricultural products. This unit also supervises the sale of surplus commodities for foreign currencies. The money realized may then be used in that country for various purposes, including market development.

AGRICULTURAL STABILIZATION

The Department of Agriculture activities discussed so far are more or less noncontroversial, and many of them have been pursued by the Department since its inception. The general term "agricultural stabilization" is, in itself, noncontroversial; but the methods chosen to achieve stability have been hotly debated for the past twenty-five years.

The parity concept. Traditionally, agriculture has occupied a less favorable economic position than manufacturing in the matter of coordinating production with prices received for its products. The hazards of weather, the multiplicity of the producing units involved, the impossibility of applying industrial cut-back methods, the dependence on the world market—these, among other factors, underscore the farmer's disadvantage. Surplus agricultural commodities meant falling prices for the farmer's product, but not necessarily a decline in the prices of the industrial goods which he had to purchase.

The Agricultural Adjustment Act of 1933, in attempting to insure fair prices for basic agricultural commodities, introduced the parity concept. "Parity" price is a price for a commodity which will give it the same purchasing power in terms of the commodities farmers buy that it had in some

---

[1] Most of the food for the School Lunch Program is bought in the open market.

base period when price relations were considered reasonably satisfactory. The base period, 1909-1914, was used for most of the commodities covered by the 1933 act. Farmers who cooperated by curtailing production—another technique to raise prices—were to be given "parity" payments to make up the difference between the current market price and the parity price of their products. Parity payments were to be financed out of taxes levied on the processors of the commodities. However, in 1936 the Supreme Court found the method of payment unconstitutional on the grounds that the processing tax was not for the support of government, but was a levy upon one group for the support of another.[2] Nevertheless, production controls were continued to a degree under the Soil Conservation and Domestic Allotment Act of 1936, in which production control was made incidental to soil conservation. Farmers were granted "soil conservation" payments out of the general treasury for planting soil-building instead of soil-depleting crops.

The Agricultural Act of 1938, which continues to be the primary basis of current farm legislation, reworked the voided program and added certain new features. This time the legislation was tied to the power of Congress over commerce. Production control was secured indirectly by a system under which non-cooperating farmers could not market (interstate commerce) their commodities without paying a penalty tax.[3]

During the war years and for two years thereafter, price supports were made mandatory for the basic commodities at 90 per cent of parity and permitted for nonbasic commodities. Actually, market prices during this period were generally above parity prices; and, as a matter of fact, the government granted financial benefits for increasing production.

Since 1948 the farm program has been a continuing political issue. Some critics, even in Congress, insist that any form of guaranteed price supports is uneconomical; self-defeating as far as curtailing production is concerned, since surpluses continue to mount; and contrary to "natural" economic laws. As a practical political issue, however, the controversy has turned on the point of flexible versus rigid supports. In general, the proponents of the flexible parity concept argue that high rigid supports stimulate overproduction; those who favor high rigid supports maintain they are necessary to assure adequate production and to give the farmer a fair income.

In general, Republican-controlled Congresses have favored a flexible support program, ranging from 60 to 90 per cent of parity, depending upon the amount of individual commodities produced. Usually Democratic-controlled Congresses have supported a more rigid support system, with a usual guarantee up to 90 per cent of parity. In the last years of the Eisenhower

---

2 *United States* v. *Butler,* 297 U. S. 1 (1936).

3 The 1938 Act was upheld by the Supreme Court in *Mulford* v. *Smith,* 307 U. S. 39 (1939). *Wickard* v. *Filburn,* 317 U. S. 11 (1942), sustained a penalty imposed for producing wheat in excess of a prescribed quota, even though the excess was consumed on the producing farm.

were chartered under the Farm Credit Act of 1933. Their original capital was largely furnished by government production credit corporations. Beginning in 1957 the functions of these corporations were merged with the federal intermediate credit banks. As of 1956, farmer-members owned over $100 million of capital stock in the production credit associations which had outstanding loans totaling $863 million.

The federal intermediate credit banks were established in 1923 to serve as discount banks to finance agricultural and livestock loans made by commercial banks, agricultural credit corporations, and other financial institutions. Ten years later their lending authority was extended to cover production credit associations and banks for cooperatives. The intermediate credit banks are wholly owned by the United States.

Banks for cooperatives were created in 1933. The thirteen banks were originally capitalized by the government, but eventually the entire capital stock will be owned by the cooperative associations. These banks make loans to farmer cooperative associations engaged in processing or marketing agricultural products, purchasing farm supplies, or furnishing farm business services. The government investment in the capital stock of the system is approximately $147 million; the cooperatives investment is approximately $20 million.

Farmers Home Administration. The Farmers Home Administration was established within the Department of Agriculture in 1946. It makes credit available for a number of purposes. Direct and insured farm ownership loans are made to farm tenants, farm laborers, and sharecroppers who are unable to secure credit elsewhere on reasonable terms. Direct loans at four and one half per cent interest are made up to 100 per cent of the value of the farm, with the repayment period not to exceed forty years. Other types of loans include (1) operating loans to farmers and stockmen, (2) direct farm housing loans to owners of farms who cannot secure reasonable credit for this purpose, (3) direct and insured soil and water conservation loans, and (4) a disaster loan revolving fund.

Rural Electrification Administration. R.E.A. was established in 1935 to make loans for the extension of electric service to rural people. It became a part of the Department of Agriculture in 1939. Since 1949 it has been authorized to make loans for the purpose of furnishing and improving rural telephone service. When the agency was set up, only 10.9 per cent of the farms in the United States had electric power. In 1964 approximately 96 per cent of the farms had electricity, due in large measure to R.E.A. activities.

THE FARM PROBLEM

Even though the national government has acted in many ways during the past 30 years to improve the economic position of the farmer, not even the most optimistic observer claims that a permanent solution to the "farm problem" has been attained. A major problem area is the matter of mounting surpluses. Production continues to outstrip demand. One can verify this fact by an examination of the operation of the Commodity Credit Corporation in buying or making loans in order to support prices. In 1951 the total value of the commodities owned and loans outstanding was $1.7

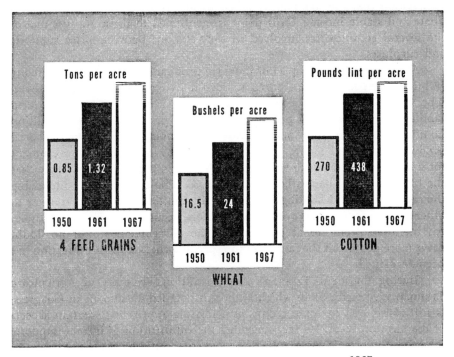

YIELDS PER ACRE FOR MAJOR CROPS, PROJECTED TO 1967

The rise in production per acre during the past 10 years has been especially spectacular in the major crops—wheat, cotton, and feed grains. This trend will continue. Feed grain yields may approach 1.5 tons per acre by 1967. Average wheat yields of 27 bushels per acre or more should be expected on an acreage as large as was harvested in 1961. Cotton yields by 1967 may be somewhere near one bale per acre.

billion; in 1954 the amount had risen to slightly more than $6.0 billion; by 1959 the figure had reached $8.6 billion. It costs the government millions of dollars each year to store the commodities which it has purchased. At the same time, other government funds are spent on research aimed at increasing the yield per acre of many crops. So far, at least, no satisfactory plan has been developed which would permit the government to dispose of the bulk of its surplus commodities without drastically affecting market prices at home or abroad and so creating international problems. One advantage of a "free market" for agricultural commodities is that it acts to a degree in a self-regulatory fashion when a particular commodity is in over-supply. For example, if corn is a glut on the market, then some farmers would shift from corn to soybeans. If the government is maintaining price supports for corn, however, the voluntary transfer to soybeans is not as apt to occur. This is not to suggest that a return to the "free market" is the solution to the problem; government became involved in price support operations for the very reason that the free market failed to supply the farmers with an adequate and stable income. This point is mentioned to illustrate just one of the several complexities involved in the relations between price supports and surpluses.

Another important aspect of the farm problem is the fact that too many full-time farm families are trying to earn a living with too few resources. The chief beneficiaries of higher farm prices are the two million farm families who sell over 85 per cent of all farm products. Almost a million families, mostly in the South, divide the remainder of the agricultural production. Even if money is made available by the national government for small farm operators to enlarge their holdings, there is no guarantee that the land itself will be available for purchase. The alternative to increasing the capital and land holdings of these small families is to urge a transfer to other occupations. Some voluntary transfers occur of course at all times. An intensive promotional program by the government would no doubt move more people off the farms, but no specific program in this direction has been developed.

During President Truman's Administration, Secretary of Agriculture Brannan suggested a plan which, although it failed enactment in Congress, is still considered by some groups as a feasible approach to certain aspects of the farm problem. He recommended the substitution of income supports for price supports. Direct production payments would be made to farmers in order to bring their incomes up to a parity standard, but the commodities would sell at the free market price. Theoretically the consumer would benefit from such an approach, while the government would not be plagued by surpluses. Benefits to any one farmer would be limited to $26,000 a year. The American Farm Bureau Federation vigorously opposed the Brannan Plan, labeling it "socialistic" in character. The Eisenhower Administration succeeded in having Congress pass legislation with respect to wool which embodied the Brannan concept, but it did not choose to try a similar approach in any other area.

Because of the diverse nature of American agriculture and because of the strength of the various commodity groups in Congress, a comprehensive frontal attack on the farm problem is going to be difficult to achieve. Until such an attempt is made, however, the "farm problem" is going to continue to be in the news.

CONSERVATION

It was not until the beginning of the twentieth century that the preachments of "conservation conscious" individuals began to have any telling effect upon national governmental policy. Perhaps Theodore Roosevelt was the individual most responsible for turning the machinery of the national government toward planned conservation programs. The importance of the subject today is attested to by the considerable number of national and state governmental agencies engaged in specialized aspects of conservation activity. Most of the federal agencies concerned with conservation are located in the Department of the Interior; but the Department of Agriculture, the Department of the Army and certain other agencies, such as T.V.A. and the Federal Power Commission, also have important roles. There is a great deal of cooperation between federal and state governments in the conservation area.

Conservation policies have engendered some of the most bitter political debates in American history. For almost a century much of the controversy resolved around the question of how the national government should dispose of the public domain. The Homestead Act of 1862 was a victory for those who believed that a pattern of family ownership should be encouraged. In the twentieth century many types of political conflicts have made a comprehensive and unified approach to conservation problems difficult if not impossible. Sometimes the struggle has arisen over policies which were advocated by the government but which were opposed by powerful economic groups. Public power versus private power, as illustrated by the history of the T.V.A., may be mentioned in this respect. Grazing privileges and the right to cut timber on the public domain has been subject to much debate. The tidelands oil controversy focused on whether the national or the state governments (backed by private economic groups) should exercise control over a vital segment of the nation's resources.

The executive and Congress have frequently been at cross purposes in conservation matters. A National Resources Planning Board functioned between 1934 and 1943, but congressional fear of excessive centralization in the executive and of possible interference with its traditional prerogative of distributing largesse through rivers and harbors appropriations, led to the termination of the agency. The Army Corps of Engineers, due to its role with respect to rivers and harbors legislation, has generally won its point with Congress over the opposition of other executive branch agencies, even to the President himself, in various jurisdictional disputes. The Bureau of Reclamation (Interior) has frequently clashed with the Army Corps of Engineers; the Bureau of Land Management (Interior) has often differed with the Forest Service (Agriculture) over logging and grazing policies. To complicate matters even more, independent agencies such as the Federal Power Commission and T.V.A. play important conservation roles.

Conservation practices vary because conservation measures applied to one type of resource may not be identical to the procedures employed to conserve other resources. In the case of timber and water, conservation calls for programs to promote renewal of the resources. Because minerals, coal, and oil do not renew themselves, new deposits must be developed, inferior grades utilized more effectively, and substitutes must be developed from those resources which we have in abundance.

LAND AND FORESTS

At one time within the continental United States the national public domain, i.e., land owned by the national government, was 80 per cent of the total acreage. More than a billion acres have been sold or given away, but the national government still controls over 21 per cent. In Alaska the national government owns all but an insignificant percentage of the land.

Bureau of Land Management. Located in the Department of the Interior, the Bureau of Land Management exclusively administers approximately 470 million acres of public domain lands, about 290 million acres of which are in Alaska. It is responsible for the management and disposal of the land and its natural resources, including range grasses, minerals, gas and oil, and timber.

The conservation job of the Bureau is an important contribution to America's resource development. In 1959 the resource harvest from BLM lands included enough timber to build more than 100,000 average homes, enough oil to heat more than five million homes for the next year, enough forage to feed more than eleven million livestock and big game for an average of four months. The Bureau turned in more than 136 million dollars to the United States Treasury in the same year.

Bureau of Reclamation. The Reclamation Act of 1902 authorized the Secretary of the Interior Department to construct and operate works for the storage, diversion, and development of waters for the reclamation of arid and semiarid lands in the United States. Today, federal reclamation projects are capable of furnishing water for more than seven million acres of land through water conservation facilities in 17 states. The facilities include approximately 140 storage dams and reservoirs, 105 diversion dams, approximately 24,000 miles of canals and laterals, and about 7,600 miles of drains. Through 1959 the total value of crops produced in reclamation project areas since 1906 was $14.2 billion, nearly five times the net federal investment in reclamation.

National forests. Management of the national forests is under the direction of the Forest Service, an agency within the Department of Agriculture.

The 181 million acres of national forests are located in forty-one states and Puerto Rico. They now have more than one-third of the remaining saw timber in the United States. The cutting of timber from the national forests is done by private companies under governmental supervision. Stock-grazing is permitted but controlled. The forests must be protected against fire, insects, and disease. Wildlife resources must be looked after. Watersheds are managed for the regulation of stream flow, flood control, and varied uses of water. The national forests are prized recreational areas for millions of Americans.

Other activities. Soil conservation, which has already been discussed, is one of the most important activities with respect to the land. The National Park System, T.V.A., and other agencies—some of which will be discussed below—have significant roles in the conservation and use of land and forests.

WATER AND ELECTRIC POWER

Many sections of the country are confronted with water shortage problems. The problems give promise of becoming more widespread and acute in the years to come. About the same amount of water is available, but more is being used. Approximately 17 per cent of available water is put to use; about one-fourth of this consumed during use, with the remainder available for reuse. A partial solution to the water shortage problem may be found in more effective water storage facilities on the surface, and the replenishment of underground supplies. The federal government continues systematic research to develop economical methods of converting saline and brackish waters into fresh water.

Bureau of Reclamation projects provide water to 106 municipalities and 68 industrial entities in 32 project areas scattered throughout the West. The importance of this aspect of the reclamation program is indicated by the fact that about eight and one-half million persons live in these areas, including the large metropolitan areas of Los Angeles and San Diego.

One of the most important political issues which continues to confront the American people is the role the government should play with respect to the generation and sale of electric power. This is particularly true in the western states where a majority of the government's multi-purpose dams are located. Slowly, but surely, the federal government is expanding its proportion of the nation's capacity to generate electric power. The construction of multi-purpose dams has been justified on the grounds of conservation, flood control, irrigation, navigation, and national defense needs. The nub of the controversy is primarily whether the government should compete with private utilities. T.V.A. is the best example of a government agency competing directly with private enterprise in the sale of electric power. Many government owned hydro-electric projects furnish power to privately owned utilities, which in turn service other customers.

Supervision of federal power projects is scattered among several agencies. The Tennessee Valley Authority is an independent government corporation; the Department of the Army through its Corps of Engineers is involved; and the Department of the Interior has its Bureau of Reclamation and three specific power administrations[5] active in this area. The Federal Power Commission's work is discussed in another connection.[6]

MINERALS

Mineral resources are irreplaceable assets to our nation's prosperity and security. Although the United States is the greatest consumer and producer of coal, iron, and oil in the world, World War II requirements showed how rapidly reserves in these vital resources could be reduced. Hoarding will not solve the problem of short supply for future generations. Technological advance, leading to more efficient extraction and use of basic materials and to the creation of new mineral assets, appears to be our best course. The two Department of Interior agencies discussed below bear considerable responsibility in insuring that our mineral resources will meet the nation's future requirements.

Bureau of Mines. Various studies are being conducted by the Bureau of Mines to improve ore recovery of copper, lead, zinc, tin, and iron as well as to develop new and improved methods of obtaining light metals such as aluminum and titanium. It continues to make advances in coal research, among which the coal-to-oil studies are perhaps best known. An eleven-year research and development program has taken oil shale to the threshold of economic utility. Intensive research is conducted with respect to the production, transportation, storage, and refining of petroleum and its by-products.

Geological Survey. The Geological Survey has been in operation since 1879. It is responsible for seeking out new supplies and appraising known sources of mineral and mineral fuels, classifying public lands, mapping the surface features of the United States, and evaluating the quantity and quality of our water supplies.

OIL AND GAS

Only about two per cent of the oil produced in the United States comes from the national public domain. A political controversy which simmered for

---

5 These being: The Bonneville Power Administration whose primary function is to market the electric power produced at hydroelectric projects operated by the Army Corps of Engineers and the Bureau of Reclamation in the Pacific Northwest; the Southeastern Power Administration which markets surplus power produced by Department of the Army projects in nine Southeastern states; and the Southwestern Power Administration which markets surplus electric power from a number of federal dams in six Southwestern states. The Bureau of Reclamation markets power from its hydroelectric projects which do not fall within the jurisdiction of any of the above.

6 See p. 480.

years concerned the question of whether the national government or the states should control the rich fields on the continental shelf between the low-water mark and the three-mile limit. The Supreme Court decided that the fields were within the domain of the national government, but the states most directly involved, backed by the oil companies, pressed Congress for the right to control the area in question. President Truman vetoed a bill in 1952 which would have turned over the fields to the states; one of the key issues in the 1952 presidential election turned on this point, with the Republican party favoring state control. Following the Republican victory, President Eisenhower signed legislation in 1953 vesting in the states title to submerged lands and resources within their "historic" boundaries. In May of 1960, the Supreme Court decided that Texas and Florida were entitled to develop submerged lands as far as nine nautical miles beyond their coasts, but that Alabama, Louisiana, and Mississippi were restricted to three nautical miles. The federal government has jurisdiction over the continental shelf beyond the "historic" boundaries of the states. In the future the resources here will probably be more valuable than those controlled by the states.

Since a preponderance of oil resources is owned by private interests, the national government has found it difficult to exert direct conservation controls. In the early 1930's some of the states tried, through interstate compacts, to discourage over-production and wasteful practices. Quotas were agreed upon among the states, and laws were passed within each state forbidding shipments exceeding fixed production quotas. At first, the interstate compact approach had little effect, since most of the oil-producing states were not members, and shipments were made in violation of member-state laws. In 1933 Congress sought to aid the states in their enforcement policies by authorizing the President to prohibit the transportation in interstate or foreign commerce of petroleum products shipped in violation of state law. However, the Supreme Court ruled the national legislation unconstitutional in 1935, saying that Congress had granted excessive legislative powers to the President.

Urged on by Congress, the number of states participating in the interstate oil compact increased until at present it includes twenty-three states. Congress also passed legislation in 1935 directly forbidding shipment of petroleum in interstate or foreign commerce in violation of state regulations. Thus a measure of control over petroleum production has been achieved.

The national government does not control the amount of natural gas which is taken from the fields owned by private enterprise or the states. The Federal Power Commission has the power to set the rates at which the gas is sold in interstate commerce.

Office of Oil and Gas. The Office of Oil and Gas is the staff agency of the Department of the Interior which assists and advises the Secretary of Interior and the Assistant Secretary for Mineral Resources in the discharge of their responsibilities concerned with the development, coordination, and management of petroleum and gas programs assigned to the Department by the President and Congress.

In addition to its domestic activities, it has important international duties, particularly in support of NATO planning and in providing petroleum guidance in connection with development of U. S. foreign policy. This office is the focal point for coordination and leadership in governmental oil and gas activities. By keeping abreast of oil production, refining, transportation, storage, gas transmission and distribution in the United States and the rest of the world, it is in a position to provide detailed guidance on problems and policies having an impact on petroleum and gas supply.

FISH AND WILDLIFE

The Fish and Wildlife Service is a part of the Department of the Interior. Its central objective is to insure the conservation of the nation's wild birds, mammals, fishes, and other forms of wildlife both for their recreational and their economic value. The Service administers a federal grant-in-aid system designed to aid the states in the development of fish and wildlife habitat. It is responsible for the conservation of migratory birds pursuant to the Migratory Bird Treaty Act with the governments of Canada and Mexico. The operation of fish hatcheries is an important part of a program in maintaining inland fisheries. Through its commercial fisheries program the Service seeks to develop the potential wealth of marine fisheries. Over 280 wildlife refuges have been established under national control.

Many of these activities mentioned are generally known and appreciated by the public; on the other hand, it is not often realized how much basic research is conducted by the Fish and Wildlife Service in order to carry out its responsibilities more effectively.

SUMMARY

For over a century the national government has aided agriculture in countless ways such as research activities, crop and market reporting, and technical assistance. Since 1916 credit facilities for farmers have been created and expanded. It was not until the 1930's, however, that the national government embarked on programs designed to raise farm income through a system of government loans, guarantees, and production controls. But the "farm problem" is the subject of much discussion and frequent action at almost every session of Congress. The present operation of the price support system requires the government to buy commodities in order to keep the market price up. The government warehouses bulge with surplus commodities, because even on less acreage the farmers produce more and more of the basic crops. Another area of concern on the farm front is the fact that the drive to increase farm income has brought comparatively little benefit to the large number of families tilling small unproductive plots of land. This low-income group has no future on the farm, but how are they to be persuaded to leave?

The abundance of America's natural resources long retarded any serious consideration of conservation practices by the national government. From the first decade of the present century, federal conservation activities have expanded steadily but in a rather haphazard pattern. The Department of Interior has responsibility for administering the majority of conservation programs, but several other agencies are also involved.

Conservation practices cover a wide range of activities including: (1) research which makes possible a fuller knowledge of the extent, character, and utilization of various national resources; (2) management of renewable resources to insure efficient use of a sustained yield basis; (3) prevention of waste in the development and use of mineral and water resources through new techniques and new programs to insure full utilization; and (4) preservation and enlargement of scenic, wildlife, and recreational resources.

BIBLIOGRAPHIC NOTE

The Department of Agriculture publishes a multitude of specialized studies the titles of which may be found in a *List of Available Publications of the United States Department of Agriculture* (Washington, D. C.: Government Printing Office, 1960).

For a comprehensive historical study of national government activities with respect to agriculture, one may consult Murray Benedict, *Farm Policies of the United States, 1790-1950* (New York: The Twentieth Century Fund, 1953). Rainer Schickele's *Agricultural Policy* (New York: McGraw-Hill Book Company, 1954) stresses more recent policy. An intensive examination of the operation of the price support system and other facets of the commodity programs is found in Murray Benedict and Oscar Stine, *The Agricultural Commodity Programs: Two Decades of Experience* (New York: The Twentieth Century Fund, 1956). Also see Willard W. Cochrane, *Farm Prices, Myth and Reality* (Minneapolis: University of Minnesota Press, 1958).

Several books deal with the political forces shaping agricultural policy and administration. Charles M. Hardin's *The Politics of Agriculture* (Glencoe, Ill.: The Free Press, 1954) is an excellent account of the interrelations of interest groups and government agencies in developing and administering soil conservation programs; Grant McConnell's *The Decline of Agrarian Democracy* (Berkeley, Cal.: University of California Press, 1953) includes a detailed history and analysis of the Farm Bureau movement. Also on the Farm Bureau, see O. M. Kile, *The Farm Bureau Federation Through Three Decades* (Baltimore, Md.: The Waverly Press, 1948). The activities of both rural and urban pressure groups on farm legislation are considered in Wesley McCune's *Who's Behind Our Farm Policy?* (New York: Frederick A. Praeger, Inc., 1957). Also see *The Farm Bloc* (Garden City, N. Y.: Doubleday, Doran Co., 1943) by the same author.

William H. Peterson's *The Great Farm Problem* (Chicago: Henry Regnery Company, 1959) is a plea for a return to the free market concept. Other analyses and recommendations concerning the farm problem may be found in *Economic Policy for American Agriculture* (New York: Committee for Economic Development, 1956); L. Soth, *Farm Trouble in An Age of Plenty* (Princeton, N. J.: Princeton University Press, 1957); Murray Benedict, *Can We Solve the Farm Problem?* (New York: The Twentieth Century Fund, 1955).

One of the most controversial proposals with respect to agricultural policy is given an objective treatment in Reo M. Cristensen's *The Brannan Plan* (Ann Arbor, Mich.: University of Michigan Press, 1959). Lowry Nelson's *American Farm Life* (Cambridge, Mass.: Harvard University Press, 1954) covers many aspects of present-day farm life, including relations with national and local governments.

The most complete inventory of the nation's material resources is found in the President's Materials Policy Commission, *Resources for Freedom* (6 vols., Washington, D. C.: Government Printing Office, 1952). For an analysis of the problems, policies, and criteria for judging effective conservation policies, see S. Von Ciriacy-Wantrup, *Resource Conservation: Economics and Policies* (Los Angeles: University of California Press, 1952).

The inevitability of politics in conservation policies is stressed in Norman Wengert's *Natural Resources and the Political Struggle* (Garden City, N. Y.: Doubleday & Company, Inc., 1955) and Judson King's *The Conservation Fight from Theodore Roosevelt to the Tennessee Valley Authority* (Washington, D. C.: Public Affairs Press, 1959). For the role of the Army Corps of Engineers in water resources development, see Arthur Maass, *Muddy Waters* (Cambridge, Mass.: Harvard University Press, 1951). Other studies dealing with various aspects of water resources include William Leuchtenberg, *Flood Control Policies* (Cambridge, Mass.: Harvard University Press, 1953); R. E. Huffman, *Irrigation Development and Public Water Policy* (New York: Ronald Press Co., 1953); Ben Morrell, *Our Nation's Water Resources: Policies and Politics* (Chicago: University of Chicago Law School, 1956); and *The Report of the U. S. President's Water Resources Policy Commission* (Washington, D. C.: Government Printing Office, 1950).

Land and forest resources are discussed in E. Louise Peffer, *The Closing of the Public Domain* (Stanford, Cal.: Stanford University Press, 1951); M. Clawson and B. Held, *The Federal Lands: Their Use and Management* (Baltimore: Johns Hopkins University Press, 1957); and Arthur H. Carhart, *The National Forests* (New York: Alfred A. Knopf, 1959).

For a balanced treatment of the tidelands oil issue, see E. R. Bartley's *The Tidelands Oil Controversy* (Austin: University of Texas Press, 1953). An account of the government's conservation policies in a region is given in Charles McKinley's *Uncle Sam in the Pacific Northwest* (Los Angeles: University of California Press, 1952) in which the author states the case for the creation of a Columbia River Valley Authority. Two studies in defense of the Tennessee Valley Authority are David Lilienthal's *TVA: Democracy on the March* (New York: Harper & Brothers, 1944) and Gordon B. Clapp, *The TVA* (Chicago: University of Chicago Press, 1955).

The *Annual Reports* of the Department of the Interior contain a great deal of statistical and other information relating to natural resources.

25

Labor

A UNIQUE feature of the political party system in the United States is the absence of a strong socialist or labor party. "Big" labor, in the sense that organized labor is a powerful economic and political force in our contemporary society, achieved its status within the framework of our traditional two-party system. However, more than two-thirds of the workers in the United States do not belong to unions. Non-union members are much more dependent than union members upon specific legislative enactments at the national and state levels guaranteeing reasonable wages, hours, and working conditions.

The fact that the United States has a federal system has been extremely important in the development of labor unions and the passage of labor legislation generally. For almost a century the organs of the national government were merely onlookers with any governmental decisions affecting labor being made at the state level. Today, of course, there are many national laws and Supreme Court decisions concerning labor matters, but a surprising number of workers, unions, and labor problems remain subject to the states' jurisdiction.

THE LABOR FORCE

The government defines the potential labor force to include all persons of fourteen years or over who are not institutionalized (homes for aged, prisons, etc.). At the beginning of 1964 this potential force numbered slightly more than 127 million persons. The actual labor force, those working or seeking work, amounted to 74.7 million. Excluding armed forces personnel, the civilian working force stood at 73 million; of this number 68.7 million people were actually employed.

Technology, urbanization, increasing educational opportunities, the changing status of women in the economic life of the nation, modification of cultural patterns, the impact of the social security concept, and many other factors have contributed to marked changes in the composition of the labor force in the twentieth century. Within the last fifty years, the number of white-collar workers has increased by nearly 200 per cent; the number of

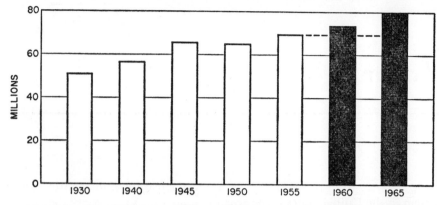

TOTAL LABOR FORCE FROM 1930 TO 1965 (INCLUDING THE ARMED FORCES)

manual workers in industry has increased by approximately 75 per cent. On the other hand, the number of agricultural workers has decreased by about 50 per cent.

In 1900 less than one worker in five was a woman; in 1940 the proportion had risen to one in four, and by 1955 one out of every three was a woman. Of the ten million increase in the labor force expected between 1955 and 1965, more than half will be women.

Projecting 1955 trends through 1965, the Labor Department makes the following calculations with respect to the occupational structure in the latter year. The professional and technical group which includes the scientists, engineers, lawyers, teachers, physicians, and nurses will increase by more than one-third. An increase of over one-fifth is indicated for proprietors and managers; clerical and sales personnel will increase by more than one-quarter; craftsmen and operators, the skilled and semi-skilled workers who man the factories, build homes, roads and buildings are destined to increase by nearly one-quarter. Service workers—barbers, hotel

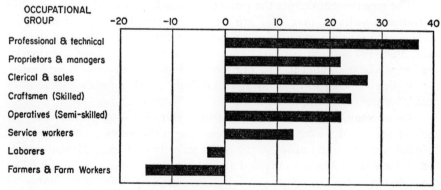

EMPLOYMENT IN MAJOR OCCUPATIONAL GROUPS PER CENT CHANGE FROM 1955 TO 1965

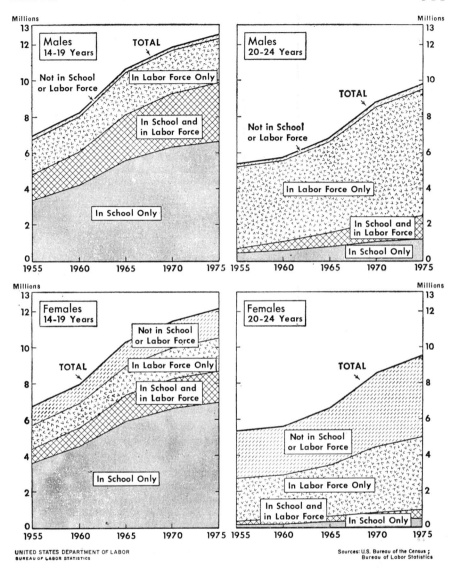

SCHOOL ENROLLMENT AND LABOR FORCE STATUS OF POPULATION

employees, policemen, and firemen, as examples, will increase between 10 and 15 per cent; unskilled laborers, farmers, and farm workers will continue to decline.

LABOR UNIONS

The fact that Americans accept labor unions as a normal part of our society is an extremely significant development. During the nineteenth century the dominant view was quite different. Although the national government did not by statutory law place obstacles in the way of union development, federal and state courts interpreted the common law to the disadvantage of the struggling labor organizations. Eventually, the courts interpreted the Sherman Act, aimed at the regulation of business, as applicable to unions in certain situations. Still later, when the public conscience and the power of the unions persuaded Congress to enact legislation of a positive type in favor of unions, the courts found certain of these acts unconstitutional. Particularly from the 1930's until the present, the national government has concerned itself with the passage of many comprehensive labor laws. Some of these laws are considered restrictive by the unions, but their total effect is to give recognition to the union as a legal institution necessary to the general welfare of the workingman in a capitalistic society.

Early union activities. Labor unions have a long history in the United States. Even before the Declaration of Independence, skilled artisans in certain handicraft industries combined into benevolent societies primarily in order to provide members and their families with financial assistance in the event of serious illness, debt, or death of the wage earner. Before the turn of the nineteenth century, the scope of activities engaged in by labor organizations had begun to increase. Unions through collective action sought higher wages, minimum rates, shorter hours, and even the closed shop in some cases. The rudiments of collective bargaining appeared especially among the printers and shoemakers in Philadelphia and New York. The strike was employed as a means of securing labor demands in a number of instances before 1830.

During the 1830's union groups were formed by crafts on a city-wide basis in a number of localities. Organization of groups beyond a single local area was first tried in 1834 when city central bodies from seven cities met in New York to form the National Trades' Union. In 1835 and 1836 a number of crafts endeavored to set up country-wide organizations, but these experiments collapsed following the panic of 1837 and the period of depression and unemployment which followed.

Unions as conspiracies. Employers viewed the rise of labor organizations as a threat to their economic well-being. During the formative period of union development, there were no statutory laws aimed at restricting labor organizations, but frequently in the first decades of the nineteenth century, public prosecutors were induced to proceed against unions under the common law doctrine of criminal conspiracy. In its most rigid form the doctrine ". . . held that labor unions themselves were illegal, that although an individual employee might attempt to secure wage increases and improved working conditions, a number of workers who came together to organize into a union constituted an illegal conspiracy. What one could do legally, numbers joined together could not legally do. The union itself under this rigid interpretation, became an illegal organization." [1]

However, the more general interpretation of the conspiracy doctrine distinguished between the organization itself and the means employed by the organization in seeking to achieve its objectives. Thus the union itself could be considered a legal organization, but if it sought, let us say, to enforce a closed shop rule, the latter activity would constitute criminal conspiracy.

Organized labor's cause was given a strong push forward as a result of a decision by the Massachusetts Supreme Court in the case of *Commonwealth v. Hunt* in 1842. The court held that labor unions, as such, were legal organizations, and that "a conspiracy must be a combination of two or more persons, by some concerted action, to accomplish some criminal or unlawful purpose, or to accomplish some purpose not in itself criminal or unlawful by criminal or unlawful means." The court also denied that an attempt to establish a closed shop was unlawful or proof of an unlawful aim. As other state courts began to follow this precedent, the doctrine of criminal conspiracy lost its force as a weapon against unions by employers.

Doctrine of civil conspiracy. All was not smooth sailing for the unions, however, for another formula—the doctrine of civil conspiracy—was applied by the courts against the unions. Professor Chamberlain has written:

> . . . the courts began to examine the motivation behind the demands that unions were making. They continued to examine labor unions with an eye to the impact on the individual and with an eye to the impact on the community; but in doing so they examined, not the labor union itself, but rather the particular demands which it was making, the objectives which it was seeking, the purposes which it was after. Whereas under the criminal-conspiracy doctrine it had been the public prosecutor who brought the charge, and the penalty had involved fine and imprisonment, under the doctrine of civil conspiracy it became the aggrieved party, the employer himself, who took the initiative, and the penalty usually came in the form of money damages.[2]

Eventually, the injunction came to be used in civil conspiracy cases. Now instead of the employer having to await the commission of an act which damaged him and then entering a suit for the recovery of damages, he could petition the court for an injunction to stop the union action before it occurred. If the union leaders ignored the restraining order, they could be held in contempt of court. Unions complained that this procedure, in effect, meant that agencies of the government (courts) were being used by employers to nullify legitimate objectives of labor organizations as, for example, when an injunction prohibited picketing, which in turn destroyed the effectiveness of strikes.

---

[1] Neil W. Chamberlain, *Labor* (New York: McGraw-Hill Book Company, Inc., 1958), p 17.

[2] *Ibid.*, p. 21.

Union activity from 1840 until 1886. Following the panic of 1837, many workers turned toward the formation of producers' and consumers' cooperatives. Others were attracted toward various cooperative community schemes stimulated by the "utopian" ideas spread by the followers of the French Socialist Charles Fourier and the English reformer Robert Owen.

In the 1850's several national unions were founded. This decade was also marked by many strikes involving almost every known craft in a majority of the cities throughout the country.

The Civil War stimulated the formation of many new industrial concerns, and improved transportation facilities brought the different parts of the country closer together. Unions were spurred to new activity. In 1863 there were approximately 80 local unions in 20 northern states; a year later, these same states had almost 300 locals. In the fifteen years following the war fourteen new national unions were formed. There were three unsuccessful attempts to unite the various craft organizations into national labor federations. As was true in earlier periods union membership rose and fell with the economic cycle. For example, union membership rose to 300,000 by 1872, but then dropped to 50,000 by 1878.

In 1877 railroad strikes spread throughout the country bringing in their wake riots, martial law, and the intervention of state and federal troops. Although the unions failed for the most part to gain their immediate objectives throughout this period, there was developing within the labor movement a consciousness of solidarity and common purpose. Unskilled workers—on the railroads, in the mines, in the textile mills—participated in the industrial conflict and thus the organized labor movement was no longer identified exclusively with the skilled groups.

The 1880's saw the peak strength reached by the Noble Order of the Knights of Labor founded in 1869 by Uriah S. Stephens. Under the leadership of Terence V. Powderly, the Knights of Labor grew in membership from 10,000 in 1879 to over 700,000 members throughout the country in 1886. The broad aim of the organization was the replacement of a competitive society by a cooperative one in which workers might fully enjoy the wealth created by their hands. Specifically, the program called for such things as the eight-hour day, equal pay for equal work by women, abolition of convict and child labor, public ownership of utilities, and the establishment of cooperatives. Educational and political methods were relied upon rather than collective bargaining. Strikes were employed only as a last resort.

The American Federation of Labor. In 1881 six prominent crafts unions —those of the printers, iron and steel workers, molders, cigarmakers, carpenters, and glassworkers—established the Federation of Organized Trades and Labor Unions. Its leaders were Samuel Gompers and Adolph Strasser. For five years the organization was overshadowed by the Knights of Labor. When the Knights refused to agree to respect the jurisdiction of the large craft unions, the latter groups established the American Federation of Labor with Samuel Gompers as its President. Starting with a membership of 138,000 in 1886, the new Federation doubled that number within twelve years.

Perhaps the most striking characteristic of the American labor movement up until the 1880's was the readiness of the workers to abandon their unions in the face of depressions for the promise of relief offered by political panaceas. From the first the American Federation of Labor stressed "pure and simple" unionism. It avoided long-range reform programs but concentrated on immediate gains. It was committed to the wage system, in contrast to many of the earlier unions, and meant to improve the lot of its members within that system. Its leaders prided themselves on the organization's lack of an ideology and its avoidance of commitments on broad social objectives. The American Federation of Labor did not eschew politics, but it did avoid tying itself to any particular party or seeking to organize a labor party. Its dictum was to defeat labor's enemies and to reward its friends.

By the end of World War I, the American Federation of Labor's membership had passed the four million mark. From 70 to 80 per cent of all union members were within its organization in the period from 1890 to 1920. The 1920's witnessed a general decline in the membership of the American Federation of Labor as well as the independent unions. In the depression years at the beginning of the 1930's, total membership in all labor unions had dropped to below three million.

Rise in labor union membership under the New Deal. The enormity of the "Great Depression," heralded by the stock market crash of 1929, shook the social and the economic foundations of American society. Social and economic reforms advocated by many diverse groups for decades found strong support in the New Deal era of Franklin D. Roosevelt. It became fashionable in many quarters to blame the business community for economic conditions. One theory held that business had failed to distribute enough of its earnings as wages resulting in a lack of purchasing power by consumers, and thereby contributing to the depression; stronger unions were considered a possible antidote to such a situation.

With the support of the national government, organized labor's ranks swelled rapidly. Membership jumped from less than three million in 1933 to over seven million by the end of 1937. Organized labor had become a major force, pressing demands upon the government with the sanguine expectation that favorable responses would be forthcoming.

The CIO. The American Federation of Labor had originated on the basis of craft unions, i.e., carpenters, bricklayers, shoemakers, and so forth. Through the years it had come to accept unions organized on an industry-wide basis such as the United Mine Workers, but its leadership remained craft oriented. Organization in the mass-production industries was hampered because of the reluctance of established craft unions to surrender jurisdictional claims and permit organization on an industrial basis. Advocates of industrial unionism within the American Federation of Labor organized a

Committee for Industrial Organization in 1935 with John L. Lewis, leader of the United Mine Workers, as president. Under this group's leadership an intensive organizing drive was undertaken, and striking gains were made in steel, automobile, rubber, and other hitherto unorganized fields. CIO unions

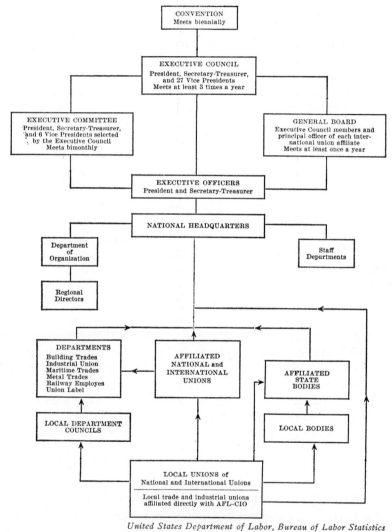

United States Department of Labor, Bureau of Labor Statistics

STRUCTURE OF THE AFL-CIO

were suspended, and, in 1938, expelled from the American Federation of Labor. In the latter year the CIO changed its name to Congress of Industrial Organizations and established itself on an independent basis.

The CIO never surpassed the AFL in numbers, but it was nevertheless much more broadly based—appealing to the whole of the non-management labor force. From the first the CIO took a broader interest in public policy matters than had the AFL. It was much more active in political campaigns, consistently supporting Democratic presidential candidates and extending its campaigns to state and local elections.

AFL-CIO merger. For a period of seventeen years, the AFL and CIO remained apart. As time passed, however, factors were at work which were to make a merger possible. Broadly speaking, the CIO leadership moved a bit toward more conservative goals while the AFL shifted its political philosophy nearer to that of its principal rival. The AFL unions, finding themselves in competition with the CIO, were pushed into manifesting interest in unskilled workers and industrial unions. Thus the craft versus industrial union issue became less important. Opposition to the Taft-Hartley Act of 1947, viewed by the unions as a definite setback to labor, furnished a focal point for unity. In 1952 William Green, president of the AFL, and Phillip Murray, president of the CIO, died within two weeks of each other. They were succeeded by George Meany, who had previously been secretary-treasurer of the federation, and Walter Reuther, president of the United Automobile Workers. Each of the new presidents faced grave problems with respect to certain component units within his organization. There were rumors that the Teamsters, the largest organization within the AFL, and the Steelworkers, affiliated with the CIO, might join with the United Mine Workers to form a third federation. A merger of the AFL and CIO would enable both to withstand better any possible divisive actions. In the fall of 1955, a merger was effected under a title which combined both names. In 1959 the AFL-CIO accounted for about 13.5 million of the approximately 17.5 million union members in the United States. Perhaps the most important effect of the merger was to give a psychological lift to organized labor. Whether the economic power of the unions was immediately enhanced is open to question, since collective bargaining is exercised by the constituent unions within the federation. It is, however, likely that the consolidation of organizing drives will constitute a gain for the unions. It appears reasonable to expect, although this point has not yet been proved, that the political activities of the merged organizations will be more effective than they were under the old order.

NATIONAL LABOR LEGISLATION

Sherman Antitrust Act. The Sherman Antitrust Act, passed by Congress in 1890, was hailed as a first step in federal regulation of business organizations, but labor unions were soon brought within its purview through judicial interpretation. The hatters of Danbury, Connecticut, organized a national boycott in an attempt to secure recognition of their union by an employer. Customers were urged not to patronize stores in which the hats of this particular manufacturer were sold. The United States Supreme Court held that the boycott prevented the flow of hats of the manufacturer across state lines, and that the union had therefore been guilty of restraint of trade in interstate commerce under the Sherman Act.[3]

The Clayton Act. In 1914 the Clayton Antitrust Act was passed in order to clarify the Sherman Act both with respect to business and labor union practices. It contained a declaration that "the labor of a human being is not a commodity or article of commerce." It also included provisions regulating the procedure in the issuance of injunctions in labor disputes. Organized labor hailed the labor provisions of the act as "Labor's Magna Charta," maintaining that their organizations were now exempted from the provisions of the Sherman Act. That this was true, however, was disclaimed in the congressional debates even by congressmen who were friendly toward labor. In a number of decisions the United States Supreme Court interpreted the act as being largely a codification of existing law, except with respect to those sections limiting the use of injunctions in labor disputes, and even here indicated that there was no absolute ban on the use of injunctions.

Railway labor legislation. The first federal labor relations law was enacted in 1888 providing for arbitration and presidential boards of investigation in railway labor disputes. Ten years later the Erdman Act, providing for mediation and voluntary arbitration, superseded the earlier statute. In addition the new law prohibited "yellow dog" contracts in the railway labor field. Thus railroads were forbidden to require as a condition of employment an agreement not to join a labor union. However, the section of the Erdman Act relating to "yellow dog" contracts was declared unconstitutional by the Supreme Court in 1908.[4]

Legislation in 1920, 1926, and 1934 also dealt with labor-management relations in the railway field. The Transportation Act of 1920 restored railroads to private ownership after a brief period of government operation (1917-1920) occasioned by World War I. The Railway Labor Act of 1926 established a definite procedure for collective bargaining and set up machinery for mediation, arbitration, and fact-finding. If negotiations for new contracts could not be settled by collective bargaining, the law provided that the matter be referred to a Board of Mediation. When mediation proved unsuccessful, the board was to use its influence to get both sides to agree to arbitration. If arbitration were once agreed upon, the decision of the arbitrators became binding and enforceable in the federal courts. Failure to adjust differences by any of these methods could lead to the creation of an emergency board by the President to investigate the dispute. For thirty days after its report, no change except by agreement could be made by the parties to the dispute. The 1934 amendments to the Railway Labor

---

3 *Loewe* v *Lawlor,* 208 U. S. 274 (1908).
4 *Adair* v. *United States,* 208 U. S. 161.

Act went still further in protecting worker rights. Company unions were forbidden; the railroads were required to negotiate in good faith with labor representatives certified by the Mediation Board (now called the National Mediation Board); a number of specified labor practices such as the use of "yellow dog" contracts, were prohibited to the owners. The 1934 legislation also established a National Railroad Adjustment Board whose primary function was to iron out differences over disputes growing out of grievances concerning the interpretation or application of agreements with respect to rates of pay, rules, or working conditions.

The Norris-La Guardia Act. Even before Franklin D. Roosevelt's New Deal legislation came to the aid of organized labor, the Norris-La Guardia Act of 1932 pointed to a change in the climate of congressional opinion toward labor. "Yellow dog" contracts were made unenforceable in federal courts. The use of the injunction in labor disputes was drastically curtailed and even where it was permitted numerous procedural protections were afforded labor organizations. The legislation also limited the liability of unions and their officers and members for unlawful acts of individual officers, agents, or members. The Supreme Court upheld the constitutionality of the legislation.[5]

The National Labor Relations Act. Under the National Industrial Recovery Act (NIRA) of 1933, declared unconstitutional in 1935, famous section 7 (a) guaranteed labor's right to organize and bargain collectively. This legislation also made possible, through the adoption of codes in industries, regulations fixing minimum wages, maximum hours, and prohibiting child labor. Within two months after the Supreme Court had voided the NIRA, Congress enacted the National Labor Relations Act (Wagner Act).

The Wagner Act required employers in interstate commerce to bargain collectively with their employees, and outlawed as unfair methods of dealing with employees which might interfere with their independence in bargaining. Among the specific unfair labor practices prohibited to employers were: (1) interference with the rights guaranteed the employee in the Wagner Act; (2) domination or interference with the formation of any labor organization or contributing to the financial support of a union; (3) discrimination against employees because of union membership; (4) discrimination against an employee who had filed charges or testified under the provisions of the Act; (5) refusal to bargain collectively with employee representatives.

In a very significant decision in 1937, the Supreme Court upheld the right of Congress under the commerce power to pass the National Labor Relations Act.[6]

National Labor Relations Board. The National Labor Relations Board,

---

5 *Lauf* v. *E. G. Shinner & Co.*, 303 U. S. 323 (1938).
6 *National Labor Relations Board* v. *Jones and Laughlin Steel Corp.*, 301 U. S. 1.

practices, and labor-management collusion against the interests of the employees. Hoping no doubt to head off further restrictions on unions by Congress, the AFL-CIO expelled the Teamsters, its largest union, and several smaller unions. However, the investigations continued and congressional sentiment mounted in favor of legislation designed to curb abuses revealed by the special committee. After an extremely bitter struggle extending over a two-year period, Congress passed the Labor-Management Reporting and Disclosure Act of 1959.[7] Broadly speaking, the legislation provided a number of new requirements with respect to the internal affairs of unions, and added certain amendments to the Taft-Hartley Act primarily aimed at preventing "unfair" union practices with respect to employers and the public.

Provisions affecting internal union affairs. A detailed "bill of rights" seeks to foster democracy within labor unions. Union members are guaranteed equal rights and privileges to nominate candidates, vote for union officers, and to participate in union meetings. Any union member whose rights under the bill of rights section is infringed may file a federal suit for relief. Elections of officers must be held at least once every (1) five years for national or international unions, (2) four years for general committees, systems boards, joint boards, joint councils, or their intermediate bodies, (3) three years for local unions. Officers, including executive board members, must be elected by secret ballot among members in good standing. However, for national or international unions, there is an alternative—that is, election at a convention of delegates chosen by secret ballot. Unions and officers must comply with all reasonable requests to distribute campaign literature to members at a candidate's expense. Unions must provide adequate safeguards to insure a fair election, including the right of any candidate to have an observer at the polls and at the counting of ballots. Procedures are also provided for the removal of officers and the negation of an invalid election.

Unions and their officers must comply with an elaborate reporting system. All unions are required to adopt constitutions and by-laws and register them, and other information with respect to their financial and organizational structure, with the Secretary of Labor. Annual reports are called for detailing assets and liabilities, receipts and sources, payments to employees receiving more than $10,000, and possible "conflict of interest" financial transactions with employers or employer "middlemen."

Other provisions of the law require that officers handling union funds be fully bonded and make it a federal crime to embezzle, steal, or otherwise misappropriate union funds.

Taft-Hartley amendments. The Taft-Hartley Act made it an unfair practice for a union to persuade the employees of any business to stop working for the purpose of forcing the management to cease dealing with another firm. This provision did not prevent unions from urging supervisory

---

[7] See p. 314.

personnel—not defined as employees in the Act—to stop working. Neither was there any provision in the law to prevent the union from approaching the employer directly and asking him to stop doing business with another firm, perhaps threatening his business with labor troubles if he did not comply. The new law made it illegal for a union to influence supervisors to stop work in order to get their employer to cease business transactions with a second firm; it also made it unlawful for a union to coerce or threaten (but not to persuade) an employer to stop dealing with another employer.

A "hot cargo" contract between a union and an employer would state that employees would not be required to handle goods headed to or from a struck shop. While an employer did not have to sign such a contract, he was under pressure to do so in order to "get along" with the union. The 1959 law with certain exceptions outlawed the "hot cargo" contract.

Another amendment to the Taft-Hartley Act was aimed at so-called "blackmail picketing." The type of picketing possible was restricted; if, for example, another union had won a NLRB election or if there had been an NLRB election within the preceding twelve months even though another union had lost the certification election. Restrictions were also placed on picketing for longer than thirty days if the union had not asked the NLRB to hold a certification election within that time.

The National Labor Relations Board has always refused to handle certain types of labor disputes over which it had jurisdiction on the basis that they were too small to warrant the expense. A Supreme Court decision ruled that state agencies could not take action in such cases because Congress had pre-empted the labor-management field involving interstate commerce. Thus, there resulted a "no man's land" in which the NLRB did not act and where the states could not act. Under the new law states were permitted to assume jurisdiction in such cases.

SETTLEMENT OF LABOR-MANAGEMENT DISPUTES

Governmental agencies at all levels have long used their offices to secure voluntary settlement of labor-management disputes. Most states have established machinery for the purpose of mediating industrial controversies involving employees and employers. *Arbitration,* in which both parties agree to submit the dispute to a third party with both sides agreeing to accept the decision, plays an important role in labor-management relations at the state level.[8] However, arbitration is not used very often for making major settlements. Its use is usually associated with the interpretation of existing contracts. Frequently, compulsory arbitration has been suggested as a means of protecting the nation's economy against disastrous strikes and lockouts. Traditionally, organized labor and management have combined to oppose the idea of compulsory arbitration.

---

8 Under federal law arbitration may be used in railway labor disputes. See p. 518.

Federal Mediation and Conciliation Service. In 1917 the United States Conciliation Service was formally organized within the Labor Department. Up to 1947 the Service had successfully settled over three-fourths of the disputes referred to it. The Taft-Hartley Act separated the Service from the Labor Department, creating an independent Federal Mediation and Conciliation Service. The agency possesses no law enforcement authority. Its mediators, located throughout the United States, rely wholly on persuasive techniques to perform their duties. The Service offers its facilities in labor-management disputes in any industry affecting interstate commerce either upon its own motion or at the request of one or more parties to the dispute whenever in its judgment such dispute threatens to cause a substantial interruption of commerce.

Injunctive process. The Taft-Hartley Act also provided a procedure which may be used to delay strikes or lockouts which "imperil the national health and safety." In such an instance, the President may appoint a board of inquiry to ascertain and report the facts. Following the report the Chief Executive may instruct the Attorney General to petition a federal district court to enjoin a strike or lockout for as long as eighty days. In the meantime the Mediation and Conciliation Service works to effect a settlement. The fact-finding board will also be reconvened to continue its work and to make a second report by the sixtieth day. If the dispute remains unsettled, the employer's last offer is to be submitted to the employees for a secret vote to determine whether or not it is acceptable. If unacceptable a strike would not be illegal. The President may then report the facts to Congress "with such recommendations as he may see fit to make for consideration." The Supreme Court upheld the section of the law dealing with the injunctive process in 1959.

Labor has been more critical of the Taft-Hartley injunctive procedure than has management. Unions have suggested that management has more to gain by "freezing" the status quo through injunction than does labor. It has also been pointed out that the emergency provisions have almost completely failed to avert critical strikes. The procedure has been criticized as distorting and putting undue pressure on the normal collective bargaining process. On the other hand, the threat of legislation to end the dispute, implicit in the Taft-Hartley law, no doubt was an important factor leading to the settlement of the long drawn-out steel strike in 1959.

PROTECTIVE LEGISLATION FOR THE INDIVIDUAL WORKER

Much of our discussion up to now has been concerned with legislation affecting labor organizations rather than with the legislation affecting individuals as such who may or may not be members of labor unions. By and large, the protective measures discussed below benefit non-union members more than those who belong to labor organizations. For example, in the area of minimum wages, a strong union through the collective bargaining process is almost sure to secure for its members (and incidentally for non-union workers in the same industrial unit) a higher wage than called for by minimum wage laws. At one time (even as late as the early 1930's), the American Federation of Labor opposed minimum wage laws for fear that such legislation might weaken unions' bargaining positions.

Wage and hour legislation. The national government was slow to enact legislation bearing on wages and hours other than for its own employees. This reluctance was due in part to the notion that the national government had no business becoming involved in local matters, partly because of the probability that such laws would be declared unconstitutional, and also because the American Federation of Labor did not support the concept of governmental guarantees to individual workers. Congress did provide a basic eight-hour day for railway workers in 1916, this area of transportation obviously falling under the commerce power.

Around the turn of the nineteenth century, some of the states began to pass legislation, based on their police powers, for the purpose of protecting workers from employer exploitation. Frequently, these laws were nullified by both state and national courts as depriving both employers and employees of due process of law. For example, in 1905 the United States Supreme Court used this reasoning to void a New York State statute that prohibited workers in bakeries from toiling for more than 60 hours a week. According to the Court, the statute interfered with the right of contract between the employer and employees; the general right to make a contract in relation to business was considered as a part of the liberty of the individual protected by the Fourteenth Amendment.[9] Nevertheless, three years later the Supreme Court upheld a ten-hour day for women in Oregon as bearing a reasonable relation to the state's power to regulate the public health, safety, and morals.[10] A further extension of the state's power to regulate working hours was recognized by the Court in 1917 when an Oregon statute providing a ten-hour day for all industrial workers was upheld.[11]

The Supreme Court sustained an Oregon minimum wage law in 1917,[12] but then in 1923 it invalidated a similar statute in the District of Columbia.[13] Following this decision other state laws were negated. Finally, in 1937 the Supreme Court once more reversed itself and upheld the minimum wage statute for women in Washington State. Mr. Justice Hughes, writing for the majority, noted:

> In each case the violation alleged by those attacking minimum wage regulation for women is deprivation of freedom of contract. What is this

---

9 *Lochner v. New York*, 198 U. S. 45.
10 *Muller v. Oregon*, 208 U. S. 412.
11 *Bunting v. Oregon*, 243 U. S. 426.
12 *Stettler v. O'Hara*, 243 U. S. 629.
13 *Adkins v. Children's Hospital*, 261 U. S. 525.

freedom? The Constitution does not speak of freedom of contract. It speaks of liberty and prohibits the deprivation of liberty without due process of law. In prohibiting that deprivation the Constitution does not recognize an absolute and uncontrollable liberty. Liberty in each of its phases has its history and connotation. But the liberty safeguarded is liberty in a social organization which requires the protection of law against the evils which menace the health, safety, morals and welfare of the people. Liberty under the Constitution is thus necessarily subject to the restraints of due process, and regulation which is reasonable in relation to its subject and is adopted in the interests of the community is due process.[14]

Today a majority of the states have passed wage and hour legislation applicable to workers not covered by federal law.

Federal Fair Labor Standards Act. Comprehensive federal legislation concerning wages and hours was first attempted in the early days of the New Deal, but when the NIRA was declared unconstitutional a fresh start had to be made. In 1936 the Walsh-Healey Act required that all federal contracts involving expenditures of $10,000 or more must limit working hours to eight per day or forty per week except as permitted by the Secretary of Labor. The statute provided that rates of pay in such cases should not be less than the prevailing minimum wage of the industry as determined by the Secretary of Labor.

The Fair Labor Standards Act, passed in 1938, embraced many more workers. It was based on the commerce power and was designed to eradicate sub-standard labor conditions from interstate commerce.[15] It prescribed a maximum work week of forty hours and required the payment of time and one-half for overtime work.[16] In the beginning, hourly wages were fixed at 25 cents, but were raised to 30 cents in 1939, 40 cents in 1945, 75 cents in 1949, and $1 in 1956. A new minimum wage law, with strong support from President Kennedy, passed Congress in 1961. It provided for a minimum wage of $1.25 an hour, the increase coming in steps, to be completed by 1963 for some workers already covered and by 1965 for the remainder. The new law applied to many workers in retail, service, and construction industries, heretofore not included.

Child labor legislation. Since children are considered as special wards of the states, there was never any serious question as to whether the state could regulate the conditions of child labor. However, the states were slow to act in this area for fear of placing their industries at a competitive disadvantage with those in other states. Shortly before World War I, Congress took cognizance of this state of affairs by forbidding the transportation in interstate commerce of products of mines employing children under sixteen and the products of factories employing children under the age of fourteen.

---

14 *West Coast Hotel Co.* v. *Parrish,* 300 U. S. 379.
15 Upheld by the Supreme Court in *United States* v. *Darby,* 312 U. S. 100 (1941).
16 To take effect in the third year after its passage.

The Supreme Court held the law unconstitutional as not being a true regulation of commerce, but an attempt by Congress to regulate the internal affairs of the states.[17] Another attempt was made in 1919 to restrict child labor by imposing a ten per cent tax upon the annual net profit of mines or factories which employed children contrary to regulations established in the law. The Court ruled this law unconstitutional on the ground that it was not a tax but a penalty designed to accomplish purposes beyond the powers of Congress.[18] A constitutional amendment was then proposed by Congress dealing with the subject of child labor, but it received the approval of only twenty-eight states.

Ultimately, the Walsh-Healey Act and the Fair Labor Standards Act included provisions with respect to child labor and were upheld by the Supreme Court. The latter law is the more comprehensive of the two. It prohibits the labor of children under sixteen years of age except under provisions laid down by the Bureau of Labor Standards (originally by the Children's Bureau). A number of areas of employment are completely exempt from the Labor Standards law. These include retailing, personal service, motion pictures, newspaper delivery, agriculture, and situations in which children work for their parents—except in manufacturing or mining.

Unemployment insurance. The depression in the 1930's pointed up the necessity of providing a nation-wide system of unemployment insurance. The states were unable or unwilling to handle the problem until Congress, in the Social Security Act of 1935, pushed them into action. Congress imposed a tax on employers at the rate of three per cent of their workers' pay in jobs up to $3,000 per worker a year. However, if states established insurance plans which met federal requirements, nine-tenths of the tax could be paid directly to a state fund for unemployment benefits. Actually, each state has its own unemployment insurance plan guided by the necessity of meeting federal standards.

The tax falls on the employer alone save in two states. After being employed for a few weeks, a worker is ordinarily eligible for benefits within a week after losing his job. The benefits vary from state to state, the national average being $30 a week for twenty weeks in 1958. In 1961 President Kennedy requested emergency legislation to provide up to 13 weeks of supplemental benefits to jobless workers. Congress authorized a temporary increase in the tax rate to accomplish this purpose, but rejected the President's recommendation for a permanent increase.

Workmen's compensation. The chance of an accident is always a potential threat to the economic security of a worker and his family. Common-law rules, developed in the early days of the industrial revolution, made it extremely difficult for the employee to collect damages from the employer

---

[17] *Hammer* v. *Dagenhart,* 247 U. S. 251 (1918).
[18] *Bailey* v. *Drexel Furniture Company,* 259 U. S. 20 (1922).

even if injured on the job. In the twentieth century, statutory law gradually replaced common law in this area giving fairer treatment to the worker. All states now require employers to carry compensation insurance of some type. Usually, state boards or commissions make findings in accident cases which become the basis for the payment or rejection of the employee's claim. About three-fourths of the states have enacted legislation providing full medical benefits to workers injured on the job. A few states require insurance plans which give benefits to workers who are unable to work because of illness.

Aiding workers to find employment. In a complex economy there is always the problem of matching the worker with the job. Before the advent of the New Deal this problem was generally handled unsatisfactorily. Some states had established public employment agencies before this time, but the task was left primarily to private agencies who sometimes charged exorbitant fees and misrepresented wages and working conditions.

In 1933 the Wagner-Peyser Act initiated a system of federal grants to states for the establishment of state employment offices provided the states conformed to the standards set up by the federal government. During World War II all state offices were taken over by the national government only to be returned to state control in 1946. The Bureau of Employment Security (Labor Department) coordinates the activities of the various state systems and operates a special veteran's employment and farm placement service, as well as a general placement service for the District of Columbia.

Migratory farm workers. Migratory agricultural workers are employed in almost every state in the nation. Significant numbers of these workers move, work within the state but away from their homes during the season. In addition, clearly identified groups move in seasonal migratory patterns from their homes in the South, Southwest, and Far West to work in northern states, returning home in the fall. The number of persons (including family non-workers) moving intra- and interstate is estimated at 350,000 to 400,000. In addition to available local and migratory domestic workers, about 450,000 foreign workers were hired in labor shortage areas as temporary farm labor in 1957. Of these, 436,000 were Mexican nationals.

Laws regulating child labor, minimum wage payments, workmen's compensation, and unemployment insurance have traditionally exempted agricultural workers from their coverage. In 1954 the President established a Committee on Migratory Labor to provide a coordinated federal approach to improving the social and economic welfare of domestic migratory agricultural workers and their families. One of the Committee's outstanding achievements has been the development of standards for the safe transportation of migratory workers.

The Labor Department has undertaken a number of programs to assist the migrants. Many of these are aimed at giving leadership to and securing the cooperation of state agencies concerned with the problem. One of the

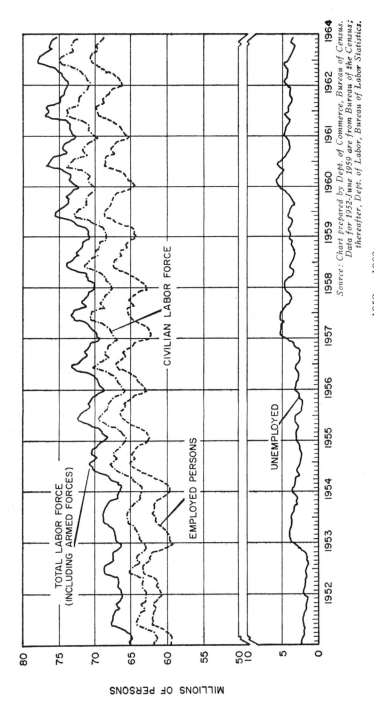

TRENDS IN THE LABOR FORCE: 1952 TO 1963

Source: Chart prepared by Dept. of Commerce, Bureau of Census. Data for 1952-June 1959 are from Bureau of the Census; thereafter, Dept. of Labor, Bureau of Labor Statistics.

most ambitious projects, carried out in cooperation with the Mexican government, is concerned with recruiting Mexican workers, operating reception centers, providing transportation from migratory centers in Mexico to reception centers with subsistence on route, and supervising labor contracts with employers.

THE DEPARTMENT OF LABOR

The idea of a Department of Labor was first proposed by labor leaders in 1865, but the first official action was taken in 1884 when President Arthur established a Bureau of Labor within the Department of the Interior. In 1888 the bureau was given independent status as a Department of Labor but without cabinet rank. This unit was absorbed in the Department of Commerce and Labor, established in 1903, and then in 1913 the two were separated with the Department of Labor accorded cabinet rank along with the Department of Commerce. The purpose of the department, as stated in the organic act, is "to foster, promote, and develop the welfare of the wage earners of the United States, to improve their working conditions, and to advance their opportunities for profitable employment." The term "wage earners" has customarily been interpreted to include salaried workers. The department serves both organized and unorganized labor equally. Certain functions performed by units in the Labor Department have already been discussed. There follows a brief statement of the principal functions performed by some of its more important bureaus.

Bureau of Labor Statistics. The Bureau of Labor Statistics is the federal government's principal fact-finding agency in the field of labor economics. It has no enforcement or administrative functions. All of the data it collects from workers, businessmen, and governmental agencies are supplied voluntarily. It collects and publishes statistics and other facts relating to a number of fields such as employment and the labor force, earnings and wages and hours, prices, cost of living, work injuries, productivity, labor-management relations, and occupational outlook.

Bureau of Employment Security. The Bureau of Employment Security carries out the national government's responsibilities in connection with the administration of two programs operated by the national and state governments on a cooperative basis—namely, the public employment service program and the unemployment insurance program. Delegated to the bureau also are certain responsibilities with respect to the skill development, utilization, and emergency management of the nation's manpower resources in the event of a national emergency.

Wage and Hour and Public Contracts Divisions. The Wage and Hour and Public Contracts Divisions are responsible for the administration of the Fair Labor Standards Act and the Walsh-Healey Public Contracts Act.

DEPARTMENT OF LABOR

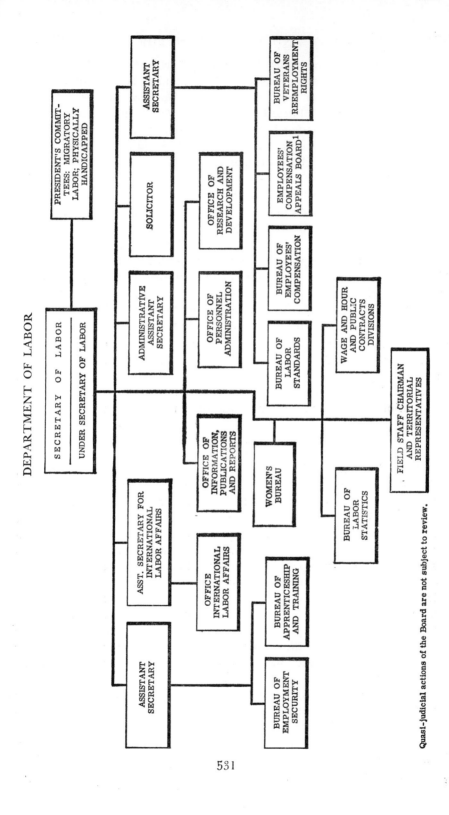

Quasi-judicial actions of the Board are not subject to review.

Bureau of Labor Standards. The Bureau of Labor Standards is a service agency to state labor departments and officials, and to labor, employer, and civic groups interested in the improvement of working conditions. It promotes industrial safety and health, develops desirable standards in the fields of labor legislation and labor law administration, and in cooperation with the Office of International Labor Affairs assists in implementing international labor standards. The Bureau is responsible for developing and recommending to the Secretary of Labor standards for inclusion in child labor regulations under the Fair Labor Standards Act.

Bureau of Employees' Compensation. The Bureau of Employees' Compensation is responsible for the administration of several federal laws providing workmen's compensation and related benefits in connection with job-related injuries for approximately three and one-half million workers. These workers include all civil officers and employees of the United States, and certain other groups such as members of the Coast Guard Reserve, Reserve Officers' Training Corps, longshore and harbor workers, and other persons in maritime employment on navigable waters of the United States.

Women's Bureau. The Women's Bureau seeks to advance the status of women as workers and as citizens, and helps them to increase their contribution to the economy. Its basic activities are fact-finding, analysis, reporting, and furnishing advisory assistance. The Bureau analyzes trends in the employment of women, their income, education, and job training.

SUMMARY

Organized labor achieved status in the New Deal period. Before this, with few exceptions, labor unions found little sympathy for their goals in the halls of Congress or in the courts. The National Labor Relations Act of 1935 ushered in a new era in labor-management relations. It was then that the law became a positive force in support of the unions. Collective bargaining, the closed shop, and the protections afforded organization activities caused union membership to increase spectacularly. The political and economic strength of labor unions became a force to be reckoned with in political campaigns and in legislative decisions. The pendulum of public and congressional opinion swung toward the views of management in 1947. In that year the Taft-Hartley Act modified certain provisions of the Wagner Act more to the liking of the business community. The provision outlawing the closed shop was resented most by organized labor, but attempts to effect repeal have been futile.

Revelation of unsavory and fraudulent practices with respect to the internal organization of some unions resulted in the passage of the Labor-Management and Disclosure Act of 1959.

The majority of the American labor force is not included in labor unions. Legislation by the states affecting wages, hours, and working conditions, long delayed by unfavorable court decisions, is now the rule. The basis of national legislation in this area is the Fair Labor Standards Act of 1940, applicable to employees in interstate commerce activities.

The concern of the national government with stable labor-management relations is reflected in the work of the Federal Mediation and Conciliation Service. Strikes and lockouts affecting the national welfare are subject to delay under the injunctive procedures of the Taft-Hartley Act.

BIBLIOGRAPHIC NOTE

Neil W. Chamberlain's *Labor* (New York: McGraw-Hill Book Company, Inc.. 1958) is an excellent general book on American labor unions, including material on their growth, aspirations, relations with government and management, and internal organization. Another work covering a broad range of topics but with emphasis on trade union history is Harry A. Millis and Royal E. Montgomery, *Organized Labor* (New York: McGraw-Hill Book Company, 1945). Good one volume histories of the American labor movement include Selig Perlman and Philip Taft, *History of Labor in the United States, 1896-1932* (New York: The Macmillan Company, 1935) and H. U. Faulkner and M. Starr, *The Labor Movement in America* (New York: Harper & Brothers, 1945). Two recent publications dealing with important periods in union development are Marc Karson, *American Labor Unions and Politics, 1900-1918* (Carbondale, Ill.: Southern Illinois University Press, 1958) and M. Derber and E. Young (eds.), *Labor and the New Deal* (Madison, Wis.: University of Wisconsin Press, 1958). Richard E. Lester's *As Unions Mature* (Princeton, N. J.: Princeton University Press, 1958) is an analysis of the status of labor unions in recent years in America. For another analysis of the power of modern unions, see Donald R. Richburg, *Labor Union Monopoly: A Clear and Present Danger* (Chicago: Henry Regnery Company, 1957).

A number of studies treat the relations of government and labor. Among these are Harold W. Metz, *Labor Policy of the Federal Government* (Washington, D. C.: The Brookings Institution, 1947); H. A. Millis and Emily C. Brown, *From the Wagner Act to Taft-Hartley* (Chicago: University of Chicago Press, 1950); G. W. Miller, *American Labor and the Government* (New York: Prentice-Hall, Inc., 1948); and Charles Killingsworth, *State Labor Relations Acts: A Study in Public Policy* (Chicago: University of Chicago Press, 1948).

For a comprehensive coverage of mediation and arbitration procedures, see Kurt Braun, *Labor Disputes and Their Settlement* (Baltimore: Johns Hopkins University, 1955). Other works pertinent to the settlement of labor-management disputes include Vincent I. Breen, *United States Conciliation Service* (Washington, D. C.: The Catholic University of America Press, 1943) and Harold L. Enarson and R. W. Fleming, *Emergency Disputes and National Policy* (New York: Harper & Brothers, 1955). For a discussion of two aspects of labor-management relations against which labor struggled for years, see Felix Frankfurter and Nathan Greene, *The Labor Injunction* (New York: The Macmillan Company, 1930) and Joel I. Seidman, *The Yellow-dog Contract* (Baltimore: Johns Hopkins University Press, 1932).

An authoritative account of internal union management is presented by Philip Taft in his *The Structure and Government of Labor Unions* (Cambridge, Mass.: Harvard University Press, 1954). Arthur J. Goldberg describes the "great" merger in *AFL-CIO: Labor United* (New York: McGraw-Hill Book Company, 1956).

The *Labor Review,* published each month by the United States Department of

Labor is filled with statistics concerning employment, unemployment, wages and hours data, etc. On farm labor see the *Farm Labor Fact Book,* a publication of the United States Labor Department, Washington, 1959. For the problems of migratory laborers, one may consult *Migratory Labor Notes,* issued periodically by The President's Committee on Migratory Labor. On laws relating to workmen's compensation, see H. M. Somers and Anne R. Somers, *Workmen's Compensation: Prevention, Insurance, and Rehabilitation of Occupational Disability* (New York: John Wiley and Sons, Inc., 1954).

26

Health, Education and Welfare

THE rejection of the laissez-faire philosophy by American public policy-makers is nowhere so apparent as in the education and welfare fields. The social security concept is now deeply embedded in our governmental policies. There are those who warn against policies which move toward the creation of a "welfare" state; but actually, the question now is what degree and what varieties of "welfare" state activities the American public will demand that their government assume.

The United States was one of the last of the great industrial countries to adopt comprehensive social security programs. The laissez-faire philosophy played no favorites with respect to an individual's liberty. He was free to make a million dollars or to starve to death, with little interference from the national government in either case. Under our federal system, however, the states have always furnished meager public assistance in extreme hardship cases. Paupers were sometimes cared for in county poor houses, even when the general attitude was that only the shiftless or lazy would have gotten themselves into such straitened circumstances. By the twentieth century most states had also made some provision, although rarely adequate, for helping old people, widows and orphans, and persons too disabled to work. The Great Depression spurred the states to increase the scope of their welfare activities, but the magnitude of the problem dwarfed state and local efforts. Haltingly, at first through loans, then through grants, and later by action on many fronts, the national government entered the picture. The Social Security Act of 1935 clearly affirmed the responsibility of the national government to support a comprehensive system of social welfare assistance in the many areas necessary to the well-being of individuals in a modern, industrial and interdependent society.

Education and public health activities by government at both the state and national levels are of long-standing acceptability. The past quarter of a century, however, has seen the national government giving more and more positive assistance to the states in both of these areas. Yet in both cases, events are pushing forward the time when further vital decisions will have to be made as to whether the national government should assume additional responsibilities with respect to education and health.

THE SOCIAL SECURITY ACT

The Social Security Act consists of nine distinct programs, all with the same basic objective. The cardinal aims of social security are to keep individuals and families from destitution, to keep families together, to give children the opportunity of growing up in health and security. The Act itself is federal law, but the federal government operates only one of the programs—old-age, survivors, and disability insurance. The other eight programs are operated by the states with federal cooperation.

Old-age, survivors, and disability insurance. Progress in public health has resulted in an increasing proportion of the population reaching old age. In an industrial society the aged have fewer chances to earn their own living, since factories and offices require full-time workers who can maintain a relatively fast pace. Increasing living costs, including higher taxes, and higher standards of living make it difficult for the average worker to provide adequately out of his private resources for himself and his dependents following retirement. Obvious hardships to dependents result when the wage earner is disabled or dies.

Old-age, survivors, and disability insurance, administered by the Social Security Administration, is the modern approach to alleviating these difficulties. Originally restricted to wage earners in private industry and com-

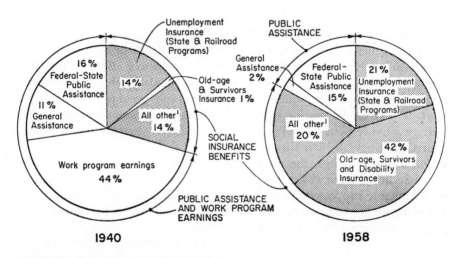

1940   1958

¹Railroad retirement, Federal civil service retirement, other Federal contributory and noncontributory retirement programs, State and local government retirement programs, State and railroad temporary disability insurance, workmen's compensation.

THE SOCIAL INSURANCE PROGRAMS   Social insurance programs account for four-fifths **of every** dollar expended under public income-maintenance programs, excluding veterans programs.

merce, the law was amended in 1950 to cover persons self-employed in non-farm and nonprofessional work, regularly employed agricultural and domestic workers, and under certain conditions, employees of nonprofit institutions, state and local government employees, and some federal employees. Subsequent amendments brought in farm owners and professional personnel. With few exceptions, the law now covers all people who are gainfully employed or self-employed. The principal exclusions are federal civilian employees under another retirement system, doctors of medicine, and employees of state and local governments and nonprofit organizations that have not come into the system voluntarily. The program provides regular monthly benefits for insured workers and their families when the wage earner reaches retirement age (65 for men, 62 for women), for eligible survivors when the worker dies at any age, and for disabled workers aged 50 to 65 and their eligible dependents.

Financing the program. Each payday every worker in a covered job, regardless of age or benefit status, pays a small percentage of his wages—not counting wages over $4,200 a year through 1958[1] or over $4,800 for 1959 and later years—as a social security tax for his old-age, survivors, and disability insurance. The contribution is deducted from the worker's pay by his employer, and the employer himself pays an equal sum. In the beginning the rate was one per cent, but it was gradually raised becoming two and one-half per cent in 1959 and three per cent in 1960. At three-year intervals, the rate is scheduled to increase until in and after 1969 it will be four and one-half per cent.

The employer sends both contributions and a report to the Treasury Department. This report, made out once each year by farm employers and four times each year by other employers, shows each worker's name, social security number, and the amount of his earnings. The contributions are deposited in a trust fund, ear-marked for benefit payments. The reports are forwarded by the Treasury Department to the Social Security Administration which keeps a record for each worker.

A person whose annual net income from covered self-employment is $400 or more reports his earnings and pays the social security tax when he files his federal income tax return. The contribution rate for self-employed income was three and three-quarters per cent in 1959 and is scheduled to increase until it reaches a maximum of six and three-quarters per cent in and after 1969.

Retirement benefits. If at the time of retirement a worker has enough quarters of coverage to be fully insured, he is eligible for retirement benefits. Anyone with forty quarters of coverage is fully insured for life. However, it is possible for as few as six quarters of coverage to fully insure certain persons depending upon their age and when they entered the program.

---

[1] Until 1954 the tax was only on the first $3,600 of annual earnings.

Earned income up to $1200 per year is permitted without affecting the amount of benefit payments. After the age of seventy-two, there is no limit upon the amount a person may earn and still receive the full benefit payments. The amount of the benefits payable are based on the worker's average monthly earnings in covered employment or self-employment. The following table gives examples of the different types and amounts of benefit payments.

Unemployment insurance. A second type of social insurance program which came into existence as a result of the Social Security Act deals with unemployment insurance. During the year ending June 30, 1959, about 44 million persons, on the average, were in jobs covered by the federal-state unemployment insurance program. Another one million were in covered railroad employment. Together, they represented about 77 per cent of the total average employment of wage and salary earners in the United States. Most of the jobs not covered are on farms, in state and local governments or non-

AVERAGE PAYMENTS UNDER OLD-AGE, SURVIVORS, AND DISABILITY INSURANCE, UNEMPLOYMENT INSURANCE, AND PUBLIC ASSISTANCE: 1940 TO 1963

[As of December, except as noted. Includes Alaska, Hawaii, Puerto Rico, and Virgin Islands]

PROGRAM	CURRENT DOLLARS					1963 DOLLARS [1]				
	1940	1950	1955	1960	1963	1940	1950	1955	1960	1963
OLD-AGE, SURVIVORS, AND DISABILITY INSURANCE										
Average monthly benefit in current-payment status:										
Retired worker	$22.60	$43.86	$61.90	$74.04	$76.88	$49.55	$54.20	$71.25	$76.65	$76.88
Aged widow	20.28	36.54	48.69	57.68	66.84	44.45	45.15	55.10	59.70	66.84
Widowed mother and 2 children [1]	47.10	93.90	135.40	188.00	[2]191.60	103.30	116.05	153.15	194.60	[2]191.60
Average monthly old-age benefit of worker retired in 1940[1]	22.60	41.40	51.60	55.00	55.00	49.55	51.15	59.40	56.95	55.00
UNEMPLOYMENT INSURANCE (STATE PROGRAMS)										
Average weekly benefit for total unemployment	10.88	20.78	26.10	34.18	35.78	23.85	25.70	30.05	35.40	35.78
PUBLIC ASSISTANCE										
Average monthly payment per recipient:										
Old-age assistance	20.26	43.95	53.93	68.45	77.03	44.45	54.35	62.05	70.85	77.03
Medical assistance for the aged [3]				195.84	201.20				202.75	201.20
Aid to families with dependent children	9.85	21.13	24.35	30.07	31.75	21.60	26.10	28.00	31.15	31.75
Aid to the blind	25.38	46.56	58.08	73.17	82.03	55.65	57.55	66.85	75.75	82.03
Aid to the permanently and totally disabled		45.41	56.18	67.64	75.74		56.15	64.65	70.00	75.74
General assistance (per case)	24.28	46.65	55.03	71.62	68.01	53.25	57.65	63.35	74.15	68.01

[1] Rounded to nearest five cents.
[2] As of June.
[3] Program initiated Nov. 1960 under the Social Security Amendment of 1960.

Source: Dept. of Health, Education, and Welfare, Social Security Administration; unpublished data.

TRENDS IN SELECTED WELFARE PROGRAMS—1940 TO 1963

profit organizations, in the domestic service, or in small firms excluded under most state laws. Farmers and other self-employed persons also are not covered by unemployment insurance laws because of the problems involved in determining objectively whether their unemployment is involuntary and beyond their control.[2]

Public assistance to the needy. In earlier days, towns or counties carried the whole responsibility for those unable to support themselves. Later some of the states began to help the local units of government provide public assistance. The Social Security Act brought the financial resources of the national government to bear on the problem. The federal government and the state governments now share in paying for public assistance and in seeing that it is properly administered. To obtain federal funds, a state must submit and have approved a plan of operation that meets certain requirements of the Social Security Act.

Within this general framework each state initiates and administers its own public assistance programs, including the determination of who is eligible to receive assistance, how much can be granted, and under what conditions. Periodic reviews are carried out by federal authorities to assure that federal funds are spent for the purpose for which Congress appropriated them.

Federal sharing in state assistance costs is based on each state's average monthly payment times the number of recipients in each program. National law fixes maximums on the amount of payments to be shared and sets the ratio of federal contributions. The states may make higher payments by using their own funds. In old-age assistance, aid to the blind, and to the permanently and totally disabled, federal funds provide four-fifths of each monthly payment up to $30 per recipient. In aid to dependent children, the federal share is fourteen-seventeenths of each payment up to $17 per recipient.

Federal grants vary for the part of the average payment between $30 and the $65-maximum for federal sharing in the adult programs, and between $17 and the $30-maximum in aid to dependent children. The federal government provides 50 per cent in states with average per capita income equal to, or above, the national average. In states with less per capita income, federal grants increase proportionately to 65 per cent. Administrative costs are shared equally by the federal and state governments.

Old-age assistance. All of the states provide old-age assistance for needy persons 65 years of age or over. The payments to these old people are made only on the basis of need. They are not to be confused with benefits under Old-age, Survivors, and Disability Insurance, which are based on wages received and taxes paid during years of work in covered employment. Almost 2,500,000 persons, about one in six persons in the country 65 years of age or

---

2 For a more detailed discussion of unemployment insurance, see p. 527.

over, received old-age assistance in June, 1958. This total has been gradually decreasing and will continue to decrease as more and more workers become eligible for the old-age and survivors insurance payments. Most states require that a person must have lived in the state at least a year in order to receive

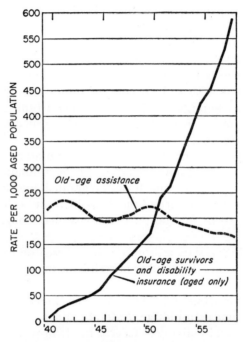

OAA RECIPIENTS AND OASI AGED BENEFICIARIES PER 1000 POPULATION—AGE 62 AND OVER, JUNE 1940-1958

old-age assistance, with a number of states requiring a five-year residence period. As of 1958 the national average monthly payment per recipient for old-age assistance was $61.39. Monthly payments ranged from a low of $29.85 in Mississippi to a high of $106.40 in Connecticut.

Aid to dependent children. Financial assistance under this program is provided for needy children when the father or mother is dead, disabled, or absent from home. To be eligible the children must be living with a parent or relative. The main object here is to permit children to remain with their families in their own homes. The federal government participates in payments to dependent families until the child is 18. Some states terminate the assistance when the children are between 16 and 18 years of age unless they are attending school. Most states require that a needy child live in the state for a year before any application for assistance is accepted. As of June, 1958, over 2,700,000 dependent children were receiving public assistance. This number represented 3.3 per cent of all children in the nation under the age of 18. The national average monthly payment per recipient was slightly more than $27.

Aid to the blind. All of the states have aid to the blind programs which are financed in part by federal funds. In general, payments are made to needy persons who are totally blind or who have so little sight that they cannot earn a living. In most states the blind may also qualify for additional assistance under other programs. In determining the need and amount of assistance, states must disregard up to $85 a month of earned income in order to encourage and assist blind persons to become self-supporting. Approximately 108,000 persons were receiving payments in 1958. The national average assistance monthly payment was about $66 in the latter year, but the range of payments was from slightly less than $37 to slightly more than $113.

Aid to the permanently and totally disabled. Since 1950 the federal government has aided the states in financing payments to needy persons 18 years of age or over who are permanently and totally disabled. Such disability is interpreted to mean a physical or mental impairment, disease, or loss that prevents an individual from holding a job, making a home, or filling some other position that would ordinarily be within his competence. Over 300,000 persons received aid in 1958. The national average payment per month was approximately $60.

Services for children. There are three programs within the Social Security Act providing specific types of aid for children. These are: (1) maternal and child health services, (2) services for crippled children, and (3) child welfare services.

Through consultation and through grants of funds appropriated each year by Congress, the Children's Bureau of the Social Security Administration helps the states extend and improve their services for mothers and children. These health and welfare programs are service rather than cash income programs. Under their provisions no money is paid to any mother or child; all grants go to state agencies. To take full advantage of the federal assistance, states must meet part of the cost of the programs.

As far back as 1921 Congress provided appropriations for maternal and child health services. The service has since been incorporated into and expanded under the Social Security Act. Typical health protective services are prenatal clinics, child health conferences, immunization services, and health services for children of school age. Doctors, dentists, nurses, medical social workers, and other health workers are helped to get post-graduate education in maternal and child care.

Each state has a crippled children's agency. The agencies are able to provide medical and surgical treatment, hospitalization, and other services for the physical restoration and social adjustment of many children.

The Social Security Act also provides for the development of child welfare services to help the least secure children—those who are homeless, dependent, or neglected and those who are in danger of becoming delinquent. Federal funds in combination with state contributions may be used for district, county, or other local child welfare services, for developing state services, or for the encouragement of the use of adequate methods for community child welfare organizations.

FEDERAL BENEFITS TO PARTICULAR GROUPS

In addition to the various benefits which flow to the general public through the social security system, the federal government has assumed responsibility for providing certain benefits and services for particular groups in the United States. Outstanding examples in this category are legislative enactments applicable to veterans and Indians.

Veterans benefits. The story of veterans benefits in America started in colonial days. By the time America had secured its independence, the concept of veterans benefits was well established. One of the first steps taken by the first Congress was to pass a federal pension law. By 1819 a Bureau of Pensions had been created; it has continued in some form ever since.

VETERANS, BY ESTIMATED AGE AND PERIOD OF SERVICE: 1963 [In thousands.]

AGE IN 1963	All veterans	KOREAN CONFLICT		World War II	World War I	Spanish-American War	Other [1]
		Total	No service in World War II				
All ages	22,166	[3] 5,663	4,567	[3] 15,100	2,343	22	134
Under 25 years	13	1	1				12
25 to 29 years	906	867	867				39
30 to 34 years	3,316	3,090	3,018	275			23
35 to 39 years	4,508	1,025	631	3,863			14
40 to 44 years	5,025	369	36	4,979			10
45 to 49 years	3,189	178	11	3,167			11
50 to 59 years	2,449	113	3	2,433	(³)		13
60 to 69 years	1,816	19		364	1,442		10
70 years and over	944	1		19	901	22	2
Average age [4] years	44.2	33.8	31.9	44.0	69.1	85.3	37.5

[1] Includes former members of the (peacetime) Regular Establishment who were receiving Veterans Administration disability compensation and veterans of the Indian Wars.
[2] Includes 1,696,000 veterans who had served both in World War II and the Korean conflict.
[3] Less than 500.
[4] Computed from 1-year age groups.

Source: Veterans Administration; unpublished data.

LIVING VETERANS IN CIVIL LIFE, JUNE 30, 1963

Medical benefits of various types were established for veterans following the Civil War. World War I saw the enactment of a greatly expanded program which included programs of disability compensation, insurance for servicemen and veterans, family allotment provisions, and rehabilitation measures for the disabled. In 1930 various activities affecting war veterans were brought together within the newly-formed Veterans Administration. During and following World War II, the federal government has been extremely generous to veterans as a group.

Number of veterans. In 1959 almost 23 million veterans were still living, representing about one out of every eight persons in the United States. Over 81 million people are veterans, members of veterans' families, or dependent survivors of deceased veterans. This means that of the nation's total population, 45 per cent are men, women, and children who are present or potential beneficiaries of programs administered by the Veterans Administration.

Medical care. The VA operates the largest chain of hospitals in the world, the number in 1959 reaching a total of 171. In addition the agency operates a nationwide system of domiciliaries and clinics. Where necessary it authorizes hospital care in non-VA hospitals, domiciliary care in state homes, and outpatient care by private practitioners. In general, medical and dental care to veterans is provided at government expense for those who are needy or who have service-connected disabilities.

Compensation and pensions. In terms of money expended, compensation and pension payments are by far the largest single cost item in VA's annual budget. During fiscal year 1959, more than three billion dollars in benefits were paid to veterans and their dependents. It is expected that pensions and death benefit payments will reach their peak about the year 2000, when the total cost is expected to be at least five and one-half billion dollars a year. Compensation benefits are paid to veterans for service-incurred disabilities and to dependents of deceased veterans where the veteran's death is attributable to service in the armed forces. In 1959 payments for disabilities were $225 per month for 100 per cent disability with larger amounts for certain disabilities such as paraplegia, loss of legs or arms, or blindness. Most of the pension benefits are paid to permanently and totally disabled war veterans and dependents of deceased war veterans whose incomes are below an established level. A large proportion of the pension payments are to World War I veterans and dependents of deceased World War I veterans.

Education and training. Nearly eleven million persons have been the beneficiaries of VA education and training programs. Vocational rehabilitation programs assist World War II and Korean Conflict veterans with service-incurred disabilities to prepare for, find, and hold suitable employment. The training needed to achieve rehabilitation is provided in colleges, schools below college level, business establishments, and on farms. By 1959, more than 600,000 World War II veterans had taken training under this program.

The heart of the "GI" bill, passed during World War II, is designated as "Readjustment Training." The purpose of this program was to afford vocational readjustment and restore lost educational or vocational opportunities to veterans whose careers were interrupted or impeded by service in the armed forces during World War II, and by subsequent legislation to Korean Conflict veterans. Financial assistance has been provided to veterans while they pursue a course of training of their own choice in colleges, schools below the college level, business and industrial establishments, or on the farm. Nearly eight million World War II veterans have been assisted by the readjustment training program. More than two million Korean Conflict veterans have taken readjustment training.

A program of educational assistance for war orphans is not expected to reach its peak until the mid 1960's. The objective of this program is to give war orphans an opportunity to obtain the education they might have received if their veteran parent had lived. Educational assistance is provided to children of persons who died from injury or disease resulting from military service during World War I, World War II, or the Korean Conflict. These educational programs may be pursued in schools of higher learning or a specialized course may be taken in schools below the college level. As much as thirty-six months of educational assistance may be provided.

Through 1959 more than twenty billion dollars had been expended by the Veterans Administration for education and training activities. The total effect of the program can never be precisely measured. Disabled veterans have been aided in leading a more complete and productive life. Certainly, too, the program has raised the educational and professional levels and the technical proficiency of the nation's labor force.

Veterans' insurance. Over six million policies are now in force covering servicemen from World War I, World War II, and the Korean Conflict. Maximum coverage for any one veteran is $10,0000. Since the federal government bears the entire administrative costs out of separate appropriations, and since the program is not designed to make a profit, the cost of the policy to the veteran is very low compared to what he would have to pay for the same amount of insurance with a commercial company.

Veterans' loans. The Veterans Administration guarantees or insures home, farm, and business loans made by private lenders to veterans of World War II and the Korean Conflict. Loans are made for a variety of purposes, such as buying or building a home, conducting a business or farming enterprise, buying livestock, machinery, tools, and other equipment, and for working capital.

The American Indian. Seventy or eighty years ago Indians were treated as "wards of the government"—confined to their reservations by Army troops and furnished with government rations. In 1924, however, citizenship was conferred on all Indians by act of Congress; today they enjoy the same rights as other citizens.

The great majority of the more than 250 tribes in the United States now live on 53 million acres of reservation land and other Indian holdings located chiefly in the western states. About 40 million acres of these lands belong to all the members of a particular tribe. The other 13 million acres are "allotted" lands. These are tracts which were allotted to individual tribal members. Today, as a result of inheritance, many of them are owned jointly by a large number of individual Indians. The government serves as trustee for both tribal and allotted lands.

When Columbus discovered America, the Indians are believed to have numbered nearly one million. From then until about 1900 their number declined to an estimated 250,000. Since that time, however, their number has been steadily increasing until now it is around 500,000. Of the total, about

350,000 receive special services from the federal government. Whether an individual Indian wishes to remain on or leave a reservation is exclusively a question for that Indian to decide. In fact, the federal government now has a voluntary relocation program to assist Indians who want to leave reservations which do not provide good employment opportunities.

At present the Department of the Interior's Bureau of Indian Affairs, which is the principal federal agency concerned with Indians, and the U. S. Public Health Service are together spending about $150 million annually on programs for the Indians for whom the federal government has responsibility.

These programs, which vary in extent with conditions and needs of the individual tribes, are aimed at three prime objectives: (1) to raise the Indians' educational standards through the provision of more and better schools; (2) to improve their health through ample medical and hospital services; and (3) to better their economic and social conditions through the stimulation of new job opportunities in agriculture and industry.

Over half of the Indian Bureau's appropriation goes for reservation schools or to help pay for the Indians' education at nearby state-supported schools. The remainder goes for a dozen other services like law-and-order, welfare, soil conservation, irrigation, relocation, roads, and forestry. Considerable money has to be spent on managing Indian trust property, a matter which has become increasingly complicated through the inheritance of allotted lands. The Bureau operates through ten area offices in the western United States and Alaska which, in turn, supervise the work of sixty-nine field offices.

THE NATION'S HEALTH

A few statistics reveal the remarkable progress made in protecting the health of the American people in recent years. The average length of life for the entire population increased from 66.8 years in 1947 to 69.6 years in 1954, but the figure has remained practically unchanged since then.[3] The infant death rate dropped 18 per cent, from 32.2 deaths per 1,000 live births in 1947 to 26.3 in 1957. The maternal mortality rate for 1957 was 3.9 per 10,000 live births, compared with 13.5 in 1947—a 71 per cent drop. Scarlet fever and streptococcal sore throat, diphtheria, whooping cough, and measles caused about eight deaths for every 100,000 youngsters under 15 years of age in 1947. In 1957, however, these diseases were responsible for only about one death per 100,000. The death rate for tuberculosis was 7.8 per 100,000 in 1957, compared with 33.5 in 1947. On the other hand, the chronic diseases characteristic of the latter part of life continued to take a heavy toll of lives. Together, diseases of the heart and blood vessels and cancer ac-

---

[3] In 1900 the figure was 49.2 years.

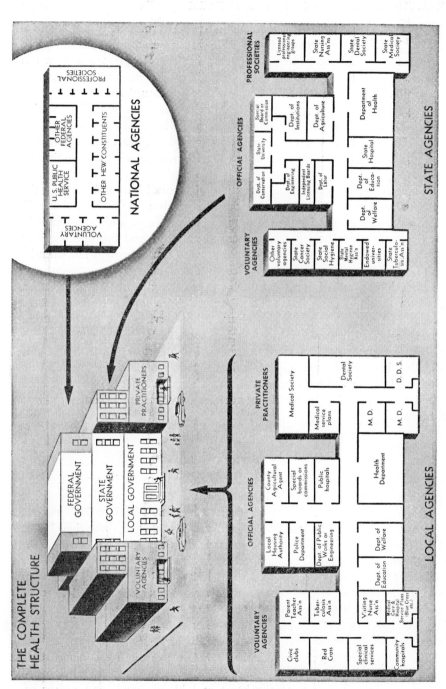

THE COMPLETE HEALTH STRUCTURE

NATIONAL AGENCIES

PROFESSIONAL SOCIETIES

VOLUNTARY AGENCIES

U.S. PUBLIC HEALTH SERVICE

OTHER FEDERAL AGENCIES

OTHER HEW CONSTITUENTS

FEDERAL GOVERNMENT

STATE GOVERNMENT

LOCAL GOVERNMENT

VOLUNTARY AGENCIES

PRIVATE PRACTITIONERS

STATE AGENCIES

PROFESSIONAL SOCIETIES

Licensed professional engineering groups

State Nursing Ass'n

State Dental Society

State Medical Society

OFFICIAL AGENCIES

State University

Special Board or Commission

Dept. of Conservation

Dept. of Engineering

Independent Licensing Boards

Dept. of Institutions

Dept. of Agriculture

Dept. of Labor

Department of Health

Dept. of Welfare

Dept. of Education

State Hospital

VOLUNTARY AGENCIES

Other voluntary agencies

State Cancer Society

State Social Hygiene

State Mental Hygiene Ass'n

Endowed universities

State Tuberculosis Ass'n

LOCAL AGENCIES

PRIVATE PRACTITIONERS

Medical Society

Medical service plans

Dental Society

M. D.

M. D.

D. D. S.

OFFICIAL AGENCIES

County Agricultural Agent

Special boards or commissions

Public hospitals

Local Housing Authority

Police Department

Dept. of Public Works or Engineering

Dept. of Welfare

Dept. of Education

Health Department

VOLUNTARY AGENCIES

Parent Teacher Ass'n

Tuberculosis Ass'n

Visiting Nurse Ass'n

Medical Care & Hospital Service Plans (Blue Cross etc.)

Civic clubs

Red Cross

Special clinical services

Community hospitals

PUBLIC HEALTH AGENCIES

546

counted for 70 per cent of all deaths in 1957. The death rate for the majoi cardiovascular-renal diseases was 523.7 per 100,000 in 1957, compared to 491.0 in 1947. The 1957 cancer death rate was 148.7, substantially higher than the 132.2 rate of a decade earlier.

The accompanying chart illustrates the degree to which all levels of government and a variety of voluntary and professional groups contribute to the improvement of the people's health. Local boards of health or health departments were common by the beginning of the nineteenth century. After the Civil War, state health departments were established. At present, state and local public health agencies perform a multitude of functions including regulation, information, and the provision of many sanity and health services.

The Public Health Service. The Public Health Service, the oldest of the organizations which compose the Department of Health, Education, and Welfare, is the principal health service of the federal government. It dates from 1798, when the Marine Hospital Service was created to provide medical and hospital facilities for merchant seamen. The scope of its activities has gradually increased until a quarter of a century ago, since which time its functions and responsibilities have multiplied rapidly. Appropriations for the Service rose from less than $150 million in 1945 to over $800 million in 1959.

The work of the Public Health Service falls into three major categories: research, medical and hospital services, and public health practice. The Service also administers financial grants to the states for general and special public health services and for the construction of hospitals, health centers, and other medical facilities. Grants are also made to public and private nonprofit research institutions for medical research and the training of scientists.

Research. The National Institutes of Health are the center of research activities in the Public Health Service. Although basic research in the Service is more than a half-century old, the seven constituent units of the National Institutes are of recent origin, beginning with the creation of the National Cancer Institute in 1937. They are the outgrowth of the increasing emphasis in medicine and public health upon the diseases that are now the major causes of death and disability in the nation. Other institutes have been established in the fields of mental health, dental research, arthritis and metabolic diseases, neurological diseases and blindness, heart disease, and microbiology (allergies and infectious diseases).

Other divisions of NIH coordinate additional research activities of the Public Health Service, all focused on contemporary health programs. Highly qualified scientists conduct the studies in facilities of the Public Health Service, in the field, and in laboratories of other institutions under cooperative arrangements. Fellowships and traineeships are awarded so as to increase the number of medical and public health scientists. Public Health Service research grants augment the nation's medical research effort. These grants

DEPARTMENT OF HEALTH, EDUCATION AND WELFARE

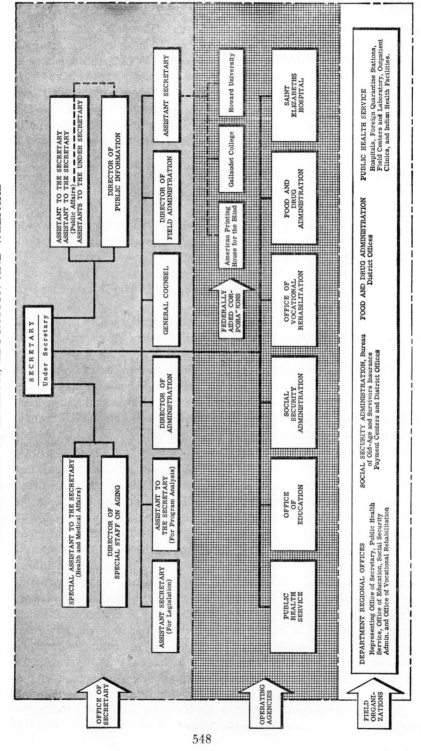

help support the investigations of research scientists in their own institutions. Grants are also made for the training of professional personnel in certain specialized fields, such as mental health, cancer, and heart disease.

Medical and hospital services. The Public Health Service provides medical and hospital care only for certain groups of people whom Congress has made eligible to receive such care. Among these are seamen of the American Merchant Marine, personnel of the United States Coast Guard, certain Indians, and civilian employees of the government. The last-named group receives care only for disease and injuries contracted in connection with their employment. Hospital services are also provided to persons with leprosy, voluntary patients who are addicted to narcotic drugs, and federal prisoners.

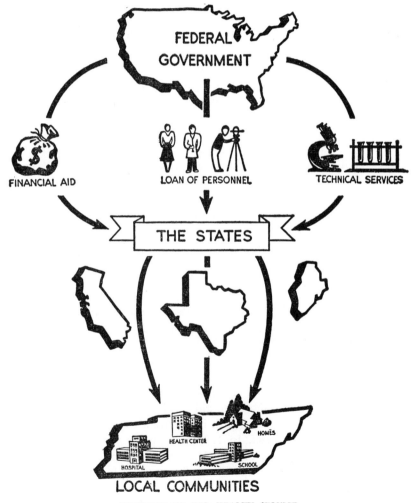

GRANTS-IN-AID FOR HEALTH SERVICE

Since 1948 the federal government has provided funds to aid the states and local communities with hospital construction projects. Over an eleven-year period the average annual appropriation for such purposes has been slightly less than $100 million. The total cost of projects undertaken under the program has averaged about three times the federal contribution. There is no question but that the federal program has encouraged construction of hospital facilities, where without federal aid, they would not have been undertaken. Many persons feel that the program should be expanded, pointing out that during the last decade new construction has been offset materially by increases in population, by obsolescence, and by the abandonment of old facilities as new facilities are constructed.

Public health practice. In the field of public health practice the Service provides leadership and technical assistance to states and local communities. It develops and promulgates standards for the protection of the public from milk- and food-borne diseases. In cooperation with state and local health departments, it develops and tests new methods in the prevention and control of disease. It licenses the manufacture of biologics and assists states and communities in dealing with such new problems as water and air pollution and radiological contamination. It collects and distributes the nation's vital statistics and conducts special studies of health data. It provides teams of public health experts to help communities suppress epidemics and prevent the spread of disease in times of disaster. Broad responsibility for the health aspects of civilian defense programs has been delegated to the Service. In its cooperative programs with the states, the Service helps communities through demonstration of new and improved methods, through the loan of personnel and equipment, and through the conduct of training programs for state and local health workers.

Health insurance. Although certain groups receive hospital and medical care at government expense, most families must depend upon their own resources to pay medical and hospital bills.[4] Individual and group insurance plans give millions of families some protection, but in many cases the costs are much greater than the benefits provided by the insurance.

A proposal for national compulsory health insurance sponsored by President Truman was rejected by Congress. The suggestion was opposed vigorously by the American Medical Association, private insurance companies, drug manufacturers, and others who saw in the recommendation a positive step toward "socialized" medicine. A more modest recommendation by President Eisenhower designed to aid low-income families through a federal underwriting of voluntary health insurance also failed to pass Congress.

Medical aid for the aged. In 1960 Congress authorized a program of medical assistance for the needy aged, augmenting existing federally supported state old-age assistance programs financed by federal-state matching

---

[4] Not, of course, in the case of accidents on the job covered by state and federal law.

grants. Participation is optional for each state and the type and extent of medical assistance is determined by each state.

One of the bitterest legislative battles of the second year of the Kennedy Administration involved the President's recommendation to provide medical and hospital care to persons over sixty-five as a feature of the social security system. The American Medical Association called the proposal unnecessary, too expensive, and socialistic. Other opponents insisted that the 1960 legislation should be given a fair trial before a new approach was tried. Some Democratic Senators objected to the way the measure was handled in the Senate, since the medicare proposal was added to a bill already passed by the House so as to bypass the Senate Finance Committee. In July, 1962, the Senate in a close vote turned down a compromise version of the President's medicare plan. Thirty-one Republicans joined by twenty-one Democrats— most of them from the South—voted against the plan. The President immediately determined to make medicare a primary issue in the 1962 congressional campaign.

FOOD AND DRUG ADMINISTRATION

By the turn of the century food processing was moving from the home kitchen and the small shop to large factories and processing plants where it was impossible for the individual to satisfy himself about the wholesomeness of the product. Conditions in many of the food processing plants were primitive by modern standards. Books and magazine articles alarmed the public with shocking exposures of filthy, fraudulent, or dangerous products. Such disclosure led Congress to pass the original Pure Food and Drug Law of 1906. Enforcement was vested in the Bureau of Chemistry of the Department of Agriculture. In 1927 the Food and Drug Administration was established as a separate unit with the latter Department. FDA is now a constituent unit within the Department of Health, Education, and Welfare.

The original Pure Food and Drug Law was completely rewritten and modernized in 1938, under the title of the Federal Food, Drug, and Cosmetics Act. An important amendment, added in 1958, gave still more protection to the consumer in the area of food additives, by requiring food and chemical manufacturers to satisfy FDA of the safety of their products *before* they were marketed.

FDA acts in many ways to police the purity, quality, and labeling of food, drugs, and cosmetics. Among other activities, the agency: (1) makes periodic inspections of food, drug, device, and cosmetic establishments and examines samples from interstate shipments of these products; (2) enforces the law against illegal sales of prescription drugs; (3) checks the manufacturers' evidence of the safety of all "new" drugs (about 40 each month) before they are put on sale to the public; (4) issues and enforces regulations specifying the kinds and quantities of new food additives that may be used in or on food products; (5) establishes the amount of pesticidal residues that

may remain on food crops without injury to consumers, and polices shipments to see that residues are within safe limits; (6) checks imports of foods,
drugs, devices, and cosmetics to make sure they comply with United States
law; (7) cooperates with state and local officials in the inspection of foods
and drugs contaminated by disasters, such as floods, hurricanes, explosions,
and fires, and in the removal of dangerous items from the market.

PUBLIC EDUCATION

The United States has long prided itself, with justification, upon the
accomplishments of its public school system, directed by the states and local
communities. The educational system has been a basic instrument in realizing the democratic ideal of equality of opportunity. In the past few years,
however, almost no other topic in national life has called forth so much
discussion of the system and whether it can furnish the quality product
which our society will require from this point on. An important aspect of
this question, though certainly only one of the significant facets, is whether
our educational system can supply the scientists and technicians who are so
vital for the national security. But beyond this:

> . . . a society depends on achievement at many levels. Whether it is
> the general capabilities needed to man our industrial apparatus, or the
> more highly trained abilities required to staff the specialized functions of
> our society, or the supremely important achievements of creative thought,
> the need is for an unprecedented degree of individual effort and accom-
> plishment. Not only must we have wise leadership in all areas of our na-
> tional life, cultural as well as political, ethical as well as technological;
> not only must we have competent people in a wide range of key profes-
> sions; but underlying it all we must also have an informed citizenry.
> Among the tasks that have increased most frighteningly in complexity is
> the task of the ordinary citizen who wishes to discharge his civic respon-
> sibilities intelligently.[5]

Much of the discussion about education in America concerns what is to
be taught and how. Sooner or later, however, most questions lead to the
basic problem of financing. School population has soared. The school age
population grew at a rate twice that of the total population in the period
between 1946 and 1958. Public school enrollment increased by 49 per cent
in the period from 1946 to 1959. Because children are staying in school
longer, high school enrollment is rising at an even faster rate than total enrollment. In 1946 only 17.5 per cent of the population between 18 and 21
was attending college; by 1959 the comparable figure stood at 40 per cent.

Expenditures for public elementary and secondary schools rose from
$5.0 billion in 1948-1949 to $14.5 billion in 1958-1959. It has been estimated
that $30.0 billion will have to be spent in 1968-1969 just to keep our present

---

5 Rockefeller Brothers Fund, Inc., *The Pursuit of Excellence: Education and the
Future of America* (New York: Doubleday and Co., Inc., 1958) p. 11.

pace in education. But even now serious teacher and classroom shortages exist. There is great disparity in the ability of the individual states to finance educational systems. This obviously affects the quality of education, since 96 per cent of the costs of our public elementary and secondary schools is borne by state-local tax dollars. As a consequence, the pressure on the federal government to assume a greater share in school financing is mounting.

Educational activities of the federal government. Even before the present Constitution, the Northwest Ordinance of 1787 specified that the 16th section of land in all townships in the Northwest Territory be reserved for the maintenance of public schools. During the administration of Andrew Jackson, $47 million was distributed by the federal government to the states for the purpose of building classrooms. The Morrill Land-Grant Act of 1862 granted to each state 30,000 acres of public land per congressman for the support of a college which would have as its primary purpose the teaching of agriculture and mechanical arts. Provisions were also made for military training.

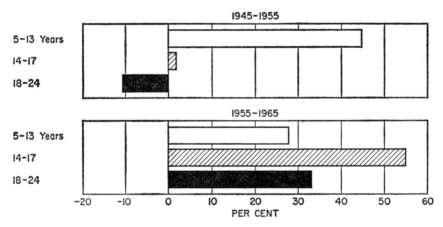

SCHOOL AGE POPULATION PER CENT CHANGE IN SIZE OF AGE GROUPS

Congress has passed a number of acts for the purpose of encouraging vocational education. The Smith-Hughes Act of 1917 provided grants for promoting vocational education in the public schools and for encouraging special education for teachers of vocational subjects. Subsequent acts have increased the scope and the funds available in the field of vocational education.

Since 1946 statutes have provided for the distribution of funds and federally purchased foods to schools, public and non-public, to be used for school lunches. Beginning in 1954 surplus milk was made avaliable to non-profit elementary and secondary schools, as well as child care centers, settlement houses, and summer camps.

Generous assistance has been granted by the national government to school districts on which activities of the United States have placed serious financial burden. Funds are provided to help cover current operating expenses and school construction. Funds are furnished toward the education of children who reside on, or with a parent employed on, tax-exempt federal property.

Since World War II the federal government has furnished millions of dollars for various types of research activities carried out by universities and other research institutions. The National Science Foundation, established as an independent agency in 1950, coordinates and encourages basic research in the physical sciences through grants and a fellowship system. As a result of this and other legislation, many universities find that a greatly increased percentage of their total budget derives from federal research grants. For example, in a recent year federal funds amounted to 77 per cent of the total expenditures at Massachusetts Institute of Technology, 29 per cent at Columbia University, 28 per cent at Princeton, 82 per cent at the California Institute of Technology, and 16 per cent at the University of Michigan.

The role of the federal government with respect to educational assistance to veterans has already been mentioned.

The Office of Education. The Office of Education was created just after the Civil War to collect information concerning education, provide that information to the people, and in other ways promote education in the United States.

The functions of the Office include the provision of various services such as research and studies, professional consultation, cooperative research with states and institutions, and the administration of certain grants. It collects and disseminates information on education in the states and territories to make possible intelligent comparison and wise decisions on programs and operations. The Office presents proposals for improving practices and the adoption of educational standards which are arrived at by cooperative planning and research.

More federal aid to education? The arguments in favor of more direct federal aid to the states and localities for education may be summed up as follows: The nation as a whole must assume responsibility for the education of its citizens; only the federal government can offset qualitative differences in education arising from the fact that the nation's wealthiest states have three times the per capita income of the poorest states; the soaring costs of education will in the future tax the resources of even the wealthier states; that only the national taxing power can guarantee quality education for the many. The long history of the land-grant college is cited as evidence against the contention that federal aid means federal control.

Opponents to additional federal aid marshal many arguments in support of their position. Perhaps the most significant one is that education is a traditional state and local function and that increased federal support will ultimately lead to federal control over the curriculum, teacher qualifications, and other standards. It is suggested that with funds flowing from the national treasury for educational purposes, some states will contribute more in proportion than they receive in return. Another approach is to recommend that the states reorganize their tax structures so that they can bear the increasing costs. It is argued that federal administrative costs are too high, that the federal tax dollar will not go as far as the local tax dollar. Another objection is that greatly increased federal expenditures in this area will cause the federal budget and the national debt to go even higher.

At least two additional obstacles have arisen when aid to education bills have reached the floor of Congress. Sometimes the proposals have become enmeshed in the controversy over segregated schools. Southern representatives in Congress oppose legislation which appears to make federal funds contingent upon the acceptance in all communities of the integration principle. Whether to extend aid to parochial schools has been a divisive factor, raising as it does the constitutional issue posed by the First Amendment.[6]

While the arguments, of course, continue, now the real question seems to be *what kind* of aid rather than *whether* additional federal aid is to be forthcoming. Legislation passed in 1958 seems to bear out this change.

The National Defense Education Act of 1958. Although as the title indicates, the Defense Education Act is tied in with national security needs, it represents the broadest approach to the question of federal policy in education matters since the 1862 Morrill Act. It is estimated that nearly 900 million dollars will be expended under the law over a four-year period. The act sets up a system whereby gifted and needy college students may obtain loans of $1000 a year for five years, with provisions for repayment extending for ten years following graduation at the low interest rate of three per cent. Priority is given to those who intend to teach in the public schools and to those whose academic records show superior attainment in science, engineering, mathematics, or modern foreign languages. If a graduate teaches for five years in a public school system, he is required to repay only one-half of the loan.

Another section of the law established a program of fellowship grants to enable more college graduates to obtain their Ph.D. degrees. Ultimately, the program calls for the financing of over 5000 graduate fellowships. Each award carries a stipend of $2000 for the first year of graduate study, $2000 for the second year, and $2400 for the third. There is an additional payment of $400 for each such year for each dependent. Each college or university involved in the program will receive up to $2500 for each graduate fellow studying at that particular institution.

Funds are also provided for additional guidance, counseling, and testing services in the nation's public schools. About one-third of the anticipated funds are earmarked for the purchase of equipment suitable for use in

[6] For an excellent account of the efforts to enact aid to education legislation since 1948, see Robert Bendiner, *Obstacle Course on Capitol Hill* (New York: McGraw-Hill, 1964).

providing education in science, math, and modern languages, and for minor remodeling of laboratory or other space used for such material and equipment. Still another part of the act calls for the establishment of language centers and language institutes.[7]

The National Defense Act states specifically: "Nothing contained in this act shall be construed or authorize any department, agency, officer, or employee of the United States to exercise any direction, supervision, or control over the curriculum, program of instruction, administration, or personnel of any education institution or school system." An apportionment system assures that all of the states will be enabled to share in the program.

Prospects for additional federal legislation. For several years Congress has given serious consideration to bills which would provide for federal aid in the construction of schools and for teachers' salaries. The House of Representatives in 1962 rejected a Kennedy recommendation which would have given federal aid to public but not private or church schools, for salary and construction. Both House and Senate did pass bills which would have authorized funds in grants and loans over a five-year period to public and private colleges for classrooms and libraries. But the legislation failed to go through when the House rejected a revision in the Senate bill that provided some $600 million for student loans.

PUBLIC HOUSING

Except for scattered activities during World War I, the federal government did not concern itself with housing problems until the depression years of the 1930's. Federal guarantees of one type or another have made it possible for persons to own homes, who a few years ago, could never have secured the down payment required under a strictly private lending operation. In 1956 three out of every five American families owned, or were in the process of purchasing, their own dwellings. Nevertheless, there remained some spots to mar the American housing picture. Thus, in the country as a whole as of 1956, about 24 per cent of all dwelling units were dilapidated or without private toilets, private baths, or hot running water. In central cities of metropolitan areas, this condition existed in approximately 14 per cent of the dwellings and in farm and rural non-farm housing it was true in almost 40 per cent.

Providing decent houses for minority groups is a continuing problem. Negroes, Latin Americans, Puerto Ricans, and Orientals are perhaps the specific groups most in need of improved housing facilities. Another persistent problem, which overlaps others to some degree, is that of providing adequate housing for those with insufficient incomes.

Housing and Home Finance Agency. Several programs for improving housing in the United States are joined under the Housing and Home Finance Agency which was established in 1947.

Federal Housing Administration. The Federal Housing Administration

---

[7] In 1964, amendments to the act expanded the number of areas in which special attention could be given to include history, civics, and other humanities.

was established to encourage improvement in housing standards and conditions, to provide a system of mutual mortgage insurance, and to exert a stabilizing influence on the mortgage market. The agency does not make loans or build houses but operates insurance programs. In other words, provided the housing construction meets FHA standards, it insures the loans made by private lending agencies up to a certain per cent of the appraised value of the property. For example, a typical FHA insured mortgage for a single family dwelling may be as high as 97 per cent of the first $13,500, plus 85 per cent of the next $2,500, plus 70 per cent of the remainder of the appraised value of the property. Similar, but not exactly the same type of mortgage guarantees are made available for cooperative housing, rental housing, armed services housing, and urban renewal area projects. Through 1958 FHA had helped almost 5 million families to own homes, aided more than 22 million families to improve their properties, and had assisted in providing housing for about 800,000 families in multi-family projects.

Public Housing Administration. The low-rent public housing program, authorized by the United States Housing Act of 1937 as amended, provides for federal financial and technical assistance to local housing authorities organized under state enabling legislation. The law sets forth: (1) that the Public Housing Administration may lend financial and technical assistance to Local Housing Authorities so they might develop low-rent housing; (2) that Local Housing Authorities pay, out of rents, all operating expenses and, to the extent possible, the yearly payment on capital costs of the development; and (3) that the Public Housing Authority will, from appropriated funds, make up the difference between the yearly cost of amortizing the capital indebtedness and the amounts available to the Local Housing Authorities out of operating income to meet such costs.

Loans are generally repaid with interest by the Local Housing Authorities from the proceeds of the sale of long-term bonds to private investors. The bonds are guaranteed by the full faith and credit of the federal government which, through the Public Housing Administration, makes annual contributions toward their retirement, thereby guaranteeing the low-rent character of the program.

Low-rent public housing developments are initiated, planned, constructed, owned, and operated by the Local Housing Authorities, with the support and approval of the local governing bodies.

All but four states have adopted necessary enabling legislation permitting the establishment of Local Housing Authorities empowered to contract with the federal agency in accordance with the requirements of the United States Housing Act.

The Housing Act of 1959 provides that income limits for occupancy and rents are to be fixed by the local authority and approved by FHA after taking into consideration (1) the family size, composition, age, physical handicaps, and other factors which might affect the rent-paying ability of the family; and (2) the economic factors which affect the financial stability and solvency of the project. Under the federal law, income limits for occupancy and rents must be set to ensure that a gap of at least 20 per cent will remain between the upper rental limits for admission and the lowest rents at which private enterprise is providing a substantial supply of decent, safe, and sanitary housing.

Federal National Mortgage Association. Most of the funds for the construction of housing are provided by banks, insurance companies, building and loan associations, and other private lending institutions. These companies frequently sell the mortgages they hold in order to obtain cash or to make other investments. The federal government created the Federal National Mortgage Association to provide a nationwide general secondary market for FHA insured mortgages. Subsequently, FNMA was authorized to purchase certain types of VA mortgages also. But the agency also exerts influence over the secondary mortgage market by selling as well as buying. For example, in 1958 the increased availability of funds for investment in home mortgages resulted in "Fannie Mae" stepping up sales of FHA-insured and VA-guaranteed mortgages and slowing down purchases. In other words, the agency buys when the market is tight and sells when the market eases.

Urban Renewal Administration. The Urban Renewal Administration is responsible for aiding localities through a system of loans, grants, and technical assistance in projects to clear and redevelop slum areas and to rehabilitate and improve blighted areas. The initiative for participation in the urban renewal program must come from the local areas. By 1958 fifty-six metropolitan areas, urban regions, and special areas were receiving federal assistance.

Community Facilities Administration. The Community Facilities Administration is not entirely concerned with housing. It makes loans to state and local governments for the construction of various types of public works such as gas, water, and sewage projects. A major responsibility of the agency in cooperation with state and local governments is the development of a reserve of planned public works which can readily go into construction to satisfy varying economic and community needs. The agency may also aid in the financing of housing and service facilities undertaken by institutions of higher learning.

Housing Act of 1961. President Kennedy sponsored housing legislation in 1961 provided for more liberal federal participation by grants and loans to various housing and related programs. Congress passed most of the President's suggestions, including increased funds for urban renewal, long-term loans for rental and cooperative housing, subsidies for rehabilitation of slums, grants for the construction of new public-housing units, additional aid for metropolitan planning, and guaranteed loans for low- and middle-income homes.

Other federal aids to housing. The Veterans Administration operates the VA-guaranteed loan program for the construction of homes for veterans. Although VA makes direct loans to eligible veterans in rural areas and small cities and towns remote where VA-guaranteed loans are not readily available from private lending sources, the primary emphasis of the program is a guaranty system which encourages private lenders to make the loans. Since 1950 over one and one-half million homes have been constructed under this program.

The Federal Home Loan Bank System makes loans to building loan associations, cooperative banks, savings banks, and other types of institutions that make home loans to individuals.

The Federal Savings and Loan Insurance Corporation insures the safety of savings and credited earnings up to $10,000 for each investor's account in an insured institution. All federal savings and loan associations, and those state charted building and loan, savings and loan, and cooperative banks which apply and are approved are insured.

SUMMARY

The Social Security Act of 1935 epitomizes a remarkable change in the attitude of the national government with respect to its responsibility in the field of social legislation. It brings the collective forces of the national and state governments to bear on problems which had plagued American society to some degree throughout our history, but which had become chronic and acute with our rapid industrialization. Of the nine distinct programs covered by the social security law, the national government is solely responsible for only one—Old-age, Survivors, and Disability Insurance. Seven of the eight remaining programs are joint federal-state affairs, with the national government aiding in the financing through complicated grant-in-aid formulae and exercising a degree of supervision by other means. Unemployment insurance is primarily a state undertaking, but according to standards approved by the national government.

Health problems are receiving more and more attention from the national government. A large proportion of the Public Health Service's energy and funds are devoted to cooperating with state, local, and private agencies in research projects, clinic and hospital construction, the training of technicians, and the like. President Truman was unsuccessful in establishing a compulsory health insurance system. In 1960, Congress passed legislation for government sponsored health insurance for the needy aged.

A significant issue at present concerns the role of the national government in public education. Despite the tradition of local responsibility, the time appears near when the federal government will assume a share of the financial burden for school construction and the payment of teacher salaries.

BIBLIOGRAPHIC NOTE

The *Report* of the President's Commission on Intergovernmental Relations (Washington, D. C.: Government Printing Office, 1955) contains a great deal of information on public health, education, and welfare programs. The *Annual Report* of the United States Department of Health, Education, and Welfare summarizes the current activities of all of its constituent units.

Two books by Eveline M. Burns discuss the general subject of social security in the United States. The first, *The American Social Security System* (Boston: Houghton Mifflin Company, 1951) is primarily descriptive; the second, *Social Security and Public Policy* (New York: McGraw-Hill Book Company, Inc., 1956) is more concerned with current and future problems. On the latter point, see James E. Russell (ed.), *National Policies for Education, Health, and Social Services* (Garden City, N. Y.: Doubleday & Company, Inc., 1955). John D. Hogan and Francis A. J. Ianni in their *American Social Legislation* (New York: Harper & Brothers, 1956) emphasize the sociological patterns leading to social legislation.

A crucial area, and one which is almost bound to become a major political issue, is that of economic security for the aged. On this point consult John J. Corson and J. W. McConnell, *Economic Needs of the Older People* (New York: The Twentieth Century Fund, 1956). A series of monographs published by the University of Minnesota Press, Minneapolis, 1951-1952, examine in detail the operation of three programs: See Ruth Raup, *Intergovernmental Policies in Social Welfare;* L. Wyatt, *Intergovernmental Policies in Public Health;* and Francis E. Rourke, *Intergovernmental Policies in Employment Security.* For a comprehensive study of the history, general philosophy, administrative problems, and practical aspects of public assistance, consult H. M. Leyendecker's *Problems and Policy in Public Assistance* (New York: Harper & Brothers, 1955).

For an inventory of the health resources of the nation for the first half of the twentieth century, see George W. Bachman and associates, *Health Resources in the United States, Personnel, Facilities, and Services* (Washington, D. C.: The Brookings Institution, 1952). For a contrasting inventory there is the President's Commission on the Health Needs of the Nation, *Building America's Health* (5 vols., Washington, D. C.: Government Printing Office, 1952). A good general survey for the period covered is found in Harry S. Mustard's *Government in Public Health* (New York: The Commonwealth Fund, 1945). An important factor in the government's future role in health insurance depends upon the adequacy of voluntary health plans. On this score, see O. W. Anderson and J. J. Feldman, *Family Medical Costs and Voluntary Health Insurance: A Nationwide Survey* (New York: McGraw-Hill Book Company, 1956). Oscar A. Anderson, Jr., describes the early years of food and drug regulation in his *The Health of A Nation: Harvey W. Wiley and the Fight for Pure Food* (University of Chicago Press, published for the University of Cincinnati, 1958).

For a brief but provocative analysis of America's needs in education, see Rockefeller Brothers Fund, Inc., *The Pursuit of Excellence: Education and the Future of America* (Garden City, N. Y.: Doubleday & Company, 1958). Hollis P. Allen, *The Federal Government and Education* (New York: McGraw-Hill Book Company, 1950) surveys the past experience of the federal government in education. Richard G. Axt's *The Federal Government and the Financing of Higher Education* (New York: Columbia University Press, 1952) treats such topics as federal research grants, the two Morrill Acts, and the GI Bill. A plea for cooperative efforts by national, state, and local governments to solve problems in education is contained in Dawson

Hales' *Federal Control of Public Education: A Critical Appraisal* (New York: Columbia University Teachers College, Bureau of Publication, 1954). The politics of recent efforts to enact federal aid to education are covered in Robert Bendiner, *Obstacle Course on Capitol Hill* (New York: McGraw-Hill, 1964) and in H. Douglas Price, "Race, Religion, and the Rules Committee," in Alan Westin (ed.), *The Uses of Power* (New York: Harcourt, Brace & World, 1962).

Aspects of the housing problem are considered in Edward C. Banfield and Morton Grodzins, *Government and Housing in Metropolitan Areas* (New York: McGraw-Hill Book Company, 1958). On government and the veteran, see the President's Commission on Veterans Pensions, *Veterans Benefits in the United States* (Washington, D. C.: Government Printing Office, 1956).

27

National Defense

THE responsibility for national defense has always been a major function of the national government. The delegates who assembled in Philadelphia in 1787 to consider strengthening the Confederation and the drafting of a constitution gave careful attention to national defense. Independence had recently been won and this naturally highlighted the importance of national defense. Moreover, there was the pressing problem of dealing with the Indian tribes of the West. All in all, the very existence of the country in a world which even then was not considerate of small and weak nations depended in no small measure upon defense power. So, though the regulation of commerce received a single clause in the Constitution, the framers took pains to draft nine different provisions relating to national defense. There was general agreement that the states were not in a position to deal effectively with this matter and consequently defense was placed more or less exclusively in the hands of the national government. In order to give every opportunity for adequate exercise of this function, the hands of the national government were left relatively unfettered in dealing with the problem.

SCOPE OF THE NATIONAL DEFENSE POWERS

The national defense powers are broad in scope both as a result of the provisions of the Constitution and the various acts which have been placed on the statute books by Congress. They include the organization and control of armed forces based on land, sea, and air operations. Congress is given power to "lay and collect taxes, duties, imposts, and excises" to "provide for the common defense." [1] Congress may "declare war, grant letters of marque and reprisal, and make rules concerning captures on land and water." [2] Congress may "provide for calling forth the militia to execute the laws of the Union, suppress insurrections and repel invasions" [3] and may also "provide for organizing, arming, and disciplining the militia, and for govern-

---

[1] Art. I, sec. 8.
[2] *Ibid.*
[3] *Ibid.*

ing such part of them as may be employed in the service of the United States." [4] In most of these there are no limitations, though appropriations to support the army cannot be for a longer term than two years. But these formal provisions of the Constitution give only a partial picture of the national defense power. Under national defense legislation the President may take over the transportation facilities of the country, occupy industrial plants in which the management refuses to cooperate in national defense programs, prohibit transactions in foreign exchange, freeze assets of foreign countries in the United States, close down radio stations, and establish a system of censorship. These are but a few of the steps which may be taken for the welfare of the country during a national emergency. That is not to say that all of these steps will necessarily be taken even after a declaration of war. But the President may go far in dealing with the situation if he deems it prudent and necessary to do so. The national defense powers of the United States may not be all-inclusive—certainly there are limitations and public opinion plays a role—but it is obvious that they are far-reaching.

NATIONAL DEFENSE MACHINERY

Office of the President. As commander-in-chief of the armed forces of the United States, the President is the top agent in the national defense machinery. He may not be a professionally trained military man, and indeed rarely is, and hence he may not actively direct the military forces of the United States in person. However, as commander-in-chief, he possesses the legal responsibility for the operation and policies of the armed forces and this, like his authority in the foreign relations field is a very grave one indeed. All Presidents depend heavily on their military and civilian assistants in carrying out such functions, but as holders of the office, they cannot escape the legal responsibility of directing the national defense themselves. Some Presidents naturally take a more active role in the details and day-to-day operations than others, and the burden is far heavier in times of national emergency than during periods of normalcy. Nevertheless, every President bears a heavy load in connection with his role as commander-in-chief.

Key White House advisors appear to have increased their importance in defense policy-making in recent years. Thus, President Kennedy relied heavily on his brother Robert in several military crises. President Johnson likewise appears to rely on personal staff as much as on the formal machinery outlined below.

National Security Council. During most of its history the United States has depended upon the President and the departments of the Army and Navy to handle national defense matters. But the disturbed international situation following World War II and the development of new types of weapons and tactics of a far more deadly variety has led to an overhauling

---

[4] *Ibid.*

and expansion of the defense machinery. The National Security Act of 1947 provided for a National Security Council to give continuing attention to the problems of national defense. Headed by the President himself, the National Security Council is made up of various *ex officio* members and attaches. The Vice-President and the secretaries of Defense and State are *ex officio* members of the National Security Board. The chairman of the Joint Chiefs of Staff, the director of the Central Intelligence Agency, and others attend the meetings to give professional advice. The National Security Council met regularly every week during the Truman and Eisenhower administrations. Both Kennedy and Johnson dropped regular meetings, but called occasional sessions. It is assisted by a staff of administrators and experts and by a Planning Board. The Planning Board prepares reports, proposals, and the like which provide the basis for the deliberations of the National Security Board. An Operations Co-ordination Board, until eliminated in 1961, had the task of carrying out the decisions adopted by the National Security Board or at least seeing that they were implemented by the service departments and other agencies. The director of the Central Intelligence Agency is present to make reports on various critical situations throughout the world. The chairman of the Joint Chiefs of Staff represents the Joint Chiefs of Staff and the service departments.

One of the chief responsibilities of the National Security Council involves the preparation of an annual top-secret document known as "Basic National Security Policy." This document which runs to 25 or so pages is supposed to set forth the overall national defense policy of the United States for the year. A great deal of time and effort on the part of the Planning Board, the staff of the National Security Council, the National Security Council itself, and others is expended on drafting this document. It is supposed to be the guide for the Joint Chiefs of Staff, the Defense Department, the State Department, and indeed the entire government in matters of national defense. But despite the enormous amount of consideration given to the preparation such a policy statement and guide, agreeing on a clear-cut statement has not proved an easy matter. National defense problems have become so incredibly complex and there are so many major differences of opinion, that it has become almost impossible to set forth a meaningful basic policy. General M. D. Taylor, former Chief of Staff of the Army who was Chairman of the Joint Chiefs of Staff in 1962, and subsequently ambassador to Vietnam, once said, "The Council has never provided a Basic National Security Policy sufficiently clear to guide the Joint Chiefs and the Defense Department." [5] Not everyone would perhaps agree with such a conclusion, but it is clear that the task of the National Security Council is a most exacting one under existing conditions.

Joint Chiefs of Staff. During World War II the Joint Chiefs of Staff came into being to make decisions in regard to strategic movements, the

[5] See his article entitled "One Defense Chief," *Look,* December 22, 1959.

use of the armed forces, and other matters vital to a successful prosecution of the war. Headed by the Chief of Staff of the President and including in its membership the Chiefs of Staff of the Army, Navy, and later the Air Force, this body made so great a contribution that it seemed logical to make it permanent. This was done when the National Military Establishment was set up after the war. In 1949 the position of Chief of Staff of the President was allowed to lapse and a new position as chairman of the Joint Chiefs of Staffs came into being. Made up of the chairman and the three service chiefs with the Marine Corps chief participating on occasion, the Joint Chiefs of Staff occupies a position at the very top of the military hierarchy. On the basis of the "Basic National Security Policy" document of the National Security Council, it is charged with drafting a national defense operational plan for the United States every year. It also directs military operations through its authority to furnish the basic directives to commanding generals and to assign unified commands in strategic areas. The Joint Chiefs of Staff depends on a fairly sizable group of officers who carry on the preliminary work of strategic and logistic planning and providing intelligence information. It is represented at the sessions of the National Security Council by its chairman and its chairman ordinarily works closely with the Secretary of Defense in administering the military program of the country.

The Joint Chiefs of Staff has been reported to be far from unanimous in its decisions, but this is apparently not true in most routine matters. In fact a member has revealed that in all but 23 instances between October 6, 1955 to March 31, 1959 the Joint Chiefs were unanimous in their actions.[6] However, on a number of great issues, the representatives of the service departments have vigorously supported varying concepts of what the national military policy should include, particularly whether reliance should be placed on guided missiles and other nuclear weapons or whether a more balanced program, giving a greater role to the surface forces in limited military operations, should be followed. In such cases of disagreement the matter is referred to the Secretary of Defense for decision. He seems to depend in large measure on the recommendation of the chairman of the Joint Chiefs of Staff, following his recommendation in 18 out of the 23 cases. The Department of the Army, being favored in only three of the disputes, naturally feels underprivileged. Prior to becoming Chairman, General Taylor urged the dropping of the Joint Chiefs of Staff and the substitution of a single Defense Chief of Staff to deal with operations and a Supreme Military Council for advisory purposes.[7]

Department of Defense. The National Security Act of 1947 and a supplementary act of 1949 provided for a single Department of Defense to unify or at least co-ordinate the military operations of the United States.

---

[6] See *Lock*, December 22, 1959.

[7] *Ibid.*

DEPARTMENT OF DEFENSE

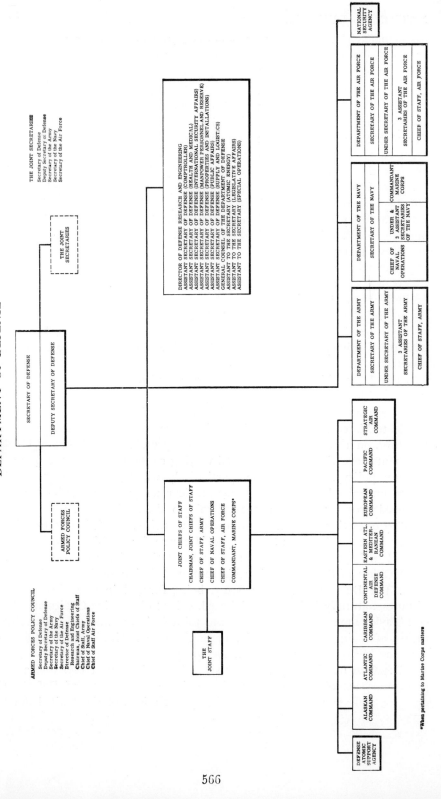

Departments of the Army, Navy, and Air Force continue to exist, but they are subordinate to the Department of Defense whose head represents all of the defense agencies in the President's cabinet. Various alterations have been made in the Department of Defense, since its inception shortly after the end of World War II, in order to make its work more effective; but its path has been far from an easy one. Service rivalries growing out of long-established traditions have been difficult to control at times. However even more important problems have developed as a result of the divergent concepts of the role of the various services in the national defense program of the future. Budgetary pressures have contributed to ill-feeling and even bitterness in certain quarters; and personality factors have, of course, played a role. In a formal sense much has been accomplished by setting up a Department of National Defense; it can hardly be denied that the step was a necessary one. Just what the concrete achievements have been it is not always easy to ascertain. Certainly some measure of increased co-ordination has resulted, but a good deal of disagreement if not dissension remains. The Kennedy administration has accelerated the rate of integration in spite of the continued opposition of the three services and the expression of doubts by some leading members of congressional committees.

Army, Navy, and Air Force departments. The Army, Navy and Air Force departments remain as the operating organizations of the ground, sea, and air services of the United States. The Department of the Army, formerly the War Department, traces its history back to the Act of 1789 or even to a department existing before the adoption of the Constitution. The Department of the Navy dates from 1798. The Department of the Air Force was provided for by the National Security Act of 1947, though the air force had long existed as a part of the War Department. All three of these departments are headed by civilian secretaries who, prior to 1947, held seats in the President's cabinet but at present are just below cabinet rank. Prior to 1949, the secretaries had direct access to the President, but the Act of 1949, in order to further co-ordination, provided that the secretaries of the Army, Navy, and Air Force Departments must go through the Secretary of Defense when dealing with the President. Each of the service departments has an under secretary and assistant secretaries who are also civilians to deal with general administration. Below that level there are numerous operational, planning, and logistic divisions which are usually headed by military personnel.

ATOMIC ENERGY COMMISSION

The Atomic Energy Commission, established by the Atomic Energy Act of 1946, is an independent agency of the government rather than a part of the Department of Defense. Many would have liked to see the Atomic Energy Commission placed under military control because of the intimate relation of atomic research and development to national defense, but public sentiment favored civilian control for several reasons. In the first place, the tradition of civilian as against military dominance in the United States seemed to point in the direction of civilian status for any atomic energy agency. In the second place, atomic energy has great potential possibilities in the industrial and health fields in addition to the military application and it was argued that a civil agency could best develop an overall program for such use. The Defense Department maintains a Military Liaison Committee with the Atomic Energy Commission. With a very large budget the five-member Commission, to which members are appointed by the President with the consent of the Senate, carries on an elaborate program which is, for the most part, very carefully guarded against publicity. The Atomic Energy Act of 1946 prescribed four program divisions to deal with research, production, engineering, and military application. Other subdivisions have been authorized by the commission itself. The Atomic Energy Commission carries on research activities at the Oak Ridge National Laboratory in Tennessee, the Los Alamos Scientific Laboratory in New Mexico, the Argonne National Laboratory in Chicago, the Brookhaven National Laboratory on Long Island, New York, and the Knolls Atomic Power Laboratory at Schenectady, New York. It produces fissionable materials at Oak Ridge and at Hanford, Washington. It also arranges with private research institutions and international research agencies to carry on certain projects.

CENTRAL INTELLIGENCE AGENCY

Prior to 1947 the record of the United States in the intelligence field was spotty and a great deal of severe criticism resulted. Vital information which should have been available seemed to be lacking. It was charged that intelligence officials in the armed forces were frequently wanting in professional background and imagination. Techniques often seemed to be obsolete and there was competition and duplication of effort on the part of the intelligence sections of various departments of the government. The National Security Act of 1947 provided for a single integrated intelligence agency, known as the Central Intelligence Agency. This agency does not have a monopoly on intelligence collection and analysis and the armed services and certain other public organizations continue to have their own intelligence branches. The Central Intelligence Agency is a sort of super-intelligence organization which to some degree co-ordinates the work of the other agencies and supplements their efforts with additional programs. The operations of the Central Intelligence Agency are not of course carried on in the limelight; even Congress is at times sensitive because it may be unable to find just what is going on. It is public knowledge that CIA is administered by a director who is appointed by the President with the consent of the Senate and who reports directly to the President. One of the chief responsibilities of the Central Intelligence Agency is to advise the National Security Council. Its director attends the meetings of the Council. In recent years the Agency has been involved in heated controversy over its alleged lack of coordination with State Department directives.

INDUSTRIAL MOBILIZATION

National defense requires the use of vast quantities of supplies of one kind and other. This means that adequate national defense necessitates the gearing of industrial production into the operations of the military agencies. During World War II a succesion of agencies, including the Office of Emergency Management, the Office of Production Management, the War Producton Board, the Office of Price Administration, the War Manpower Commission, the War Food Administration, the Office of Defense Transportation, the War Shipping Administration, the Office of Economic Stabilization, and the Office of War Mobilization were set up to control production, labor supply, prices, agricultural production, transport, raw materials, and other important aspects of the industrial system. After the war came to an end, these were liquidated either at once or as soon as reconversion had been accomplished. The international situation since 1950 has led to the creation of other agencies for industrial mobilization. A stockpiling program was authorized by the National Security Act of 1947; many items essential to national defense but not readily available in domestic markets have been purchased and stored to meet possible emergencies in the future. At the end of 1950 the President set up an Office of Defense Mobilization to "direct, control, and co-ordinate all mobilization activities of the executive branch of the government, including but not limited to production, procurement, manpower, stabilization, and transportation" [8] as a part of the executive office of the President and it reported directly to the President. The agency was abolished by President Kennedy during the first year of his administration. Its functions—already greatly reduced—were transferred to the Department of Defense in September 1961.

THE ARMED SERVICES

National Guard. Every male citizen between the ages of eighteen and forty-five years is legally a member of the national militia, but only a comparatively small proportion of these are organized into members of the National Guard. The states provide armories, appoint officers, and have general control over the National Guard units during peace time. However, the expenses are in large part borne by the national government which in turn exercises the constitutional right to specify training methods and to determine equipment. When the occasion demands, the President may call out parts or all of the National Guard for active service; control by the

---

[8] The office of Civil and Defense Mobilization in 1958.

states then gives way for a time. In periods of war the National Guard is federalized and becomes part of the national forces.

The Army. The ground forces of the United States are known as the Army, though this distinction has broken down to some extent in modern warfare; the ground forces may at times operate in the air. The Army is the oldest fighting arm of the government, dating back to the first year of the new republic or even before. It has experienced all sorts of treatment and encountered a great array of problems during its long history. Prior to 1939 it was ordinarily a small force of professionals during peace time and an expanded force of regulars and non-professionals during wartime. Since the end of World War II its size has been substantial and it has been composed of both professional members and selective service trainees. The Army is generally administered by the Department of the Army, but its particular role is determined by Congress, the National Security Council, the Department of Defense, and the Joint Chiefs of Staff. The President serves as its formal commander-in-chief, but its operational head is the Army Chief of Staff. A General Staff, a vice Chief of Staff, and two deputy Chiefs of Staff for administration, plans, and combat operations have important roles. The General Staff is elaborately organized into various subdivisions to deal with personnel, intelligence, logistics, plans and operations, organization and training, women's corps, and so forth. Special staffs include national guard and reserve divisions, an office of judge advocate general, an office of inspector general, and an historical division. There are special administrative services such as the adjutant general's department, the office of chief of chaplains, the office of provost marshal general and special services. Finally, there is a complex of technical services: medical department, chemical corps, corps of engineers, signal corps, ordnance department, quartermaster corps, and transportation corps.

The Navy. The Navy, like the Army, has had a long history, dating back to the very early days of the republic. Like the ground forces, it has had its ups and downs; but, because of the difficulty of sudden expansion and reduction, it has perhaps been more stable than the ground forces. Nevertheless, the contrast between the naval forces during peace time and wartime is spectacular. The Navy has general responsibility for the national defense activities on the water, but this also involves non-water units such as airborne units based on carriers. The Navy is generally administered by the Department of the Navy and has a large stake in the work of the Department of Defense. Its basic responsibility is determined by the National Security Council and the Joint Chiefs of Staff. Its commander-in-chief is the President, but its operating head is a Chief of Naval Operations who is assisted by a vice chief, five deputy chiefs, an inspector general, and various assistant chiefs. It has subdivisions which deal with medicine and surgery, personnel, ordnance, ships, supplies and accounts, yards and docks, aeronautics, research, legal matters, and the Marine Corps. Like the Army, it currently depends upon both professional sailors and national service trainees to operate.

The Marine Corps. Although not a separate service and without its own major department of the government, the Marine Corps has a long record of effective service behind it. It also has an aura of daring and romance not enjoyed by any other section of the fighting forces. Organized as a branch of the Navy, the Marine Corps enjoys a considerable degree of autonomy, with its own commandant who represents it on the Joint Chiefs of Staff when matters pertaining to the Marines are under consideration. Traditionally a land force operating as an arm of the Navy, the Marine Corps during recent years has been adjusting itself to an air age, though it insists on maintaining its old traditions of vigor and striking courage.

The Air Force. Starting out as a section of the Army, the Air Force increasingly came to a position of prominence in the national defense of the United States. During World War II it played a very important role that it came to operate to some extent at least autonomously. It has its own Chief of Staff who participates in the deliberations of the Joint Chiefs of Staff. Shortly after the end of World War II, when it was decided to create a National Defense Agency, the Air Force came into full majority with a separate Department of the Air Force to administer its far-flung activities. With the coming of the so-called air age, the Air Force has naturally assumed a commanding if not dominant position in the national defense of the United States. It currently has the largest number of officers and enlisted personnel of any branch and receives the biggest share of defense appropriations. It operates many types of air services and has maintained that it should have the general responsibility for air defense, though admitting the claim of the Army and Navy to the use of certain air-borne craft. Like the Army and the Navy, the Air Force has had to adjust itself to drastic modifications as traditional aircraft have become obsolescent and guided missiles have received recognition. It has argued that it should have primary responsibility for the development and use of guided missiles despite the claims of the Army and Navy to share in this field.

CIVIL DEFENSE

One of the many controversial questions pertaining to national defense is that of civil defense in a day and age when the use of atomic weapons might result in the destruction of millions of civilians through radioactivity, if not from direct exposure. Since the Civil War at least the United States has had the good fortune to keep its continental territory free from active fighting or invasion, bombing, or other primary military injury. However, a future world war would presumably involve the United States in heavy attacks from the air, possibly with little or no warning. There is a considerable difference of opinion as to the exact extent of damage which would result, some predict the death of the bulk of the people along with the destruction of most industry, while others take a somewhat more optimistic view. It is generally agreed that the dropping of nuclear weapons would cause the destruction of most of those within a radius of ten miles or more and that radioactivity might lead to the serious maiming if not total destruction of many living in outlying areas unless adequate civil defense measures are undertaken. Until now there has been a spate of talk, the setting up of a good many agencies by the states, the creation of the Federal Civil Defense Administration, and little in the way of civil defense protection. Responsibility for civil defense was transfererd to the Department of Defense in 1961 with a good deal of fanfare about new programs. Relatively little has happened since the change, however, and the talk of greater activities has died out. For a number of conflicting reasons Americans and their government refuse to take the need for civil defense seriously.

NATIONAL AERONAUTICS AND SPACE ADMINISTRATION

In 1958 Congress, at the urging of President Eisenhower, established the National Aeronautics and Space Administration (NASA). This agency was created to coordinate the efforts of the various developmental agencies in the space and missile field. It was also intended to assure civilian control over this important field. At the same time it provided for Department of Defense representation on the governing board. Further, the law provided that the military would remain in charge of "activities peculiar to or primarily associated with development of weapons systems, military operations or defense." In case of conflict between NASA and agencies of the Department of Defense the President would be called upon to decide which group had jurisdiction. After some early jurisdictional disputes that the President had to settle, the various agencies have worked together without difficulty.

Of high public interest is the Agency's program for manned space flight including the well covered launchings of American astronauts. At the same time that NASA was being established the Senate adopted a resolution creating the Senate Committee on Aeronautical and Space Sciences.

MILITARY AND MARTIAL LAW

The Constitution authorizes Congress to "make rules for the government and regulation of the land and naval forces." Congress has done this in the form of military law. Members of the armed forces are not immune from the civil rules and regulations either of the United States or of foreign countries when they are stationed abroad, but their general conduct is regulated by a special type of law which is enforced by military police and courts-martial. Minor infractions of the provisions of military law are punished by various penalties, including loss of privileges, imprisonment in a guardhouse, and deductions from pay. More serious offenders may be sent to a military prison or even condemned to death. The Army, the Navy, and the Air Force have legal branches headed by judge advocate generals and manned by professional lawyers who are attached to the various divisions and field areas. Under the supervision of these men, courts-martial are set up to pass on offenses committed by members of the armed services in connection with their professional duties.

Somewhat similar to military law in its general spirit but quite different in scope is another type of law known as martial law. If war operations, labor troubles, or natural catastrophes such as earthquakes and floods carry in their wake difficulties that the civil authorities are not able to cope with, martial law may be proclaimed. As far as the national government is concerned, the proclamation of martial law is a rare happening, since most of the events which would lead to such a state are local in character and hence call for action by the governor of a state rather than by the President or the Congress of the United States. Only in instances of serious internal disorder, invasion, or actual warfare is martial law authorized by the Constitution and then it is not intended that it apply beyond those areas immediately affected. Martial law was proclaimed in Honolulu in December, 1941 after Pearl Harbor and was maintained in Hawaii for a fairly extended period during the war.

When a proclamation of martial law has been made, the ordinary civil authorities and laws are at once subordinate to the military officials designated by the President or Congress, though they will probably not be supplanted entirely in practice. The rules of martial law apply to all civilians within a designated area and may also affect military personnel. Unlike ordinary law or military law, martial law is not an established system, since it depends upon the judgment of the military officer named to administer it. In other words, the rules of martial law may vary from place to place and from time to time. Even within a single area under martial law it is possible to have changes made from day to day to meet new conditions at the discretion of the officer in charge. Martial law is drafted in such a manner as to meet the local needs as seen by the military official in charge. Hence if the situation calls for drastic control, the rules may be very harsh indeed, even to shooting on sight within particular areas. Martial law, as proclaimed by the national government, does not carry with it the suspension of the writ of habeas corpus unless actual military operations in the vicinity require this extreme step.

MILITARY GOVERNMENT

Military government is not to be confused with military law. Though directly related to the effective operation of the armed forces, it is not intended to apply directly to those forces but is rather an instrument through which the military forces control foreign territory which is occupied by the United States. The immediate purpose of military government is to assist in the prosecution of war by relieving the tactical forces of the responsibility for certain problems. Thus military government is given the assignment of keeping the civilian population in an occupied area out of the way of the tactical forces as far as possible. In addition, military government is used to secure resources which are available in occupied areas and which are needed by the fighting forces. After the conflict has ended, military government then proceeds to its secondary purpose which is to control the occupied area until some permanent provision has been made to return it to a foreign government or it is set up under a civil administration.

It is a basic principle of military government that the existing governmental system and laws will be used as far as is consonant with military necessity and the policies of the United States. That is because it has been conclusively demonstrated that it is more effective to use what is already in existence as far as possible. Thus military government does not, except in cases of extreme emergency, operate the local government services itself. This would require more military personnel than are usually available, and in addition military government officers do not have the familiarity with local conditions which is essential to direct operations. The incumbent officials are screened and those found unsatisfactory are replaced by new personnel acceptable to military government. Likewise, the old laws are retained in so far as they do not conflict with military government policy. In the latter instance military government laws, which supersede the objectionable local regulations, are issued.

Prior to World War I the military government operations of the United States were carried on by regular non-specialized military personnel. The problems involved were comparatively simple in character; the areas were not extensive; and the period of control was fairly brief. During the occupation of the Rhineland following World War I a more elaborate system of military government was developed. But it was not until World War II that military government operations were implemented by the assignment of specialists trained in civil affairs schools. Several thousand military government officers were sent out to control German, Japanese, and other territory taken over by the tactical forces of the United States during the war. While certain aspects of the military government program came to an end with the completion of hostilities, a good deal remained to be done after V-E and V-J Days. Military government in Germany actually continued until mid-1949, when it was succeeded by an Allied High Commission, and in Japan even later, or until a peace treaty was made by the United States with Japan in 1951.

THE THORNY PROBLEM OF AN INTEGRATED NATIONAL DEFENSE POLICY

In the field of national defense there are almost inevitably divergent opinions as to what should be done and what policies should be adopted by the United States. In the past there have been bitter differences of opinion as to the role of aircraft in military operations, the division of responsibility between the Army and Navy, the employment of conscription in raising military forces, and many other matters. Presidents have made many speeches on the subject; Congress has devoted long hours to debate; military officials have argued vigorously in favor of a certain policy and strongly opposed another course, even to the point of surrendering their commissions. So it is hardly surprising that there should be differences of opinion today as to the exact national defense policy which should be adopted by the United States. It may be that the complexity of national defense in an atomic age under cold war conditions occasions even greater divergencies of opinion than during previous periods, but any difference is largely a matter of degree. During recent years there has been widespread discussion and counter-discussion of many thorny issues and it has been extremely difficult to arrive at an integrated national defense policy which is generally acceptable.

A good deal of the controversy has raged over the question of whether reliance should be placed more or less solely on nuclear weapons or whether it would be wiser to prepare for both nuclear warfare and limited war of the more conventional type. Advocates of the former maintain that the security of the United States depends largely upon its store of nuclear weapons and that since the cost of procuring these is very heavy the resources available should be concentrated to this end. Opponents of such a policy argue that nuclear war is unlikely, because it is recognized as equivalent to national if not universal suicide and that any conflicts are likely to be of the limited war variety where conventional methods are employed along with possibly limited use of atomic weapons. The matter of cost has come in for a great deal of debate. Some argue that the United States has come near the point in spending for national defense at which the ordinary economy is seriously endangered. They add that it would be futile to carry national defense expenditures to such a point that the very thing which is being defended perishes. Others believe that a much larger proportion of the national income could safely be devoted to national defense. Some of them declare that the United States is blindly pursuing a course of easy living in preference to a course of adequate national defense. Some would go so far as to advocate a garrison state in which national defense becomes the primary aim of the state and all other public activities are relegated to a secondary status to be supported on an austerity basis.

Other differences of opinion have grown out of the role of the services. The Navy, with its long tradition of pride, looks with disfavor on certain new programs that would reduce its relative status. The Army, which has been left with the most severe reductions in staff and budget during recent years, finds it difficult to accept such sacrifices calmly, especially when it strongly believes that the future will bring limited wars where ground forces are likely to be very important. There has been argument as to how much emphasis should be placed on guided missiles and how much on aircraft, what type of guided missile should be relied upon, how much attention should be given to space flights and research, on the role and feasibility of an alert system which would warn of hostile actions by another country, on the extent to which world disarmament is possible and how it can be achieved, on whether the suspension of nuclear tests is in keeping with the national defense of the United States, and various other thorny issues. The net result has been to make a clear-cut, integrated national defense policy far from simple to attain. Some would go so far as to maintain that with all of the divergence of opinion there has been no real national defense policy for several years; others, while recognizing the difficulty of bringing about agreement in these matters, are less pessimistic.

SUMMARY

The national defense authority given by the Constitution to the President and Congress is very broad in scope. It has been interpreted liberally and Congress has passed supporting legislation which gives the national government far-reaching power to take all necessary steps toward protecting the country. National defense responsibility is lodged primarily in the President, with Congress exercising a fundamental supporting role. During recent years a National Security Council has been set up to assist the President in drafting a national defense policy for the United States. A Joint Chiefs of Staff is provided to draft an operational plan based on the policy laid down by the President. A Central Intelligence Agency has been established to furnish the essential intelligence information, both as a result of its own operations and the co-ordination of intelligence collected by other agencies. The Department of Defense is the administrative arm of the government in providing defense facilities. It is charged with co-ordinating the efforts of the ground, naval, and air services.

With the spectacular advance made in the field of nuclear physics, an Atomic Energy Commission has been created as part of the national government to develop a national program which will be cognizant of both military and civil needs. The increasing importance of missile and space exploration has been emphasized by the creation in 1958 of an overall agency, the National Aeronautics and Space Administration, to coordinate developmental work in this field. A Veterans Administration, with a budget of many billions of dollars, is responsible for the care of injured veterans and administers the many programs relating to veterans. After a considerable amount of discussion of civil defense, comparatively little has been done to date in providing specific civil defense protection. The very nature of national defense makes a clear-cut, integrated national defense policy difficult to achieve and there are so many controversial problems involved in national defense today that such a policy is more than usually hard to arrive at.

BIBLIOGRAPHIC NOTE

The literature in the various subdivisions of national defense is extensive. But a good deal of it is obsolete or at least obsolescent under the conditions which prevail today. Many of the historical monographs are primarily of interest to those who are concerned with the Civil War and other earlier periods in the history of the United States. A good many of the books readily available are either too elementary or too technical in emphasis to be very useful to students in a basic course on American Government.

Though published many years ago, C. A. Berdahl's "War Powers of the Executive of the United States" (*University of Illinois Studies in the Social Sciences,* Vol. IX, Urbana, 1921) is still worth consulting on the general responsibility of the chief executive in this field. The role of the military in the United States is discussed in various works including S. P. Huntington, *Soldier and the State* (Cambridge: Harvard University Press, 1957); L. Smith, *American Democracy and Military Power* (Chicago: University of Chicago Press, 1951); W. Millis and others, *Arms and the State* (New York: Twentieth Century Fund, 1958); W. Millis, *Arms and Men* (New York: Putnam, 1956); and R. E. and T. N. Dupuy, *Military Heritage of America* (New York: McGraw-Hill, 1956). The general organization of the Department of Defense and the National Security Council is dealt with in P. Y. Hammond, *Organizing for Defense* (Princeton, N. J.: Princeton University Press, 1961).

Treatises dealing with specific services include: R. E. Dupuy, *Compact History of the United States Army* (New York: Hawthorn Books, Inc., 1956); J. A. Isely and P. A. Prowl, *U. S. Marines and Amphibian War* (Princeton: Princeton University Press, 1951); C. E. Hammond, *Marine Corps* (New York: Viking, 1958); M. O. Hyde, *From Submarines to Satellites* (New York: McGraw-Hill, 1958); and R. G. Hubler, *SAC: The Strategic Air Command* (New York: Duell, Sloan & Pearce, 1958). W. H. Riker's *Soldiers of the States* (Washington, D. C.: Public Affairs Press, 1958) deals with the National Guard.

Industrial mobilization is discussed in G. A. Lincoln and others, *Economics of National Security* (New York: Prentice-Hall, 1954) and W. G. Campbell and others (eds.), *Economics of Mobilization in War* (Chicago: R. D. Irwin, Inc., 1952). Charles Fairman, *The Law of Martial Rule* (rev. ed., Chicago: Callahan & Company, 1943) is the standard treatise on martial law. Military government is discussed in various studies, including S. Connor (ed.), "Military Government," *Annals of the American Academy of Political and Social Science,* February, 1949; C. J. Friedrich and associates, *American Experiences in Military Government in World War II* (New York: Rinehart & Company, 1948); and Harold Zink, *American Military Government in Germany* (New York: The Macmillan Company, 1947) and *The United States in Germany, 1944-1955* (Princeton, N. J.: D. Van Nostrand Co., 1957).

For various attitudes relating to the overall problem of national defense, students may be referred to the following: E. S. Furniss (ed.), *American Military Policy* (New York: Rinehart & Company, 1957); J. M. Gavin, *War and Peace in the Space Age* (New York: Harper & Brothers, 1958); H. A. Kissinger, *Nuclear Weap-*

ons and Foreign Policy (New York: Harper & Brothers, 1957); R. F. Osgood, Limited War (Chicago: University of Chicago Press, 1957); T. K. Finletter, Power and Policy (New York: Harcourt, Brace & Company, 1954); W. W. Kaufmann (ed.), Military Power and National Security (Princeton: Princeton University Press, 1956); and G. C. Reinhardt, American Strategy in the Atomic Age (Norman, Okla.: University of Oklahoma Press, 1955).

The increasing concern for military alternatives short of nuclear war are reflected in T. N. Greene, The Guerrilla and How to Fight Him (New York: Praeger, 1962), and "Unconventional Warfare," The Annals of the American Academy of Political and Social Science, Vol. 341 (May, 1962). See also Morton Halperin, Limited War in the Nuclear Age (New York: Wiley, 1963).

Two recent works of interest are Allen Dulles, The Craft of Intelligence (New York: Harper and Row, 1963) by the first director of the CIA, and Harold Stein (ed.), American Civil Military Decisions (University, Alabama: University of Alabama Press, 1963).

28

Foreign Relations

DURING the early years of the republic relatively little attention was paid to foreign relations, though even at that time the United States was perhaps not so oblivious to the outside world as some have assumed. But there were numerous pressing domestic problems, and these naturally absorbed the greater part of the attention and energy of the new country. Besides there was a widespread feeling, often associated with the famous words in Washington's Farewell Speech, that relations with other countries were to be minimized because there was so much maneuvering, working for ulterior purposes, and even treachery involved. So the United States sent out a small number of diplomatic and consular representatives, limiting them to the status of minister, appointed various agents to perform special missions, and otherwise remained fairly aloof from European political affairs.

After a century of development, the country was strong enough to be less fearful of international intrigue and it had carried its own domestic growth to a point at which concentrating on local problems was less essential. Increasing participation in world trade impelled a more vigorous interest in international political affairs. Nevertheless, it was not until World War I that the United States really emerged from its aloofness from world affairs. Even after this experience, it drew back when the ratification of the treaty involving membership in the League of Nations came to the Senate. Although it was not in the League of Nations, the United States found itself inevitably involved in international affairs as the years passed. Very active participation in World War II signalled full recognition of American interest in world affairs. It played a leading role in setting up of the United Nations and assumed a position as one of the two dominant world powers. There remains a certain amount of isolationist sentiment which flares up now and then, but this is perhaps largely a nostalgic looking back to the days of the past. Whether the United States likes it or not, it is now in a position where it must give a major part of its attention and energy to foreign relations.

THE ROLE OF THE PRESIDENT AND CONGRESS

The President is the key figure in the conduct of the relations of the United States with other countries. Congress naturally has more than a little interest in this field and devotes a considerable amount of attention to various aspects of international relations. Through its power over the purse, Congress can control much that relates to foreign relations. Missions of the United States abroad depend upon congressional appropriations for their operation; the joining of international organizations usually carries with it financial obligations which Congress must authorize. Elaborate programs such as those of foreign assistance depend in the last analysis upon congressional approval because of the vast amounts of public funds required. The Senate has to accept treaties before they become effective and must approve appointments to the major posts in the missions of the United States abroad. But the responsibility of the President in the field of foreign relations is paramount. The Constitution recognizes this when it provides: "He [the President] shall have the power, by and with the advice and consent of the Senate, to make treaties, provided two thirds of the Senators present shall concur; and he shall nominate and by and with the advice and consent of the Senate, shall appoint ambassadors, other public ministers and consuls . . . he shall receive ambassadors and other public ministers." [1] Congress may criticize what the President does and may refuse financial support at times for his foreign programs, but its members generally admit the constitutional role of the chief executive in determining policies, in recognizing foreign governments, and in carrying on relations with foreign governments and international organizations.

Though the President has to bear the full legal responsibility for the foreign relations of the United States, he must, in this day of international complexities, have assistance in carrying out these duties. The Secretary of State is his chief assistant in this field and plays an important role in the conduct of foreign relations. The President cannot constitutionally delegate his authority in this area, but he can and does on occasion depend heavily on the Secretary of State. On the other hand, a President may give a Secretary of State relatively little leeway in foreign relations, regarding him as subordinate to others in the presidential entourage.

All Presidents have heavy demands made on their time and energy today and must depend upon others for considerable assistance. Whether they follow the course of President Eisenhower and Secretary of State Dulles or whether they prefer the pattern of Presidents Kennedy and Johnson, depends upon their own inclinations. President Eisenhower did not and indeed could not delegate the responsibility for conducting foreign relations of the United States to Secretary of State Dulles, but he permitted Mr. Dulles a great

[1] Art. II, secs. 2 and 3.

amount of leeway and initiative and almost invariably approved his proposals and recommendations. His successors, on the other hand, have not
relied on their Secretaries of State very heavily. They have done the
routine things, sat in the cabinet, and presided over the State Department,
but they were not the chief aides in the foreign relations field. It is sometimes said that President Kennedy was his own Secretary of State. If this
means that he took unusual interest in foreign relations and gave much of
his time to such matters, the statement is relatively accurate. But even President Kennedy required assistance. Rather than use the Secretary of State,
however, he preferred to employ special agents such as his brother, Robert.
For advice he seemed to fall back more heavily on key White House advisers
than on the Secretary of State.

Today, perhaps as never before, a President is called on to take a
personal role in international affairs. He must attend various top-level international conferences at which heads of states meet. Recently there has
been established a pattern which may or may not prove permanent under
which a President makes foreign tours in order to confer with other heads
of states on their own soil, explains the aims of his country to other peoples,
and serves as an emissary of good will.

THE SECRETARY OF STATE

While some Secretaries of State have played a more prominent role than
others in the conduct of foreign relations, the formal position of this official
is always high. He sits immediately to the right of the President in cabinet
meetings and is the ranking administrative official in the government. There
have been outstandingly able Secretaries of State, a good many Secretaries
of ability, and some of mediocre qualities. But no other department can
boast of so long a line of distinguished heads as the State Department. The
roster commands respect; it includes the names of Thomas Jefferson, John
Marshall, James Madison, Daniel Webster, John Hay, Elihu Root, and
Charles Evans Hughes, to name only those whose service lies far enough in
the past to take them somewhat out of the field of controversy.

The Secretary of State is nominated by the President for an indefinite
term and his appointment is usually if not invariably approved by the Senate
on the grounds that the President should have a free hand in naming the
members of his cabinet. At an earlier period the Secretary of State had to
give much time to the routine administration of the State Department,
though some took such a responsibility more seriously than others. Now-
adays, what with an under secretary, a deputy under secretary for administration, an assistant secretary in charge of a bureau of administration, a
director general of the Foreign Service, and the like, the Secretary of State
is relieved of much of this very necessary but routine work. Unless he wants
to occupy himself with the details of administration, as some still do to some

extent at least, the Secretary of State is free to devote himself to the major problems of foreign relations. He can even delegate to the under secretary much of the work of receiving and conferring with ambassadors and other representatives of foreign countries in Washington. He can hold himself free to confer with the President on the important matters of policy, can attend to the working out of detailed policies after the President has reached a decision, spend his time on foreign journeys to confer with foreign secretaries, represent the United States at foreign ministers' conferences, and the like. If he is a man of intelligence, substantial background in the international field, fertile in ideas, and skillful in persuading the President, he may be able to leave a considerable impress on the foreign policy of the United States. Certainly the contributions of some Secretaries of State have been notable, even though they have no legal authority to decide matters of general policy themselves.

THE DEPARTMENT OF STATE

The Department of State was established almost immediately after the government began to function in 1789. Inasmuch as this agency was authorized to take over and carry on the work which had been handled by a department set up by the Continental Congress in 1781, it is sometimes considered to antedate the Constitution itself. Long a comparatively small department, sometimes described as a "club" in which the senior officials were frequently thrown into one another's paths and could transact business on a personal basis, the Department of State has expanded a great deal during recent years, particularly since World War II. It is at present served by many thousands of persons. It is still not one of the largest federal agencies in terms of staff; but, because of its age as well as the importance of its role, the Department of State stands to the fore in formal precedence.

Most countries whether large or small have foreign offices or departments of foreign or external affairs, and it surprises some observers that the United States does not follow this pattern. Though the Department of State is assigned a few domestic duties, its primary functions have to do with foreign relations. It may therefore be regarded as the foreign office of the United States. It has the role of handling the great amount of routine work and on occasion handles the less important policy formation essential in carrying out the President's responsibilities in the field. A vast amount of preliminary work must be done before the President can decide on basic policies particularly when international problems are as complex as they currently are. The staff of the Department of State collects information about these matters, embodies them in numerous reports and papers, drafts policy proposals for the approval of the President, and otherwise does the necessary work for the development of a foreign policy. After the President has reached a decision, the Department of State may then find itself with the

DEPARTMENT OF STATE

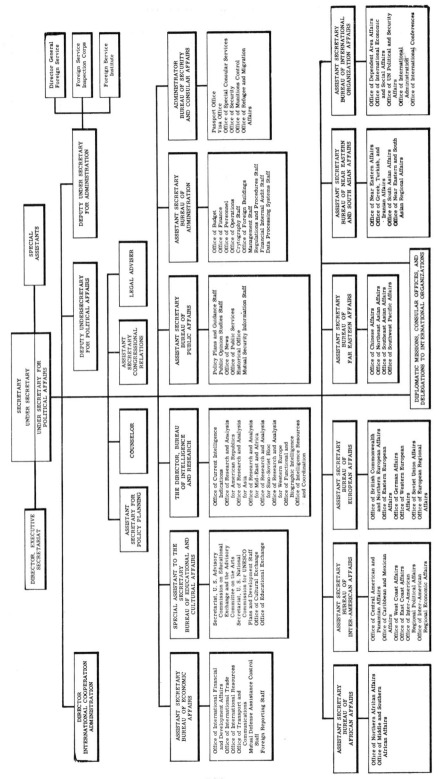

heavy burden of implementing the policy through its many missions abroad, through its representatives in international organizations, and at various international conferences. Altogether its load of work is a heavy one and its staff both at home and abroad puts in long hours, often under pressure, contrary to the impression that some have of devotion to cocktail parties, teas, and the like.

Until World War II the Department of State had a comparatively small staff in Washington, very few representatives in international organizations, and a rather modest representation in foreign capitals. War developments, the establishment of the United Nations, and the increased attention given by the United States to international matters during the postwar period have combined to bring about a striking growth. In contrast to less than a thousand staff members in Washington in 1938, the Department of State now employs many thousands, overflowing from the State Department Building into more than 20 other buildings in Washington prior to the construction of its large new addition. Foreign service personnel has also expanded rapidly during the postwar years; it more than doubled during the years 1943-1946 alone. All of this has necessitated administrative reorganization, and many changes of major or minor import have been made during recent years. It has not been a simple matter to achieve a satisfactory administrative setup and the result has been a good deal of uncertainty and at times confusion, despite the attention paid to recommendations of the Hoover Commission, the Wriston Committee, various university professors of public administration, and others.

At the head of the Department of State there is of course the Secretary of State. He is assisted by an under secretary who has general responsibility for the internal operation of the department and acts as the head when the Secretary of State is absent. An Under Secretary for Political Affairs assists in coordinating the development and implementation of United States foreign policy. A Deputy Under Secretary for Administration is responsible for the management and organization of the Department and the Foreign Service. Another deputy under secretary assists and acts for the Under Secretary for Political Affairs. A counselor with the rank of assistant secretary acts as advisor on the overall problems of foreign relations. Some ten assistant secretaries are in charge of subdivisions which attend to congressional relations, public relations, educational and cultural affairs, economic affairs, international organizations, and the five geographical divisions—European Affairs, Far Eastern Affairs, Near Eastern and South Asian Affairs, African Affairs, and Inter-American Affairs. A legal advisor heads a staff which furnishes advice on points of international and domestic law. A director of the Bureau of Intelligence and Research and an administrator of the Bureau of Security and Consular Affairs are placed at the assistant secretary level. Two units created in 1961, the Agency for International Development and the Peace Corps, are headed by an administrator and a director, respectively.

The geographical area bureaus are broken down into numerous offices, for example, Northern European Affairs within the Bureau of European Affairs. Many of the other offices are further subdivided into several divisions and they in turn are broken down into sections or other units where the work is performed. Minor organizational changes occur rather frequently.

THE FOREIGN SERVICE

Until recently there was a Department of State staff in Washington and a Foreign Service staff in the field. While both shared responsibility for carrying on the foreign relations of the United States, there frequently seemed to be a fairly wide gulf separating the two. The staff in Washington spent its time very largely in the United States and the Foreign Service staff often got back to the United States infrequently and then for brief periods. The result was that the Department of State officials did not always have a clear idea of the problems in the field and the Foreign Service officers did not always appreciate the problems of public opinion, congressional attitudes, and the like at home. Certain other governments recognized the weakness inherent in such a setup before World War II, and integrated their foreign office and Foreign Service staffs. There was discussion of the problem in the United States for some years, but little or nothing was done to deal with it because of the reluctance of the influential Foreign Service officer group to have its status changed and the lack of enthusiasm on the part of many of the Department of State staff in Washington for foreign assignments. Finally, a committee, headed by President Wriston of Brown University, was appointed to investigate and make recommendations. It took a firm stand in favor of a far-reaching reorganization under which those either in Washington or in the field involved in administering the foreign relations of the United States should be placed in a Foreign Service. This does not mean that all Department of State personnel have been given positions in the Foreign Service, for clerical, custodial, and some general administrative employees, as well as some higher officials are not regarded as primarily concerned with foreign relations. But it does mean that many of those in key positions in the Department of State in Washington now have Foreign Service status and are subject to foreign assignments periodically, and that those in the field are brought home at regular intervals for duties in the Department of State. The Foreign Service is consequently substantially larger than it was earlier.

Prior to 1924 the Foreign Service was rather inadequately established by law and entry was frequently tied up with political influence, though some able people were recruited. The Rogers Act of 1924 joined the consular and diplomatic services into a Foreign Service of the United States and provided that admission should be by competitive examination only. The Moses-Linthicum Act, which came a few years later, also brought the clerical employees attached to the Foreign Service under the merit system. The result of these acts was to provide a career service which has been a considerable asset to the country. The end of World War II saw the provisions for the Foreign Service somewhat out-of-date and hence, in 1946, Congress enacted a Foreign Service Manpower Act to authorize a much-needed expansion in personnel and a Foreign Service Act which undertook a more or less complete reorganization of the service. Under the latter act, various special staffs which had grown up during the war years were dropped and a single integrated Foreign Service of the United States was established. Two new categories were added: those of career ministers and Foreign Service reserve officers. Compensation and allowance were substantially increased.

The first category in the Foreign Service is that of Foreign Service officers. Here are eight classes together with two special classes at the top known as career ministers and career ambassadors. Nominally appointed by the President and confirmed by the Senate, these officials are actually selected as a result of competitive examinations and receive promotion on the basis of their records. It is the practice to commission these officers as both diplomatic and consular officials, and they may be shifted from one assignment to the other. On the diplomatic side they usually hold title as first, second, or third secretary; on the consular side they are consul-generals, consuls, and vice-consuls. Prior to the "Wristonization" process, the Foreign Service officer class was rather small and included only those assigned to diplomatic or consular work. "Wristonization" brought in many new officers by integration and by transfer from the Foreign Service staff corps, with the result that administrative personnel in the higher brackets, attachés doing labor, commercial, and other special functions, and the research and intelligence staff are at present Foreign Service officers.

In order to meet the special needs of the Foreign Service, reserve officers are authorized. These officials are appointed in eight grades, corresponding to those of the Foreign Service officer class below career minister, receive their positions from the Secretary of State rather than the President, and draw the same compensation as Foreign Service officers in the same grades. Appointments are limited to four years of consecutive service, and it is intended that this category include specialists who are needed for more or less temporary assignments.

The missions and consular offices of the United States abroad require large numbers of stenographers, filing clerks, code clerks, translators, couriers, and administrative and fiscal staff. These constitute the Foreign Service staff corps. Their number has been somewhat reduced recently by the transfer of many of their higher level people to the Foreign Service officer category. In addition, it has been the custom to employ a good many persons of foreign citizenship to assist in the work of the Foreign Service abroad. It is generally more economical to employ local janitors, chauffeurs, and translators.

Foreign Service Officer Schedule (Revised by 1960 Pay Act)

Career Ambassador	20,000	(Unchanged)						
Career Minister	19,800							
FSO-1	17,250	17,650	18,050	18,450	18,850	19,250	19,650	
FSO-2	14,900	15,255	15,610	15,965	16,320	16,675	17,030	
FSO-3	12,535	12,890	13,245	13,600	13,955	14,310	14,665	
FSO-4	10,645	10,945	11,245	11,545	11,845	12,145	12,445	
FSO-5	8,755	9,055	9,355	9,655	9,955	10,255	10,555	
FSO-6	7,215	7,455	7,695	7,935	8,175	8,415	8,655	
FSO-7	6,035	6,215	6,395	6,575	6,755	6,935	7,115	
FSO-8	5,085	5,265	5,445	5,625	5,805	5,985	6,165	$6,345

Foreign Service Staff Schedule (Revised by 1960 Pay Act)

FSS-1	12,655	13,030	13,405	13,780	14,155		
FSS-2	11,740	12,065	12,390	12,715	13,040		
FSS-3	10,785	11,095	11,405	11,715	12,025		
FSS-4	9,780	10,090	10,400	10,710	11,020		
FSS-5	9,025	9,285	9,545	9,805	10,065	10,325	
FSS-6	8,270	8,500	8,730	8,960	9,190	9,420	
FSS-7	7,515	7,745	7,975	8,205	8,435	8,665	
FSS-8	6,760	6,990	7,220	7,450	7,680	7,910	
FSS-9	6,005	6,235	6,465	6,695	6,925	7,155	
FSS-10	5,500	5,690	5,880	6,070	6,260	6,450	6,640
FSS-11	5,000	5,155	5,310	5,465	5,620	5,775	5,930
FSS-12	4,495	4,650	4,805	4,960	5,115	5,270	5,425
FSS-13	4,010	4,165	4,320	4,475	4,630	4,785	4,940
FSS-14	3,550	3,705	3,860	4,015	4,170	4,325	4,480
FSS-15	3,325	3,440	3,555	3,670	3,785	3,900	4,015
FSS-16	3,095	3,175	3,255	3,335	3,415	3,495	3,575
FSS-17	2,860	2,940	3,020	3,100	3,180	3,260	3,340
FSS-18	2,640	2,720	2,800	2,880	2,960	3,040	3,120
FSS-19	2,410	2,490	2,570	2,650	2,730	2,810	2,890
FSS-20	2,180	2,260	2,340	2,420	2,500	2,580	2,660
FSS-21	1,950	2,030	2,110	2,190	2,270	2,350	2,430
FSS-22	1,720	1,800	1,880	1,960	2,040	2,120	2,200

There is a curiously persistent impression that Foreign Service personnel, particularly in the officer category, must have private means. The Chief of the Division of Foreign Service Personnel of the Department of State has commented on this misapprehension, declaring, "It is more likely that his parents [Foreign Service officer's] are people of moderate means, or even poor, than wealthy. The majority of Foreign Service officers have no other incomes than their salaries and post allowances." That is not to say that private means may not be convenient at times. Social grace is not a liability in the Foreign Service, provided it is supplemented by intellectual vigor and faithful attention to duty. However, the notion that Foreign Service personnel spend most of their time attending cocktail parties, receptions, and the like is at the very least an exaggeration. There may be social demands which are taxing and certainly the chief of the mission in some capitals has to give a considerable amount of time to attending social functions of one sort or another. But the ordinary Foreign Service member, even if of officer grade, has to spend many hours in his office, attending to paper work, getting off reports to Washington, conferring with his associates and officials of the government agencies of the country to which he is sent, and the like.

AMBASSADORS AND MINISTERS

The United States maintains diplomatic missions in most of the capitals of the world—the only significant exception being a few capitals behind the Iron Curtain. Each of these is headed by a chief of mission who holds the title of ambassador or minister. During the first century of its existence the highest diplomatic representative of the United States was a minister—legislation authorizing ambassadors was not passed until 1893. For some years the more important missions received ambassadors and the missions to smaller countries were headed by ministers, but today almost all chiefs of mission rank as ambassadors. While an ambassador enjoys greater precedence than a minister and under international law represents his government, the actual roles of a minister and an ambassador are approximately the same. Neither ministers nor ambassadors are covered by the career provisions of the Foreign Service legislation, but Foreign Service officers may attain the grade of career minister or even in a few instances career ambassador. Career ministers are usually assigned to posts as counselors or economic ministers in large missions—at times they serve as consul-general—but they may also be given posts as ambassadors. Career ambassadors may be given posts as ambassadors, or occasionally as high administrative officers within the Department of State.

There is no rule requiring the appointment of ambassadors and ministers on the basis of career status or indeed on the basis of any previous experience in the international field. The President, with the consent of the Senate, may name any citizen who strikes his fancy as ambassador to some country with which the United States has diplomatic relations after formally ascertaining from that country that such a person would be acceptable. The result is that politics may have a good deal to do with the selection of ambassadors. Wealthy men who have ambitious wives or are themselves ambitious for a certain type of recognition feel that they are entitled to diplomatic posts because of generous contributions made to the campaign chests of a winning political party. Such expectations are not always realized. If such appointments are forthcoming, they may be undesirable missions and for only a year or two. For some years the majority of ambassadors have been selected from the ranks of the higher Foreign Service officers; at times three-fourths or more have come from such a group.

There is a considerable difference of opinion as to the justification of appointing non-career ambassadors. Other countries sometimes follow such a practice, but in general the accepted pattern is to place persons experienced in diplomacy at the heads of missions. It is not difficult to name non-career ambassadors of the United States who have performed effective service and are recognized both in the capitals to which they have been sent and in this country as entitled to respect. But it is easier to compile a list of non-career ambassadors who have been nonentities and even objects of ridicule. Fortunately it is comparatively rare at present to find ambassadors who make embarrassing public displays as a result of drunkenness. However, it is not so difficult to find ambassadors who cannot speak the language of the country to which accredited; this may be the case even among career ambassadors. What is more serious perhaps is that some seem to know and care very little about the institutions, cultural background, and problems of the country to which they have been assigned.

In defense of sending non-career persons to head missions, it is alleged that a fresh point of view is valuable in the post of ambassador. It is maintained that career men develop certain prejudices and set ways that make it difficult to see clearly and to accomplish far-reaching results. There may be a certain amount of truth in such observations. Certain career Foreign Service officers are somewhat limited in breadth of view, though these are probably less commonplace now than they were earlier. Despite lack of diplomatic experience, there are men of affairs who bring to ambassadorial posts new points of view and refreshing vigor. Those who advocate the use of non-career ambassadors lose sight of the fact that the foreign office officials and fellow diplomats with whom American ambassadors have to work are usually professionally trained in diplomatic traditions and usages. On occasion, they may accept a non-career ambassador who has unusual personal qualifications, even though he cannot speak their jargon, but it is more likely that they will refuse him respect and consider him a nobody. The fact that certain tactics may work wonders in the business world of the United States does not mean that they will achieve substantial results in a foreign capital. It is sometimes argued that wealthy men should be selected since the expenses incident to being an ambassador in certain capitals are well above the salary and allowances given by the United States. For the wealthiest country in the world to fall back on such reasoning is hardly something to be proud of.

On the other hand, where the non-career ambassador does bring tact, understanding, and a knowledge of the country to his job, the fact that he is a political appointee and is apt to have better access to the President than a regular foreign-service officer may make him more desirable than a career diplomat to the receiving country.

FOREIGN RELATIONS INSTRUMENTALITIES

In carrying on foreign relations, the United States makes use of numerous instrumentalities in addition to the ambassadors and the Foreign Service. Some of these are employed frequently and have been familiar for many years. Others are more recent in origin. Some are fairly routine in character, while others are more spectacular.

Notes and representation. The United States frequently exchanges notes and continuously carries on discussions with foreign governments through its representatives stationed abroad. Notes are sent by the President or by the State Department to express the views of the United States and are transmitted to the head of state or the foreign ministry of another country. They may be relatively routine in character, but they often deal with matters of considerable importance. On complex questions it is not unusual for a series of notes to be exchanged. Many other matters are discussed orally by the Department of State officials in Washington with the ambassadors and other diplomatic representatives of foreign countries or by the representatives of the United States in foreign countries with the foreign ministries of those countries.

International conferences. At an earlier period, when travel was difficult, it was not feasible to schedule international conferences except on momentous occasions. But with the world circled by airways, international conferences of one kind and another have become frequent occurrences. Complex issues can sometimes be settled around a conference table, while the use of notes and representation would require many months. Heads-of-state or summit conferences bring together the top leaders in the world, or at least some of the top men, together with large numbers of lower level representatives. Thorny issues can at times be disposed of by heads of state in conference, but the time factor makes discussion of many international problems in any very adequate manner more or less impracticable. Foreign ministers conferences are more commonplace and bring together foreign ministers of various countries, together with supporting lower level staffs. There is usually less time pressure in these meetings and this makes it possible to carry on the detailed negotiations which may be necessary to insure results. Both of these types of international conferences require a great deal of preliminary preparation on the part of the Department of State and foreign office staffs if they are to be successful. There are numerous other international conferences called to discuss trade agreements, cultural matters, and indeed almost every other conceivable subject. One or more of these is likely to be in session at any given time. They usually include officials representing the countries participating together with leading figures from the area involved.

International organizations. Closely related to international conferences are the meetings of the many international organizations to which the United States belongs. Some of these are likely to be going on at any specified time. Almost everyone is familiar with such organizations as the United Nations and NATO, but few people perhaps realize how many international organizations are currently active. Without counting the various agencies of the

TRUSTEESHIP COUNCIL OF THE UNITED NATIONS IN SESSION

United Nations and its Economic and Social Council, the United States participates in more than 70 international organizations of one kind and another. There are four international organizations in the agricultural and fisheries area; five in the commercial and financial field; 15 in the educational, scientific, and cultural realm; a dozen in the political and legal domain; some 14 in the social and health area; and ten in the transportation and communications field. Most important of all, there is, of course, the United Nations, with its Security Council, General Assembly, Economic and Social Council, Trusteeship Council, and Educational, Scientific, and Cultural Organization. Many of these find progress rather slow, but on the whole a good deal of important work is transacted. Membership in these international organizations costs the United States millions of dollars each year and some raise the question as to whether they are worthwhile. It is true that certain international organizations are more valuable than others. However, the total cost of American participation is hardly more than a drop in the bucket as compared with the expenditures for national defense. Many international organizations maintain permanent headquarters which arrange for conferences and carry out the programs adopted.

Treaties and other agreements. The United States has from its early years entered into treaties and various other agreements with one or more countries. Treaties are made in connection with peace settlements, alliances, mutual assistance, commercial affairs, arbitration, and certain other political or quasi-political matters. They may be bilateral in character when the United States and one other government are involved, or they may bring in a number of governments. Other forms of international agreement include conventions, protocols, executive agreements, declarations, statutes, provisions, arrangements, and regulations. It is sometimes difficult to differentiate between a treaty and one of these other agreements. Moreover, it is not always clear why one form has been used rather than another. However, in general, treaties are more formal in character than other types of international agreements. During the early years of the republic treaties were probably employed more commonly than were the other forms of agreements. Out of a total of more than 1400 international agreements to which the United States has been a party since 1778, more than 900 have been formal treaties. During recent years the treaty has been used less frequently. In a recent decade, for example, there were only 18 treaties among the more than 300 international agreements.

Treaties and certain other international agreements must be ratified by the Senate, but executive agreements are not submitted to the Senate. Executive agreements are less formal than treaties and may be characterized as "international understandings." There is some controversy as to whether executive agreements are authorized by the Constitution, but they have been used fairly frequently during recent years. There seems to be little objection to them as long as they are confined to routine matters, such as the International Postal Union, pilot licenses, exchange of information, and the registration of trade marks. However, agreements like those made at Yalta and Potsdam, which involved highly important political issues, have aroused not a little controversy. Well over one thousand executive agreements have been entered into by the United States, most of them dating from 1900.

Special agencies. During World War II the United States set up a number of special agencies to serve as instrumentalities in carrying on activities in foreign countries. The Foreign Economic Administration, the Office of War Information, and the Office of Strategic Services may be cited as examples. Many of these performed valuable service, but the Department of State regarded them with some apprehension since they seemed to encroach to some extent upon its domain. In some instances there was conflict between the foreign service personnel and the staffs of these agencies. At the conclusion of the war most of these special agencies were dissolved. In 1949, the Hoover Commission warned against the future use of special agencies except in the most extraordinary circumstances. Only two instrumentalities of great importance have been set up since World War II—one under a variety of names to administer the foreign economic assistance program and the other to carry on an information service abroad. Both have at times been placed under the Department of State.

FOREIGN AID ADMINISTRATIONS

During the years since World War II, the United States has found it desirable to carry on a far-reaching program of economic assistance to foreign countries. The United States had the good fortune to emerge from World War II with an expanded industrial setup, a homeland which had not suffered from enemy invasion or bombing, and greater vigor than ever before. Other countries found themselves with economies more or less paralyzed and widespread destruction in their home and public works. After some months it became apparent that the recovery of many countries would depend upon outside aid and that the economic welfare of the United States was tied up with the recovery of its allies. Consequently the United States embarked on a course of providing large amounts of money every year to assist other countries in getting back on their feet. To begin with, this aid was given mainly to European countries which had been allies of the United States during the war, but as the years passed Germany was included and underdeveloped countries in Asia and Africa were added to the list. The early efforts were largely confined to the economic area; but, as time has passed and European countries have forged ahead of even pre-war records in industrial production, attention has been given to military assistance and to industrial development in underdeveloped countries.

To administer the famous Marshall Plan, a special agency known as the Economic Co-operation Administration was created by Congress. Headed by an administrator who was appointed by the President with the consent of the Senate, ECA allocated many billions of dollars to finance the European recovery program and to a lesser extent other economic programs. From 1955 until 1961 the agency for operation in this field was known as the International Cooperation Administration. In 1961 its functions were absorbed by a new agency within the Department of State known as the Agency for International Development (AID). AID has responsibility for carrying out nonmilitary U.S. foreign assistance programs and for continuous supervision and general direction of all assistance programs authorized by Congress. The agency works through a number of programs such as development loans, development grants, and investment guarantees. A special "Alliance for Progress" program is designed to provide technical and financial cooperation among the American Republics.

THE PEACE CORPS

The Peace Corps was established within the Department of State in 1961.

This latest mechanism for carrying out the United States' policy of aiding newly developing nations of the world is staffed by volunteers, carefully selected and well trained, who serve for periods of two years, teaching or working in a number of other fields, in the communities to which they are sent. While in service, the volunteers do not receive salaries, but of course their living expenses are paid. At the end of their service the members of the Peace Corps are paid a modest amount based upon the number of months of service.

INFORMATION AGENCIES

The great attention paid by the Soviet Union to foreign information and propaganda programs has perhaps been at least partially responsible for the West's current attention to the importance of information agencies in foreign countries. Most of the countries of the world, whether large or small, now seek to make information about themselves available in other countries. The various diplomatic missions and consular establishments of the United States have not been oblivious to such a need and indeed have long undertaken a certain amount of activity of this sort. But experience seems to indicate that a special agency either within or outside the Department of State is required for a reasonably effective program. Foreign service personnel have too many other responsibilities to provide anything like the concentrated effort essential to an effective program in the information field.

Whether an information service should be placed under the general direction of the Department of State as a somewhat autonomous subdivision or whether it should be set up as an independent agency has been a controversial question. The result has been that at times the Department of State has had overall responsibility and at other times there has been a separation. At present the United States Information Agency is an independent agency reporting to the President. Whether such an operation is placed within the Department of State or in an independent position, it is of course important that there should be a high degree of co-operation between the Foreign Service staff in the field and the staff of the information agency.

The United States Information Agency has the heavy responsibility of interpreting American foreign policy as well as the American way of life to other peoples of the world, especially to those in sensitive areas. The Voice of America broadcasts programs in many languages to various parts of the world. News summaries, political commentaries, and discussions of current issues of the day are combined with musical, cultural, and entertainment features. In the capitals and other large cities of the world, information centers are maintained to provide news services to newspapers and journals and to make material emanating from the United States available to public officials, business concerns, scholars, and others who are interested. Libraries are operated in many large centers of population to make books, periodicals, newspapers, and other printed materials from the United States available. Various books from the United States are brought out in cheap editions in the language of the country. Cultural programs involving the personal appearance of musicians, dramatists, and other artists from the United States may be scheduled, though the sending of major symphony orchestras and Broadway theatrical companies is usually a part of the cultural relations program of the Department of State. Exhibitions of paintings and other works of art from the United States may be put on. English instruction may be given. One of the programs attempts to facilitate the importation of university textbooks, technical publications, and the like at prices which the local residents can afford to pay. Many observers consider the ramified informational program as one of the most effective instrumentalities now being used by the United States in its foreign relations. Proposals to curtail such services often bring forth numerous protests under letters to the editors of foreign newspapers bearing the heading "How to Lose Friends."

FOREIGN POLICY OF THE UNITED STATES

It is not simple to acquire an accurate understanding of the foreign policy of the United States through the years. Indeed some complain of the difficulty of obtaining anything like a clear-cut view of the foreign policy at any given time. National attitudes have undergone changes, sometimes of a drastic character, through the years. This may make it hard to reconcile the position at one period with that of another. A country made up of such diverse elements of population as the United States and giving such an important role to public opinion and the desires of interest groups necessarily finds it far from easy to issue clear-cut statements of its foreign policies. Some degree of compromise of points of view is almost bound to appear and at times there may be indecision because of the conflicting interests.

Isolation. The warp upon which the United States wove its intricate pattern of foreign policy during many decades was isolation. From the early days of the republic, when George Washington delivered his famous words dealing with entangling alliances, to Pearl Harbor in 1941, there was a deep-seated desire on the part of many Americans to avoid more than routine relations with other countries. As individuals the American people have been fond of traveling outside of their own country and at times, during the nineteenth and early twentieth century, public opinion rather reluctantly supported active participation by the United States in international affairs. When the outcome of such participation turned out to be disappointing and especially when it appeared that the United States had been duped by other countries, however, the general suspicion of international diplomacy found support. The isolationist attitude was doubtless based in part on the geographic location of the United States in relation to other world powers.

Moreover, the fact that its natural resources made the country self-sufficient to a degree far beyond that of most other nations entered in. But World War II demonstrated the illusion of American geographical isolation and for various reasons brought the United States to a position of active participation in international affairs, though support for isolationism continues in some quarters.

Hemisphere security. Despite the isolationist sentiment in the United States and indeed to some extent as a result of it, the United States at an early date insisted that the western hemisphere be posted against European aggression. In 1823, President Monroe sent a message to Congress in which he declared: "We owe it therefore to candor and to amicable relations existing between the United States and those powers [the European countries] to declare that we should consider any attempt on their part to extend their system to any portion of this hemisphere as dangerous to our peace and safety." This doctrine, known as the Monroe Doctrine, was long interpreted as reserving the western hemisphere as a sort of sphere of influence to the United States and as such was sometimes resented by the Latin American countries. But what position should the United States take with respect to a Communist regime, more or less locally spawned, as in Cuba? Certainly Castro's original revolution found support in many Latin American countries. The abortive attempt by the United States to support an overthrow of the Castro government indicated indecision on our government's part in the face of such a dilemma. When actual Soviet missiles were uncovered in Cuba, however, it was fairly easy for the United States to obtain cooperation from Latin American states in defending this hemisphere against "outsiders."

Imperialism. In contrast to the attachment which many people of the United States had for isolationism, certain elements of the population have at times been anxious to have the government acquire additional territory and support economic penetration of other countries. The pressure for colonial expansion influenced American foreign policy at various periods. After the war with Mexico, extensive areas were taken from Mexico and incorporated into the states of Texas, New Mexico, Arizona, and California. At the turn of the century the Panama Canal Zone, Puerto Rico, and the Philippines were acquired. Even after the urge to acquire additional territory had largely subsided, there was still considerable pressure to have the military forces of the United States protect the investments of its citizens in certain foreign countries, particularly in Central America and the Caribbean. The last marine detachment was withdrawn from the Caribbean region as recently as 1934. The USSR continues to charge the United States with economic imperialism, maintaining that its foreign aid and other programs are disguised forms of imperialism, but the basis for such allegations does not appear very substantial.

International co-operation. During recent years and particularly since World War II, the United States has placed great emphasis upon international co-operation. The United States played a leading role in the establishment of the United Nations. Not only was the organizing conference held in San Francisco, but New York City was made the general headquarters or capital of the United Nations. The United States has taken an active part

A SESSION OF THE UNITED NATIONS GENERAL ASSEMBLY

in the many international organizations which have been set up by the United Nations and contributes more heavily to their support than does any other country. On occasion it is true that the United States may have seemed to bypass the United Nations, though it has never failed to give general recognition to the importance of international co-operation in the world. In its quest for international co-operation, the United States has sometimes been charged with failing to exert the decisive leadership which some regard as essential. In its desire to co-operate it has at times overlooked the non-democratic character of political regimes in other countries, especially in the Latin American area, thus giving them support which has been bitterly criticized in certain circles.

Regional co-operation. The Charter of the United Nations recognizes the need for both world-wide co-operation and regional efforts to promote peace. The United States has been active during recent years in supporting various regional groups, including the North Atlantic Treaty Organization (NATO), the South East Asia Treaty Organization (SEATO), and the

Organization of American States. To what extent the aim has been to strengthen international co-operation and to what extent such participation has been based on national defense considerations may not be entirely clear. Both factors have perhaps been present in the various regional groups, with co-operation more dominant in the case of the Organization of American States and security playing a primary role in NATO and SEATO.

Fear of communism. For many years the United States has had a widespread apprehension about communism as manifested in the Soviet Union and other so-called "red" regimes. It required many years for the United States to recognize the communist regime in Russia and then relations were hardly cordial. During World War II the attitude seemed to alter for a time; President Frankin D. Roosevelt and at least some of his associates attempted to follow a new policy which was based on a belief that the United States and the Soviet Union could work together as allies both during the war and after. But the course of events after the war steered American policy back to the earlier attitude of distrust. The experience in the Korean War hardened this policy, with the result that the United States has refused to recognize the People's Democracy of China or to countenance its admission to the United Nations. Some observers have concluded that the basic foreign policy of the United States during recent years has been dominated by this apprehension of communist regimes; others would not go so far, but it seems clear that this attitude of concern has had a considerable influence on the overall foreign policy of the United States as well as on many specific items. Thus the emphasis on NATO, on making allies rather than probationers out of West Germany and Japan, and on European affairs rather than Asian affairs has been closely tied to the fear of communist threats to destroy political systems based on a capitalist economy.

How to reconcile such apprehension with a desire to promote international co-operation has been one of the most complicated issues confronting the policy-makers. The policy of fear has brought a cold war which, in the eyes of many, might eventually develop into a holocaust involving mass destruction. A more positive attitude, which would promote international harmony by recognizing co-existence and make some relief from the heavy burden of national defense possible, has tremendous appeal. Certain statements from the communist countries to the effect that there is room in the world for the two systems gives support to such a positive policy. But communist spokesmen have also threatened to root out capitalism and capitalist states. It is difficult to know how far the recent conciliatory words can be trusted. Are these sincere or are they devices to beguile and eventually lead to destruction? If they are ignored, the way seems discouraging indeed, with indefinite cold war perhaps leading to atomic destruction whether intentional or not. But if they are accepted at face value and result in an unpreparedness which might be the occasion of western destruction, the prospects are even blacker. The dilemma is not a simple one.

A free world. Foreign policy statements by the United States during recent years have announced the "four freedoms," the right of every people to manage their own affairs, without interference from other countries, and the general desire of the United States to see a free world established. Some of these statements have merely announced the desire on the part of the United States for free elections everywhere, but others have at least implied that the United States followed a policy of containing the communist regimes to their present status, if not one of pledging itself to the eventual liberation of the satellites of these regimes. Few would perhaps question the wisdom of enunciating the principle of free elections and a free world in the western sense. Many on the other hand have expressed doubt as to the wisdom of a policy based on containment or the feasibility of a policy which commits the United States to liberate the peoples of Hungary, Czechoslovakia, Bulgaria, Poland, and other satellite countries.

Economic assistance. There has been an increasing recognition of the relation between democratic political systems and viable economies during recent years. At an earlier period it seemed enough to institute democratic forms, but experience has indicated that such forms are not likely to flourish in the absence of stable economic conditions. Even in the countries which have had experience with democratic institutions, certain difficulties have been apparent as a result of economic deficiencies. While the foreign policy of the United States has wavered as to what should be done in establishing a free world, it has followed a reasonably consistent path in the matter of economic assistance, although Congress annually carries on lengthy debates as to the exact amount of foreign aid to be extended.

Military strength. In his State of the Union Message in 1961, President Kennedy observed that "we are moving into a period of uncertain risk and great commitment in which both military and diplomatic possibilities require a free-world force, so powerful as to make any aggression clearly futile." Thus a basic instrument of our foreign policy remains that of maintaining a military force second to none.

Disarmament. The United States and the Soviet Union agree that disarmament may offer the world its only hope for a lasting peace. Any disarmament agreement among nations will have to proceed piecemeal. After the Soviet Union, first, and then the United States resumed atmospheric testing of atomic weapons, disarmament talks stressed the possibility of banning the testing of most types of atomic weapons. The United States took the position that such an agreement to be effective would require freedom for inspection teams to travel within the territory of all nuclear powers, a proposition opposed by the Soviet Union. Improvement in devices for detecting atomic explosions led to a modification of the United States' position with respect to inspection teams, and in 1963 the United States, the Soviet Union, and Great Britain signed the Test Ban Treaty. It is too early to know whether further disarmament will follow this first step.

SUMMARY

The President is charged with the primary responsibility for the conduct of foreign relations. Congress through its power over the purse and the authority of the Senate to ratify treaties and confirm ambassadors has considerable influence in this field. The President is assisted in the carrying on of foreign relations by the Secretary of State who may or may not be given a good deal of leeway. Preparatory work, conduct of negotiations, and implementation of foreign policies decided upon by the President are performed by ambassadors and ministers, by the Foreign Service, and by the State Department staff, as well as White House staff members.

The United States carries on relations with other countries through personal representation in foreign capitals, the exchange of notes, international conferences of various sorts, membership in international organizations, the making of treaties and other agreements, and through the use of agencies to administer its foreign aid and information programs.

BIBLIOGRAPHIC NOTE

General discussion of the conduct of foreign relations may be found in a number of books, including: Elmer Plischke, *Conduct of American Diplomacy* (rev. ed., Princeton, N. J.: D. Van Nostrand Company, Inc., 1961); J. L. McCamy, *The Administration of American Foreign Affairs* (New York: Alfred A. Knopf, 1959); Harley Notter, *Postwar Foreign Policy Preparation* (Washington, D. C.: Government Printing Office, 1950); R. H. Farrell, *American Diplomacy* (New York: W. W. Norton & Company, 1959); W. A. Williams (ed.), *Shaping of American Diplomacy* (New York: Rand McNally, 1956); K. London, *How Foreign Policy Is Made* (New York: D. Van Nostrand Company, Inc., 1949); *Governmental Mechanism for the Conduct of United States Foreign Relations* (Washington, D. C.: The Brookings Institution, 1949); and John Gange, *American Foreign Relations* (New York: Ronald Press, 1959). Though published many years ago, E. S. Corwin's *The President's Control of Foreign Relations* (Princeton, N. J.: Princeton University Press, 1917) remains a standard study of the basic role of the President. The place of the House of Representatives is canvassed in H. N. Carroll, *House of Representatives and Foreign Affairs* (Pittsburgh: University of Pittsburgh Press, 1958). The general role of Congress is treated in R. N. Dahl, *Congress and Foreign Policy* (New Haven: Yale University Press, 1949).

On the particular place of Secretaries of State in the conduct of foreign relations, students may consult the volumes in S. F. Bemis (ed.), *American Secretaries of State and Their Diplomacy* (rev. ed., New York: Pageant Book Co., 1958). For a detailed analysis of the Department of State, see Graham Stuart, *The Department of State; A History of Its Organization, Procedure, and Personnel* (New York: The Macmillan Company, 1949). Special administrative problems of the Department of State are discussed by one of the specialists called to advise on administrative reorganization, A. W. Macmahon, in *Administration in Foreign Affairs* (University: University of Alabama Press, 1953). J. R. Childs deals with the Foreign Service in *American Foreign Service* (New York: Henry Holt & Company, 1948). A particularly interesting survey of the problems of the field, with a number of points of view represented, is the report of the American Assembly entitled *Representation of the United States Abroad* (New York: Columbia University, 1956). Elmer Plischke's *Summit Diplomacy* (College Park: University of Maryland, 1958) discusses the role of high level international conferences in international relations. J. Mervyn Jones analyzes treaty-making in detail in *Full Powers and Ratification: A Study in the Development of Treaty-making Procedures* (New York: The Macmillan Company, 1947). Two recently published works are particularly useful. Seven participants in a conference of the American Assembly have set forth their ideas in Don K. Price (ed.), *The Secretary of State* (Englewood Cliffs, N. J.: Prentice-Hall, 1960). R. E. Elder in *The Policy Machine* (Syracuse, N. Y.: Syracuse University Press, 1960) deals with operations within the Department of State and the relations of this agency with the National Security Council.

General textbooks on American foreign policy include the following: T. A. Bailey, *A Diplomatic History of the American People* (rev. ed., New York: Appleton-Century-Crofts, 1957); R. J. Bartlett (ed.), *The Record of American Diplomacy* (rev. ed., New York: Alfred A. Knopf, 1954); M. M. Knappen, *Introduction to American Foreign Policy* (New York: Harper & Brothers, 1956); H. W. Barber, *Foreign Policies of the United States* (New York: The Dryden Press, 1953); E. S. Furniss and R. C. Snyder, *Introduction to American Foreign Policy* (New York: Rinehart & Company, 1955); *Major Problems of U. S. Foreign Policy* (Washington, D. C.: The Brookings Institution, 1954); L. L. Leonard (ed.), *Elements of American Foreign Policy* (New York: McGraw-Hill Book Company, 1955); J. W. Pratt, *History of U. S. Foreign Policy* (New York: Prentice-Hall, Inc., 1955); C. O. Lerche, *Foreign Policy of the American People* (Englewood Cliffs: Prentice-Hall, Inc., 1958); and Dexter Perkins, *The Evolution of American Foreign Policy* (New York: Oxford University Press, 1948). D. G. Acheson, *Power and Diplomacy* (Cambridge: Harvard University Press, 1958) and G. F. Kennan, *Realities of American Foreign Policy* (Princeton, N. J.: Princeton University Press, 1954) are very interesting expositions of certain aspects of foreign policy by former high level officials in the Department of State. B. C. Cohen, in *Political Process and Foreign Policy* (Princeton: Princeton University Press, 1957), traces the relationship between political forces and foreign policy. The report of the American Assembly conference *International Stability and Progress* (New York: Columbia University, 1957) presents various points of view in regard to economic assistance programs. C. L. Sulzberger, in *What's Wrong with U. S. Foreign Policy* (New York: Harcourt, Brace & Company, 1959), discusses the weaknesses of American policy as seen by a senior representative of the New York *Times* who specializes in international problems.

Three recent publications of note are: Norman A. Graebner, ed., *An Uncertain Tradition: American Secretaries of State in the Twentieth Century* (New York: McGraw-Hill Book Co., 1961); Wilson P. Dizard, *The Strategy of Truth: The Story of the U. S. Information Service* (Washington, D. C.: Public Affairs Press, 1961); and Warren F. Ilchman, *Professional Diplomacy in the United States: 1779-1939* (Chicago: University of Chicago Press, 1961).

The whole question of disarmament has caused considerable interest among writers in the field of foreign affairs. Two recent collections that can be profitably consulted are David H. Frisch (ed.), *Arms Reduction: Program and Issues* (New York: The Twentieth Century Fund, 1961) and Seymour Melman (ed.), *Disarmament: Its Politics and Economics* (Boston: The American Academy of Arts and Sciences, 1962).

29

The Territories and the District of Columbia

WITH the admission of Alaska and Hawaii as states and the establishment of the Philippines as an independent nation, territories have lost the limelight which they enjoyed earlier in United States history. Nevertheless, they can hardly be cast aside as unimportant even though their numbers and areas have been greatly reduced. The rapid development of Puerto Rico during recent years has added considerable interest to territorial administration. In contrast to the notable progress made in dealing with territorial problems either by admission as states or by creation of autonomous commonwealths, as in the case of Puerto Rico, little has been achieved in placing the District of Columbia on a sounder basis. Although the prospects appear somewhat brighter than they did before, this problem, which has aroused discussion for decades, appears to be one of the most complicated ones to be found on the list. Despite severe criticism of the existing arrangement, agreement as to change seems most difficult.

The relationship of Congress toward the territories of the United States is unitary rather than federal in nature. This means that the territories enjoy only the powers of government that Congress is willing for them to exercise. They do not have any residual powers, nor do they have any inherent rights of self-government. Congress has the power to retract any grants of governmental power which it may have allowed the territories.

TERRITORIAL HISTORY

A century ago the United States had vast territorial holdings in the North American continent. As a result of the Spanish American War, World War I and II, and the purchase of Alaska from Russia, other areas both on the continent and outside were added. Aside from the District of Columbia all of the continental area has now been organized into states. The Philippines have been given independence; the Hawaiian Islands have been set up as a state; the remaining territorial areas, except for Puerto Rico, consist of bits and pieces which are small in area and population and which are scattered over the world. Despite this record the United States is sometimes accused of being a colonial nation, grasping and avaricious and anxious to exploit the resources of helpless people. In some of the Latin American countries the reputation of the United States in this respect has been and perhaps to a considerable extent is still quite lurid. The United States is regarded as the "Colossus of the North," a gigantic ogre which has developed a taste for gobbling up smaller countries. Even now that few territories remain, the United States is sometimes charged with carrying out nefarious colonial ambitions indirectly—through puppets which in theory are independent but in reality depend upon the United States for orders.

At first it may appear that such charges are too ridiculous to warrant any attention whatsoever, but the persistence of the charges and the genuine apprehension to be observed in certain quarters makes a brief look at the record desirable. Much of the reputation seems to stem from past events. It is not often remembered in the United States that a generous portion of the republic was taken by force from Mexico. The land included in the states of California, Texas, New Mexico, and Arizona was once either entirely or largely owned by Mexico. The United States then secured these areas and added them to round out her borders. Puerto Rico and the Philippine Islands were separated from Spain as a result of the Spanish American War. The Panama Canal Zone affair was handled more from behind the scenes, but there is a widespread feeling in the Latin American countries that it represents another case of aggression.

The United States is sometimes charged with intervention in and exploitation of other countries. Indeed at present the greater part of the allegations made arise from such alleged American activities. It is charged that the United States gives economic and military aid to regimes that will take orders and uses various pressures to pull down regimes that it dislikes. Programs like the Marshall Plan have done a good deal to convince many observers of the falsity of these charges. The willingness of the United States to surrender bases in countries like Morocco, where it has expended hundreds of millions of dollars, also indicates to some erstwhile critics that the United States is basically not a colonial power. But the past record has not been unblemished and it is not easy to live down the past. The role of the United States in the affairs of the post World War II world makes it possible for diverse interpretations to be offered as to its purpose and goals.

TYPES OF TERRITORIES

Two formal types of territories have been recognized under the law and in the courts of the United States; they are unincorporated and incorporated. In addition, some areas have a special status and do not readily fall into a definite category. The Supreme Court of the United States has held that the constitution does not automatically follow the flag[1] and that Congress has broad discretion under the provision of the Constitution which reads: "The Congress shall have power to dispose of and make all needful rules and regulations respecting the territory or other property belonging to the United States; and nothing in this Constitution shall be so construed as to prejudice any claims of the United States, or of any particular state." Unless Congress ordains by law or a treaty provides otherwise, a territory is regarded as being unincorporated. This means that Congress may set up any form of government that it pleases if reasonable attention is paid to the general principles underlying the Constitution. The inhabitants of unincorporated territories are not citizens of the United States; nor are they entitled to the constitutional rights of jury trial, grand jury indictment, and related personal freedoms. Unincorporated territories are not a part of the United States, at least technically, and hence import duties may be levied upon goods sent from them to the United States, much as it is levied on foreign products.

An incorporated territory, on the other hand, is part of the United States. Its inhabitants are recognized as citizens of the United States. As far as is applicable, the Constitution applies to it. Alaska and Hawaii, before admission as states, were regarded as incorporated territories in every sense. The distinction between incorporated and unincorporated territories is perhaps less significant at present than it was in the past. With Alaska and Hawaii admitted as states and Puerto Rico occupying an autonomous status, handling its own affairs in general though attached to the United States, the fairly elaborate reasoning of the Supreme Court, that differentiated between incorporated and unincorporated territories and even goes so far as to divide unincorporated territories into classes, does not seem to have the practical significance of an earlier day.

Special types of territories may now present more problems than the traditional variety. Okinawa and the other Pacific islands, which were part of Japan and were occupied by the United States during World War II, do not fit well into the ordinary system of territories and their future status may be uncertain. The air and naval bases in the Atlantic and Pacific, which came to the United States during World War II, also have special status. The latter usually have few native inhabitants and may present little in the way of administrative problems, but Okinawa in the Pacific has a sizable local population which has to be dealt with.

ADMINISTRATION OF TERRITORIES

The United States has not seen fit to make any uniform arrangements for the administration of its various territories. Prior to the 1930's it was

---

[1] See *Balzac* v. *People of Porto Rico*, 258 U. S. 298 (1922).

customary to consider territorial administration as primarily related to military administration. The Philippines were long handled by the War Department. The Navy Department assumed responsibility for Samoa and other Pacific insular territories other than Hawaii. It was perhaps natural at the time to emphasize the national defense aspect of territorial administration, but growing criticism was generated by the secondary attention given to the welfare of the peoples of the territories. The result was the transfer of general oversight of the territories, except for a few tiny areas in the Pacific, to a Division of Territories and Island Possessions in the Department of the Interior.

The military departments continued to display an interest in the territories which were significant from the standpoint of national defense and of course controlled bases and military installations. But the Department of the Interior carried the main responsibility for civil affairs. Though far from perfect, this new arrangement resulted in substantial improvement in many areas. The local inhabitants felt more satisfied; greater emphasis was placed on education and public welfare.

World War II interrupted the transfer of territorial administration from military to civil auspices. Hawaii and Alaska were both very important in the Pacific war and the military departments naturally felt entitled to major authority during the war years. With the end of the war, Alaska and Hawaii again resumed their places under the Department of the Interior, but there were various areas taken over from the Japanese which remained under military administration. Nevertheless, some progress has been made recently in moving toward civil administration of the remaining territories. Guam, for example, long under military rule, was given a civil government and placed under the Department of the Interior in 1950.

THE FUTURE OF THE TERRITORIES

For many years prior to 1959, there was lively discussion about the future of the territories. Alaska and Hawaii had assumed such importance and were so anxious for statehood that the question of their future almost invariably arose in every session of Congress, in every State of the Union message to Congress from the President, and in every national political convention. The admission of Alaska and Hawaii to statehood after many years of argument had the effect of sharply reducing the discussion about the future of territories. There remained a certain amount of speculation as to Puerto Rico, with some arguing that Puerto Rico should become a state and others insisting that it should be given full independence. But such discussion tended to be desultory, since the majority of Puerto Ricans seemed to be reasonably satisfied with their autonomous position as a commonwealth enjoying substantial financial benefits without having to take on the financial burdens of complete independence. It is possible that the temper of public opinion in Puerto Rico may change and the question of admission to statehood or full independence may become a real one. However, the immediate situation is not such as to suggest this.

The remaining territories are small in area and in population and appear to be neither well suited for statehood nor for independence. At one time it would probably have been presumed that their fate was permanently to remain as military bases or at least areas where self-government was not feasible. But the events of the last decade have demonstrated the deep desire and even demand on the part of even small groups to be given

PRESIDENT EISENHOWER SIGNING THE HAWAIIAN STATEHOOD ACT

control over their local affairs at least. Obviously the United States cannot ignore this, and it seems likely that some arrangement will have to be worked out under which the inhabitants of the remaining small territories will have more of a voice in their own affairs. The former Japanese islands in the Pacific have not been forgotten by Japan and it may be that they will be returned to that country, particularly if international tensions subside. Panama periodically becomes aroused over the status of the Panama Canal Zone, and it is conceivable that some agreement will be made providing for a transfer. The military bases scattered here and there present a different problem. Some of them are under limited leases and presumably will be given up at their expiration. Others have been permanently transferred to the United States, but this permanence hardly means what it did some years ago.

PUERTO RICO

As a territory, Puerto Rico now occupies a position as a mountain among molehills. Its area is not large in comparison with that of many of the states of the United States, but it far exceeds that of other territories. Its congested and rapidly increasing population dwarfs that of any other territory and indeed considerably surpasses the populations of a number of states. Puerto Rico came to the United States as a result of the Spanish American War. For many years it held an uncertain status because the United States did not seem to know what to do with it. Although the Foraker Act of 1900 made some provision for its government, it was not until 1917 that Congress finally got around to passing an organic act which applied especially to the island. Even after the organic act was passed, the situation in Puerto Rico remained more or less critical. The population was larger than the island could support on a reasonable standard; the resources were not great and remained largely undeveloped; and the economy was by and large a stagnant one. On visiting the island after many years of American administration, a former President of the United States characterized Puerto Rico as a gigantic poorhouse. The situation was aggravated by general indifference in Washington and by a disposition to reward political worthies from the United States with appointments in the government of Puerto Rico. The Puerto Rican people were divided and often displayed great bitterness toward other factions as well as toward the United States.

It was not until the 1930's that the situation began to take a turn for the better. Instead of appointing political hangerson to positions in Puerto Rico, Washington came to realize that the very least that it could do was to send governors and others with some knowledge of Puerto Rican problems and a desire to ameliorate the tragic shortcomings. Certain of the welfare programs of the 1930's assisted by making available substantial sums for alleviating the misery in Puerto Rico. In 1944 the President of the United States promised the Puerto Ricans that they would be permitted to elect their own governor as soon as feasible. Moreover, a commission was sent to the island to investigate conditions and recommend steps for improvement. The internal conflict among the people of Puerto Rico began to subside; Puerto Rican leaders of ability began to appear on the scene; effective political party organization began to function, at first very feebly but gradually gaining strength. Finally, in 1949 Puerto Rico was set up as an autonomous commonwealth, remaining attached to the United States but given authority over internal affairs.

The achievements of the Puerto Ricans since 1949 have been striking. Primary emphasis has perhaps been placed on strengthening the economy, since it is recognized that most other developments depend upon building economic stability and improving the standard of living. It would be inaccurate to say that this goal has been completely realized, but far more has been done in a decade than had been done in several earlier decades. There is still widespread poverty, and many Puerto Ricans continue to leave their homeland for New York City to find a livelihood. But hundreds of industries have been attracted to Puerto Rico under an imaginative scheme which relieves them from normal taxes during an initial period. Elaborate schemes of public improvements have been inaugurated. Efforts have been made toward developing resources. The result is that the Puerto Rico of today can hardly be recognized by those who knew it a few years ago. Accomplishments in the fields of education, public health, public administration, and related areas have been less spectacular than those on the economic side, but they have been substantial.

The general pattern of government in Puerto Rico resembles that of a state, but one must always take into account the Latin temperament of the people which may result in rather different manifestations and end products. The governor is elected by the voters and exercises strong powers. To what extent the record of the one and only incumbent of the office since 1949 is the result of the authority vested in the office and to what extent it stems from the vigorous personal qualities of the man himself is not easy to determine. Certainly no one can deny the very great role of the governor in the progress made since 1949 or in the current operations.

There is a bicameral legislature, with a membership smaller than is to be found in many states. The members are elected by adult citizens who can pass a literacy test. Most of the members of both the senate and house of representatives are chosen on the basis of single-member districts, but in both houses several members are elected to represent the people at large. The powers of the legislature are reasonably broad, with the usual right to levy taxes, to make appropriations, and to deal with local matters. The governor may veto acts of the legislature, with repassage over his veto by a two thirds vote. The leadership of the governor in the legislative field has been notable. The President of the United States and Congress have authority to check certain types of action, but little or no use is made of such power.

The government of Puerto Rico has the administrative departments usually found in a state: education, attorney general, finance, health, agriculture, labor, and interior. The heads of the departments serve as an advisory council to the governor. A system of courts culminates in a supreme court of five members. The voters elect a resident commissioner to represent them in the House of Representatives in Washington, but he has only the right to speak there; he does not have the right to vote.

VIRGIN ISLANDS

The Virgin Islands were acquired by purchase from Denmark in 1917. They are of special interest to the United States because of their proximity to the Panama Canal. Under the control of the President for some two decades, they were given a reasonable measure of freedom in handling their own affairs by an act of Congress passed in 1936. Even before this, in 1927, the residents had been made citizens of the United States. The heady influence of recent developments in nearby Puerto Rico has given rise to discontent among the Virgin Islanders, and there is now a campaign to persuade Congress to confer broader authority over local affairs on the islands' government. A governor, appointed by the President with the consent of the Senate, heads the executive branch of the government and reports to the Department of the Interior in Washington. The territorial legislature consists of a unicameral body of members called Senators. These are elected for two-year terms, six at large, two each from St. Thomas and St. Croix, and one from St. John. There is a district court to handle the more important civil and criminal cases; local courts deal with less important cases.

GUAM

Guam is the largest of the Mariana Islands, but even so it has an area of only about 225 square miles and a population of some 38,000. It was acquired from Spain in 1898. Because of its fine harbor, it has been of interest to the Navy and has been, until recently, administered primarily as a naval station rather than as a civil territory. The Navy has taken its responsibilities seriously, but it has naturally given most attention to its own activities on the island. For some years there was a feeling, both among the people of Guam and in certain quarters of the United States, that a more adequate provision for civil government was desirable. Various official recommendations were made looking toward this end, but it was not until 1950 that Congress got around to passing an organic act for Guam. This confers citizenship in the United States on the people of Guam and authorizes a considerable measure of self-government over local affairs.

SAMOA

The eastern section of the island of Samoa became a protectorate of the United States as a result of the Anglo-German-American agreement of 1900. World War I saw Germany pushed out of Samoa and the administration shared between the United States and Great Britain. Less populous than Guam, the American part of Samoa has a population of about 20,000. As in the case of Guam, Samoa has been primarily the concern of the Navy and indeed was not formally recognized by Congress as a territory until 1929. Since July 1, 1951, Samoa has been administered by the Department of the Interior which appoints a governor and a secretary. It has a bicameral legislature. A new constitution authorizing increased self-government was drafted in 1960.

PANAMA CANAL ZONE

The zone which surrounds the Panama Canal is held by the United States on a perpetual lease from the Republic of Panama. Some in Panama maintain that such a lease was given under duress and that it should be terminated, with the area returned to Panamanian control. A strip of land only five miles wide through which runs the Panama Canal, this territory is minuscule though it has a population exceeding fifty thousand. It occupies a larger place than its size would indicate in territorial affairs of the United States because of its military and commercial importance. A governor, appointed by the President with the consent of the Senate, has the responsibility of full administration, since there is no legislative body. Laws are prescribed by Congress or by the President. There is a district court and a system of local magistrates' courts. The bill of rights of the Constitution is regarded as in effect in the Canal Zone, though it is not a fully incorporated territory.

FORMER JAPANESE TERRITORIES

At the end of World War II the United States found herself in possession of various Japanese territories located in the western and southern parts of the Pacific. The Marianas, Marshalls, and Carolines, with a total land area of less than one thousand sqaure miles, had been administered by Japan as a mandate under the League of Nations. Okinawa, the Bonin Islands, and other islands owned outright by Japan were the scene of some of the bitterest fighting of World War II and were regarded as of strategic importance. To begin with, all were administered by the United States under a military government setup. Some of the territories have been returned to Japan under the peace treaty made with the United States. The former mandated territories have been organized into the Territory of the Pacific Islands and placed under the trusteeship of the United States by the United Nations. The principal territorial problem is represented by areas considered of strategic importance, of which Okinawa is the best known. Japan would like to have these returned, but the United States is reluctant to surrender control because of the international uncertainty in the western Pacific. Both the Army and Navy have been concerned with the occupation of these islands, with the naval role paramount. Various programs have been launched to improve education and public works, to foster agricultural production, and to provide adequate housing facilities, but the inhabitants have been restive at times even after elections were authorized. The uncertain future of the islands make it difficult to plan for their permanent civil administration.

LEASED AIR AND NAVAL BASES

In concluding this brief discussion of territories it may be appropriate to refer to the naval and air bases leased from various foreign countries, though these are not strictly territories. A good many arrangements have been made with foreign countries to permit American bases to be established. Some of these call for temporary use of land; others provide for leases of 99 years, and in a few cases perpetual control has been authorized. The European and African bases fall into the former category, while the bases stretching from Newfoundland to British Guiana received from Great Britain in 1940 are held either for long terms or in a few instances perpetually. These bases are very largely, if not entirely, military in character and are administered directly by the military services of the United States. They are very small in area and have few civilian inhabitants. They have been mainly in the limelight because of the attempts on the part of some of the parties concerned, for example, Morocco and Trinidad, to terminate the leases.

THE DISTRICT OF COLUMBIA

The framers of the Constitution perceived that the rivalry and jealousy among the states was such that it would be unwise to locate the permanent seat of government within the confines of any one of them. Both Philadelphia and New York City served as headquarters of the national government for a time, but the constitutional provision giving Congress the power "to exercise exclusive jurisdiction in all cases whatsoever, over such district (not exceeding ten miles square) as may, by cession of particular States, and the acceptance of Congress, become the seat of the government of the United States," [2] indicates that the framers had other arrangements in mind as soon as they could be conveniently made. Negotiations were started shortly, and the first Congress which, convened in 1789, staged a long-drawn-out and frequently highly emotional debate as to whether the national capital should be located in the North or the South. A compromise was finally reached; the necessary land was ceded by Maryland and Virginia; and the seat of government was moved to the District of Columbia on the Potomac in 1800. Various other countries follow a similar policy in separating the national capital from the rest of the country—Argentina, Brazil, and Mexico may be cited as examples.

At times there has been some discussion of the wisdom of the decision to locate the national capital on the Potomac near the Atlantic seaboard. In light of the expansion of the country from the Atlantic to the Pacific

---

[2] Art. II, sec. 8.

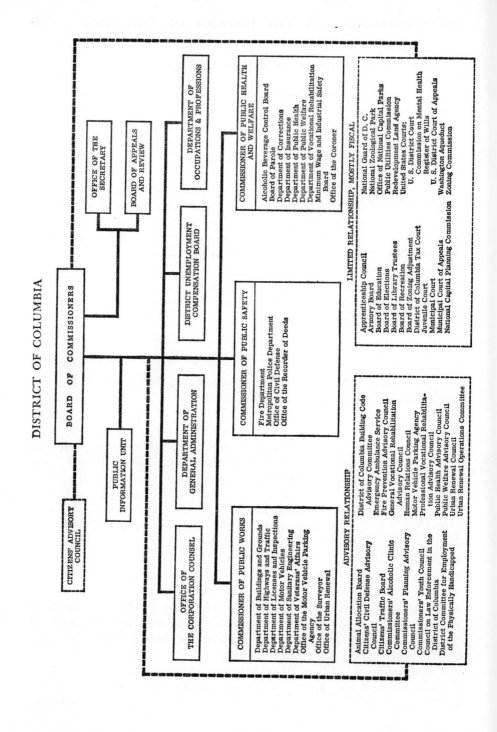

DISTRICT OF COLUMBIA

BOARD OF COMMISSIONERS

CITIZENS' ADVISORY COUNCIL

PUBLIC INFORMATION UNIT

OFFICE OF THE CORPORATION COUNSEL

DEPARTMENT OF GENERAL ADMINISTRATION

OFFICE OF THE SECRETARY

BOARD OF APPEALS AND REVIEW

DEPARTMENT OF OCCUPATIONS & PROFESSIONS

DISTRICT UNEMPLOYMENT COMPENSATION BOARD

COMMISSIONER OF PUBLIC HEALTH AND WELFARE

Alcoholic Beverage Control Board
Board of Parole
Department of Corrections
Department of Insurance
Department of Public Health
Department of Public Welfare
Department of Vocational Rehabilitation
Minimum Wage and Industrial Safety Board
Office of the Coroner

COMMISSIONER OF PUBLIC SAFETY

Fire Department
Metropolitan Police Department
Office of Civil Defense
Office of the Recorder of Deeds

COMMISSIONER OF PUBLIC WORKS

Department of Buildings and Grounds
Department of Highways and Traffic
Department of Licenses and Inspections
Department of Motor Vehicles
Department of Sanitary Engineering
Department of Veterans' Affairs
Office of the Motor Vehicle Parking Agency
Office of the Surveyor
Office of Urban Renewal

ADVISORY RELATIONSHIP

Animal Allocation Board
Citizens' Civil Defense Advisory Council
Citizens' Traffic Board
Commissioners' Alcoholic Clinic Committee
Commissioners' Planning Advisory Council
Commissioners' Youth Council
Council on Law Enforcement in the District of Columbia
District Committee for Employment of the Physically Handicapped
District of Columbia Building Code Advisory Committee
Emergency Ambulance Service
Fire Prevention Advisory Council
General Vocational Rehabilitation Advisory Council
Human Relations Council
Motor Vehicle Parking Agency
Professional Vocational Rehabilitation Advisory Council
Public Health Advisory Council
Public Welfare Advisory Council
Urban Renewal Council
Urban Renewal Operations Committee

LIMITED RELATIONSHIP, MOSTLY FISCAL

Apprenticeship Council
Armory Board
Board of Education
Board of Elections
Board of Library Trustees
Board of Recreation
Board of Zoning Adjustment
District of Columbia Tax Court
Juvenile Court
Municipal Court
Municipal Court of Appeals
National Capital Planning Commission
National Guard of D. C.
National Zoological Park
Office of National Capital Parks
Public Utilities Commission
Redevelopment Land Agency
United States Courts:
    U. S. District Court
    Commission on Mental Health
    Register of Wills
    U. S. District Court of Appeals
Washington Aqueduct
Zoning Commission

and now far to the north of the continent in the case of Alaska and well out in the Pacific in the case of Hawaii, the District of Columbia is not conveniently situated from the standpoint of the majority of the inhabitants. A location somewhere near the geographical center would be more logical, but the decision was made when few could foresee the expansion. Once the discussion was made it could not easily be altered.

Early provisions. The national capital was laid out under an elaborate plan drawn up by the famous French city planner, Major Pierre Charles L'Enfant, who had so much to do with the layout of modern Paris. Instead of following the traditional gridiron or checkerboard pattern which seems to be the favorite of many Americans, Major L'Enfant laid out broad avenues which, instead of running parallel, converge on the government buildings, particularly the capitol buildings like the spokes of a wheel. The L'Enfant plan has not been followed fully, but even so it gives to Washington a character of its own. It was considered desirable by the early Congresses that the inhabitants of the District of Columbia should be given a measure of local self-government, even if they were not entitled to elect senators and representatives. It may be of interest at this point to note that in such countries as Argentina and Mexico the people of the federal district are given representatives in the national legislature. But having fought for independence on the basis of no taxation without representation, our forefathers did not see fit to extend representation to the inhabitants of the District of Columbia. But for approximately three quarters of a century the residents of the District who qualified as voters betook themselves to the polls and elected a mayor and members of a city council who were entrusted with the usual functions of local government.

Unfortunately this arrangement did not work out very well in practice, though there is some question whether it was more objectionable than local government elsewhere at the time. The period of the Civil War and for some years after saw municipal government at perhaps its lowest level. These were the days of the Tweed Ring in New York City, the Gas Ring in Philadelphia, and notorious machines in most large cities. Corruption seemed to be the rule in urban government throughout the United States. Washington was no exception, and its local government was characterized by graft, extravagance, and general inefficiency.

From 1871 until 1874 Congress experimented with a territorial form of government for the District of Columbia; the new form of administration was composed of a governor, a board of public works, and a legislative assembly consisting of a Council and a House of Delegates elected by the people. At the same time the District of Columbia was represented in the lower house of Congress by a delegate.

Beginning in 1874 a change was made, and the District was governed by three Commissioners appointed by the President. This change was made permanent four years later.

Present provisions. Under the provisions made by Congress in 1878 and continued to the present day with rather minor modifications, Congress itself makes the necessary ordinances, levies taxes, and appropriates funds for the operation of the District of Columbia. The second and fourth Mondays of each month are supposed to be devoted to performing in the capacity of a city council for Washington. Congress has found itself so loaded down with business and so many of its members are more or less indifferent to district affairs that it actually delegates much of its authority in this field to standing committees which it has set up to deal with the District of Columbia. These committees have to have the formal approval of the entire Congress of course for most of their actions, but this is ordinarily rather routine. These committees are sometimes known as the "Washington City Council," and certainly have a great deal to do with district administration.

Three commissioners are provided to work in conjunction with the congressional committees and to carry out their decisions. Two of these are appointed by the President with the consent of the Senate from among the residents of the District of Columbia for three-year terms. A third commissioner is an officer of the Engineers Corps of the Army who is detailed by the President for an indefinite period for such service. As a group the commissioners meet to draw up routine regulations relating to public safety, health, and the use and protection of property. They appoint the officials who carry on the many functions entailed in running the district and supervise the general operation of all branches of the district government, with the exception of the schools which are entrusted to a board of education whose members are appointed by the judges of the district court. Each commissioner assumes direct charge of a section of the district administration. The engineer handles public works; a second commissioner gives attention to the protection of person and property; while a third deals with health, public welfare, and related items.

Proposed changes. The affairs of the District of Columbia have been administered with at least reasonable efficiency under the system outlined above and there has been no flagrant corruption. The public works seem to be well above the average, with adequately paved streets which are well maintained. The standards in the schools have been praised. The housing situation has been critical and particularly among the large Negro population has been critical despite the slum-clearance program. But dissatisfaction on the part of the residents has been widespread and at times there has been bitter criticism of a system under which the inhabitants have no direct voice in the handling of local affairs. The national government appropriates annually a substantial sum of money as its contribution toward meeting the costs of operating the various services, but the inhabitants often complain bitterly at the size of this contribution, alleging that they are forced to pay through property and other taxes for services which should in all fairness be borne by the government whose buildings and other properties are so numerous in the District of Columbia and which are tax exempt.

Home Rule for the District of Columbia? In the last fifteen or twenty years residents of the District of Columbia have been assiduously pressing for "home rule," in the form of an elected mayor and council with powers to enact local laws. Both political parties have endorsed in principle this idea in their national platforms. In 1959 the Senate passed for the fifth time in ten years a bill which would permit an elected mayor and council and a non-voting delegate to the House of Representatives. The Committee for the District has traditionally blocked all efforts to pass a home-rule law in the House of Representatives.

In 1960 Congress approved a proposed constitutional amendment which permits the District of Columbia to participate in the election of the President, with three electoral votes. Within a few months the necessary three-fourths of the states ratified the proposal.

SUMMARY

The stage has been reached where territories occupy a smaller place in the national scene than at any previous period. With the admission of Alaska and Hawaii as states, all of the continental area owned by the United States, except for the District of Columbia, has been removed from territorial status and indeed the boundaries of the states have been extended far into the Pacific. The remaining territories, except for Puerto Rico, are small in area and in population and in the case of Puerto Rico there appears at present to be little desire either for statehood or complete independence. The chief problem relating to territories is that of providing adequate civil administrations which will give the local inhabitants a reasonable voice in handling their own affairs, at the same time recognizing the legitimate interest of the military services in their strategic facilities. The District of Columbia presents a special problem which after many years of discussion and a great deal of local dissatisfaction has not even been partially solved. The affairs of the District of Columbia are administered by congressional committees and three commissioners named by the President. Although the standards of administration are reasonably good in general, the hundreds of thousands of local residents are critical because they have no direct voice and feel that they are forced to pay an unfair share of the costs.

BIBLIOGRAPHIC NOTE

With the Philippines an independent nation and both Alaska and Hawaii admitted as states of the union, the literature relating to territories is not as extensive as has been the case in the past. W. H. Haas, *The American Empire* (Chicago: University of Chicago Press, 1940) surveys the territorial field as it existed prior to World War II. No general survey of the scene since the far-reaching developments which have taken place since World War II is available, though the Department of State publication entitled *Non-Self-Governing Territories,* Washington, 1947, covers a section of the field.

The earlier depressing years in Puerto Rico are vividly portrayed in R. G. Tugwell, *Stricken Land: The Story of Puerto Rico* (New York: Doubleday & Company, Inc., 1947) by a sometime governor who was prominently associated with the New Deal and has served on the faculties of Columbia and Chicago Universities. Some idea of the transformation which has taken place in Puerto Rico during recent years may be gained from the series of articles in the *Annals of the American Academy of Political and Social Science* (1953) published under the title *Puerto Rico: A Study in Democratic Development.* For the most recent changes, students may consult reports of speeches by Governor Muñoz and other articles in the New York *Times* and other newspapers. Also worth consulting is Vicenzo Petrillo, *Puerto Rican Paradox* (Philadelphia: University of Pennsylvania Press, 1947). A very recent book on developments in Puerto Rico is Homer Page, *Puerto Rico: The Quiet Revolution* (New York: Viking Press, 1963).

L. H. Evans, *The Virgin Islands* (Ann Arbor: J. W. Edwards, 1945) covers developments in the Virgin Islands down to World War II, but there have been changes since. Norman J. Padelford, *The Panama Canal in Peace and War* (New York: The Macmillan Company, 1942) and W. D. McCain, *The United States and the Republic of Panama* (Durham, N. C.: Duke University Press, 1937) discuss problems of the Panama Canal Zone but again do not bring the story up to date.

The two well known books, L. Schmeckebier, *The District of Columbia; Its Government and Administration* (Washington, D. C.: Brookings Institution, 1928) and L. Schmeckebier and W. F. Willoughby, *The Government and Administration of the District of Columbia; Suggestions for Change* (Washington, D. C.: Brookings Institution, 1929) are still worth consulting despite the many years which have elapsed since their publication. The best of the recent materials on the District of Columbia is Martha Derthick, *City Politics in Washington, D. C.* (Cambridge: Harvard University Press, 1962).

Constitution of the United States

PREAMBLE

We the people of the United States, in order to form a more perfect union, establish justice, insure domestic tranquillity, provide for the common defense, promote the general welfare, and secure the blessing of liberty to ourselves and our posterity, do ordain and establish this Constitution for the United States of America.

ARTICLE I

Section 1. All legislative powers herein granted shall be vested in a Congress of the United States, which shall consist of a Senate and House of Representatives.

Section 2. 1. The House of Representatives shall be composed of members chosen every second year by the people of the several States, and the electors in each State shall have the qualifications requisite for electors of the most numerous branch of the State legislature.

2. No person shall be a representative who shall not have attained to the age of twenty-five years, and been seven years a citizen of the United States, and who shall not, when elected, be an inhabitant of that State in which he shall be chosen.

3. Representatives and direct taxes[1] shall be apportioned among the several States which may be included within this Union, according to their respective numbers, which shall be determined by adding to the whole number of free persons, including those bound to service for a term of years, and excluding Indians not taxed, three-fifths of all other persons.[2] The actual enumeration shall be made within three years after the first meeting of the Congress of the United States, and within every subsequent term of ten years, in such manner as they shall by law direct. The number of representatives shall not exceed one for every thirty thousand, but each State shall have at least one representative; and until such enumeration shall be made, the State of New Hampshire shall be entitled to choose three, Massachusetts eight, Rhode Island and Providence Plantation one, Connecticut five, New York six, New Jersey four, Pennsylvania eight, Delaware one, Maryland six, Virginia ten, North Carolina five, South Carolina five, and Georgia three.

---

[1] See the Sixteenth Amendment.

[2] Partly superseded by the Fourteenth Amendment.

617

4. When vacancies happen in the representation from any State, the executive authority thereof shall issue writs of election to fill such vacancies.

5. The House of Representatives shall choose their speaker and other officers, and shall have the sole power of impeachment.

Section 3. 1. The Senate of the United States shall be composed of two senators from each State, chosen by the legislature thereof,[3] for six years; and each senator shall have one vote.

2. Immediately after they shall be assembled in consequence of the first election, they shall be divided as equally as may be into three classes. The seats of the senators of the first class shall be vacated at the expiration of the second year, of the second class at the expiration of the fourth year, and of the third class at the expiration of the sixth year, so that one third may be chosen every second year; and if vacancies happen by resignation, or otherwise, during the recess of the legislature of any State, the executive thereof may make temporary appointments until the next meeting of the legislature, which shall then fill such vacancies.[4]

3. No person shall be a senator who shall not have attained to the age of thirty years, and been nine years a citizen of the United States, and who shall not, when elected, be an inhabitant of that State for which he shall be chosen.

4. The Vice President of the United States shall be President of the Senate, but shall have no vote, unless they be equally divided.

5. The Senate shall choose their other officers, and also a president *pro tempore,* in the absence of the Vice President, or when he shall exercise the office of President of the United States.

6. The Senate shall have the sole power to try all impeachments. When sitting for that purpose, they shall be on oath or affirmation. When the President of the United States is tried, the chief justice shall preside: and no person shall be convicted without the concurrence of two thirds of the members present.

7. Judgment in cases of impeachment shall not extend further than to removal from office, and disqualifications to hold and enjoy any office of honor, trust or profit under the United States: but the party convicted shall nevertheless be liable and subject to indictment, trial, judgment and punishment, according to law.

Section 4. 1. The times, places, and manner of holding elections for senators and representatives, shall be prescribed in each State by the legislature thereof; but the Congress may at any time by law make or alter such regulations, except as to the places of choosing senators.

2. The Congress shall assemble at least once in every year, and such meeting shall be on the first Monday in December, unless they shall by law appoint a different day.

---

[3] See the Seventeenth Amendment.
[4] *Ibid.*

Section 5. 1. Each House shall be the judge of the elections, returns and qualifications of its own members, and a majority of each shall constitute a quorum to do business; but a smaller number may adjourn from day to day, and may be authorized to compel the attendance of absent members, in such manner, and under such penalties as each House may provide.

2. Each House may determine the rules of its proceedings, punish its members for disorderly behavior, and, with the concurrence of two thirds, expel a member.

3. Each House shall keep a journal of its proceedings, and from time to time publish the same, excepting such parts as may in their judgment require secrecy; and the yeas and nays of the members of either House on any question shall, at the desire of one fifth of those present, be entered on the journal.

4. Neither House, during the session of Congress, shall, without the consent of the other, adjourn for more than three days, nor to any other place than that in which the two Houses shall be sitting.

Section 6. 1. The senators and representatives shall receive a compensation for their services, to be ascertained by law, and paid out of the Treasury of the United States. They shall in all cases, except treason, felony and breach of the peace, be privileged from arrest during their attendance at the session of their respective Houses, and in going to and returning from the same; and for any speech or debate in either House, they shall not be questioned in any other place.

2. No senator or representative shall, during the time for which he was elected, be appointed to any civil office under the authority of the United States, which shall have been created, or the emoluments whereof shall have been increased during such time, and no person holding any office under the United States shall be a member of either House during his continuance in office.

Section 7. 1. All bills for raising revenue shall originate in the House of Representatives; but the Senate may propose or concur with amendments as on other bills.

2. Every bill which shall have passed the House of Representatives and the Senate, shall, before it becomes a law, be presented to the President of the United States; if he approve he shall sign it, but if not he shall return it, with his objection to that House in which it shall have originated, who shall enter the objections at large on their journal, and proceed to reconsider it. If after such reconsideration two thirds of that House shall agree to pass the bill, it shall be sent, together with the objections, to the other House, by which it shall likewise be reconsidered, and if approved by two thirds of that House, it shall become a law. But in all such cases the votes of both Houses shall be determined by yeas and nays, and the names of the persons voting for and against the bill shall be entered on the journal of each House respectively. If any bill shall not be returned by the President within ten days (Sundays excepted) after

it shall have been presented to him, the same shall be a law, in like manner as if he had signed it, unless the Congress by their adjournment prevent its return, in which case it shall not be a law.

3. Every order, resolution, or vote to which the concurrence of the Senate and House of Representatives may be necessary (except on a question of adjournment) shall be presented to the President of the United States, and before the same shall take effect, shall be approved by him, or being disapproved by him, shall be repassed by two thirds of the Senate and House of Representatives, according to the rules and limitations prescribed in the case of a bill.

Section 8. 1. The Congress shall have the power to lay and collect taxes, duties, imposts, and excises, to pay the debts and provide for the common defense and general welfare of the United States, but all duties, imposts, and excises shall be uniform throughout the United States.

2. To borrow money on the credit of the United States.

3. To regulate commerce with foreign nations, and among the several states, and with the Indian tribes;

4. To establish an uniform rule of naturalization, and uniform laws on the subject of bankruptcies throughout the United States;

5. To coin money, regulate the value thereof, and of foreign coin, and fix the standard of weights and measures;

6. To provide for the punishment of counterfeiting the securities and current coin of the United States;

7. To establish post offices and post roads;

8. To promote the progress of science and useful arts, by securing for limited times to authors and inventors the exclusive right to their respective writings and discoveries;

9. To constitute tribunals inferior to the Supreme Court;

10. To define and punish piracies and felonies committed on the high seas, and offenses against the law of nations;

11. To declare war, grant letters of marque and reprisal, and make rules concerning captures on land and water;

12. To raise and support armies, but no appropriation of money to that use shall be for a longer term than two years;

13. To provide and maintain a navy;

14. To make rules for the government and regulation of the land and naval forces;

15. To provide for calling forth the militia to execute the laws of the Union, suppress insurrections and repel invasions;

16. To provide for organizing, arming, and disciplining the militia, and for governing such part of them as may be employed in the service of the United States, reserving to the States respectively the appointment of the officers, and the authority of training the militia according to the discipline prescribed by Congress;

17. To exercise exclusive legislation in all cases whatsoever, over such district (not exceeding ten miles square) as may, by cession of particular

States, and the acceptance of Congress, become the seat of the government of the United States, and to exercise like authority over all places purchased by the consent of the legislature of the State in which the same shall be, for the erection of forts, magazines, arsenals, dockyards, and other needful buildings; and

18. To make all laws which shall be necessary and proper for carrying into execution the foregoing powers, and all other powers vested by this Constitution in the government of the United States, or in any department or officer thereof.

Section 9. 1. The migration or importation of such persons as any of the States now existing shall think proper to admit, shall not be prohibited by the Congress prior to the year one thousand eight hundred and eight, but a tax or duty may be imposed on such importation, not exceeding ten dollars for each person.

2. The privilege of the writ of *habeas corpus* shall not be suspended, unless when in cases of rebellion or invasion the public safety may require it.

3. No bill of attainder or *ex post facto* law shall be passed.

4. No capitation, or other direct, tax shall be laid, unless in proportion to the *census* or enumeration hereinbefore directed to be taken.[5]

5. No tax or duty shall be laid on articles exported from any State.

6. No preference shall be given by any regulation of commerce or revenue to the ports of one State over those of another: nor shall vessels bound to, or from, one State be obliged to enter, clear, or pay duties in another.

7. No money shall be drawn from the treasury, but in consequence of appropriations made by law; and a regular statement and account of the receipts and expenditures of all public money shall be published from time to time.

8. No title of nobility shall be granted by the United States: and no person holding any office of profit or trust under them, shall, without the consent of the Congress, accept of any present, emolument, office, or title, of any kind whatever, from any king, prince, or foreign State.

Section 10. 1. No State shall enter into any treaty, alliance, or confederation; grant letters of marque and reprisal; coin money; emit bills of credit; make anything but gold and silver coin a tender in payment of debts; pass any bill of attainder, *ex post facto* or law impairing the obligation of contracts, or grant any title of nobility.

2. No state shall, without the consent of the Congress, lay any imposts or duties on imports or exports, except what may be absolutely necessary for executing its inspection laws: and the net produce of all duties and imposts laid by any State on imports or exports, shall be for the use of the treasury of the United States; and all such laws shall be subject to the revision and control of the Congress.

3. No State shall, without the consent of Congress, lay any duty of

[5] See the Sixteenth Amendment.

tonnage, keep troops, or ships of war in time of peace, enter into any agreement or compact with another State, or with a foreign power, or engage in war, unless actually invaded, or in such imminent danger as will not admit of delay.

ARTICLE II

Section 1. 1. The executive power shall be vested in a President of the United States of America. He shall hold his office during the term of four years, and, together with the Vice President, chosen for the same term, be elected, as follows:

2. Each State shall appoint, in such manner as the legislature thereof may direct, a number of electors, equal to the whole number of senators and representatives to which the State may be entitled in the Congress: but no senator or representative, or person holding an office of trust or profit under the United States, shall be appointed an elector.

[6] The electors shall meet in their respective States, and vote by ballot for two persons, of whom one at least shall not be an inhabitant of the same State with themselves. And they shall make a list of all the persons voted for, and of the number of votes for each; which list they shall sign and certify, and transmit sealed to the seat of the government of the United States, directed to the president of the Senate. The president of the Senate shall, in the presence of the Senate and House of Representatives, open all certificates, and the votes shall then be counted. The person having the greatest number of votes shall be the President, if such number be a majority of the whole number of electors appointed; and if there be more than one who have such majority, and have an equal number of votes, then the House of Representatives shall immediately choose by ballot one of them for President; and if no person have a majority, then from the five highest on the list the said House shall in like manner choose the President. But in choosing the President, the votes shall be taken by States, the representation from each State having one vote; a quorum for this purpose shall consist of a member or members from two thirds of the States, and a majority of all the States shall be necessary to a choice. In every case, after the choice of the President, the person having the greatest number of votes of the electors shall be the Vice President. But if there should remain two or more who have equal votes, the Senate shall choose from them by ballot the Vice President.[7]

3. The Congress may determine the time of choosing the electors, and the day on which they shall give their votes; which day shall be the same throughout the United States.

4. No person except a natural born citizen, or a citizen of the United States, at the time of the adoption of this Constitution, shall be eligible to the office of President; neither shall any person be eligible to that office who shall not have attained to the age of thirty-five years, and been fourteen years a resident within the United States.

---

[6] The following paragraph was in force only from 1788 to 1803.
[7] Superseded by the Twelfth Amendment.

5. In case of the removal of the President from office, or of his death, resignation, or inability to discharge the powers and duties of the said office, the same shall devolve on the Vice President, and the Congress may by law provide for the case of removal, death, resignation, or inability, both of the President and Vice President, declaring what officer shall then act as President, and such officer shall act accordingly, until the disability be removed, or a President shall be elected.[8]

6. The President shall, at stated times, receive for his services a compensation, which shall neither be increased nor diminished during the period for which he shall have been elected, and he shall not receive within that period any other emolument from the United States, or any of them.

7. Before he enter on the execution of his office, he shall take the following oath or affirmation:—"I do solemnly swear (or affirm) that I will faithfully execute the office of President of the United States, and will to the best of my ability, preserve, protect and defend the Constitution of the United States."

Section 2. 1. The President shall be commander in chief of the army and navy of the United States, and of the militia of the several States, when called into the actual service of the United States; he may require the opinion, in writing, of the principal officer in each of the executive departments, upon any subject relating to the duties of their respective offices, and he shall have power to grant reprieves and pardons for offenses, against the United States, except in cases of impeachment.

2. He shall have power, by and with the advice and consent of the Senate, to make treaties, provided two thirds of the senators present concur; and he shall nominate, and by and with the advice and consent of the Senate, shall appoint ambassadors, other public ministers and consuls, judges of the Supreme Court, and all other officers of the United States, whose appointments are not herein otherwise provided for, and which shall be established by law: but the Congress may by law vest the appointment of such inferior officers, as they think proper, in the President alone, in the courts of law, or in the heads of departments.

3. The President shall have power to fill up all vacancies that may happen during the recess of the Senate, by granting commissions which shall expire at the end of their next session.

Section 3. 1. He shall from time to time give to the Congress information of the state of the Union, and recommend to their consideration such measures as he shall judge necessary and expedient; he may, on extraordinary occasions, convene both Houses, or either of them, and in case of disagreement between them with respect to the time of adjournment, he may adjourn them to such time as he shall think proper; he shall receive ambassadors and other public ministers; he shall take care that the laws be faithfully executed, and shall commission all the officers of the United States.

---

[8] See the Twentieth Amendment.

Section 4. The President, Vice President, and all civil officers of the United States, shall be removed from office on impeachment for, and conviction of, treason, bribery, or other high crimes and misdemeanors.

ARTICLE III

Section 1. The judicial power of the United States shall be vested in one Supreme Court, and in such inferior courts as the Congress may from time to time ordain and establish. The judges, both of the Supreme and inferior courts, shall hold their offices during good behavior, and shall, at stated times, receive for their services, a compensation, which shall not be diminished during their continuance in office.

Section 2. 1. The judicial power shall extend to all cases, in law and equity, arising under the Constitution, the laws of the United States, and treaties made, or which shall be made, under their authority;—to all cases affecting ambassadors, other public ministers and consuls;—to all cases of admiralty and maritime jurisdiction;—to controversies to which the United States shall be a party;—to controversies between two or more States;—between a state and citizens of another State;[9]—between citizens of different States,—between citizens of the same State claiming lands under grants of different States, and between a State, or the citizens thereof, and foreign States, citizens or subjects.

2. In all cases affecting ambassadors, other public ministers and consuls, and those in which a State shall be party, the Supreme Court shall have original jurisdiction. In all the other cases before mentioned, the Supreme Court shall have appellate jurisdiction, both as to law and to fact, with such exceptions, and under such regulations as the Congress shall make.

3. The trial of all crimes, except in cases of impeachment, shall be by jury; and such trial shall be held in the State where the said crimes shall have been committed; but when not committed within any State, the trial shall be at such place or places as the Congress may by law have directed.

Section 3. 1. Treason against the United States, shall consist only in levying war against them, or in adhering to their enemies, giving them aid and comfort. No person shall be convicted of treason unless on the testimony of two witnesses to the same overt act, or on confession in open court.

2. The Congress shall have power to declare the punishment of treason, but no attainder of treason shall work corruption of blood, or forfeiture except during the life of the person attainted.

ARTICLE IV

Section 1. Full faith and credit shall be given in each State to the public acts, records, and judicial proceedings of every other State. And

---

[9] See the Eleventh Amendment.

the Congress may by general laws prescribe the manner in which such acts, records and proceedings shall be proved, and the effect thereof.

Section 2. 1. The citizens of each State shall be entitled to all privileges and immunities of citizens in the several States.

2. A person charged in any State with treason, felony, or other crime, who shall flee from justice, and be found in another State, shall on demand of the executive authority of the State from which he fled, be delivered up to be removed to the State having jurisdiction of the crime.

3. No person held to service or labor in one State under the laws thereof, escaping into another, shall, in consequence of any law or regulation therein, be discharged from such service or labor, but shall be delivered up on claim of the party to whom such service or labor may be due.

Section 3. 1. New States may be admitted by the Congress into this Union; but no new State shall be formed or erected within the jurisdiction of any other State; nor any State be formed by the junction of two or more States, or parts of States, without the consent of the legislatures of the States concerned as well as of the Congress.

2. The Congress shall have power to dispose of and make all needful rules and regulations respecting the territory or other property belonging to the United States; and nothing in this Constitution shall be so construed as to prejudice any claims of the United States, or of any particular State.

Section 4. The United States shall guarantee to every State in this Union a republican form of government, and shall protect each of them against invasion; and on application of the legislature, or of the executive (when the legislature cannot be convened) against domestic violence.

ARTICLE V

The Congress, whenever two thirds of both Houses shall deem it necessary, shall propose amendments to this Constitution, or, on the application of the legislatures of two thirds of the several States, shall call a convention for proposing amendments, which, in either case, shall be valid to all intents and purposes, as part of this Constitution when ratified by the legislatures of three fourths of the several States, or by conventions in three fourths thereof, as the one or the other mode of ratification may be proposed by the Congress; Provided that no amendment which may be made prior to the year one thousand eight hundred and eight shall in any manner affect the first and fourth clauses in the ninth section of the first article; and that no State, without its consent, shall be deprived of its equal suffrage in the Senate.

ARTICLE VI

1. All debts contracted and engagements entered into, before the adoption of this Constitution, shall be as valid against the United States under this Constitution, as under the Confederation.

2. This Constitution, and the laws of the United States which shall be made in pursuance thereof; and all treaties made, or which shall be made, under the authority of the United States, shall be the supreme law of the land; and the Judges in every State shall be bound thereby, anything in the Constitution or laws of any State to the contrary notwithstanding.

3. The senators and representatives before mentioned, and the members of the several State legislatures, and all executive and judicial officers, both of the United States and of the several States, shall be bound by oath or affirmation to support this Constitution; but no religious test shall ever be required as a qualification to any office or public trust under the United States.

ARTICLE VII

The ratification of the conventions of nine States shall be sufficient for the establishment of this Constitution between the States so ratifying the same.

Done in Convention by the unanimous consent of the States present the seventeenth day of September in the year of our Lord one thousand seven hundred and eighty-seven, and of the independence of the United States of America the twelfth. In witness whereof we have hereunto subscribed our names.

[Names omitted]

Article in addition to, and amendment of, the Constitution of the United States of America, proposed by Congress, and ratified by the legislatures of the several States pursuant to the fifth article of the original Constitution.

ARTICLE I[10]

Congress shall make no law respecting an establishment of religion, or prohibiting the free exercise thereof; or abridging the freedom of speech, or of the press; or the right of the people peaceably to assemble, and to petition the government for a redress of grievances.

ARTICLE II

A well regulated militia, being necesary to the security of a free State, the right of the people to keep and bear arms shall not be infringed.

ARTICLE III

No soldier shall, in time of peace, be quartered in any house, without' the consent of the owner, nor in time of war, but in a manner to be prescribed by law.

ARTICLE IV

The right of the people to be secure in their persons, houses, papers, and effects, against unreasonable searches and seizures, shall not be vio-

---

[10] The first ten amendments adopted in 1791.

lated, and no warrants shall issue, but upon probable cause, supported by oath or affirmation, and particularly describing the place to be searched, and the persons or things to be seized.

Article V

No person shall be held to answer for a capital, or otherwise infamous crime, unless on a presentment or indictment of a grand jury, except in cases arising in the land or naval forces, or in the militia, when in actual service in time of war or public danger; nor shall any person be subject for the same offense to be twice put in jeopardy of life or limb; nor shall be compelled in any criminal case to be a witness against himself, nor be deprived of life, liberty, or property, without due process of law; nor shall private property be taken for public use without just compensation.

Article VI

In all criminal prosecutions, the accused shall enjoy the right to a speedy and public trial, by an impartial jury of the State and district wherein the crime shall have been committed, which district shall have been previously ascertained by law, and to be informed of the nature and cause of the accusation; to be confronted with the witnesses against him; to have compulsory process for obtaining witnesses in his favor, and to have the assistance of counsel for his defense.

Article VII

In suits at common law, where the value in controversy shall exceed twenty dollars, the right of trial by jury shall be preserved, and no fact tried by a jury shall be otherwise re-examined in any court of the United States, than according to the rules of the common law.

Article VIII

Excessive bail shall not be required, nor excessive fines imposed, nor cruel and unusual punishments inflicted.

Article IX

The enumeration in the Constitution of certain rights shall not be construed to deny or disparage others retained by the people.

Article X

The powers not delegated to the United States by the Constitution, nor prohibited by it to the States, are reserved to the States respectively, or to the people.

Article XI[11]

The judicial power of the United States shall not be construed to extend to any suit in law or equity, commenced or prosecuted against one

[11] Adopted in 1798.

of the United States by citizens of another State, or by citizens or subjects of any foreign State.

Article XII[12]

The electors shall meet in their respective States, and vote by ballot for President and Vice President, one of whom, at least, shall not be an inhabitant of the same State with themselves; they shall name in their ballots the person voted for as President, and in distinct ballots, the person voted for as Vice President, and they shall make distinct lists of all persons voted for as President and of all persons voted for as Vice President, and of the number of votes for each, which lists they shall sign and certify, and transmit sealed to the seat of the government of the United States, directed to the President of the Senate;—The President of the Senate shall, in the presence of the Senate and House of Representatives, open all the certificates and the votes shall then be counted;—The person having the greatest number of votes for President, shall be the President, if such number be a majority of the whole number of electors appointed; and if no person have such majority, then from the persons having the highest numbers not exceeding three on the list of those voted for as President, the House of Representatives shall choose immediately, by ballot, the President. But in choosing the President, the votes shall be taken by States, the representation from each State having one vote; a quorum for this purpose shall consist of a member or members from two thirds of the States, and a majority of all the States shall be necessary to a choice. And if the House of Representatives shall not choose a President whenever the right of choice shall devolve upon them, before the fourth day of March next following, then the Vice President shall act as President, as in the case of the death or other constitutional disability of the President. The person having the greatest number of votes as Vice President shall be the Vice President, if such number be a majority of the whole number of electors appointed, and if no person have a majority, then from the two highest numbers on the list, the Senate shall choose the Vice President; a quorum for the purpose shall consist of two thirds of the whole number of Senators, and a majority of the whole number shall be necessary to a choice. But no person constitutionally ineligible to the office of President shall be eligible to that of Vice President of the United States.

Article XIII[13]

Section 1. Neither slavery nor involuntary servitude, except as punishment for crime whereof the party shall have been duly convicted, shall exist within the United States, or any place subject to their jurisdiction.

2. Congress shall have power to enforce this article by appropriate legislation.

---

[12] Adopted in 1804.
[13] Adopted in 1865.

Article XIV[14]

1. All persons born or naturalized in the United States, and subject to the jurisdiction thereof, are citizens of the United States and of the State wherein they reside. No State shall make or enforce any law which shall abridge the privileges or immunities of citizens of the United States; nor shall any State deprive any persons of life, liberty, or property, without due process of law; nor deny to any person within its jurisdiction the equal protection of the laws.

2. Representatives shall be apportioned among the several States according to their respective numbers, counting the whole number of persons in each State, excluding Indians not taxed. But when the right to vote at any election for the choice of electors for President and Vice President of the United States, representatives in Congress, the executive and judicial officers of a State, or the members of the legislature thereof, is denied to any of the male inhabitants of such State, being twenty-one years of age, and citizens of the United States, or in any way abridged, except for participation in rebellion, or other crime, the basis of representation therein shall be reduced in the proportion which the number of such male citizens shall bear to the whole number of male citizens twenty-one years of age in such State.

3. No person shall be a senator or representative in Congress, or elector of President and Vice President, or hold any office, civil or military, under the United States, or under any State, who, having previously taken an oath, as a member of Congress, or as an officer of the United States, or as a member of any State legislature, or as an executive or judicial officer of any State, to support the Constitution of the United States, shall have engaged in insurrection or rebellion against the same, or given aid or comfort to the enemies thereof. But Congress may by a vote of two thirds of each House, remove such disability.

4. The validity of the public debt of the United States, authorized by law, including debts incurred for payment of pensions and bounties for services in suppressing insurrection or rebellion, shall not be questioned. But neither the United States nor any State shall assume or pay any debt or obligation incurred in aid of insurrection or rebellion against the United States, or any claim for the loss or emancipation of any slave; but all such debts, obligations and claims shall be held illegal and void.

5. The Congress shall have power to enforce, by appropriate legislation, the provisions of this article.

Article XV[15]

Section 1. The right of citizens of the United States to vote shall not be denied or abridged by the United States or by any State on account of race, color, or previous condition of servitude.

---

[14] Adopted in 1868.
[15] Adopted in 1870.

Section 2. The Congress shall have power to enforce this article by appropriate legislation.

ARTICLE XVI[16]

The Congress shall have power to lay and collect taxes on incomes, from whatever source derived, without apportionment among the several States, and without regard to any census or enumeration.

ARTICLE XVII[17]

The Senate of the United States shall be composed of two senators from each state, elected by the people thereof, for six years; and each senator shall have one vote. The electors in each State shall have the qualifications requisite for electors of the most numerous branch of the State legislature.

When vacancies happen in the representation of any State in the Senate, the executive authority of such State shall issue writs of election to fill such vacancies: *Provided,* That the legislature of any State may empower the executive thereof to make temporary appointments until the people fill the vacancies by election as the legislature may direct.

This amendment shall not be so construed as to affect the election or term of any senator chosen before it becomes valid as part of the Constitution.

ARTICLE XVIII

Repealed by 21st Amendment[18]

After one year from the ratification of this article, the manufacture, sale, or transportation of intoxicating liquors within, the importation thereof into, or the exportation thereof from the United States and all territory subject to the jurisdiction thereof for beverage purposes is hereby prohibited.

The Congress and the several States shall have concurrent power to enforce this article by appropriate legislation.

This article shall be inoperative unless it shall have been ratified as an amendment to the Constitution by the legislatures of the several States, as provided in the Constitution, within seven years from the date of the submission hereof to the states by Congress.

ARTICLE XIX[19]

The right of citizens of the United States to vote shall not be denied or abridged by the United States or by any State on account of sex.

---

[16] Passed in 1909; proclaimed 1913.

[17] Passed 1912, in lieu of paragraph one, section 3, Article I, of the Constitution and so much of paragraph two of the same section as relates to the filling of vacancies; proclaimed 1913.

[18] Submitted by Congress, December, 1917; proclaimed January, 1919.

[19] Proposed in 1919, adopted in 1920.

The Congress shall have power by appropriate legislation to enforce the provisions of this article.

ARTICLE XX[20]

Section 1. The terms of the President and Vice President shall end at noon on the 20th day of January, and the terms of Senators and Representatives at noon on the 3d day of January, of the years in which such terms would have ended if this article had not been ratified, and the terms of their successors shall then begin.

Section 2. The Congress shall assemble at least once in every year, and such meeting shall begin at noon on the 3d day of January, unless they shall by law appoint a different day.

Section 3. If, at the time fixed for the beginning of the term of the President, the President elect shall have died, the Vice President elect shall become President. If a President shall not have been chosen before the time fixed for the beginning of his term, or if the President elect shall have failed to qualify, then the Vice President elect shall act as President until a President shall have qualified, and the Congress may by law provide for the case wherein neither a President elect nor a Vice President elect shall have qualified, declaring who shall then act as President, or the manner in which one who is to act shall be selected, and such person shall act accordingly until a President or Vice President shall have qualified.

Section 4. The Congress may by law provide for the case of the death of any of the persons from whom the House of Representatives may choose a President whenever the right of choice shall have devolved upon them, and for the case of the death of any of the persons from whom the Senate may choose a Vice President whenever the right of choice shall have devolved upon them.

Section 5. Sections 1 and 2 shall take effect on the 15th day of October following the ratification of this article.

Section 6. This article shall be inoperative unless it shall have been ratified as an amendment to the Constitution by the legislatures of three-fourths of the several States within seven years from the date of its submission.

ARTICLE XXI[21]

Section 1. The eighteenth article of amendment to the Constitution of the United States is hereby repealed.

---

[20] Proposed in 1932, adopted in 1933.

[21] Proposed in February, 1933, and received the approval of the requisite three-fourths of the states by November, 1933.

Section 2. The transportation or importation into any state, territory, or possession of the United States for delivery or use therein of intoxicating liquors, in violation of the laws thereof, is hereby prohibited.

Section 3. This article shall be inoperative unless it shall have been ratified as an amendment to the Constitution by convention in the several States, as provided in the Constitution, within seven years from the date of the submission hereof to the States by the Congress.

Article XXII[22]

Section 1. No person shall be elected to the office of the President more than twice, and no person who has held the office of President, or acted as President, for more than two years of a term to which some other person was elected President shall be elected to the office of President more than once. But this Article shall not apply to any person holding the office of President when this Article was proposed by the Congress, and shall not prevent any person who may be holding the office of President, or acting as President, during the term within which this Article becomes operative from holding the office of President or acting as President during the remainder of such term.

Section 2. This Article shall be inoperative unless it shall have been ratified as an amendment to the Constitution by the legislatures of three-fourths of the several States within seven years from the date of its submission to the States by the Congress.

Article XXIII[23]

Section 1. The District constituting the seat of Government of the United States shall appoint in such manner as the Congress may direct:

A number of electors of President and Vice President equal to the whole number of Senators and Representatives in Congress to which the District would be entitled if it were a State, but in no event more than the least populous State; they shall be in addition to those appointed by the States, but they shall be considered, for the purposes of the election of President and Vice President, to be electors appointed by a State; and they shall meet in the District and perform such duties as provided by the twelfth article of amendment.

Section 2. The Congress shall have power to enforce this article by appropriate legislation.

Article XXIV[24]

Section 1. The right of citizens of the United States to vote in any primary or other election for President or Vice-President, for electors for President or Vice-President, or for Senator or Representative in Congress, shall not be denied or abridged by the United States or any state by reason of failure to pay any poll tax or other tax.

Section 2. The Congress shall have power to enforce this article by appropriate legislation.

---

[22] Adopted in 1951. [23] Adopted in 1961. [24] Adopted in 1964.

Table of Cases Cited

Index